William Sever Lincoln

Life with the Thirty-Fourth Mass. Infantry in the War of the Rebellion.

William Sever Lincoln

Life with the Thirty-Fourth Mass. Infantry in the War of the Rebellion.

ISBN/EAN: 9783337122232

Printed in Europe, USA, Canada, Australia, Japan

Cover: Foto ©ninafisch / pixelio.de

More available books at **www.hansebooks.com**

LIFE

WITH THE

Thirty-Fourth Mass. Infantry

IN THE

WAR OF THE REBELLION

BY WILLIAM S. LINCOLN,
Late Colonel of the Regiment and Brevet Brigadier General U. S. Volunteers.

WORCESTER:
PRESS OF NOYES, SNOW & COMPANY,
1879.

COPYRIGHT.
WILLIAM S. LINCOLN,
1879.

TO MY COMRADES

OF THE

34TH MASSACHUSETTS INFANTRY.

I dedicate to you this imperfect narrative of our "*three year's service.*" You will require no apology for the minuteness with which our life in its early and most uneventful period has been detailed. Rather, you will share my regret that it has been impossible to give an equally minute account of the stirring incidents of our later days' service. I have made no attempt to give a connected narrative of our military life :— on the contrary, at the risk of being tedious, I have endeavored to weave together extracts from familiar letters and diaries in such manner as to review, more fully than could otherwise be done, the fast fading recollections of our soldier life. The labor will be amply repaid if only partial success attend it.

The work has been done at *your* request, and for *your* gratification. Had it been intended for the general public, much might have been omitted — and many things been varied in the telling. Such as it is, it is committed to you, in the hope that you will pardon its faults — overlook its defects — and accept whatever of good there may be in it as a slight, but heartfelt tribute to your worth as soldiers by one who is proud to have been your Commander in the past, and to subscribe himself, now, your warm and grateful friend,

THE AUTHOR.

TO MY READERS.

Years ago I was honored by my associates of the Regimental Association with a request to prepare for publication a history of the 34th Massachusetts Infantry. Various causes combined to delay the execution of what thus became a duty. What *seemed* easy to be done was found to be, in reality, difficult to do. All the official and many private papers connected with the organization and early service of the Regiment were destroyed, or lost, in the hurried evacuation of Martinsburg and Harper's Ferry, consequent upon the advance of the Rebel Army under Early, in the summer of 1864. The members of the Regiment were confidently relied upon to furnish material facts and incidents connected with our service, more especially during the period when my own enforced absence deprived me of opportunity of personal observation. The residence of many of the men, however, was unknown;—many, probably, to whom circulars were addressed, were not reached at all;—and of those who were reached, most made no response. Necessity, therefore, compelled me to draw more largely from my own "Diary," and letters written to personal friends, than under other circumstances would be excusable. I am, however, under very great obligations to Major Willard, Capts. Elwell and Soley, and more especially to Lieut. Judd, for aid, without which the work would not have been completed, even in its present form;—and for which did I not make this public acknowledgment, I should be ungrateful, indeed. I have appended to the public life of the Regiment, at the risk of seeming egotism, a narrative of my own individual experience while a prisoner in the hands of the enemy, and also during the long and anxious days of my successful escape. For this, the requests of valued friends among the old members of the Regiment must be my excuse. Bespeaking a large measure of indulgence for the imperfections of the work, I am most respectfully,

THE READER'S HUMBLE SERV'T.

TABLE OF CONTENTS.

CHAPTER I.

ORGANIZATION, RENDEZVOUS, &C.,   13-26

General Orders No. 17, May 29, 1862 — Special Order June 3 — Lieut. Col. William S. Lincoln — Charles W. Elwell — Recruiting — Capt. M—— — Camp Opened — Charles P. Trumbull — George W. Marsh — Capt. Potter — F. B. Rice — Charles H. Howland — Samuel F. Woods — Squad-drills — Recruits — Pay and Bounty — Muster In — Public Meetings — Recruits — Lieuts. Lincoln and Cobb — Capt. Cooley — Capt. Holden — Charles B. Cutler — Recruits — Enfield Rifles — Battalion Drills — Rejected Recruits — Public Meeting in Worcester — Recruiting — Number of men in Camp — Censure — The man of the snakes — Explanation — In readiness to move — Regiment Reviewed — Enfield Rifles — Flag Presentation — The Colonel's Horse — Marching Orders — Springfield Muskets — Dress Parade — The Paymaster and Roster — Good-byes — March — Finn of "A" — New York — Jersey City — Philadelphia — Baltimore — An Invitation — Bedlam — The Colonel's Compliments.

CHAPTER II.

WASHINGTON, ARLINGTON AND ALEXANDRIA,   -   26-38

Washington — En Route — Maj. Bowman — Our Rear Guard — My Office Bell — Tents Pitched — Policing the Ground — Marching Orders — Marching Orders again — Alexandria — Lieut. E.'s Experience — Reveille Call — Camp — What we Escaped — Cloud's Mills — R. G. O. — Old Troops — Our Drills — Visitors — Little Mac — Inspection — Pure Water — Our Fare — Obtaining Supplies — Trains — McDonnell's Division — Orders — Our Work — The Sick — Serg't Fitzpatrick — Tents — Visitors — A Review — A Scare — A new Camp — A little Milk — An Interview — The Brigade.

CHAPTER III.

FORT LYON,   38-50

Our Camp — R. G. O. — On Fatigue — A little Scare — A Council of Administration — A little Vain — Reveille — Dress Coats — What a Noise! — A new Uniform — Transferred — Capt. Chandler — Guard Duty — Our Front — A Serenade — Monthly Inspection — Old Double Quick — A Sanitary Measure — Gen. Banks — Company E — Sickness — A Soft Thing — Lieut. E. — Our Teams — A Walk through Camp — Our Sutler — Sickness — Mule Driving — A Drill — Armorers' Tools — A Detail — Sickness — Review — General Order — Promotions — The Weather.

CHAPTER IV.

FORT LYON,   50-57

Our Sick — What's that Noise? — Inspection — Our Sick — A strange Note — Movements of Troops — Games — Our Equipage — Our Sick — Winter — A conscientious Feeder — Our Sick — Troops Moving — Our Hospital — Our Camp.

CHAPTER V.

FORT LYON,   -   57-69

A Skirmish Drill — Great News — Thanksgiving — Our daily Life — A Prisoner at very hard Labor — Winter Quarters — A new kind of Stuffing — Capt. Willard — Joe Bolio — The Convalescent Camp — The Boys are Chuckling — Visitors — Redoubt A — Our Sick — F Company — Blank Cartridges — A Band — Christmas — The Shovel and the Hoe — Mince Pie — Our Darkeys — A Scare — Peace Reigns.

CHAPTER VI.

FORT LYON, - - - 69–77

A Wine Party — Fatigue Duty — Small Pox — In Arrest — A House Warming — A Trial — An Inspection and Review — Brigaded at Last — Dandy Soldiers — Guide Right — "'Tis n't what I thought it was going to be" — A Noisy Family — I want Four Dollars — Commissions — A Fatigue Party — A Review — An Inch Taller — The Weather — More Visitors — Our Fund.

CHAPTER VII.

FORT LYON, - - 77–87

Brigade Headquarters Guard — The Weather — More Visitors — Officers' School — I should n't take that Job — Sentences of Courts Martial — The Ripley House — A Queer World — A Good Story — An Excitement — A Tailor's Shop — A Cripple Brigade — A Shoe Shop — A Wood Party — A Good Joke.

CHAPTER VIII.

FORT LYON, - 87–91

Target Practice — Marching Orders — Lieut. Lincoln in Arrest — Setting up in State — Lieut. Lincoln's Discharge — Paid off — A new Brigade — Assignment of Companies — A Luxurious Allowance.

CHAPTER IX.

UPTON'S HILL, - 91–98

Marching Orders — Historic Ground — Our Camp — Our Things — Sweeping — Our Medical Staff — Fort "All Hazards" — "The Boys" — Our Shops, &c. and Our Fund — Drills — Injunctions to Vigilance — Pay Day.

CHAPTER X.

WASHINGTON, - 98–105

A Marching Salute — Details for Duty — Our Quarters — Details of Officers — Capt. Meigs — Our Guard — A Good Joke — Our Guard — Details of Companies — Sickness — The Heat.

CHAPTER XI.

WASHINGTON, - - 105–109

Resignations — Lieut. Lovell on Duty — Cases of Punishment — Details for Duty — Dr. Mary Walker.

CHAPTER XII.

WASHINGTON, 109–117

Capt. Camp — Maj. Sherburn — Marching Orders — A Guard Relief — Movement of Troops — Resignations — Fourth of July — Marching Orders Again — Off at Last — An Accidental Death — Run to Sandy Hook — Maryland Heights — Brigaded — Waste of Property — Our Strength — Bull Beef — Rebel Working Parties.

CHAPTER XIII.

HARPER'S FERRY, 117–122

Crossing of the Potomac — Our occupation of Harper's Ferry — Our Camp — "Who killed the Bull" — Details of Officers — The Sutler — The Brigade — A Merry Evening — A Reconnoitering Party — Some of our Officers — Transferred — What's to be Done — Transferred Again.

CHAPTER XIV.

HARPER'S FERRY, - 122–129

The 9th Maryland — Records of Courts Martial, &c. — A Tableaux in E — Reasonable Requests — A Little Unpleasantness — A Busy Night — A Storm on the Picket Line — Our Work — The D——l to Pay — Charlestown — What shall we do — Our Strength — A Recruiting Party.

CONTENTS. 7

CHAPTER XV.

HARPER's FERRY, 129–141

A Review — Alarms — Our Sick — A Raid — Special Orders — An Inspection of Camp — A Scrape — Reviews — And Inspections — Deserters — Milking — Winter Quarters — Clothing Account — The Chaplaincy — An Applicant for a Commission — Off Duty — On the Rampage — Commissions — Fatigue Duty — Drills — Commissions — Deserters — An Alarm — A Promising Recruit — No Drill — An Alarm — A New Post Commander — Sound of Guns.

CHAPTER XVI.

BATTLE OF RIPON, - - 141–164

Artillery Firing — Regiment turned out — Ordered to move — Companies F and C Skirmishers — Lieut. Cobb Dangerously Wounded — Lieut. Goodrich — Miners' Wheel Horses — A Message from Cole — Company H — Our Killed — Capt. Bacon — An Order from Gen. Sullivan — Our Force — 9th and 10th Maryland — Trophies — Prisoners — Our Loss — Cease Firing — Continue the Same — Never Fear Mr. Adjutant — Capt. Chandler — Lieut. Cobb — The Flag — Surgeon Clarke — An Alarm — Lieut. Cobb — Mr. Phelps — Rejoined for Duty — A Compliment — Bi-Monthly Inspection and Muster for Pay — A Minister — Our Wounded — Another Alarm — Deserters — Our old Minister again — Another Alarm — Visitors — A Queer Incident — The 10th Maryland — Complaining Citizens — Some Recruits — Red Tape — Orders — Our Sick — More Commissions — Corps d'Afrique — A Grand Ball — A Parade — Post General Order — Our Ball Room — A Suggestion — Lieut. Lincoln — Lieut. Hall — Death — Passes — Thanksgiving and the Ball — The new Commissioned Officers — Surgeon Thorndike — Our Cripples — A new Rule — Our Wood and old Flagg — The Weather — More Recruits — A Coolness — Woods, A. A. G., and the Lieut. Col. Col. Wells — Marching Orders — Lieut. Bacon — Who may Go — Who left Behind.

CHAPTER XVII.

THE VALLEY EXPEDITION, 164–174

Forward — The 12th Virginia — The 34th Massachusetts — Boyd's Cavalry — Furst's Battery — Berryville — Winchester — The Left Wing — Capt. Soley — Reveille — Why this Delay — Newtown — Middletown — Cedar Creek — Strasburg — The Trinity — Gen. Rosser — Grouse and Buffalo Meat — Headquarters Mess — Our Lines — Boyd — Orders — Contrabands — The Train — Brigade General Orders — On the Move — Woodstock — Amusing Scenes — Edinboro' — Mt. Jackson — A Cavalry Picket — An Incident — Another Incident — Capt. Stearns — The 34th — New Market — Harrisonburg — Orders — The weather — "Get under Arms" — Information — Gen. Early — A line of Log Heaps — The Acting Brigadier — Our Line of Fires — Forward, Boys.

CHAPTER XVIII.

THE VALLEY EXPEDITION, 174–135

An Incident — Our Night's March — New Market — A Patrol — 12th Virginia — Mt. Jackson — Edinboro' — Boyd's Report — On the Road — Speculations — Enquiries — Woodstock — Halt — An Encounter — Information — Strasburg — The Road is Clear — Cedar Creek — Half Rations — Hard Tack — The Country People — On the March — Our Prisoners — The Weather — Middletown — Winchester — Relief — Reports — In Bivouac — Orders — Company B — Capt. Potter — The 34th — The Creek — Waiting — Halt, Now — Home — An Instance of Punishment — As a Military Movement — The Prisoners — The Sergeant — The Refugees — Pillaging — To us of the Shoulder Straps — The Men — Gilmor and McNeil.

CHAPTER XIX.

HARPER'S FERRY, - 185–195

Home Again — Capt. Chandler — Maj. Pratt.. Col. Wells — Our Sick — Commissions — Hash — A Ball — Gen. Sullivan and a Call — An Order — A Compliment — More Clothing — A Curious Affair — An Order — A Recruit — Our Wood and Old Flagg — Orders — The 12th Virginia — All Quiet — Bartlett of K — Howard of B — Assistant Surgeon Thorndike — The 12th Virginia — Thanks — The

Chaplaincy — The Ball — Mishaps — The Brigade Moves — Early — The weather Sport — Our Condition — The Artillery — Early — Averill — Assistant Surgeon Smith — A. S. Thorndike — Rebel Deserters — Our Position — Lieut. Hall — Lieut. Lincoln — A Fall of Snow — A Note from Gen. Sullivan — Lieut. Col. Lincoln — 10th Maryland — Reports — Lieut. Elwell's Telegrams — Maj. Pratt — An Order for the Regiment — Maj. Cole — Companies A and G — Lieut. Horton — Recruits — Our Force — Transferred — Capt. Leach and Snicker's Gap — Capt. Chandler — Transferred Again — Capt. Pratt — New Brooms Sweep Clean — Lieut. Col. Lincoln — Capt. Bacon and Lieut. Murdock — A Guard — The Band, and what means this — Dr. Thorndike — A Raiding Party — Early — Re-enlistment.

CHAPTER XX.

CUMBERLAND AND RETURN, 195–209

Our Orders — Verbal Orders — Capt. Willard and Lieut. Goodrich — At Cumberland — New Orders — An Alarm — In the Mud — The 12th Virginia — The Band — Time idled Away — New Orders — In bad Odor — Our Recruits — The Small Pox — Lieut. Walker of "A" — A Detail — Furloughs — A Missionary — The Paymaster — A new Detail — Hurley of "G" — Grady of "H" — A little Song — An Old Friend from Maine — An Alarm — Serg't McIver — A Flag of Truce — On Leave of Absence — Our Recruits — Discharges — A Memorial — Our Invalids — An Examining Board — The Weather — Our Strength — "If 't was a Hod ye 'd lend us."

CHAPTER XXI.

HARPER'S FERRY, 209–219

The 22d of February — Our old Missionary — Despatches — Orders to Major Pratt — A Cheery old Brother — Major Pratt's Reports and Gen Sullivan's Orders — More Commissions — A new Assignment — Maj. Gen. Kelley — New Orders — Our Strength — An Explanation — In a state of Excitement — Our old Friend again — Capt. Soley and his Expedition — On Leave — Inspection — Capt. Potter — Snow — Col. Wells — Lieut. Col. Moody Inspecting Officer — Lieut. Lincoln — Our Sick — The Surgeons — More Orders — More Commissions.

CHAPTER XXII.

POINT OF ROCKS AND MARTINSBURG, - 219–227

Our Orders — Point of Rocks — In bad Odor again — Gen. Sullivan — The 18th Connecticut — Capt. Thompson — Lieuts. Elwell and Belser — Martinsburg — A new Brigade — Our Trains — Assignment to Duty — Our Recruits — Incorrect Accounts — Apropos to this — A Storm — Our Sick — Lieut Platt — Recruits — New Tents — Capts. Potter and Thompson — Capt. Chandler — An Order — Dress Parade — 123d Ohio — Sweeney of "C" — Gen. Sigel — Capt. Potter — Lieut. Lincoln — The Pioneers — Our Cook Houses — Lieut. Macomber — The Sutler — A Detail — An unofficial Note — Capt. Soley and Lieut. Hall — Capt. Pratt and Lieut. Cobb — Gen. Wheaton — A Story — Marching Orders — Martinsburg and our Patrol — Serg't King.

CHAPTER XXIII.

MARTINSBURG, 227–236

Lieut. Col. Chandler — Capt. F.'s new Uniform — Capt. Bacon — Lieut. Ammidon — Our Camp — Tierney of "A" — A Caution — Our Details — Some Beer — A Storm — Fuller of "F" — Our Standing — Miner in Trouble — Orders — A Parade — Lieut. Lincoln on Duty — Our Sick List — Marching Orders.

CHAPTER XXIV.

ON THE ROAD — AND AT THE FERRY, 236–247

Our March — Its History — Command turned over — An Interview — An Order and a Bivouac — Another Order — In Camp — The Signal Corps — Capt. Pratt — Major Pratt — Capt. Bacon — "Who'll do the Policing?" — Lieut. Elwell — Lieut. Walker — 19th U. S. Colored Troops — Volunteering — More Troops — A fair-sized walking Army Wagon — A Story — A Death in "E" — Gen. Max Webber — Our Neighbors of the 18th Conn. — Our Parade.

CONTENTS. 9

CHAPTER XXV.

HARPER'S FERRY AND MARCH TO MARTINSBURG, 247-259

Our Dogs — Capt. Leach — What's to Pay? — Chaos again — A new Brigade — An Alarm — Our March — Capt. Bacon — An Alarm — Lieut. Murdock — A Joke — In a Muddle — The Col. in Command — Dr. Allen, Surgeon — Another Alarm — An Inspection — Our Parade — "Dispatches, Sir" — A Garrison Review — Marching Orders.

CHAPTER XXVI.

SIGEL'S CAMPAIGN, - - - 259-273

On the Road — Bunker Hill — Muster for Pay — Our Strength — The Country — On the Road again — Winchester — Our Army — Our Transportation — Stripped Naked — "Look at Us now!" — Red Tape — A Drill — Some of our Officers — Our Sick — Major Pratt Detailed — Another Drill — Field of "G" — New Orders — Our Teams.

CHAPTER XXVII.

SIGEL'S CAMPAIGN, 273-280

March to Strasburg — General Orders — Lieut. Macomber — Woodstock — A Halt — Tumbling Creek — Our Sutlers — Our Camp — A queer Story — Roast Veal — The Assembly — A Forced March — Col. Boyd — An Artillery Duel — In Bivouac — Capt. Fox.

CHAPTER XXVIII.

BATTLE OF NEW MARKET, - 280-292

Col. Moore and Orders — Companies B and I, Capt. Potter — Line of Battle — Capt. Chauncey — Col. Wells — Company G, Capt. Leach — A Charge — Our Dogs — Lieut. R. W. Walker — The Enemy Staggered — 54th Pennsylvania — An Order to Retreat — Bacon's Voice was Heard — Our Left Flank and Rear — The Color Company — Lieut. Col. Lincoln — The Retreat — Col. Wells' Report — From Gen. Imboden's Report — Strength of the Opposing Parties, and their respective Losses — Our own Casualties — Letter of Major Pratt — How came the Disaster? — Sigel's Removal — Rhudes Hill — Detail of our March in Retreat — In Camp at Cedar Creek — In Advance — Major Pratt in Command — Adj't Woods.

CHAPTER XXIX.

GEN. HUNTER IN COMMAND, 282-299

General Orders — Inspection — Marching Orders — A Frolic and an Incident — An Advance — Our Wounded at Mt. Jackson — Rhudes Hill — Our Strength — New Market — Mrs. Rupert — Our Dead — The Battle Field — Foraging — Lieut. Platt — Harrisonburg — Our Wounded — The Hospital Supplied and Robbed — Signalling — Marching Orders — Line of March — A Train of Wagons Burned — Port Republic — In Bivouac.

CHAPTER XXX.

HUNTER'S EXPEDITION, 299-305

Battle of Piedmont — Our Colors — Terrible Loss — A Charge — Company I — Our Loss — An Incident or Two — A Man of "E" — Two of "F's" Men — Gallant Conduct of Lieut Elwell — After the Battle — A March — Staunton — On the Road — Our Wounded — Property Destroyed — Gens. Crook and Averill — Col. Wells and the 1st Brigade — Col. Moore — The 34th, Capt. Thompson — Assignment of Officers to Duty.

CHAPTER XXXI.

HUNTER'S RAID, - - - 305-310

Destruction of Property — Finn of "A" — On the Road — Our Destination — A Supply Train — Fairfax — On the Road again — Our Columns — Near Lexington — In Bivouac — Crossing the James — Our Camp — Property Destroyed — This Region — The Weather — Re-enforced — The Work of Destruction — Gen. Duffie — Marching Orders — Our Route — Our Bivouac — A little Foraging — On the Way — Liberty — The River — Encamped.

CHAPTER XXXII.

HUNTER'S RAID, 310-317

On the Road—Lynchburg—Averill—Crook—Our Work—In Bivouac—An Advance—Gen. Breckenridge and some Telegrams—The Enemy—Fortifying—We are Roused—The Ball Opened—Our Scouts and Skirmishers—Gen. Early and his Corps—We are not Whipped—Our Hands Full—Major Pratt's Letter—Our Loss—In Retreat—Lieut. Goodrich—A Night March—Liberty—A Skirmish—Our Orders—On the Road to Salem—Suffering—Allowed to Rest—The Column in Motion—The Prospect Ahead—Our March Interrupted—We Halt—Crook's Rear Guard—Our Train—Newcastle—Guerilla Attack—Some One had Blundered—A pretty good March—An hour's Halt—On the Road again—In Camp—We rest, for a wonder—A leisurely March—Encamped again.

CHAPTER XXXIII.

HUNTER'S RAID, 317-322

A Wagon Guard—Sweet Springs—A good Rest—Our Camp—Red Sweet Springs On the Road—White Sulphur Springs—On Short Rations—Five Dollars for a Hard Tack—Green River—A Ford—Major Pratt's Letter—On the Road—Meadow Bluffs—A Halt—A Ration of Meat—A Halt—A Heartache—Big Sewall Mountains—Up with Headquarters—"How the Boys are Cheering!"—Actual Starvation—On the Way again—A Rain—In Camp—An agreeable Change—"It seems hard!"—On the Road—Gauley Mountain—Hawk's Nest—The Enemy—Gauley Bridge—Fording.

CHAPTER XXXIV.

HUNTER'S RAID, 322-325

We Breathe Easier—Our Camp—An Incident—"The Critter rode extremely well"—Major Pratt's Letter—Serg't Blake's Letter.

CHAPTER XXXV.

HUNTEY'S RAID, 325-331

At Rest—Our Rolls—Marching again—Camp Piatt—Sad News—On the Kanawha and Ohio—Looking Back—An occasion for Discipline—"Guns must Shine!"—Plundering—A notable Instance—"It means War!"—On the River—By Rail to Cherry Run—The Command—Orders.

CHAPTER XXXVI.

THE RACE GROUND, 331-338

On the March—Our Camp—On the March again—A glad Welcome—In Camp—Harper's Ferry—Old Friends—In Motion again—To Knoxville and Hillsboro—Skirmishing—Orders from Gen. Crook—Resting—To Snickersville—A Sharp Engagement—Our Loss—A Blunder—Cross the River again—To Winchester—Manœuvring—Off for Martinsburg—Skirmishing—A Duel—"I did n't hit him!"

CHAPTER XXXVII.

THE RACE GROUND, 338-344

Boonsboro—In Camp—On the Road—In Camp—No Rest—At Halltown—A Drill not laid down in "Casey"—Something Wrong—To Burkettsville—In Camp at Wolfsburg—The Heat—Our Strength—The Monocacy—Capt. Potter—An Execution—Marching Orders—The Weather—Knox's Ford—Paid Off—Berryville—In Camp—Front Royal—On the March—Middletown—Skirmishing—In for it again.

CHAPTER XXXVIII.

THE RACE GROUND, 344-348

Skirmishing again—In Camp—To Winchester again—To Berryville and Charleston—In Camp—Some Red Tape—Major Pratt—News of Col. Lincoln's Escape—Marching Orders—More Skirmishing—Off for Halltown—Another Skirmish—A Barricade—Charlie Thurman—A Reconnoisance.

CONTENTS.   11

CHAPTER XXXIX.

THE RACE GROUND,   348-352
Our Rolls — "Feeling Tip-top" — To Berryville — A Skirmish — More Skirmishing — Hard at Work — Everybody Cross and Ugly — More Cheerful — Marching Orders — At Summit Point — On the Move again — Unpleasant Weather — Weather Mixed — Weather Pleasant — All sorts of Weather — Weather continues the same — Foraging — Gen. Sheridan — Leave to go in.

CHAPTER XL.

THE BATTLE OF THE OPEQUAN,   352-360
Movement of Troops — Our men dismissed to boil their coffee — The Battle Field — The Sound of Battle — Discussing the Situation — "Don't be Impatient!" — Our Call — Encounter the Enemy — Standing Ready — We join in the Charge — And drive the Enemy — Changing Direction — The Field in our Front — An Advance in Line — We march right on — "Lie down! Lie down!" — "That was a close shave, boys!" — "It seemed an age!" — "Forward! It was Forward!" — Capt. Thompson — From our Cover — Parker of "I" — A Lieutenant of Dupont's Battery — An Advance — The day was warm — The Cavalry — Crook's Command — It was twilight — In Bivouac — Capt. Soley — Col. Wells — Major Pratt — Lieut. Col. Wilds — Capt. Chamberlain — Lieuts. Dissoway and Cobb — Our Loss.

CHAPTER XLI.

THE BATTLE OF THE OPEQUAN,   360-365
Some Incidents — Col. Harris and Capt. Soley — Capt. Elwell — Hines and Burnham — Hospital Steward Fairbanks — Dr. Smith — A brother of Capt. Thompson.

CHAPTER XLII.

THE BATTLE OF FISHER'S HILL,   365-371
Marching Orders — Cedar Creek — In Bivouac — Strasburg — Fisher's Hill — Gaining Position — Crook's Command — Its Movement — In Position — The Attack — The Rebel Earthworks — The Fighting — The Work Done — Trophies — The Charge — The 34th — Col. Wells — Our Loss — An Accident — Death of Major Pratt — Our Work — On the March — In Camp — On the Move Again — Harrisonburg — Our Duty There — Down the Valley — The Work of Destruction — In Camp at Cedar Creek — A Reconnoisance — No Hostile Force Near.

CHAPTER XLIII.

THE RECONNOISANCE,   371-376
Boom! Boom! — A New Kind of Salute — Under Arms — The Rebel Force — The Ground Marched Over — How it Seemed — Outflanked — Orders to Retreat — Col. Wells Wounded — Lieut. Cobb — Surrender of Capt. Willard — Col. Wells' Death — Gen. Early — Lieuts. Cobb and Cailigan — Libby Prison — Gen. Thoburn — A Late Commission — Our Loss — A Flag of Truce — Capt. Elwell's Letter — An Army Correspondent — Another Reconnoisance.

CHAPTER XLIV.

BATTLE OF CEDAR CREEK,   376-380
Disposition and Movement of the Rebel Troops — The Surprise — Our Route — The 19th Corps — Further Retreat — The 6th Corps — A Scene of Confusion — Matters when Sheridan Rode up — An Advance along the Whole Line — The Charge Successful — The Cavalry — Arms Stacked — Our Loss.

CHAPTER XLV.

CEDAR CREEK,   380-385
Capts. Soley and Dr. Smith — Old Zeke — Our Lost Marker — The 34th — On the Opequan — Our Oct. and Nov. Rolls — A New Flag — Marching Orders — On the Way — Aikens Landing.

CHAPTER XLVI.

BEFORE RICHMOND, 385–390

24th Army Corps — Our Condition — Lieut. Col. Potter — Capt. Leach — Our Duty — Our December Rolls — Clothing — Our January Rolls — Our February Rolls — General Orders — The Corps Badge — Renewed Activity — On the March — Sheridan's Troops — Our Route to Hatcher's Run — Entrenching — Skirmishing — Our Loss — More Skirmishing — Our Strength.

CHAPTER LXVII.

BEFORE RICHMOND, - - 390–393

First of April — Battery Gregg — The Assault — Our Loss — Lieut. Rowley's Letter — The evacuation of Petersburg — On the March — A Halt — General Orders behind Richmond.

CHAPTER XLVIII.

BEHIND RICHMOND, 393–396

On the Rebel Flank — Rice's Station — A Skirmish — Col. Kellogg — Our Loss — Farmsville — Double Quick — A White Flagg — The Surrender — In Camp — Gen. Devens — From a Richmond Paper.

CHAPTER XLIX.

TO LYNCHBURG AND RICHMOND, - - 396–400

Appomatox Station — Marching Orders — Lynchburg — Col. Potter — Property Destroyed — On the Road Again — Richmond — Reception — Col. Lincoln — Our Camp — Muster out of our Officers — April Returns — Our Duties — Rebel Flags — Surrender of Rebels — Disabled Men — Seine Fishing.

CHAPTER L.

IN RICHMOND, - 400–407

Honors to the 5th Corps — Postponed — Our Picket Detail — Capt. Chauncey — Paying Honors — The Army of the Potomac — Custer's Division of Sheridan's Cavalry — Sherman's Army — Gen. Gibbon, and his Order — An Avalanche of Orders — Billet Doux — Preparations for our Muster Out — An Arrest of a Man of E — Our Recruits — Visitors — New Clothing — Our Strength.

CHAPTER LI.

IN RICHMOND, - - 407–414

Orders for Promotion — Our Examining Board — A Division Review — The Weather — Order for Corps Review — Our March — Order Countermanded — Bronze Medals — Our Recruits — Our Rolls — An Act of Insubordination — Court Martial — Walsh of A — A Corps Review — Presentation of Medals — Farewell of Maj. Gen. Gibbon.

CHAPTER LII.

JOURNEY HOME AND DISCHARGE, 414–421

Our Muster Out — On the Journey — Our Recruits — Down the James — Baltimore — Philadelphia and Breakfast — Our Surgeon and his Horse — New York — Hon. D. W. Lincoln — Our route Onward — Our Parting — Providence — Gen. Burnside — Readville — Gen. Pierce — Quarters Assigned — Theory and Practice — Regimental General Order — Our Losses — Assembly at Readville — Final Pay — One Exception — Discharge and Final Adieus — The White Flag — Acknowledgments to Medical Staff, Quartermaster, Adjutant.

ERRATA.

The worst are particularized below:

Page 15, "Charles W." should read Charles *H*. Howland.
Page 129, a "Non-commissioned" should read a *promising* recruit.
Page 190, "three to four hundred" should read *three to four thousand*.
Page 228, "2d Lieut Cutter" should read 2d Lieut. *Cutler*.
Page 286, In Imboden's report, the "13th" should read the 18*th* Regiment.
Page 387, "F. W. Van Loan" should read *L.* W. Van Loan.
Page 394, the word "*Filing*," on the 11th line should precede the word *to*, on the 10th line.
Page 401, hurried and "hasty" should read hurried and *hearty*.
Page 409, omit, in the 26th line, the words "the result of."

CHAPTER I

ORGANIZATION, RENDEZVOUS, ETC.

THE promulgation of General Order No. 17, Headquarters, Boston, May 29th, 1862, while it communicated, officially, to the People of this State, the fact that "a call had been made "upon the Commonwealth, by the President of the United "States, for thirty Companies of Infantry, to serve for three "years, or during the war;" also made known that "ten of "these companies will go to compose the 34th Regiment," "which will be recruited in the Counties of Worcester, Hamp- "den, Hampshire, Franklin, and Berkshire, and will go into "Camp at the Agricultural Fair Grounds, near the City of "Worcester; said camp to be designated Camp John E. Wool, "in honor of Major General Wool, of the U. S. army."

The order provided for the selection and commissioning of the line officers by His Excellency; directed the immediate recruiting of the men; gave directions as to the character, and amount of expenses which would be allowed; as to the transportation of recruits to camp; the procurement of all necessary blanks and papers; the age of recruits, the formalities attending the enlistment of minors—and announced that the officer to command the camp would be designated by subsequent Special Order. On the 3d day of June, by "Special Order," said Headquarters, William S. Lincoln, of the City of Worcester, was designated and appointed Lieutenant Colonel of the 34th Regiment; and directed to assume command of said Camp John E. Wool; to use his utmost exertions for the speedy organization of said regiment; and for that purpose, he was authorized to make requisitions upon the Adjutant General for such camp "equipage, clothing, subsistence, and transportation, as he might require, and as was provided in General Order, No. 17, present series."

Clothed with this authority, after a personal interview with his Excellency, Lieutenant Colonel Lincoln addressed himself to the task before him. There were upon the files of the Executive Department at the State House, letters from gentlemen, in many towns of the territory within which the regiment was required to be raised, the writers of which asked to be commissioned in the service, and pledged themselves, in case their wishes were granted, to forward to camp without delay, some whole companies, others, more limited number of Volunteers. Letters were at once written, and forwarded to these gentlemen, and correspondence opened with others, with a view to secure their influence and services in the work. Charles W Elwell, of Greenfield, who was met at the State House, whither he had gone with a modest request to be allowed to recruit for the regiment, *without* exacting promise of reward, was given the authority he sought, and was the first person actually at work. Applicants for such authority crowded fast upon the heels of each other, and in a very short space of time, a competent force was engaged. At the outset it was deemed best to confine each officer to a certain specified territory, within which the recruits for his particular company were to be secured; but the repeated complaints that these territorial limits were disregarded in the zeal to obtain volunteers, soon led to the countermanding of the order, and thereafter recruiting went on without reference to town or county lines.

Authority to recruit for the regiment was given every person who applied therefor, but each was distinctly informed that success in securing a given number of Volunteers would not, *of itself*, entitle the party to a commission. On the other hand, *all* were made to understand that they would, in turns, be called into camp after it was opened, and that the granting of commissions to any rank would depend largely upon their ability to drill, discipline and command men. The wisdom of this rule was shown by its practical working. As an instance; among the letters and files in the Executive Department, was one from a worthy gentleman, setting forth his ability to bring into camp at a short notice, a full company of men, and requesting authority to recruit, and also a commission as captain. He received the authority to recruit. Weeks passed, and although aided by two Lieutenants, he had but the merest skeleton of a company. He was called upon to come into camp for duty. Soon after reporting, he was detailed as "officer of the day." "What's this?" asked he of his lieutenant, showing his little triangular billet! "That! that's a detail!" "A detail! and what's a detail?" "why" said E, as he opened it, "this is a detail for you as officer of the day for to-morrow," "Officer of the day! officer of the day! What's that?" and as E began to explain, Captain M's head began to ache, and he took the next train for home, and was never again seen in a camp of the 34th.

Headquarters were established and camp opened, on the 12th day of June, because of representations by the recruiting officers, of the difficulty of holding their men after enlistment, for want of suitable facilities for feeding and housing them. Charles P Trumbull, of Worcester, was appointed Quarter Master Sergeant; and George W Marsh, of Leominster, Commissary Sergeant. By the midnight train from the West, on the next day (13th), Captain Potter, of Pittsfield, reached town with thirty men, and marched them into camp.

Meantime an unpleasant state of affairs existed, in reference to the position of Quarter-Master. This had been offered by the Lieutenant Colonel commanding, to F. B. Rice of Worcester; who, furnished with his letter of appointment, went down to the State House for confirmation, and to be commissioned. But His Excellency had already designated and commissioned Charles W Howland of Plymouth, as such officer, and Mr. Rice returned with such report. Remonstrance was made to His Excellency. It was urged that while the western counties were looked to to furnish the men to compose the regiment, it was but sheer justice that the officers should come from the same territory; and further, that inasmuch as this officer would form a part of the military family of the commanding officer of the regiment, it was his right to designate him. But remonstrance was of no avail, and Rice was subsequently attached, in the same capacity, to the 36th.

Samuel F. Woods of Worcester, was appointed at the same time to be adjutant, and was commissioned accordingly.

On the 17th day of June squad drills were ordered, and guard was mounted at the entrance of the camp. 21 tents were erected. By the 27th of the same month, the number of men had so increased that all the regular duties of camp were initiated.

June 29th. The number of men in camp to-day was between one and two hundred; composing parts of seven companies and occupying forty-three tents. Sentinels were placed around the camp to-day for the first time.

Recruiting, though progressing fairly fast for the season of the year, and in a region so largely agricultural as was this from which the men of the 34th were to be drawn, was yet far too slow for the ardor of the Governor; and tables, prepared by his direction, were, July 7th, issued, showing the number of men each city and town should raise to meet their proportion of the call which had been made upon the State. In addition, the Mayors of cities and Selectmen of towns were authorized to act as recruiting agents, as well for the new organizations as for those already in the field, and were urged to the most strenuous exertions to fill the quotas assigned to them. A premium of $2 was authorized to be paid to every person who should bring in an accepted recruit.

July 2d. To secure more rapid enlistment, *one* month's pay and $25, or one-fourth of the governmental bounty was authorized to be paid to all recruits at the time of their muster in.

7th. Religious services were held in camp to-day for the first time, Rev. Dr. Hill officiating.

10th. Dr. R. R. Clarke, of Whitinsville, was appointed surgeon to the regiment, and ordered to report at camp without delay.

14th. One hundred men were mustered into service to-day by Captain Graham, U. S. A.

For the last week or ten days many public meetings to encourage recruiting have been held, and bounties ($100 generally,) offered to such as would volunteer for the service. Under this stimulus, recruiting has been quite active; and now, the 19th day of July, there were in camp belonging to the 34th, between four and five hundred men. In addition, there were a goodly number enlisted for the 35th, besides some for the 36th regiments, all of which were ordered to report to the commanding officer of the 34th. In all there were sixty-six tents up. Seventy-three recruits, from the town of Westfield, under escort of the Westfield Fire Engine Co., preceded by the Westfield Cornet Band, the whole commanded by Rev. Mr. Bowler, of the same town, caused quite an excitement as they marched through the streets of the city, to camp.

Besides these, twenty-three were received from Pittsfield; twenty-two from Millbury; sixteen from Shirley; eleven from North Adams, and smaller parties from Holyoke, Southbridge and Springfield.

21st. "Lieutenants Lincoln and Cobb are commissioned as mustering officers for the regiment; and henceforth we shall have less difficulty in holding men who repent after enlistment, and run away before we can get a regular officer to muster them."

On the 22d, twenty-two men came in from Westfield; Captain Cooley brought in eighteen from Pittsfield, and sixteen were added to Captain Holden's Company.

Charles B. Cutler, of Worcester, appointed Sergeant Major, reported for duty.

23d. Eighty-six recruits came in to-day from Berkshire County; this, exclusive of forty-five from Pittsfield, for the Allen Guard, Capt. Cooley, In addition, there were eighteen from Grafton, and seventeen from Southbridge; not all of these, however, were for the 34th. We received thirty-two recruits from Spencer, who were escorted by the Leicester Fire Engine Co., preceded by the Leicester Cornet Band, all under command of Luther Hill, Esq., Selectman of that town. After being mustered in, they were assigned to Company E, and given a furlough for a few days to enable them to arrange suitably for their absence.

Captain Potter's Company numbered seventy-five; Captain

H. W Pratt's, (the Worcester Light Infantry), 70, and the Company from Westfield, 70.

The men, although unarmed, were now exercised in movements of the company. We have had in camp for some time, Enfield rifles, which have been sent up for our use; but the Lieutenant Colonel Commanding keeps them boxed up, refusing to issue them until it is established certainly that Springfield rifles cannot be procured.

"Companies A, B, and I, are full; the number of men has so increased (amounting to 600), that battalion drills are ordered.

Some of the recruits from Southbridge were rejected upon examination of our own officers; as the newspapers *will have it,* "for the most trivial defects, *loss of teeth* and *stiff joints of fingers.*"

" For the purpose of encouraging recruiting generally, and
" more especially filling its quota, a public meeting of the citi-
" zens of Worcester was called for the afternoon of this day,
" the 26th. All places of business were closed, many of them
" being profusely decorated with flags; and amidst the firing
" of guns, and the ringing of bells, thousands gathered on the
" public common. The Mayor called the meeting to order;
" spirited and eloquent addresses were made by Governor
" Andrew, Hon. A. H. Bullock, John B. Gough, and others.
" Colonel Wells, late of the 1st Massachusetts, who had come to
" the city to visit the regiment, which, it is understood he is to
" command, was introduced to the meeting, and received with
" loud and hearty cheers. In his address the Colonel alluded to
" the losses in the old regiments, as the result, not so much of
" disease and battle, as of what *he called* the *wasting processes.*
" Men in the first regiments were not examined with sufficient
" care, and have been sent home because of physical disability,
" which should have caused their rejection."

Aug. 1st. Owing to the influence of the many public meetings held in the different towns, and to the activity of the municipal officers, recruiting has been going on with great success, and during the past few days large accessions have been made to the regiment. The number reported to-day was nine hundred and twenty. But there has been greater zeal shown to fill the quotas assigned to the various towns, than judgment displayed in selecting the recruits, who are sent into camp. This has operated hardly upon the officers of the organization, and subjected them to a great deal of *undeserved* censure. For instance, a man who had enlisted in another regiment early in the war, who became crazy, and had been committed to a hospital for the insane in August 1861, being discharged therefrom only about four months ago, was rejected by the proper regimental officers, after examination. This was spoken of in the daily press as an *unwarranted* stretch of *authority*, and the case was described as that of a man who, "from the effects of a slow fever, had been *for a few days out of his mind*." Again the same authority stated that "*half* of the Westfield Volunteers, and some thirty of those from Pittsfield, had been rejected;" while the truth was that but *three* of the Pittsfield men were rejected, and those, not by the Medical, but by the mustering officers; while *all* of the Westfield recruits, *save one who had "snakes in his boots,"* were accepted. Again, it was charged that "Granby raised her full quota of eleven men, and sent them to Worcester last week, and had eight men rejected by the "*numbskull examiner;*" while in fact, only *four from Granby* had presented themselves to the proper officers of the regiment, *all* of whom had been accepted.

The "*man of the snakes*, is causing us some trouble. Rejected by us, after a careful examination, he tramped over the highways to his home, and was taken by the town authority to Boston, where he was presented to the Governor, as a man who was anxious to enlist, but "*whom the 34th wouldn't have*." The Lieutenant Colonel commanding was summoned to headquarters for explanation. The truth of the whole matter was this: On one side was the surgeon, a man of mature judgment, of long practice, of acknowledged professional skill, and in good repute; who had had experience in the army, and knew the wants of the service; and who knew well that many men who enlisted in the first regiments, were unfit for duty, when they were mustered in; and that they were discharged for disabilities which existed at the time of their enlistment, after the government had sheltered, paid, doctored, nursed and fed them for months.

"There is perfect accord in this matter, among the officers who are charged with the duty of raising the regiment; and the course adopted in examining and accepting recruits, will be adhered to as long as the responsibility rests upon them."

21st. Two men, *accepted* by the Regimental Officers, were rejected to-day by Captain Cooley, U. S. A. mustering officer, after examination. Instead of "*snakes in their boots,*" they had "*fits.*"

We had two recruits to-day, from territory assigned to the 33d Regiment. They are brothers and were admitted to this regiment by virtue of a special dispensation in their favor, issued from the office of the Adjutant General of the State. "They would not enlist in the 33d, and unless they could have "a *situation* in the 34th, would remain at home." Inasmuch as the situation they stipulated for was merely a place in the *ranks of a good company*, there was no difficulty in acceding to their wishes. They are good looking, well meaning, but somewhat *queer;* and have reported with a goodly supply of *citizen's* clothing, a nice, *large iron bound trunk* and a *new cotton umbrella* for each.

"We are to be in readiness to move next week. Our mustering officer pronounces "the 34th to be the finest looking body of men ever organized into a regiment in this State; they being "*all picked men,* selected with care, after a rigid examination." This commendation, by one who knows of what he speaks, goes far to satisfy the examining and mustering officers of the regiment of the wisdom of the course adopted by them."

6th. The regiment was reviewed to-day by the Governor, who was accompanied by the members of his staff, and Colonel Wells. Meanwhile the men are still unarmed. The Enfield rifles are still unpacked, and another attempt is being made to exchange them for those of Springfield make.

12th. "The day has been an eventful one to us, marked as it was, by the presentation of a national flag to the regiment, by our lady friends in the city. The delivery was prefaced by an eloquent address from Hon. Alexander H. Bullock. The flag was received by the Colonel with appropriate remarks, and, as it was given to the hands of the color bearer the regiment welcomed it with hearty cheers. Hon. Judge Russell took advantage of the opportunity to present to the Colonel a horse, suitably caparisoned, the gift of his friends and late associates of the "Boston Bar." While the men were embodied, "Orders" were promulgated directing the regiment to march to-morrow. "Even now the Enfield rifles are in their boxes and the men without arms; but the Springfield guns are on the way to us, and upon their receipt to-night, will be at once distributed."

13*th*. The regiment did not move to-day, as ordered. Tents were struck, camp and garrison equipage was upon teams; much of it had, in fact, been delivered at the railroad station; every needed preparation had been completed, and the men *in line*, ready to march, when, at 2 P. M., a special order was received, countermanding the movement. Precisely the reason for this, nobody seems to know, though gossip has it, that the 33d couldn't get ready, and it wasn't quite "*en regle*" to allow the 34th to precede it. Probably this does not fully account for it. As the men were embodied, the opportunity was improved, and the first "Dress Parade" of the regiment was had.

14*th*. Had we moved yesterday, as ordered, "the boys" would have been compelled to march away, carrying with them the broken promises of the Government. "As it is now, everything is right." The pay master arrived after our line was dismissed, and paid off six companies of the regiment, and is now engaged in paying the remaining four companies. "We of the Field and Staff, are to live a while longer *on faith*, as there is no money for *us*." Notwithstanding, we move to-morrow according to orders just received.

The following is our muster roll of officers:

FIELD AND STAFF.

Colonel, GEORGE D. WELLS.
Lieut. Colonel, WILLIAM S. LINCOLN.
Major, HENRY BOWMAN.
1st Lieutenant, SAMUEL F. WOODS, *Adjutant*.
1st Lieutenant, CHARLES H. HOWLAND, *Quarter Master*.
Major, ROUSE R. CLARKE, *Surgeon*.
1st Lieutenant, WILLIAM THORNDIKE, *1st. Assist. Surgeon*.
1st Lieutenant, CYRUS B. SMITH, *2d Assist. Surgeon*.
EDWARD B. FAIRCHILD, *Chaplain*.

NON-COMMISSIONED STAFF.

Sergeant Major, CHARLES B. CUTLER.
Quartermaster Sergeant, CHARLES P. TRUMBULL.
Commissary Sergeant, GEORGE W MARSH.

LINE OFFICERS.

Co. A.
HARRISON W. PRATT, *Captain*.
JOHN A. LOVELL, 1st *Lieut*.
ROBERT W. WALKER, 2d *Lieut*.

Co. B.
ANDREW POTTER, *Captain*.
WILLIAM L. COBB, 1st *Lieut*.
LaFAYETTE BUTLER, 2d *Lieut*.

Co. C.
ALONZO D. PRATT, *Captain*.
FRANK T. LEACH, 1st *Lieut*.
HENRY BACON, 2d *Lieut*.

Co. D.
GEORGE W THOMPSON, *Captain*.
JAMES W. SMITH, 1st *Lieut*.
J. AUSTIN LYMAN, 2d *Lieut*.

Co. E.
WILLIAM B. BACON, *Captain*.
GEORGE MACOMBER, 1st *Lieut*.
LEVI LINCOLN, JR., 2d *Lieut*.

Co. F.
———— ———— *Captain*.
CHARLES W ELWELL, 1st *Lt. C'g*.
THOMAS W RIPLEY, 2d *Lieut*.

Co. G.
———— ———— *Captain*.
CHAUNCY R. CHAUNCY, 1st *Lt .C'g*.
JERRE HORTON, 2d *Lieut*.

Co. H.
HENRY P. FOX, *Captain*.
ALBERT C. WALKER, 1st *Lieut*.
MALCOLM AMMIDON, 2d *Lieut*.

Co. I.
DANIEL HOLDEN, *Captain*.
ALEXIS C. SOLEY, 1st *Lieut*.
GEORGE E. GOODRICH, 2d *Lieut*.

Co. K.
WILLIAM H. COOLEY, *Captain*.
LYMAN W VAN LOAN, 1st *Lieut*.
SAMUEL H. PLATT, 2d *Lieut*.

15th. We have eaten the goodly and bountiful collation furnished for us by our Lady friends of the city, and with hearts stirred by varied feelings have said our last "*good byes,*" and now stand in line for the last time upon our Camp ground, 1,027 strong. We wait only for the appearance of our Colonel to move. Preceded by a band of music, we are to march in column of companies, to "*the Common,*" where we are to take transportation for Washington. Our route through the city is by way of Agricultural, Elm, Chestnut, Harvard, and Main Streets. The " Spy " shall tell the story : —

" Along its whole march, the Regiment was greeted by the
" waving of handkerchiefs, and by hearty hurrahs, and by all
" the evidences of profound sympathy, and universal admira-
" tion which men receive who enter a contest by all their coun-
" try's wishes blest. Our streets were not thronged as on some
" former occasions, when regiments have left us, only because
" this went off on such short notice. The brief notice also pre-
" vented that full preparation on the part of the railroad
" which would have been had, and which had to do with the
" wearisome delay of the troops on the Common. All thought
" the officers of the regiment, on the whole, made a creditable
" appearance. Of the Lieutenant-Colonel [Lincoln], no word is
" required in Worcester. In courage and conduct, he will never
" be wanting; nor would we omit a reference to Captain H. W
" Pratt of Company A, another of our citizens. He won
" laurels, as Captain of the Infantry, in the three month's ser-
" vice, and has always been true to every occasion since. Such
" a past is a guaranty for the future. Major Bowman has also
" been tried by battle, and the severe ordeal of the prison.
" His promotion is conclusive of the honorable manner in which
" he endured both, and also of his military ability. The
" Colonel [Wells] too, seemed the right man in the right place.
" The universal feeling is, that he has really earned the place he
" holds. Where there is fighting to be done, we know, and his
" men know he will be there. He knows also, we have good
" reason to believe, that he has under him a body of men worthy
" of a brave and high-souled leader. That God's blessing may
" be upon him and them, is the fervent prayer of every loyal
" heart."

The delay upon the common above alluded to was trying in the extreme, and withal, in a degree demoralizing. Well wishing and sympathetic friends crowded upon the ranks, in too many instances distributing "pocket pistols" loaded with ammunition not prescribed in the service. Quarter-Master McKim of the United States, and Reed and Brigham of the State service, were present to see to our embarkation. There was disagreement between these officers and those of the railroad, as to the manner of our transportation; the former desiring to divide the train, the latter insisting that the regiment should be forwarded in *one* line of cars. Quarter-Master Brigham *cut the knot* by separating the first nine cars, and at once dispatching them, having on board the right wing, under charge of the Lieutenant-Colonel. The remainder of the regiment followed close behind. The run to Norwich, and by steamer across the sound, was rapid, pleasant, and easy; the men, with very few exceptions, being quiet and orderly. In the darkness of the night, Finn, of A., took French leave of us sometime between leaving the cars at Norwich and embarking on the boat. As we passed by the cities of Brooklyn and New York, the whistles of the boats on the water and cheers from the throngs which crowded the banks of the East river, and the various tug and ferry boats were enough to frighten the living and waken the dead. Gliding steadily on, we reached our dock at Jersey City and disembarked without delay. Here a long line of close box cars was drawn up to receive us, and clambering up, and in, we were soon again on our way. All through New Jersey our passage was greeted by hearty cheers. Philadelphia was reached in the afternoon. The regiment was warmly received and cordially welcomed at the "Cooper's shop refreshment rooms," where its members were greatly refreshed by baths and supper. At 9 P. M., through streets darkened by clouds of dust, we marched to the Baltimore depot, and seating ourselves again in box cars, were sped on our way. Bivouac fires along the track, and picket posts at bridges, and switches, served to remind us of the existence of war.

Early on the morning of the 17th we reached Baltimore,

and, disembarking at the President Street depot, formed column of companies, and, to the horrid rub-a-dub of our untrained drum corps, made our way across the city by the route made memorable by the massacre of the 19th of April of the last year. It was as if it were a city of the dead. There were no greetings, no cheers, nothing to break the silence which became oppressive. No flags waved from house-tops, or windows. Hardly a white person was seen on this long line of march. Lieutenant Lincoln, in command of the rear guard, was occasionally lost sight of, and some little anxiety was occasioned thereby. But we experienced no interruption, and in due time reached the Washington depot. The regiment here received an invitation to breakfast, which was accepted; and at its close our Colonel received another invitation, this time to make a requisition upon the Government Quartermaster for the breakfast which we had been invited to, which *he* also accepted, although a little ungraciously. Again we *packed* into *still worse* box cars than any occupied before, and were moved on our last stage to the Capital.

Our train was a long one, and the engine of insufficient power, and we failed occasionally to make the up grades. While the engine was stopping at one of these grades, as the boys said "to catch breath," *bedlam broke loose*. While in camp Wool, many of the boys, disregarding friendly warning, had spent their money in purchasing revolvers, and now amused themselves by a little target practice, firing from the doors and the roofs of the cars.

"Sergeant Major," said Colonel Wells, "give my compliments to the officer of the day, and tell him to go through this train and confiscate every pistol he can find in the possession of an enlisted man." The fusilade ceased suddenly, and gradually a large pile of weapons, of every imaginable pattern, was gathered, to be stored by the Quarter-Master.

CHAPTER II.

WASHINGTON, ARLINGTON AND ALEXANDRIA.

Washington was reached in the afternoon, and the regiment quartered for the night at the "Soldier's home." The next day, to the music of the "Marine Band," in heavy marching order, we moved to our destined camp of instruction in Virginia. On our passage by Willard's, we paid to General Corcoran of the 69th New York, who had just returned from imprisonment in Libbey, the honor of a marching salute. We halted to be addressed by him. Here we parted with Major Bowman, who not having been yet exchanged, declined to go farther. Soon resuming our march, we passed over Long Bridge, where the band was dismissed, and in the heat, and through clouds of dust, which nearly stifled us, late in the evening reached our camping ground. Lieut. Lincoln, with the rear guard, impressing into service a goodly number of hackney carriages, for the transportation of those who from the heat and dust couldn't or wouldn't walk, had hard duty to bring up the stragglers, and harder still to get rid of the *jehus* whose teams had been impressed. Tired and dirty, we closed to half distance, stacked arms, and spread our blankets for our first night's bivouac. Assistant Surgeon Thorndike caused no little merriment, as starting from his blanket in the dead of the night he enquired *if his office bell didn't ring.*

Tuesday, Aug. 19th. Tents are ordered to be pitched; the order of the camp, conforming to the restricted space assigned to us. We are near "Hunter's Chapel" so called; upon ground occupied by the rebel pickets, immediately after Bull Run, about midway between Arlington, and Munson's Hill. Blenker's division was encamped here last winter, living in a sort of dog kennel fashion, in holes, dug some two or three feet deep in the ground, into which they must have *crawled.* The roofing having been removed, the eye falls upon an accumulation of rubbish and filth perfectly indescribable. The country around presents a picture of utter desolation. Houses in ruins, fruit trees stripped of foliage and bark by animals which have been picketed among them; acres upon acres of forest trees, with their bare limbs and brown trunks, are tangled in inextricable confusion, as they were felled to clear the range for the guns mounted upon the neighboring fortifications.

Here is to be established a camp of instruction, (called camp Casey,) to which all new regiments from the East are to be ordered for drill and discipline. In our front, are already three Pennsylvania regiments, and one from New York; on our left is our own 33d.

Our first business is to police the ground, and squads are detailed for that purpose, as also to dig wells; those formerly existing having been filled up by these Dutchmen, at their departure. There is *no water* within a mile and a half of our camp.

19*th*. The work of cleaning our position, and getting into comfortable condition still goes on. Everybody, apparently, is bringing into camp *boards* to floor their tents, some procuring them by purchase, others not quite so legitimately. Lean, lank, gaunt visaged Virginians are thronging headquarters with complaints of depredations upon their premises.

All work is stopped by receipt of orders to march in the morning, with two days cooked rations.

At dress parade, Colonel Green of our 14th, and General Whipple were present, and complimented us upon our appearance.

20*th*. The colonel, who left for Washington immediately upon receipt of yesterday's marching orders, returned early this morning, accompanied by Maj. Bowman, who has been duly exchanged and transferred to the command of our 36th. The order for us to move is countermanded. This, upon the representation of Colonel Wells, and Maggi, of the 33d,—which regiment was included in the order — that raw, undisciplined, and undrilled as are the men of both commands, it would be little less than murder to send us into action.

21st. Orders to march at once for Alexandria, there to take transportation for Catlett's station, reporting to General Banks, were received during the night, and this morning, all is bustle. Tents are struck, wagons loaded, ammunition distributed— that is, *all we had*—forty rounds of ball cartridges to a man, for by some singular fate, we find ourselves almost in the face of the enemy, *without a percussion cap.* We march; first despatching the Quarter-master to Washington, with a requisition for this indispensible part of a soldier's equipment. Winding among the ravines, our flag betrays our origin, and as we pass fort or encampment, the men of the different commands exchange hearty cheers.

We reached Alexandria soon after noon: the boys suffering much from the combined heat and dust; a few falling by the way; and the colonel rode to the city to report in person our arrival. There was much lamentation at being compelled to leave our lumber, at least so much of it as had been paid for; the officers of company F being chief mourners.

22d. The night has passed unconfortably enough, the boys lying upon their arms, on the embankment of the railroad, and the officers seeking the cover of box cars, or our own wagons, parked near by. A mule corral was in close neighborhood, and to judge by the noise it was "full opera" night with the animals. One of the line officers, Lieutenant E. tells his experience of the night, thus. It commenced to rain, and as he had no *umbrella*, he crawled under one of the wagons for shelter. Rolling up in his blanket, with a stick of wood for a pillow, and getting into a little hollow, into which he just fitted, he was, after a while, lulled to sleep. Waking in the morning, he found himself hemmed in by a fellow lodger on each side. "A man and a brother" lay snoring in front, and behind, a large dog was curled up against him. With his sword, the Lieutenant rapped the darkey across his shins, who, starting up with a howl, crawled hastily from the cover of the wagon, closely followed by the Lieutenant and dog. As they confronted each other, the darkey's eyes opened, he screeched out, "Lord *God, it's an ossifer!*" and, with one bound disappeared round an adjoining building, the dog, however, a little ahead.

Reveille call showed that some of the boys were absent, and Lieutenant G. was detailed, with a small party to patrol the neighboring streets, and arrest any of the regiment whom he might find. Coming across one of B's men who refused to halt when ordered, the Lieutenant fired, wounding the man slightly, and brought him into camp upon the arms of his party. A great deal of excitement was caused by the act, and arms were seized, and loud threats made by the men. But the drums were ordered to beat "to the color," "fall in" was shouted by officers, line was formed, and discipline prevailed. Tents were now ordered to be pitched, camp guard was mounted, and all became quiet. A large force, under the command of the Lieutenant Colonel, was now dispatched to patrol the neighboring streets and close all places where intoxicating liquors could be procured.

Late in the evening the Quartermaster returned from Washington, with a supply of percussion caps for our muskets, and we learned from him, that the rebels raided upon Catlett's Station last night, capturing the baggage and part of Head Quarters staff, and killing or taking prisoners most of the guard at that point.

What an escape for us! Had transportation been furnished for us upon our arrival here, we should have been *there without the means of firing a shot.*

23*d.* Our orders to report to General Banks are still in force; but we are furnished no transportation. We have moved out from Alexandria, about three miles, and are encamped near Cloud's mills, directly upon the line of the railroad. On our left flank, stands Fort Ward; to our right, is Fort Ellsworth; while on our right, but in the rear rises Fort Lyon, largest and most formidable of the three. A corn field in our rear furnishes the only sign of cultivation within sight. From this, in spite of the protestations of the owner, our boys draw their supply of *roasting ears and potatoes.* Regimental General Orders, "Camp Worcester," directs squad and company drill in the morning; Battalion drill to be followed by dress parade, for every afternoon.

26*th.* Regimental General Orders require in future *all*

Line officers to be present at reveille and tattoo roll calls, and when not actually engaged on other duty, at *all drills*. Two days rations of hardtack and cooked meat to be kept in haversacks, and forty rounds of ball cartridges, with ample supply of caps in the cartridge boxes. At each roll call, the men are to appear fully armed and equipped; and commanders of companies are to make *personal* inspection of arms, equipments, cartridge boxes, cap pouches and haversacks, previous to each day's parade.

We are required to furnish a daily detail of two full Companies, for patrol duty in Alexandria, and one Company is detailed for our own camp guard.

We are now completely surrounded by the veterans of the Army of the Peninsula, who have gathered round us for the past few days. The railroad is occupied by long trains, and the turnpike beyond constantly clouded by dust from columns of troops moving slowly out to Centerville and Manassas. In the evening the scene to our front is indescribably beautiful. Every hill and valley is sparkling with bivouac fires. The signal lights which rise far to the front and are repeated from station to station, till met by answering flashes from the great dome of the Capitol, throw a veil of enchantment over the whole scene. The songs of the men in near by encampments, are loud and harsh, but from far off bivouac fall upon the ear, sweet and mellow.

The 15th Massachusetts marched by this afternoon, and is in bivouac about a mile to our front. Some of our officers have gone out to give their acquaintances greeting. In the ranks they found Captain B's brother Frank, whom they brought back with them; without shoes, stockings or shirt, having had nothing to eat for the last three days but two pieces of hard tack, his condition was pitiable. But he was the same gallant, plucky fellow he ever was, and with his necessities supplied from our stores, he went his way in good spirits.

28*th*. Our drills, which of necessity were suspended by the occupation of all available ground by McClellan's army, are now resumed, though under difficulties, as the many dead horses and mules which lie festering on the ground, form "obstacles in front," and the innumerable sinks give occasion for frequent movements by the flank.

Lieutenant Colonel Underwood, with Lieutenant Vose, and Colonel Maggi with Captain Wyman, all of them belonging to our 33d, made us a visit to-day, and looked over our camp. The two latter remained to sup with the Field and Staff. Of course, discussion followed upon the events of the last few days, and naturally enough, opinions differed as to the merits and general capacity of the late and present commanders of our army. Wells, an ardent friend and warm admirer of the present one, was thoroughly convinced that now matters would all go smoothly and well; while Maggi was equally sure that "McClellan was not fit to hold a Corporal's warrant in the 33d."

31st. We were all a good deal excited yesterday by the heavy canonading in front, which continued all day, the last report being heard about 8 P. M.; and the marching and countermarching of troops by our camp for the past day or two has given rise to much speculation. Long columns, of all arms, on their way to the front, fairly darkened the "pike," until night before last, when staff officers and orderlies passed out from the city, and soon the weary men were retracing their steps. "Little Mac," as the "boys" call him, rode out and met the troops as they were marching back. As he was recognized, caps were thrown up, blankets and shelter tents were waived, and the air fairly shook with the cheers given for him.

To-day the railroad is burdened with broken engines and cars partly burned by the Rebels a night or two ago, at Manassas, and now being drawn back to the city. A train of rebel prisoners has passed by on its way to Alexandria. Destitute as our boys from the Peninsula were, they were clothed in fine linen, compared with these fellows.

To-day we have been "inspected and mustered for pay."

An order from the military Governor of Alexandria read to the regiment, at parade, afforded us all much amusement.

Just in rear of our camp is a race way or canal, broad, *uncovered*, and full of water. The men of the Peninsula army, covered with dirt, sat down on its banks to pick from their bodies the vermin which infested them, and wash themselves and their dirty clothes in its water.

The overflow from the *sinks* of all these thousands of troops runs into it. Within stones' throw, in plain sight, upon its banks, lie *now* the swollen and decaying carcasses of more than twenty horses and mules, to take no account of the score or more which lie rotting upon the plains near by. And the order of the military Governor, after reciting that from this source alone, the city draws its supply of *pure* water, threatens with severe punishment, any of our command who shall be found guilty of polluting it.

The men are now served with soft bread in lieu of hard tack. The line officers fare well; some of them living quite sumptuously. Company E's officers live like fighting cocks; Captain Bacon having brought with him from the 13th, his negro servant, a capital cook, good waiter, and most adroit and successful forager. The Field and Staff get along pretty well, considering all things. Breakfast, dinner, and tea resemble each other so much, that, were it not for the *hour*, any one might doubt to which he was called. Coffee at each, and salt mackerel and potatoes at nearly all. The Colonel and Chaplain have thus far been masters of the butter, which is, nevertheless, decidedly strong; but the rest confess themselves beaten. Milk we get in small quantity at ten cents a quart; cheese from the "Sutler," at forty cents the pound.

The Chaplain has been afflicted with a severe cold, for a day or two past, although he keeps about. He is a good deal disturbed, however, by a little difficulty he has experienced in obtaining supplies, as witness; "Colonel," said he at the mess table this evening, "Colonel, I wish you would issue an order that I should wear shoulder straps." "What for? what rank do you claim? what need have you for shoulder straps?" asked one or another. "Well, I draw pay equal to that of a Captain of Cavalry, and "——"Hold there,—"You can't rank me!" interrupted the Adjutant,—"And I can't get any whiskey unless I wear shoulder straps," continued the Chaplain. "Can't get whiskey unless you wear shoulder straps! How's that? and what do you want whiskey for?" "Why Colonel, the Surgeon prescribed whiskey and molasses for my cold. I have a hard one, you know; and this morning I went to Alexandria to get my flask filled. Going into a saloon, I asked for some, and was refused, with the statement that they did not sell any. But *that* I did not believe — so I hung round there, and pretty soon I saw a Lieutenant go in, hand out his flask and get it filled. I then went in, and asked again to have mine filled — and was again refused. "We don't sell whiskey here," said the barkeeper. But, said I, "you just sold some to that officer!" "Oh, yes! We sell to officers, but we can't let enlisted men have any." "Ah, well, if that's all the trouble, I am an officer." "You an officer! Of what? Where are your straps? That story won't pass muster, here." And so, Colonel, I couldn't get my whiskey, and I want an order to wear straps." And he got his order — and ———

Sept. 2d. Immense wagon trains are passing from the front into Alexandria; and, in the distance, we can see the glittering bayonets of a large column of troops, moving, as rumor has it, toward Washington.

A strong guard of "ours" is stationed on the Pike, with orders to stop and turn back all stragglers from the army. McDowell's division, only, is allowed to march past us to the rear.

Orders just received, direct us to be in readiness to move at a moment's notice. The Colonel has left for Washington. The boys are putting their arms in order, and the cooks are busied round their fires, preparing the rations for our haversacks. Still, in the midst of the preparation for our anticipated movement, and the excitement consequent upon the late fighting so near us, all suspend labor to gather around some straggling soldier or contraband from the front, and listen to his story.

5th. Bank's division has moved; and *we* are still here. All eyes turn anxiously toward each rider who approaches, in hopes of receiving orders to report to that General for duty.

Our work here has been, and is severe, irregular, and irksome. Our *regular* daily detail for patrol in the city is for three hundred men and ten officers. Yesterday we were called upon for five full companies in addition; a requisition we were unable to fill. And we furnish, almost daily, large parties *for fatigue* in Alexandria. Besides, we are required to picket a line some three miles long, in advance of our position.

Thus far the weather has been very pleasant, but the nights are becoming chilly. Diarrhœa is somewhat prevalent among us, and we have a few cases of Dysentery. We have lost *two* men by death, and *one*, Sergeant Fitzpatrick, of company D, by desertion. Though not much of a soldier, the Sergeant's singular ideas, and quaint forms of command, afford us much amusement.

Once before, he has been absent without leave; and to the reprimand of his Captain, delivered himself as follows: "Indeed, Captain, I presume there might be cases, in which *you* would much prefer that a man should take upon himself the responsibility of running guard, rather than trouble you with an application for a 'pass;' as, for instance, where the man felt a necessity for leaving camp, and you an obligation to refuse him the privilege." We are bound to suppose that to the mind of the Sergeant the emergency has arisen.

5th. Yesterday we sent to Alexandria four companies for duty; one of which was forwarded to Washington, as part escort at the burial ceremonies of General Stevens, killed in one of the recent engagements. Those of us who remained in camp were much gratified to have from our Chaplain, at dress parade, an assurance that "if we lived pure lives, and did our duty faithfully, we would all be remembered, upon our return home, by being elected Selectmen or Overseers of the Poor of our respective towns." We have 'struck' our Sibley tents, in anticipation of an order to march, and the boys are under their 'shelters.' But, as we can't procure storage for our Sibleys in Alexandria, unless marching orders reach us soon, we shall pitch them again, as the nights are getting very chilly. We have lost two more men. As much as we were blamed for our rigid examination when recruiting, we have quite a considerable number of men whom we ought not to have accepted into the Regiment, and whom we must soon send home.

7th. Hon. Henry Wilson, P Emory Aldrich, and Henry S. Washburn, of Worcester, and Messrs. Marshall and Nourse, of

Westboro, visited us to-day. These latter gentlemen are on a tour to the various Massachusetts Regiments, bearing comforts to the men in the hospitals. Their faces served to gladden those of us who yet remain well. The Regiment, under command of the Lieutenant Colonel, made its first appearance in Alexandria to-day; being ordered there for review and inspection by the Military Governor of the city. It received complimentary notice from General Slough for its good appearance.

The Colonel, who during its absence from camp had returned from Darnestown, left again for Washington and a visit to General Banks.

9th. By the departure of older troops we are again left in advance, and have to 'picket our front.' A 'scare' in the city led to orders to us to 'fall back behind the guns of Fort Ellsworth; and we now tenant "*Camp Slough,*" so called, not so much in honor of the General of that name, as because of the character of the ground we occupy. It has been occupied as a camp for Cavalry, and the amount of dirt and filth accumulated upon it, would astonish one unacquainted with the army. By sweeping, shoveling, and carting away, it has been made endurable.

12th Broke camp and moved about a mile to the front, under orders to report to General Grover—our own, the 33d Massachusetts, 11th New Jersey, and 120th New York, all new regiments, are to form a new brigade.

Our quarters are upon ground formerly belonging to General Cooper once our own, now, Adjutant General of the rebel army.

The remains of former fruit and vegetable and flower gardens can be traced; but not a fence, nor a tree, nor a shrub is left. My own tent is pitched where formerly was a strawberry bed; the Surgeon's stands upon what is left of an extensive rhaspberry plat; feeble shoots of flowering shrubs struggling through the hard trodden soil, betray the extent of former ornamental grounds.

As has been our lot hitherto, with one exception, our camp is upon ground heretofore occupied by Cavalry; and the luxuriant growth of "pig weed," suggests to "the boys" its appropriate name: although by orders from headquarters it is officially named "Camp Grover."

A mile to the rear stands a large brick building, noted before these sad days as "Fairfax Female Seminary," now used for a hospital, and fitted with 2,500 beds. Close to our front is a small unpainted house, occupied for a while last winter by Colonel Meagher with his wife, but now tenanted by a low down white and his family, who claim to be union.

With no crops of any kind to harvest, no horse, no cow, no hay, no grain, no pig, no poultry, no fire wood, nor any means of getting any, they look calmly and indifferently to the coming on of cold weather.

"Can I get a little milk of you?" asked Lieutenant S., to-day, of the good lady of the house. "Milk! milk! and where would the milk come from," asked she in her turn, "when we've got *na'ry cow*! No, we don't have any milk now, but there's some whiskey you can have if you want." "Oh! then you keep a little whiskey, do you?" asked the Captain. "Oh, yes! we always keep that, said she; there's near a barrel full over there!" "A barrel full of whiskey! A barrel full!" exclaimed the Lieutenant. "That's a pretty good supply, is'nt it?" "Well! what's a barrel full of whiskey in a family where there's no cow!" asked she, and the Captain gave it up, *the conundrum*, I mean, not the whiskey.

How those of us who were at headquarters at the time, enjoyed an interview which has just terminated, between Colonels Wells and Maggi. The 34th was the first regiment to reach this new ground, and Colonel Wells at once made headquarters in this house of General Cooper's. Maggi, who soon rode up, came hurrying in, bustling about, now up stairs, now down, from one room to another, till at length he addressed Wells with the remark that *he* had selected his quarters, and suggested that perhaps he (Wells), had better choose rooms for himself. "Ah!" asked Wells, "which rooms do you propose to occupy, Colonel Maggi?" "*These two*," said Maggi, pointing to "them." "Those two," said Wells, "why, those are the very ones I have just taken for my own use!"

"Well, yes!" said Maggi, but *then* I had not come up! *now*! "But *now*," said Wells; "Why, Colonel, I suppose you won't dispute my right to the first claim as ranking officer;" "Ranking me! ranking me!" fairly screamed Maggi, "and *I* commanding the 33d, while *you* have the 34th! But upon comparing proofs, Wells' commission was a day the oldest, and Maggi, in a rage, flung himself out of the house, and mounting his horse, spurred away toward Washington, leaving us of the 34th convulsed with laughter.

16*th*. The brigade is broken up! Maggi returned from Washington yesterday, with orders to report, with his command, to General Slough for provost duty in Alexandria.

CHAPTER III.

FORT LYON — COUNCIL OF ADMISTRATION — GUARD DUTY — SICKNESS — A SCARE — MULE TEAMS — GENERAL REVIEW — PROMOTIONS.

General orders of this date assign Colonel Wells to the "command of Fort Lyon and its defences." In communicating the order, Colonel Wells directs "Lieutenant Colonel Lincoln to move his command at once, and occupy the ground lately occupied by the 69th New York." Here we now lie, in what Wells calls a camp of magnificent distances. For the first time, we are not cramped for room. Company streets are thirty feet wide; one side covered by the Sibleys; Cook houses are forty feet to the rear; Line officers tents still forty-five feet in rear of these, and the Field and Staff about midway between these and the parapets of the Fort. To the left and in rear of these last, are pitched the hospital tents. On the right and in line with the company cook houses, are the Sutler's quarters. At the left flank are the guard tents; in rear of these the qartermaster and commissary store houses; and still in rear of these are the stables. The ground covered by our camp has been thoroughly policed; that occupied by the men's tents spaded deep and turned over. Numerous springs bubble up in the ravines near camp, but the water is not good, and the men of the companies are engaged in digging wells near their cook houses. At short distance in front run the sluggish waters of Hunting Creek. Regimental general orders directing the internal economy of the camp, provide for its daily sweeping from guard line to line of parade; burying outside of our lines of all cooks refuse; daily cleansing of stables, and grounds adjoining; and the covering of all excrement in the sinks with fresh earth each morning. All this to be done by occupants of the guard house, if any, if not, by detail from each company.

20th. We have occupied our present camp four days; have scraped up, and carted off twenty-seven four-horse wagon loads of filth and rubbish. Yet, although the camp in its whole extended surface, is daily thoroughly swept, we are not clean. The 33d laugh at our continued policing, but just at present, cleanliness is of more account than godliness.

Two hundred of our men, with proper compliment of officers, are daily employed in digging a line of rifle pits, connecting this post, and Forts Ward and Worth; it having been discovered, now twelve months after their construction, that the valley between them is not commanded by the guns of either of these works. Nothing however is allowed to interfere with our regular daily company and battalion drills.

23d. We had quite a little scare last night. About midnight, a cavalry man dashed into camp and reported that our picket line had been forced. The men were turned out at once, and stood to their arms, till day light. Our own officers, this morning, report that a cavalry vidette, hearing a noise in his front, and unable, on account of the darkness, to ascertain the cause of it, discharged his piece; his companion fired at the flash of his comrade's carbine, and both, wheeling their horses, rode in upon the Infantry line; one continuing his race till he reached our camp. An alarm so needlessly given is provoking, but the prompt and steady conduct of our men is gratifying. A council of administration is appointed by General Order of this date; members composing it, Lieutenant Colonel Lincoln and Captain Wm. B. Bacon.

To this council is given the determination of what articles the Sutler shall keep, and the prices he may ask for each. While it is not of much consequence at what price he disposes of fried pies, dougnuts, apples, cigars, cheese, butter &c.; for these the men may or may not purchase, as they feel inclined, it is of importance that advantage shall not be taken of their necessities, and that exhorbitant prices shall not be asked for oil, emery cloth, blacking, brushes, &c., and the other articles which the men require for the proper care of their arms, equipments and clothing.

25th. Grover, acting Major General, has applied to have us attached to his, formerly Hooker's Division, paying us the indirect, but high compliment, of offering for us the "Excelsior Brigade." Perhaps we are getting a little vain, but the flattering comments made by the many officers who visit our camp, watch our drills, and inspect our parades, and the hearty and oft repeated applause given by the old soldiers who throng our line, excuse, if they do not justify such feelings on our part.

Especially are we complimented for the beauty, order, and cleanliness of our camp, and its surroundings. A critical inspection of this is made every morning. Immediately after guard mounting the whole surface of the camp, from the guard line, past the parade, is *swept* by the prisoners, or, if there are none, by a detail from the regiment, and the rubbish is carted to a distance. The refuse of the cook houses, kept for the time in tight barrels, is carried away daily, emptied into holes dug for the purpose, and carefully covered with fresh earth.

General Orders "Headquarters defenses of Washington, south of the Potomac," just received, prohibit "the sounding of reveille before sunrise." Now *when* is sunrise? And how determined, if like that of to-day, the morning is cloudy? Alexandria has been searched in vain for an almanac, and the Adjutant and chief Bugler each seem to have an extra wheel, to keep in, or take out of their watches, according to the length and soundness of their morning naps.

Dress coats are being issued and the Colonel is having his tent floored, and the two things look as if we were *settled here.*

Hark! what a noise! It seems as if Bedlam had broken loose!

The Corporal of the guard salutes, and reports that his senior Lieutenant had sent up a prisoner whom he could do nothing with.

It was Anderson of "B" who, from having been one of the very best soldiers of the company, has become utterly indifferent to, and negligent of duty, and dirty in person and clothing. He had thrown away his pants, substituting therefor his blouse, into the sleeves of which, he had thrust his legs. The body of this garment was indifferently secured around his person, by a broad belt of light blue cloth. Pieces of red flannel were pinned to his shirt, and on each shoulder, as marks of imaginary rank. His countenance was rigid as if cut from marble, and his appearance drew roars of laughter from the boys, who turned out to look at him, and perhaps to notice his reception. "Ah! Anderson is this you? What dress is that?" "An uniform of my own, Colonel!" "Your own, is it? Well, Mr. officer, enter upon the guard book that it is not to be changed in any particular, except by express orders from these Headquarters." "But Colonel, I am sick!" "Sick, are you? Well! orderly, give Dr. Clark my compliments and ask him to report here at once!" The Doctor could detect no evidence of sickness, but, as the result of a consultation, adminstered a powerful emetico-cathartic. It was swallowed, but with a wry face, and the poor fellow has been kept occupied in more ways than one ever since.

27th. Anderson reports himself as better this morning, indeed, as feeling quite well; so he is at work, under guard, picking up the thousand and one little pieces of paper lying about camp. The wind is blowing raw and cold, and his new pattern of pants leaves uncovered a most substantial part of his body. He has preferred a request to be allowed to exchange *his own* for *our* uniform; but *we are not issuing clothing, just now.*

29th. We are transferred from Grover's command, and ordered to report to General R. O. Tyler, of the 1st Connecticut Heavy Artillery. This, much to the disgust of most of the officers, though the Colonel says, "this is just what I have been working for." Captain Chandler, promoted from a 1st Lieutenancy in the 1st Massachusetts Infantry, to the command of "F" of ours, reported to-day for duty.

Regimental General Order directs that the guard be instructed daily, by relief, in the proper discharge of their duty; the Lieutenant Colonel personally to superintend the instructions, at least once daily. This officer is also notified by the same order that he will be held personally responsible for the manner in which this duty is hereafter done. The order was issued in consequence of the following: The Surgeon had occasion, some little time ago, to visit the Hospital after dark, the Hospital itself being outside of the camp limits. As he approached the lines, he was challenged by the sentinel (a man of "A"), who, as he brought his musket to 'the charge,' scratched with his bayonet the Doctor's breast. "I don't know anything about military duty," said the Surgeon, when representing the matter, "but I do know that I don't want to be run through. If that is the proper way to challenge a man, all right; only just tell me how to avoid being *stuck* in a dark night; if it is not the proper way, just alter it; either way I am satisfied. The Doctor is assured he shan't be run through, and to secure that end, this order is issued. As guard duty has been done by Company, it was easy to place the responsibility in this case, and Company "A," principally complained of, will change its practice.

We still picket our front, the line being some four miles out. One post is upon the estate of Mason, of Mason and Slidell notoriety; a princely place, so our officers say, confiscated by our government, and held in joint occupancy by a Colonel Dulaney, a sort of deputy, under "Pierrepont," governor of West Virginia, and *seven* Secesh women, all of these being wives or widows of Rebel officers.

The Colonel, accompanied by two officers of Hooker's Staff, and a young lady from Boston, over whom we are all raving, returned from Washington, where he has been for the last day or two. During his absence, some of the officers of the 33d, with their band, came up to serenade Headquarters. It was considered a sure thing that they would be dry after their long and dusty walk, but the united Field and Staff could not furnish enough to even wet their lips. So, by way of excuse, we told them that they couldn't wonder that our supply was short, knowing, as they did, that we could procure nothing but what they allowed to pass their lines, and none knew better than themselves how little that was.

30*th*. Monthly inspection to-day showed a very marked improvement in the appearance of the men, and the condition of their arms and equipments.

Oct. 2d. Eight batteries and seven regiments of Infantry, with a long train of ambulances, have passed by camp on their way to participate in a review by Major General Sickles of his (Hooker's old) division. As the men of the 1st Massachusetts and the 26th Pennsylvania were marching by our drill ground, where we were hard at it, they recognized our Colonel, who, for a time on the Peninsula, had commanded each of these bodies, and their loud shouts of "*there's old double quick!*" drew from him responsive salute, and from us, cheers.

3d. Orders just received direct the breaking up of camp. Many are the speculations as to the reason, but really it is a sanitary measure only; it being thought advisable that ground so long covered with canvass should have the benefit of sunlight, and thorough airing. In spite of all our care, some queer revelations were made by this striking of tents; not the least astonishing being the amount of medicine which has been concealed. One tent disclosed nearly a *quart of pills*, prescribed and given out at Surgeon's call, but not taken. The surgeons look aghast, but it must be confessed the rest of us enjoy the joke. Yesterday a man of F, carelessly fired his piece and lost two fingers of his right hand in consequence. To-day one of B's men discharged his musket in attempting to *draw* the load. The ball passed through the palm of his hand, but without injuring any bone.

General Banks honored us with a visit. He desires to have us as a part of an expeditionary corps now being organized by him, and is assured such service would be very gratifying to the regiment.

8th. Company E, Lieutenant Macomber in command, on picket in our front, has sent in a request to be allowed to remain out another day, having discovered traces of the passage through our lines of a rebel spy whom they hope to capture. The request is granted.

Our Quartermaster is down with typhoid fever, which prevails among us to a good extent, but luckily of a mild form. He has been moved to the house of a Mr. Roberts near by, where he will be tenderly cared for. The measles have broken out among the men, and for the present we shall be tabooed in consequence. Reports from company commanders show that we have over three hundred men who have never had this disease. Captain Fox, who has been sick for near six weeks, reported for duty to-day. Captain H. is on the morning sick list, but S., his 1st Lieutenant, says he is down only from *too much Battalion drill.*

10th. Company E is still on picket. Its term of duty expired a day or two ago. The spy whose traces were discovered, and to capture whom its commander desired to be allowed to remain, failed to put in an appearance as expected. The Lieutenant now reports the discovery in the brush near his line, of fresh horse dung, and thinking that he has both a sure and a soft thing in hand, asks to be allowed to remain another twenty-four hours, that his company may have the eclât of the capture. Of course his request is granted, and the rest of us are now anticipating much sport at his expense.

12th. Lieutenant E., of F is detailed as Acting Regimental Quartermaster, during the absence of Howland, who goes home to-day on sick leave.

A heavy rain, which, commencing yesterday, has continued since with undiminished violence, has transformed our camp into a mortar bed, and we wish we were anywhere but on the north-east side of a steep clay hill, in open tents, without floors, and the wind blowing, one moment a hurricane from the north-east, and the next *great guns* from the north-west. The Colonel goes to Washington to-night, having been called there by Governor Andrew. All hands are making every possible effort, to guard against this terrible weather, and officers' servants are scouring the country for old stoves, stove pipes, and pieces of sheet iron.

Our teams are employed in drawing into camp, *bricks* with which to build ovens for the companies, and such chimnies and walks as are desirable. We gather them wherever they can be found. I wonder how each owner is hereafter to identify his property ! A walk through the camp discloses a great variety of ingenious ways of keeping comfortable. If an officer is rich (and whoever has for a servant one of these " contrabands " is so,) in the possession of a little box stove, with a piece of stove pipe, he rivets together, back to back, two tin mess plates, which, inserted in a slit made in the side or roof of his tent, makes a primitive thimble for the passage of his pipe. This fellow is an aristocrat. If he is poor in this sense, and unfortunate in having no stove, he takes an iron pot, turns it bottom side up, over a hole in the ground, which serves as a fire-place. From this a trench is dug across his tent, which is covered with boards, and terminates outside in a chimney formed by four or five pork barrels, set one above the other.

Beds vary still more. A. spreads his blankets upon his tent floor, of dirt or wood, as the case may be, and uses his boots for a pillow; B. nails up a long narrow box, strongly suggestive of that unpleasant, black looking shell, in which we all sleep our last slumber; another makes his couch of small cedar or arbor vitæ twigs, carefully laid one upon the other; while he who is more fastidious, drives into the ground four forked sticks, rests upon them two slender poles, to which a proper number of barrel staves are fastened cross ways, and, spreading his blankets, enjoys a spring bed, as luxurious as any which crowd the warehouses at home.

15*th*. A telegram from "Headquarters defenses of Washington" was received last night. It informed us of the movement in this direction, of a large body of Rebel Cavalry. Our picket line was strengthened by an additional Company, and the Regiment slept upon its arms. A few shots were exchanged by the pickets, but the night in camp passed quietly. Our Sutler furnished much amusement to us all in his anxiety to find a place where he would be actually safe in person, for he professed indifference as to what became of his stores. "What a fool I was, ever to come out," said he. "There was no need of it. I was confortable enough at " home, a nice woman for a wife, a good house to live in, all " paid for, hot and cold water in every room, and nothing " to worry about. If they will only let me alone this time! " Say, tell me, isn't their some place that's safe, that a man " can go to? For God's sake if there is, say so, quick!" And upon a suggestion, he hurried up the hill as fast as his short legs could carry him, in search of a bomb proof in the fort.

We lost, last night, one of our men by desertion.

Lieutenant Ripley is laid up with rheumatism, and Lieutenant Goodrich off duty by an accidental injury to his foot.

Fevers, chills, and new cases of rheumatism exhibit themselves daily; and with the measles, cases of which show occasionally, our sick list is becoming fearfully large. The Surgeon has just returned from Washington, where he went to procure, from the sanitary commission some comforts for the sick, not issued by the Government. He is a "queer stick," reserved and taciturn to a fault, but in his intercourse with the sick, kind, tender and sympathetic. He and his assistants are all splendid fellows, and we are fortunate, indeed, in our medical staff.

In addition to these officers our hospital corps is composed of a steward and assistant steward, five nurses, two cooks and one man who does the washing.

16th. "Only think, Colonel," said Lieutenant E. to.day, "only two years and nine months *longer to serve!*" The ludicrous aspect of the matter so stated, caused a shout of laughter from all who heard him.

The column of Rebel Cavalry which was cause of alarm to us a night or two ago, is reported to have been yesterday within a few miles of Chain Bridge, and their presence has put the whole line from Harper's Ferry to this place on the *qui vive*.

In exchange for the two four-horse teams, taken from us a few days ago by officers of the Quartermaster's department, we now have the offer of two *six mule* teams. As the mules are unbroken, we decline the offer. Other regiments near us have made such exchange, and a funny time they are having in breaking these animals to harness. One man is at the head of each leader, another is on the near wheeler, while still another acts as a skirmisher. The mules go along, braying and kicking as if possessed by a thousand devils. Now they go plunging into a ravine, and over goes the wagon; this righted, they bound up a steep bank, and another overturn is occasioned; once more in order, crack go the whips, and with mingled yells from the driver and braying of the mules, a narrow causeway is approached. "Hi! hi there," shouts the manager to the driver of an ambulance, whose team is slowly plodding along ahead. "Hi, there! get out of the way!" "Get out of the way yourself," comes answering back. "All right," shouts the muleteer, "*your* team goes where *you* drive." "*I* ride where *my* mules take me; if you don't care, I don't." A collision seems unavoidable. The party of the ambulance looks anxious; the mule rider triumphant; when, just as a crash seems inevitable, swoop go the mules from the causeway, over goes the wagon, and all are neck deep in the water. The laugh is with the ambulance party, now. Hours pass away sometimes before the mules can be made to move; and we turn congratulating ourselves that we are not yet serving Uncle Samuel as mule drivers.

21*st*. Our drill this afternoon was honored by the presence of a large number of officers, from Brigadiers to Lieutenants, who rode out from Alexandria to witness it. The boys did admirably, and won much well deserved applause.

22*d*. Precisely how he brought it about is not clear; but E., our Acting Quartermaster has returned from Washington, bringing with him a complete set of *armorer's tools*, which are denied to all regiments furnished, *as we are*, with Springfield muskets. Of course this possession of tools necessitates the detail of some one as armorer, which is done. A General Order of the day constitutes the Lieutenant Colonel, Regimental Trial Officer, to try and determine. all cases such as have formerly been sent to Regimental Court Martial which last named are abolished from this date.

Another case of measles showed to-day, although sixteen days have passed since the last one appeared. This will fasten us here, undoubtedly, for a long while, as however anxious officers may be to strengthen their commands with new regiments, none of them fancy new diseases.

Another of our boys, Perry of C, died to-day. He was taken down, seven weeks since, with typhoid fever, from which he was slowly recovering, when he was attacked with the measles.

23*d*. Well! we are tired enough to-night. On the 21st we received a dispatch from General Sickles, who has Hooker's old division, advising us that General Banks, who commands the defences of Washington, accompanied by the President and Secretary of State, would review his troops; inviting us to join his command for the occasion, and tendering us the honor of acting as immediate escort to the reviewing party. Our Column, in platoon front, covered the street from curb to curb, and our marching and appearance drew oft-repeated cheers from the many soldiers and civilians who thronged the sidewalk. Surrendering the Reviewing party, we took the place assigned us in line. The Drums rolled, the Bands played and arms were presented to the General-in-Chief. Galloping to the right the Reviewing party rode slowly along the front, every Regiment save one, at the approach of the dignitaries coming to the Present, and so remaining till the reviewing party had passed. The 34th alone, stood at the "shoulder." After marching in review in column of companies, the troops were dismissed. Colonel Wells, who during the day had been on duty with the General Staff, made to us, on the field, a little speech, saying that "he felt grateful *to* us, thankful *for* us, and proud *of* us, and that among the many regiments *he* had seen, *he* had never seen one which, on such an occasion, appeared better."

24*th*. The order at "Parade" to-night was varied by the reading of the following from General Sickles:

"The Major General commanding, besides the President and "Major General Banks, takes great pleasure in complimenting "the soldiers of his division, for their appearance, their skill in "marching, and efficiency in the manual of arms; and particu-"larly to the 34th Massachusetts Regiment, who performed "escort duty for the President, he expresses his highest appre-"ciation. Never before has he seen a *new* regiment that "appeared so well; their marching, the oldest regiment being "unable to excel."

25th to 27th. Regimental General Order published to-day, announces the promotion of Captain H. W Pratt, of Company A, to be Major; 1st Lieutenant F. T. Leach to be Captain: 2d Lieutenant Wm. L. Cobb to be 1st Lieutenant; and Sergeant H. T. Hall, to be 2d Lieutenant. The 1st District of Columbia, and the 153d New York, are encamped in our front, and our surrounding is again looking warlike. We are having the most terrible storm yet experienced. The rain is now, and has been for the past twenty-four hours, coming down like a deluge, and the wind blowing a perfect hurricane.

CHAPTER IV.

RECRUITING.— INSPECTION.— ELECTION.— A CONSCIENTIOUS
FEEDER.— HOSPITAL.

30*th*. Our sick list is becoming fearful; there being over two hundred and twenty in hospital and in quarters. By death, desertion, and discharge, we are reduced to the round one thousand. Lieutenant J. W Smith has this afternoon welcomed to camp his wife, and has sent up a request to be allowed to take temporary quarters outside our lines. A little irregular this, but what less could be asked, — or granted?
"Hark! What's that noise? Do you hear it? What a squalling!" "Pshaw! that's absurd! It sold P singing coronation." "Well, let's find out about it. Good morning Captain P, So you're recruiting, are you?" "Recruiting, sir! recruiting! Company C isn't doing anything of the kind!" " But Captain, your company has got a new member in camp." "A new member in my company, and *I* not know it! How's that? *when* sir? *where* sir?" "In your company cook house, *now* Captain." "Who? what? I don't understand sir." " A Baby! Captain! a Baby!" "A baby, sir! a baby in my company *without my order!* Lieutenant, what does this mean? Find out sir, and report sir, at once." With a bound the Lieutenant is at the cook house, and as he opens the door, y-a-h, y—a—a—a—h goes the baby. The captain stood straighter than ever, and looked aghast at the confirmation of the charge. The matter is easily explained. The man's wife has come out to be near her husband, and walks daily to and from Alexandria to pass the time with him when not on duty.
Such devotion deserves reward, and orders are issued to pitch a tent just outside the lines for her use.
31*st*. To-day is the last of the month. In the absence of

the Colonel, who is sick, the regiment was reviewed, inspected, and mustered for pay by the Lieutenant Colonel. This inspection and mustering for pay is no child's work either, and this, whether one looks at it from the standpoint of an inspecting officer, or the inspected men.

To take into ones hands, and examine critically one thousand stand of arms; to inspect closely the appearance and condition of the men, their clothing and equipments, and the manner in which the same are put on and worn, or rather, are packed in the knapsacks; inspect the ammunition, its quantity and quality; to verify each company roll and see that each man, whether present or absent, is accounted for; to examine the condition of the camp, the quarters of the men, the company books, and manner of keeping, &c., &c., is no light task. Nor is it an easy thing for the men, drawn up in line, to stand *motionless*, head and eyes to the front, disregarding everything but each man his own soldierly position. In the heat of the day, with a fly marching his beat from the tip of a man's nose to his cheek, there is a terrible temptation to brush him away.

The least movement of a white glove along that line of dark blue, is plainly seen, and woe to the unlucky fellow who yields to temptation! He won't want for *time* to meditate, under the shelter of the guard tent, on the uncertainty of the things of this life, and the unreasonableness of all human enactments. If, after all was done, there was any prospect that the pay master would appear, men and officers would be better pleased.

Nov. 1st. The Quartermaster reported for duty to-day, just in season to allow Lieutenant E to take his company on drill, as Captain Chandler has given up sick. Doctor Smith is confined to his bed, and Dr. Clark is quite unwell. Our sick list numbers to-day two hundred and eighteen. Two of G's men died to-day. Our disease is mainly of a typhoid nature.

A strange note has just been handed in to Head Quarters, written by a Mr. Mason, whose house is near by, and who is a brother to him of Slidell notoriety. The writer states " that he " is poor, and his family sick; that he has hitherto been "furnished with a guard to protect his person from insult, and "his property from injury; and that by the marching away of "old troops, from his immediate neighborhood to-day, he is left "exposed." Wherefore, "he requests the commanding officer "of the 34th Massachusetts Regiment, this being the command "nearest to him, to furnish him with such a guard as shall "ensure his protection;" and concludes with the still more cool request, "that the guard shall bring his own rations."

A plain refusal was returned, but General Patterson, in command, who was appealed to, has sent down an order directing us to comply with the request, and there is no help.

Our own position continues unaltered, although there is great change among the troops stationed near us. The 15th Virginia is now marching on to ground just vacated by Sickles' division. The 33d Massachusetts has gone to join Sigel, and the 123d New York have marching orders.

The 12th and 13th Vermont moved a night or two ago, and the 14th, 15th, and 16th regiments, from the same State, are now marching past us to the front.

The Colonel, who has been in Washington for the past few days, returned to-day.

Candles, hard-tack, and salt horse, as the boys call it, which were shipped to the Peninsula for the use of McLellan's army, are now being issued to us; neither seem to have received any benefit from the journey.

4*th.* Yesterday, battalion drill was dispensed with, and the boys enjoyed a good game of foot-ball; wing playing against wing. To-day is Election day, and we are to vote for Governor as if at home. The camp has been very quiet; no speeches have been made, except one by the chaplain, who mounted a pork barrel and harangued in favor of the re-election of Governor Andrew. The vote was light, standing 145 for Andrew, 345 for Devens, and 5 for Wells.

Our requisition for lumber has been returned, *dis*-approved, and we send out a strong foraging party, daily. It is now returning with a lot of logs, etc., for our stables, which were got by pulling down some out-buildings found unoccupied.

Our equipage is to be reduced seriously by General Orders

received to-day. *Three* wall tents only are allowed the Field and Staff officers, instead of the *thirteen* under which we are now sheltered. Each Company is to be allowed two *Wall* instead of the five *Sibley* tents they now have; and the Line officers are put each to his own "tent *d'abri*."

The regiment has attained a good degree of proficiency in the movements laid down in the School of the Battalion, and the Colonel, who watches from the shadow of his tent its progress, expresses entire confidence in the result of a competitive drill with any regiment in the service, *whether new or old.*

Warriner of A, a student at law, in the office of Mr. Gillett, of Westfield, at the time of his enlistment, died to-day.

Lieutenant Lovell and Orderly Stiles, of "A," are on the sick list to-day, and Fairbanks, of H, died this morning. Finn of A, who left the ranks at Norwich, on our way out, and Grady of H, are both sent to general Court Martial for trial.

Winter is upon us, but we are illy prepared to meet it. Desirous of flooring our tents, we make a requisition for lumber, which is returned, *refused,* "because the 34th is not in garrison." Another one for straw is refused, "because the 34th is not on the march;" and so red tape bids fair to kill both soldiers and horses.

At Surgeon's call this morning it almost seemed as if a majority of the regiment put in an appearance. Men with heart disease, with hernia, with diarrhœa, with measles, with rheumatism, with backaches, headaches, and aches all over; all obstinately refusing to get *better* or *worse.* Take the case of one. He has been "*sick in quarters*" nearly all the time we have been out; never sick enough for the hospital proper. He is in "*pain all over;*" the Surgeons can discover no actual disease, but tender hearted as they are, they regularly, each morning, excuse him from all duty. But see what a *conscientious feeder* he is. His chief of section watched him closely this morning. He had before him at breakfast his regular ration, which he attacked vigorously, and conquered admirably. This was at 7 A. M.; at 9 he visited the sutler's and made way with a loaf of bread, a large piece of fried salt pork, three sausages, six hard boiled eggs, a large slice of cheese, a fried pie, and two tin cups of coffee. At noon he was ready for and ate his regular allowance. And he is "sick in quarters," and has not done a day's duty for more than two months!

Upon the above statement of his *dis*-ability, a special Regimental Order put the man upon a course of battalion drill, at 2 P. M., and a liberal allowance of "double quick" promises to work a cure; at least, at roll call this evening, he says he is feeling much better, and the wonderful properties of the new prescription have been reported to the medical staff for their information.

6*th*. About three inches of snow lie upon the ground this morning.

11*th*. In the absence of Colonel Wells, and Lieutenant Colonel Singis, who commands the N. Y. battalion of artillery, which forms the inner garrison of the fort, the command of the post devolves upon Lieutenant Colonel Lincoln. We are having issued to us again hard-tack, which was shipped to McClellan's army, at the White House; nearly all of it mouldy or wormy, and the whole worthless.

Three new cases of measles showed to-day.

Company A will be on duty to-morrow, without even a Sergeant in command. The wives of more of our men are appearing, prepared to stay, and some old tents, which we have gobbled up, are to be pitched for them.

13*th*. Troops, new regiments, mostly nine months men, are again moving past us to the front. Grover is ordered to report to Banks, and Heintzleman is relieved from command of the defenses of Washington. Our nearest neighbors, the New Jersey — Colonel McAllister — marched to-day, and thus we are left veterans of the field. The Rebels are retiring behind the Rappahannock, as it looks now, and our army is pursuing the old, old way, of keeping between them and Washington. Why the powers at Washington should persist in adhering to this route, seems strange to all whose opinion we hear. All officers whom we hear speak of the matter, agree that an advance by the James, on the south side of Richmond, will have to be made eventually. It is reported to-day in Alexandria, that at Banks' request, we are assigned to him; although it is stated with equal confidence in Washington, that we are to report at Harper's Ferry to Grover.

So far as depends upon ourselves, we are getting into condition for winter.

The private horses of the command, are now housed in comfortable log stables, and the like are being put up for the animals belonging to the government. Sixty men are detached daily as "choppers." They are making sad havoc with a beautiful grove of oak and hickory trees, of about one hundred and sixty acres, from which we procure fuel for our fires, and stockading for our tents.

We have been remodelling our hospital. Heretofore it has been composed of one Sibley tent for convalescent and special patients, another for cook-house and wash-room, two others united, one used as dispensary, the other for quarters for the steward, and three "hospital tents." ranged in line, each capable of accommodating ten patients. It has been impossible to keep these tents comfortable, with Sibley stoves, the only means provided for heating them. One would almost roast at the end near the stoves, while he would be near freezing at the other extremity of the tents. To remedy this and other troubles, we have had dug at the northern end of this range of tents a wide and deep pit, which, covered over with iron and earth, constitutes the fire box, and is large enough to receive a half cord of wood at a firing. From the rear of this pit, or fire box, a trench about two feet square, dug in the center, extends the whole length of the range of tents, and enters a chimney built of sods and brick, about thirty feet high, at the south end of the hospital. This trench is covered with plates of iron beaten from old locomotive boilers, which the Rebels have wrecked in their various raids upon the railroad, and these iron plates are in turn covered with boards in the walks between the ranges of cots.

Ventilation is secured by ripping short spaces in the seams of the canvass roof, which are kept open by cross sticks of wood. The storm is effectually kept out by a "Fly," which covers all. It was fired up yesterday, and proved to be a complete success. Cold as the weather was last night, the thermometer showed but three degrees difference at the two ends of the tents. In consequence we feel indisposed to part with our sick, whom thus far, unlike any Regiment near, we have managed to keep with us, in spite of warnings from Medical Inspectors, and circulars and orders from Medical Directors at division Headquarters. A party of medical officers from department Headquarters, some of whom were Regulars, have spent hours to-day in examining the hospital. They came down to supervise in person the removal of our sick to general hospital. A removal which they had more than once directed, but which we had never made. After a close examination of our arrangements they left us undisturbed; not only so, but gave us many compliments for the ingenuity shown, and the care and skill exercised by us.

Our Vermont friends encamped near by, scrutinize closely these and the various other little arrangements we have made for our comfort. "Give me the Massachusetts boys," said one to his companion, as the two strolled through our camp to-day, "for getting fixed up comfortably. By gorry, Jim; look there! See, they've got a regular old fashioned well sweep. Don't that look like home?" One of our boys was brought into camp this afternoon, wounded in the arm by a charge of ball and buck shot, received while plundering a neighboring turnip field. In retaliation, some of his company made an excursion without leave, and meeted to the owner of the vegetables their measure of justice. Upon complaint made by the plundered party, Headquarters has taken a hand in the affair, and as a result we have a large family in the guard tent.

Lieutenant Lovell was taken down to-day with fever.

CHAPTER V

A SKIRMISH DRILL.—EVENING IN CAMP.—VERY HARD LABOR.
—WINTER QUARTERS.—AN ARREST.—A GOOD JOKE.—
HEAD-QUARTERS DINNER.—OUR BAND.

15th. For some time past the non commissioned officers have been drilled, by themselves, in the movements of the skirmish line the commissioned officers having been required to be present, although not to participate in the drill itself. Of late the drill has been directed by bugle call; the officers being required, if necessary, to supplement the call by verbal order. But this morning the *entire* regiment had its first lesson in these movements. The color-guard, strengthened by details from each company, formed the reserve. The regiment was deployed in line, and, as extended, covered nearly a mile of ground. All things being arranged, at an intimation from the Colonel, the chief bugler sounded "the forward." Our advance "is stopped, as we catch the warning call to "lie down;" and "this is sounded at Headquarters, with no regard to the con- "dition of the ground on which our temporary beds are to be "made. While lying, many of us in uncomfortable positions, "we get the order to commence firing, and, as we use nothing "but caps, there is no damage done. The order to "rise up" is "soon sounded, and, in fear of an imaginary enemy, we get a "new one to "rally by fours;" then "by sections." The alarm "is found not to be serious, and again we go forward, deploy- "ing as we advance. The bugle almost talks to us. Up and "down steep inclines — across ravines and morasses, through "thickets almost impenetrable, we move in obedience to that "imperative note which seems to say "nine miles farther," "nine "miles farther," as plainly as if it spoke. Sweating, puffing, "and a little tired with this onward rush, we welcome the "new notes sounding "the retreat," plainly telling us to "get "out of that!" "get out of that!" The call to disperse, liber-"ally interpreted, sounds like—"spread out a little." That to "rally, "hurry up, hurry up, hurry up, boys." Associating "familiar phrases, like the above with the calls, they become "strongly impressed upon the memory." We were out some two hours and a half, and for a first performance, the drill was a great success.

16th. We inaugurated, yesterday, a new morning drill, and henceforth two Companies are to go to the fort for instruction in the school of Artillery, with both Field, and Siege guns. General Barnard, Chief of Artillery, visited our camp to day, and inspected the post, and garrison. He says that we are not to be ordered away.

A Pedler, who supplies us with the daily papers, gave us much amusement for a few moments, to-day. "Here I am again, boys," he shouted, as he rode his diminutive little mule into camp. "Here I am again, with that double-breasted news-"paper, the Philadelphia Enquirer. I've got news for you,— "glorious news, this time. We've got the rebels now! no "mistake about it!! What's that, Corporal? Tell you the "news? Well, you buy my papers first! buy a paper, and I'll "tell you a piece of news that is not printed yet! genuine! "glorious!— no mistake about it!! Thank you, Corporal!— "thank you! *there's* your paper, and *here's* your change! And "now for the news! McClellan has been heard from! Yes, "sir, "little Mac" has been heard from! He has reported for "duty,— to — his — wife!!" and putting spurs to his mule, he trotted away, shouting "here's the great double-breasted news-paper! Great news! glorious news!"

The inimitable manner, in which the story was told to the gaping crowd around him, was too much for the gravity of any of his hearers, and the camp echoed and re-echoed to the roars of laughter which continued long after he rode off.

27th and 28th. For days past long trains of army wagons and pontoons have occupied our drill ground, en route from Washington to Fredericksburg. The roads are well nigh impassable by reason of deep mud. Two squadrons of the 1st Massachusetts, one of the 1st Maine, with three regiments of Vermont (9 months), men have passed us to-day on their way to Sigel; and the 1st Massachusetts battery and 26th Pennsylvania are now passing to the same destination. An enormous train of Ambulances, under protection of an entire regiment of cavalry, has also passed on the Mt. Vernon road, to the front. Yesterday was Thanksgiving Day at home, and was in a manner observed by us. All duty, save dress parade, which was had at 10 A. M., was suspended. By contribution of the officers, a generous supply of oysters was furnished the men for dinner. All the officers, save the Colonel, who had accepted an invitation to dine with General Heintzleman, in Washington, enjoyed a dinner nicely cooked by our good friend, Mrs. Roberts, near by. All our teams were sent up to Washington, early in the morning, to bring down any boxes which might have reached that city by express, for any of the regiment.

Look over the camp with me and notice how the men spend their evening hours. Here can be seen a bright eyed, flaxen haired young man, whose education at home this call to arms has interrupted, pursuing by the dim light of the regulation candle the study of his favorite Latin author—while, some few tents removed, by the glimmer of a like dip, a group of more thoughtless comrades are deep in the mysteries of old sledge or euchre. Withdrawn to a remote corner of the camp, a party of earnest and devoted ones join in devout supplication for grace and support in the trying scenes which may lie before them, while others, more self-reliant, indulge in comments upon the latest movements of the army, or growl about the order just issued from Regimental Headquarters. The smothered voice of some home-sick volunteer, asking in broken notes " Do they miss me at home," is fairly drowned by the thundering chorus of a party of rollicking ones who leave " John Brown's body mouldering in the grave, as they go marching on."

Such are the scenes of our every day life.

But when, as to-night, school don't keep, the officers come in for their share of the fun. Here the scraping of the fiddle gives warning that Captain F. has a dancing party to-night, where booted feet will shuffle in the rapid whirl of a 'gander' waltz or quadrille; there, a little way removed, the sonorous voice of old P is heard as he pitches the key note to Coronation for his assembled friends. Old Tom is heard counting fifteen-two, in the game to which he has challenged his bosom friend Charley, and Captain W is offering to go one better with H., who is positive himself, and is trying to satisfy others that *he* '*knows his little biz.*' As befits their dignity, the Adjutant and Assistant Surgeons, higher up the hill, are warbling strains from the last opera, while high over all the loud cry, " Corporal of the Guard, post thirteen," leads to a wondering enquiry from all, what the Lieutenant Colonel is up to now. In the momentary lull caused by this last disturbing cry, comes from the tent of the "old he Doctor," the cheering direction to "continue the same." And so go the hours till taps strike. Then, as by magic, all noises cease; all occupations are suspended; all lights are put out, and silence settles upon the camp, broken only by the monotonous tramp of the sentinel who wearily paces his lonely beat.

There has been an accession to our garrison in the person of an Austrian nobleman, Count Engleheim; sent by General Court martial to serve out a sentence of three months to hard labor. An officer in the Austrian service, when the news of this Rebellion reached him, he obtained leave of absence from his command, and reaching here, tendered his services to our government. A position on the Staff of General Blenker was given him. When Blenker's command was disbanded, this young officer, acting by the advice of General Stienwhar, enlisted in a new organization then being formed, and was soon after commissioned and assigned to staff duty. As Sigel's command was marching through a small village on its route, it was fired upon by persons in the houses by the way side, and Engleheim, with others of the Staff, was directed to search out and arrest the offenders. In one of the houses, a man was found with a musket in his hands, the barrel of which was warm from its recent discharge. Drawing his sabre, Engleheim struck a blow which inflicted a serious, though not mortal wound. For this he was arrested, brought before a court martial, found guilty, and sentenced to "three months hard labor at the Brooklyn Navy yard." Sigel approved the finding of the court, but directed the sentence to be carried out at this Post, the nature of the hard labor to be specified by the Commandant. If you visit the garrison the Count receives you with a pleasant smile, and draws and presents to you a glass of "Lager;" (every cask of which it has been made his duty to draw and distribute,) with the remark in his broken English, "Very hard labor! Very hard labor! indeed." He is a very pleasant, gentlemanly fellow, a most accomplished officer, and skilled swordsman and horseman; and though cheerful, in reality chafes under his enforced absence from the active duties of army life.

30th. The Colonel returned from Washington late last night to enjoy his cabin, 12 x 20, made of hewn logs, and fitted in all the magnificence of a panel door and side lights of 6 x 8 glass, which the Pioneer corps put up for his use during his absence. The fly of his former tent forms the roof of his new house. With the exception of the Colonel, and Quartermaster, who is now having a cabin built of logs, the Field and Staff will winter under canvass. The men will "stockade" their tents, orders for doing which have been issued. This stockading is done by setting on end, in a shallow trench of the circumference of the Sibleys, slabs split from logs, set six feet above ground, to the tops of which the walls of the tents are securely fastened. These slabs are hewn smooth on the inside, the space between filled in with clay, and the whole completed by hanging on the side facing the street, upon hinges made from old boot legs generally, sometimes upon those made from wood, doors made from hard-tack boxes, or lumber, if to be procured.

One of our streets is a sort of 5th avenue; the doors of the tents being paneled and grained to imitate black walnut and mahogany. These particular ones were a gift from the boys of those regiments which have recently moved. But there is room for suspicion that we do not hold all our possessions by so good a title.

In the center of these tents is placed a Sibley stove; above which, and around the stove pipe, the arms stand in racks made for the purpose. Two tiers of bunks are run around the wooden wall, the lower one made broad enough to form a comfortable settee. Knapsacks carefully packed, and blankets closely rolled, are at the head of each bunk. If the men are luxurious, they collect cedar boughs, which, when carefully spread, form quite a soft bed — springy and elastic. The boxes, received from home, are half buried in the ground, beneath the lower tier of bunks, and form cellar and store-house for the good things each man possesses.

Nearly all the residents in our neighborhood are indebted to abandoned camps, for most of the comforts they possess. Dinah takes away on her head lumber enough to build a shanty; while Sambo picks up, and hides, chairs, stools, pails, stoves, bedsteads, or what answered for such, and in fact, any, and everything, which his observation leads him to hope he can sell to the troops who next occupy the ground. Vain delusion! for the boys are quick to detect the ear marks of army ingenuity, and are ready to appropriate, without compensation, whatever of the kind, they find and fancy.

Among other things which reached camp to-day from home, was a large box for H., holding *one hundred turkies*, intended for Thanksgiving. A goodly sized bottle of whiskey, closely stowed inside, formed a *new kind* of *stuffing*, for one of the turkies.

Dec. 2d. Our monthly inspection, which has been postponed on account of continued rain, was had to-day; at which we welcomed Wells Willard, a former Lieutenant and Acting Adjutant of the 21st Massachusetts, *now* Captain, and assigned to Company "A" of ours. How we laugh, as we catch, rolled out in the sonorous voice of one of "I's" men, "Attention the universe! By kingdom, right wheel! Where in h—ll, old Abe, are you going with your States, now?" all in imitation of a little incident which happened in one of our late drills. Yesterday, we sent our Pioneer corps and wagons, out on a foraging expedition, after some evergreen trees, with which to screen from observation, our "sinks." They were fast cutting down, and loading some beautiful Pines, from a grove of young trees, when the owner, a thorough going union man, as is everybody here, when his property is touched, appeared, and hailed them with, "What are you doing here? Who are you? What regiment do you belong to?" etc., to which Bolio, a ready witted teamster, replied: "The 16th Virginia!" "I reckoned so!" said the irate Virginian. "Here have I been ever since the breaking out of the war, surrounded by troops from all parts of the country, and not a stick of wood have I lost, till you d——d Virginians camped here. I'll report you for a d——d low-down thieving set, as you are; and I'll see if I can't get you ordered away."

4th. Queerly enough, our neighbors, the 16th Virginia, moved to "Upton's Hill" yesterday, and we wonder did the affair of "the pines" have anything to do with this order.

Our guards arrested to-day some old soldiers, tenants of the "Convalescent camp," as it is called, who were caught in carrying away part of the abattis, which protects the approaches to this fort. In defence, the prisoners state that there was but forty cords of wood issued the last week to their camp of over 16,000 men; (our own consumption is from ten to fifteen cords weekly); that they were nearly freezing; thoroughly chilled through, and that they had no fire with which to do their cooking even. Of course, discipline required that they should replace the wood they had attempted to carry off. But humanity equally demanded that they should be discharged, with no more than a reprimand. Their camp, which is near by us, is in a shocking condition. No one who has not seen it can conceive of its uncleanliness, nor of the suffering of the poor fellows. In a warm day thousands of them can be seen, wandering over the country in search of chips and twigs with which to boil their coffee, or heat water to wash their shirts in.

The boys are having a good laugh at the expense of the Lieutenant Colonel.

On drill (skirmish) yesterday, some men of F. fell behind the line, and were indifferent to the bugle calls, which directed the various movements. Their negligence was so marked that the orderly Sergeant was ordered by the Lieutenant Colonel in command, to send to the guard tent at the close of the drill, one whose name was given, and another described as wearing a ragged blouse, particularly *torn and out* at the elbows. There being but one man of F among the prisoners at the guard tent this morning, Sergeant B. was called upon to explain. "How happens it, Sergeant, that the order, given you yesterday on drill, has not been obeyed?" "I could not pick out the man you wanted Colonel." "Couldn't recognize one of your own company? How's that, Sergeant?" "Why Colonel, you remember that he was a good distance from us, when you gave me the order for his arrest, and, as you only designated him, as wearing a ragged blouse, badly out at the elbows, and, as most of our men wore *just that kind of garment*, I could not be sure which one of them all you wanted." "Oh, very well, Sergeant! that will do for *this time*, after this we'll find an ear mark you will be sure to recognize." And so now "the Boys" are chuckling not a little.

7th. Snow, to the depth of over three inches, lies on the ground, from the storm of day before yesterday. The thermometer stands at eight degrees and the Potomac is frozen over.

12th. We are having many visitors to our camp, persons unable to get to "the front," partly from the difficulty of procuring transportation, more perhaps from the General Order, just issued, prohibiting the presence of civilians in the lines opposite Fredericksburg. As small compensation for their disappointment, we admit them within the fort, and order out the boys for drill.

Of course we invite them to our fare. "Sit down with us to table. We can't plead that it's washing day, in excuse for our *boiled dinner*. Let me help you to a slice of this boiled pork; it would be good, if it were better done. You don't like it? Well, try a piece of this tongue. What! you won't? Well, then, try this turnip; don't be afraid! You can't mash it? well! here's something which is softer. What is it? Why, it looks as if it were cabbage; as if it might now be thickened grease; I guess it's cabbage soup! You won't take any? Well, help yourself to anything you see, which you think you'll like, and don't stand upon ceremony! There, in front of you, is salt; here are pepper and vinegar, and there —— cook, bring the mustard! Here is what *was* hard-tack, when first shipped to the Peninsula, — take it quick, or it will run away! and here is what the sutler calls butter! You don't eat, gentlemen! well, then, Orderly, set out the sardines and lemons, for dessert. I am sorry you don't like our fare! it is the best we've got, however. Just now we take what we can get, and are thankful we can get anything.

The work upon the new fortifications, in the throwing up of which two hundred of our men have been engaged for weeks, is progressing satisfactorily, and shows finely. Redoubt "A" is completed, and guns are being placed in position to-day. Apropos to this, there is circulating among us a good anecdote in connection with this line of forts, which is known as the "Defences of Washington." Alluding to those now being built, as well as to those long since constructed, some one asked General McClellan if they could be of any possible use: "Oh, yes!" responded the General, "of incalculable advantage, in a POSSIBLE *contingency!*" To illustrate: you might ask of what possible use is a man's breast? but, if a man should happen to have a baby, don't you see he might possibly find use for his bosom? And so of these forts, if the rebels should happen to take Alexandria or Washington.

We lost two men, by death, last night; making four this week. Out of seven students at the Westfield Normal School, who enlisted and joined us at Camp Wool, *five* have died, *one* has been discharged by reason of disability, and the remaining *one* is now in hospital, very sick. With such a result, the authorities at home must feel compelled to grant that our examinations were none too rigid.

16th. We buried to-day the second of two brothers. Four days ago he appeared for the first time at Surgeon's call; complained only of being chilly, but told the doctor he knew he should die, and dead he is. Another of the men confined for a long time, and given up by the Surgeons, told them he should live, and he is now *on duty.*

We have placed five guns in position in the new "redoubt" A, and the platforms for the other six are nearly completed. This is to be garrisoned by five Companies, under the Lieutenant Colonel; three Companies under the Major are to hold "C," and two under one of the Captains, are to occupy "B."

19th. "F" lost one of its Corporals last night by desertion, and in him the regiment lost one of its color bearers. He was magnificent in phisique, being tall, burly, broad shouldered, looking every inch the soldier. But, being Selectman of his town at date of enlistment, and dissatisfied at the slow rate of promotion in the regiment, he has gone. We lost to-day another of G's men. This Company has now lost by death and desertion twelve men.

Mrs. Judge Russell, escorted by Captain Rice of the 1st Massachusetts, rode out this forenoon to witness our skirmish drill. In compliment to her, blank cartridges were issued to the men, which added much to the interest of the exercise. We (that is the officers), who are assessed, and who are also to contribute monthly, according to rank, are organizing a band. The instruments have been purchased, and the members detailed as musicians. Sibley tents, which we "gobbled," have been stockaded and otherwise prepared. As a sanitary measure, we hope much from it.

21st. The troops, comprising the garrison, were paraded for review and inspection by Acting Brigadier General Wells to-day. Crowds of officers rode out from Alexandria to witness the ceremony.

27th. Christmas, on the whole, passed off well. The Colonel, attended by Lieut. Colonel Wetherell, of Governor Andrew's staff, who had been with us a day or two, left for Washington to attend a party at Heintzleman's quarters. All drills were suspended by order, and none but necessary duty performed. Our officers, in return for many civilities received, invited the officers of the Dutch garrison to a collation in our camp. Apples, cheese, sandwiches, and lager constituted the spread. The ill humor of the men to the Sutler, at one time threatened an outbreak, which would have seriously affected our fair name, but a determined front on the part of a portion of the officers soon quieted all outward manifestations of ill feeling.

The weather is like summer, and we sit with our tent doors open, and without fires. The traveling, however, is horrible. By orders just issued we are to complete the fortifications upon which a portion of our men have so long been laboring, and to-morrow the whole Regiment are to take up the "shovel and the hoe." Not much to their liking.

One of our men received to-day a box intended for Christmas, so badly packed that its contents made one great *mince pie*. Sugar, cheese, chestnuts, cranberries, pickles, apple sauce, plum cake, and roast turkey were all jammed into one general *hash*. To wile away time, which otherwise would hang heavy, the boys spend some of their spare hours in hunting and killing the rats which swarm in the camp, having their homes in the holes they have dug in the banks of the ravines adjacent. One row of twenty dead ones lies on our right flank; victims of this forenoon's sport.

Our darkies furnish us with a good deal of amusement. From what distinguished families they come! "Jeff Davis" is called to brush the Captain's (Bacon's) boots; "Zollicoffer" to bring an armful of wood; "Beauregard" to draw a pail of water. But they devote every *spare* moment at their command in learning to read: all of ours going nightly to a school kept at Fairfax Seminary for the especial benefit of their race. They all have a "*misery at the heart*" whenever sickness of any kind attacks them. The remedy is as unvarying as the complaint is universal, and consists in wrapping head, body and feet in as many blankets as they can procure, and sweating and sleeping away the ill feeling.

28*th*. Garrison review to-day was a great success, our band making its first appearance. To-night the boys are sleeping on their arms; one company of the Artillery Battalion garrisons "Redoubt "A:" *F* of ours, Captain Chandler, holds "B:" an armed sentinel walks his beat in each street of our camp. Mr. Mason, our old acquaintance from Occoquan, broke in upon us this afternoon with the statement that, while at his dinner, a party representing themselves to be of the 17th

Pennsylvania cavalry rode up to his house, having been driven from their post by a force of rebel cavalry and artillery; and that as he was hurrying to bring us the information, another portion of the same command, some of them wounded, rode up reporting that the whole line had been driven in. While listening to his story, an orderly galloped into camp, bringing the compliments of Colonel Zagony, and the information that *his line* (Infantry) had been driven in. We have sent out advance posts, and are waiting. Now, at 11 P. M., a party of telegraph operators are seeking the shelter and protection of our camp. From them we learn that the 17th Pennsylvania is badly cut up; and that the rebel force is at "Pohick church," about 8 miles away.

29th. Peace reigns in our camp, and to all appearance "quiet on the Potomac." Alexandria had a big scare last night. The post commissary started off all his beef cattle for Washington, and employed his entire force in removing his other stores. At midnight, General Slough routed his command and marched them out some two miles on picket.

CHAPTER VI.

WINE PARTY — BRIGADED AT LAST — AN ORIGINAL WAY OF GIVING ORDERS — PAY DAY — COMMISSIONS RECEIVED — A "FATIGUE" PARTY — REVIEW AND INSPECTION — MORE VISITORS.

Jan'y 1st, 1863. Lieutenant Colonel Singis, of the New York Artillery Battalion, sent a very polite invitation to the officers of the 34th, to attend a "*Rhine Wine*" *party*, to be given by himself and his officers, at 11 o'clock this forenoon. Cold ham, corned beef, pigs feet, bologna sausage, potato salad, Swietzer cheese, very good, and Limberger cheese, not so good to an uneducated palate, wine and lager formed the entertainment. Count Engleheim acted as cup-bearer in accordance with his sentence. The conversation was limited, so difficult was it for us to understand or make ourselves understood; but all could join in camp songs. Distant firing occasionally broke upon our ears, rendering some of us, at least, a little nervous, and the party soon broke up.

8th. This is the tenth day that the entire Regiment has been at work upon the new line of fortifications. We have accomplished a large amount of work, and the engineer in charge, Lieut. Schenck, is profuse in his compliments as to the manner in which the work has been done. Company "B" has, during all this time been employed in the construction of "gabions." But the labor is irksome enough, and it is getting to be a little difficult to keep the boys steadily and faithfully at it. The habitual shirks are formed into a company by themselves, and a little more particular supervision results in a day or two, in their being remanded to their own companies. The few hard cases are treated to a "barrel shirt," and a march backward and forward under special escort, with perhaps a night in the guard house, always effects a cure.

A detail of men from the parole camp, for work on these new fortifications has been ordered of late. These old soldiers are guarded by a company of the 26th Michigan, in their march to and from their own camp. But at the trenches, an overpowering unwillingness to work seizes every devil of them, and down go the tools, and out come the "*cards,*" and all go in for a little "*old sledge.*" The remonstrances of the officers of the guard are of no avail. "Away with yees, away with yees; and shure how can you want a man to work all day, just for the trifle he gets to eat, when there's no drink at all, at all!" Gen. Barnard, with a party of engineers, has been occupied to-day running the lines for an additional Fort, to be connected by covered ways and rifle pits, with the redoubts we have been constructing; and Lieutenant Schenck communicates the not very agreeable information, that the 34th will be required to build the new works. Colonel Wells chafes at this, and says that if we continue our work as we have begun, we shall be converted into a regiment of Engineers.

To our dismay, the " small pox " has made its appearance among our negro servants. A General Order directs that every man of the command be at once vaccinated, and that every negro servant be removed from the camp. After the lapse of four weeks, we have three new cases of measles.

Lieutenant B, of "B," is in arrest, and charges prefered against him. His offence being, that, as officer of the guard, he gave passes to two Sergeants of his company to go to Alexandria, communicating to them also the countersign for the night.

9*th.* Colonel Wells, having been summoned by special message, has left for Washington. " F's " officers have finished their cabin, and give a house warming this evening. Doughnuts (two large pans of which grace the table, with large reserve in the rear), sage cheese, smoked halibut, etc., form the repast. We have had returned an application to be furnished with copies of " Artillery Practice," with the disapproval of General Barry (chief of that arm), endorsed thereon. Not to be balked, we have purchased them from our regimental fund.

One of our Sergeant's, M. of B., is now being tried by Major P., acting as trial officer, for the third time. He was drunk and noisy, in the streets of A, while there on a pass a few days since, and was arrested by the Provost Guard, and confined in what used to be known as the "slave pen." Upon being released, on his return to camp, he was arrested by our own authority, and charges were preferred against him. Upon trial, he was adjudged guilty, and a fine of five dollars imposed. The proceedings were disapproved, and the matter returned to the Major for reconsideration. This resulted in his being sentenced to pay a fine of seventeen dollars, and now again a disapproval of the proceedings follows, and he is to be tried anew.

An inspection and review is ordered for this afternoon, in honor of Hon. Charles R. Train, James G. Grinnell, and Charles G. Davis, all of Massachusetts, who are present in camp. An order "Headquarters defences of Washington," just received, informs us that the regiment and its camp are to be subjected to inspection by an officer of the regulars, on the 18th. The condition of the command, and the cleanliness of the camp, is best judged by the fact that not the slightest preparation is to be made for the ceremony. What a terrible change in the weather! Friday and Saturday were as warm as June, but last night the thermometer fell to 18°, and to-night the weather is still colder.

We lost another man to-day, this one from K.

17*th*. Agreeably to a notice sent down to us yesterday, we were inspected to-day, by an officer of the Regular Army, detailed for the purpose. It was uncomfortable enough, the thermometer standing at 18°.

Another of K.'s men died to-day.

19*th*. We are fairly brigaded at last. The 1st and 19th Connecticut, 14th and 34th Massachusetts, forming the new command. Our brigadier is Robert O. Tyler, a graduate of West Point, formerly Colonel of the Connecticut 1st, and said now, to be one of the best artillery officers in the service.

According to him, to form a really good regiment, the men should be what are called "Dandy soldiers." He calls his men the "Dandy regiment;" and *so, the best* of the army. Notwithstanding which, we arrested to-day one of his men, who was hanging round our camp, drunk, and noisy, and returned him under guard, with our compliments to his Colonel.

In the intervals of *our* drills, we watch the efforts of Lieut. Colonel Singis in drilling his men, as Infantry. Marching in column of companies to-day, where, of course, the *guide* is left, somehow, probably by accident, Captain Stultz, who commands the right company, and led the column, gave the order "Guide right." At once, the Colonel shouted, "*halt!*" and thus broke out: "What for, Captain Stultz, you shall give the order guide right? You be the first company in the — in the — what you call 'em — yes, that's it, in the column. You shall guide *left!*— you shall *no* guide *right!* When you shall march in review, then you shall guide right; but, by g—d, you shall guide right, not at no other time, except once — when you are last, and shall be first;—*then* you shall guide right also."

It was an original way of directing that the guide should be right, when the column was marching left in front.

Elwell, of F., makes us all laugh at a story he tells of one of his men. "Lieutenant," said the man, "I thought I'd come up and have a little talk with you. The fact is, I've just had a letter from one of my folks, and they want to know when I'm coming home; they want to see me proper bad, and I kind 'o hanker after them; and so I thought that I'd just tell you, that after we are paid off, I guess I'll just go back." "Go back! why? what do you want to go back for?" "Well! the fact is, Lieutenant, *this is'nt just what 1 thought it was going to be*; and so, I guess I'll just leave you, when I get my money." To the Lieutenant's suggestions that he had better see the Captain about the matter, the poor fellow replied, "that he calculated *that wan't of no account.* He didn't feel much acquainted with the Captain, and guessed he (the Lieutenant) would do just as as well.

A Regimental General Order, of to-day's date, inaugurates a

school for the commissioned officers. Hours, from seven to nine each evening, from date of order, except Sundays.

24th. A noisy family of some twenty-five of the boys are in the hands of the guard this morning. Offences, drunkenness, and running the guard. Soley, Lieutenant of yesterday's guard, had a hard time of it; a little rebellion in his family, during the night, giving him active employment. He proved to be the right man for the time, and the place. The immediate cause of the row was the presence of the paymaster; who, however, pays us only to November. Sitting around the table during the payment, was the Lieutenant Colonel Commanding, the Adjutant, prepared to exchange with the men his check upon a bank at home for their money; and the sutler, anxious to receive from the paying officer the amount of any little bills he may have charged. "Here, I want four dollars from that man!" he exclaimed, as, in answer to the call of his name, the man stepped forward. "Sorry for you," was the reply of the paymaster. "Deducting stoppages, charged against him on the roll, there is thirty-six dollars and six cents due; ten dollars monthly has been allotted by the man to his wife. You can have the *six cents*, if you are quick about it."

The Colonel has gone to Washington to attend the wedding of one of his friends. Commissions were received to-day for Soley, Captain, Vice Holden, resigned; Lincoln to be 1st Lieutenant, Vice Soley, promoted; and Orderly Sergeant Stiles, of A, to be 2d Lieutenant, Vice Lincoln promoted.

Our drills (during our temporary relief from fatigue duty at the redoubts, granted on account of the frozen condition of the ground), have been resumed. This afternoon, however, we had an interesting little fatigue party of our own, to vary the monotony of our life. Outside of our lines, though in front, and near to our camp, is a thick growth of brush; and although we have always dug suitable *sinks* for the command, which have been kept clean by daily covering of earth, the boys have used this ground till it has become offensive. So, it was determined to give such a lesson as would prevent any recurrence of like trouble. Shovels, in sufficient number to properly arm the whole command, were borrowed for the occasion, and thus provided, the men were moved against the offensive position. There was an involuntary recoil of the line as the work of the afternoon was disclosed, but escape was hopeless, and the result is that the ground is thoroughly policed. There is general belief that no occasion will arise to take the boys out for like duty again..

An order from General Tyler, just issued, contains the following announcement: "The garrison of Fort Lyon will be inspected on Saturday next. An inspecting officer will be detailed from these Headquarters. The troops will be allowed the whole of the day previous, to get ready." Whew! I guess we shall survive.

Since we were paid the very devil seems to be to pay. A thorough search has been made in all the houses and suspected places near us, but to little purpose. We find no rum, and no signs that any is kept. Nevertheless, it is all drunk,—with some woman. We are fairly non-plussed. But an unusual expanse of crinoline on the persons of some apparently innocent apple women, excited suspicion; suspicion led to search; search disclosed a string of canteens secured to the waists of the frail ones, beneath the exuberance of petticoat and flounce, and we breath free once again.

28th. A violent north-east snow storm broke upon us last night, and has continued to rage all day. Our sentries have been withdrawn from all posts, save at the guard tent and Headquarters, and these are relieved hourly. Spite of the severity of the weather, we are compelled to send out our teams, and a small fatigue party, to keep our fires going. In the bad state of the roads, our teams (four horse), can bring in but about two and one-half feet at a load, and they are kept constantly employed in consequence. Three of our horses died last night. Lieutenant Lincoln, while following through the brush some citizens of Alexandria who were hanging around the camp, and supplying our men with whiskey, was suddenly seized from behind, overpowered, and deprived of his revolver.

29th. Two ambulances, each drawn by four horses, in which were Colonel Wells, Adjutant Woods, Lieutenant Bacon,

Captain Potter, and Sergeants Clark and Pomroy of B as witnesses, with Lieutenant Butler the accused, have just left camp, for fort Richardson, at which place the Court, before which Lieutenant B. is to be tried, convenes to-day.

31st. The regiment was reviewed and inspected to-day by Lieutenant Colonel Kellogg of the 19th Connecticut, detailed for that purpose, from Brigade Headquarters.

The day was beautiful over head, but, under foot, perfectly horrible. "All very nice for those who ride, but pretty rough for us poor devils who foot it," could be heard, in under tone along the line. We had donned all our finery for the occasion. The boys sported white gloves, purchased from the regimental fund, and the officers were in holiday attire. But the muskets were bespattered with mud, and the sashes showed a kind of ashes of roses color, as the rich underground of scarlet showed faintly beneath the thick upper crust of the sacred soil. Notwithstanding the intimation contained in the General Order directing the inspection, not a minute had been given for special preparation. We appeared, as we could appear any day, with ten minutes notice. The inspection was very rigid, everything belonging to us being subjected to close scrutiny.

In the absence of General Tyler, we found consolation in the presence of Captain Wyman of the 33d, and Hon. Dwight Foster and Judge Russell of Massachusetts, and our old friend Grinnell from Washington.

Feb'y 1st. "I do not believe," says Colonel Kellogg in his official report of his inspection, made yesterday, "I do not "believe that there is another regiment in the whole service, "that can show so many guns, in such good condition. My "own regiment, which I think a good deal of, is nowhere in "comparison, and though I think the 1st Connecticut has *two* "companies that can beat anything I have seen to-day, *as a* "*whole*, the regiment won't compare with you." *We stand* an inch taller in consequence of this, and all we ask now is for an opportunity to *drill* with this dandy 1st. When the mud is dried, and the country more passable, we are to invade the quarters of this crack regiment, moving as skirmishers, by bugle call solely: — A thing General Tyler says he has never known a regiment, as a whole, able to do.

6*th*. A severe snow storm from the northeast set in yesterday, but this morning, the wind changed to the southwest, and brought rain instead of snow. A photographer from A. visited us to-day, for the purpose of getting a picture of our camp. *Three* views were taken; one of the camp merely, one with the regiment in column of companies closed in mass, and another with the regiment in line as for parade. In each of the two last the encampment formed the background of the picture. By general order, all the troops in and around Washington, including those garrisoning Alexandria and the neighboring forts, are to compose the "22d Corps," under Major General Heintzelman.

5*th*. The thermometer has been, for the past few days at 18°; our snow changed to rain last night, but the wind has again changed, and warm rain is now falling.

A train of *fifteen* wagons, procured from the Post Quartermaster at Alexandria yesterday, was employed with our own *six*, in drawing wood into our camp; but the whole amount drawn, will hardly keep our fires an equal number of hours. The Colonel is detailed on a Court of Enquiry, to investigate charges preferred by Gen. Slough, against Capt. Wyman of the 33d, Provost Marshal of Alexandria.

T. W. Hammond, wife and son, of Worcester, and Mrs. Pierrepont, wife of Rev. John, made us a flying visit to-day. Mrs. Hammond left a bundle of stockings, to be given to any of the boys who were in need. Samuel Smith, city clerk of the same city, Hon Mr. Washburn, M. C., and Mr. Purple, both from Franklin County, also made us a short visit.

16*th*. The birds are with us; and those farmers, who think that the heavy foot of war is not to be placed again upon their fields, are busily engaged in planting and seeding. We have procured, by appropriation from the Regimental Fund, boxing gloves and foot balls for each company in the regiment; and the camp is noisy with the shouts of the men engaged in these games. The band is also playing at Headquarters.

CHAPTER VII.

BRIGADE H'D-Q'RS—GUARD — MORE VISITORS — SCHOOL — COURT MARTIAL — THE ADJ'T — AN ALARM — A CRIPPLE BRIGADE — LIEUT. LINCOLN'S WOOD PARTY — A JOKE.

We are furnishing our quota of men for Brigade Headquarters Guard. One Sergeant and *three* privates, selected by each captain from those of his company most proficient in drill, reported to the Lieut. Colonel commanding. From this number was selected a Sergeant at large, and *one* private from each company, as our contribution to this body. Yesterday morning the General took it into his head to inspect his guard. He is reported to have gone down his line, tossing his head, and saying to his A. A. General: "A-d-j-u-t-a-n-t, — a-h! — here's a thing— that won't do — won't do at all — send it back! and, a-h — here s another — bah! send them both back — and get others!" So this morning, a man of F, and one from G, were conducted into camp by a Sergeant, who bore a letter from the A. A. A. General, communicating the intelligence that the men "*would'nt do*;" and directing others to be detailed in their stead. The men "*that would'nt do*" had been selected for their thorough knowledge of guard duty, and proficiency in the manual, as well as for their general good character as soldiers. No reason was given for their rejection. So, recalling the general's predilection, we decided to humor it. He had rejected *good soldiers*. We returned to him *swell fellows*, who sported white chokers and oiled their hair and whiskers; and, if he is satisfied with the exchange, we shall be.

17*th*–20*th*. The weather, which yesterday was delightfully warm and pleasant, changed during the night, and a storm of snow, followed by rain, has raged all day. Spite of the severity of the weather, troops have been moving *in* round us. Girney's Brigade, from Upton's Hill, has encamped near by, and Cowdin's, although not visible to us, is closely adjoining. Among our visitors of the last few days, have been Gen. Calvin Pratt, Judge Chapin, and Henry C. Rice, of Worcester, and H. B. Staples, of Milford. They all walked from the city to camp; the last two passing safely *over* the ground, *in* which the Judge, but a few hours before, had seen his overshoes swallowed.

Dr. Thorndike has left for home, on leave obtained at the War Department, spite of the disapproval of Gen. Heintzelman.

Lieut. Smith, of D. has sent up again his resignation; this time "immediate, and unconditional." His former one, although approved at Regimental Headquarters, was *dis*-approved by the General Commanding the Defences.

Camp life is just now softened by the presence of the wives of Surgeon Clark, Capt's. Pratt and Cooly, and Quartermaster Howland. The snow of the past storm, lies some seven or eight inches deep, rendering drills impracticable. The officers are exercising their ingenuity in constructing all kinds of indescribable things, which answeras poor substitutes for sleighs, and "the Boys" are amusing themselves in match games of snowballing, where even shoulder straps do not secure exemption from,—let us be wise and call them *stray balls*. It is high carnival with all, save the occupants of the guard tents, who are kept busy shoveling paths across the camp, which, out of regard to the *crinoline*, are dug some seven to eight feet wide.

Our sick list is complicated with a few cases of scurvy; and, since the government issues no vegetables, the Regimental Fund has been drawn upon for the where-withal to purchase a supply of onions, for the men, all of which are eaten raw.

The school for "officers," which has been running now for some months, closed its first term last evening. No doubt the officers will enjoy their vacation, as much as if they were scholars of more tender age. Strange as it may seem, it can't be truthfully said, that they hunger and thirst for education's sake. No instance has occurred, as yet, of pining because of enforced absence from camp, during school hours, nor are they all found listening anxiously for the bugle call which summons them to this duty. There are some cases of habitual tardiness, and instances of attempts at absenting themselves altogether. Apropos to this is the following: "Orderly," said the Colonel, a night or two ago, "Orderly, give my compliments to Capt. C. and tell him the school is waiting his arrival." And no one seemed to envy the Captain his situation when he put in his appearance. "Now, gentlemen," resumed the Colonel, "now that we are all together, we'll take up our lesson, which is upon fortifications." "Lieut. S, how would you go to work to construct a magazine?" The answer, satisfactory so far as it is given, is interrupted by putting to the next in position the question "In what manner should the roof be constructed so as to render it 'bomb proof?'" This officer hesitates,—becomes confused,—"Next," calls out the Colonel. "I pass, sir," is his reply, perhaps forgetting that he is not playing euchre. And the Colonel turning to hide the smile playing upon his lips, says: "Well, Capt. P, how would *you* go to work?" "I should not take the job, Colonel." And no one more heartily than the Colonel joins in the roar which is excited by this answer.

Again, "Capt. C., suppose the regiment is ordered out for inspection, where would you place the Commissary Sergeant?" "The Commissary Sergeant?" asked the Captain seeking by the question to gain time for thought. "Yes Captain, the Commissary Sergeant, what would you do with him?" "Send him to his quarters, Colonel." And again, in the laugh that followed, the Colonel's voice drowned all others.

Lieut. Macomber, who has been confined for the last six weeks with a severe attack of inflammatory rheumatism, and who had applied for "leave of absence," based upon Surgeon's certificate, approved by his commanding officers, had his application returned to-day, *dis*-approved, but accompanied with a pass admitting him to officers hospital in Georgetown.

In the matter of Orville Young, tried for striking the Orderly Sergeant of his company, the sentence of the Court is: "that "he be confined at hard labor at the Rip-raps for three years, "without pay, and then be dismissed the service." Farley of

I. tried by the same Court, for *desertion*, is sentenced " to hard " labor, without pay, for the same term, and at the expiration " of that time, to be *branded on the left shoulder, with the* letter " D." The sentence of Lieut. Butler is not as yet promulgated.

28th. To-day is bi-monthly inspection, and muster for pay. S. D. Harding, of Worcester, temporarily a visitor, was invited to accompany the Lieut. Colonel in the discharge of this duty; but, like a wise man, he allowed his discretion to get the better of his zeal, and made an early retreat from the severity of the weather.

To-day's mail brought details for the Lieut. Colonel and Major, as members of a Court Martial, ordered to assemble in Alexandria.

March 3d. The sensation among the officers to-day, is the formal opening of the "Ripley House" so called; a small, but select place of entertainment, under the immediate supervision of Lieut. Ripley, of F, where the officers of that company, are to board those of E, and a portion of those of A and B.

During the temporary absence of Adj't Woods, who has left to deliver at fort Delaware our two men sentenced to hard labor at the Rip-raps, Lieut. Lincoln acts as Adjutant.

We are growling over our weather of to-day—rain, hail, snow, thunder and lightning, and sunshine, each striving for mastery.

4th. What a queer world is this of ours! Here is our Colonel, an original anti-slavery man, and free soiler, and our Lieut. Colonel, an uncompromising "old line" Whig; the former giving a halting support to the late proclamation of the President, while the latter adopts it without any reservation. To make the matter still more singular, the latter, as a member of a General Court Martial, is to sit in judgment upon Lieut. Col. Beecher, of the 153d N. Y. Infty, (said to be the son of Henry Ward Beecher,) upon a charge, among others preferred, of disloyalty. Specification, in this, that " he, the said Lieut. " Col. Beecher, said that he would not fight to restore the " government,—he would let the South go, slaves and all,—he " would not fight to uphold the proclamation. If that was " what was wanted of him, he would join the South! He " should fight where they paid best," and other like expressions.

There are additional charges of "insubordination,"—"dis-"obedience of orders," and "conduct unbecoming an officer "and a gentleman." Summarily stated, they all stand for *general good for nothingness.*

7th. The regiment was reviewed by Hon. Amasa Walker, of North Brookfield, yesterday. Our boys are *furloughed* by threes and fours, for all sorts of reasons, and for no reason at all; save that they "want to go home;" but thus far, nearly all applications for "leave of absence," made by officers, have been returned disapproved at Department Headquarters. Should this course be continued, it will almost pay to be "reduced to the ranks." In spite of disapproval at Headquarters, however, and through the influence of the member of Congress, from his district, a ten days leave of absence has been granted by the War Department, to Lieut. Smith, of D. The Chaplain, who left for home long ago, taking the remains of his little brother, who died in camp, has so over-stayed his time, as to be reported this morning "absent without leave."

Lieut Hall, who has been on "sick leave" for months, returned to-day, a picture of perfect health.

The Adj't also reached camp from his trip to Fort Delaware. He reports that at every stage of his route, he received the highest compliments for the appearance of his guard.

He tells also a good story: Before leaving the boat to turn over his prisoners, he gave each of them a glass of whisky. Tears started to the eyes of one of them, as he swallowed his portion; and, to the Adjutant's inquiry if it was too strong, "Not that, Adjutant! not that," he replied. "Well! what are you crying for then?" "Why! why! Adjutant! I was thinking as how it would be *three years before I got another taste!!!*"

Capt. Cooley, of K., is off duty, by reason of loss of voice. We have also, ten or twelve men unable to speak a loud word; but in these cases, the loss of voice follows a long seige of typhoid fever; whereas the Captain's attack is sudden, and without apparent cause.

We had a pretty little excitement, about tattoo to-night, occasioned by the discharge of a musket in camp, and the unpleasant whiz over head of a missile of some sort. I thought it passed over *my* head. The Surgeon, on the right, insists upon it that it grazed his tent. The Adjutant, Colonel, Quartermaster, and all on the left declare it passed near them. The Sentinel in the rear, says he was "*near being hit*," while the line officers, lower down the hill, just *barely escaped*, if their statements are to be relied on. The explanation is, that the senior officer of the guard while inspecting the relief, about to be posted, ignorant that the junior officer had previously inspected, snapped the lock of a musket, and the man's *ram-rod* went flying diagonally over the camp.

His officer will have hard work to account for it, as expended in service.

15th. The second term of our "School for Officers," commenced this evening. Our first review and inspection, by Gen. Tyler in person, was had yesterday. Lieut. Jarvis, of the Massachusetts 14th, reported to-day, under orders to establish a signal station at this fort.

The men received their *extra pay* yesterday, for work done upon the new defences.

25th. The Adjutant, with a guard of one Sergeant, and fourteen privates, left to-day for Fort Delaware, having in his custody twelve prisoners, sentenced to be kept there, at hard labor, for different periods.

We have purchased, from the regimental fund, all necessary appliances, and to-day have started a tailor shop, having detailed seven men to repair *old*, and fit and re-make *new* clothing, for the men of the command.

Lieut. Macomber, having recovered his health, reported to-day for duty.

28th. About 9 P M. last night we were disturbed by a cry of fire given in Alexandria; soon after a second alarm was given for a fire in Fairfax Seminary Hospital, and a third for one a short distance in our own front. This last proceeded from the burning of an unoccupied building, upon the estate of George Mason, near by, and was undoubtedly incendiary. The camp was alarmed, and the officers of the guard, with a portion of the command went out to it. The result to us was, that Redoubts A., B. and C., were each occupied by one company of ours, and that Lieut. Cobb, with twelve picked men, was sent out on picket, at the junction of the Fredericksburg, and Mt. Vernon roads.

And this is probably all that it will amount to, although we are now again in front; not a picket between us and the Accotink, and our seven hundred and fifty effective men are the only support to works, which would require as many thousands, to hold against determined attack.

29th. "All quiet on the Potomac" and "raining like blazes." Our alarm of last night aroused the 142d New York, 26th Michigan, and 1st District of Columbia, encamped about a mile from us. Alexandria was in a perfect fury of excitement; and this morning the walls of many of the houses in that city are adorned by huge placards, having at their head, the imprint of a *lone star*, of the first magnitude; with "no levity — Watch — the 30th is the day!" in large print beneath.

Our sick list is frightful; and, after deliberation, we have organized what is termed by some "Lincoln's Cripple Brigade." "What's that?" "Well! it is composed of men, who, like him of F, 'don't find it just what they thought they should,' and 'want to go home.' Some who feign sickness; some who, really sick at first, don't relish being returned to duty; malingerers many — shirks, all of them.

Under orders to furnish a guard for the large amount of government property in the camp just vacated by the 27th Maine, and wholly unable to spare able bodied men for this duty and perform the other duties required of us, we have had a medical inspection of sick in quarters, and have selected the deaf, the moon blind, the lame of one leg, and those others, so afflicted with lameness as actually to halt on both limbs, and, assigning to the command of the body, non-commissioned officers marked for fidelity to duty, and strict obedience to orders, have determined to entrust to these men the safety of the property in question. As line was formed in front of the Adjutant's quarters, many a bent form straightened, and more than one eye brightened, in anticipation of the discharge which these fellows flattered themselves they had tired us into granting them. How faces lengthened, as orders were issued to them to pack their knapsacks, and report again in *light* marching order. Sad, but laughable were the interviews at Headquarters, between many of these men and the commanding officer! "Where are you going to send me, Colonel? I can't do duty! I have been excused for months." "Well, yes! but the duty will be light — almost nominal — merely to guard the property in the camp of the 27th Maine!" "But, Colonel, I can't do that! I can't 'walk beat!' You see I have to use a cane!" "Never mind about that! you may have a seat! it isn't your legs which are wanted! only your eyes, this time!" "But, Colonel! if the rebels should come!" "Then you'd be in the right place! you can't run! you'd *have* to fight!" "Well, Colonel! if I must go, can't I ride there in the ambulance?" "Not a step, sir! you must walk there! our able bodied men have done your duty long enough! They are, and have been overworked, and you must march, and remember, you will draw no rations till you reach your new camp!" Support was promised them, in case of an attack, and with many and loud mutterings, the long procession straggled from the camp. It is literally true, that one man, upon being deprived of his cane, hobbled off limping on his well leg.

Now, in none of these cases, can the surgeons, after the most careful examination detect any real disease. The *deaf* readily hear the *sick call;* the moon blind find no difficulty in making their way any where about camp, at any hour. They all sleep well, — they all eat well; — and really, it seems as if there was nothing they couldn't do, except do duty. What a *sell* it would be if the Rebels should actually gobble them up! But we shall make good soldiers of the most of them, yet. To-morrow we are to resume our labors on the new fortifications, five companies being ordered for the duty.

Dr. Clark and wife, Capt. Pratt and wife, Capt. Cooley and wife, Quartermaster Howland and wife, Capt. Leach, Dr. Smith and Lieut. Macomber, who has just returned to duty, after his protracted sickness, have gone to-day on a visit to Mount Vernon.

April 2d. Lieut. Smith, who has been long away on leave of absence, appears on the morning report as a *deserter*.

We have purchased, by appropriation from the Regimental fund, complete kits and a lot of sole leather, and have organized a regimental shoe shop, where repairing is to be done at a cost to the men of the bare expense of the materials.

A general Court Martial, Lieut. Col. Lincoln, President, is to assemble to-morrow for the trial of Lieut. Schaumberger, 3d Battalion, New York Artillery, for disobedience of orders and unmilitary conduct, in refusing, when thereto ordered, to take the Company under his command upon fatigue duty, to wit: the fortifications upon which *we* have so long been at work, basing his refusal upon the ground that as Artillery men his command was not liable to do such duty.

Our weather the past few days has been severe. Violent rains, have alternated with severe snow storms, each accompanied with high winds. For some time past our teams have been unable to draw wood enough to supply the daily demands of the camp, and what has been accumulating in the Quartermaster's hands has now become exhausted. Anticipating this state of things, requisition for fuel was made some days since upon the Post Quartermaster at Alexandria. The requisition was approved, and *we* were ordered to furnish a party of eighty men to proceed by rail towards Centreville and load a train of cars, *thirteen of which were for our own wants.* After loading these cars, the entire train was run by our camp to Washington, where the wood was unloaded, and our party, under Lieut. H, were left to walk back, some eight miles, to our camp.

Upon the report of these facts by this officer to Headquarters, a second requisition was made. As before, we were answered that "thirteen cars would be furnished for the use of the 34th Massachusetts, which would be required to detail a party of eighty men, properly officered to accompany the train, and load it for the use of the regiment." Lieut. L. was selected to command this party. The most express orders were given him to load the train, and "*see to it*," that the wood was left at the crossing in front of our camp.

Having completed the first part of his duty, the Lieutenant was asked by the conductor of the train, where he wished his party to be left. "At our camp, of course, with the wood," was the reply. "But I shall carry the wood to the city," said the conductor. "But the train was provided for our use, and upon our requisition," said the Lieutenant. "I don't care for that, I shall run the train to Alexandria." "And I shall obey my orders, and stop it at the crossing," said the Lieutenant. — As the train rolled along, the Lieutenant inquired of the conductor, if he would stop at our crossing, but received no reply. The speed was gradually increased, till the rate of running, as it neared our camp, was frightful. At a signal given by the Lieutenant, his party applied the brakes. It was friction against steam, with the advantage in favor of the former, and the train came to a dead stop, *before* our crossing was reached. "What does this mean, Lieutenant?" asked the conductor. "That the train has stopped," said the Lieutenant. "Well, I order you to take off the brakes, and let it go on." "Not unless you will promise to leave our wood at our crossing." "I'll report you at Headquarters, for *obstructing a train.*" "Report, and be d——d; I have obeyed my orders!" So the engine was detached, and the conductor, denouncing in unmeasured language the soldiers in general, and this party in particular, steamed away, leaving our party in possession of the field, and its trophies.

A good joke is current in the Brigade, while though not strictly correct, perhaps, is nevertheless substantially true. An order from the office of the War Department directed that the *Republicans* in the 1st and 19th Connecticut Volunteers, R. O. Tyler, Acting Brigadier General, commanding, to the number of four hundred, be granted furloughs in order to go home and vote at the election soon to be held in that State. Now, Gen. Tyler and Col. Abbott of the 1st, and Lieut. Col. Kellogg of the 19th, are each Democrats, and the deuce is to pay. Col. Kellogg, upon receipt of this order, left his command, and tendered his resignation. This was returned to him unaccepted. So he summoned to his presence Major Smith, his next in rank, and required him to receipt for the Regimental property. This he declined to do; thereupon the Lieutenant Colonel showed (some say kicked), the Major out of his tent, wrote and forwarded his resignation a second time, packed his valise, and departed for home. Notwithstanding this, the work of furloughing the men is going bravely on.

CHAPTER VIII.

PRACTICE WITH SHOTTED GUNS — MARCHING ORDERS — LIEUT. LINCOLN IN ARREST — PAID OFF — INSPECTION — NEWLY BRIGADED. — ASSIGNMENTS OF COMMANDS — ALLOWANCE OF STATIONERY.

Our men have had their first practice with shotted guns; twenty pounds parrotts, with shell. The targets were at distances of three quarters, and one and three quarter miles away. As a whole, the firing was good, the shots all being good line shots, but many of them falling short, the fuse being bad, requiring to be cut two inches long, when one and three quarters should have been sufficient. Three, only of our twenty five shots, hit the target.

12th. In the absence of the Colonel, at 6 A. M., orders were received for the regiment to move to-morrow morning, with seven days rations, three cooked; three wall tents allowed the field and staff, and a shelter tent to each line officer. Baggage to be confined to a small valise to each officer.

Gen. Tyler, reporting to Headquarters, "that the 34th Massachusetts from its acquaintance with the surrounding country, its good drill and discipline, and especially its proficiency in the school of Artillery, is of more value than any troops which can be sent to replace it," asks to have the order countermanded, which is done.

Capt. Cooley, who has received leave of absence on account of aphonia, will leave for home at once. He takes with him Mrs. A. D. Pratt and his own wife, Mrs. Dr. Clark having left some time since. Lieut. Macomber is still too unwell to accompany us. Lieut. Butler, awaiting sentence of general Court Martial, and Lieut. Stiles in arrest, and to be tried, are both to be left behind.

Lieut. Lincoln is placed in arrest for his conduct as commander of the "wood party," by orders from Gen. Heintzleman, and Gen. Tyler is ordered to investigate and report upon his conduct in the affair.

18*th*. We still remain; no orders to move having reached us, though other regiments have left.

All applications by our men for furloughs have been returned refused. Walsh, of A, while walking with a companion along the banks of Hunting Creek, was struck by a ball fired by one of the 153d New York, City Guard. Notwithstanding the wound, which is serious, the abdomen being pierced, the man walked into camp, and to the hospital. Upon examination the surgeons pronounce the wound fatal.

By orders from Headquarters defences of Washington, we have been ordered to detail a company to guard the property left by the 3d (Abercrombie's,) Brigade, which has marched away. Company I, Capt. Soley, has been selected for the duty, and he maintains regal state at his Headquarters near Cloud's Mills.

Our former Sergeant, Tannatt, called upon us to-day, sporting the dress of a 2d Lieutenant.

23*d*. Upon the report of Gen. Tyler, Lieut. Lincoln is released from arrest, and returned to duty. In communicating the discharge, the Regimental General Order compliments the Lieutenant "upon his exact compliance with his orders, and his good conduct in the affair" for which he was complained of.

It is raining a perfect flood, and Hunting Creek, in our front, has overflowed its banks. The water upon the road is above the beds of our wagons.

24*th*. We have been paid off up to March 1st, and the money seems to burn in the pockets of some of the men. "A" has nine in the guard house, drunk, and eleven other absentees from tattoo roll call. B is striving hard not to be outdone. A patrol, from the guard quarters, has just brought into camp one of A's men, who was found drunk, sitting down in the mud, and water, on the banks of the creek, *waiting*, as he said, "for the plaguey stuff to run out."

27*th*. Our man Walsh is improving, and will get well.

At the close of the inspection to-day, the Brigadier-General commanding rode into camp, as the companies last inspected, C, E and G, were about to be dismissed. At his request, they were again ordered to "prepare for inspection," and were subjected by him to a critical examination, at the close of which he exclaimed: "Beautiful! beautiful!"

28th. Gen. Tyler, of late in command "of the Defences of Washington, south of the Potomac," has been relieved, and Col. Tannatt, of our 14th, assigned temporarily thereto. Col. Abbott, of the 1st Connecticut, is placed at the head of our brigade, and our Col. has mounted and ridden away to Washington.

30th. General orders, "Headquarters Defences of Washington," just received, assign "Col. G. D. Wells, of the 34th Massachusetts Infantry, to the command of Forts Worth, Ellsworth, and Lyon, and Redoubts A, B, C, and D; the whole to be designated the "2d Brigade, Defences south of the Potomac," and the A. B. G. is directed to garrison the Redoubts immediately.

By brigade orders of same date, "Lieut. Col. Lincoln, commanding the 34th Massachusetts, is directed, at once, so to dispose of his command, as to comply with said general order." Accordingly, Companies A and F, Capt. Chandler commanding, are assigned to Redoubt "C," Companies E and G, Capt Bacon commanding, to Redoubt B, and B and D, Capt. Potter commanding, to Redoubt "A." The remaining companies under the immediate command of the Lieut. Colonel will encamp in rear of this line of Redoubts. These earth works have been constructed by us, and the men feel a commendable pride in them. A spirit of rivalry, between the several commands, is already apparent, and even now, men from each redoubt are scouring the country, in search of sound turf, with which to sod their magazines, bomb proofs, and parapets. If only they are permitted to remain in occupancy long enough, these redoubts will be little jewels in the line of defences, of which we may well enough feel proud!

This change is especially welcomed by our medical staff, as it puts us upon high land, away from the malarial influences of the creek, near which we have so long been encamped, and to which much of our sickness is undoubtedly owing.

To unable us properly to meet our new responsibilities, the Quarter-master laid upon our tables our allowance of stationery for the ensuing quarter. See how luxuriously our necessities are supplied! For instance, the Government's allowance to the Regimental Commander is *two* quires of letter, and *one* quire of fools-cap paper; twenty-five envelopes, one pen-holder, and ten steel pens, one lead pencil; two sticks of sealing wax, one-fourth ounce wafers, and (*only*) one piece of *red tape*, and yet, in any and every official communication he forwards, he is required to use at least a half sheet of paper.

CHAPTER IX.

Upton's Hill.

HISTORIC GROUND.—POLICING CAMP.—REGIMENTAL GROWTH. DISCHARGES FROM REGIMENT.— FORT "ALL HAZARDS." SPORTS.—REGIMENTAL FUND.—INSPECTION.—DRILLS. —INJUNCTIONS TO VIGILANCE.—PAY DAY.

May 4th. While busily engaged in preparing for occupation the new redoubts upon which we have so long labored, in obedience to orders of the 1st instant, other orders reached us after taps last night, which directed us to march at once, and occupy this post. Notwithstanding our unsettled condition the regiment was reported "in line," ready to march in two hours, after receipt of its new order.

We find the 11th Massachusetts Battery, Capt. Jones, in position here, occupying a small earthwork, near the house of a Mr. Upton, for whom the hill is named, and in which, Col. Wells, commanding post, takes up his quarters. The 34th will pitch its tents upon ground lately occupied by the —— Brigade, Pennsylvania Reserves; so soon as it can be policed sufficiently to be habitable. At present the filth is abominable.

We are upon historic ground. "Munson's Hill," an eminence on our left, is famous for having opposed insurmountable obstacles to McClellan's advance at an earlier stage of the war. Our position commands it, and is itself, in turn, commanded by "Miner's Hill," to our right. Old Rebel earthworks are visible all around us. We have pickets out in all directions, our position being an isolated one, in advance, and Mosby hovering about. We left at Fort Lyon the Surgeon and Quartermaster, to make arrangement for the proper disposal of the hospital and camp. Macomber, who is sick, Stiles and Butler who are in arrest, and the Chaplain were all left behind. Sergeant Wood's wife, alone of all our woman kind, accompanied the regiment on its march. The men stood the march well, spite of their heavy knapsacks, one of which, and that carried by one of our smallest men, actually weighed ninety pounds. Our chief tailor rather than trust his "goose," with the equipage left behind, put it into his knapsack, and actually backed it the whole way.

7th. We are enjoined, in orders, to the utmost vigilance, permitting no one to go through our lines, unless provided with a pass from Headquarters at Washington. Our drills are resumed, both company and batttalion.

The work of getting our camp clean is as yet incomplete. How filthy these Dutchman were! The holes they dug in the ground, and covered with their " A " tents, are reeking with old shoes, clothing, rotting straw, and half decomposed meat, bones and bread.

Our camp is laid out in the shape of a parallelogram; on one side in orderly streets, are the tents of the men; directly opposite are those of the line officers; the quarters of the field and staff are at one end, opposite to which is the entrance to the camp, flanked at one side by the quarters of the guard. The open space between these is reserved for our parades and guard mountings.

Lieut. Butler rejoined us to-day. At the request of Col. Wells, the sentence imposed upon him has been remitted, and he restored to duty. The Chaplain also rejoined us. We have enjoyed a good laugh at his expense, he having engaged in and enjoyed a game of ball last *Sunday,* having *forgotten what day of the week it was.*

9th. The Quartermaster rejoined us to-day, having completed the transfer of government property, for which he was accountable, at Fort Lyon. How *stuff* accumulates in camp; or, to put it in another light, *how a regiment grows?* One week ago to-night we left our old quarters, with *three* of our wagons well loaded. Since that time, these teams have made *one,* and sometimes *two* trips daily; and to-day, we had a government train of *twenty-one four-horse teams,* loaded down with "*our things;*" and the whole are not here yet. Besides, we have stored in Alexandria our company camp ranges, or cook stoves, which cost us $50 each; and turned over to the Post Quartermaster at Alexandria, about two hundred and fifty cords of wood, one hundred and fifty muskets, and a considerable quantity of ammunition and rations.

At parade to-night, the first since leaving Fort Lyon, cheer upon cheer were given by the boys of the 11th Battery, who had assembled to witness our movements. This Battery is to report in Washington, on the 18th, preparatory to being mustered out. The Colonel, who has been in Washington the past few days, returned to-night, bringing information that orders are to be issued for our junction with the Army of the Potomac; Gen. Hooker in his request for more troops, having specially designated the 34th Massachusetts as wanted by him.

11th. The sun scalds down oppressively upon the bare space which our tents enclose; and the dust, which fifty sweepers raise upon our parade ground is unendurable. The fact that the wind blows strongly towards Headquarters, probably is an inducement to every sweeper to use his broom vigorously. Surgeon Clark reached camp to-day, bringing up all the sick that could be removed, and twenty!! wagon loads of Hospital tents and stores. He has discharged *five* men this last week, and sent *ten* to general hospital, all of which will probably be discharged.

Our rolls show our strength to be eight hundred and sixty-seven, rank and file.

Up to this time, we have kept our sick with us, and the unremitting care and attention of our medical staff has probably saved us many whom otherwise we should have lost. At one time, our sick list was frightful. Rheumatism, Fever, (mostly Typhoid,) Measles, Small Pox, Homesickness, and a thousand and one ills, mostly indescribable, weighed us down; and medical inspectors, examined our reports, and medical directors ordered the transfer of large numbers of our men to general hospital. But still we held to them all; enlarging our accommodations and adding new comforts and conveniences to our hospital. Bodies of green sashed officers descended in person upon our camp, to see, with their own eyes the execution of their orders; and, after inspecting our sanitary arrangements, left with high appreciation of the skill and attention of our surgeons, and well deserved compliments for the perfect working of the means our ingenuity had adopted for the comfort and recovery of our patients. So that, till the movement to this post, we have lost no men by having them swallowed up in these general hospitals. Alas! that it can be no longer so!

Oh, dear, the horrors of war! We have no market, and the country round is literally bare of everything. How we of the shoulder straps envy the boys, whom the government provides liberally with hard tack and pork; while our caterer leaves us to laugh and grow fat upon our regular dish, at all meals, of sardines and lemons.

Companys I and D, Capt. Thompson commanding, have just marched out to occupy Fort "Buffalo;" or, as the boys call it, Fort "*All Hazards*," from an expression used in the order detailing them to the occupancy of the work.

14*th*. Phew! how it blows, and how cold and raw it is! A terrible storm is raging, with such gusts of wind as threaten the safe standing of our tents.

17*th*. What a change in our camp since reaching this post! One wouldn't know the boys to be the same. Songs, stories, ball playing, mock parades, are the order of the day! At reviellié this morning, our eyes were greeted with a "Sibley stove," mounted on a "tripod," the pipe directed to the tents of the line officers. The boys were photographing the officers as they made their appearance on the parade. The pantomime of putting in front of the stove a piece of board, on which was roughly drawn a charcoal sketch, using it for a negative, covering it with a shelter tent, and running for dear life behind a blanket, suspended near by, as a screen; pouring a pailful of water over it, and re-appearing and submitting it to the inspection of the bystanders, was side-splitting.

To-night the whole camp has been convulsed with the imitation of the Light Battery drill, by the boys, under the immediate management and command of Anderson of B, who will be remembered as the owner of a peculiar uniform, of his own designing, at Fort Lyon.

We have put into full operation again, our tailors, shoemakers, blacksmiths, and armorers shops, all with complete outfit of tools, and such stock as is necessary; and all, save the armorers, purchased with the money raised among ourselves. In addition we have bought our Band instruments, boxing gloves, and foot balls, besides checker and back-gammon boards for the hospital, and have over five hundred dollars in the Regimental Fund. All this money has been raised by monthly assessment upon the officers, in amount, proportioned to their rank.

17th. To-day was occupied by another inspection, the third within a week, all of them by orders from Washington. This finished, the boys hurried to witness the drill of Jones' Battery. It was perfect.

19th. In return for the gratification afforded us by the drill of the battery, the forenoon was occupied by battalion, and the afternoon by regimental skirmish drill, by request of Captain Jones and his officers. W C. Smith of H, left us to-day, commissioned to one of the regiments of colored troops, now forming at home.

23d. At the request of "the Boys," all drills have been suspended, that they might engage in a regular game of football; wing against wing, the Lieutenant Colonel acting as umpire. The weather was intensely hot; the game sharply contested; and, in their desire to win, many of the boys reduced their clothing to shirts, drawers, and stockings. The Colonel, who has been absent in Washington a day or two, drove into camp with a party of lady friends, but turned away at seeing the condition of the men, and subsequently administered a sharp reprimand for what he was pleased to call the "indecent exhibition."

Jones' Battery is relieved by one from Michigan.

Col. DeRussey succeeds to the command, from which Col. Tannett has been relieved; and by his orders, our pickets are largely increased, Alexandria having been badly scared last night, by a Rebel force, on the Mt. Vernon road. The inhabitants of the neighboring farms are thronging Regimental

Headquarters, (the post commander being absent), asking for guards to protect their property. But all applications of the kind are refused.

26th. We have been blessed with the always welcome presence of the Paymaster, to-day, who pays up to the first of this month. Robert J. Hamilton of I received his discharge to-day, to accept his commission in the Massachusetts 54th.

Renewed injunctions to "strengthen our pickets," and to "increased vigilance," reach us from Headquarters at Washington.

Rapid artillery firing, and the quick galloping into our camp of a party of light artillery men, caused us to stand to our arms, last night, but nothing came of it.

27th. A special messenger from Washington brings renewed injunctions "to the exercise of the utmost vigilance." The authorities there seem to be panic stricken. Our pickets have just brought in an officer of the 12th Michigan cavalry, on his way to his command. He was without the countersign, having been officially informed in Washington that *our* pickets had been gobbled.

What a heap of trouble attends pay-day; and how sure is liquor to be had wherever troops are stationed. How it is procured so readily, puzzles us all. Within a circle of a half mile there may be *six* houses. Our men leave camp, and in a short time return so drunk that it is a wonder how they manage to get back at all. Last night a drunken fracas in "B" was settled by sending *three* of her men to the guard tents. "A" soon made a contribution of *four* to the same quarter; then "B" added another in the person of one who, after being paid off, visited Alexandria without leave; and "A," not to be outdone, contributed still another to this well established hotel; altogether, there was too much whiskey; Clary of A was tied to a post at the guard tent. Being the first punishment of this nature, the boys, already excited, lost themselves, and loud cries of "fall in," "fall in," "cut him down," "cut him down," attracted attention. Capt. B, officer of the day, jewel of an officer that he is, was quickly upon the ground, and soon quieted the disturbance.

The bugles now sounded the assembly, and a drill followed, long enough and sharp enough to take any superfluous *vim* out of these fellows; but A., Lieutenant of the Guard, has just reported that the mutterings in camp are loud, and to enquire if he shall not call for an addition to his guard. He gets no comfort beyond the assurance that he is responsible for the quiet and order of the camp. Now, at tattoo, another Lieutenant commanding reports one of his Sergeants beastly drunk, unable to stand, or answer to his name, and asks for advice as to his own course in the matter. There is but one rule in such cases, as he is reminded. But the Sergeant is the son of rich and influential parents, who aided largely in getting up the company, and whom the Lieutenant dares not offend. So it is plain that Headquarters must act, and the stripes are torn from the man's arm.

31st. We are guarding a camp occupied by hundreds of contrabands, of both sexes and all ages, which has been lately established on our flank. The poor creatures are grateful enough for the safety which our uniform guarantees to them.

All work is suspended in camp, and a large detail of the boys, armed with axes mostly, some with pick or shovel, are hard at work obstructing the highway leading to our position, and by *slashes* and otherwise, so blocking all wood-paths and by-ways as to render them impassable for Cavalry. This, in pursuance of orders from Gen. Heintzelman, who, with his staff, is this side the river, superintending in person the obstruction of the approaches to Washington. Notwithstanding all this, and other indications of a *scare* in that city, the Lieut. Colonel commanding, and Capt. Fox, are detailed as members of a Court Martial ordered to assemble to-morrow at Fort Anthony, seven miles from here.

CHAPTER X.

WASHINGTON.

A MARCHING SALUTE.—DETAILS FOR GUARD DUTY.—OUR QUARTERS.—DETAILS OF OFFICERS.—CAPT. MEIGS.—OUR GUARD.—A GOOD JOKE.—OUR GUARD.—DETAILS OF CO'S TO DUTY.—CASES OF SICKNESS.—THE WEATHER.

June 2d. Everything like labor was suddenly suspended yesterday, by receipt of orders to hold ourselves in readiness to move, the moment we were relieved by the "Brigade of Pennsylvania Reserves, now in motion." Our march of the day was one of only nine miles; but the sun was burning hot, and the dust stifling. The road was obstructed, in many places, by huge trees, placed, abattis like, across the way, which rendered our progress difficult and tedious. , Proceeding through Georgetown, and down the avenue, as we neared the White House, the bugles sounded "attention." The gaunt form of the President was discovered at the gate, in front of the White House, and orders were sent down for a marching salute as we passed. Our army of dogs being sent back to the cover of our wagons, the regiment formed in column of companies, the band struck up a patriotic march, and with lines beautifully dressed, and arms glittering in the sun, the regiment looked and marched splendidly.

Judge of the unutterable disgust with which, as drawing near to the President, in the conceit that our appearance could not fail of eliciting complimentary notice, we heard him enquiring, "What regiment is it?" "Where is it from?" "And how dare they disobey the order mustering out of service, all regimental bands!"

Gen. Martindale, to whom we reported, paid us the compliment of saying, that "he had ordered us into the city, in consequence of the flattering reports made to him of our excellence in drill and discipline." In the hurry of our getting off, Anderson of B, and Thurman of D deserted.

4th. Our duties here commenced yesterday, by sending to the "Carroll Hill" and "Old Capitol" Prisons, a guard of one hundred and twenty-five men each.

To-day, we detail fifty men to the depot of the Baltimore & Ohio Railroad.

Capt. Cooley returned to us yesterday, not having regained his voice, as we hoped he would.

Lieut. Smith, who left us last March, was returned to us to-day ironed, and in custody of an officer specially detailed, in Boston, to see to his safe delivery to us. Charges of desertion are to be preferred against him, and he will be sent to Court Martial. We occupy wooden barracks, erected upon a square on East Capital Street, a few rods from the Capitol itself.

Companys "A" and "F," "C" and "E," and the Q. M. occupy the buildings on one side of the square. Opposite them are "G" and "K," "D" and "H," and "I" and "B." Headquarters are in a low building next the street; and at the other extremity is the hospital. This is on the second story, occupying a room about twenty-five by forty, well lighted and ventilated, suitably provided with comfortable bunks.

We have raised, in the center of this room, a framed platform, upon which are roses, geraniums, and other plants, in full bloom.

After moving from these quarters many wagon loads of old boots, shoes, bones, and other abominations, we are comfortably clean and sweet.

The boys are put *upon honor*, for the most part, in the matter of leaving camp. "Passes" are furnished, almost without stint; the men being required to present themselves at the Guard Quarters, upon going out and returning to camp; shoes, belts, &c., polished,—clothes brushed clean, and the number of the regiment, and the letter of their company conspicuous on their caps. One hundred and forty-four visited the city yesterday, all of whom returned sober, and many of them before the expiration of their allotted time.

Col. Wells is detailed as member of the Board to examine applicants for commissions in Regts. of colored troops, and Lieut. Col. Lincoln is president, and Capts. Bacon and Fox members, and Lieut. H. Bacon, Judge Advocate of General Court Martial, to sit daily.

7th. The wives of a goodly number of our men have reached us, and more are coming; for whose accommodation tents are pitched, on land near, but outside Regimental quarters.

The compliment of an order from General Headquarters, directing the Provost Guard of the city to report all passes issued from our own Headquarters, has been paid us.

In spite of a cold Northeast wind which rendered us all uncomfortable, we had our regular inspection, and evening parade; at the latter of which, a large number of spectators, many of them in uniform, were present.

Capt. Meigs, who has general supervision of the State prisoners, and their guard, during a call to-day, amused us much with an account of his experience with one of our sentinels. In going his accustomed rounds, he dismissed the Sergeant, who had formed his escort, and continued his way alone. As he proceeded, "You can't pass here, sir," fell sharply on his ears; accompanied with the ring of the metal, as the musket was brought down. Turning upon the sentinel, the Captain asked, "What are your instructions?" "None of your business, sir!" Attempting to advance, came the sharp "halt, or I fire!" "What are your instructions guard, that you stop me in my rounds?" asked the Captain. "None of your business," was again the answer. "Straightening myself, with a dignity becoming my position," said the Captain, "I ordered 'Recover your piece!' I am your commanding officer; and must pass." Sentinel: "I don't know you sir! My Lieutenant is my commanding officer, and *I am yours, now;* so, stand back!" Captain — "What are the bounds of your beat?" Sentinel — "None of your business!" Captain — "Where does this passage lead?" Sentinel — "none of your business!" Captain — "Are there other guards near you?" Sentinel — "None of your business!" Captain — "Well, I am Capt. Meigs, and my business is to superintend this prison, and its guard, and I order you to let me pass." Sentinel — "I've heard tell of Capt. Meigs, but I don't know him, nor any one but my own officer, while I am sentinel, so stand back, sir!" "And," said the Captain, "By Jove, Colonel, I backed down, for the first time in my experience, and used your guns as a mirror by which to curl my moustache."

Our pieces are indeed brought to a high degree of polish; so highly polished are they, that we have been charged with having them silver plated. With these, and the scales, which we are to don to-morrow, by general order, and the white gloves, and well blacked equipments, of old date, we shall indeed be the "*Dandy Soldiers*" Gen. Tyler would have us.

Our eight hundred men replace the eighteen hundred, or thereabouts, of the Brigade of Penn Reserves, (*Bucktails*), which we relieved. Capt. Parker, of Gen Martindale's Staff tells us, that the General asked, as a personal favor, that we might be ordered to report to him for duty.

Connected with our duty at the railroad station, a good joke has occurred. While on duty there, Lieut. Horton in command, heard the sentinel, on post at the door, call "Turn out the guard;" and as he thought, add, "Officer of the day." The men sprang to their arms, and the Lieutenant placed himself at their head, to do the proper thing. Seeing no *officer*, nor, in his opinion, any person who was entitled to a salute, he brought his men to an "Order," and stepped to the door, to see for himself, who was approaching.

"Why didn't you salute the President, Lieutenant?" asked Capt. Mix, who has the station in charge. "President! what President?" asked H. "I havn't seen anybody who looked like a President!" "Look there, then" said the Captain, pointing to the long, lean figure of "Old Abe," who, with uncovered head, was bowing to the guard, as he shuffled down their front. Poor H. felt bad enough; but was consoled by the statement of Capt. M. that the honest old soul could not tell "*Present arms*" from any other movement; in proof of which, said he, "look at him, returning to your men, his acknowledgements for the salute, they ought to, but have not, paid him."

A detail, just ordered, takes from camp *every man fit for duty*.

Emerson (Sergeant) of K was discharged to-day, to accept promotion in colored troops.

10*th*. We, in camp, were startled to-day by a musket shot, which, upon inquiry, was found to have been fired by one of our sentinels, at the old Capitol Prison; an honest, straight forward, well meaning young fellow, but green as grass; and the following is the man's own account of the matter, as told to a comrade after reaching quarters.

"Now Bill" he says to his comrade, "I vow, I don't know
" what got into me. You see, I had never been on that beat
" before, and the fellow who was there when I was posted,
" only told me not to let any body pass. But he never told me
" how to stop 'em, least wise he never told me to fire. So, when
" I see a fellow, with his head and shoulders out of the
" window, I told him to halt, but the plaguey fool did n't, and
" I up and called out Corporal of the guard! Upon that the
" confounded Rebel he thought he'd *get back*, and I ordered
" him to halt again, and sung out for the Corporal of the guard!
" But before he'd got along — the Corporal, I mean — Joe
" Webber — you know him Bill — and an all-fired lazy fellow he
" is, too — Capt. Meigs, he came along — confound him, he's
" just like our Lieut. Colonel, down right on to a fellow before
" he knows it; and says he, guard! what are you making such a
" noise about? What are you calling the Corporal of the guard
" for? This is n't your camp! Well no! Capt. says I. I guess I
" know that, but what shall I do? — and just then, the d——d
" old Reb., he caught sight of the Capt. and tried to slip back,
" and I sung out *halt!* and the Capt. says he, what's that for?
" and then he caught sight of the grey back, and says he, shoot
" the cuss! and says I, *what for?* and the Capt. he looked me
" over, and says he, where did you come from? and I told
" him from old Massachusetts? and I belonged to the 34th,
" Col. Wells! and I guessed Col. Wells knew what was what,

"as well as any Capt. there was!—So then, the Capt. says he, "Guard, what are your instructions? and I told him the fool "didn't give me any. Well, says he, if any person tries to "pass your beat, you stop 'em, and if any prisoner tries to get "out, you shoot 'em! and I told him I would,—just so.

"Well, a little while after this, I caught sight of that same "eternal, all fired, mean Reb., sticking his head out of the "window again, and I told him just to put it back, but he "didn't mind, and I up and let drive at him, but the old gun "didn't shoot straight. I swan, I got just as good a bead on "him as you ever saw, but it was an all fired mean place "to shoot in!

"Well, when I found I didn't hit, I tell you Bill, I felt "cheap enough! I couldn't get reconciled, no how! I knowed "that Capt. would be along, and I was thinking what to tell "him, when sure enough, he popped on to me, and says he, "guard, what in hell are you doing! What are you wasting "ammunition for? I a'int doing no such thing Capt. says I;— "I was trying to see how near I could come to that Rebel's "head and *not hit it*, and says I, Capt. I'll bet anything the "ball just singed him! Confound your singeing, says he! I "don't want any guard of mine should miss, when he fires! "Don't you now, Capt? don't you really? If I'd only just "known that before! just let me draw another bead on him, "if that's the case, and he's a gone 'er! I can shoot some, Capt. "I *can that!* and you just get the fool to put his head out "again, and you'll see who can shoot, and who can't!"

There was not so much in the story itself, but the man's manner of telling it was inimitable.

Lieut. Lincoln with "I," and Lieut. A. C. Walker with "H," Lieut. Lovell with "A," and Lieut. Macomber with "E," guard the "Old Capitol" and "Carroll Hill" prisons, on alternate days. Lieut. Horton with "G," alternates with Platt and the men of "K" at the Railroad Depot. Lieut. Bacon, with thirty men, goes to-morrow to Philadelphia, having charge of a party of deserters from the Rebel army, who, having taken the oath of allegiance to Uncle Sam, are assigned to that city as an abiding place. Lieut. Hall with thirty men is now absent on similar duty in New Jersey. Lieuts. Butler and Van Loan have charge of invalid detachments, at two of the neighboring hospitals. Lieut. S. of "D" is in arrest, waiting trial on charges preferred against him; Lieut. S. of "A" waiting sentence of Court Martial, and Lieut. L. of "D" has complied with request from Headquarters, and sent in his resignation, which has gone forward, approved.

E lost a man to-day under peculiar circumstances. He was taken sick yesterday, and excused from duty; answered at Surgeon's call this morning, and was ordered into hospital, where he died this afternoon.

12th. We sent out to-day a detail of one commissioned and two non-commissioned officers and twenty men, as guard over a large party of wounded, but convalescent soldiers, en route to hospital in New Jersey. Our party looked splendidly,— all leather as black as the ace of spades, all brass brighter than a new dollar, and the guns,— well, as Capt. P. says, one wanted *smoked glass* through which to look at them.

One of E's men was missing at morning roll call; his clothes, watch and money, still at the head of his bunk, seemed to indicate a somnambulistic leave taking. A man of A also disappeared in the night, but as he left the guard house and walked off with the iron wristlets with which he was adorned, we concluded *he* knew what he was about.

Again our last man is taken from camp, by orders to relieve a guard from the 157th New York, which regiment is ordered to the front.

16th. We were called upon this afternoon for a party to be marched instantly to the "Soldiers' retreat," to quell a disturbance made by some men, who, their time of service having expired, refused to obey the orders of any one. Lieut. Cobb in command, succeeded admirably in carrying out his orders, and quiet was speedily restored.

18th. At inspection to-day two of the boys were so overcome by the heat as to drop in their places. The thermometer was at 108°. Notwithstanding the heat, our parade was had at an earlier hour than usual, to gratify the inspecting officer, and other officers from Gens. Heintzleman's and Martindale's Headquarters, who desired to witness it.

CHAPTER XI

WASHINGTON.

LIEUT. LOVELL'S EXPERIENCE—TWO CASES OF PUNISHMENT—A CASE FOR "FURLOUGH."

The resignation of Lieut. Lyman has been accepted; and the Chaplain for *general* reasons, and Capt. Cooley, on account of impaired health, have forwarded theirs for approval. Capt. Soley and Lieut. Elwell returned to duty to-day, having been off on leave of absence. Capt. Lovell had quite a lively little affair while on duty yesterday, as officer of the guard, at the prison.

Among the persons confined there is a large, muscular masculine looking woman, reported to have served as Orderly Sergeant in some Rebel organization. She is noisy and troublesome, and steadily sets at defiance all the rules for the government of the prison. A carpenter having been sent into the entry, where her room is, to make some needed repairs, she flew into a passion, threw his tools out of one of the windows, and then turned upon, and actually kicked him out of the entry. The guard called his Corporal—the Corporal his Sergeant—and the Sergeant his officer. Lovell ordered her to be quiet, and she laughed at him; he ordered her to her room, and she snapped her fingers in derision; he threatened to iron her, and she dared him to do so, adding that there wasn't a Yankee living who could do that. Waiting his opportunity, Lovell caught her; she clinched; there was a struggle and a fall—a succession of kicks and shrieks, and she was left—free to rise—adorned with a pair of bracelets not usually worn for ornament! Sullen and crestfallen, she retired to her room.

21st. Distant cannonading was distinctly heard to-day, reported to be at Chantilly. We have a little army of old and young, grave and gay, ugly and pretty, all of them happy — wives, among us. For the most part, they take life as it comes; making the most of what is agreeable, and accepting the unpleasant as inevitable. But a little incident of camp life disturbed the even current of the day, and afforded to the lookers-on a good deal of amusement.

Wagner, of I, a great, burly Dutchman, too fond of liquor to be included in the prison guard, and therefore retained in camp, had got roaring drunk, somehow, and was made into what is technically called a "spread eagle." It so chanced that he was seen in this situation, by Mrs. Marth, the wife of a Corporal of G., and a fellow countryman. Almost frantic with excitement, the woman rushed to Headquarters with a complaint against the man's Captain, which she accompanied with a threat of carrying her complaint to Gen. Heintzleman, unless the man was instantly released. She was dismissed from Headquarters at once; her threat, alike with her complaint, being disregarded. Camp was made hideous with her howling, and her husband was called and directed to take her to her quarters outside the camp. And now came the fun! She 'd no idea of being controlled, *least of all*, by her husband; and, therefore, resenting his interference, she turned upon him, threw him into the gutter, and pounded him soundly. Was it in retaliation for this, we wonder, that he deserted last night? More of our boys' wives made their appearance to-day, one of whom had to give the conjugal embrace to her husband, in the guard house, in presence of an appreciative and sympathizing party of comrades.

22d. Capt. Soley, with fifty men, and Lieut. Ammidon, with thirty, are off on special duty. Lieut. Cobb, with twenty-five men, starts for Philadelphia to-morrow, having in charge a body of rebel prisoners, to be delivered in that city. Lieut. Bacon, in command of a like squad, on similar duty, returned from that city to-day. He reports that the appearance of his party excited much attention. Capts. Fox and Pratt, and Lieut. Lyman, whose resignation has been accepted, left for home to-day; the two former on short leaves of absence.

June 23*d*. While sitting in my quarters to-day, a faint rap sounded on my door. In answer to my "come in," a young, as the sailors would say, "hermaphrodite-rigged" form appeared, and approaching with extended hand, in a pleasant, subdued voice, said: "This is Col. L., I believe. *I* am Miss Dr. Walker, U. S. A."

She was dressed in a close-buttoned, blue cloth frock, the skirts falling to her knees; tight fitting black pants, and congress boots; and, twirled in her hands, an ivory handled sun shade. A jaunty little hat was perched upon a small, but well formed head, down each side of which long cork-screw curls were flowing. Beautiful eyes, a fair complexion, and a pretty chin, helped diminish the unfavorable impression produced by thin, pursed-up lips, and a sharp, almost transparent nose. "You have a private, Col., in your hospital, by the name of R——s, in whom I have taken an interest,—not for himself, precisely, but because of his health. He ought to have a furlough—in fact, *he must* have one. Can't you give it to him?" "I fear not, madam." "Then one must be procured through my influence," she continued. "I am very patriotic—and the officers know that I never ask of them anything improper to be granted. I spend my time in the hospital—am just up from "Acquia Creek," where I have been for the last two months, and where I became much interested. Now Col., I don't *know* how it is, but I am afraid *you don't know* Mr. R——s, and I will tell you all about him." "On the contrary, Dr., I do know him perfectly well." "Yes, Col., as a *soldier* perhaps." "As a *soldier*, and *patient* both, Dr." "As a patient, Col.? Is it possible?—what is his disease?" "Why Dr., the man has been in hospital under treatment, for months; first for measles, then for aphonia, and he now labors under a severe attack of what we call commission fever, for which time is the best and only remedy." "Oh, Col.! Oh, Col.! how can you say so? I assure you, upon my honor, that Mr. R——s is an extremely conscientious man, who wouldn't, for the world, practice any deception! And I *know* he ought to have a furlough!" "Yes, but Dr. our Surgeons decline to give the necessary certificate." "But Col., *I* am a Dr., you know, and I have prepared a certificate of the necessity of a furlough, to the recovery of the man's health." "Unfortunately, Dr., *you* are not *our* Surgeon!" "True, Col.! but you must be aware that the rules only require a certificate of ill health from *a* surgeon, and not, by any means, from *the* particular regimental Surgeon."

"Certainly, my dear doctor, you state the requirement correctly; but if the officers of the 34th have a weakness, it is of confining among themselves, everything relating to the morale, and discipline of the regiment."

"How then, Col.! Don't you send charges to General Court Martial?" "Oh! now my dear miss, you "touch us on the raw!" *If we like a man*, no little matter can separate us. If circumstances arise, which require a little extra attention to him, the Captain takes him in hand! If the disease is beyond the Captain's skill, or power, to cure, he falls into Headquarters' hands! Only, when we have made up our minds, that the interest of the 34th requires a permanent separation, do we send a man to General Court Martial!" "Well, Col., I thank you for your frankness; but I see, in this case of Mr. R———s, you will force me to appeal to those of higher rank!" "How I shall regret that, my dear doctor! To have it said, that a *lady* had been *forced* to anything by an officer of the 34th, would mortify the whole command!!" I wish I could describe her look at this reply! She tore a leaf from her diary, and remarking that she was "at home" every afternoon after five, handed me her address, and bowed herself from my quarters.

CHAPTER XII.

WASHINGTON.

CAPT. CAMP— MAJOR SHERBURN— MARCHING ORDERS—RESIGNATIONS— 4TH OF JULY— MARCHING ORDERS AGAIN— OFF AT LAST— AN ACCIDENTAL DEATH— RUN TO "SANDY HOOK"—MARYLAND HEIGHTS—NEWLY BRIGADED —WASTE OF PROPERTY AT EVACUATION OF POSITION—OUR GOOD NAME TARNISHED.

Capt. Camp, in charge of the railroad station, writes us thus: "I must insist upon your not relieving the guard at this station. For the two years I have had charge of it, I have never had duty performed so satisfactorily." He refused to allow the guard on duty, to be relieved by the new detail; and has suceeded in procuring an order from General Headquarters, directing "the party, now on duty, to remain as *permanent* guard." His success has induced Capt. Meigs, at the old Capitol Prison, to prefer the same request.

Maj. Sherburn, our inspector of the 18th, reports in writing, as follows;

"This Regiment is in the very best condition, as regards "drill and discipline;— its quarters perfectly neat;— its hos-"pital arrangements perfect;— and it has never been my lot to "inspect a regiment, whose arms and equipments were in such "splendid order."

Are n't we justified in feeling proud? when it is remembered that not one moment of time was spent in preparing for this inspection, save such as was required to "pack knapsacks."

Capt. Leach, returned from "absence with leave" and reported for duty to-day.

26th. " The 34th Regiment. Massachusetts Volunteers, will hold itself in readiness to move at a moment's notice." Such is the order which reached us this evening; and we are only waiting the relief of our various guards. This work goes on slowly and slovenly; being done by the employees of the Quartermaster's department, who, as report goes, are organized, equipped, and well drilled; ready to do duty as soldiers, in case of need. Judge how well founded this claim, in their behalf, is, by the following: A squad of these fellows, under command of a Captain, was marched up to relieve a guard on duty, and received the following orders: "*halt,*" "*front.*" " Order arms." There being some delay in the execution of this last order, the commanding officer broke out in this most approved military fashion? "Lay your guns down on the ground, d—n your souls!!"

27th. Our order to be ready to move, is countermanded, and we have resumed duty as before. I have been up to the Old Capitol Prison, to look at some five hundred rebel prisoners, who, under guard of two companies of ours, are to be transported to Fortress Monroe. In physique, these men are everything one would desire for soldiers; and, except for clothing, need shun comparison with no body of men in the service; — " Though, to be sure," as our Adjutant remarked, " They have n't each got two pairs of white gloves, and a stock in his knapsack."

28th. 10 *P M.* Again an order to hold ourselves in readiness to move.

29th. Still here; though ready to fall in, at the first tap of the drum. A rebel force is raiding between here and Baltimore. The 39th Massachusetts moved last night to Fort Alexander; and the 14th New Hampshire to Fort Massachusetts. Hooker is relieved, and Meade ordered to the command thus vacated. My boy, Jim, has just laid upon my table an immense bouquet. "Why, Jim? where did you get that?" " Well, Colonel," said he, touching his cap, "that ar was confisticated from a yallar gal, what has just seceded!"

30th. To-day was Bi-monthly Inspection and muster for pay. The resignation of the Chaplain has been accepted. We lose, also, to the great regret of every person in the command, Capt. Cooley; his health being such as to forbid his remaining in the service.

July 3d. We are ordered to report at 9 A. M., to-morrow, in front of the City Hall, to form part of the escort in the municipal celebration of the day.

July 5th. Our work of yesterday, escort to the procession in the municipal celebration of the day, was fatiguing enough. The weather was intensely hot, and some of the boys were sun-struck. We moved on to line, at the City Hall, at 9 A. M. All our details for guard, except one relief at each station, were called in, and thus increased, our regiment outnumbered, by double, any other command on duty. We were greeted with cheers at several points in the line of march. The day's duty was closed by a "march in review," before Gens. Martindale's and Heintzleman's Headquarters; officers from the staff of each of whom have ridden out to-day to compliment us upon our "splendid appearance," and as they are pleased to say, "our triumph over all other regiments on duty." We are accused of having had our arms *silver-plated*, and more than one bet was won and lost on this point.

Fatiguing as the service was, it was not without its amusing incident. On our homeward march the Colonel was desirous of showing us off to a bevy of ladies, chief of whom was Miss U—, with whom he had made an intimate acquaintance. So he despatched the Adjutant along the line to put us on our good behaviour. Arms were brought to the shoulder, and in column of companies, to the inspiring notes of "the Girl I left behind Me," he led us by her residence, ignorant of the appearance he himself made, as with pants slipped above his knees, thus disclosing the bright scarlet of his close fitting drawers, he proudly reined his prancing bay charger before the eyes of the lady of his love.

At our evening parade the whole square was densely packed. Officers, citizens, ladies on foot, on horseback, and in carriages, so filled the avenue that the boys had to wait on line some time after the parade was dismissed to allow the crowd to disperse.

8th. At the request of Hon. B. B. French, our band was allowed to go out last evening, to serenade the occupants of the "White House," and this morning's papers speak of the performance "by the Matchless Band, of the 34th Massachusetts, Col. *Peck.*" Such is fame! Capts. Fox and Pratt, and Lieut. Lovell, made their appearance to-day, much to our joy, for we are very hard worked.

9th. The afternoon and evening have been full of excitement. Soon after dinner, the Col. who had left camp in the morning, returned in haste, and exchanging his uniform for citizen's dress, left camp without communicating with any one. In phrase familiar among us, the Judge was absent, the Col. at home.

About 4 P. M., Capt. Potter A. A. A. G. Headquarters Defences, dashed up, and in an excited tone and manner, demanded "*why* the regiment was not under arms." Simply Capt. was the reply, "because we do not move without orders!" "But your orders were issued long ago!" "That may be so, Capt., but none have been received." "Where is Col. Wells?" "He was here a short time ago, Capt." was the reply, and the orderly was directed to look for him, and say to him, that Capt. P. desired to see him. The Capt. however with, "well Col.," call in your guards, pack your knapsacks, and get ready to move at once, put spurs to his horse and rode off. All guards, with the exception of those over the state prisons, were at once ordered to camp, and the hospital and Quartermaster's department put in readiness to move, the latter by the efficiency of the Quartermaster Sergeant, as the Quartermaster himself was absent. We were resting thus, when an aide de camp of Gen. Martindale dashed up, his horse all in a foam, with an inquiry for Col. Wells, and learning his absence, for Col. L. Upon the latter presenting himself, he received an order to "move the command." "What Capt. as it is? I have 'nt half the regiment with me!" "You have had ample time Col! Why are you not ready?"

"You were ordered to call in your guards, long ago, Colonel! Why did you not obey?" "I could not imagine, Captain, that it was intended that I should take the guards from the government prisons, and leave the rebels there unguarded! All my other guards were called in, and are ready to move now." "But, are you not relieved at the prisons?" "No, sir!" and off *he* dashed.

That no possible blame should attach to the Regiment, all guards, *not on actual post* at the prisons, were ordered into quarters, to pack knapsacks; and this done, the sentinels on duty were relieved for the same purpose; and the whole guard were at their posts, ready to join the command as it should move on its way. Messengers were despatched in all quarters for the missing Colonel and Quartermaster. Now, at near 9 P. M., Capt. Potter again galloped up, and angrily demanded to know "why we were not under arms. By G–d! Colonel, we have looked upon yours as the *best* regiment ever on duty in this city; but this is inexcusable!" The storm of abuse, which was breaking over my head, was suspended by the arrival of an Orderly, with written orders, which he handed me. They proved to be the ones which had been issued *hours before;* and the lightning flashed at the orderly instead of at me.

"Still," said the Captain in more civil tone, "Still, I cannot understand why you are not ready to move!" "I am ready to move this moment Captain, if directed, and—" "Get your men under arms at once, Colonel!" was his order. How our bugles rang out their "call to the color," in the hope that in the stillness of the summer air, our missing officers would hear, and hearing, recognize them! Our line showed small, as it was formed. "Where is your regiment, Colonel?" broke from the Captain, as saluting, I reported it ready. "It is a strong one; and yet you muster here, *not* more than two or three hundred men." "Captain, every man, subject to my orders, stands in line! It is not our fault that other men, detailed by Superior Headquarters, are not present." "But you reported yourself as ready to move!" "True, sir; and I am ready." "Where are your details, Colonel?" "At the Government prisons, Captain." "Why are they not relieved?" "I wish I could tell you, Captain. They have orders to come in as soon as relieved, and I have no doubt they will do so."

The Capt. sat his horse for a few moments; his low muttering indicating, pretty plainly that *some one would catch it*. But his patience gave way before long, and, in response to his sharp command, the order to march was issued. As we drew near the prisons, we were directed to "halt." The work of relieving our guard was going on, with all the slow awkwardness so peculiar to the employees of the Quartermaster's Department. This accomplished, the men fell into line, and, to the inspiring music of our band, beneath the light of a nearly full moon, we marched through deserted streets, to the railroad station, where a train of cars was in waiting for us. Here our Col. joined us.

It was past eleven P M., when the long train of cars moved out from the station, in the direction of Baltimore. We left behind Lieut. Elwell, charged with the proper disposition of our own and the Government property, and first Asst. Surgeon Thorndike in charge of the hospital, its sick and supplies. The Relay House was not reached till after sunrise the next morning, and our stay there was long. At length we started; our running was slow. Many of the men had clambered upon the roofs of the box cars, there being no provision made for them to sit down inside. As we neared Ellicott's Mills, we were all startled by a cry that a man had fallen from the train. It was Fitzgerald, one of F's best men. His body, horribly mangled, was left in charge of a brother soldier from his own company, who was directed to see to its proper burial; and, saddened by the occurrence, our route was resumed. It was evening when we reached Frederic Junction. Crossing the Monocacy on a frail wooden bridge, in place of the splendid iron one destroyed by the rebels last December, and rolling along through a most lovely valley, the train came to a stand at "Sandy Hook," about 9 P. M. Disembarking, the regiment threaded its way through almost countless trains of cars, and army wagons. Thick, heavy clouds obscured the moon, and, in almost Egyptian darkness, we felt our way. Our route lay along a narrow road between the canal, on our left, and Maryland Heights, which towered to a great height, on our right. In the darkness one man fell into the canal, but was rescued with the loss of his musket only.

It was past two o'clock when, having reached a plateau midway up the mountain, we laid down, as we were halted, for the sleep and rest we needed.

Upon trains close following our own, were the 39th Massachusetts, a Pennsylvania regiment of heavy Artillery, and two light batteries, the whole under the temporary command of Col. Wells. Our bugles roused us early on the morning of the 12th, and soon afterwards, Cols. Sprague and Studley, Lieut. Harkness, and others of the 51st Massachusetts, gave us a warm and pleasant greeting.

We were tired and hungry. Foraging parties soon unearthed from beneath wood piles, and other places of concealment, near the few farm houses in sight, boxes of hard tack, and barrels of pork, which there was little hesitancy in pronouncing "contraband." Our "shelters" are pitched upon a little triangular plot of clear ground, some two hundred feet from the river side of the mountain. To the east, rise the Heights proper, now held by six regiments of Infantry, and two batteries of Artillery. To the west, is "Fort Duncan," garrisoned by our own 46th; a part of the 51st lying in support. On the opposite side of the river rise Loudon and Bolivar heights, between which, are the ruined villages of "Harper's Ferry," and "Bolivar," now held by Rebel forces. Lee has escaped, and with these others, we are sent up here *to lock the stable.* By orders of Gen. Negley in command, the 34th and 39th Massachusetts, the 173d Pennsylvania, with a squadron of Michigan, and another of Pennsylvania cavalry, are brigaded under Col. Wells.

The 39th has been detached, and with the 8th, 46th, and 51st, Massachusetts, the whole under command of Brig. Gen. H. S. Briggs, marched last night, en route for Boonsboro, and the "Army of the Potomac."

What a frightful waste of property attended the evacuation of this position! Dried apples, hard tack, rice and sugar, all mixed and jumbled together, lay in heaps, from two to three feet deep, and this, although the Rebels have drawn away large quantities, and all the farmers from the near country, have take away large supply for present and future wants,

Piles of Sibley tents, *as good as new*, save that each has been slit once from top to bottom, and heaps of Springfield muskets, many of them with broken stocks indeed, but many entirely uninjured, and for which our boys have left their own, in exchange, lie scattered about. One huge one hundred pound rifled Parrott gun lies on the mountain side, down which, after being dismounted, it was hurriedly thrown. Everything shows a hurried, and ill considered, and ill planned evacuation; between which, and its re-occupation, it is said, just *four* days elapsed. All told, *we* number six hundred and fifty men present for duty. Two companies are on picket, and two others support the garrison at fort Duncan. Every able bodied man of ours is *on fatigue*, to-day, engaged in drawing up to fort Duncan two thirty-two pound pieces.

14*th*. For the first time the fair fame of the regiment is tarnished. Two Sergeants, C. of "C," and Mcl. of "G," passed our picket line to-day, and shot, dressed, and cut up, a bull belonging to a farmer near by; leaving the meat to be brought in after dark. Strange taste which makes *bull beef* stolen, sweeter than Uncle Sam's rations regularly issued! Complaint was made at Headquarters,— investigation followed — the guilty were placed in arrest, and all are waiting the close of proceedings.

Rebel-working parties are visible in Harper's Ferry, attempting to throw a bridge across the Shenandoah. They are covered from fire, from this side, by females, or males dressed in female apparel.

CHAPTER XIII

Harper's Ferry.

CROSSING OF THE POTOMAC—OCCUPATION OF HARPER'S FERRY
— CHANGE OF CAMP—"WHO KILLED THE BULL"—
DETAILS OF OFFICERS — A MERRY EVENING — OUR
OFFICERS — TRANSFERRED — POST GENERAL
ORDER — TRANSFERRED AGAIN.

15*th.* In the early morning, an order was received, to "detail *one hundred* picked men, as sharp shooters, without rations, in light marching order, ready to move at a moment's notice." This was superseded, almost instantly, by one for the entire regiment to be got ready to move, in similar order.

Without delay, we descended the heights, crossed the canal, and drew up on the river-side, partially covered by the trees upon its banks.

"Pontoon" boats floated in the waters of the canal, in charge of a party of the engineer corps, and "scows" near by, indicated that a crossing was to be attempted. Gen. Negley, in person, superintended the operation. The Potomac was to be crossed from two starting points. F company on one boat, with Col. Wells, A. B. G., from the ford proper, and B company on another, with Lieut. Col. Lincoln, commanding the regiment, from a point lower down, preceded slightly by picked men from E and I companies, under command of Capts. Bacon and Soley, and Lieuts. Lincoln and Cobb, and closely followed by the remaining companies of the regiment pushed out. The 17th Indiana battery, Capt. Miner, shelled the opposite shore, from which, concealed in the brush which covered Loudon Heights, and half hidden in the ruined buildings of Harper's Ferry, Rebel skirmishers poured an annoying but harmless fire.

The crossing was quickly effected, and the breast works on "Camp Hill" occupied without delay. A few prisoners were taken. The pontoon bridge was speedily laid; a squadron of Connecticut Cavalry crossed, and was pushed forward in pursuit of the enemy; Company "D," Capt. Thompson, following in support. The rebels, slowly retiring beyond "Bolivar," were sharply engaged at Halltown by Maj. Farnum, who was taken prisoner, but whose party, in turn, captured a Col., one Capt., one Lieut. and two privates of the 12th Va. Cavalry.

At 11 P. M. our wagons came up, bringing the first morsel of provisions we had had since breakfast; and after eating, we laid down with neither shelter or covering.

16th. Chaos reigns supreme; our order of encampment having been changed *three* times since our crossing, at the whim of the General commanding. Just now, our line faces the Shenandoah, stretching along the spur which divides the waters of that river from those of the Potomac. At the extreme right are two pieces (rifled six pounders) of the battery which covered our crossing; next our right wing; then *two* more pieces of artillery; then our left wing, which is also flanked by *two*, the remaining pieces of this battery. Regimental Headquarters are to the rear of the color company, behind which lies in bivouac Col. Curtis with two squadrons of the 1st Massachusetts cavalry. "Gregg's" Division of Cavalry, about 5000 strong, lies about a mile to our right front.

16th to 20th. We have moved, and now lie behind the breastworks on Camp Hill, so called. Miner's battery, is on our right, and the line of defence extends from the cliffs on the banks of the Potomac, to the Shenandoah on the left.

We have used the strong arm, and have seized and now occupy for a hospital the wooden Church in Bolivar, just below and in front of the earthworks which constitute the only line of defences for this place.

The "Army of the Potomac" is again in motion; Buford's division of cavalry crossing the Potomac yesterday, at Berlin," and the 12th corps, lying in bivouac, last night, on the road, opposite us, at the foot of Maryland Heights.

Yesterday, the twenty-five dollars assessed upon companies C and G for the value of the bull killed by two of the Sergeants of those companies, while we were upon Maryland Heights, were paid to the owner of the animal. So was secured indemnification for the past; Regimental General Orders of the day, reduce to the ranks the offending non-commissioned officers, which guarantees the future.

Ours is the only Infantry force this side of the river, and all approaches to the place are held by pickets from our command, with the most strict orders to allow no communication with the post, on the part of any persons, beyond the lines. One of our officers on duty at the Shenandoah crossing, is so strict a constructionist that he refused to permit the passage of market men of Loudon county, upon whom the citizens of the place are dependent for their daily supplies; and the consequence is that there are no dinners in the village, to-day.

Capt. Potter of "B" is appointed Provost Marshal of the post, one company acting as provost guard. Lieut. Ripley is placed as A. A. D. C., and Adj't Woods A. A. A. G. on Brigade staff. For the only time in our service, the Col. has held council with his officers as to our position; Gen. Sickles having expressed a desire to secure the regiment in his Division, and having offered our Col. the command of a Brigade. We unanimously advised an acceptance of the offer, but the Col. refused it, and so we stay here.

Gen. Negley is relieved, and Gen. Lockwood, of the "Potomac Home Brigade," a body of brave men, *"who will fight to the death, if the Rebels invade Maryland,"* but *who decline to " cross the river to prevent such invasion,"* is appointed to the command of this place.

Our Sutler, now, eight days since our departure from Washington, came up to-day, bringing as supplies precisely one hundred papers "fine cut," and one half box "navy tobacco," one gross matches, *six* phials of oil, and *one half* dozen sheets of emery cloth. Liberal supply, indeed, for the wants of six hundred men! Capt. Fox left us yesterday, on sick leave, for hospital in Washington,

22*d*. Our brigade is united again, the 173d Pennsylvania and the remaining squadron of cavalry having crossed the river yesterday, making our garrison 1767. Gen. Gregg having moved his command last night, the two remaining squadrons of cavalry, supported by two companies of infantry, picket our front, the Rebels being within one-quarter of a mile of our advanced posts; Ewell, with his corps, lying only eight miles distant from us. Gen. Lockwood, leaving his home brigade in safe quarters, on "the Heights," has in person crossed the river and taken his quarters in one of the abandoned houses on "Camp Hill."

23*d*. The Quartermaster's stores, which day before yesterday were moved to this place, are now being moved back to "Sandy Hook," and with them have gone the persons of the commanding General and staff.

A reconnoitering party, Capt. Bacon commanding, marched into Loudon yesterday, but without any definite result, beyond discovering an encampment of *three* Rebel regiments.

Yesterday, for the first time since leaving Upton's Hill, the regiment was out on battalion drill, to-day on skirmish drill.

Our evening has passed right merrily. Just before tattoo. Dr. Clark escorted to Regimental Headquarters, which are in an abandoned house, without door or window, and with no flooring, except on the second story, a bevy of ladies, young, but, ah me! not fair! All chairs we had were occupied, and temporary seats were made of trunks, and valises turned on end. The Ladies sang patriotic songs.— The Band was called upon for its choicest airs, and to crown all, the boys roared out their army glees! all went merrily! Additional interest was given to the affair, by the presence in the party of Miss ———, a young lady from Bolivar, who, at the occupation of the village by the Rebels, in answer to their demand upon her to haul down and surrender the national flag flying from her father's house, wrapped it round her person, and, *pistol in hand*, bade them "come and take it."

Two companies, "C" and "E," A. D. Pratt commanding, in answer to orders, garrisoned *three* "monitor cars," each armed with *two* howitzers, and loop holed for musketry, for a trip to the front, on the Winchester Railroad. The condition of the road was such as to render an advance impossible, and after proceeding about three miles, the expedition was abandoned.

The 173d Pennsylvania, a nine months' organization of drafted men, has left for home and muster out. In its place the 9th and 10th Maryland, *six months' troops*, are added to the Brigade; but they are across the river and *prefer* Maryland soil.

The sentence of Lieut. Stiles, "dishonorable dismissal from the service," is to-day promulgated to the Regiment.

Lieut. Smith, in arrest and turned over to the "Provost Guard" at Washington at our hurried departure from the Capitol, has been permitted to resign, although under charges, and has been *honorably* discharged.

Lieut. Butler is under arrest again; this time for abandoning his post as Officer of the Guard. He sent in his resignation, which has been forwarded "approved."

We are transferred again; this time from the Department under command of Gen. Couch to the "Middle Military Department under Gen. Schenck. Maj. Pratt and Lieut. Horton start to-day for home, on fifteen days' leave.

August 3rd, Sunday. Post General Order forbids the moving of Government trains on Sundays. "What's to be done?" asks the Commissary; "we've no bread!"

It's "root hog, or die." Trains to be used in spite of the order, or the Boys to go hungry! So the trains were ordered to "Sandy Hook" for rations; and Capt. Blakely of the Cavalry, being without forage, took courage from our action, and despatched his wagons for hay.

6th. We are transferred again; this time to "the Army of Observation, Mountain Department," Major-Gen. Kelley commanding; Headquarters at Cumberland. The same command formerly held by Banks and Fremont.

CHAPTER XIV

THE 9TH MARYLAND — RECORDS OF COURTS MARTIAL, ETC. — TABLEAUX IN "E" — REASONABLE REQUESTS — UNPLEASANTNESS AT DIVISION HEADQUARTERS — A BUSY NIGHT — A STORM ON THE PICKET LINE — OUR WORK — CHARLESTOWN — RECRUITING.

The 9th Maryland, Col. Simpson, have so far overcome their scruples as to cross the river to-day for the purpose of being reviewed and drilled by the "Born Chieftain," as Gen. Lockwood is called by his staff. Well! well! well! such a sight, and such work!!! The officers were gotten up as lady killers! Such length of sashes! such breadth of belts; such gorgeous shoulder straps! On the part of the men, such slouching appearance! such disregard of time and step in marching! such entire want of even the look of soldiers! Going down the line, the General came to one of the men leaning on his musket in an attitude of heavy loafing, and thus addressed him: "My dear man! do you know that if you allow yourself to indulge in such an attitude you will never make a soldier?" "Have'nt I got the order to *rest?* and don't I know how to take it easy?" was the answering question.

7th. Sent down through the regular channels, came to-day, a large bundle of orders, mostly records of courts martial; which, after being read at Headquarters, it is ordered, *shall not be read* at the head of the Regiment, as is customary. What a mess our soft-hearted President makes, in the exercise of his pardoning power! Deserters, sentenced to *be shot*, have the sentence commuted to "*loss of two months pay!*" Spies, convicted and sentenced *to be hung*, in one instance, now of record before me, have the sentence disapproved, and commuted to "*being sent through our lines!*" Drunken Officers, *cashiered* by vote of brother officers, get *remanded to duty* by their tender hearted Commander-in-Chief! Officially to promulgate such action, at the head of a Regiment, is to destroy all discipline!

This matter of discipline is delicate in the extreme. To illustrate: By Post General order, it is forbidden to any soldier to cross the Shenandoah River. Yet yesterday, three of our men *forged* the name of the Lieut. Colonel commanding, to a pass allowing them to cross the river; and this morning the officer who recognized the pass, is in arrest by order of the Post Commander; and the men who committed the forgery, in our Guard House, under charges preferred by the Captain of their Company. The mail has brought for one of these men, a commission in the line of the State of New Jersey, and an appointment on the staff of his brother, the General; and his Captain now prefers a request to be allowed to withdraw the charge against this man, based upon the statement that the "forgery was committed in a frolic;" and that the "princi-"pal offender now holds a commission, and should not, therefore, "be longer detained in the Guard House." This request has been returned *refused;* with the endorsement, that the forgery was no less a *serious* offence that it was committed in a frolic, as evidence of which, is the arrest of the officer who regarded it; and also, that the man, although he holds in his hands a commission, and appointment to staff duty, is still a member of the 34th; undischarged, and, of course, amenable to our discipline.

Just look at this tableau in Company E!

Two men are playing checkers, with corn and beans, upon a board chalked out on the floor of the piazza to Headquarters; near by, four others, seated on boards supported on bricks placed on end, are playing euchre, with a drum head for table; to the left stands a man with a dirty rag in his pocket, a piece of hard soap in one hand, and brush in the other, ready to shave his customer, who, with legs wide apart, and head thrown back, stands leaning against a tree.

8*th*. The day has passed with but little of incident.

Two damsels, who desired to "search the camp for a couple

"of saddle horses" they had lost, presented themselves at Headquarters early in the forenoon; but, inasmuch as they declined the escort of an officer, their request was refused. With an air of triumph they soon re-appeared, presenting an order from the Acting Brigadier, allowing them to go through the camp, unaccompanied. Notwithstanding the order, a Sergeant of the Guard was directed to attend them. The animals were not found, however. A lady from "Bolivar" soon after made a call, preferring a request that " our Sergeant of Patrol "might be directed to call at her house, and *whip one of her negroes*," too big for her to handle. And, later in the day, a man from the same village, who exhibited permission from the Post Commander to " give an evening entertainment for the benefit " of a newly wedded pair, *provided the party should be con-* "*ducted in an orderly manner*," made his appearance, and preferred his request that he might be furnished with a guard from the Regiment, to secure the quiet of the assembly.

12*th*. A little unpleasantness occurred to-day at Division Headquarters, which is of interest mainly as some of our men were concerned.

It was necessary, yesterday, that some writing should be done at an unusually early hour. For some cause the clerks were not within call. So, Boone, the A. A. G. stormed; and with Massey, A. A. D. C., reported to the "Born Chieftain" the indignity. Orders were thereupon issued that "thenceforward the orderly should call the roll of the clerks each morning at 6 A. M." So this morning the roll was duly called; but no clerks responded, and report thereof was made. "Send them to the Guard House!" thundered the General, which was done; and the staff officers sat down to perform the duties for which the clerks had been detailed. Orders were at once forwarded to the Regiment to detail other men competent to act as clerks. Report was made that "all such were already detailed." In this dilemma a council was called, and after deliberation the offending clerks were summoned before the General, who, expatiating upon the pleasures incident to the position they filled, and commenting upon the enormity of the offence, gave them the option of remaining at his headquarters in the enjoyment of the attending blessings, coupled with that one of attending morning roll call daily at 6 A. M., or of being returned to their Companies. To the consternation of the General and his staff, who were utterly unable to understand such perversity, the clerks chose to be returned to their Companies, where they now are. Meanwhile, there is an agreeable lull in the shower of orders which has been pouring upon the Regiment.

Many of our men are having their wives come out, and for their accommodation the military arm has been used to dispossess some others, temporary residents of the tenements they occupy; after all, with no more right than our own men.

15th. We have had a busy night. A scare at headquarters led to the issue of orders about 10 o'clock P. M., directing two companies to report, at once, to the officer of the day. The force marched in exactly *six* minutes from the time the order reached headquarters. A second order for a large detail to strengthen the Provost Guard was soon afterwards received; and yet again another directing a reinforcement of a full company to the Picket on the left flank.

Ours is still the *only* Infantry Regiment at this Post, and we are worked to death. It has *more than once* happened that at night, officers are ordered out for a twenty-four hours' service, who, in the morning of the same day, were relieved from a term of duty of equal length.

There has been a storm on the picket line, but fortunately without injury to anyone. Gen. Lockwood, *unaccompanied*, dressed in citizen's pants, with an army blouse, and his head covered with an old palm leaf hat, rode up, attempting to pass the line. His demand to be allowed to ride to the front was refused by the sentinel, and an orderly was despatched with orders to Col. Wells, in command of the Post, to report at once. Upon reaching the ground, the General read him a lecture upon what he was pleased to term "the insubordination of the sentinel." At this stage the commanding officer of the Regiment was ordered also to the ground, and the lecture was transferred to him. "But, General, your own orders are that *no one* is to be allowed to go to the front unless he presents a pass from the *Provost Marshal.*" "Yes, Col.; but I announced my name and rank." "Anybody might have done the same, General; and how was the sentinel to know you, being without uniform, mark of rank, or the least thing to confirm your statement?" The matter terminated by an assurance from the General that he had simply desired to test the fidelity of the sentinel, *who, he was pleased to find, knew his duty.* We are equally well pleased.

Capt. Leach, with Companies "A" and "G" was ordered to the banks of the Shenandoah, to resist an attempt at crossing by a guerilla force, which has been hovering round us for a few days past.

Captain Bacon, with his squad, who had crossed into Loudon to arrest some parties there, returned, bringing with him *four* prisoners.

Yesterday was the anniversary of our leaving Worcester; and the officers of the left wing, in order that it might not pass entirely without notice, invited their brothers of the right wing to a little entertainment, which consisted mainly in treating such as they could catch unawares, to a good, healthy tossing in a blanket.

20*th*. *We* hold this place, *aided* by a Battery of *six* pieces, and about *one hundred and fifty* Cavalry, where the garrison formerly has varied from four to thirteen thousand men. Mark how we are worked! Company "F" has but *six* men not on duty; "H" has but *ten;* "D," *twenty,* and "A," "G" and "E" were ordered out last night and are still absent. There are now in camp *one hundred and thirty-eight* men and *four* officers only, who have not been on duty the past twenty-four hours. Capt. Fox returned to-day from his leave of absence.

21*st*. The d——l has been to pay since yesterday, when the Regiment was paid off. As a whole our boys are splendid fellows. A few of them will get drunk when they can, but the most of them are, at all times, unexceptionable in their behavior. Three of "F's" men threatened the life of their Captain, last night. *They* are coming to their senses in the Guard House. Another man struck the Officer of the Guard a very severe blow, and *he* is admiring the looks of iron bracelets upon his wrists.

26*th*. We have been adding to the otherwise good appearance of our camp. Bowers of evergreen cover each company's street, giving comfort to the men, as well as beauty to the camp.

"The King of France, with 40,000 men,
"Marched up the hill, and then, marched down again."

And almost the same performance was required of us yesterday. In pursuance of orders received late in the evening of the 24th, *five companies* of the Regiment—"C," Lieut. Cobb, "D," Capt. Thompson, "E," Lieut. Horton, "H," Capt. Fox, and "I," Lieut. Lincoln, the whole under the Lieut. Col., marched on to line at 4 A. M., of the 25th, and almost immediately left for Charlestown, under orders to report to Col. Simpson of the 9th Maryland, who was stationed with his command, about four hundred strong, in that place. Capt. Bacon of "E," Pratt of "G," and Soley of "I," were on special duty for the time being. *Our* march was undisturbed; although, but the day previous, a wagon train on its way to that place had been attacked and compelled to return. We came *unchallenged* upon the pickets of the 9th, stationed about half a mile outside the village; and narrowly escaped receiving their fire. *That Regiment itself was drawn up hastily and confusedly in front of the Court House, as we were marched by.* Our route through the village took us by the Court House in which John Brown was tried, and which the 9th now occupied as barracks, to the cupola of which a Union Soldier was lashing a flag-staff, from which already the Stars and Stripes were floating; past the jail in which the old hero was confined, now used as a stable for the horses of a small squad of Cavalry; and in plain sight of the spot on which was erected the gallows, from which the soul of the martyr went marching on. Passing on, we drew up on a beautiful estate, occupied by a Mr. Ransom. At the order to halt, all windows were shut, all blinds drawn to, and doors violently slammed and bolted. Mr. R. himself seemed in an unhappy state of mind, at what he termed "an unholy violation of his privacy;" actually refusing to allow the boys to draw water from his well, but willing enough to sell them milk at sixteen cents the quart. "*He* "was a gentleman!—*he* was!" "The ladies of his family were "delicate and refined!—*they* were!" "His family were in deep "grief, on account of the recent death of a loved member! "And, oh dear! what shall we do." "Why, my dear sir, what "*is* the matter?" "My dear little grandson is fretting at being "deprived of his daily walk!" "Well, why don't you let him walk, if he wants to?"

"His dear mother can't trust him alone! and she can't come out of the house this morning!" "Why not, sir? what prevents?" "Why Col., you must know that no Southern lady can venture among your Northern soldiers, rough and rude as they are!" "Not even to spit upon the bodies of the dead and dying, who have laid on the streets of your village sir?" was the inquiry.*

Of course the day was monotonous. The officers, seeking relief from the sun, gathered under the trees near the house and resorted to the inevitable pipe and cards, to while away the hours; some few streched themselves upon the floor of the piazza, and courted sleep.

Suddenly, loud groans disturbed us, and our friend was seen wringing his hands, and giving other unmistakable signs of inward disturbance.

"I fear you are seriously ill, sir," was the remark! "Oh no! not that! but look at those soldiers! what could tempt them to invade that garden? See! there is one now, just taking hold of that rose-bush! How can he do it? Why is it permitted?" It was true, some of the boys were in the garden, but they were walking in the paths, occasionally stooping to examine and enjoy the flowering shrubs and plants, which made the place so beautiful, *but not even breaking one blossom from its stem.* *No order* was issued to disturb their enjoyment. So passed the time, till late in the afternoon, when Col. Wells and staff rode up, and, in response to orders, we retraced our steps, reaching camp about 7 P. M.

28th. Our rolls show our strength to be eight hundred and fifty-four, and of this number at least one hundred and fifty men are unfit for active service. After a long trial, we have succeeded in obtaining leave to send home a recruiting party, and Lieut. Elwell starts to-day for Massachusetts, with ten men, to try and fill up our ranks. Each company contributes, from its "savings" fund, twenty dollars, toward the incidental expenses of the party.

---

* In allusion to an occurrence which actually happened.

CHAPTER XV

REVIEW — ALARMS — SICK — INSPECTION OF CAMP, &C. — COMMISSIONS — A RAMPAGE — BRIGADE DRILLS — A NON-COMMISSIONED RECRUIT — AN ALARM.

Sept 2*d.* The various commands were reviewed yesterday, preliminary to being mustered for pay. The 34th was simply perfect; the 10th Maryland, Maj. Pratt of ours, inspecting officer, was so, so; the batteries, inspected by the Acting Brigadier, were in fair condition; and the Cavalry, well, *bad* is no word to use, in describing their condition. Their appearance justified the remark of our Adjutant, A. A. A. G. on the brigade staff, that the "only two persons, in the command, who were in uniform, were the Captain and Lieutenant, and they were in *shirt sleeves.*"

Leave was granted to such of our officers as were off duty, to ride out to Charlestown, to witness the ceremony of a flag presentation to the 9th Maryland. Spear of I, a private, who has been on the sick list for weeks, walked the distance *out and back,* and at his return was *marched on to duty.* Sergeants Dempsey of B, and Walker of H, promoted to Lieutenants, were mustered in as officers.

The last few days have been hard upon us. Alarms, given from Charlestown, led to the hurried march of one wing, Major Pratt commanding, to that place; and during their absence to the movement of three companies to "Loudon" and "Snicker's gap." Lieut. Lincoln is on leave of absence; Capt. Willard goes to-day on sick leave; Lieut. R. W. Walker is reported absent without leave, having overstayed his time. A large party of Virginians, claiming to be *Union men,* came into the post yesterday, to avoid, as they said, a Rebel conscripting party, which was scouring Jefferson County.

6th. Our sick list is increasing again rapidly. In answer to a note from Headquarters requiring explanation of his absence from this morning's roll call, Lieut. Hall writes " that of the past *thirteen nights* he had been on duty *six*; that he was on picket the night of the 8th; and being the only officer present for duty, with his Company, was called in to command it on the occasion of the Review on the 9th by the Acting Brigadier; that the heat of the day, or want of proper rest brought on a diarrhœa which kept him up till nearly morning, when he fell asleep and failed to hear the call." Such is a not exaggerated statement of the manner in which we are worked; and to all the remonstrances from Regimental Headquarters, the powers that be turn a deaf ear. We have drawn for and received an issue of "Sibley tents," which has rendered a new laying out of the camp necessary. To render themselves comfortable, the boys have *drawn* a lot of boards, all official requisitions upon the Government for lumber proving ineffectual.

The tents are now all well floored; some of them comfortably fitted with bunks and doors. The regular morning inspection of the camp showed that a few more doors and windows were necessary to make *all* comfortable, and the Pioneers—a handy set of fellows—were directed to leave camp after taps, to procure the few articles we needed. This course was taken to prevent indiscriminate pillaging by the men. The raid was a successful one, and the boys are enjoying the fruits of it.

10th. Lieut. R. W Walker who has been detained by sickness in Mass., returned to-day, and Lieut. Goodrich starts to-night for home, on ten days' leave.

12th.

HEADQUARTERS 1ST BRIGADE,
HARPER'S FERRY, *September* 11, 1863.

SPECIAL ORDER, No.

"You are hereby ordered, *personally*, to make thorough examination of the camp of "the 34th Massachusetts Infantry, *for boards*, alleged to have been taken by the men "of your command, from the unoccupied and partially destroyed government build- "ings in Harper's Ferry; and to arrest, and place in confinement, to be properly "dealt with, *all* the occupants of *any* tent, in which any such government property may be found.

"By order of the Colonel Commanding

S. F. WOODS, A. A. A. G.

"To Lieut. Col. W. S. LINCOLN,
 "Commanding 34th Massachusetts Volunteers."

Whew! Hard times these, for the poor fellows who are worked half to death, and want a dry place to sleep on when they come in from duty! "Ah! Good morning, Capt," as responsive to my "come in" the officer of the day presented himself for instructions. " Sit down, Capt. What's the news? The Boys are pretty comfortable, now they have got their Sibley's, aren't they?" "Well, yes! I guess they want a few more boards, though, to finish up with." "*Your* Company is all right, is n't it, Capt?" "Oh, yes, Col! my boys are all *hunkey!* but then, some of *them* are a little short." "Well, Capt., I've no new instructions for to-day; but I'll be obliged to you to call — say in an hour from now — and accompany me through the Camp. Complaint has been made, at Brigade Headquarters, that the Boys have been *stealing Boards,* and I am directed *personally* to search the Camp and arrest the occupants of every tent in which I find any; and I desire you to accompany me on the search." "In about an hour, did you say, Col.?" "Yes, Capt." "You won't take notice of *any small pieces,* I suppose?" "Oh, no! only *floor boards.*" And so, when the examination occurred, it happened, curiously enough, that nothing could be found save pieces from three to four feet long; and as there was no ear mark by which to identify Government property, report was made of the facts, and the Boys were undisturbed.

But we were hardly out of this scrape before a new one threatened. A citizen of "Bolivar" presented his complaint that some soldiers, as he charged of the 34th, had been seen by him, the past night, carrying away the doors and windows from an unoccupied house in that Village which belonged to his brother. Alas! here, were our pioneers coming to grief! But they must be protected, also. "Well, my dear sir, allowing it to be true that your windows and doors were stolen, what makes you charge our boys with the theft? Don't you know Miner's men lay side of us? and that they all are a set of thieves? Penitentiary convicts?" "Yes, Colonel, I know they *call them* so; but these fellows were *Infantry* men." "Well, don't you know that Miner's Caissons are full of Infantry and Cavalry jackets?" "That may be, Colonel, but then *they* can't cheat me! I found out these fellows right easy."

"No doubt you found out that the thieves were soldiers, but how dare you charge the theft upon the men of the 34th?" "Look here, now, Colonel; mind I don't say they were *your* men; I don't say any such thing; only, that the thieves were Massachusetts men, and I don't know any Massachusetts troops here, but yours." "Yes, I see, but how did you make them out to be Massachusetts men at all?" "Oh, right easy, Colonel, right easy; I knowed them by their talk. When I told them to let the windows alone, one of them turned round and asked "*Be these your windows?*" and I knowed them right off!" Did n't I laugh at such evidence of citizenship? Confident in the success of a defence against such proof, if the charge was carried farther, the complainant was dismissed to the safe conduct of the Officer of the Guard, with a serious warning of the danger he incurred in attempting to thus injure the good name of the command.

On the 11th, at the close of a General Review and Inspection of the Garrison, by Gen. Lockwood, the 34th was required to go through various Batallion movements, and to exhibit its proficiency in the manual, followed by an exhibition of its skill as Skirmishers. Its movements, being directed by bugle call only, drew from the Reviewing Officer the highest praise; from the Acting Brigadier, the exclamation, "By Jove, Adjutant, "the boys can't be improved;" and from the men of the other organizations, deafening cheers.

On the 12th an order came down to move the entire command. This was subsequently modified so far, that Companies "C" and "E" only, in support of one section of Miner's Battery, the whole commanded by Maj. Pratt, were required to march hastily to Charlestown, in answer to a call from Col. Simpson, who reported the presence of a force of Rebel cavalry, near him.

A Review and Inspection of the Regimental Transportation at 5 A. M., and of the Regiment at *six*, on the morning of the 14th, by Quartermaster Gen. Meigs; a Brigade drill on Maryland Heights, in the afternoon of the same day; (drawing from him the flattering remark, that "it was the finest Regiment he ever saw);" all this, added to our heavy daily details, have occupied us fully, the past week. A General Order received to-day, "dishonorably dismisses Lieut. Butler from the service."

Deserters from the Rebels come in daily, averaging from *six to twelve* in number, and one day this last week, amounting to thirty. A member of Gen. Ewell's staff, who is in our charge, states that if any certainty existed that this region would be held permanently by our forces, thousands of the Rebel army would desert at once. Packard, of "F," taken violently sick yesterday, immediately after bathing in the river, is given over by the Surgeons, who report that he can hardly live through the night. Babbitt, of "E," who suffers from sun-stroke, received on our duty of the 4th of July, is in Hospital, very low. A detail of one officer and ten men is ordered from us to-day, as guard over some Rebel prisoners, who are to be sent to Baltimore.

Judge Russell and wife are in camp, on a visit to our Col., and are now, we hope, enjoying a serenade by our band.

We are a good deal annoyed by the presence in, and around camp, of the cows owned in the neighborhood; in the absence of pasturage, our swill barrels furnishing a good deal of food. Our boys endeavor to draw pay in kind, although, owing to the wildness of the animals, they are not always successful. To render the operation of milking an entire success, a soldier holds fast each horn; *one* has firm grip of the animal by the nose; *another* grasps the tail, while others, at each side, pull away at the teats. The little milk got in this way is much relished.

18*th*. To-day we begin to prepare our winter quarters. We have placed some *twenty* of our horses in the basement of what was one of the most expensive and elegantly finished houses in the village.

An order of Gen. Lockwood's, just received, directing an additional detail for picket, headed "Headquarters *Defences Maryland Vols.*," excites hearty laughter among us.

21*st*. The pay master is with us again, and his visit has additional interest, from the fact that the "clothing account" of the men, for the year, is to be settled. The Government allows to each man, on this account, forty-two dollars; and while some of the boys have not drawn so much, others have so far exceeded the amount as to have absorbed some three months additional pay. As a whole, the clothing has been well made, and of good material; but there is much complaint of that now issued.

Lieut. Hall returned from Washington to-day, bringing up some *fifteen* of our men, who were transferred to general Hospitals, at our hurried departure from that city in July. For a long time, these men have written, expressing their desire to rejoin us; having been detailed as *clerks*, *cooks*, nurses, or in some like capacity, about the hospitals in which they were detained. All applications to the Surgeons in charge have been invariably returned, endorsed that "the men were unfit to be discharged." A representation to the Secretary of War direct, setting forth the facts, led to an order from that Department, directing the Surgeons in charge of these hospitals to "turn over to any officer, detailed from the regiment to receive them, any man of the 34th within their control."

Letters from home are almost daily received at Headquarters, naming different individuals as suitable persons to join us as Chaplains. But our reply is, that *by their works*, we should like to know them. The mania, for Commissions over colored troops, rages among the men with great violence, and various means are resorted to to insure success. But the most singular is the one just made known to us.

It was forwarded to Headquarters by Gov. Andrew, to whom it was addressed, bearing His Excellency's endorsement "that Lieut. Col. Lincoln would express his opinion whether the man was adapted to and qualified for a command over Colored Troops."

The letter was from one of our Sergeants, who wrote to the Governor that "he could have easily procured *fifty men*, and *so* " *claimed a commission;* but that he enlisted as a private from a " sense of duty, not feeling entirely qualified to command; but " that his situation is now changed. A year in the ranks has " qualified him for the situation of a commissioned officer. The " certificate of Hon. Mr. D., Member of Congress from his dis- " trict, will bear testimony to his standing in society." He further " states " that he abandoned a good business to join the Regi- " ment; that as a citizen of the town of K., he cast his vote in " favor of offering a bounty for volunteers, having also given

" liberally from his private means; that he led the way in vol-
" unteering on Saturday, and on Monday was in Camp with the
" full quota of his town; that he was Post Master, storekeeper
" and member of the Republican County Committee; that he
" was of the convention when the Governor was first elected;
" that he listened to the address made by His Excellency in
" which *his own ideas and opinions were expressed exactly*, but
" that the ideas then entertained were now strengthened ten-
" fold." Wherefore, and by reason of the foregoing, a hope was
expressed that " the Governor would give to the writer of the
" letter a commission over some Colored Troops, and enable him
" to put to a better use the talents which were now wasted."

Now it was easy enough to write that this man was well
drilled as a soldier; was of good habits; attentive and faithful
to duty, and of value to us *in the ranks*, all of which was true.
But precisely this was not what was asked. The fact was, that
though a good soldier, he had proved to be a poor non-commissioned officer. Ignorant of what standard of qualification the
Governor had set up as rendering a man " adapted for a command over Colored Troops," the only thing was to state the
foregoing facts *with the addition* " that he would not do as an
officer for us."

Capt. Pratt and Lieut. Lincoln, both speaking in their natural
tones and with their usual strength of voice last evening, are off
duty this morning, each unable to speak above a whisper.

Our " Born Chieftain " has been on the rampage again.
Accompanied by his full staff, he visited certain houses where
liquors are supposed to be sold; and certain others of bad repute
otherwise; and, as a result of his raid, a medley of whites and
blacks adorn the Provost Guard House this morning; not one
of ours, however, is among the number. Returning triumphantly
from this foray, he fell upon our Patrol at Bolivar, and our
Picket lines beyond, winning neither laurels nor victims. " Are
" you out with the knowledge of your Colonel ?" he asked of
a Captain of the 10th Maryland, whom he met and arrested on
the street. " I am out *with my Colonel*," was the reply. So
the Colonel was hunted up, and thus accosted; " Colonel, are
" you out of your camp with the sanction of your superior offi-

"cer?" "No, General." "Then why are you away at all?" "Because, General, as Colonel of a Regiment, I claim the right " to be anywhere I please, within the limits of my Brigade!" and *he* was allowed to pass. Not long after, the Colonel was roused from sleep by the beating of the long roll in his camp, and starting out, found his men hurrying on to line, in presence of the General, who, having ordered the alarm, was going down the lines, counting the files, to determine that the men of the command were present. Now this *was no joke*. In anticipation of any such little game upon us, Regimental General Orders have been issued to the Officers of the Guard, that whoever of them shall allow a "General alarm to be given in the camp of " the 34th, except by orders direct from our own Headquarters, " or in consequence of the near presence of the enemy, will be " at once arrested, and brought to court martial."

Commissions have reached us for 2d Lieut. Ripley as 1st, and Sergeants Belser of E, and Kinnicutt of H, as 2d Lieutenants.

For some unknown reasons there has been committed to the immediate charge of our own Regimental Camp Guard, two *Rebel officers*, claiming to be of Gen. Ewell's staff. Our guard tent is also graced by the presence of *two young ladies*, also entrusted to our safe keeping, by higher authority.

In addition to all former duties, we now send out a large fatigue party to procure timber for stockading our tents, and wood for our fires, our requisition for fuel having been returned, with an order " that the 34th will provide for all wants of this kind from the country near by." We have drawn, in consequence, two hundred axes, and it won't be our fault if we don't have ample supply for all our wants.

The Acting Brigadier persistently orders all brigade drills on " Maryland Heights," in deference to the Marylanders who don't like Virginia soil, thus requiring from us a long and toilsome march to and from the mountain. Of late some of the boys who don't really hanker after this additional fatigue, after marching on to line, have fallen out before crossing the river, and returned to camp. As a consequence of such performance to-day, nine men of " A " occupy the Guard House. Wilson of that company has deserted. A sharp little affair between

Mosby's men and Cole's Cavalry, in which the latter suffered the loss of *fifteen men*, led to Company " C " being despatched, at a double quick, across the Shenandoah, arriving, however, too late to render any assistance.

30th. Our usual brigade drill was suspended to-day, it being monthly inspection for the 34th, and pay-day for the 10th Maryland.

Calligan, Corliss, and Allen, of " F," are sent to general Court Martial upon charges preferred by their Captain; they having threatened to shoot him.

We hear from Lieut. Elwell that he has recruited for us *eleven men*, five of whom have been forwarded to us.

Sergeant Pennell of E, has applied and been recommended for a commission in some " Colored Regiment." He complains of our inactivity. Thus far, no one from our regiment has been rejected by the Examining Board. *Two*, who, having received promotion, left us at Upton's Hill, sleep their long sleep in the sands of Morris Island.

Oct. 3d. Pursuant to orders, at half-past eight the regiment took up its march for Maryland Heights, where the Brigade was reviewed by Major Gen. Kelley, commanding the " Army of Observation." The 34th secured his especial commendation.

At the close of the parade, some of the officers rode out to Charlestown, where the 9th Maryland still is, in a state of nervous excitement. Application made by us to be allowed to exchange places with it, meets with a decided negative at brigade Headquarters. Firing, in that direction last night, kept us on the *qui vive*, and now, rockets from the direction of Key's ford furnish occasion for new anxiety.

Gen. Lockwood is relieved from command here, and is to be succeeded by Brig. Gen. Sullivan, a son-in-law of Gen. Kelley. We get " King Stork " in exchange for " King Log." Wilson, who deserted a few days since, was returned to us, in arrest, to-day. Also Fuller of "A," and Smith of " K," two deserters from us while in Washington. In consequence of an affair in front, in which Capt. Somers, one of our best Cavalry officers has been killed, orders are received " to hold the entire Regi-
" ment ready to move, at a moment's notice. Company " E,"

"with one piece of Artillery, Capt. Bacon in command, is "directed to move at once." Quartermaster Sergeant C. P Trumbull, and Orderly Sergeant Pennell of "E," are directed, by orders from the War Department, to proceed at once to Washington, for examination for commissions in the colored troops. Another order from the same quarter, "requires the "commanding officer of the 34th Mass. Infantry to explain "without delay, why Field of "G" has not been discharged "from the Regiment, that he might accept a commission, in "accordance with General Orders to that effect." Inasmuch as no order to that effect had ever been received at Regimental Headquarters, there was no difficulty in making the explanation demanded.

12*th*. We have to-day thirteen recruits in camp, eight of whom were brought up a day or two ago, by Lieut. Belser. These men, particularly the "Veterans," open wide their eyes at the amount of duty required from us. With a total effective force of six hundred and six, exclusive of warrant officers, our daily detail is for three hundred and sixty men. One of our recruits has had, since he reached us, *seven fits!* rather promising, that, at $700!

14*th*. Yesterday was marked in white to us, by its being pleasant, and NO *Brigade Drill;* also, by the arrival of our new commander, Gen. Sullivan; and the military order for a Grand Review, by both the out-going and in-coming Generals, supplemented by receipt about midnight, of additional orders "to move "at once to Maryland Heights."

Just three months have passed since we crossed the Potomac, and occupied this place. All last night was spent in removing to "Berlin," by rail and wagon, the property of the Government stored here; the men of the 34th standing to their arms, and the Battery "limbered." Early this morning we were required to furnish a Fatigue Detail, to assist in removing the "General Hospital." Couriers have been riding in hot haste between this place and "Charlestown." Trains filled with Government stores of all kinds are passing by from "Martinsburg." And now come orders directing us to pack everything, as we "*leave not to return*." It is too bad! Our tents are all stockaded;

timber nicely hewed — each tent banked round, and nicely sodded — Company streets thoroughly crowned, worked, and paved with brick. It was, an hour ago, a jewel of a camp! but now everything is bare and naked. All property, both Government and Regimental, is loaded on to our wagons, and the Regiment waits only for orders to move. At 2 P. M., orders came down to send our entire transportation to report to Capt. Patten, Post Quartermaster. Our wagons were unloaded, property piled in camp, Guard placed over it; and we waited till late in the evening, when, in absence of further orders, the men were directed to "*lie* upon their arms."

15th. The order of yesterday from Brigade Headquarters to " be ready to march at a moment's warning," was renewed at an early hour this morning. But at noon we were directed to unpack everything and resume our former situation, furnishing patrol and sending out pickets as before this grand scare. By General Orders " Headquarters Defences of the Potomac," Col. Wells is assigned to the command of this Post *and* of the 1st Brigade, 1st Division, "Army of Observation." He sweeps clean, as all new Brooms do. His first general order directs the closing of all places of business at *nine P. M.*; prohibits all soldiers from being on the streets after that hour, and citizens from being out of doors after *ten P. M.*, under penalty of arrest; prescribes full uniform, dress coats, scales and white gloves to be worn by all Patrol and Headquarters Guards; allows but two men from each Company to visit the Ferry at the same time; and directs that every one so visiting the town shall be in full uniform and with side arms.

As a relief to the monotony of our daily battalion drills, the Regiment has commenced the bayonet exercise, Col. Revere, of the 10th Maryland, instructor.

17th. The sound of heavy guns rings on the ear from the front. Our situation is not pleasant. How often we have heard the cry of Wolf! We wonder now, whether the animal is really prowling about, or whether all this alarm, of the past few days, is a ruse of the Generals' to ensure the removal of a portion of the immense amount of stores which have been gathered here since our occupation. The Regiment is in splendid condition, and there is a great expression of hope that if the enemy desires our position, we may be allowed to try and hold it against them. Many people, from the near front, crowd our camp daily, giving utterance to expressions of surprise at the comparatively feeble garrison now here. Among them are the Messrs. H., father and son, Worcester County men, now living near Halltown. The father, in conversation to-day, made the statement that at the time of the surrender of this Post last year, General Ewell, with his staff, made Headquarters at his house; and, that to an assertion of his that the Rebel troops could not take the place, Ewell's A. A. G. replied, that the place would be in the possession of the Confederate troops by noon of the day succeeding, and *that too, without firing a gun.* And it proved to be so.

CHAPTER XVI.

BATTLE OF RIPON.

19*th*. We have had our "baptism of blood."
Yesterday, at Reviellé, a single discharge of artillery was heard from the direction of Charlestown, to which no especial attention was paid. When returning from breakfast, however, *three* other distinct reports were heard, and turning I hurried to Brigade Headquarters. *All were in bed.* "We have no artillery in Charlestown, Col." "What you've heard, must be practice firing at Martinsburg." Now, inasmuch as Charlestown was but *eight* miles away in one, while Martinsburg was *twenty-two* miles distant in another direction, this explanation was not quite satisfactory. But, in justice to the Col. commanding, it ought here to be stated (what was not learned till after the affair of the day was over), that the reason why no attention was paid to the report of the firing, was, that as late as two o'clock of that morning, a courier had brought, from Col. Simpson, at Charlestown, a written report that "his cavalry had just come in from a scout, and that there was no rebel force within *twenty* miles of him." This information was not communicated, however, and, dissatisfied with my reception, I hurried to camp, and caused the regiment to be turned out, in *complete marching order.* Hearing nothing farther to cause alarm, the companies were allowed to stack their arms, and the men to separate, with the caution not to put off their equipments. The reliefs, from the provost and patrol guard, coming into camp at this time, for breakfast, were sent back, with orders to return at once with their arms and equipments. No other preparation *could* be made, and, in company with several officers, I took position on the breastworks, where a look-out could be had over the pike. While engaged thus, a single heavy gun

was heard again, and soon a horseman turned the heights of "Bolivar." Our glasses showed us that he *wore our uniform,*—that he was *bare headed,* and that he was urging his jaded beast with spur and sabre. Messengers were at once despatched to the officers on picket, "*to send in every man, not on actual post;* and all turned to watch the horseman, who, galloping through the camp, had already reached brigade Headquarters.

The tranquility reigning there was not disturbed; and orders were about being issued to dismiss the men, when "Look there, Colonel," exclaimed Capt. Bacon; and directing our glasses again to the front, another mounted soldier was seen, *bare headed,* and hurrying at speed toward us. Without waiting his arrival "the Assembly" was sounded. Meanwhile the messenger had gained Brigade Headquarters, and, dismounting, disappeared from our sight. In an instant, Orderlies, mounted and on foot, hurried away in all directions. The one sent to us with orders to get under arms, without delay, was directed to report the "regiment on line ready to march." So soon as the Battery could harness, we were ordered to move.

At "Halltown" a halt was ordered that "canteens" might be filled, and arms loaded. Here the Battery passed us, at a sharp gallop; and Company "A," Capt. Willard, was detached in support.

The regiment followed at a quick step, and again *three* Artillery shots fell upon the ear. A messenger from Major Cole, commanding a small squad of Cavalry, which had been hurried from camp in Bolivar, now rode up with information that he (Cole) had struck the enemy, who had fallen back into "Charlestown." Another Orderly soon followed, reporting that the enemy was in force, consisting of mounted Infantry and Cavalry, with *six* pieces of Artillery, the whole commanded by Imboden; that they were already in retreat; that he, Cole, was harrassing them, but was nearly out of ammunition. The sharp crack of Miner's rifled pieces was soon heard, and the boys, responding with a cheer, broke into a "double quick." As we neared Charlestown, overturned wagons, scattered papers, broken muskets, cast off equipments, and, saddest of all, bodies of dead soldiers, at which swine were already rooting, and upon which, from the doors of near dwelling houses, beings in female garb were steadily gazing, lined the road. We marched through the Village, out on to the pike leading to "Berryville," soon coming up with "A," halted by the side of the road, about a mile out. Word now reached us from Cole that he could not hold the enemy, but was himself forced to give ground; so forward we pushed, *again at a double quick.*

Company "F," Capt. Chandler, was sent to the left, and Company "C," Lieut. Cobb, to the right, in order as skirmishers; while the Regiment advanced by the Pike. Here Capt. Bacon, who had been on duty as Field Officer of the day at the Ferry, joined us and assumed command of his Company. (Capt. A. D. Pratt, who on account of sickness had been off duty for weeks, having volunteered to relieve him.) "Shell" now began to fly over our heads, and soon we heard the reports of our own rifles as the skirmishers got engaged. The country over which we were advancing was rolling; wooded knolls covered with timber, open enough, however, for the passage of artillery, with intervening hollows of cultivated land at short musket range distance, offered favorable positions for a retreating force, and we gained *one* hill after a stout resistance, only to find the enemy in possession of the *next*, and awaiting our advance.

The resistance was becoming more stubborn, when word was brought that Lieut. Cobb was dangerously wounded, and Lieut. Goodrich was despatched to assume command of the Company, and send Cobb to the rear. Our advance was now by the pike. As the head of the Regiment topped the crest of a knoll on the left of which Miner, with *one section*, was wheeling into position, a shell struck the ground, but without exploding, within a few feet of our leading files, a second followed, bursting over our heads, but doing no injury; and a third came, taking off the hind legs of both of Miner's wheel horses. From another gun, away to the right, came chunks of railroad iron, pieces of chains and bundles of horse shoes bound together with telegraph wire, making most devlish screeching as they cut their way among the branches of the trees. A rapid flank movement on our part with a purpose of cutting off this last piece, a *twenty-four pound-*

er, was discovered, and the Rebels, rapidly limbering up, withdrew it in safety. A turn in the road brought us again out on the pike, and, as the leading files showed, shells and shot from the Rebel artillery struck, and covered us with dirt and stones. Again we crossed into the fields and advanced in line.

Here a message was received from Cole, to the effect that he was overpowered, and compelled to give ground, coupled with a request that we would hurry to his assistance. The messenger, assuring us that our movements would be covered from observation, by high ground on the right, remained with us to pilot our movement. Coming out on to the pike, we were advancing at a double quick, anxiously looking for the whereabouts of Cole, when the protecting ground to our right, fell off, leaving the head of the column uncovered. As the leading company, "E," was exposed, the Rebels, who were in position, secured from observation by the timber on our right and front, met us with a fire from *three pieces* of his artillery, and a deafening volley from his muskets. To halt and form, was the work of but a minute. But we were none too quick; for a body of cavalry suddenly charged upon us, perhaps expecting to find us in confusion from the unexpected fire to which we were exposed. Dressed in our uniform, and slowly falling back towards us, when first seen, they were taken for Cole's men. As they neared us they discharged their carbines, and wheeling, fled. But company H, facing about, was quick enough with its fire to empty *four or five* saddles. The contest, at this place, was sharp, for some moments; the 34th alone contending for the ground. Here, and at this time, fell Corp. Gage of "E," bearing the white flag of the State, shot through the heart; and Clark of "K." of the color guard, *hit in the breast*, each dying without a word. McDaniels of "E," hit in the foot, sat down, cut out the ball with his jackknife, and resumed his place and firing. A ball passed through the pants of the Lieut. Col. commanding, just grazing the flesh of the thigh, and lodged in the saddle blanket.

Company E, which had advanced entirely beyond the protection of the high land which covered our approach, was for a moment, a little demoralized,—its members crying out "*Gage is killed! McDaniels is wounded! Clark is dead!*" But they were recovered by their gallant Capt. Bacon,— who, in facing the storm of bullets falling thickly round him, called out, "shut up your mouths, boys, and let your rifles do the talking for you." He was conspicuous for his cool and daring conduct throughout.

Miner now came up, and shelled the woods in which the enemy had been posted, and, under cover of his fire, we advanced, to find Imboden again posted on the crest of a knoll still farther to the rear. Here again the contest was renewed. Slowly, and in this manner, we gained ground; every inch of the way stubbornly contested, until about 5 P. M., when an Orderly from Gen. Sullivan, at the Ferry, reached us, bringing orders to cease the pursuit, and we laid down to rest. Our force engaged was the 17th Indiana Battery, Capt. Miner, *six six pounders, rifled;* Maj. Cole's Maryland Battalion, about one hundred and fifty strong, with about thirty Cavalry scouts; and the 34th Massachusetts, about four hundred and fifty men, Lieut. Col. Lincoln, commanding; the whole under Col. Geo. D. Wells, Acting Brigadier General. Of the rest of the Brigade, the 9th Maryland, Col. Simpson, had been surprised and nearly all captured early in the morning, the Field Officers only escaping; and the 10th Maryland, Col. Revere, ordered out at the time we were, but having about *two miles* farther to march, did not "get up" till after the pursuit was ordered to be stopped. In their advance upon the road we had fought over, they discovered, and brought down from trees by the wayside, four or five Rebels, who, from their elevated posts, had signaled to Imboden the changing position of our forces, and thus enabled him to get such exact range of our column.

We secured as trophies, a Cavalry Forge—one wagon loaded with sabres,—other arms and equipments, bags of flour, etc., and divers papers of the command, among them a muster and pay-roll of a company of "White's Battalion," for the last month.

Rebel prisoners state their force at 2,500, under Imboden in person; consisting of Cavalry, mounted Infantry, and *six* pieces of Artillery—one twenty-four pounder, two twelve pounders, and three rifled sixes.

The official return of our Brigade shows a loss of seven

killed, forty-two wounded, exclusive of the 9th Maryland, which regiment had *one killed, three wounded*, and two hundred and seventy-three captured. Our own loss was two killed, one dangerously, and seven slightly wounded. At this, our *first* engagement, our boys were a good deal excited, firing at random. Particularly was this so, at the moment, when, while moving to Cole's support, we so unexpectedly met that awful storm of fire from the concealed enemy. To recover them the order to "cease firing," was given. The advantage of cover, possessed by a portion of the command, was pointed out, and they were admonished of the necessity of loading leisurely, aiming carefully, and firing deliberately. Soon they were themselves, when firing was resumed, and from this time they were steady enough; the boys greeting with a hearty laugh one little fellow who, jumping on to the top of the bank, behind which he had been protected, leveled his musket, and with the exclamation "Continue the same," blazed away.

The pursuit was not without its amusing incidents. The A. A. A. G., at one time in advance of the line, rode in, escorting a Rebel soldier whom he had captured, and turned him over to an Irishman, with directions to keep a close watch of him. "Niver fear, Mr. Adjutant, niver fear! If the spalpeen runs I'll prod him with this little tooth-pick," at the same time shaking his bayonet. Another of our boys, also an Irishman, seeing two Rebels crossing his path, jumped behind a tree, and, leveling his piece, called to them to halt. As they stood at his challenge, he thus broke out: "Well, what are you going to do now?" "Surrender!" they cried out. "Why don't you do it, then? throw down them murdering guns, or by the holy Moses I'll shoot you both!" and, in an aside, "the poor craythurs don't know she aint loaded."

Capt. Chandler, with his Company, had an opportunity of testing *our* movement, "Cavalry! rally by Company!" His men, deployed as skirmishers, had been advancing through a field of standing corn; and, as his line reached "the opening," he caught sight of a body of Rebel Cavalry "coming for him." There was no time to reach his reserve, even if he could have seen precisely where it was; so, giving the order above, his men rallied round him at a run. The Cavalry recoiled before the circle of bristling bayonets, fired their carbines without injury to us, and wheeling, fled. It was Chandler's turn then, and, at his order, a bright flame poured from his pieces, and as the smoke cleared, *five* riderless horses were galloping away.

Lieut. Cobb, dangerously wounded, the ball having entered the head between the eyes, carrying with it from his cap the lace number of his regiment, was left in a farm house at Ripon, *unconscious*. Bringing off the bodies of our dead, and all our wounded, we commenced our homeward march about 6 P. M., reaching camp without a straggler, near midnight; having marched in *fifteen* hours, *thirty-six* miles, without food, fighting over six miles of the way.

The flag given to the Regiment by the ladies of Worcester, shows marks of being struck by six bullets.

21*st*. Surgeon Clarke went out to Ripon yesterday, and brought in Lieut. Cobb, wounded in the affair of the 18th. He is still unconscious.

The men are sleeping upon their arms to-night, and an order to move is (now, half past 1 A. M.,) momentarily expected. Lieut. Belser left us to-day to rejoin our recruiting party in Massachusetts.

25*th*. Lieut. Cobb is more comfortable, and we now have hopes of his recovery. His friend and nurse, Mr. Phelps, of Boston, has gone to Headquarters at Clarksburg, hoping to obtain sick leave for him.

Two of our men who, at our hurried departure from Washington were transferred to general hospital, rejoined us a day or two ago, and reported for duty. To-day a letter was received at Headquarters, from a Captain of Company——of the Invalid Corps, reporting them as deserters from his command, and asking the commander of the regiment to arrest and return them to Harrisburg, for trial and punishment. Now, these men have been borne upon our rolls to the present time; no notice of any transfer to any other organization having ever been communicated to us. They state that, upon their arrival at Harrisburg, learning their fate, they were disgusted, and took French leave; setting out and walking to this place. With tears in their eyes they profess their ability to serve with us, and they beg, most earnestly, not to be sent back. They will not be surrendered, except upon the imperative order of the War Department.

A communication from the Secretary of War to Gen. Sullivan, complimenting him that for once, "Harper's Ferry is garrisoned by a force, and under a commander who *dared march to find an enemy*," has been received, and made public. Our drill to-day, changed to a skirmish, from Battalion, at the request of officers of other commands, drew crowds of applauding men and officers from neighboring camps. So much for gratification. As set off, a starving damsel, *fat, not fair,* but forty at least, besieged Headquarters, loudly complaining against some of the boys, who, she alleged, had carried from her premises, "a *small piece of plank, and three* cabbages."

In contrast to this, appeared the smiling faces of seven of the boys, with applications that quarters might be provided for their wives just arrived.

The weather is cold; ice forming an inch thick in camp.

The Acting Brigadier, called to-day, as he said, to tell us that he thought the camp the prettiest thing of the kind which he had ever seen.

Nov. 1st. Yesterday was our bi-monthly Inspection and Muster for pay. Visitors from Massachusetts were with us. "Why Col.," said one, Mr. W T. D., of Greenfield, "your arms are in most splendid condition, and look, to me, as well as if just from the armory!" It was intended as a compliment, but it was mortifying beyond measure; and we sent the Quartermaster for some which had never been issued, that he might see the contrast — about what there is between a most highly polished piece of cutlery, and a well finished shovel.

We have had in camp for a few days past, a one-horse minister, accredited by the Christian Commission "to the army in the field." As a whole, little benefit has resulted from the presence, among us, of this class of men. Failing to understand, as nearly all of them do, their proper duty, they secure neither respect nor consideration from officers or men. The offer by this one to officiate at our evening parade on Sunday next, was gladly accepted; but, perceiving how ignorant he was of all camp life, its routine and duty, he was informed that if the weather should continue damp, drizzling, and chilly, as it then was, he must not be disconcerted at an order to the men to "remain covered," during his service. "What!" he exclaimed, raising his hands in horror at the intimation, "What! approach the throne of Almighty God, in prayer, with covered heads!" "As well so, sir, as with unbended knee; our first duty is to preserve the health of the command, and if the heart is right, what matter where the cap is?" But, spite of his offer, he was not present. In his absence, the Rev. Mr. F., also of the Commission, introduced himself, and volunteered for the duty. His prayer was short, but touchingly eloquent. Pointing to our flag, upright before our eyes, and riddled with balls, he spoke of our recent baptism, asking God's blessing upon the flag and all engaged in its defence.

The *old* fellow, who watched the proceedings from his room, at a little distance, thus alluded to the matter: "I was sorry, "Col., that I could not be present at your parade, for I couldn't "bear to disappoint 'the boys,' as you call them. How did "you get along?" "Oh! nicely, sir, nicely! We had a very "touching service." "Service, Col.! Service! Why, how was "that? I watched your movements, and I don't see how you "could have had any. It must have been very short." Yes, sir, "short; not longer than five minutes, but eloquent and impres- "sive." "Five minutes! Five minutes! Why, Col., I couldn't "have got through my introduction in that time!!!" "Oh! "my dear sir, it's just the introduction that we were afraid of. "Standing in the cold and wet, we don't want any of that."

Our wounded are doing nicely. Lieut. Cobb has left for home, on sick leave. *Howe*, shot in the breast, and *Mockly*, in the thigh, will both be out shortly. *McDaniels*, hit in the foot, will be confined longer.

5th. Another night alarm, and the regiment ordered to Halltown, where it bivouacked, returning this morning. So quietly was our move conducted, that Miner, of the battery, whose Headquarters are within our lines, knew nothing of it.

Deserters and contrabands are coming in, in considerable numbers, daily. These, with prisoners who are sent in by the cavalry in front, agree that Imboden is chafing under the affair of the 18th, and is moving down the valley, for this post, and its garrison. Post General Order of to-day forbids any person leaving the village, in any direction.

Our old Minister, the one who couldn't pray when our heads were covered, affords us all much amusement. In his wanderings, he has come across an uninhabited house, which he thinks would accommodate the men of *two* companies, and which he is anxious the men should be allowed to occupy, being so much more comfortable than our tents. He has no idea of the necessity of keeping embodied, nor does he understand, why, if there is anything comfortable within reach, it is not appropriated at once. If I should listen to him, I should let loose the boys to do as they pleased. In contrast to what he advises, I show him an order from Brigade Headquarters, reciting complaints against the men, for plundering; and directing the camp to be thoroughly searched, and the inmates of any tent, where should be found *any boards* used for flooring, to be arrested and punished. "Is that possible?" he exclaimed! "When it is *so muddy, too*? Well Col., I must have done wrong then, as I have just been telling some of the men, where they could find some *good ones*. I guess I'd better go right back, and tell them not to touch them at all."

He was not quite pacified by an assurance that I would take care of the boys, for said he, "Col. *there* are the boards, and *here* are your orders!" "True! but the officer, who makes the search, will be instructed to take no notice of any short pieces he may see, and it will somehow happen that he won't find *any but short pieces*." "I see! Col." said he, with a merry twinkle of his eye, "*I see*." And I think the old fellow actually thought it was a righteous way of executing the order.

He speaks of our men as a band of devoted Christian brothers; and seems astonished at the assertion, that rigid discipline has made, and keeps them what they are; inasmuch, as he says, that he can discover nothing which looks as if it ever had been, or was now practised.

6th. Another night alarm; and for the Regiment, another night's bivouac at Halltown. Surgeon Clark greeted his wife, upon her visiting camp to-day. They, with the Quartermaster and his wife, are to have quarters in an unoccupied house in the village.

7th. Imboden, as our scouts report, is at Berryville, and our cavalry are in motion. A note from Gen. Sullivan's Headquarters, gives us warning "*to be ready to march to-night.*"

A queer incident, showing how much more strange truth is than fiction, happened to-day. Last August, one of K's men was granted a furlough. Over-staying his time, he was reported as a deserter. After a while, he was heard of as being in the city of Albany. His "descriptive list" was sent to the Provost Marshal of that place, and the man was identified, arrested, and forwarded to general rendezvous, in the City of New York. Soon after, we received notice, that the man was at the camp of distribution. An officer was sent for him, but was informed that no such man was in the camp. Not long after, an official letter, from the Quarter-master at that camp, was received at Headquarters, containing charges for clothing, delivered to the man. This was returned with the endorsement that as the man was not present to be surrendered upon our demand, that fact would be regarded as evidence that the clothing could not have been issued to him. So the matter has stood for months. But to-day, the man presented himself at Headquarters, bearing a letter from the selectmen of Pittsfield, endorsed by Captain Cooley, his former commander, containing the statement, that the man had expressed a desire to rejoin the regiment, and, at their request, the Provost Marshal had forborne to arrest him; and concluding with a hope that we should not feel under obligation to inflict punishment upon him.

According to the man's story, he reached Baltimore, on his return to the regiment, at the expiration of his furlough; and soon after, found himself in Albany, where he was arrested and sent to New York; that *he was forwarded* to the "*Camp of Distribution,*" near Alexandria, which he left, and *walked in his uniform, without hindrance,* back to Pittsfield, where friends advised him to return to us; and he had done so. He is in the Guard House, to await final determination of his case. What an infliction we have been called upon to endure! At parade to-night, we were dreadfully bored by our old minister, who still hangs around; and who preached to us for more than a half hour, by the watch, upon the *doctrine of predestination.*

The men had such dreadful coughs, before the close of the service, that a stranger might have had serious alarm for the health of the command. But we have only about sixty under surgeon's care.

The 10th Maryland returned from Baltimore, to-day, where it was ordered, that its members might vote at the election, just had in that city. Upon arrival here, it was ordered to proceed to Martinsburg. The 1st Virginia Battery, (Furst's) *six Napoleons*, moved up close to our breastworks, this afternoon; their horses being left harnessed.

10*th.* The day is beautiful; a light snow fell last night, and the weather is quite cold. All day long, a crowd of complaining citizens have thronged Headquarters. Every old woman who loses a cabbage, and every man who misses a brick, or piece of board, goes straightway to Brigade, or Division Headquarters, and forthwith comes an Orderly, bearing a despatch, calling the attention of "Lieut. Col. Lincoln, commanding the 34th " Massachusetts Infantry " to the alleged " ill doings of the men "of his command." Pretty hard, this! at least on the part of the Acting Brigadier, who knows, as we all do, that the men of Miner's Battery are pardoned penitentiary convicts; and that straggling Cavalry men, without discipline, or control of any kind, are continually ravaging the country ! Besides, *our tents are floored, now,* and have been for some time; and we don't want any more *boards.* Two deserters were returned to us to-day; one, arrested in Massachusetts last June, and the other left by us, under charges, at our departure from Washington.

13*th.* Six recruits reached us to-day, making *twenty* whom we have received. *Three* of them are given to *fits;* are entirely worthless, not having done a day's duty since joining; and the worst one of the lot cost the most, being what is termed a "Vet-" eran Recruit," at $700. Two of our boys received commissions by to-day's mail; *one* as Captain, the other as 1st Lieutenant in the 9th United States Colored Troops. Thus far, we have furnished *seven* commissioned officers to other Regiments; and have in camp now another man, carrying in his pocket a commission, and awaiting an order, from the War Department, directing his discharge from the Regiment.

Orders from Brigade Headquarters direct, that in future, our fatigue party of wood choppers shall be armed, and that no wagons be sent for wood unless under suitable escort.

Just now we are victims to red tape. Just previous to our departure from Washington, three of our officers, having just received promotions, were sent up to General Headquarters to be *mustered in*. In the excitement consequent upon Gettysburg, or perhaps from the *hurry* of sending off troops, the mustering officer could not attend to them; and, without being mustered, they were assigned to duty in accordance with their rank. Two of them, some time since, visited Department Headquarters to be mustered, but were ordered back, with the information that a proper officer would be detailed to visit the Regiment, for the performance of this duty. So, on the 27th of August last, a regularly appointed mustering officer appeared among us, and all three of these officers were duly mustered to the rank to which they were commissioned, *as of date the 9th of July*, the day on which they received their commissions, and were assigned to duty.

But to-day's mail brings an order from the War Department, setting aside the action of this officer, directing the muster of *two* of them to date from *August 27th*, and *absolutely revoking* the muster of the third one.

So also of Carr, a Sergeant of ours. He holds a commission as Lieutenant in the —— Regiment, New Jersey Infantry; a letter from the Adjutant General of that state to his brother, Genl. Carr, now serving with the Army of the Potomac, and still another letter, from the General himself, forwarding the commission and notifying him of his appointment to a position on his (the General's) staff. All these documents were duly forwarded from Regimental Headquarters, with an application from Carr, approved, asking his discharge from the 34th, to accept promotion in the New Jersey line. But they were returned by Maj. Genl. Kelley, commanding Department, with the endorsement: "*Denied. There is no evidence that there is any vacancy, to fill which this commission is issued.*"

Upon the heels of all this comes an order from Gen. Sullivan forbidding any soldier from appearing with the badge of a rank to which he has not been properly mustered. What shall poor ——— do? He was mustered *out* as a Sergeant, and mustered *in* as a 2d Lieutenant; assigned to duty as such officer; acting as such even now, although his muster has been revoked by the War Department. The revocation of his muster *in* as 2d Lieutenant does not cancel his muster *out* as Sergeant. Besides, his place as Sergeant is filled. He is to us *Lieutenant* or *nothing*. *He* don't want to leave *us*. *We* don't want to spare *him*. *He* can't resume his chevrons, nor wear his bar, according to Sullivan. What shall he do?

Various parties of Guerrillas are hovering near us, and orders from Brigade Headquarters forbid our sending out teams for wood except under strong escort, and direct all chopping details to be armed.

16*th*. Our work is severe and harassing beyond description, and nearly beyond endurance. Two of our very best men were taken down to-day; the Surgeon's report, from *overwork*. We lost a man in hospital last night, as the Doctors say, from *mince pie*, he having bought and eaten the whole of one. Sergeant W., of A has taken to himself a girl from the village, to be Mrs. W., *No.* 2. Col. Wells is detailed to Court Martial, and the command of the Brigade is assigned by Genl. Sullivan, to Lieut. Col. Lincoln; Col. Simpson of the 9th Maryland being under a cloud from the affair of the 18th of Oct., at Charlestown.

What a host of applications are pouring in from the boys to be allowed to appear before the Examining Board at Washington! Corporal Granville and Sergeants Hull of K, and Rhodes of A, already commissioned, leave to-night. G.'s life, as detailed by him, has been a checkered one, indeed. He formerly lived in Boston, was engaged in trade, lost largely and failed; left secretly for the west, first writing a note to his wife that his body would probably be found in Charles River; was prospered in his new home, and after awhile returned and compromised with his old creditors; engaged as a school teacher in W., and enlisted from that town as a private in the 34th; was soon advanced to be a Corporal, and is now commissioned a Captain in the 9th Regiment U. S. Colored Troops.

Corporal Wiswall of "C," now one of our Recruiting party in Massachusetts, is, by order from the War Department, received to-day, "relieved from farther duty in the 34th, and "directed to report immediately to Maj. Gen. Banks, for duty "in the 'Corps D'Afrique.'" Capt. Pratt, of that Company, in answer to a note from Headquarters, directing him to forward the name of some suitable person, to fill Wiswall's place, writes thus: "I have the honor, in obedience to orders from Head-"quarters, to forward the name of a man, who will use his "energy in procuring Recruits for the 34th, instead of, for him-"self, a commission in any 'Corps D'Afrique.'" The Paymaster is here, and all are made happy by his presence.

21*st*. The officers are making plans for a grand ball, on Thanksgiving night; and, at their request, two of our teams have been employed in bringing into camp evergreen boughs, with which to cover the charcoal sketches upon the walls of the Lockwood House, in which the ball is to be held.

23*d*. A note from Gen. Sullivan, giving information that he, with his staff, and the ladies of his family, would be present at parade to-night, leads to its being ordered in all the blaze of dress coats, scales, white gloves and sashes.

• 25*th*. *Post General Order* commits Lieut. B——, of Miner's Battery, under charges for highway robbery, to the custody of the 34th, "to be held *as close prisoner;*" and the Lieutenant Colonel commanding is notified that "*he* will be held personally "responsible for the appearance of the prisoner, when called "for." Rather unpleasant for the Lieutenant Colonel; and decidedly hard lines for the Lieutenant, who, of course, must be subjected to the mortification of being guarded by an armed sentinel. Our ball-room, decorated with wreaths, and branches of evergreens, is looking beautifully. A spread eagle, made of twigs and sprays of evergreen, is neatly done, and attracts much attention. There has been much anxiety, and a good deal of discussion as to the entertainment. A caterer from Baltimore suggests *cold meats, raw and pickled oysters, and cheese!* A little Nig. about camp, says, "Poick," as he terms pig, and "Cologne Sausage."

Lieut. Lincoln, commanding a guard of twenty men, has left

for Wheeling, to deliver to the authorities there, thirty-five Rebel prisoners. Among them are the A. A. G., and the I. G., and chief of staff of Gen. Pemberton.

Lieut. Hall, with proper guard, goes to Washington, having in charge nine deserters from our forces, who have been arrested here; and is under orders to bring back seven recruits for us, now in that city, waiting transportation hither.

We had a sudden death in hospital to-day. The man had been sick about a week, but not enough to be confined to his bed. He complained only of a pain in the head. He ate his meals regularly—and his supper to-night; yet soon afterwards he dropped off without moan or struggle.

26th. Thanksgiving at home! and in honor of the day, no drills, nor fatigue, but permission given to about one hundred of the men to visit the village. Passes to do so are always granted early in the morning, and distributed at guard mounting; the number determined by the Regimental Commander. But this morning, Wells, newly appointed to the command of the Post, sent down an order forbidding more than two men from each company being away from camp, at the same time. On the whole, it was concluded not to recall those already issued for to-day, but obey the new order to-morrow. Soon a rap, and, from the orderly, "The Col's. compliments, and he desires you to report at his quarters instantly," which being done, "How's this, Col? didn't you receive an order, this morning, restricting the number of passes from your camp!" "Yes, sir!" "Well, I've just returned from the village, and I saw, on the street, double the number of your men, that that order allows." "You couldn't have seen near all of them, Col., if that is your count, for there's more than three times the number down there!" "And yet you received my order?" "Oh, yes, sir! But my boys were down town before your Adjutant was out of bed. If you want an order obeyed the *day it is issued*, you must get your family out of bed earlier. The Col. laughed, and admitted *we had him*, concluding the interview by requesting the Parade to be had at 3 P.M., for the gratification of Gen'ls. Kelly and Averill, who were present in town. Our line was formed at the appointed hour, but no

Generals appeared. As the Parade was dismissed, an orderly rode up, with a request to hold the regiment, for the arrival of the Generals, who, with a bevy of ladies, were, at the time, inspecting the camp. Upon their appearance, the parade was repeated, its close being marked by many expressions of praise from the Generals; Averill being especially complimentary.

27th. Thanksgiving has come and gone; and with it the ball given by our officers; Gens. Kelley, Averill, and Sullivan, and acting Brigadiers Wells and Maulsby, of the renowned " Potomac Home Brigade," with the officers of their respective staffs, honoring the affair with their presence. Kelley is a tall, angular looking personage, with a thin, hatchet-like face, and grayish hair and whiskers; from 55 to 58 years of age. He was dressed in an old seedy grey suit, and looked like a Quaker, run to seed. Sullivan, about 35, large size, stout built, with a just springing black moustache, and keen black eye, looked more the soldier than he actually is. Averill, a spruce little fellow, about 30, light and wiry, full of life and activity, dressed in a close-fitting cavalry jacket, is to all seeming the beau ideal of a dragoon. Wells, you know. Maulsby made his appearance in the glare and glitter of lace and bullion, enough for a hundred officers like him. A splendid sash of orange silk, interlaced with gold threads, and belt thickly embossed with gilt leaves, circled his body. A pair of heavy bullion epaulettes ornamented his shoulders, and seemed to weigh him down with their gorgeous magnificence. No officer, other than he, showed in any but the plain shoulder straps pertaining to his rank.

The ladies, God bless them! were there in large numbers. And oh! the dresses! and ah! the *un*-dresses! Sprigged muslins, and other gauze-like fabrics, floated round forms of 200 pounds, at the least, of good solid adipose matter; and heavy, stiff black silks stood out from and helped cover skeletons, whose bones could almost be heard rattling an accompaniment to the music of the dance. Flashy calicoes contrasted with heavy, glaring red merinos. High-necked and long-sleeved dresses, jealously guarded from, perchance, a too searching eye, the least particle of flesh, dry and withered too often, it is true; and again, there were other dresses so cut and disposed as to reveal the rich amplitude of shoulders and bosom to any who *would not turn away.*

The rooms looked beautifully. A chandelier, made by a circle of bayonets, suspended from the ceiling, being particularly admired.

For supper we had three varieties of cake, piled upon broad, shallow, white crockery dishes, *sweet water grapes, carefully picked from the stem,* stewed oysters, and a whitish, lumpy looking compound, unrecognizable by taste, but announced as chicken salad. *This by a fashionable caterer from Baltimore.*

Owing to the thoughtfulness of the married ones among us, and by great exertion, some well known earthen necessities were procured. Our own band furnished music most delightful, playing the latest and most fashionable airs. On the whole, the affair was a great success; reviellé from the bugles in camp bringing the signal to disperse.

31*st.* The non-commissioned officers, not to be outdone by their superiors in rank, have arranged, by permission, for a ball on New Year's Eve, and every spare man in camp is busied in preparation.

Assistant Surgeon Thorndike, who both as officer and man has won the esteem and love of the whole command, has been commissioned as full Surgeon in the Massachusetts 39th, Col. Davis. His personal gain, from this promotion, don't at all reconcile us to our loss.

We are making preparations to get rid of our cripples; though red tape in large abundance hampers our every movement to that end. Among them is included Schrock of "A," a "Veteran Recruit," procured at a money cost to the Government of seven hundred dollars, who has been with us *five weeks* and has had *six fits,* without doing a single hour's duty since joining us.

A new rule for the encouragement of the boys has been promulgated. It has been the custom for the officer of the day to select at guard mounting, each morning, from among those who are most soldierly in their bearing, and whose dress and equipments bear the best inspection, *three* men to be Orderlies at Headquarters. The new rule exempts from *all* guard duty *for a fortnight* such men as may be selected as such Orderlies, four times in a month. And this morning the Adjutant reports that eight men are enjoying the benefits of such exemption. As a whole, the regiment never made so perfect an appearance as now.

Three more men leave us to-day for Washington, and the Examining Board.

Piled near camp are three lines of wood, altogether amounting to some *three hundred cords*, product of our muscle, mostly obtained from the estate of a Mr. Lucas, who lives on a princely place near "Halltown," which has been stripped of every rod of fence by the men of both armies in former years, and from which we have cut, and are now cutting, every growing tree. This wood is kept for the days when the rain and the mud will combine to prevent any use of our teams; and fatigue parties are now cutting and bringing into camp what suffices for actual daily consumption.

The weather is just now intensely cold; and the General commanding is out of fuel; the medical director is out of fuel; A. A. G. Boone is out of fuel, and old Flagg, the Post Quartermaster, upon whom all these officers have made requisitions for fuel, hasn't a single spare stick on hand. Our pile is remembered, and a long train of Gov't wagons was driven into camp this morning, with the intent to raid upon our possessions. We are old enough in service, to get what we can, and good enough soldiers to keep what we get. So Flagg's train is turned about, and sent away *empty*. "Why, you've got two hundred cords at least, in your camp!" "Oh yes, more than that;" "and you won't let us have any?" "Not a stick!" "Well then, you shall chop all the wood wanted at the post;" and so now comes an order for a detail of forty men, to cut wood for the Post Q. M.; which we can't help.

4th. The weather is still intensely cold; the wind blowing so fiercely as to make it impossible for the sentinel, on the parapet, to stand against it.

Our sick list is complicated by a case of *scarlet fever.*

Lieut. Elwell, chief of our recruiting party, reports a total gain of *forty* men. Willard asks that Elwell may be informed he prefers to "*give his men fits,*" instead of having them bring them with them. For the first time, an application of one of our men to be allowed to appear before the Examining Board, has been forwarded *dis*approved. The applicant came out as a Sergeant,— was reduced to the ranks for intoxication — after which he was promoted to corporal; and now presents this application, approved by his captain, who is a thorough-going "*teetotaller.*"

For the first time, too, since the organization of the regiment, a coolness exists between the Col. Commanding Brigade, and the Lieut. Col. commanding the regiment. Cause as follows:

While the Col. was on Court Martial in Cumberland, his orderly visited the camp, and stole from a member of his company, a sum of money,— about thirty dollars. Of course, his arrest followed. Charges were preferred against him by his Captain, which were approved, and referred for trial to Major Pratt. Meanwhile the man was held in our guard house. Upon the return of the Col., which was by the mid-night train, he called loudly, but in vain, for his orderly. Learning his whereabouts and the cause of his absence, he wrote and sent down the following unofficial note: "Dear Col., I want my Orderly. Yours, G. D. W.;" to which was returned: "Dear Col., I've got him; when I'm through with him, you can have him. Yours, W S. L." An explanation followed, and the fact of the theft, arrest,— and progress towards trial, was communicated. Thereupon was issued the following: "Headquarters 1st Brigade. In future, whenever charges are preferred against a man of the 34th Massachusetts Infantry, the same shall be referred to these Headquarters for consideration, and final disposition." "By order of Geo. D. Wells, Col. 34th Massachusetts Infantry, Commanding Brigade." "S. F. Woods, A. A. A. G."

This is serious! Who is responsible for the command, its

drill and discipline? the Lieut. Col. actually in command, or its nominal head, who is away, and exercising a distinct and separate authority? Would the Acting Brigadier presume to send such an order to Miner, of the Battery? or to Curtis, of the 12th Virginia? or would he submit to such interference were his situation reversed? These are questions demanding consideration. A large detail from the regiment, under Maj. Pratt, and Lieuts. Macomber and Ammidon, is engaged in a thorough re-building of the road leading from Shenandoah street, past Camp Hill, to Bolivar, and beyond. To-day there isn't a solitary man left in camp, liable to detail.

Five more of our men are ordered to Washington, for examination as commissioned officers.

A case has arisen to-day, which, calling for the action of the Regimental Commander, renders necessary a determination of the course to be adopted in reference to the Brigade Order, when charges are preferred against men of the 34th. To yield obedience, is to surrender a high duty, the prerogative of the Regimental Commander; to give control of the discipline of the regiment to an officer in no way accountable therefor; to forfeit all claim to respect from others, and more than all else, to lose one's own self respect. Therefore, a letter was sent from Regimental Headquarters acknowledging receipt of the Brigade Order, protesting against its legality, and respectfully declining obedience. That done, an hour was given to Gen. Sullivan, who, with his wife, thoroughly inspected the camp. At a late hour of the day, the presence in camp, of Woods, A. A. A. G. was observed. He came with instructions to place the Lieut. Col. commanding under arrest, not to be executed however, if that officer would withdraw his refusal to obey the Brigade Order in question. This was declined, unless the order which called forth the refusal was first withdrawn, and so the matter now stands. Gen. Lockwood, commanding at Baltimore, has asked of the Department that the 34th may be ordered to that city, for provost duty. God shield us!

9th. Everything is progressing as usual. An unexpected visit to the camp was made to-day by Col. Wells. After a thorough inspection, he spoke in most complimentary terms of its appearance, the condition of the regiment, and the good conduct of the men at all times, and on all duty. At leaving, in reference to the almost constant near presence of raiding parties of the enemy, he expressed a desire that the command should be "at all times kept ready to move at a moment's notice." No allusion whatever was made by him to the little existing unpleasantness between the heads of the respective Headquarters; nor was there the most remote intimation given of any movement then ordered, or in contemplation.

Judge then, with what surprise, shortly after taps, a request to report immediately at Brigade Headquarters was received; and upon reporting, to receive orders to draw rations for fifteen days, and 50,000 rounds of ball cartridges *immediately*. "What, to-night, Colonel!" "Yes, sir, to-night;" and at a still later hour, to be told in person, "you will hold your command, Col., in readiness to move at a moment's notice." A written order sent down at 2 A. M., directed as follows: "Eight wall tents only will be allowed to the Field and Staff, and Line officers; one wagon only for the transportation of all needed hospital tents and supplies, and Officers' baggage. This last will be strictly confined to blankets and mess equipage."

In striking contrast to this was the furnishing of Brigade Headquarters; upon whose four four-horse teams were loaded mess-chests, trunks, chairs, *bedsteads*, *feather-beds*, and *sheets*, and a *cooking-stove*, besides something for the inner man, more appetizing than hardtack and coffee! Under the direct supervision of Lieut. Henry Bacon, Acting Quartermaster, the matter to be transported was suitably loaded; a large supply of axes, picks, and shovels, being included. The command was turned out, and closely examined; the able-bodied of the Guard relieved, and their places filled by those who would be liable to break down, and encumber the expedition. The strife among the men now was to see *who might go; not*, who *could stay behind*. To leave our Sibley tents, with all their many contrivances for comfort, and to go out on a fifteen days' march, in the middle of December, is no joke. Yet the men prefer it to being left. Dr. Thorndike, commissioned Field Surgeon to the 39th Massachusetts,— Lieut. Platt, Assistant Provost Marshall,— Lieut. Horton, on duty at Division Headquarters, —Capt. Pratt and Lieut. Lincoln, off duty, by reason of "Aphonia,"—and to whom the charge of the camp is to be committed; Capt. Leach, on court martial,— and Quartermaster Sergeant Trumbull are to remain behind. And so, our preparations are made. Now, 3 A. M., comes the order directing the movement at 7 A. M.; and, as it is made known to the Regiment, the shouts of "Hurrah for Baltimore!" and "Bully for Washington!" ring upon the air.

CHAPTER XVII

VALLEY EXPEDITION.

START AND MARCH TO BERRYVILLE — WINCHESTER — TO STRASBURG — OUR CAMP THERE — BRIGADE ORDERS — WOODSTOCK — AMUSING SCENES — MT. JACKSON — INCIDENTS ON THE MARCH — OUR PICKET — NEW MARKET — HARRISONBURG.

10th. Reviellé roused us at an early hour, knapsacks were packed and breakfast eaten, and at five minutes before seven the regiment was in line, ready for the order "Forward." The 12th Virginia reported in *light marching* order, and a delay was occasioned by the necessity of sending across the river for their blankets and "tents, d'abri." The stampede of a part of Miner's horses occasioned still further delay, and it was not till half past eight o'clock that the order to move was issued. The 34th led the column; next came the battery, next a train of some forty wagons, the 12th Virginia closing the column, which stretched out nearly two miles long. Our route was through Bolivar, Halltown, and Charlestown, over the scene of our October engagement with Imboden. At Charlestown, Boyd's 1st New York Cavalry, and a section of the 1st (Furst's) Virginia Battery joined us. At near sundown we made our bivouac in a grove of oak wood, just outside of Berryville, the cavalry going on in advance. Our march this day was 19 miles.

11th. Off about 8 A. M., to-day, the 12th Virginia leading the column. Our route was through "Berryville," a place formerly of considerable pretension, but now with little signs of life, and none of business; over a country where farm buildings were in ruins; where there were few fences and no crops. Fording the "Opequan," with water about knee deep, we soon after made our noonday halt. Resuming our march, we soon came in sight of Winchester, and the breastworks thrown up on every eminence by one or the other of the armies which in past time have occupied, or fought to gain possession of the place. Before entering the town our left wing was detached, under Maj. Pratt, and with the drum corps and the U. S. Flag, moved as a separate organization. But it's doubtful if anybody's eyes were blinded by the arrangement. And so, marching through the principal streets, by the Court House and other public buildings — all scarred by the fire of contending armies — where none but the negro population greeted our progress, we pitched our camp upon a field where our companions of the 12th had fought the summer before, under Milroy; and where cast off equipments lay mouldering, and bones of deceased soldiers lay whitening in the sun. Capt. Soley had charge of our rear guard, and had the usual trouble incident to the duty of bringing up the stragglers of a column. Upon making his report, he was furnished a proper guard, with orders to close up one or two drinking saloons, the proprietors of which had disregarded his orders. He did his work effectually, confiscating and bringing into camp a supply of knives, forks, cups, plates and spoons sufficient to establish Headquarters mess; and a small quantity of passably good whiskey, of which there was not a drop in the Regiment. Pickets were established, and under orders to resume the march at an early hour in the morning, we dropped asleep.

12th. Our Bugles sounded the Reviellé at 6.30 A. M. Breakfast was soon swallowed, and our men in line. But why the delay? In the raw cold of a December morning, men won't stand shivering in line, at least, without grumbling! John Mack, driver of one of the Brigade wagons, was helplessly drunk. He had found Headquarters' stores, and appropriated a part to his private use. So *he* was to be sent back; a few men were also found unable to march farther, *two* only of whom were *ours*. A new issue of rations was made to the whole command, that wagons might be obtained in which to send back the disabled. This done, the column moved; the 34th in advance. Passing over ground where Shields and Jackson had manœuvered and fought; through "Newtown," and "Middletown," small villages, whose poor, dilapidated buildings lined long, ill-conditioned streets, at the corners of which stood grey-headed, gaunt-looking men and women; on—on—over the Mac-adamized pike, till, having forded "Cedar Creek," we went into camp, at 4.30 P. M., in thick woods, upon a hill to the east of, near to and overlooking the village of "Strasburg." Not a single able-bodied man had been seen during the day. Our march, the *distance to be made each day*, the *places at, or near which we were to encamp nightly*, had been directed, by orders from the "Trinity," (as Halleck, Stanton, and "Old Abe," are somewhat irreverently called,) previous to our starting; and *at this place*, in pursuance of orders from Headquarters, that same command at Washington, we are to remain encamped *four* long days.

The Rebel General Rosser, with a force largely in excess of our own, laid against us, on the other side of the Shenandoah. Perhaps from this fact, our line of encampment was frightfully extended. As the troops were well covered from observation by the woods, from our bivouac fires alone could any idea of our strength be gained. Our pickets were well out in all directions; beyond the circle of which, no one was allowed to go. No hindrance was offered to the coming into camp of such as might desire to visit us; but, "once in, stay in," was the order. Previous to the march, Captains Bacon and Soley, Lieut. Kinnicut, and the Lieutenant Colonel commanding, had been boarding at a private house in the Ferry, and the orders to march were so peculiar in the manner of delivery, that no arrangement for subsistence upon the expedition could be made; so that up to this time, those officers had lived upon charity. While awaiting the return of some men, sent out to make purchases, a present of some *"grouse* and *buffalo meat"* was sent up to Regimental Headquarters, for supper; and it was none the less relished, that the meat of the first was *white*, and tender, with a flavor very like chicken; and that the taste of the latter was much *like veal!* The return of the foragers with liberal supplies of milk, butter, bread, turkies, and sheep, put the above named four on their feet, so far as commissariat was concerned. But the tables were turned at Brigade Headquarters, where, notwithstanding all their appliances of bedsteads, beds, sheets, chairs, and cooking stoves, the officers were living on short rations of hams and hardtack. The Pioneers were detailed to cut wood, which the drummer boys were set to bring in, and pile in a heap, for the fires, round which most of the officers gathered.

13*th*. The morning is chilly, with indications of rain. Extended as we were yesterday, the order to-day is to "*stretch our lines still farther.*" We are all occupied in preparations to keep comfortable for the days we are to remain here. The men are suffering a good deal from badly blistered feet, but there is no complaining. "Boyd" is scouting our front, and has sent in a considerable number of prisoners for us to guard.

14*th*. The storm which had threatened, broke upon us last night with fury. Rain, snow, and wind combined to make our position uncomfortable, though the thick cedars and pines which screen us from observation, also afford us partial protection from the severity of the weather.

Orders from Headquarters direct the 34th to furnish a guard of fifteen, to be detailed from the "*poorest, lamest, deadest, men*" of the command, who are to be sent back to the Ferry, as guard over the prisoners now in our keeping, numbering over ninety.

Many a man, with sore and swollen feet, pleads hard to be allowed to remain with the column; and the final detail was governed, quite as much by the morale of the men, as by their physical condition.

15*th*. "Contrabands" throng the camp, with wild stories of the movements of Averill, who is *raiding* near "Saltville;" and to create a diversion in favor of whom, our column is moving. Refugees from Rebel conscription, from their hiding places in the mountains, in considerable numbers, and some residents near by also, come in, seeking safe conduct to our lines under the protection of our column.

The train is to be repacked, that wagons may be procured in

which our prisoners and guard can be transported to the "Ferry;" and huge piles of hard tack, in boxes, are stacked in camp, exposed to the rain, which has poured now for *thirty-six hours* in a continuous stream.

We resume our march to-morrow, taking with us *six days'* rations of bread, and *three* only of pork, the men being put on *half rations*. We carry only *thirty* out of the 50,000 rounds of ball cartridges with which we started, and are light enough to move quickly if we are driven to it. I could not help enjoying myself to-day at the condition of things at Brigade Headquarters, where I had been ordered to report. Their mess was reduced to hard tack and ham, and the wry faces of the members, as the Quartermaster dismounted from a foraging expedition he had undertaken for their relief, bearing under his arm a peacock as the only trophy of his raid, were funny enough. Our own larder, at the time, was amply supplied with live sheep and turkeys, besides mutton and chickens, sufficient for several days, and I made merry at their expense.

Returning to my own quarters, I found a group of officers anxious to obtain permission for their servants to leave the column, on to-morrow's march, for the purpose of procuring supplies. To their request, I could only point to the order of the day, just issued from Brigade Headquarters, "forbidding any "soldier to leave the column on any pretext," and directing the officers "to shoot any man who should be found away, attempt- "ing to approach, with the purpose of entering, any house upon "the route." "But what shall I do, Col.? My mess hasn't a mouthful to eat!" "Wait, Capt.! The Col. don't know that I have any supplies. I'll make the same request for myself. If it is granted, he can't very well refuse you; if it is refused, I will share with you of my abundance." So my note was dispatched at once, and was brought back by the Orderly, who carried it, with the following endorsement: "Respectfully "returned, *disapproved*. Lieut. Col. Lincoln's attention is "called to orders Brig. Headquarters this date, prohibiting any "man's leaving the column, on the march. Commanding offi- "cers of separate Battalions and Batteries will be held to the "most exact personal responsibility for the observance of the "above order." With a smile, I threw the paper to the Captain. 'Twas better for him to take a carcass of mutton from my store than to indulge in grumbling; and, shouldering his meat, he started off.

16th. Our original order had directed us to move, by prescribed marches to "Strasburg," (where we now are,) to remain there *four* days; then to resume the advance up the valley, by similarly prescribed marches, reaching Harrisonburg on the 18th; to hold that place till noon on the 19th, avoiding a fight if possible, and this done, to return to the Ferry. Upon reaching Strasburg, report of the threatening position of the Rebel Gen. Rosser's command on our flank, had been made, but produced no change in our orders; so, through the drenching rain, which still continued to fall, the boys moved on to line, at half past seven, and soon after, the bugles sounded "forward," the 34th taking its turn in the rear. Our route, still upon the Mac-adam was without obstructions, save such as were caused by gullies, down which the water rushed, often, up to the knees of the men.

We reached "Woodstock" by the middle of the afternoon, the day's march, about twelve miles. The train was carefully parked; artillery placed in position for any emergency; strong pickets thrown out, completely girdling us, and more than usual precaution taken against surprise. Where is Rosser? and what will he do? are questions of considerable interest to all of us.

17th. The wind changed in the night, and this morning blows piercingly cold, from the north-west. At half past seven, without beat of drum, or blast of bugle, the men moved on to line, ready for the march. The scenes of the morning, though sad, were amusing enough. Everything had been thoroughly soaked in the rain of yesterday, and, upon reaching camp, all hands had turned their energies to drying themselves, their clothing and equipments. Some taking off their boots, or shoes, had placed them by the fires to dry; and now found them a "*world too small;*" others had laid down with their feet to the fire, and so the leather had been scorched to a crisp. Officers, magnificent in their long legged and stylish boots, were hunting for privates with whom to exchange for the regulation shoe; and all, of whatever rank, unable to trade for shoes of size large enough to slip over their blistered and swollen feet, slit the uppers, from instep to toe, or cut out the whole front of the shoe leather. Many of *large understanding*, wrapped their sore feet in bandages made of pieces torn from their shelter tents, or woolen blankets. With all these discouragements, the column cheerfully limped along its difficult road. The rain, of the preceding days, had washed from the Pike all dust and loose dirt, and the sharp grit of its frozen surface, wore away the soles of our shoes, as a rasp would wear away paper. "Jordan was a hard road to trabble." The spirit of good natured rivalry between the men of the two Infantry commands, was such, that neither would falter, and, from one or the other, could always be heard the merry jest or patriotic song. "Co boss! Co boss!" in allusion to the bounty of "*seven hundred dollars and a cow*," as the boys said, our old veterans would call out to a faltering recruit, less inured than themselves to fatigue and hardship; but generally there was little opportunity for such good natured crowing. All bore themselves gallantly, and many unflinchingly trod the rough pathway with *bare and bleeding feet*.

Passing through "Edinboro," a place of small consequence, we halted for the night, at "Mt. Jackson," (a neat village of some pretension), going into camp in a piece of thick woods, on a hill, in rear of some large hospital buildings, erected after the first Bull Run, and near the unfenced burial ground attached thereto, where swine were rooting over, and tossing about the head boards which had marked the last resting place of representatives from nearly every state in the Union.

Sending forward a Cavalry picket of *two Companies* from Boyd's command, which now kept but little in advance, to hold the bridge which spanned the north fork of the Shenandoah, just the other side the village, we prepared to pass the night.

To-day's march showed us that every live animal had been driven before our advance by the inhabitants near our route.

An incident, which occurred during a temporary halt to-day, strongly illustrates the accuracy with which one familiar with moving bodies of troops, can estimate the strength of a column. Ever since since leaving "Strasburg," the females, who came to the doors to gaze upon us, had been eloquent with scoffs and jeers, and full of prophecies that we were marching a road over which we should not be able to return. Rumor preceding us, gave our number as *twenty-five thousand strong;* and, as we halted for a brief rest, a young, scornful-looking damsel, standing in a doorway, was heard, in reply apparently to a question asked of her, by an inmate of the house, to say: "Well, "if there is over *seventeen hundred* of them, I won't reckon "again." We actually numbered seventeen hundred and forty-two.

Another incident was full of excitement. Attached to the person of the Commander of the column was a party of about *twenty* mounted men, mostly from Cole's Battalion of Maryland Cavalry, under a grim old Sergeant of Boyd's 1st New York. While out scouting on our flank, these fellows flushed a party which, under a dashing young Lieutenant of Fitz Hugh Lee's command, had came down to bushwhack us. Our party was the strongest, and the Rebels sought safety in flight. Selecting the Lieutenant for his victim, the old Sergeant pushed closely on his track. The chase, with its windings and doublings was in plain view from the elevated road along which we were moving. Once or twice the old Sergeant raised his pistol, as if fearful of losing his man; but, resisting the temptation to fire, he steadily pressed on, at last making him prisoner, at a high rail fence, up to which the Lieutenant boldly rode, but over which he was unable to force his beast. No words can properly describe the peculiar air of satisfaction with which the old Sergeant turned his captive over to us for safekeeping; and, after exchanging saddles, galloped away upon the back of the animal he had so gallantly ridden down.

18th. The attack upon and disaster to our Cavalry picket, at the bridge across the Shenandoah last night, was made known to us at an early hour this morning, by Capt. Stearns, who commanded the party, and who was fortunate in making his escape. His party had been surprised, with a loss of *fifteen* men and *twenty-six* horses. It seemed almost a necessity that the bridge should be held by us, as the current was swift and deep, and the banks high; but we were too weak, especially in Cavalry, to spare a sufficient force to ensure its being held.

So, with a warning to the Villagers, that they would be held responsible in person and property for its preservation, we moved, leaving it unguarded. The 34th was again in the rear, having in charge about one hundred prisoners, all of whom had been captured and sent in to us by Boyd's command, since leaving Strasburg.

Reaching New Market, we came to a halt in the main street, which extended the whole length of the Village. Nothing indicated the existence of war, but the entire absence of able bodied males. There was no lack of aged men and women, and young children of both sexes, between whom and "the boys" many a jest was exchanged; and the belief, not always good naturedly, expressed that we should not be able to march back over the same route. The prisoners indulged in loud boastings that the tables would be turned upon us, and they soon be guarding us with our own muskets. Indeed, on all sides could be heard the confident assertions that we were marching to certain defeat.

As we neared Harrisonburg, a halt was ordered, while our commander communicated his orders for the disposition of the troops, during the night. This done, surrounded by his staff and body guard, he put spurs to his horse and galloped, out of sight, to the front. Marching on, at almost sundown, we reached our designated camping ground, in a dense wood, to the left of the pike, almost a mile outside of the Village.

The Artillery being posted, with Infantry in proper supporting position, arms were stacked, and the men ordered to prepare their coffee. A large body were at once detailed to cut down trees, and another and larger one to roll them together, for our bivouac fires. The weather was intensely cold. Its severity may be judged from the fact, that, at this time, almost every man's canteen had become useless; the water in them, having frozen hard enough to split them open. The work of preparing for our fires was interrupted by an Orderly, who brought orders to our Lieut. Col., directing him "to get under arms, and hold the column ready to move at a moment's notice." Quietly the orders were promulgated; and the line was quickly formed. What did it all mean? We were left to conjecture, for no farther communication reached us. Standing inactive, the cold was hard to bear, and was fast reducing us to an unserviceable condition. Now, our A. A. A. G., who had accompanied the Col. commanding on his ride to the front, and had conferred with Boyd, of the Cavalry, came in, giving us the information that we had nearly run into the arms of the Rebel General Early, who, having failed in his attempt to intercept Averill on his retreat, had turned his attention to our column. As but a few miles intervened between us and his command, and, as it would be folly for our small body to attempt to contend with his full corps, we concluded that our hurried retreat would be ordered. But no orders came to us, and as by this time the severe cold was telling upon the men, arms were again stacked — axes distributed — and while some were chopping, others, and a larger party, were engaged in rolling into huge piles, the fallen logs and limbs; the object being to build a long line of fires, under cover of which, to slip off, if, as was conjectured, such should be the final determination of our leader. Our situation now became generally known, and the Boys worked with a will till they had rolled together a long line of log heaps.

Riding on to the ground, and catching at a glance the apparent disobedience of his orders, in that the men were not in line, the Acting Brigadier, in no very measured language, demanded an explanation? "A statement of what was being done, was received, with thanks for the conception, and execution of the idea; and a direction that it should be carried to completion." That done, Col., said he, "you will get the column under arms, move out on to the Pike, without delay; set your face towards the ferry, and, mind, unless you see me, or get a note, which you can swear is in my hand-writing, don't you stop, till you get to the ferry, for now, Col.,—it's *legs or Libby*."

The huge piles of logs, extending in long line, were quickly fired, and between 7 and 8 P. M., after a day's march of *twenty-three* miles, encumbered with our prisoners, and a number of families who hoped, under the protection of our column to reach the Union lines, in the cold and the darkness we commenced our retreat. The 34th in its turn had the advance. The Colonel joined us before we had been long on the road, and his sharp "Forward, boys!" uttered as he rode past to the head, imparted renewed life to the column.

CHAPTER XVIII

VALLEY EXPEDITION.

AN INCIDENT — OUR NIGHT'S MARCH — EDINBORO' — A HALT AND IMPORTANT INFORMATION — THE ROAD IS CLEAR — BIVOUAC AT WINCHESTER—WELL, HALT NOW!—HOME AGAIN — A PUNISHMENT — MORE INCIDENTS.

An incident of the day's march is too interesting not to be given. Among our prisoners we had a Lieutenant of Fitz Hugh Lee's command, a smart young fellow, with a bright new uniform; the same, who, driven from the ambush from which he had intended to bushwhack us, had been run down by our grizzley old Sergeant of New York Cavalry. On the day's march a temporary halt had been ordered; the head of the 34th resting just opposite a house, some little way, back to the left, from the pike. "I'm right glad it ain't so! I'm right glad it ain't so!" uttered in a loud tone, broke upon our ears; and turning, we saw a tall, gaunt, gray-headed old man, with uncovered head, and hat swinging in accompaniment to his exclamation, striding toward us. Repulsed in his attempt to pass the line of sentinels which fenced in the prisoners, he appealed to the Officer of the Guard, and by him was referred to the Lieut. Col. Commanding. His request to be allowed to pass the Guard and speak with one of our prisoners, was denied. "But he is the only boy left to my old age, and he left home only yesterday!" "*No matter!*" "Well, Colonel, where did you come from?" "Massachusetts." "Massachusetts! Massachusetts! from what part?" "Worcester." "Worcester? God bless the old county! There's where *I* was born; I came from Dudley; my name is

Baker; *I'm a Union man;* my oldest boys are in your army, (that is, if they are alive; for I've heard nothing from them since I run them through the lines), and now, you've got the youngest. I wanted to run *him* off, too; but his old mother could not part with him, so I got him detailed to help me on my farm, to get him rid of the conscription. But they gave him a Lieutenant's commission, and so got him away from me. And when he heard you were coming up this way, *nothing would do him* but he must go out to meet you. We, his old mother and I, plead hard against it, but we couldn't stop him. So I gave him my best mare, and he got some boys together and rode off; and when I saw one of your men this morning riding by on "old Blaze Face," (I knew the mare to oncet,) I reckoned it was all up with the boy. But you've got him among your prisoners, and for the sake of his old mother, for love of the old State!—let me to him, Colonel!" The appeal was successful.

Rushing past the guard, the old man hurried on, with outstretched arms, exclaiming, with broken voice, "Hulloa, John! "How did this happen? I thought 'twas all up with you when "I saw old 'Blaze Face' going by this morning! I knew the "critter right off! And, John, they told me you was killed! "but I'm glad it ain't so! I'm right glad you are *here.* You "mustn't feel so smart, boy! you mustn't feel so smart! "These Yankees are pretty cute, too!"

"Yes, damn it! father," broke in John, "the Yanks have got "me now. I thought the critter could run away from any "Yankee horse that ever was foaled; but, curse them, they "were too fast for her; and they've got *me,* and the *mare, too!* "But never mind; they can't take me out of the Valley! I'm "a prisoner now, but they won't keep me long!"

The old man's request to be permitted to take his boy up home, that he might take leave of his mother, and get a change of clothes, and some provisions, was refused, with the remark "that he would have the same rations as our men had, and that "his mother saw him yesterday!" "Yes; but Col., *hard bread* "*isn't as good as soft biscuit!* and his old mother's heart is most "broken for her baby. Let him go, Col., for the sake of the old "flag which my boys are fighting under! You need n't fear; "I'll bring him to you again, *sure!*" Knowing well the risk, yet somehow feeling confident all would turn out right, he was allowed to take him; yet not without the accompaniment of a faithful guard.

Minutes passed, and the prisoner did n't show! "Forward!" was sounded from the bugles, and still there was no appearance; but, as the head of the regiment neared his home, our prisoner, provided with a good large bundle, with his father and the guard, awaited our approach. The prisoner, as he stepped within the guard, turned, and, with an air of bravado, said: "Never, mind, old man! Don't fret! I'll be home again in a day or two!" "God bless and keep you, Col.!" said the father, "you and your "brave boys. *Keep my boy safe!* You've got him, and all I "ask is, that you'll keep him till the end of the war;" and, wringing his hands, the old man turned away, partly, perhaps, to hide the tears which were streaming down his face.

It is an interesting fact, that the young man, upon our return to the Ferry, was delivered to the provost guard there, was confined afterwards at Ft. Warren, and was not liberated till hostilities closed.

We found butter here at seventy-five cents the pound, small sized loaves of bread seventy-five cents each; whiskey ten dollars a quart; corn six dollars the bushel. Cassard our Brigade Commissary, sold the hides, from two two-year old steers, for fifty dollars. Matches were sold by the men, at two dollars the card; and one man refused one hundred and sixty dollars for his boots; but this last price was in Confederate bills. After leaving Strasburg, the men were on half rations. We carried nothing but grain, for our horses; which, for seven days, had no other forage.

Monday 19*th.* Our last night's march was one which none of us will ever forget. We had marched twenty-three miles to reach Harrisonburg. This, in broad day, when one could choose the path for his sore and blistered feet, was bad enough; but, in the darkness of the night, no one could choose his road, and it was literally true that our night's march could have been tracked by the bloody footprints of the men. In spite of all this, however, it was conducted swiftly; and, but for the dull rumbling of the wagons and artillery, not a sound proceeded from the column, except when an occasional misstep drew a suppressed oath from the poor sufferer, or a smothered command was passed from officer, to officer, along the column. We reached "New Market." at 4 A. M., and, filing on to a hill overlooking the Village, stacked our arms. Permission was here given the men to light their pipes and kindle fires. Poor fellows! they were too tired to care for either; and except such as were detailed for the night picket, all laid down, and slept upon the ground they occupied, in line. All were not permitted to enjoy this rest, however, for upon the complaint of a citizen, — Dr. Hinckle, that men from the Artillery were breaking open and plundering stores, a Patrol from the 34th was marched into the Village to put an end to the outrages complained of.

Morning dawned all too quickly; and at 8 A. M. we were again in motion; the 12th Virginia, which prided itself especially upon its powers of marching, leading the way. In the anxiety, lest we were pursued by Early, all make good use of their legs. We passed "Mt. Jackson;" reached "Edinboro'" in good season in the afternoon; and having encamped in order of battle, in case of being overtaken and attacked before morning, breathed more freely.

Here, in the evening, Boyd joined us with his cavalry; expressing great admiration for what he laughingly called our "*unbounded capability for retreating.*" *He* had been left at Harrisonburg, with orders to keep up our fires, and conceal, as effectually as he could, and as long as possible, our departure. His force had been driven into H. before we left; and, during the night, he abandoned the town, falling back so as to cover our intended camp. The account he gave of his own, and the rebels' movements the morning after we left, amused us greatly. The smoke, still rising from our long line of fires, betrayed our supposed position. Throwing out a long line of skirmishers, the enemy began a cautious advance. By skilfully manœuvring, now showing a line dismounted, now appearing in column, Boyd caused them to halt. A careful reconnoisance was made by the enemy; his line of skirmishers was strengthened; and about 11 A. M., it gallantly charged, and captured—our smouldering fires. Boyd's purpose being accomplished, he gathered his small force, and galloped sharply after us.

Tuesday, 20th. The order of march, issued last night, directed a movement at *three*, A. M. As we, having moved on to the Pike, were waiting for the train and artillery, many and various speculations were indulged in by men and officers. Was Early after us? and if so, could he out-march us? Was Rosser in our front? From the 12th Virginia could be heard, "Can the 34th keep out of the way?" for it was our turn to lead.

Our night's march had given us an advantage in the race, which all felt was to be engaged in. If only we could maintain what we had gained!!

We reached "Woodstock" at sharp day-break. "Halt!" was ordered in the main street of the town. The iron axle of one of our wagons had broken short off, at the shoulder,— and our Col., like a good soldier as he was, determined to leave nothing for the enemy. So the 34th was called upon for blacksmiths; while the B. Q. M. rode up and down the village searching for a forge, at which the axle could be welded. The men leaned upon their muskets, in the street; and the officers grouped together upon the sidewalks. As I stood, having dismounted to stamp some warmth into my feet, I was rudely jostled by a female, who approached unperceived from my rear, and passed hurriedly on. The force with which she struck me, precluded the idea that the collision was accidental. Who was she? and what did she mean? These questions were puzzling me, when I perceived that she had turned in her walk, and was retracing her steps. Her course was directly towards me. I braced myself for the meeting. Another step, and she would be square against me. But, with a side step, she brushed past; her hand caught mine, and, by a dexterous manipulation, she left in my grasp, a piece of paper, folded closely. With no sign of recognition, she pursued her way; and turning the corner of a street, near by, passed out of sight. This was queer enough! I moved away some distance, before I ventured to look at the note. The paper was without signature, or date; but it gave information of the whereabouts of Rosser, and of his then hurried march to intercept us. Springing to my horse's back, I gave the note into the Col.'s hands, with a statement of how I came in possession of it.

"Send your Pioneers here, Colonel, and cut and burn this wagon!" was his order, as he read the note. This accomplished, our march was resumed. During this halt, a few hard looking, middle-aged men glared at us, from the corners of the streets; and, as the column filed from the ground where it halted for breakfast, a party of about forty fired a few shots upon our rear guard. One of "Furst's" Napoleons, well charged with grape and cannister, sent back our compliments, and we were troubled no more.

At near noon, we approached Strasburg. The note, so strangely delivered at Woodstock, warned us of danger here. So, halting at Fisher's Hill, our scouts were pushed out in front, and on flank. Slowly and cautiously we followed. The head of "the narrows" was reached, and again we halted, to give time for a thorough observation in front. Hurrah! the road is clear!! Catching the signal that there was no enemy to dispute our advance, with lightened hearts, and quickened step, we passed through Strasburg, and at 1 P. M., re-occupied the camp, we had formed on our march up the valley.

Two miles in front was Cedar Creek. Once across that, all felt there would be safety. As we must get wet in fording it, the men desired to cross it at once, that they might have the advantage of their bivouac fires at which to dry their clothes, rather than to cross to-morrow morning with a day's march, in wet clothing, before them. But the Col. commanding wouldn't listen to the suggestion.

The men had been on half rations, since leaving this camp. Leave was granted to issue the reserved rations, which amounted to eight *hard tack*, and a goodly sized piece of bacon, per man; all of which was speedily disposed of. The horses too, which had been confined to short allowance of grain, for the same time, now enjoyed long forage, which was dealt out to them.

Scattered around, lay the carcasses of a number of cows, killed, as the villagers insisted, by having eaten greedily of the "*hard tack*," we had left on the ground, when marching away.

Pickets were thrown out as before, but now, free communication was allowed to the country people, many of whom came in, "*toting*" their little all, with a fixed determination of leaving the valley with us.

21*st*. Our march was resumed *early* this morning; the 12th Virginia heading the column, and leading off at a pace which kept our teams to a pretty steady trot. Upon reaching "Cedar Creek," it was found that our prisoners, with their Guard (a Company of the 12th,) were behind, in the village of Strasburg. A halt was of course necessary till they could be brought up, and turned over to Company "F," of ours, Capt. Chandler, whose turn it was to take charge of them.

The weather was very severe; a cold north-east wind swept across the level, and blew up clouds of dust which enveloped the column. We halted at noon, for dinner, in the village of "Middletown;" and, marching with a quick step through "Winchester," went into bivouac in the wood, by the banks of the "Opequan." A supply train of wagons, with medical stores, and ambulances with Surgeons, met us just before we reached "Winchester." Reports had reached the Ferry of serious disaster to the column; not only by reason of exposure to the extreme severity of the weather, but also in consequence of an encounter with the Rebels; and relief in this shape was sent forward to us. Seated round our camp fires, we listened to the wonderful accounts of our exploits, which had reached those in authority; and were none the less contented, that there was so little foundation for the most of them. The evening passed merrily! A shot fired upon one of our pickets, on the "Winchester" side, causing us to spring to our arms, disturbed our repose for a moment; but other than this, "all went merry as a "marriage bell."

24*th*. Orders, issued last night, directed "one Company of "the 34th to be sent forward at an early hour, to throw a foot "bridge across the Opequan;" and Company "B," Capt. Potter, was detailed for the work, with directions to move at 3 A. M.

At 4.30 A. M., the 34th led the column, on what was felt to be the last day's march. The water was high in the creek, with a body of thin ice extending some distance from the bank.

The troops crossed upon the rude bridge of logs, which Capt. P's men were finishing when we came up; and ascending the steep bank, there halted for the train. Our horses were all smooth shod; and the water, which froze as it dripped from the animals and vehicles, rendered the task of climbing the hill slow, and difficult. The men were impatient in their long waiting in the cold; and when, at length, the Bugler sounded "forward," Capt. Willard, whose Company formed the advance guard, led off, rapidly. One, two, and three miles were passed over, in the exact time of sixteen, seventeen, and sixteen and a half minutes each, when, sounding faintly from the rear came the "halt," and the Colonel commanding rode up, laughingly enquiring, "if we were running away." "Oh, no, Colonel," was the reply, "but you know the 12th boast that they have "never met troops who could march fast enough for them; "and we are trying to please them!" "Well! halt now," said he, "and let them get up, and say how they like it, so far!" We breakfasted near "Berryville;" passed through "Charlestown at noon, where we dropped Furst with his Artillery; (Boyd having been left at "Winchester,") and marched on to line, in our own camp, at 4 P. M., bringing with us, ninety-eight prisoners, besides a goodly number of refugees, and contrabands, with their families. The conduct of the men of the 34th, for the whole time, was worthy of the highest praise.

Once only, during the expedition, was there an occasion for punishment in the regiment. Upon our return march, a Sergeant of ours left the column, with the purpose of entering a house, in disobedience of orders. For this offence the stripes were torn from his blouse, he was marched in arrest for the rest of the day, and at night, regimental special order sent him to duty, *as a private*, in the ranks. It is due him, however, to say that his previous conduct, as a warrant officer, was unexceptionable, and that he was led to this act of disobedience by his sympathy for a comrade, who, being sick, desired to obtain some soft bread for the hard tack issued to him.

As a military movement, this expedition was hazardous enough to be termed fool-hardy. To attempt, in the dead of winter, to penetrate, with a column of 1,700 men of all arms, the enemy's country, to a distance of more than 100 miles, cutting away from a base of supplies, with no hope for support, would be sufficiently venturesome under the most favorable circumstances. What shall be said of such a movement when, as in this case, the order of march, the day for starting, the distance to be passed over each day, the four days' tarrying in encampment, midway of the advance, are all prescribed by Headquarters far distant from the scene of the movement, where neither the nature of the weather, nor the obstacles to be encountered, could by any possibility have been foreseen.

To have successfully accomplished the movement, escaping from a force of ten times our number, without the loss of a man, bringing with us every prisoner, and encumbered by a cloud of refugees, evinced a skill, and endurance, and pluck, not always heretofore exhibited by our troops. Had Rosser, whom we left on our flank, succeeded in crossing the Shenandoah, and so fallen upon our rear, or laid in wait to oppose our retreat, the result would not have been so favorable. But he was prevented from crossing by the high water in the river; and when at length he did move to cut off our return, our night's march down the Valley had been so rapid as to bring us in advance of him.

During the entire route, every person with whom we could hold communication, according to his predilection, expressed the hope, or fear, that we were marching to certain defeat and capture. The prisoners were entirely unconcerned at their situation; bantering their guard by confident assurances that, in a day or two, the tables would be turned, and they be holding our own muskets over our heads. More especially was this true on our hurried homeward march; and each grove and pass, every ford and bridge, was closely searched by them, as if from out of each their deliverance was to be effected.

The loyal among the inhabitants gave us hearty welcome. The contrabands flocked to our camp by night, in some instances communicating information of importance; and such of them as accompanied us in (and but from the fact that we *could not well stop on our return*, the number of these would have been much larger) were extravagant in their demonstrations of joy.

Many refugees from the ruthless conscription of the Rebel officers, hurried from their hiding places to the protection of our flag.

No one who was near can ever forget the feeling caused in our ranks by the loud cries and wild yells of a party of these people, who, in this way tried to attract our attention, hoping to reach our column. With no covering for their heads, or feet, their bodies but partially protected by wet, torn and dirty quilts, their long hair hanging down over their faces, unshaven, half starved, they staggered up to us, tears streaming from their eyes, and prayer and thanksgiving pouring from overflowing hearts. One could hardly conceive of such misery.

On our upward march, before reaching Strasburg, there was an amount of pillaging which would have done *honor* to Gilmer or Mosby, but which was disgraceful to a disciplined command.

A cavalry scout would dash up to the column, enveloped by a lot of turkeys, geese and hens, tied to every spare point of saddle or trapping, followed by a second, flourishing a *steel square*, or a pair of *steelyards* in his hand, and wearing a woman's *bonnet* over his cap; while a third held in his arms a kettle of apple sauce, smoking hot, as it was snatched from the fire, or a loaf of bread, taken half baked, from the oven. The caissons of Miner's Artillery revealed looking glasses, feather pillows, and articles of wearing apparel of no use save to persons of the other sex.

All this was stopped, however, by the General Order issued before leaving Strasburg, which forbid any soldier leaving the column while on the march, and entering any house, under penalty of being shot; and thenceforth fear kept these rag-a-muffins decent.

To us of the shoulder straps, there was privation enough. Bread was one dollar the loaf, small at that, and not always to be had at any price. No one on the route would sell an article of any kind, for any price, to a *d—d Yankee nigger*, as these people called our black servants. The men fared better, as their rations were regularly issued; and moreover, they could always trade away to the people their *coffee grounds* for bread. Through the whole expedition the men were in heavy marching order; a portion of the time on half rations, many without shoes, and marching in stockings; others with feet but partially protected by bandages made from strips of their blankets or shelters, and leaving the bloody footprints of their swollen and blistered feet upon the frozen pathway; and in such condition accomplishing a night march of twenty-one miles, resting only an hour and a half, immediately upon one of twenty-three the preceding day, and all this without a straggler. Gilmer and McNeil hung round us during the trip, but with no disastrous results, if the loss sustained by the Cavalry Picket at the bridge, near Mt. Jackson, is excepted.

CHAPTER XIX.

Harper's Ferry.

HOME AGAIN — PROMOTIONS — GEN. SULLIVAN — A CURIOUS AFFAIR — OUR WOOD-PILE — NEW ALARMS — THANKS — A FAILURE — AN ALARM AND A MOVEMENT — ANOTHER ALARM AND MARCH — RECRUITS — TRANSFERRED — AN EXPEDITION — TRANSFERRED AGAIN — NEW ORDERS — OUR BAND.

25th. No duty was required from the men, from the hour of their return yesterday, till parade this evening, the call for which gave the first intimation to them of the intention to have them out. Stiff and lame as most of the men were, their march was not so springy as usual; but on line they were the same soldiers as ever, their arms glittering in all their customary splendor, and the manual being perfection itself. One thing, only, marred the beauty and pride of the parade. Lieut. D. had so far forgotten what was due to himself, and the regiment, as an officer, as to appear on line in a state of intoxication, for which offence he was at once placed in arrest. Capt. Chandler of F, has received a leave of absence for fifteen days. Major Pratt is detailed on General Court Martial.

28th. Col. Wells has left for Cumberland, having been detailed as a member of a General Court Martial to assemble there.

We shall lose *one* man from K, in consequence of the hardship and exposure of our late expedition. He made no complaint till on our last day's march, when he was put into one of the wagons. Upon getting into camp, he was sent to the hospital, where he now is, delirious and fast failing.

Upon our return commissions were found waiting for Sergeants Pennell of E, and Farwell of A, to Lieutenancies in Colored regiments. Recommendations of *four* applicants for examination by the Board in Washington, and of *two* men to Governor Andrew, to be commissioned by him, in regiments now being raised at home, were forwarded to-day.

Each company has purchased a patent "meat chopper," also wire toaster or gridiron, substitute for the everlasting frying pan, which Uncle Sam. issues. Henceforth we can enjoy broiled, instead of fried beefsteak; and can luxuriate in *hash*. As a necessary consequence, there will be considerable increase of company savings. The Regimental fund has been drawn upon for the means with which to procure like articles for our hospital. The line officers are making arrangements for a ball, to come off on New Year's Eve; our absence at Christmas having prevented the one intended for that time.

29th. Gen. Sullivan made a congratulatory call, at Head-quarters, this P. M., being very profuse in his compliments to the regiment, and leaving a written order directing "Lieut. Col. Lincoln to take command of the brigade, in the absence of Col. Wells;" a course rendered necessary, by the presence, at the post, of Col. Simpson of the 9th Maryland, ranking officer, whom Sullivan refuses to recognize.

In a full and free conversation about various bodies of troops and their manner of performing duty, he remarked, that "the 34th was the only regiment he had ever seen, which was as well entitled to commendation for real work, *as for style*" as he was pleased to call it; adding that "when he assumed command here, he made up his mind that we could not be equalled on parade, but that probably we were worthless in every other respect. Yet to his surprise, he found on trial, that we were most excellent in every place, and for every duty."

The re-clothing of the men throughout, although just previous to the late expedition, we had issued an entire outfit, was completed to-day.

Nearly all the articles now furnished by the government, the shoes, especially, are of very poor quality, not only as regards the manufacture, but also so far as the material is concerned. Men, with clothing drawn a week ago, are actually more ragged than some whose clothes were issued months since.

If only the boys could get at the contractors! There would be no one here at any rate, to pity or take their part.

We had a curious affair last night. Our outer pickets are from a squadron of Pennsylvania cavalry, one post, of six of its men, being at "Keyes' Ford," on the "Shenandoah," two or three miles in front. The Sergeant in charge, last night, having posted his sentinel, laid down by the fire with the rest of his party, and *all slept*. A little fellow by the name of "Mobbly," from White's battalion, Rebel Guerillas, stole upon this party, and securing their arms, actually *kicked* them to wakefulness. Securing the sentinel, he marched the whole party to the banks of the river; and learning from their statements that they were *six months men*, and that their time would expire on the fifth of next month, he released them with the not very complimentary remark, that he "*reckoned they were n't of much account to either party*." An order, Headquarters Gen. Sullivan, constituting "Lieut. Col. Lincoln commander of the post, with orders to report, in person, for instructions," covered by a personal note, giving information of the near approach of *Early*, and advising to increased watchfulness, was received to-day.

Some of the prisoners brought in by us have enlisted into the U. S. Service, and are full of fight and revenge.

One of them a South Carolinian, has joined the ranks of the 34th, and seems already at home beneath the white flag of old Massachusetts.

30th. We left in camp, at our departure upon the late expedition, *three* tiers of fire-wood, each 160 *feet long* and *six feet high*. Old Flagg gobbled it all while we were away, and our daily detail of sixty choppers, is making sad havoc with the beautiful oak groves of Mr. Lucas's estate. He pleads earnestly that we should spare a part, but in vain.

Now, at midnight, an orderly brings dispatches directing the 34th and Miner's Battery to be in readiness to march early to-morrow morning, to Charlestown, in support of Boyd, who is in camp there, with all our available cavalry; and which place is threatened by Early. The 12th Virginia is to cross from Maryland Heights, and hold the breastworks behind which we are encamped.

31*st.* The historic "all quiet on the Potomac" is not, as yet, disturbed. Bartlett, of K, died to-day, from typhoid fever, brought on by the exposure and fatigue of the last expedition. Howard, of B, who, however, did not accompany us, is very low with the same disease.

We have, to-day, but eleven officers of the line reported "present for duty." Assistant Surgeon Thorndike has received his commission as Surgeon of the 39th, and is to leave us forthwith, very much to our regret. We shall be fortunate indeed if we secure a successor who comes any way near filling his place.

It has rained violently, and without any intermission, all day.

The 12th Virginia, which has been standing to its arms since early morning, without blankets or rations (the Major in command giving as a reason that his orders did not require him to take either,) has just now, 7 P. M., received orders to "draw two days' rations *and make themselves comfortable* where they are." In the absence of any direction how this last part of the order is to be executed, *we* have volunteered to vacate a tent in each company street for their occupation.

We are, as we have been all day, ready to fall in at a moment's notice, and Miner still has his horses in harness.

A general order, "Headquarters 1st Brigade," has just been sent down by Col. Wells, "thanking the command for their "patience and endurance in the late expedition, with the state-"ment that the conduct of the troops had merited and received "the warmest encomiums from both division and department commanders."

The day's work closes for me, by a letter to Gov. Andrew, acknowledging the receipt of his dispatch, communicating the fact that D— B— had been named to him as a suitable person to fill the place in the staff made vacant by the resignation of our late Chaplain. While admitting the irreproachable conduct and character of private B., in fear that his past service in the ranks would much weaken the respect in which such officers should be held, and so impair his usefulness, the benefit of the proposed favor was respectfully declined.

"The Ball," arranged by the officers, to come off last evening, proved to be a failure; partly by reason of the severity of the weather, and somewhat on account of our unsettled condition. The ladies of the neighborhood, with few exceptions, sent in during the afternoon, little notes, expressive of their regret at feeling compelled to withdraw their previous acceptance. Those who did not so decline, started on their way, but, without an exception, failed to reach the ball room.

In the almost total darkness of the night, Capt. B——, having in charge the Misses S——, was driven over a cellar-wall, his ambulance over-turned, and his party spilled into the mud and water, of the cellar, from which, after much trouble, they were extricated, with no other damage than a thorough wetting. Yielding to entreaties, he turned, and landed his fair companions safely at their own houses. Notwithstanding this desertion by the ladies, the officers resolved into a "Gander party," and made a "night of it," by themselves.

Jan'y 1, 1864. After two days continuous heavy rain, the storm broke about midnight, and this morning the sun shines brightly. Early in the day, orders from Sullivan's Headquarters, directed "Lieut. Col. Lincoln, to move his brigade, at once, to Bolivar Heights, and occupy that position; holding it unless firing should be heard in front, in which case, he would move rapidly in the direction thereof, without waiting for specific orders." Rations were at once issued, and the command marched to the designated point. The Redoubts, on each side the Pike, were occupied by the Artillery; and the Infantry was drawn up in support, sheltered, so far as was possible from the severity of the weather. Headquarters were established under the lee of a pile of brush, where, wrapped in our blankets and cloaks, we could watch the country for miles around.

So far as the eye could reach, the Pike was occupied by the Quartermaster's department of the Cavalry force at Charlestown; and a perfect mob of camp followers, hurrying confusedly to the protection which our position was supposed to offer.

All manner of stories were told by these fugitives. What was certain was, that Early, in force, was advancing and threatening Charlestown, and a brush seemed imminent.

In the bitter cold of a biting wind, with no shelter, and without a stick of wood within reach, the Infantry was fast becoming benumbed, and unserviceable. The men of the 12th Virginia, mountaineers principally, started some rabbits from among the weeds, and brush, and pursued with wild halloos. This had the good effect of restoring circulation, at least; and the 34th, stacking their arms, joined in the exciting sport. Deployed as skirmishers, the men swept along in a wild chase after the frightened animals, and *run down* and caught more than a hundred of them. The day was thus passed; and towards night, the troops were re-called by an order from Division Headquarters, which order also directed the command to be continued in readiness to move upon receipt of orders. "So severe was the cold, that one man in the bivouac of the Cavalry perished from exposure.

2*d.* Our condition remains the same, couriers from Boyd, in front, bringing intelligence that Early, with his force, is between Berryville and Winchester. In the interregnum, the regiment was mustered for pay. A rigid inspection showed that we were in readiness for whatever might be in store for us.

3*d.* The weather still continues intensely cold; our condition the same, with the exception that at noon to-day all the Artillery of the Brigade moved out to Halltown, where Wheaton's Brigade, the 3d of the 6th Corps, three to four hundred Infantry (which reached here by rail yesterday), is encamped.

Early lies in bivouac from Summit Point to Bunker Hill. Averill, with his Cavalry, has reached Martinsburgh from his late raid.

Assistant Surgeon Smith, for a long time Acting Post Surgeon, has been relieved and returned to us, much to our joy. Thorndike still remains with us, Maj. Gen. Kelley refusing his muster out to accept his promotion in the 39th, on the ground "that the exigencies of the service require his presence in this department."

4th. A good many Rebel deserters come into this post daily. They represent their sufferings as having been dreadful. Averill is hanging on Early's rear, and is reported to have driven him yesterday back to Strasburg.

Our own position is unchanged. The 12th Virginia left at noon to-day, by rail, under orders to report at Cumberland.

Lieut. Hall, having in charge our rolls and a party of prisoners, left for Washington to-day; and Lieut. Lincoln is detailed again for to-morrow to escort another lot of Rebel prisoners to Wheeling.

5th. We had a light fall of snow last night, and to-day, although the snow has changed to rain, the cold is becoming more severe.

A note from Gen. Sullivan, in response to an application addressed to his Headquarters, stating "that the present is an opportune moment for Lieut. Col. Lincoln to avail himself of the leave of absence granted some days since, as there is no enemy near," led to preparations for departure by that Officer on the night train; but the arrival of the 10th Maryland, about *two hundred and fifty strong*, suddenly hurried from Baltimore by orders from Washington, led to a change of purpose.

Reports were current in that city that Martinsburg had been taken, and Harper's Ferry seasonably evacuated; its garrison having succeeded in escaping to Maryland Heights. Halleck had ordered all troops, which could be spared, to be hurried from Baltimore to the defence of this place.

Lieut. Elwell telegraphs that *ninety* recruits for us left Boston on Saturday last.

6th. In the absence of Lieut. Col. Lincoln, who left to-day, the command of the regiment devolved upon Major Pratt.

9th. An order, received at Headquarters at 5 A. M., calling out the entire regiment, was promptly responded to. *In ten minutes* from the time of its receipt, the boys filed out from camp on a hurried march to support Cole, who, for weeks past, has been scouting Loudon County, with success; and whose camp was surprised, about 2 o'clock this morning, by about three hundred from White's and Mosby's bands of guerillas. The first knowledge Cole had of the presence of the enemy was from a volley fired upon his men, sleeping in their tents; and although taken unawares, he succeeded in rallying his command, attacked in turn, re-possessed his camp, and repulsed the enemy, who left upon the field three officers and four privates killed, with a large number of wounded. The distance to Cole's camp was some *three miles;* and, although the regiment moved at a quick step, its arrival was too late to be of any service,

Leaving Companies A and G in temporary support of Cole, the Major conducted the balance of the regiment back to the Ferry. Lieut. Horton, by order of the War Department, has been *detached* from the regiment, and appointed Commissary of Musters, 1st Division, Department West Virginia.

14*th.* Ninety recruits reached us to-day in charge of Capt. Bacon, who had been sent to Washington for them.

Our force, at this post, is lessened by the departure for home and muster out of the 21st Pennsylvania Cavalry, six months' men.

16*th.* The "1st Brigade, 1st Infantry Division, Department of West Virginia," is, by General Order of this date, dissolved, and "the 34th" is temporarily attached to the 3d (Wheaton's) Brigade, "6th Army Corps, Army of the Potomac." The change is welcomed at Regimental Headquarters, and will be a relief to the men.

Capt. Leach, in command of one hundred men, has been despatched, with five days' rations, to scout through Loudon County, towards Snicker's Gap. In imitation, perhaps, of the example set on the occasion of our Valley Expedition, the hour of setting forth, the place for the respective night's bivouac, the time of reaching and leaving the Gap, and the route to be followed both going and returning, is prescribed in Division General order. Capt. Chandler, F Co., returned to-day from his late leave of absence.

20*th.* General Order "Division Headquarters," of this date, detachs from Wheaton's Brigade, the 34th Massachusetts Infantry, and directs that it "form an independent command, "to report directly to Gen. Sullivan, commanding the Division."

Capt. A. D. Pratt has left for home on a twenty days leave of absence.

21st. "New brooms sweep clean." Instance: "One Cap-
"tain, two Lieutenants, with forty men, and a bugler from the
"34th Massachusetts Infantry, henceforth daily, will report to
"Gen. Sullivan, in person, for duty as patrol."

"Any soldier on the street, in the day time, without a pass
"from his Regimental or Battalion Commander, is to be arrested.
"If Cavalrymen, they are to be dismounted, and their horses
"turned over to the Post Quartermaster. Any citizen or
"soldier on the street after 6½ P. M., is to be confined in the
"Guard House. Officers, if without the countersign, are to be
"placed in arrest." Such is the order promulgated yesterday.
In consequence, the Guard House is literally *crammed* with prisoners, among them being a Lieutenant of the 102d New York,
and the entire body of teamsters attached to the Post Quartermaster's Department.

Lieut. Col Lincoln returned to-day from his leave of absence,
and Capt. Bacon and Lieut. Murdock left on leave.

An order from Division Headquarters directs us to furnish
a "guard of one hundred men at the Pontoon Bridge."

With this, came an order directing "the band of the 34th
Massachusetts regiment, to report this evening at Division
Headquarters. Now, while the members of the band are
enlisted men, liable to duty as such in the ranks, they are
musicians, only by a little private arrangement known to
themselves, and the officers of the regiment. To us, they are
musicians, performing upon instruments either purchased by
themselves, or by appropriation from the Regimental fund; but
to the world they are soldiers — and soldiers only. Unwilling
to recognize Gen. Sullivan's authority over them "*as a band*,"
Regimental Special Order directs each member, by name, to
report in full uniform, with side arms, but without instruments,
at Division Headquarters, this evening, at the hour designated
by Division Order.

No "sound of revelry was heard" where fair ladies and
brave men had gathered to make the eve "pass merrily as a
marriage bell;" but instead thereof, "how dared he" do this?
"Send for him, to report at once," and upon the appearance of
the representative of the 34th: "What means this Col? How

dared you disobey my order?" "What order, Gen.?" "What order? What order? You know very well sir! Mrs. S—— desires to have a little dance, and I ordered you to send down your band, to furnish the music; instead of which, a dozen or so of private soldiers report with their side arms, but without instruments." "Where is your band?" "I recognize General, your authority over me, and the men of the 34th regiment; but the musical instruments of our band, are private property, belonging to the musicians themselves, or the officers of the regiment, used for our own gratification, by contract with each man, for which we pay from our own pockets. These men are enlisted soldiers; as such, and only as such, are they subject to your order, and——" "But they have played at my quarters before this, Col., at my request?" "Certainly Gen., and will again, when you *request* it!" "It's the *order* then, you object to!" "Only that, Gen.!" "Well, Mrs. S. wants the music! will you see that she is gratified?" "With pleasure, sir." And so the affair terminated.

31*st*. Dr. Thorndike left to-day, for his new position, as Surgeon of the 39th.

A raiding party has been sent out, with orders to search every house, and seize all liquor found. We hear by deserters, who come in daily, that "Early" is encamped at Woodstock.

A paper is being circulated, and has been signed by about a third of the boys, containing an agreement to serve for three years longer, provided the government will accept the service, and allow us the usual furlough home; the order of the government, in regard to such re-enlistment, not applying to the 34th, as there is more than twelve months of our original term unexpired.

CHAPTER XX.

Cumberland and Return.

OUR ORDERS — AT CUMBERLAND — NEW ORDERS — AN ALARM — IN THE MUD — FURTHER ORDERS — IN BAD ODOR — RECRUITS — HURLEY OF G — GRADY OF H — A LITTLE SONG — AN ALARM — A FLAG OF TRUCE — DISCHARGES.

Feb. 1st. 11½ A. M.: The Regiment is in marching order, with *three* days rations, and *sixty rounds* ball cartridges. We are to move without tents; officers without horses; and wait, only, the making up of a train, in which to be transported to Cumberland; where Kelley, in anticipation of being attacked by Early, is concentrating troops. It is raining hard.

1 P. M. Orders are just handed in, directing "the commanding officer of the 34th Mass. Infantry to move, at once, with *five hundred men*, to the railroad station, to take transportation for Cumberland." *Twenty* sergeants, *forty-five* corporals, and *three hundred and eight* privates, being every man of the command, in camp, fit for duty, and subject to Regimental order, were moved. Upon reaching the station, the Patrol and Provost guard, were urgent in their request to be taken into the line. Representing to the Gen. this desire of the men, he gave his consent to our drawing *one hundred men* from the guards at the Ferry. While the men were being embarked, Gen. S. communicated his orders verbally thus: "You'd better put one or more reliable officers, upon the engine, Col! I shall hold you responsible for the train, and the command. These conductors, and engineers, are all d——d rebels; you must watch them closely, and upon the slightest evidence of their

unfaithfulness, you must blow out their brains, and run the train yourself."

"Be very careful, as you near 'Clear Spring;' you will probably be fired upon there; and should you be, you will land your force, and burn every building in the neighborhood. At all hazards, Col., you will force your way through;" and, with a significant look, he added, "mind, and remember, that I don't want you should bring me any live prisoners." "Let me have your orders in writing, Gen., if you please." "There is no time for that, Col.; every minute is precious; your train is ready. Good-bye."

Capt. Willard and Lieut. Goodrich were placed upon the engine, with directions to look closely after the engineer, and off we steamed; our comrades left on duty, waving and shouting farewell greetings. Nothing interrupted our rapid run. All went, and promised well. Nearing "Clear Spring," our speed was slackened; and, steam being shut off, we approached with caution, and with no noise, save the rumbling of the train. The station was reached; and instead of rebel bullets, a despatch from Gen. Kelley was received, urging all possible speed in reaching Cumberland. With open throttle the engine was urged forward; and at 7 P. M. the Regiment was reported, at Department Headquarters, as "present for duty." "Go back to your command, Col., at once. Keep your men together. Don't leave them a moment; orders are now being made out. We shall send you to 'New Creek,' or 'Patterson's Creek,' both of which places are threatened." Hours passed, and no orders came. We were crowded, compelled to stand in close box-cars, which had been used for the transportation of cattle; and which were offensive, and filthy; not having been cleaned at all since having last been so used. Is it any wonder that the men grumbled? or that no one, when morning dawned, was in very good humor? The Adjutant, despatched to Gen. Kelley's quarters, returned with information, that orders would reach us, so soon as it was determined to what point we were to be sent! While waiting, an engine whizzed by us, from the east. *The Guard, (a company) at Patterson's Creek, had been captured, and the bridge across the stream had been burned, during the night, by the rebels*. The horse had been stolen; yet the stable could be even now locked; so the 113th New York was hurried off, by special train, to guard *what had been destroyed*, and *we* were soon after disembarked. Halloa! what does this mean? Officers, mounted and spurring for dear life! "Col. Lincoln," said Col. Wells, "the General directs you to move your Regiment at double quick, to Black's Hill!" "Where's that?" "Overtake that Battery, you are to support it," and turning, he dashed away. By a short cut, across the fields, we passed the Battery as it ascended the hill, and, filing to the left, drew up in line, on its crest. Here Gen. Kelley and staff, Col. Campbell, Post Commander, and staff, the Post Q. M. with his clerks, Col. Wells, with other officers, members of the Court Martial in session here, all constituting a cavalcade, formidable in *members* at least, rode up, and gave the necessary orders, for the disposition and unlimbering of the Artillery.

What did it all mean? Vague rumors of the *near* and *threatening* position of the enemy were flying among us, when suddenly the circle round the General was broken, and out from the group, his horse bounding madly under the spur, dashed our Colonel with orders to send, at a double quick, a company deployed as skirmishers through the woods *in our front*. "Soley" stripped his men to light order and was off in a twinkling. Wells had hardly rejoined the circle of officers when, turning, he galloped again towards us, his clear voice ringing out the order to send *to our right flank* another Company also as skirmishers. "You're in for it," exclaimed he, as in obedience to the order A, (Capt. Willard), started, deploying as it went. "What is it, Colonel?" "The enemy in force are advancing in this direction; one of *your* men has been captured by them; has escaped, *but with the loss of his musket*." "One of ours? captured by the enemy! I guess not, Colonel; *who* is he? *where* is he? *what's* his name?" "I can't tell his name, but—(as the circle of officers around Kelley just then broke, showing the soldier standing in bold relief), *there he stands!*" What a laugh broke from us as the fellow was recognized. "What is there to laugh at?" asked Wells. "To think how you've been *sold!*" "Sold! Sold! how, and by whom?"

16

"Only, Colonel, that I'll bet there is'nt another officer in the command who would n't have known that miserable devil, at sight!" "What do you mean, sir, by such a remark?" "This, Colonel, that in your informant, stands Malcolm Smith, the greatest liar among us; a man for whom a party has been scouring Cumberland all the morning; who slipped away from his company sometime last night, leaving his musket behind him, which his Captain, and not the Rebels, has got. I'll wager, Colonel, the man is drunk; and when you have got from him all the information you desire, we've a little account against him to be settled." Wells rejoined Kelley; the Officer of the Day claimed S—— as his prisoner, and Orderlies were despatched to recall Capts. Soley and Willard, who, conducting their Companies cautiously through the woods, had just caught sight of and were preparing to pick off the pickets of our friends of the 12th Virginia, on post in our front. The affair caused much merriment among us, and we were still enjoying ourselves over it, when the Colonel rode up and very gravely gave Gen. Kelley's instructions that "S—— should be kept in arrest until our return to the Ferry, when charges would be preferred against him before General Court Martial. "For what? Colonel," was the enquiry. "For what! why, for creating a false alarm in camp; a most serious offence!" "I guess I would n't, Colonel, it won't sound well, will it, for the General commanding? Better leave him to us." "Well, you have the General's order," were his parting words as he turned and joined the Cavalcade, which was on its way to town. We were left to ourselves, in the mud and water of the cold and spongy soil.

Late in the evening our good friends, the 12th Virginia, now in barracks, generously sent for our comfort their tents and stoves, without which we should have had a night of much suffering, as we were forbidden to cut down any standing trees for our fires.

3*d*. A note, from the Col., requesting that the Band might be ordered to report to him, for the purpose of serenading some ladies in the village, was returned, with the information that it was not with us. His request that it should be sent for, was declined, in view of the uncertainty of our stay *here*, and final destination. But, by order of Col. Wells, direct, it joined us this afternoon.

6th. We have laid in the mud and water for a week; no enemy nearer us at any time than the raiding party at " Patterson's Creek," and no alarm more serious than that created by Malcolm S—'s drunken performance. The time has been idled away by us. An attempt at drill was made,—the intention being to surprise the good people of " Cumberland," by the invasion of their village, by the regiment on skirmish drill. But the state of the fields was too bad to warrant the attempt, and we laid quietly in camp. No good, so far as we can perceive, has come to any one by our presence here, save, perhaps, what may have resulted from the nightly playing of the band beneath the windows of the female members of a traveling theatre company performing in the town.

7th. At 6 P. M., orders came to take cars for transportation to the Ferry. The camp was struck at once, and, leaving our stores, of all kinds, in charge of Quartermaster Sergeant Trumbull, the regiment was marched to the line of the railroad. Here a line of close box cattle cars, the floors of which were ankle deep with the droppings of their last living freight, was pointed out for our occupancy. This was too much! On our way up we had submitted to such transportation without a murmur. Under orders to move *towards* the enemy, nicety as to the mode of going seemed in bad taste. But now it was different. A day's difference in the time of reaching the Ferry could not be of much account, and orders to march were withheld. An interview was sought with the commanding General. Representations of the filthiness of the cars provided for us, fell upon listless ears. Permission to march to our destination was asked and denied ; and it was only after an explicit refusal to order the regiment into the cars which were provided for us that any attention was given to the remonstrance. A train of box cars, *clean, however*, was at length furnished, and at a little after 8 we were started on our way.

8th. We reached our camp after a run of about three hours, last night. We found *forty* additional recruits, who arrived during our absence, waiting assignment to their companies. We found, also, that we were in bad odor at Division Headquarters. All because of the number of men taken to Cumberland.

Our original order specified *five hundred* as the number to be taken. Three hundred and seventy-three only were in camp subject to the order. Seeing the anxiety of the men of the various guards at the Ferry to accompany us, the General himself had given verbal permission to take with us *all who desired to go*. The members of the band had joined us after we reached Cumberland. An attempted explanation of the unintentional disobedience of orders was cut short by the General's—" No "matter! No matter about it *now!* Let it all go! I damned "you enough for it while you were gone!"

We left in hospital, at "Cumberland," one of our men, sick from wet, cold and exposure. While there, a man who had suffered for months from "aphonia," upon being spoken to by the doctor, at surgeon's call, answered in his former loud voice, and quickly disappeared from his wondering companions, in seeming fright at the unwonted noise. How queer, such cases!

9th. The assignment of all our recruits to the companies of their choice is at length completed, and the rolls of such disabled men as we desire to discharge from the regiment, has been made out. Mainly, these are fit subjects for the invalid corps.

The 14th New Hampshire, attached to Wheaton's brigade, sent to fill our place, while we were in Cumberland, and whose quarters are *in the grave yard*, near our camp, is now ordered out to Halltown. Just previous to leaving Washington, this regiment received *ninety drafted men, or substitutes therefor*, and lost *fifty* of them by desertion, before roll call, the next morning.

Their drills, guard mounting, and parades furnish much amusement to our boys. At parade, if a head itches, off comes the cap, that a good scratching may be had; *noses* get many a brush and buffet, as intrusive flies light upon and tickle such members; and many a time, a good natured fellow turns upon his heel to exchange a friendly word with his rear rank neighbor. It is hard to realize that our boys, who now stand like carved statues, under all such provocation, could ever have been such undrilled and gawky fellows as these men are.

10th. The small pox, which has of late been somewhat prevalent among us, is abating; but the measles threaten us instead, having been now, as when we were at Fort Lyon, introduced into camp, by men on their return from furlough.

Lieut. Walker, of A, has sent in his resignation, which has been forwarded, approved.

An order from A. A. A. G. Nims, Gen. Sullivan's staff, directs "Lieut. Col. Lincoln immediately to detail from the 34th Massachusetts infantry, a competent non-commissioned officer, to *take command* of a *colored pioneer corps*." This was done, and the officer reported himself at Division Headquarters. There being no "*pussons*" there, from whom the corps could be formed, new orders were issued, directing the Sergeant "to take a file of men, and scour Bolivar, and the Ferry, and impress all niggers found running at large."

For "fatigue," we send daily to the village, all soldiers who know *how* "*not to do it*," instead of those who fancy they must do an honest day's work, no matter of what nature it is. *We were green once*, but have got all over it, and none of us fancy an order to *scrape the streets*.

We are sending home our men as fast as possible, on furloughs of ten days time, in view of a more active service in store for us, having now *fifty* absent. As an inducement to good conduct, preference is given to applications coming from men unexceptionable in deportment.

A gray headed, simple, but well meaning old man, bearing the broad seal of the Christian Commission, *detailed*, as he says, for six weeks, "*to do good in the army*," came to us to-day. His great anxiety seems to be to find some building, in which to gather together the *Masons* of the regiment, " to teach them morals," as he says. "Ah, Col., you're not a brother," he remarked, as inability to furnish any assistance in his search, was expressed.

11th. The Paymaster has settled with us, and now, *midnight*, all is quiet; not a soul in the Guard House.

A new detail of fifty men is called for from the regiment, for fatigue in the Ferry, to be under the command of Lieutenant "McOrmber," as he is designated in the order.

The startling announcement was made, at reveillé roll call this morning, that Hurley, of G, had been found in his bunk, *dead*. He answered to his name at tattoo call, last night. Upon inquiry, it came out that he, with Wagner of the same Company, left camp in the evening and purchased at a house of an Irishman near by, a bottle of whiskey, Hurley, as his companion says, drinking the largest half of the liquor.

In consequence of this, a party was despatched from camp, with orders to "search every house in the neighborhood, seize "all liquor, and arrest every party in whose possession any spir- "its should be found."

Apropos to this: Who of us will ever forget Grady, of H. Ignorant, stubborn, but well meaning on the whole; when sober, a good soldier; when drunk, which is too often the case, a terrible nuisance. As the boys say, "he is one of 'em." As a rule, we are chary of giving him favors, but he has been behaving so well lately, that he was allowed a pass to the village to-day. Returning in good season, but a little mellow, he thus accosted the Captain: "Well, Captain, when are you "going to let us roughs go home?" "Never, Grady!—never— "until you learn to keep sober." "Sober, is it; sober, is it, you "mane? Well, then, let me ask you a bit of a question. Don't "you give furloughs now to your best soldiers, Captain? Don't "you do it, I ask?" "Certainly, Grady, certainly! and if you "had let whiskey alone, you'd have had your furlough long "ago." "Well now, Captain, see here! I ain't the worst sol- "dier you've got, am I? say now, Captain, am I?" "Well, no, "Grady; you're one of the best when you let whiskey alone!" "Well, then, Captain, see here now; I'll tell you how 'tis!—and "we'll fix it. You just let Grady go home, like a good fellow "as ye are, and—as for the whiskey—the whiskey 'tis, Cap- "tain, ye mind!—why, don't ye give that a furlough at all, at "all!!"

And here's another.

"Lieutenant," said Capt. W., "where can a man get a drop,

just a drop to rinse out his mouth?" "I can't tell, Captain."
"Oh, come now, be a good fellow, *I'm so dry*. I'd give a dollar—that is, I would if I had one, for just one swallow! The least mite of a taste would do me." And E., who knew, weakened and told, adding "that there was but a drop in the canteen, and he didn't believe he could get that." "You come along and see," said W., and off they went. "Good morning, good morning, Colonel." "Good morning, Captain, take a seat; what can I do for you this morning?" "Nothing special, Colonel; its a friendly call; its pretty cold weather, Colonel; yes! It's dry, too—very dry!—yes! The boys are behaving pretty well now, Colonel! yes, very well." "A little noisy, perhaps?" "Not bad. They sing a good deal, Colonel; yes, sometimes. I sing a song or two, myself, Colonel; perhaps you would like to hear me now;" and a willingness being expressed, the Captain, in a voice anything but musical, in a slow strain at the start, but increasing his time gradually, till the last line, which was rattled off at a double quick, thus broke out:

> Between you and me, I really think,
> Between you and me, I really think,
> Between you and me, I really think,
>   It's just about time to take a little drink.

The Colonel surrendered; the canteen was produced, and W took his swallow. Civility required that he should not now hurry away. So general conversation was kept up for some time, till W., *dry again*, essayed another performance, this time concluding his stanza with, "Its time now to take *another* drink." But it didn't work so well as at first, and the party separated.

Our old friend from Maine called again to-day.

"I have called upon you, Colonel, to inform you that somebody, a good Congregationalist Clergyman, from the hills of Berkshire, has arrived, charged particularly to look after the well-being of the 34th." "Well, my dear sir," was the answer, "I am very glad to hear it; that is, if the man has got any common sense, which you will remember I have said was not, in my opinion, the richest possession of the men of your cloth."

"You are more than half right, Colonel, in that; and, if *you* say so, I'll sound this fellow, and if he is'nt the right thing, I'll come up myself on Sunday, and preach to you." "Good! we shall be glad to have you. You're one of the right sort, and if you'll promise to be here certainly, the parade shall wait for you."

The only drawback to this old gentleman is his extreme anxiety as to the number of Masons, or as he terms them, "*Brothers*," among us.

Told, by way of joke, that Miner's men,— *hard cases*,— *roughs all of them*, were of the fraternity, "Ah! well," was his pleasant rejoinder, "there are always found Tares among Wheat."

12th. Another alarm last night, causing the whole command to be turned out and kept under arms. It was occasioned by a party of Rebels, under Gilmer, who, striking the railroad at Duffield, tore up the track, causing the up night train to be thrown off. This done, Gilmer distinguished himself by indiscriminate robbery of all the passengers, male and female, taking all they had of money, watches and jewelry.

With a consideration altogether unusual, Gen. Sullivan, instead of sending us, on foot, after these mounted robbers, got together the patrol and despatched them, by special train, to the scene of disaster.

And in this connection occurred one of those little incidents where a well meaning man, by an excess of zeal, gets himself into trouble.

Sergeant McIver, of G, at the time of this alarm was waiting at the station for the down train, on which he was to take to Baltimore the remains of Hurley, of his company.

Leaving "the dead to bury their dead," he borrowed a musket, and joined the party sent up to Duffield. Upon his return this afternoon, he found the corpse which he had left uncared for on the platform, in charge of another of his company, and an officer in waiting to conduct him to the Guard House. We hope to save him from the wrath of the Gen. commanding.

A party of one Lieutenant and five privates, *Greybacks*, riding upon "McLellan" saddles, on horses branded "U. S.," having with them an ambulance lettered "*5th army corps*," displaying a white cotton rag fastened to a stick, under escort of a squad of New York cavalry, was stopped at our breastworks, to-day, till the pleasure of Gen. Sullivan could be ascertained. Their professed object was to obtain permission to remove the body of a Rebel Colonel, killed a year ago, and buried at Shephardstown, twenty miles north of us. Having nothing to verify the character and object of the party, save Rosser's pass, reading: " Guards and pickets will pass Lieut. Allen and party through the lines, to remove a body," the officer and his party were turned over to the care of the Provost Marshal, the ambulance to the medical purveyor, and all the horses to the Post Quartermaster.

14*th*. Capt. Bacon and Lieut Walker have returned from their leave of absence, and Capt. Pratt and Lieut. Lincoln, away on sick leave, have had their time extended.

15*th*. The Rebel party which came in, two or three days ago, " to *procure a body*," is ordered to be sent through the lines, " *via Hillsboro*," thus making a complete circuit of our posts. We have received recruits in such numbers as to exceed the maximum number allowed a regiment, and have been carrying them along until we could make a place for them, by discharging some of our disabled, about which there has been no little difficulty.

But to-day a departmental general order has been received, directing us to "drop from our rolls" the names of forty-seven of our old men, and send the men so dropped to Washington, by rail, to-night, thus affording us the desired relief.

Among those absolutely *discharged*, is Schrock, of A, a veteran recruit, costing, in the language of the boys, "$700 *and a cow !*" who joined us in October last, and in *eighteen* days had *fourteen* fits; once falling upon a red-hot stove, without the power of getting away.

His rations being deemed *more than equivalent for any service he has rendered*, he is discharged "without final statement."

It has cost us a good deal of trouble to get rid of this fellow.

His "discharge papers" were made out, some weeks ago; signed by the proper Regimental officers; approved at both

Brigade and Division Headquarters, and sent up to Gen. Kelley for his final order. That officer, by the chief of his medical staff, returned the discharge papers "*disapproved,*" and directed that Schrock should be sent to General Hospital, in Frederic, with a suggestion, that it was probably a case of *malingering.*

Upon the return of the papers thus endorsed, a memorial was addressed to the Secretary of War, setting forth the facts, complaining of the unwarrantable action of Department Headquarters, and asking for redress. This memorial, signed by the commanding officers of the Company, was forwarded, *approved* by the Regimental, and Brigade Commanders, and by *Sullivan, without comment.* Kelley returned it to Sullivan, for *his* approval, or disapproval. Sullivan to *his* medical director, for *his* opinion. Medical Director Hays to Surgeon Clarke, for *his* opinion, (each of these last officers had signed the man's discharge papers.) The Regimental Surgeon re-forwarded the paper, endorsing the representation made by Capt. Willard; Medical Director Hays, "coincided in the conclusions of Surgeon Clarke;" Sullivan expressed "confidence in the opinions of Drs. Hays and Clarke, and the representations made by the company and Regimental Commanders, and his conviction that an investigation of the conduct complained of should be had." The paper, thus fortified, was received by Gen. Kelley, and he, instead of forwarding it to the War Department, to which it was addressed, referred it to his Medical Director, the very officer, whose action was complained of, who wrote thereon, "Let this man be discharged," to which Kelley added, "without pay," and then appended the sweeping endorsement that "whatever man of the 34th is pronounced by "Surgeon Clarke, Lieut. Col. Lincoln, and Division Medical Director Hays, *unfit for service,* will hereafter be at once discharged." And so *we* are content; and join in the laugh which is raised at Division Headquarters over our triumph.

16*th.* Our invalids (forty-nine in number) left us last night; and a sad parting it was. Great men wept, like children, over the enforced separation.

Howard, of I, who had a short time before married a Harper's

Ferry girl, had, of course, to leave his wife behind; and Angell, of E, one of the $700 Veteran Recruits, who joined us in Oct., but who has ever since been an inmate of our Hospital, found himself, by this move, compelled to defer the consummation of his marriage, with one of the Bolivar damsels.

Davis, of G, discharged, by order of the War Department, to enlist as Hospital Steward in the regular service, also left with the party.

"A Board, consisting of Gen. Wheaton, Medical Director Hays, Lieut. Col. Lincoln, and Surgeon Clarke, is directed to convene, without delay, for the examination of all Recruits alleged to be unfit for service. Eight of ours, among them, *one* weak in body and mind,— but *fourteen years* of age, as he claims;— another, a lad of *fifteen*, whose pulse is carried to one hundred and thirty, by a brisk walk across a room;— and the throbbing of whose heart beneath his buttoned overcoat is plainly visible at the same distance;— and another so devoid of understanding as to be pronounced idiotic — all sold by step-father, or selectmen of towns, for the thirty pieces of silver, are to be sent before the board for examination. *Three*, who joined us in October, have already been discharged; and we have sent to the "Invalid Corps," sick men more fit for active duty, than some of the recruits now with us. A beautiful new "State Flag," reached us to-day, in exchange for our old one, which we are directed to return to the State House in Boston.

17*th*. The wind of yesterday increased in violence during the night, and to-day is so intensely cold and windy, that it is necessary to relieve the sentinels at the breastworks, every forty minutes, instead of once in two hours; and only four are on post at a time, instead of thirteen.

20*th*. What fluctuations appear in our strength! A few days since we were up to the maximum number allowed; the next day we were short by *two;* the day but one after, we were short forty-nine; and now we lack fifty three of our full quota. Our recruits, especially the "veterans," think our labors severe and altogether hard to bear. In particular, do they complain of the little requirements preliminary to leaving camp. Two, whose application for leave had been refused, yet who nevertheless walked away, and were absent at roll call, can now be heard, as they slowly pace the guard parade, with their knapsacks full of bricks,—" Indade, my back is most broke! I'm kilt entirely with backing these bricks! oh! holy mother! Lieut., ease up a little, can't ye? Bedad, if this is the way ye use a boy for taking a bit of a walk without leave, my throat will go dry a long while before I trate it again to a drop! *If 'twas a hod, now, ye'd lend us!* *'Twould be so much nater!*"

CHAPTER XXI.

Harper's Ferry.

22D OF FEBRUARY — OUR OLD MISSIONARY — DESPATCHES, SIR, IMMEDIATE — A CHEERY OLD BROTHER — MAJ. PRATT, AND NEW ORDERS — PROMOTIONS — ANOTHER TRANSFER — MORE ORDERS — AN EXPLANATION DEMANDED — OUR OLD FRIEND AGAIN — CAPT. SOLEY — THE WEATHER — OUR SICK — ORDERS.

22d. The usual, and every day duties required in camp, have been suspended by order from Division Headquarters. The batteries on the heights have thundered forth their morning and evening salutes, in honor of the day; and *we* have celebrated it by a street parade, paying to Gen. Wheaton the compliment of a marching salute. Lieut. Ammidon, with a guard of twelve men, escorted a squad of Rebel soldiers to Wheeling; and another squad was brought into the Ferry to-day, by a party of "Boyd's" cavalry.

I have been much amused by a call made to-day by the Reverend Mr. P., our good old missionary from Maine.

"Good morning, Col.; a glorious day! a day to be commemorated in all time! I called Col., to beg a favor." "What is it, sir?" "Well Col., the *brethren* have made arrangements to celebrate the day, by procession to "Bolivar," and an address there, and I have ventured to promise them the benefit of the Massachusetts Band! Did I promise too much, Col.? Can they have it, sir?" "Well, my dear sir, if you mean the band of the 34th, you promised altogether too much; you can't have that!" "Indeed, Col., I am very sorry to hear you say so; the *brethren* will be much disappointed! Can't we arrange it some how? Do you want it yourself, may I ask?" "I do sir!" "At what hour, do you think?" "I can't tell, precisely. I propose to make a street parade, at a time yet to be fixed, and shall want the band, for that purpose." "Oh, indeed, Col.! Well, that'll be just the thing then, for us! Instead of the band I can hope the regiment will favor the *brethren* by escorting them to Bolivar!" "No sir, I think not! I should object decidedly to order the regiment to such duty." "That is a disappointment indeed, Col! I don't see what we shall do! But what hour, may I enquire, shall you return to your camp?" "It is impossible to say, sir; there may be delay in paying our proposed compliments to the General!" "Well then, Col., in the situation, I think I had better hurry back to the *brethren*, and have them wait, where they are, until you are on your return march; then we can fall in procession in your rear, and take your escort." "In the situation, my dear sir, I can't object to your *hurrying back to the brethren*, but I have a decided objection to your stealing the escort, which I have already told you I can't give to you." "Indeed Col., that's bad! I thought we might get under your wing, somehow! How unfortunate *you're not a brother!* Would it be too much, under the circumstances, Col., if I was to ask you to excuse from your parade, *all the* "*brethren*" in the regiment, that they might join our procession?" "Well, my dear sir, I regret that I must refuse you that, also." "I am very sorry, Col.! very sorry indeed; I was in hope of establishing, to-day, in your regiment, a branch *lodge*, and had prepared an address, calculated, I felt sure, to make converts, to what, I am prepared to prove, is the oldest and best of all the institutions of the day."

But without stopping to hear the reply, the old gentleman hurried himself out.

The parade was had afterwards, and the boys, in their best clothes, looked and marched their best. Nothing could have been done better. After our return to camp, our old friend marched by, heading his procession to Bolivar, and looking as proud as if he headed a Division.

Midnight. The quiet of the camp was broken by clatter of

hoofs and clank of sabre, as drawing up at Headquarters, an Orderly presented himself, announcing, "despatches, Colonel, *immediate!*" "Two full companies to report, instantly, at "Division Headquarters, with two days' rations, and 60 rounds "of ball cartridges to a man;" and every line officer, save those on guard, away at a ball given by the Staff of Gen. Wheaton; "Orderly, send the Sergeant-Major here; then wake up Chase "and tell him to saddle, and ride, like the devil, to the 'Island,' "with my compliments to Capts. Chandler and Fox, and their "Lieutenants, and request them to report at Headquarters, for "duty, immediately." "Sergeant-Major, direct 'F and H' to arm as quickly as possible, and be ready to fall in, with rations, at tap of the drum."

How rapidly, and by what slight stir, a regiment is roused from slumber! Heads are thrust from different tents, and anxious inquiries, "what is it?" "who goes?" "where to?" are heard, and then sleep comes again quickly to all but those who are to march — to what, no one can tell.

By the time "F and H" were ready to fall in, their officers reported; but, by that time, also, a second order was received, calling for "four companies, the whole under Major Pratt." E and G were now roused, and their officers summoned from the ball-room.

No need of longer caution. The *long roll* could be heard from Wheaton's camp, and his Brigade was roused. Our own four companies were the only ones which, in fact, moved; and they were sent by rail to Monocacy Junction, under orders " to "entrench and hold their position, *at all hazards.*"

23*d.* Orders were received this morning, to forward to Maj. Pratt two additional day's rations. Our application for transportation thereof, made to the Post Q. M., was peremptorily refused. *Red tape* is in the way, some where; and how to cut it is the question. But the consideration of that question was interrupted, for the time, by the arrival of our cheery old brother from Maine.

"Well, Col.," he broke out, "your Regiment appeared finely yesterday, *finely!* *I* was very much pleased with it; and I consider myself a good judge of such matters; for, as long ago as 1832, *I was a Corporal in our State Militia*, and was quite posted up in the drill! But I have not done much at it since. However, that has nothing to do with what I come up to talk with you about.

"I'm going, on Sunday, to dedicate the old Brick church in the village; and I want your men to get some evergreen boughs for me, so that the charcoal sketches, on the walls may be covered up. They are not very appropriate drawings, you know. Can you let me have the men, Col.?" "Where do you propose to get your evergreens, Sir?" "Oh, anywhere, Col.! Across the Shenandoah, I guess. The boys tell me there is enough over there." "I guess there's enough *there*, sir; but, unfortunately for your purpose, there's a Post General order which prohibits the Boys from crossing the river." "Oh! indeed, Col., is that so? I'm not a military man myself, but that seems to me a very strange order! Isn't it? However, I see I shall have to give it up."

"But, Col., there's one thing there can't be any difficulty about! I've got some boards for seats; and have built a nice broad platform for the officers, and the ladies of the village; and I want very much to feel sure of having a good audience at my first service. So, may I ask that you will dispense with any little duties of the camp, and let your men come down and fill the seats?" "I regret to say that I can't even do that for you, sir; as a General Order from Superior Headquarters prohibits me from granting permission to more than *three* men to a *Company*, to go down town, at the same time." "Well! I seem to run against some order every step I take! but this one seems strange, very strange indeed." "It's very true nevertheless, my dear sir." "Does the order apply to officers, Col.? and can't you, and your officers attend my service?" "As for myself, sir, I never leave camp except on duty; but, besides, to-morrow is our regular Inspection; and the Boys will all be required in camp, for that!" "But the inspection might be put off, might it not, Col.? And, by the way, why is it that your inspections are had on the Lord's day?" "Well, my dear sir, you must go for an answer to that question to those who *make* our orders! All *we* have to do is to obey!" "But, Col., think of it! such wickedness ought to be done away with! Its monstrous!—its awful!" "Well, sir, perhaps not much can be said of the practice. It is something, after all, like the family Sunday cleaning, and washing, and dressing of the little ones; a little more thorough than what takes place on other days!" "Yes; yes, Col.! perhaps so!" "But now, my dear sir, as we can't go down and hear you, in your little church, suppose you come up and *see* us; and *preach* to us, too, if you've a mind. We've *no Chaplain*, and no one can tell how much good you may do!"

"I'll come, Col.! I'll come! That is, if I feel well enough; for you see, I've got a bad cold, and I should not like to add to it by being out in bad weather." "I hope you'll come, sir! We shall all be glad to see and hear you; and let me give you a little warning, now. Don't be disturbed, in case the weather should remain as it now is, at an order to the boys to remain *covered* when you offer prayer!" "You don't mean it, Col.! You can't mean to invoke God's blessing while you stand with heads covered! do you?" "Most certainly, I do; that is, if the weather should continue wet and chilly, as it now is!" "Well, well, Col., I said I'd come, and I will; but your ways are all strange! and we can all hope it will be fair, can't we?" And so we parted.

24*th.* A telegram from Maj. Pratt, at the Monocacy, states that "there had not been, was not now, and probably would not be, any Rebel force near him," and asking further orders, and for tents, *if he was to remain*, was received at Headquarters, this morning. Upon making known its contents, Gen. Sullivan's direction was received to forward to the Major orders to acquaint himself with the nature of the country near him; particularly to reconoitre the roads leading to his position, on *each side* of the river, but, on no account, *to cross* it. Also, to inform him that he would remain some days where he was, but would not be provided with tents.

Sergeant Pitts and Corporal Jameson, the former as Captain, the latter as Lieutenant, received commissions in some regiment of colored troops, to-day. Adams, Aldrich and Chickering, of

C, are now before the Examining Board for positions in like organizations.

Thorndike, now with the 39th, in the Army of the Potomac, writes, that that regiment is required to furnish a picket of *one hundred* men, for *two days' duty, once a week*, which is all the work required of it. How different from what is exacted of us! To-day, for instance, after sending out the old details, the regiment has not men enough to fill the new ones just called for.

An order, received to-day, re-assigning us to "Wheaton's (3d) Brigade, 6th Army Corps," has made us all happy.

25th. Major General Kelly reached this post last night, on a tour of inspection; and to-day at 11 A. M., is named in Division Orders, as the time at which all officers of all organizations stationed here are *ordered* to pay their personal respects to him.

While engaged in this duty, the Lieutenant Colonel commanding was handed a Special Order "to hold seventy-five men, with five days' rations, blankets, arms, and fifty rounds of ammunition, ready to march at a moment's notice." Captain Soley, with his Company, "I," strengthened by picked men from "B" and "D," was detailed. *Route* and *number of miles* for each day's march, and *hour of starting*, and route of return, prescribed by General Order. Destination, Snicker's Gap!

It's raining hard, with a high wind, and the night is dark as Egypt.

There are but one hundred and twenty-eight men left in camp fit for duty, and these all came off a twenty-four hours' tour this morning. Capt. Willard is officer of the day at the Ferry; Capt. Lovell ditto at camp, and Capt. Thompson is the only officer by whom these can be relieved.

Of course, under such circumstances, some of the men and one of the officers will fail to be relieved.

And now rides into camp an Orderly, with directions to the commanding officer of "the 34th regiment to report in person, forthwith, at Gen. Wheaton's headquarters, *to explain his neglect to send out a detail directed* by Brigade General Order of this morning."

"You command the 34th Massachusetts, Colonel, do you?" asked the General, after my introduction. "I have that honor,

General." "You received an order from my headquarters for a detail from your regiment this morning?" "Yes, sir." "And you have not obeyed it!" "No, General; I ———" "That will do, Colonel." "But, General, allow me to explain. I *could not* obey it." "Could not, Colonel? And your regiment almost one thousand strong! I don't understand." "I mean to say, General, I had not the men. I could not even relieve a portion of my men who were on duty the day before." "Then there must be mismanagement in your camp, Colonel." "All details from the regiment, General, except my own orderly and Headquarters guard, are by order from superior Headquarters; and all my remonstrances against such excessive details are now, as they have always been, entirely unheeded." "Have the goodness, Colonel, to bring to me your morning report, and all orders calling upon you for details for duty." This was done. "Why haven't you complained to the War Department, Colonel? I never saw or knew such abuse of men! You have an order, I see, to send *one hundred men* to your right flank, opposite the pontoon bridge; is that number necessary there?" "We had but *ten* men there for months, General." "Reduce that detail, then, to the former number. Here are *sixty* called for on your left; how is it at that point?" "Our guard at that point has been increased from *twenty*." "Take off forty, then. Is it necessary, Colonel, that *the patrol* should be so large?" "I furnish, General, no more than I am ordered to." "Well, you have been here since July last, I understand, and can judge of the necessity of all these details, and of the number required at each point. Forward to me a written report of your opinion, that your men may be relieved of this load. It's shameful!"

26*th.* Camp was roused about five this morning by the arrival of Major Pratt, who had marched his command from the "Monocacy," during the night.

We have been in a great state of excitement to-day in consequence of an act of highway robbery committed in broad day, on the public street near our camp, upon a man of the Pennsylvania Cavalry, by Lieut. Berry, Sergeant Green and private Berry of Miner's Battery; and the committal of the prisoners to the custody of the 34th, whose commander is ordered "to place a guard with loaded musket over them," with orders "to shoot either who may attempt to escape."

Our old friend, Mr. P., has been round again.

"Good morning, good morning, Colonel! I called in to say how sorry I was to disappoint you at your service last Sunday. Your boys, I find, don't have much religious instruction!" "No, sir, not much; and though sorry not to see *you* at parade, we got along quite nicely." "But without any service, Col.?" "Oh, no sir; we had service." "Why, I watched your movements, Colonel, from my window, and though I didn't understand them all, I didn't see any which looked like religious service. Who officiated, Colonel, if I may ask?" "I don't know, sir; a young man who introduced himself as a minister. I didn't ask his name." "Well, it's strange! Was he gifted?" "He made a very beautiful address, sir, and closed with an impressive, though short prayer." "Well, Colonel, I'll hunt him up for you; if he is all right, I'll report to you."

28*th*. Capt. Soley, with his party, returned to-day; the object for which he was sent out un(?)accomplished. He did one thing, however, which probably was not contemplated; that is, he captured and brought in *two* blockade runners, with one saddle and three team horses, and a wagon loaded with dry goods, groceries, etc., packed in boxes, marked to a Mr. Riddle, formerly in trade here, now a Custom House officer in Baltimore.

This was the fourth expedition of the kind which we have sent out, in as many weeks. In each case, the order directing the movement, prescribed alike the hour of starting from camp, the routes to be taken, going and returning, the length of each day's march, and the place of each night's bivouac. Permission for the officer in command to deviate from his instructions, according to his discretion, had been asked and refused. Before his departure on this last expedition, the danger of a rigid adherence to this unvarying programme had been discussed with Capt. S. A hint to such an officer was enough; and it is remarkable that now, when, for the first time, our party was *precisely where*, according to its order of march, *it ought not to have been*, a capture should have been made.

Recognizing that "to the victors belong the spoils," the Captain was allowed to retain the captured saddle-horse for a pack animal, while the wagon and its load of goods was turned over to the Provost Marshal.

Capt. Soley and Lieut. Hall leave to-morrow, for fifteen days' absence. Capt. Bacon has presented his resignation, the acceptance of which has been declined. Our Band is to go, to-morrow, to "Frederick," to help along the festivities in that city, consequent upon the public reception of Cole's Battalion, the men of which, having re-enlisted for "during the war," go home on a thirty days' furlough.

Brigade orders assign to the 34th, as inspecting officer for to-morrow, Lieut. Col. Moody, of the 39th Pennsylvania, of Wheaton's Brigade, which regiment is to be inspected by Lieut. Col. Lincoln, of the 34th.

29th. We lose, to-day, three more of our men, in consequence of being appointed to "commissions in colored regiments."

Capt. Potter, of B, is brought down, to-day, the surgeons say, with an attack of small-pox; happily of mild form.

March 1st. Snow has fallen all day, and it is now seven or eight inches deep. Our men are suffering, actually suffering, in consequence of the unremitting duty required of them. Colds and fevers are very prevalent.

Col. Wells, relieved from duty on court martial, at Cumberland, returned to the Ferry to-day. He has been relieved as A. B. G., but declined to resume command of the regiment, and has left for Baltimore, but in citizen's dress. Before leaving, he sent down various letters addressed to him as commanding the regiment, requesting that they should be answered. Among them were three, from different clergymen at home, asking for themselves the appointment of Chaplain; and *one* from Gov. Andrew, in relation to the same office, all which are easily enough disposed of.

"Come out, gentlemen, each of you, and live with us a while, "on trial! If you are worth anything, we shall find it out, and " will give you a *call,* but we take no second one on trust."

Lieut. Col. Moody returns to the officers commanding companies, their muster rolls, with comments like these: To Capt.

B.: "What is Bemis doing among the G's?" To Capt. F.: "Your rolls bear marks of carelessness and hurry unbecoming an officer." To Capt. L.: "Your rolls are so defective that new ones must be made out." On reference to Regimental headquarters, after a careful inspection, barring ink blots and an occasional grease spot, it is concluded that the Col. is a little over critical, and, in some points, in actual error, and they are returned to him unaltered.

3*d*. Lieut. Lincoln returned from his extended leave of absence to-day, but without having recovered his voice.

Seventeen men were taken down sick yesterday, and all sent to hospital. Our list of "sick in quarters" is increasing rapidly, and the disease, whatever it may be, is alarming. At retreat, for instance, a man appears on parade, and by morning, some times by tattoo, he is raving in delirium. All drill has been dispensed with to-day, on account of bad weather and deep mud.

Our Surgeons have united in a written recommendation that the Sutler be allowed to keep and sell *Beer* to the men, under proper restrictions. A somewhat hazardous proceeding; yet, perhaps, justifiable in our overworked condition.

4*th*. Sergeant Blackmer, of H, died last night, delirious to the last moment of his life.

5*th*. The Regiment is ordered to proceed, by rail, to Point of Rocks, and picket the line between that place and the Monocacy. This, in consequence of a telegram from Washington, giving information of the movement, in that direction, of a large Rebel force. Pitts, of A, and Jameson, of the same company, received, to-day, commissions—the former as Captain and the latter as Lieutenant—in a regiment of colored troops.

CHAPTER XXII.

"Point of Rocks" and Martinsburg.

OUR ORDERS—IN BAD ODOR AGAIN—GENERAL SULLIVAN—NEW ORDERS—MARTINSBURG—ASSIGNMENTS TO DUTY—PROPER ACCOUNTING—DRESS PARADES—SWEENY OF C—NEW TENTS—OUR OFFICERS—A GOOD STORY—POST ORDERS.

The orders to move to the Monocacy were given by General Sullivan, in person. "Get together, Colonel, all the men you "can, withdrawing from your pickets such numbers as you "think best; see that they are completely armed and equipped; "take three days' rations, and report with your force to me as "soon as possible." Upon reporting: "How many men have "you, Colonel?" "I don't know, General." "Find out then, "and let me know. You will take with you *five hundred effec-*"*tive* men: Send back to your camp all over that number, if "you have any." A count by the adjutant showed 534 men, *including* buglers, drummers, and officers' servants, and upon reporting, orders were given to get off, *as we were,* without delay.

Point of Rocks was reached: *Four companies,* Capt. Bacon commanding, were sent to the "Monocacy," with instructions to the Captain to establish pickets, and hold his ground, if attacked; telegraphing for support, if needing any. The fords, in the neighborhood, were covered by artillery, supported by infantry details; the banks of the river picketed; and scouting parties of cavalry established to keep open communication from post to post. Communication with us was opened by Colonel Maulsby, of the "Potomac Home Brigade," Headquarters at

Frederic, and arrangements made for mutual support, should it become necessary. And so *we* waited and watched.

8th. Our service has been a monotonous and weary one.

> By our watch-fires, dimly burning,
> The sods with our bayonets turning.

There hasn't been even the *ghost* of a Rebel raider to disturb our quiet.

A despatch from Gen. Sullivan, informing us that the "18th Connecticut will relieve the 34th," which is to "proceed to Martinsburg by the train which brings the 18th," was received early this morning. A letter, delivered at about the same time, informed us that we were in bad odor again, at Division Headquarters.

It seems that upon our departure from the Ferry for this place, Gen. Sullivan concluded that the streets leading to his quarters were too muddy; and determined they should be at once cleaned. So an Orderly was despatched to our camp, with orders for the officer left in command to report to the General. Capt. Chandler reported himself, and Sullivan thus addressed him: "Captain, how many men have you in camp?" "I don't know, General." "Well, find out then!" "I don't know how I can, General." "Don't know how you can? *I'll* tell you, then. Have the roll beat; the men all turned out; count them, and report." So back to camp went Chandler, routed the boys, and found in line, under arms, 235. Reporting the result, the General, pencil in hand, delivered himself thus: "The Regi-"ment has 1,000 men; you report, in camp, 235; Col. Lincoln "has with him 534; that leaves more than 200 men unaccounted "for, and I'll be d—d if I'll stand it. I'll get rid of you alto-"gether; I'll send you to Martinsburg, and see how you will "like that."

So by afternoon, down came the 18th Connecticut, with Boone, A. A. G., bearing orders for us to proceed, by rail, to Martinsburg on return train.

We were nothing loth to try the change. At the Ferry, when the train stopped, request was made that it might be delayed long enough to enable us to send to camp for regimental papers, shelter for the officers and our private property, and clothing, but this was refused, and we were hurried away as we were.

We left Capt. Thompson sick, in quarters, with varioloid; and just caught sight of the faces of Lieuts. Elwell and Belser, who, with the members of our recruiting party, had returned that day.

9th. Martinsburg. We reached this post, about 9 P. M., and marching on to the public square of the village, reported for orders. In the absence of the post commander, we were directed by his second in authority, to occupy the ground vacated by the 18th Connecticut, and were marched to the outskirts of the village, where, spreading our rubber blankets, we laid ourselves down for our night's bivouac.

Col. Wells is appointed to the command of the post, and Acting Brigadier General, having for garrison the "116th," and "123d Ohio," "34th Massachusetts," all infantry, "and the 5th (regular) U. S. battery.

10th. A careful examination in the early morning led to the selection of camping ground, apart from all the other commands, and never before occupied for such purpose.

Our train came up to-day, and with it such of the command as had been left in camp at the Ferry. Our army of dogs and Company E's cow brought up the rear. General Orders assign Woods, our Adjutant, to be A. A. A. G.; Capt. Chandler of F, to be A. I. G.; Quartermaster Howland to be A. B. Q. M.; Dr. Clarke to be A. B. S; Lieut. Ripley to be A. A. D. C.; every officer, but one, on that staff, taken from our regiment. Lieut. A. C. Walker is detailed as Acting Adjutant, and Lieut. H. Bacon A. Q. M. of the regiment. Capt. Bacon has gone to Washington on a five days' leave, to settle his affairs; he persisting in his purpose to resign.

Our recruits are awkward enough, some of them. To aid them, the Inspector, as they step off, pronounces the words *left, right; left, right.* One of them, on duty to-day as camp guard, thus soliloquized while pacing his beat: "Left, right, left, right from the country, and green — left, right, left, right, left a d——d good home."

Company I lost a man (Truesdale), to-day, very suddenly. Cause — brain fever.

Two more men of F received orders to appear before the Examining Board at Washington.

Our Quartermaster has been notified by the proper accounting officers at Washington, that his accounts, filed for approval, are found to be incorrect, in this, that he has issued to the commissioned officers of the command *three* lead pencils in excess of the number to which they were entitled. His credit is dis-allowed to that extent, and pay stopped till the discrepancy is satisfactorily explained.

Apropos to this is the experience of two officers in neighboring commands. One, a Captain, almost constantly on the move, has failed to account for a *hatchet* which had been issued to him, and was notified that unless he made proper returns, without delay, his pay would be stopped. Now what had become of the hatchet the Captain did n't know, and could n't tell. So he wrote back, asking the price of the article, and expressing his willingness to remit the required amount. To this he received a reply that "the department had no hatchets to sell." Whereupon he bought one, at the nearest hardware store, and forwarded it to the Quartermaster-General, with a letter expressing his regret that the government was so short, and concluding with a hope that affairs would go on smoothly, now that the missing hatchet was replaced.

And another, a Lieutenant commanding, (who had long neglected to attend to the repeated calls to send forward his accounts for the third quarter of 1863,) having been notified that he had been reported for neglect, and a request made to the proper authority to stop his pay, wrote back enquiring "what the proper authority said to the request?"

11*th*. A storm of unusual severity is raging, and, spite of all our exertions, the men are suffering for want of suitable shelter and fires.

Barr, of I, taken sick en route to this place, and left in post hospital at the village the night of our arrival, died to-day.

Lieut. Platt, relieved as assistant Provost Marshal at the Ferry, joined his company, K, to-day.

Thirteen recruits, from general rendezvous at Galloup's Island, Boston, Mass., also reached us to-day.

Everything indicates the near approach of active operations; and, in anticipation of a move from this place, the wives of the men are ordered from camp.

Our requisition for tents has been allowed; and we are to have an issue of new "A," or wedge tents.

Capts. Potter and Thompson, recovered from varioloid, arrived and reported for duty.

12th. Capt. Chandler, of F, has been appointed to the Lieut. Colonelcy of the 57th Massachusetts. The day previous, he had accepted the tender of a like position in Wild's D'Afrique Brigade. Thus *we lose*, and the 57th gains, a most accomplished soldier and gentleman. A good deal of feeling has been roused in the regiment, by an order from the A. B. G., which "forbids "any officer of the command from visiting the village, unless "under a permit from his headquarters!" and in consequence, the officers of the 34th have been notified that no request for leave to go to the village will receive approval at Regimental Headquarters; but that permits to leave camp at any time can be obtained from the Adjutant, by any officer, upon his leaving word at headquarters of the probable length of his absence.

13th. Dress parade was had at 4 P. M., that we might visit the "123d Ohio," and witness their manner of conducting the same ceremony, at a later hour. This regiment leaves to-morrow, to relieve the 116th, which has for four months past been distributed along the line of the B. & O. R. R. as its guard. At Winchester, under Milroy, last summer, it lost by capture, its Col., five other officers, and all but one hundred and fifty of its rank and file, and although the men have been exchanged, its officers are still held by the Rebels.

Their parade was more elaborate, than good. Line being formed, a company was detailed to escort the colors, which were received with all the honors. The manual, as such, was fair, the marching good, but the general appearance of the line bad. Hardly any two men on line, were dressed alike. Infantry frock coats, and blouses, cavalry and artillery jackets, with their yellow and red braid, and white, drab, yellow and black slouched hats, and the regulation cap, were all jumbled together.

How our men have shouted, at intervals, to-day! Sweeney, of C, wanted his wife, who has been with us almost since we first came out, to go back to Massachusetts, since she could no longer be allowed to remain in camp; but she refused to go, and appealed to Headquarters. Although she could not be forced by the military arm, to go to Massachusetts, she was informed that the order excluding her from camp would be adhered to. In her rage, she threw into her husband's arms, her baby, and he, poor fellow, as he totes the child back and forth in the camp, is subject to all manner of ridicule.

These wives have been doing a brisk business with us; washing for the men, whom they require to furnish *soap*, and coaxing fuel and food from the Quartermaster, by the fiction winked at by the Capts., that they are company laundresses, their earnings have exceeded the pay of their husbands. And then, till now the family tie has been unbroken. No wonder, spite of the many inconveniences they endure, they hate to leave.

Our new issue of tents were received to-day. They are "A" shaped, about five by seven feet, and by regulation, are to hold six men each. The camp has been newly laid out, to correspond with the new order of things.

May 14th. Gen. Sigel, now in the command of the Department, is on a visit to the Post.

Capt. Potter is appointed Provost Marshal; Lieut. Lincoln, assistant do.

The Pioneers are building stables for the horses of the command.

Details from each company are putting up log cook-houses.

Lieut. Macomber returned from his leave of absence last night.

The Sutler joined us, and set up his tent to-day.

They are setting up *for state*, at Post Headquarters; requiring the new officer of the day, when reporting for instructions, first to inquire whether the commander is ready and willing to receive him.

We have had a detail of thirty men occupied all day in cleaning the Court House, which has been heretofore occupied by the garrison here, as Patrol Headquarters. The amount of dirt removed is perfectly enormous.

Our orderly has brought in an unofficial note from Col. Wells, with information of the presence in the vicinity, of bodies of rebels, and advising precautionary measures for our safety; and in consequence, Lieut. Goodrich, with *fifty* men, is sent to picket our front and flanks.

15*th*. Capt. Soley and Lieut. Hall, returned from their visit, in Mass., last night.

Capt. Pratt, and Lieut. Cobb, are the only officers away from the command, if we except those on duty at Post Headquarters.

The former, temporarily incapacitated for duty in the field, by Aphonia, makes a model Provost Marshal, at the Ferry; and the latter is still suffering from the wound received at Ripon, in October last.

We hear, from the Ferry, that Wheaton, disgusted with life there, has applied to be returned to the Army of the Potomac. He was in a rage at the fact, and the manner of our removal to this place; as, although attached to his Brigade, the orders directing our march to the Monocacy, as also from there hither, were issued to us direct from Division, instead of through his Headquarters. And when, upon a report reaching him that the rebels were threatening "Charlestown," he sent orders to the 34th to move in support of the troops at Halltown, his orderly returned, with information that the 34th was in Martinsburg, his language, in commenting upon the proceedings at Sullivan's Headquarters, is said to have been more forcible, than complimentary to that officer.

And, in connection with the movement of our Brigade to this place, the following, told at Division Headquarters, brings a laugh from every one. Just previous to issuing the orders to the Brigade, Boone, Sullivan's A. A. G. wanted to communicate with one of the officers whom he knew to be in Baltimore. So the telegraph was called into requisition, and message after message despatched. But no acknowledgement was returned, and, in despair, Boone thus broke out: "Adjutant, where the devil is your Col.?" "In Baltimore." "Are you sure?" "Yes!" "Well, it's strange I can't reach him! I've telegraphed till I am tired." "Where to? to the Eutaw and Barnum's? Pshaw! *you* don't know the ropes! see how quick I'll bring him." Send him that!" and the following message was sent over the wires:

"Corporal Jones, at Guy's Hotel.

"The Regiment is under marching orders. Return at once, or you will be reported absent without leave," and Corporal Jones, alias the Colonel, was on the next train. Pretty well, from an Adjutant to his Colonel.

16th. Martinsburg is fairly groaning under the iron heel of its new Commandant. Every place of business is temporarily closed, and the town girdled with a chain of picket posts. All ingress, as well as egress, is for the time, stopped. All trade is suspended, and to secure a removal of restriction, each dealer forwards for inspection, samples of the articles he has in store; so that Post Headquarters, with its cases of liquors, boxes of cigars, demijohns of brandy, jugs of wine, and cases and jars of jellies and preserves, looks like a great Sutler's caravan.

The citizens complain of our Patrol as more rigid than any they have been heretofore subjected to; hard to be borne by its proper inhabitants who are thoroughly loyal, but well deserved by the large army of traders, blockade-runners, spies, bushwhackers, etc., who make their temporary abiding place here.

Sergeant King, most unexpectedly and unaccountably recovered his voice to-day; returning to him as suddenly as it was lost, it caused him no little surprise.

CHAPTER XXIII

MARTINSBURG.

LIEUT. COL. CHANDLER — CAPT. F.'S NEW UNIFORM — CAMP NEWLY LAID OUT — A WARNING — DETAILS — THE SUTLER'S ALE — OUR DRILL AND PARADE — CAPT. WILLARD — MINER AND HIS BATTERY — MARCHING ORDERS — A STREET PARADE — LIEUT. LINCOLN AND HIS FEMALE FRIENDS — MARCHING ORDERS AGAIN.

18th. Capt. Chandler received to-day his commission as Lieutenant Colonel of the 57th Massachusetts, and was mustered out of service with us. As he is to leave this Department, he invited the officers of the 34th, with those of the other commands here, to a reception at Headquarters. All who were not on duty were anxious to attend. Among others, Capt. F. of ours, was especially desirous of being present. Of course, etiquette required an appearance in full uniform; but the Captain, by some accident, had got one skirt of his uniform coat torn beyond repair. He had no change with him. For in obedience to a recent order which required all line officers "to pack and send to the rear, all superfluous clothing," and prohibiting them from retaining any baggage save such as they could carry on their persons, he had kept only the uniform he had upon his back. And while he could not bring himself to attend the festivities in rags, he had equal difficulty in making up his mind to deny himself the enjoyment of the many good things he knew were provided for the entertainment. So, after due consideration, he called upon the regimental tailor, and directed him to cut off both skirts of his uniform frock. Then arraying himself in this nondescript garment, neither cavalry jacket nor infantry blouse, he mingled with his brother officers. As the eagle eye of the Colonel fell upon the tall, commanding form of his subordinate, thus grotesquely arrayed, the following colloquy ensued:

"Ah! Capt. F., allow me to inquire what uniform you are wearing?" "Certainly; Colonel! Its the new pattern, prescribed by the last general order for officers of this command." "Indeed, Captain, what order do you refer to?" "General Order No. ——, these Headquarters, dated April ——, 1864." "Are n't you mistaken, Captain? Those orders have no reference to uniforms of any kind." "I beg your pardon, Colonel; here they are, and you'll see by reading them that I have conformed to the requirement, exactly." "Perhaps so, Captain, but I don't perceive the clause." "Why, look here, Colonel; listen, if you please!" and he read: "And all unnecessary baggage and *superfluous clothing* shall be immediately packed and 'sent to the rear,' and for want of transportation, and because they were superfluous, I've cut off my coat tails, and "——" That will do," said the Colonel, as he joined in the general roar which followed, under cover of which the Captain was escorted to the refreshment room.

18*th*. The resignation of Capt. Bacon has, though with reluctance, at last been forwarded, approved. The proceeding cannot be justified by regard to the good of the service; and can only be excused by the serious nature of the Surgeon's certificate, upon which it is founded.

Lieut. Ammidon pleads for discharge, but with little chance of favorable consideration; as business relations, merely, are at the bottom of his application.

We have completed our camp, and it is quite a little gem. Each company has sixteen "A" tents. The company streets are wide, well graded, and crowned, with gutters on each side. The cook-houses are all of the same size, made of hewn logs, but varying a little in appearance by reason of a greater or less amount of ornamental work. Every one who visits the camp is full of praise, and showers upon us compliments for its beautiful and cleanly look. The only drawback is the entire absence of water. All we use for washing and cooking is drawn by our teams, in barrels, from the creek, more than a mile distant. A well at the corner of one of the streets of the village furnishes a supply for drinking purposes; but as the inner line of pickets is between it and the camp, there is some trouble in getting a supply from that quarter.

Teirney, of A, arrested and sent to the Provost Guard House *last August*, and against whom charges were preferred for an assault upon the officer of our camp guard, and who was subsequently tried, convicted and sentenced for the offence, was returned to-day by Gen. Sullivan's orders, for duty in the regiment; *for the reason*, as stated by the Provost Marshal, that the General was unable to *find the papers in the case*. Admission to the regiment was denied him, and he was returned to the care of the Provost Marshal.

Our foot balls are worn out, and the boys have turned their attention to wrestling matches, in one of which, this afternoon, Hubbard, of F was thrown and had his leg broken.

20*th*. "Col. Stuart is on a raid, and may come this way, so be prepared to start at short notice;" so runs Col. Wells' note just received. In consequence, we have had a general overhauling of our possessions; have turned over to the Post Quartermaster everything not absolutely required for present use, and stand ready to take a double quick to front, or rear, as shall be directed. Brigade Headquarters are all packed and ready to move if necessary. Our Cavalry pickets are so often found asleep on their post by the Officer of the Day, that we continue to picket our own front and flanks. Of the *eight* regiments of Infantry here, the 34th is the only one which takes any precaution against being surprised; some of the others not even mounting a camp guard. "What queer fellows you Yankee soldiers are," said Major K, of the —— Ohio, to-day. "Why, Major?" was asked. "Why! because here I have laid by your side for weeks, and in addition to your squad and company drills every forenoon, not a day has passed that you have n't been out for afternoon Battalion drill." "That's so, Major; and during the same time you have had *no* Company, and, with one exception, *no* Battalion drill. Will your men fight, Major?"

"No, Colonel, I could n't trust them at all; how about yours?" "Why, Major, mine will go, or stand, where they are ordered, and will do, in any place, all that any men can do." "Well, that's enough; I wish I felt that mine would."

In answer to a requisition made by us months ago, we had issued to us to-day 1200 pairs of stockings, which are welcomed heartily by the boys, many of whom have been without, since January last.

22d. Gen. Stahl has arrived, and taken quarters in town. Gen. Averill is about to leave on a raid. Sullivan is assigned to the command of an expedition to operate against the enemy from the "Kanawha Valley." This leaves Wheaton in command at the Ferry. We are called upon for a detail of *three* Sergeants, *five* Corporals, and *eight* privates, who, with a like number of men detailed from the other Infantry Regiments, are to form the "Engineer Corps of the 1st Infantry Division of the Army of West Virginia," under command of Lieut. Macomber, of ours.

As these men, for all practical purposes, are to be lost to the Regiment, Commanding officers of Companies are cautioned to great *discretion* in making up their details. Our license system, or rather, the order under which our Sutler has been allowed to sell Ale to the men of the command, has thus far been attended with no objectionable result. Under the restriction of his order, his sales have been limited; and, perhaps partly from the less duty required of us, partly from change of weather, the health of this command has been steadily improving. The amount of drunkenness among the men has very sensibly diminished. But to-day, some of the boys, being without money, and wanting Beer, made a raid upon the Sutler's stores, and stole a cask of the beverage. The cask once secured, the question of interest was, *how* to get at the contents. In their impatience, the Boys knocked out the bung, and a stream of the creamy liquid, rising high in the air, betrayed them to the guard. Most of those engaged, sought safety in flight. But two preferred capture, and the attendant ills, to loss of the drink they had worked so hard to get.

A roll call, ordered in each company, disclosed the names of all absentees, who, as they return to camp, were provided quarters in the Guard Tent, where they will have ample opportunity for reflection.

25th. A very severe storm is raging, as it has raged all day, the snow melting as it falls; and, as a whole, the weather is, to use the language of the people here, quite "*blustrous.*" Fuller, of F, a Corporal of ours, was discharged to-day, having received his commission as Captain in the 39th U. S. C. Troops. In speaking of his examination, which was long and severe, he says, that when, to the question " where are you from?" he replied " the 34th Mass.," Gen. Casey, the President of the Board, remarked: " Well, sir, then you will have no difficulty with the tactics — that Regiment must be splendidly drilled."

We are enjoying here the same high reputation we have had in the other places in which we have been stationed.

27th. A large number of officers from the different commands here, with a goodly number of ladies, honored with their presence our afternoon drill and parade. The officers of the 5th U. S. Battery, (regulars) were especially profuse in their complimentary remarks.

Our late muster rolls were returned to us to-day, by Lieut. Col. Moody, 139th Pa., who inspected us at the Ferry, bearing the endorsement, "that the 34th Mass. is the *best* Regiment for drill, discipline, and general appearance, I have ever seen."

We buried one of H.'s men in the village cemetery to-day, after a sickness of two or three days only. Poor Capt. Willard, of A, wants much to be married; and asks for six days leave, in which to go to Baltimore and consummate the affair. But the powers at the head of affairs here, are hard-hearted old bachelors, and deny his request, and his grief at the refusal is heart-rending. We hear from the Ferry, that Miner is in trouble again. It seems that some of his men, having heard that an old resident was possessed of some money, way-laid and robbed him, beating him dreadfully. Sullivan, upon the matter being reported to him, was enraged. While deliberating in what way he should notice the offence, and dispose of the offenders, his attention was attracted by the noise of a rough-and-tumble fight, immediately in front of his Headquarters. Seizing his sword, he rushed on to the street, and laid about him without mercy. As the combatants separated, his eye caught Miner's uniform on the person of one of the parties. "Adjt.," said the Gen., "send these men to the Provost Marshal; and order Capt. Miner to report in person immediately." Miner put in his appearance; and the Gen. thus accosted him: "Capt. Miner! you are at the head of the most disorderly men I ever had to do with; blackguards, all of them, and a disgrace to the service; and I give you orders now, to take your command out of the Ferry,—at double-quick time." "Where shall I go to, General?" "Go to! go to! Why go to hell with it, sir!" "Go to h——e——ll! to h——e——l——l, sir!! Shall I *take my caissons there*, too, Gen.?" No answer was returned to this question, and the Capt. was soon after served with a written order to move on to Maryland Heights, where he now is.

It is but fair to say that most of this command were long ago, in their individual capacity, on the road to the place first indicated by the General.

29*th*. "The 34th Massachusetts will be ready to move at daylight to-morrow." Such is the order received late last evening; and upon enquiring, it was learned that our destination was the Ferry. The order was from Sullivan's headquarters. To resume our former service at that post, and under that officer, is to be avoided if possible; and it is with no slight degree of pleasure that we learned, that upon receipt of the order at Post headquarters, Gen. Averill started in person for Cumberland, to get it countermanded. In the probability, however, that our stay in this place would be limited, a street parade was ordered for the afternoon. Our march was through the principal streets of the village, paying, as we passed in front of their headquarters, marching salutes to Generals Averill and Wells. The Regiment was drawn up in line, on the public square for the *manual*.

Here were gathered Generals, Colonels, Lieutenant Colonels, Majors, Captains, and Lieutenants, of every arm of the service; all uniting in the request for a dress parade.

Averill, who had returned by noon train from Cumberland, came over, at the request of Wells. At the close of the parade we were complimented in the highest terms by the officers assembled; Gen. Averill saying "that it was the most perfect thing of the kind he had ever seen." He also handed to the Lieutenant Colonel commanding, Gen. Sigel's telegram, countermanding Sullivan's order for our morning's march to the Ferry. As the telegram was read by the Adjutant, the boys rent the air with cheer upon cheer.

29th. It is a dull, dark, gloomy, dismal day, the rain falling in torrents, and the wind blowing a hurricane.

Most bitter and unscrupulous of all rebels, are the females of this region; two of whom, under orders "to be sent beyond the lines" at this place, arrived here to-day from Washington. Lieut. Lincoln was detailed to execute the order, with express directions "to see to it" that they took with them nothing which would afford "aid and comfort to the enemy." The Lieutenant found these ladies surrounded by a group of sympathizing sisters, who were freely indulging in abuse of the Government and its officers. Announcing his object and his orders, he was met by a storm of invective. His request for the keys to their trunks was laughed at. "Very well, ladies; my orders to examine your baggage are imperative; if I can't unlock your trunks, I must break them open." "Oh, go on, go on, Lieutenant! *Break* them open, by all means! Carry out the decrees of your master! It's so gallant to war upon defenceless females! As for us, we are not yet slaves to your tyrant, Lincoln!" The blow upon the trunk, which impended, was arrested by screams of "There are the keys! there are the keys!" "I asked you, ladies, for the keys; not that you should throw them on the floor!" and up went the hatchet for a second blow. "Now, ladies," said the Lieutenant, as he took the keys from the hand of one of them, and turned back the lid, "if you will be kind enough to unpack!" "No! no! we shall submit to no such degradation." "All right!" said the Lieutenant. "Orderly, empty these trunks." The Orderly, under the direction of the Lieutenant, was fast piling up articles deemed contraband, or within the order, as not required for personal use, when "How dare you, sir? those are articles of wearing apparel!" "Those," said the Lieutenant, "those are what *I* call 'hoop skirts.' I see you each wear one. I allow you each a second one. These others I confiscate."

"These packages of quinine I think you won't need, and those bottles of brandy won't be absolutely necessary! if you will be good enough to repack what is left you, we can set out on our little journey!" "The trunks were *nicely* packed once, sir; you have chosen to disarrange them, we shall have nothing to do with them!" "All right, ladies! Orderly, put *these* things back into the trunks, and *those others* into a bundle by themselves, and *all* into the ambulance! And now, ladies, all's ready, and we'll go, if you please! so, driving just beyond the picket line, and stopping near a dilapidated old building, the trunks were deposited by the wayside, the ladies were assisted to alight, and touching his cap, with a wish for a pleasant journey, the Lieut. turned and drove back to town.

31st. Two companies of the 123d Ohio, left yesterday, by rail, for the Ferry, and *four* more go down to-day. McCullough, of Sullivan's staff, called upon us to-day, with the not very pleasant information, that we were also to go, the Gen., being overheard saying to himself, "I wish I had the 34th back again, and I will have it."

Our rain storm of yesterday changed during the night, to snow, of which there is now upon the ground, about six inches.

Our sick list is again quite large, and steadily increasing. Measles and mumps are the most prevalent diseases. A few cases of typhoid pneumonia exist, of very severe character.

An order of the day from Brigade Headquarters, directs that "Lieut. Col. Lincoln will move his regiment at 6 A. M., day after to-morrow, for the Ferry, *with such transportation as may be furnished him.*" This order applies to the whole brigade, although there is now at that post, three full regiments, and parts of two others, doing what the 34th alone has done the past six months.

April 1st. Acting Brigadier Wells has gone to the Ferry, and his A. A. A. G. to the city of Baltimore. An order, received early this morning, renews the marching orders of yesterday. Are we to march, or be transported by rail? In the absence of the General and his chief of staff, no information upon that head can be obtained. It is now, as it was yesterday, snowing, blowing, and raining, making it certain that our movement to-morrow, if we are to march, is to be dreaded. If the enemy threatened, no command would endure the discomfort necessarily attendant upon the movement with more cheerfulness; but, as it can be of not the slightest consequence whether we reach that place a few hours earlier or later, it is positively cruel to subject the men to such exposure.

Lieut. Bacon, A. Q. M., despatched to headquarters to ascertain, if possible, something as to our transportation, has returned, bringing the information that the A. B. G. will communicate with the regiment some time during the night.

2d. 3 A. M. An Orderly has just handed in at headquarters, the following: "Lieut. Col. W S. Lincoln, commanding " 34th Massachusetts Infantry: You will march, with the regi- " ment under your command, to the Ferry, at the hour desig- " nated in previous orders from these headquarters, with such " transportation as shall be furnished you.

"By order of the Col. commanding Brigade.

"T. W Ripley, A. D. C."

At an earlier hour of the night, A. B. Q. M. Howland had taken from the regiment two of its four-horse teams; and upon receipt of the above orders, a regimental general order was issued, directing that the wagons of the regiment would be loaded with—first, officers' baggage and such private property as the men of the command might have; second, with hospital supplies; and, third, if room was left, with Quartermaster's stores. The camp to be left standing, and a suitable guard detailed to protect it, and such government stores as we should leave behind.

CHAPTER XXIV

ON THE ROAD, AND AT THE FERRY.

OUR MARCH — IN BIVOUAC — AT THE FERRY — WHO'D DO THE POLICING? — LIEUT. ELWELL — A NEW WAY OF VOLUNTEERING — WALKING ARMY WAGONS — APROPOS TO THIS — E, LOST A MAN — A NEW POST COMMANDER — OFFICERS ASSIGNED TO DUTY.

Harper's Ferry, April 3d. We are here, having marched all day yesterday, in the rain, and hail, and snow, through mud and water, in many places over the boot legs of the men; and at dusk, when within two miles, and almost in sight of *our own tents*, standing in their place, lying down in the cold and wet, without supper, by the order of our own Col. commanding the Brigade, to "bivouac in the first piece of woods we should "come to on the march, after receipt of his order."

At 9 this morning, in obedience to orders same officer, we resumed our march, and have pitched our "*shelters*" near the "Lockwood House"; the 18th Connecticut, now occupying our old quarters. We received cordial welcome from all; particularly Capt. Pratt, of ours, who is still Provost Marshal at the place, and Lieut. Cobb, as yet but partially recovered from his wound.

Gen. Averill has gone to Washington, to prefer, in person, his request that we may be ordered to report to him, for duty, as "Mounted Infantry."

The whole history of our march hither is so peculiar, and so much blame has been thrown upon the immediate commander of the regiment, for its unnecessary and cruel hardship, that it seems proper a full and connected account of it should be written out.

As already stated, on the 30th of March an order was issued, from Brigade Headquarters, directing "Lieut. Col. Lincoln, "commanding the 34th Massachusetts Infantry, to march, with "his regiment to the Ferry, at 6 A. M. of April 2d, with such "transportation as should be furnished him." During the day of Friday, the Adjutant, and in the evening the Quartermaster, were despatched to Brigade Headquarters, to learn what they could of our movement; if we were to march, and, if so, what amount of transportation was to be furnished us; or whether we were to be sent down by rail, as we had been brought up. No one, better than the officers at Brigade Headquarters, knew how utterly inadequate to the transportation of the property of the regiment was our own four wagons. But all the information given them, was that the acting Brigadier had himself gone to the Ferry, and that, at some hour during the night, the Regimental Commander would receive a communication from him. At a late hour in the evening, the acting Brigade Quartermaster visited the camp. He brought with him an order requiring the Regimental Quartermaster forthwith to turn over to the Post Quartermaster, two of the regimental teams, incidentally remarking, that probably the regiment would be required to *march* to the Ferry. He was asked what road we should take. "Oh, the Shepherdstown road!" said he. "Yes; but which is "the Shepherdstown road? You know, Quartermaster, that we "came up by rail." "Well," said the Quartermaster, "you "know the Col.'s Headquarters in town!" "Oh, yes!" "Well, when you get there, turn short to the right; follow that "road and you can't miss your way." "All right! Now, "Quartermaster, how many wagons are we to have, and when "are they to be furnished?" "I can't tell you. I have n't "heard a word said about any transportation being furnished "you." And the interview ended.

At a little past 3 A. M. of April 2d, an orderly dismounted at Reg't H'dqr's. and delivered to the hands of the Lieut. Col. commanding, an order from Brigade Headquarters, signed by A. D. C. Ripley, as follows: "You will *march*, with the Regiment under your command, to the Ferry, at the hour designated in previous orders from these Headquarters, with such transportation as shall be furnished you." Of course, this settled one point. *We were to march;* but how about transportation? Instead of any being furnished to us, part of our own had been taken away. When it was possible to delay no longer, orders were issued to load upon our remaining wagons, first,—such property as belonged to the officers and men of the command; and second,— hospital supplies and articles necessary to be had on the march, such as axes, shovels and picks; and at the latest possible moment, as no transportation was furnished, the camp was ordered to be left standing, a suitable guard being detailed for its protection, and for the care of all Government property left behind.

And so, at precisely 6 A. M., in a driving storm of wind, rain, hail, and snow, the Regiment filed on to the road, and moved towards the village. As the head of the command entered the public square of the town, the form of the Acting Brigadier was recognized at the window of his H'dqr's. Although in heavy marching order, and moving in a drenching rain, "attention" was called, and the honor of a marching salute was paid him. This honor was acknowledged by him. Turning short to the right, as we passed his quarters, the new direction of march, conforming to information given by his own quartermaster, was taken, while he stood viewing our ranks. No effort was made to correct this error. Before we had proceeded far, the road was found to be difficult for the men, and impracticable for the teams. A halt was ordered, and the Adj't sent back to report. "Tell Col. Wells, Adj't, that his Q. M. pointed out this road as the one for us to take; that there must have been some mistake about it, as we find it impassable for our teams. Say to him, also, that I don't know in what direction to turn, and ask him for directions, and also for a guide to pilot our route." Now, the Wagonmaster rode up to report that one of his wagons had broken down, and must be abandoned. Lieut. Lincoln was despatched to Headquarters to repeat the message sent by the Adj't, and to report the accident.

Both these officers soon returned, reporting the delivery of the messages they were charged with, and the reply made by the Acting Brigadier himself, that " he no had directions to give, and no guide to furnish us."

In this dilemma, the officers were called together. " Can any of you lead us to the Shepherdstown road?" No one could do so. "Maj. Pratt, you have been field officer of the day! can't you point out the route?" He couldn't. "Well, then! can any one of you lead us to the Winchester Pike?" The Major could do that; and although this route was not without its danger, from an occasional Rebel raiding party, it had an advantage, in that it gave us a good McAdam, instead of a dirt road, on which to march.

So, with an order to the Quartermaster to turn his teams, and join us on the Pike, the regiment followed the lead of the Major, through the mud of the intervening fields. No teams were to be seen when we reached the Pike, and the Adjt., was sent off, on the road to the village, to hurry them up. The storm was raging with terrible fury. It was too severe to endure while on a halt, and the march was continued, but with slackened pace. While thus toiling on our way, looking back frequently in hope of seeing our wagons, a horseman was discovered riding furiously towards us. As he neared, he was recognized as Lieut. Ellis of the brigade staff. Drawing rein, he saluted. "Col. you will turn over to Maj. Pratt the command of the 34th, and report in person to the Acting Brigadier without delay." Maj. Pratt met the surrender of the command with the significant question. "What am I to do with it, Col?" "I wish I could tell you, Major! My orders were (and they are still in force) to march to Harper's Ferry. The road we started upon was pointed out, by the Acting Brigade Quartermaster as the right one to take; you saw that it was impassable for our teams; Col. Wells was informed of our situation, was asked to give directions for our route, and to furnish a guide to pilot us on our way, both of which requests he has denied. "We are here under your guidance; the road we are on leads through Bunker Hill, to the Ferry. If I was still in command, I should follow it, but the regiment is now in your hands;" and so saying, the Lieut. Col., wheeling his horse, started for

Headquarters. On his way into town he was met and passed by Lieut. Ripley, A. A. D. C. on the brigade staff, exchanging salutes with him as he galloped by. Entering the office of the A. A. A. G. and making known to that officer the reason of his presence, an orderly was directed to notify the fact to the Brigadier.

After some little delay the Lieut. Col. was ushered into the presence of that officer. A warm, and somewhat angry interview followed. Somebody at Brigade Headquarters had blundered. Orders intended to be given, by which transportation and guides for our route were meant to be provided, had not in fact been issued by the staff, and the regiment and its commander were the sufferers. With a promise that orderlies should report to him as guides, and an injunction to keep the men of the command out of Martinsburg, the Lieut. Col. was dismissed, with orders to "go back and take his regiment, getting on to the Shepherdstown road without delay, and march his men to the Ferry." "What, to-day, Col.? you can't mean it." "I do n't care *when* you get there, but if you halt, send an orderly forward to report that you are on the road."

Rejoining the Regiment, it was guided through fields, across ravines, to the bridge over the Opequan, and the "Shepherdstown road," where the promised orderlies were in waiting. We had now been on the march more than five hours, and were thoroughly drenched and chilled through. Our onward progress was slow, as our road was deep with mud.

Coming to a piece of thick woods, a halt was ordered, with the intention of going into bivouac; but the officers, after consultation together, knowing that our old camp at the Ferry was standing, in the hope of being allowed to occupy it upon our arrival, preferred to continue the march.

Capt. Bacon, who was suffering from lameness from an injury to his ankle, and Lieut. Lincoln, were mounted, and directed to push on to the Ferry, and report our near approach to Headquarters. They were also furnished with a requisition for coffee, and instructed to have it ready for us upon our arrival. For the first time, in our service, an official request was made that a ration of whiskey might be issued to the command.

And so, floundering through the deep mud, our march was continued. Some irrepressible spirits, among the older soldiers, would break out in occasional song, or beguile the way by calling out—"co-boss, co-boss"—whenever a tired recruit would straggle from the column.

Just before reaching Halltown, an Orderly rode up, bearing an order from our own Colonel, Acting Brigadier, directing us to "bivouac in the first piece of woods we should reach, after "receipt of his order." Leaving the Pike, which we had now struck, we filed to the right, and made our night's resting place in the wet and mud, near our winter's chopping ground, on the Lucas estate; within a half hour's march, and almost within sight of our own old home on "Camp Hill."

The whiskey asked for was soon afterwards delivered to us, by " *Tom,*" A. A. D. C., who rode into camp astride the barrel.

There was no such thing as comfort to be obtained under the circumstances; and all welcomed the morning, which broke fair and beautiful.

At about 9 o'clock, an order from the authorities at the Ferry, directing our immediate march thither, was hailed with cheers, and obeyed most willingly. We found the 18th Connecticut nominally occupying our old camp; and, in obedience to directions, we pitched our "shelters" near the "Lockwood House." Here, without the means of procuring a fire, even to cook with, the wind blowing a gale, and another storm of mingled snow, rain, and hail raging, we passed the afternoon and following night.

8th. Yesterday's storm raged all night, but is now moderating.

The property and stores of the 18th Connecticut have been collected and carefully stored by the Brigade Quartermaster, and orders from Post Headquarters permit "the 34th to take possession of their old camp." Our men, left at Martinsburg, as guard over our camp and stores, having been relieved by the 19th U. S. Colored Troops, rejoined us to-day, having come by *rail.*

Lieut. Clive, Signal Officer from Sigel's Headquarters, is in camp to select *two* of our Lieutenants for duty in that Corps.

Capt. A. D. Pratt, on duty as Provost Marshal at this post, who still suffers from "aphonia," is desirous of resigning; but his tender is peremptorily rejected.

Major H. W Pratt is off duty from the effects of our march from Martinsburg.

Capt. W B. Bacon is suffering from the same cause.

We have also *three* men in hospital, down with lung fever contracted at the same time; *one* of whom, the surgeons say, will certainly die.

"Well, Flanley!" said Lieut. Elwell, our late recruiting officer, to the man, a miserable old shirk, who had lived in the Guard House most of the time since he joined the regiment: "How do *you* get along?" "Indeed, Lieutenant, I wish my throat had been cut before ever I saw you in Worcester." "Why, you ought not to complain, Flanley; you've done no service since you came out!" "Service is it, you say, Lieutenant?" "Yes, Flanley, service! You've done none; you've been in the Guard House three-fourths of your time!" "And faith, then, Lieutenant, *who'd do the policing*, if there wasn't some of us there?" asked the old rogue; and the roar his retort drew forth, more than repaid him for all the hardships he complained of.

7th. Our Colonel is assigned, by General Orders of yesterday's date, to the command of this post. Another of our men has received a commission in one of the regiments of colored troops.

Lieut. Elwell, of F. has tendered his resignation, feeling aggrieved at the promotion of First Lieut. Chauncey, and the assignment of that officer to the command of the Company with which he (Elwell) has been identified. He is reconciled, in a degree, by the assurance that such action was taken not from any want of regard for himself personally, or from lack of appreciation of his good service as an officer. He is reminded of the fact that to prevent any questions of precedence in rank, all commissions of the original line officers were made to bear the same date; and of the standing regimental order issued, at an early day, by the Colonel of the regiment, and which the Lieutenant Colonel could neither countermand or disregard.

that no officer, under any circumstances, would receive promotion to a vacancy existing in his own Company. I may say now, farther, that which could not so properly be said to him, that upon the vacancy caused by the discharge of Capt. Chandler, in consultation with the Colonel, and at his suggestion, Lieut. Chauncey was recommended to the Governor for promotion, instead of Lieut. Elwell; and this because of the existence of the order above alluded to. 'Of course that rule should be regarded. I should not think you'd hesitate a moment; Chauncey has been doing first rate of late,' were the words of the Colonel; and I acted in accordance with them. E. was notified distinctly, that his resignation would not be considered with any favor, and I hope will be reconciled to, if not satisfied, with the situation." "We can't afford to lose him. He is too good an officer."

Lieut. R. W Walker's resignation was forwarded, "approved."

We had our first drill to-day since leaving Martinsburg.

The 19th U. S. Colored Troops, Lieut. Col. Perkins (late Captain 1st Connecticut Volunteers), commanding, of which Lieut. Pennell, late Sergeant Co. E, 34th Massachusetts, is acting Adjutant, created a sensation as they marched past our camp to-day, from Martinsburg.. They had been "*raiding*" the country for recruits, and while in M. *gobbled* about *thirty* volunteers.

The process they adopt to secure new members is as novel as it is successful. Encamping in some neighborhood where the "darkey" element is strong, they send out a scouting party, which gathers in its embrace all "gentlemen of color" it may meet on its rounds. Upon returning to camp, these "brothers" are committed to the guard-house. Here they are left awhile, to meditate upon the uncertainties of life; they are then conducted to the presence of an officer, designated for the work, who calls for "volunteers in the holy cause of freedom and the country." Generally, some of the party are ready to respond to the call; and their names are made at once to grace the rolls of the Regiment. These poor fellows are, without delay, clothed in regulation blue, and turned over to the drill master. There are some, however, in whose breasts the spark of patriotism has not yet kindled to a burning fire, and such are returned to the guard-house for *longer meditation*. In this way, time is the great agent in bringing *all*, who fall into their hands, to a realizing sense of their duty to "*volunteer*."

The 18th Connecticut and 5th New York Artillery (about 2,500) reached here to-day.

9th. Brigade General Orders of even date, direct a rigid *daily* inspection of each command; require that "each soldier shall *have at all times, and shall carry in his knapsack*, one extra pair of drawers, one extra flannel shirt, two extra pairs of socks, two extra pocket handkerchiefs, one extra pair of shoes, one rubber, besides one woolen, blanket, one overcoat, one-half shelter tent," and permits sewing materials ad libitum, and "writing paper and envelopes, not to exceed a pound in weight." Add to this, one's musket and equipments, *forty* rounds of ball cartridges, and three days' rations, and each man becomes a *fair sized walking army wagon*.

8th. Apropos to this order: At a late inspection of a command, the inspecting officer examined the cartridge boxes of his men; a thing he had not done for a long time. Coming to one known as an inveterate card player, and who had used his box as a storehouse for candles; the remnants of a good many of which were still remaining, he broke out thus: "Step one pace to the front! Now, who are you, sir?" "Corporal Jones, Captain." "Corporal Jones, is it? By the powers, but it's mistaken ye are! It's Company Cook, bedad! You've got grease enough in that box of yours to butter cakes for every man of us, ye have!" And again, to another, who perhaps wrote home as often as some of our officers, and whose knapsack was pretty full of letters: "Who are you, sir? Be pleased to step one pace to the front, and show yourself! Who are you? Sergeant Blake, is it? Bedad, you are no Sergeant at all! I think ye must be the Secretary of War, or, indeed, old Halleck himself, by all those letters!"

E lost a man last night, under the following circumstances:

A large detail from the Company was on duty at the Shenandoah bridge; and, as has been the custom, at nightfall the flooring of the bridge was removed, thus cutting off all communication between the sentinel at the eastern approach, and the relief on this side, except what could be had by walking along a plank stretched across the chasm thus made.

The night was very dark and stormy; the wind was blowing and howling furiously, and the water of the river running like a mill-race.

At the hour for posting the relief, the Corporal of the Guard, with Hunter, of "E," a capital fellow and splendid soldier, started to walk this plank. The Corporal passed safely, not missing Hunter till he had reached the other bank. Hunter fell, or was blown from the plank, and was seen no more; nor is there any trace of his body this morning. Falling from twenty-five to thirty feet, and weighted, as he was, with musket, equipments, and ammunition, he probably sunk at once.

11th. The water in both the Potomac and Shenandoah has been rising rapidly for the past few days, and a large detail from the Regiment has been employed in freeing the bridges across these rivers from the drift which has accumulated against them. But this morning finds the bridges carried away, and *one* span of the railroad bridge gone, thus cutting off all communication north and east. Brigadier General Max Webber reached here to-day, and assumed command of the Post, relieving Colonel Wells of that duty. He returns Capt. Potter, acting Provost Marshal, at his own request, to duty with his Company; and substitutes in his place Capt. A. D. Pratt, who is still suffering from aphonia. He also takes Adjutant Woods, of ours, to be A. A. A. G. on his staff.

Our friends, and now our neighbors of the 18th Connecticut, amuse us a good deal. When they were ordered to this post, after we were so summarily sent off to Martinsburg, with our camp standing, and all our "property unpacked," they moved upon a "good thing," occupying our quarters, luxurious and clean beyond all their imagining, (to judge from their own camp ground, at M., to which we were consigned, where the filth was beyond endurance). Upon being returned to this post, we longed to re-possess our own again, and asked and obtained leave to do so, inasmuch as almost that entire regiment was away on duty. Now, upon their return, they hunger and thirst after what they have lost; and stand lounging round our streets, leaning upon their muskets, indulging in ill-natured criticism of us and our doings.

"D——d paper collar soldiers, these fellows are," one says to another; "no wonder they beat us in parade and on drill! That's all they have ever done! Only let them have *one fight;* just put them on a march, and then see!" The fun of the thing comes in when we reflect how little these fellows have shown themselves to be worth; doing Provost duty, at Baltimore, for a year; then at Winchester, with Milroy, last July, where all who could do so, skedaddled; and those who couldn't, marched to Richmond with all the honors of an armed escort.

In consequence of the destruction of the railroad bridge, all trains from the west are detained at this point; and U. S. Senator Carlisle, and other dignitaries in Civil, and officials in Military life are gathered here. *We* are notified that our "parade" is to be honored with the presence of Gen. Webber, with his staff, and other gentlemen, and in return for this compliment, it is ordered to be had with dress coats, scales and sashes.

CHAPTER XXV

HARPER'S FERRY AND MARCH TO MARTINSBURG.

OUR DOGS—WHAT'S TO PAY—CHAOS AGAIN—A NEW BRIGADE—A HEARTY WELCOME—AN ALARM—CAPT. BACON AND THE 18TH CONNECTICUT—ANOTHER ALARM—A LAUGH—IN A MUDDLE—THE COL. RESUMES COMMAND—AN INSPECTION—DESPATCHES—A GARRISON REVIEW—MARCHING ORDERS.

12*th*. The "2d Brigade" has fizzled; and Wells, again plain Colonel, has left for Baltimore. Heavens! what a babel in camp! Company F is tearing down its old cook-house; and by the help of our dogs, of which we have an army, its men are having a rat hunt; one hundred and fifty-seven of the creatures, by actual count, now lying piled in one heap. Among these dogs are a few brought from home when we came out; more which have been *confiscated* by the boys, at the different stations we have occupied; and not a few coaxed into following us on our different marches. Some howl at every bugle call; all bark in chorus when the drum corps makes its presence known by its unique performances. Many are regular in their attendance at all drills, and one of these sings second, whenever our Colonel's voice is heard delivering his words of command. Some fall in regularly, and march in line for their rations; others, guerrilla like, hang on to the flanks, making stealthy approach to the cook-houses, and steal, and are off. Noble New-Foundlands, wiry terriers, mastiffs, hounds, pointers, bull dogs, poodles and mongrels of all kinds and degrees. Our stock has increased miraculously of late, and what with the regular howlings and irregular fights, over which it seems as if the boys luxuriate, as over nothing else, interference came from Headquarters, at last, in the shape of an order. The fightings were made to cease, but the dogs remained—until to-day, when the boys have corralled all they could coax, and have turned them loose again, with tin decorations to their tails. Well, they must have some fun; and if there is no whiskey in it!

Capt. Leach returned to us to-day, having, gallant soldier that he is, captured a wife during his absence in Massachusetts.

All applications for furloughs are returned from Superior Headquarters, disapproved, and notice given that none will be granted at present.

Well! what's to pay now! It seems as if bedlam had broken loose. Hark! what a roar! now a lull, during which the soft, sweet notes of our band fall with soothing influence upon the ear; now a shout drowns all other noises! The devils! They are hunting down every man they lay their eyes upon, and giving all they catch a tossing in their blankets; showing particular attention to such ones as look down contemptuously upon "such employment of their God given faculties."

Chaos seems to have come again! Orders crowd fast upon orders; now from Gen. Webber, "commanding the Post,"— now as "commanding the 1st Infantry Division,"— now as "commanding the Independent Brigade." Some come through an apparent intervening Headquarters,— some are sent down direct—some are addressed "to the Commanding Officer of the 34th,"—some to "Col. Wells,"—some to the "Lieut. Col. commanding." In the seeming confusion, one hardly knows "whether he is on foot or on horseback."

Our garrison is being strengthened; the 116th and 123d Ohio marched by us to-day, and encamped in Bolivar. *One* battalion of the 5th N. Y. Artillery is to bivouac to-night, on the glacis immediately in front of our breastworks. Miner's Battery is recalled from the hot quarters given it by Gen. Sullivan. Thus reinforced, we are to "have, in the future, Brigade Guard mounting upon the parade ground of the 34th Massachusetts; the band of that regiment furnishing the music."

16*th*. A heavy rain has been falling all night, and is still continuing.

"General orders, Headquarters 1st Infantry Division, Department West Virginia," received this morning, direct the formation of a brigade, to be composed of the 34th Massachusetts, the 116th and 123d Ohio, with the 3d Maryland (Snow's) Battery, the whole under Col. Wells, A. B. G. The brigade is ordered to take up its line of march, for Martinsburg, at 9 A. M., to-morrow.

Heaven help us! Except the 34th, this Infantry is neither drilled nor disciplined; this, however, from no fault of theirs. The bulk of the rank and file of these commands was captured at Milroy's defeat, last summer. The men were paroled soon after, and have been scattered in small squads, along the B. & O. Railroad, on duty as picket guard. The officers, however, were retained as prisoners; and many of them are, in fact, still in Rebel hands. It looks as if we were to suffer from the connection.

Capt. Pratt, Provost Marshal, and Lieut. Lincoln, on court martial, both still victims to aphonia, are to be left behind.

Our sick list is somewhat large, and we have a good many men unable to *march*, from various causes. Among these is Capt. Bacon, not yet recovered from the effects of our late march *from* Martinsburg. He is to be left in command of the camp and its guard, charged to pack, and forward by rail, such property as we cannot take on our wagons.

18*th*. Yesterday's march was severe, principally because of the deep mud of the roads. Our guide, well acquainted with the country, took many a short cut across the fields, thus avoiding much that was horrible.

At 5 P. M. we reached "Kearney-ville," and went into bivouac, in a beautiful grove of oak timber. Our Pioneers soon had a log heap, twelve to fourteen feet long, along each side of which the officers stretched their shelters. By the aid of the band, to which we all owed much, the evening passed pleasantly; many officers from the other commands gathering around our fire, and helping, by song and story, to wile away the hours. Reveillé was sounded the next (this) morning at 5 o'clock, and at 7 we were again on the march. Hearty and repeated cheers were given to the 34th, as the regiment, on its route through the village of Martinsburg, was recognized by the inhabitants. It is pleasant, now, to listen to their words of welcome. While they confess to a degree of dissatisfaction at the rigor of our patrol, they also confess that they had no reason to complain of any act of incivility on the part of the boys; and least of all, of suffering from petty plundering, as they have suffered since our departure. We passed, on our march into the town, Averill's command, which was taking passage by rail to the Kanawha. General order No. 2 appoints Capt. Potter, of ours, as Provost Marshal of the place; and directs a "daily detail from the regiment, of three commissioned, and ten warrant officers, with sixty men, to serve as Provost Guard."

Lieut. Cobb, although not recovered from his wound, rejoined us, and reported for duty.

19*th*. Col. Wells is relieved from command of the Brigade, and assigned to the command of the Post. An alarm last night, called the Regiment to arms. In *three* minutes, the Boys stood in line, ready for any emergency. Capt. Leach, with his Co., G, was sent out to picket the "Tuscarora road;" and Capt. Fox, with his own (H) Company, and B, moved to the Winchester Pike, to support the Cavalry pickets which were reported to have been driven in. *Four* Companies of the 123d Ohio were sent out, to-day, to picket the country in the neighborhood of "Sleepy Creek."

Permission has been given Capt. Leach to appear before the Examining Board, at Washington, upon his application for a position, in the field, of some "colored Regiment." Charges have been preferred against Capt. Bacon, by a Lieutenant of the 18th Connecticut; and a copy has been forwarded to the Captain. The offense, charged, is that the Capt. knocked down a man of that command, before leaving the Ferry; and the Captain's history of the affair is this:

It will be remembered, that upon our reaching the Ferry, after our march from this place, we found the 18th Connecticut in nominal possession of our old camp; and, that, as their occupancy was but nominal (all of the Regiment, save a small guard, being on duty elsewhere,) our application to *re-occupy* the camp was granted. When orders were issued, directing our march to this place, inasmuch as we could not take with us the property belonging to the Regiment, and that for which the officers were responsible, it was determined to leave the camp, and the public property in charge of a competent guard, under Capt. Bacon, who was partially disabled. When the fact that we were to move became known, these men of the 18th sniffed the plunder from afar. Like vultures, they swooped down upon our encampment, waiting only our departure, that they might pounce upon the prey. Officers and men alike envious to excel in this work of appropriation. As these fellows paid no attention to Bacon's orders to them, to desist from their plundering, he knocked one of them down. The 18th, or so many of them as were present, "*made for him.*" His guard surrounded him, and he, revolver in hand, threatened to shoot any one who resisted his authority. The 5th N. Y. Artillery, under orders to occupy the ground vacated by us, were now marching in; and, upon complaint preferred by the men from Connecticut, the Col. of the New Yorkers directed Capt. Bacon to consider himself in arrest.

"But I don't recognize your authority to give such orders," said the Capt.

"Then I will *cause* you to be placed in arrest," replied the Col. "I guess not, Col.! Do you command the Post?" "No, Capt.!" "Then you can't arrest me. I am Capt. Bacon of the 34th Mass., left by Col. Lincoln, commanding the Regiment, in charge of this camp, and, if any person attempts, in any way, to disturb me in the performance of my duty, I will shoot him, on the spot!" "That, Capt., entirely alters the case, and I apologize to you for my threat," said the Col., and so the affair dropped for the time.

But not long afterwards, Bacon detected one of the Connecticut officers walking off with a chair, and a table belonging to one of ours, and ordered him to return it. Connecticut demurred; Bacon called a guard; Connecticut, depositing his coveted prize on the ground, and seating himself, said: "I guess, Capt., I can sit here as long as you can stand there." "Shoot any person, Guard, who attempts to carry away either table, or chair," said Capt. Bacon, as he turned and walked away. For four long hours the Connecticut officer kept his seat, the guard maintaining his watch the while. At length the officer effected an ungraceful retreat, with a loss, not only of the coveted spoils, but the honor of the foray. After our train was loaded with the most valuable, and indispensible articles, what remained were given, by Capt. Bacon, to the officers and men of the 5th N. Y. Much had been obtained at no considerable money cost; all of it under some difficulties, and, taken as a whole, was a prize of high value to any command. It is no strained inference, that, but for this loss of their expected plunder, we should have heard nothing of these charges against our Captain. Meanwhile, Bacon is not, nor will he be placed in arrest; and with the forwarding of counter charges preferred by him, these Connecticut officers will learn that in War, blows are given by both sides.

21st. Camp was disturbed at a late hour last night, by the receipt of an order directing a large detail to march at once out on the "Tuscarora Road" to picket that region. Cause: the hanging round of a large body of Rebel cavalry dressed in our uniform. Lieut. Murdock in charge, is this morning, upon complaint of Lieut. Col. Wilde, 116th Ohio, field officer of the day, placed in arrest, by the commandant of the post. By the Lieut.'s written report, forwarded, approved at Regimental Headquarters, it seems, that in obedience to the orders he received, he established his reserve about three quarters of a mile from our camp, throwing out small posts in front, and on each flank; that having thus secured himself against surprise, he rejoined the reserve, and, leaving his Sergeant in charge. laid down, giving orders that he was to be called in case of need; that he was notified of the presence of the field officer of the day, but did not deem it necessary to get up, and go out to meet him. And the Lieut. charges in turn that this officer of the day, neither saw to the placing of the pickets, nor visited them after they were placed, but contented himself with riding up to the reserve.

22d. Upon the report of Lieut. Murdock, that officer is released from arrest. Lieut. Hall has, at length, been detailed from the regiment, and ordered to the Signal service. His own remonstrances, and the utmost efforts of the Lieut. Col. commanding were ineffectual to avert the transfer. Sullivan's expedition, up the Kanawha, is abandoned, in consequence of the bad state of the roads in that region; and the troops, composing the 2d brigade, are now coming by rail to this post. The 5th U. S. battery has arrived, and Averill's command are en route. Sigel holds us as in a vice, refusing all applications for furloughs, and returning "*disapproved*," every paper, no matter what its nature may be.

A joke, particularly *a good one*, is relished in camp, as nowhere else; and if it happens to be at the expense of a superior officer, the enjoyment is not at all diminished.

Our Col., just now acting post commander, good soldier that he is, is also a good deal of a martinet, and we are all enjoying a laugh at his expense. A Sergeant of the 123d Ohio, has charge of a picket post on the Winchester Pike, with the most stringent orders as to his conduct; among them being one to *detain at his post* any one, from outside the picket line, desiring to come into the village; allowing them however to forward to the commandant of the post a *written* communication, stating the object sought to be accomplished by the visit. Upon learning his orders, the Sergeant requested an allowance of pens, ink, and paper, to enable him to carry his instructions into effect. This application, to all seeming proper enough, was refused. Matters went well till this morning, when, for the first time since being on post, a countryman presented himself with the purpose of visiting the town. In the quandary in which the Sergeant found himself — unable to obey — equally unwilling to disobey his orders — he sent the man forward, under charge of a guard to report at Post Headquarters. Now the breach of orders by the Sergeant was so flagrant, that the Col. ordered his immediate arrest, and directed that he should be brought before him personally for examination. "How happens it, Sergeant, that you have disobeyed my orders?" "I could n't help doing so, Col.!" "Could n't help it! You *meant* to disobey, did you?" "No, Col., but I had no rations and so could not keep the man at my post; neither he, nor I had writing materials, so I could not comply with your orders.

Therefore I sent him up under guard, that he might communicate personally with you."

"Yes, but Sergeant," said the Colonel, "there are stores open in town where you could have supplied yourself with paper, etc."

"Ah! yes, Colonel, that's true enough; but it's no part of my duty as a soldier to furnish writing paper to the government! On the other hand, it furnishes me. I have so much pay, and am *found ;* my pay is not only small, but overdue."

And the result was that the Sergeant was returned to his duty, after being furnished with a large supply of writing materials; and, for once, as the boys have it, "the Colonel had to come down."

24*th*. Corporal Adams, of E., died last night; another victim of that "dreadful march" from this place to the Ferry. Matthews, also of E., a recruit, has been passed, by the Examining Board, at Washington, to a Lieutenancy in the 'U. S. Colored Troops.

We, that is, the commands here, find ourselves just now in a regular "muddle." Averill, who was leaving this place as we arrived, directed "Col. Taylor, of the 1st N. Y. Veteran Cavalry, to assume command of the Post;" Col. McReynolds claims the command, by virtue of seniority of rank; and Col. Wells is in actual enjoyment of the position. Each, in turn, issues orders, not always, however, in harmony with each other, and, at times, no little confusion is the consequence.

25*th*. The Colonel, relieved from command of the Post, returned to-day to the head of the Regiment.

He marked his arrival by the following;

HEADQUARTERS 34TH MASS. INFANTRY,
Martinsburg, April 25, 1864.

"REG. GEN. ORDER, NO. 40.

"The Colonel, upon returning to the Regiment, after nine "months' separation from the immediate command, congratu-"lates it, and himself, upon the able and efficient manner in "which it has been commanded during the time; and the faith-"ful devotion to duty of its officers, and the admirable conduct "of the men. It has been his chiefest happiness to see it growing in grace, and good works, and winning golden opinions in every quarter. He does not quite know, yet, whether *it is the best Regiment in the United States service*, but he does know that *it shall be.*

"By order of GEO. D. WELLS,

"Col. 34th Mass. Infantry.

"A. C. WALKER,

"Acting Adjutant."

After a two hours' Battalion drill, conducted by himself, he relinquished the command to the Lieutenant Colonel, desiring the officers to be notified to *put* and *keep* their companies in condition to march at a moment's notice.

Gen. Sigel and Staff visited the camp during the afternoon. Two Colonels also rode over to see us, both of whom are senior in rank to our own. Inasmuch as they, with their Regiments, are among the late arrivals at the Post, their presence caused Wells no little disgust, and the rest of us no little dissatisfaction.

Dr. Charles G. Allen, lately appointed Assistant Surgeon, and assigned to us, vice Thorndike promoted, reported for duty.

At 11 P. M. the camp was disturbed by the marching away of two Companies, I and G, Capt. Soley in command, sent out to support *one* from the 123d Ohio, on picket at "Harrison's Gap."

The Rebels are increasing their strength, and gradually drawing nearer to this place. A scouting party of our Cavalry was captured by them, yesterday, between "Middletown" and Winchester.

26*th*. Our supporting party marched, last night, in darkness almost tangible, and in a storm of unusual severity. After their departure the wind rose, and blew with great fury, and the rain fell in torrents. Col. Wells left, this morning, for Cumberland, having been detailed as a member of a "military commission," to assemble in that place. During the day, the regiment was inspected by Col. Thoburn, 1st West Virginia Infantry, detailed to the duty from Sigel's headquarters. It was the *fourth* inspection in as many days, by virtue of orders same headquarters. Companies I and G, returning from their night's duty on picket, caught sight of the regiment under arms, and came into camp on a "double quick." They were ordered into column, for inspection, *as they were*—anything but fair to them, but perhaps quite as well for the credit of the command. The condition of these two companies, just off duty, during a night of rain and exposure, without previous knowledge of the pending inspection, and, of course, with no opportunity of preparing for it, drew from the inspecting officer the *highest praise*. A few young men of "C," and two or three in one of the other companies, were found without "drawers" in their knapsacks, as required by late general order, and were ordered, by the Inspector, to the "Guard House." He refused to accept, in explanation of the apparent disobedience of orders, the statement that never in their past life had they worn such articles of clothing, and consequently they had not now been required to *draw* them. He claimed that they were not thereby relieved from obligation to draw for, and carry them in their knapsacks. However, they were not committed to the Guard House, as ordered by him. During the inspection, our camp was thronged with officers, of all grades, and every arm of the service. The crowd was largely increased by persons of both sexes, as the hour for our "parade" drew near. At the close, a Major in the 21st N. Y. Cavalry, a Massachusetts man, who introduced himself, said "it made his heart bound to see the old White " Flag supported by such a regiment. I don't mean to flatter " you," said he, "but I have been in the U. S. service since grad- " uating from the Military Academy. I have seen thé Dress " Parades of nearly every regiment of the regulars, and of, I " don't know how many, of the volunteer service; but this of " yours excels anything of the kind I have ever seen." Though proud as Lucifer at the compliments showered upon us by this and other officers, I contented myself with the remark that I believed we might safely call the 34th a well drilled body. " Well drilled!" was the exclamation all around; "well drilled! It's perfect! it's perfect!"

The Rev. Mr. Longley, who has been with us for some weeks, has at length made known his desire to be appointed our Chaplain. At a meeting of the officers, called for the purpose of considering the matter, it was decided, after discussion, not to extend to him the desired invitation.

27th. 4 A. M. We were roused at the above hour this morning, by a pleasant voice, announcing, "Dispatches for you, Colonel, immediate and pressing." They communicated the information that "the enemy, in force, at about ten the past evening, had driven in our outer picket line; and ordered "all infantry commanders to hold their forces ready to move at a moment's warning." Endorsing upon the back of the order an acknowledgment of its receipt, according to the new order of things, I, being tired and half sick, laid down and slept. Not a safe thing to do, as a general rule; but we had our rear, front, and flanks protected *by our own men*; and more confidence was felt in their watchfulness than in the correctness of the information, which it had taken Headquarters *six hours* to obtain and communicate. The result justified the conclusion, as no camp was disturbed.

An order for "Garrison review, by Major-General Sigel," in person, issued yesterday, directed the troops to "be on line at 2 P. M., of" to-day. *Our* distance from the place designated for the ceremony was four miles. As the head of the regiment rose the hill east of the village, near where the review was to be had, no other troops could be seen. A halt was ordered, and the staff sent out to explore; but soon returned, having failed to gain any information at the neighboring camps. Soon an Orderly cantered up, with directions from Col. Thoburn, A. B. G., to the 34th, to "take its assigned place." "Where is that?" was asked. "*I don't know,*" was the reply; and so the regiment remained where it was. Now the 54th Pennsylvania appeared; and, nearing us, was also halted. Soon the two Ohio regiments came up. But among us all, no one knew more than that there was to be a review, somewhere in that neighborhood. And so we rested, *as* and *where* we were. An hour passed, and an A. D. C. brought orders for us all to move "farther over the hill, and take position upon guides stationed there." We moved, to find the order was wrong. *Five times* we moved upon lines and to positions designated, only to be ordered elsewhere as often. While affairs were thus muddled, Gen. Sigel and staff arrived upon the field, but rode away to the cavalry, which were drawn up upon our extreme right. During their absence, Col. Thoburn, with the aid of the several regimental commanders, succeeded in getting his line formed. The review itself went off well enough, and we returned to camp at about 6 P. M.

Col. Wells returned from duty in Cumberland by the midday train, and rode on to the field in season to direct the regiment in its various movements. Our old friend, Gen. Sullivan, reached here to-day. Report assigns him to the command of the Infantry Division.

28th. The 18th Connecticut reported last night.

Commissions reached us, to-day, for Capt. Chauncey, and 1st Lieutenant Platt, and 2d Lieutenant Cutter, and they were assigned to duty accordingly.

Orders have just come down, directing the march of the troops at 5 A. M. to-morrow; the men to take five days' rations in their haversacks. We shall leave behind, Capt. Pratt, Lieuts. Woods, Lincoln, Platt, and Horton, all on duty at the Ferry; Van Loan in command of our Provost Guard here, and Cobb and Cutter in command of the sick, left to guard our camp and property. Macomber, detailed to the command of the Pioneer Corps, is attached to Sullivan's headquarters.

CHAPTER XXVI

Sigel's Campaign.

THE MARCH —"BUNKER HILL"— INSPECTION AND MUSTER FOR PAY— OUR STRENGTH — WINCHESTER — OUR TRANSPORTATION — STRIPPED NAKED — RED TAPE — A DRILL! OUR SICK — ANOTHER DRILL!! — FIELD OF G — NEW ORDERS — OUR TEAMS.

April 30th. Bunker Hill.—We reached this place about 4 P. M., yesterday; distance marched about twelve miles. The weather had changed from being uncomfortably cold to very warm, and the men suffered a great deal from the heat. At the first halt of the column, knapsacks were unpacked; contents closely examined, and the ground fairly covered with abandoned clothing. In some instances, overcoats were thrown away; in many blankets were divided, and one-half left, that the heavy burden might be lightened. To-day has been taken up in mustering for pay. We have (including the three officers and one hundred and twenty-three men left on duty at Martinsburg, but *mustered as present with the regiment*) twenty-nine officers and eight hundred and thirty-eight enlisted men. Of this number, three officers are on special duty, and thirty-seven men on extra daily duty, and one enlisted man sick. Nine Commissioned Officers are absent on duty, three of whom are away from the division. One hundred enlisted men are on detached service; four absent with leave; one without leave; thirty-six absent, sick; and fourteen away from the division. Fifty recruits are required to bring us to our maximum number. Major Generals Sigel and Stahl, and Brigadier General Sullivan, and

Colonels and Acting Brigadier Generals Moore and Thoburn are with the column.

It is the general impression that we are to await at Winchester instructions from Grant, and the hope is strong, at least on the part of *many* of the officers, that we are not to advance *far* up the Valley. We are here, twelve miles from our base, with a train of *over two hundred empty army wagons*, and the animals *without forage!* Banks, Fremont, and Shields have each, in turn, been driven from this Valley; and our present force is a smaller one than either of those Generals commanded. With all this, and the experience of Milroy the past summer, Sigel, with his present force, will be lucky indeed if he also does not have to "get out of this." The country passed over is somewhat rough and rocky; yet the soil is excellent. But there is little evidence of improvement. No orchards, (a few scattering apple trees only) not even a currant bush has been visible on our route hither, although we have marched past some princely estates, and are in the "Garden of Virginia," as this Valley is called.

Large, square, two-story buildings, mostly of brick, without blinds, unsheltered from the blazing sun, stand in the foreground; and around them, the invariable cluster of uncouth, rambling log stables, generally unenclosed.

We hear and read of "free and enlightened Virginia," yet to this time we have nowhere seen a "country school house." There are "academies" indeed, where the children of the rich and "well born" can be educated; but for the poor and those of moderate means! God help them! Virginia has not!

Winchester, May 3d. Our march of yesterday was less fatiguing than that from Martinsburg to Bunker Hill. As we moved through the streets of this place quite a number of Union flags were suspended across the street; and more, of smaller size, were waving from windows of houses, along our route. Occasionally handkerchiefs were waved by fair ladies; but more often, scowling faces, *not always bearded*, could be seen looking from behind half closed doors. We are encamped outside the town, upon ground more than once hotly contested for.

Our officers, high in place, do not enjoy the full confidence of the command. The two Acting Brigadiers — if they are to be judged by the condition of their own regiments — and is not such a fair test? are poor soldiers.

Three of our *eight regiments* of infantry were with Milroy at his surrender of this place, over a year ago; and the men of each of these regiments accuse those of the others of misbehavior on that occasion. The 54th Pennsylvania is fair; the 12th West Virginia pretty good; the rest are barely passable. In excuse for these others, it may be truly said, that such as were captured at Winchester had been without officers till a short time ago, and that they have been subdivided into small detachments, doing mere picket duty along the Baltimore and Ohio Railroad, with *little* opportunity for even company, and *none* for battalion drill. Such as it is, however, the column is here; threatening the occupation of the Valley, to create a diversion in favor of Grant — perhaps to remain where we are — perhaps to advance and occupy the country; certainly not, it is hoped, with the purpose of advancing beyond "Cedar Creek." Orders have just come down for a brigade drill. We shall now see what we shall see.

May 4th. General orders of yesterday reduced *our* transportation from *six* wagons to *three*, and every individual to "fighting trim;" the *men* being directed to pack all spare clothing in their knapsacks for transportation to Martinsburg, where they are to be stored; and the officers required to reduce their baggage to *one* small valise each — they to carry their own blankets on the march. Soon after the receipt of the order, a *train* was driven into camp to be loaded, and such a moving "you never did see." When everything directed to be sent back had been loaded on to the wagons, there was almost nothing left for future use. About midnight, with great noise of cracking whips, and loud shouts of "yah — yip, mule!" the wagons were rolled out of camp, but were recalled after being driven about two miles, and *are here now*. In the distribution of camp equipage, one wall tent falls to the Colonel; the Lieut. Colonel, Surgeon, and his two Assistant Surgeons luxuriate in the joint possession of another, while the Adjutant, Quartermaster, and their clerks, enjoy a third. Our Major, having been detailed as A. A. I. G., on Gen. Stahl's staff, is, presumably, to be better accommodated.

Look at us now! All chairs and stools having been sent back, and tables, and other conveniences of camp life having vanished, we are seated upon the ground, and eating our dinners from dishes balanced upon our knees. The Adjutant writes his orders upon a drum-head, on paper which his clerk carries in his coat pocket, and with pen and ink which *he* carries on his own person. In our tents, ranged in order, are our saddles, covered with our overcoats, poor substitutes for pillows. Carefully disposed near by are swords, belts, spurs and glasses; while hanging from the tent poles are haversacks, canteens and bridles for our horses. Each man's blanket lies, snugly rolled, upon ground where, when spread, its owner is to find his bed.

Stripped naked as we are of all carnal comforts, there is one thing we have in abundance. We fairly revel in *red tape*. For instance: Word was sent in from our left wing, out on picket, that one of our men had been suddenly taken severely sick. Under our former status, our Surgeon, upon receipt of such information, would have procured an ambulance and driven out and brought in the man. But under the existing arrangement he reports, in official form, the fact to the Medical Director; the Medical Director, endorsing said report, forwards the same to the Medical Inspector; this official, first endorsing said report, forwards the same to the officer commanding the ambulance train; this officer forwards it to the Lieutenant in charge of the train; the Lieutenant directs his Sergeant to have the man sent for; the Sergeant directs his chief of ambulances to send for the man; the chief directs the driver of some one of the many ambulances to "hook up," and report; the driver "hooks up" and reports, and there being no one else *to be directed*, the man is in a fair way of being brought in. In this case, fortunately the man had a strong constitution, and was alive when reached.

Since our arrival here, we have drawn all our supplies from Martinsburg, using for that purpose the train of wagons belonging to that post only; and notwithstanding this train fails to bring up the quantity needed from day to day, over *two hundred and fifty wagons* stand corralled here, idle and empty. We have already had *one* train captured from us by the Rebels, near Bunker Hill.

The troops are pretty busily occupied in Company and Battalion drills, and in an indescribable sort of Brigade movement; this last under the supervision of Sigel, Stahl and Sullivan, who are on the field, but who, as a rule, exercise no direct command. These Brigade drills, if such they may be called, are full of novelty to us, so different are they from any in which heretofore we have taken part. Yesterday, for instance, everything was full of the mimicry of battle. Artillery was posted; Infantry massed in column, and extended in line; and Cavalry stationed so as to protect the flanks. Everything looked beautifully! A line of skirmishers was needed to cover the front; and the 34th was singled out. "Your Regiment is drilled as "skirmishers, Colonel?' 'Yes, General.' And it moves by "bugle call?' 'Yes, General.' 'Ah, well; that's splendid! "Send your bugler to me." Various calls were sounded, by order of the General, to which the Company, sent forward as skirmishers, promptly answered in responsive movement. Rapport having been thus established, the entire Regiment was ordered to deploy as skirmishers. A "Forward" blast from the Bugler, simultaneous with an opening discharge from the Artillery, close in our rear, sent us ahead! How fortunate for us that this was playing war! and the guns unshotted! as otherwise our loss would have been fearful. During the movements of the troops, *our advance* was unchecked. Looking backward, we could see the sub-divisions of the main army rapidly changing position. Artillery, hastily limbering, made quick retreat; and, from its new position, swept, with furious discharge, the ground it had been forced to surrender. Infantry went gallantly forward, and charging, regained lines it had previously held; while Cavalry swooped down, in impetuous charge, upon an enemy supposed to be in confusion. And so the afternoon sped. The struggle behind us must have been terrible; for so engrossed with it, and the varying fortunes of the field, were its managing spirits, that the existence of the line of skirmishers seemed to have been forgotten. Over fences, through swamps, across ravines, and in wood-land, past the outer picket line, in strict obedience to that single "Forward" blast, occasionally dropping a Bugler to catch and transmit to us any new call, if any should be sounded at the far away battle field, we pushed our way on. As, after a while, the tired soldiers of the main army rested on their arms, the day's casualties footed up, killed, none; wounded, none; missing, the 34th Massachusetts Infantry; all but that *one* Bugler whose blast had carried us so far away.

Couriers skurried over the country, and overtook us moving ahead, obedient to that first and only order. Now, our own Bugler sounded the "recall;" and when our wearied boys marched into camp, it had long been dark.

Lieut. Bacon is detailed from us to duty as A. D. C. on Colonel (Acting Brigadier-General) Thoburn's Staff.

Dr. Clarke, who, upon the organization of the 2d Brigade, was appointed, and has been acting Medical Director, was returned to-day, and rejoined us. He looks as if delighted at getting back; and we are rejoiced that he is again acting with us.

The weather is very changeable; uncomfortably, almost oppressively warm by day, and cold enough in the evening, and at night, to make fires almost a necessity. Chills and diarrhœa are quite prevalent among us, though we have no serious sickness as yet.

Col. Wells is reported on the sick list. "Take your Regiment," he said to the Lieutenant-Colonel, this morning; "take your Regiment and do with it what you please. I've lost all interest in it and the service," a remark induced, perhaps, more from a sense of injustice done him, than from actual ill health.

7th. *Five* companies of ours were sent out, this morning, on a *three* days tour of picket duty.

Major Pratt left us to-day to serve as A. A. I. G. on the staff of Major-General Stahl.

Writes the Lieut. Col. under this date to a friend: "I have been quite unwell for several days, though not 'off duty;' and this morning feel quite 'down-sick,' and have been vainly trying to get rest and sleep. Among others who have dropped in upon me, has been the Col. Upon his departure, Clarke picked from the ground, a paper, and handed it to me, with the remark: 'here's a paper you have dropped, Col.' Opening it, I saw that our Brigade was under orders for a drill this afternoon." "Well, Col.!" I asked some hours afterwards, as I handed the order back to him, "what time have you ordered the line to be formed this afternoon?" "I've given no orders," was the reply. "What time will you have it formed?" "I've no orders to give about it." "But, Col.! one of us must take out the Regiment, as the Major is detailed away; and *I* feel too sick to do it." "I am sorry for that, Col.," was the reply; "but *I* won't serve under such fools; and *you* are a fool if *you* do." Just then, the drums, in the other Regiments, beat "to the color." But of course all was quiet with us. At last, but not till the 1st Virginia was moving from their camp, I ventured again to the Col.'s presence, to ask what orders had been issued. "None! so far as I know," said he. "What orders will you have issued, Col.? The other Regiments are under arms, and some of them already moving on to line," "I've no orders to give, Col.," said he. "Do with your Regiment just what you please." So I turned upon my heel, directed the Chief Bugler, near by, to sound the assembly,—the Boys responded with a cheer,—and, moving at a double-quick, the 34th stood on its appointed place, the *extreme left* of the line, second in point of time. As I rode past the Col.'s tent, his " Where's your glass, Col.? I think I'll go up to one of these knolls and watch the affair!" arrested me, only long enough, however, to give him the information he asked for. Soon, Sigel, Stahl, Sullivan, Moore,—and Thoburn, A. B. G., in actual command, each accompanied by their full retinue of staff officers, rode on to the field, and to the extreme right of the line. Riding from Regiment to Regiment, and halting at each, this imposing Cavalcade, after a long time, drew near the 34th, and the following colloquy ensued: "Col. Wells?" "No, Gen.!" "Where is Col. Wells?" "He is indisposed." "Col. Lincoln?" "Yes, Gen.!" "Can you handle your Regiment, Col.?" "I'll try, Gen.!" "I ask the question, Col., because we are going to practice some movements, this afternoon, sometimes required upon battle fields, in which every thing depends upon Battalion Commanders; and, that there may be no mistake in execution, we have come down to explain, in advance, the orders and movements. I'll now give the orders, as I shall issue them, and you will please to give close attention. "The first movement, Col., will be to change *front to rear*, upon your Battalion. The order, for this movement, you will not repeat to your command." (In this he was *wrong*.) "Next I shall give the order to wheel by Companies, to the left. This order you will repeat; next, "to close, by Battalion in mass, upon the head of column;" which order you will also repeat; next, '*right face*.' Now, presuming this to be a slip of the tongue, merely, I ventured to interrupt with "excuse me, General, you mean *left face*, don't you?" "That's precisely why I've come down here! I don't want any suggestions from Battalion Commanders! All I want from them is to listen carefully to the orders, as they are issued, and to repeat them, *precisely* as they are received." "You shall have no reason, General, to complain of me in that respect; but, at the same time, you will please excuse me for saying that your order, *right face*, will not be correct." "I don't want any suggestions from you, Col.! The order will be *right face*, and I shall expect it will be obeyed," was the remark of the General, somewhat impatiently made. "Most certainly, Gen., it shall be," was the reply; and the interview ending thus, the Generals, with their retinue, wheeled, and swept to their places in front of the line. Soon, but in a voice too faint to be heard in the distance, Order No. 1 was issued. As I sat with closed lips, I could hear my officers enquiring "what's the order? what's the order?" but regarding the instructions I had received, I gave no intimation of the intended movement.

We wheeled to the left, by company, as directed. At the order to "Close by battalion in mass upon head of column," the regiments to our rear closed *solid upon us, and upon each other*, wholly failing to maintain their proper intervals. Nor was this error noticed; or, if noticed, was it corrected, by either the proper battalion, or any of the general officers. Just then some of the line officers of the 34th, among them Capts. Bacon and Soley, inquired what the movement was to be; and upon being informed, they, with their brother officers in command, instantly, and in advance of the issuing of any general order, gave to their men the cautionary word, "*Left*." No notice was taken of this action by them. The look upon the faces of these officers, as they heard from my lips the order, "*Right!*" in repetition of it as it fell from the mouth of the officer commanding, caused me to smile. It said plainly enough: "What's the matter with you, Colonel?" Aware that each of my subordinates knew as well as myself that the order, as issued, was wrong, and fearing lest they, concluding that it was a slip of the tongue on my part, would execute the correct movement, I shouted the order, "*Right face!*" once more, which they, in turn, repeated to their astonished men. At the head of the column, as we were, we changed position in a moment. But the other organizations, after marching to the new line, were in a sort of "*town meeting*" condition. It was perfectly plain that they recognized something wrong in their position; and it was equally plain that none of the officers knew how to remedy the error into which they had been led. They were extricated at last, by the aid of the general officers. When, after a long while, the new line was formed and order restored, the cavalcade came thundering down to us, "What's the matter here-Colonel?" "Nothing, General." "Well, what's the trouble? It doesn't seem quite right to me." "Nor to me either, General." "Well, then, what's the matter with you?" "Nothing at all, General, as I said before. Only *we are in by inversion*, companies, as well as the regiment!" "By inversion?" "Yes, General. We *were* the extreme *left*. We *are now* the extreme *right regiment;* and my companies stand in line in the same manner!" "Well, Colonel, can you get your regiment back on its original line, as you were?" "Yes, General." "Oblige me, then, by doing so. Wait, if you please, till I resume my place, and then give your orders in a loud and distinct tone, so that all may hear; and when you are in position, I'll bring in the rest of the brigade." Obedient to the new orders, which were issued in as loud and clear a tone as was possible, our boys moved in a twinkling, and "rested in place." And then, such a town meeting again! With much countermarching, and indescribable confusion, and after long waiting on our part, the brigade was once more aligned. The whole affair brought forcibly to mind the trials of one of our Captains in the early days of our service. Worthy fellow that he was, getting confused one day at his inability, on drill, to handle his men "a la militaire," he gave gave them the easily understood order, "*Find your places, boys!*"

Again I straightened up to receive the general officers, who, after halting in front of the other regiments, came riding down upon us.

"This time, Col., we'll have a different movement! We'll advance by battalion, in echelon, at sixty paces, commencing the movement on the left;" and turning he rode away. Upon the receipt of the order "march," the 34th stepped forward. Turning to observe the alignment of the command, my ear caught the sound of a horse's feet, as the animal was nearing me, at a gallop. Lieut B——, A. D. C. saluting, thus addressed me. "The General's compliments, Col., and wants to know what you are doing." "My compliments to the Gen., Lieut., and tell him I am marching, as ordered;" and each of us rode our respective ways. The foot-beat of another galloping horse warned me of another approaching messenger, who put me the same question, and received the same answer. As he was wheeling to ride off, each of us saw Headquarters approaching at a rapid pace, and both of us rode forward. "How came you to be marching, Col.?" "Because of your order, General." "But *you* had no order, Col." "Excuse me, Gen., I thought I had. Your order directed a movement by battalion, in echelon, at sixty paces, the movement to commence on the left, and as the 34th was on the left, at the word march, I set my men in motion, as I ought." "No Col., you are all wrong; to have executed the movement *properly*, you should have advanced sixty paces, and *halted*; then the regiment on your right, should have moved sixty paces in advance of your new position, and halted in its turn, and so on through the line." "Pardon me, Gen., if I persist that I am right, as I could satisfy you, easily, if there was time." "You shall have time enough, Col.;—you will report yourself at Headquarters, this evening. And *now* you will halt, face about, and march your men in this direction; and when *you are where I want you*, I'll give you orders to halt." I was sincerely desirous of obeying, and had no idea of showing the slighest disrespect to my superior officers.

Impressed with the fact, that, under the new directions given us, I was to march my men to some unknown spot, in their then rear, I shouted to the regiment, far in front, the order, "*Right about, march!*" "What's that, Colonel; what's that order? There is no such order in the book!" "Oh, yes, General!" "No, Colonel, you can't find any such order in the school of the Battalion!" "But I can, General, in the school of the Company; and I have used it because it is adapted to the movement you directed." "Yes, but, Colonel, there is a proper way to do these things! You should have first halted your command; then faced it to the rear, and then taken up your march in this direction." "I have been taught, General, the very great importance of rapid movements by infantry. Had I ordered a halt, every officer would have attended, at once, to dressing his line; then at the "*About*," they would have done the same thing again; and so a good many minutes would have been wasted; whereas, by the order actually given, the march to the rear was taken up without the loss of a second of time, and the line was dressed while the march was progressing." While thus engaged in conversation, the regiment, in its new direction of march, reached and passed the ground we occupied, and the A. B. G., without indicating, in any way, the spot where he desired the regiment to be halted, rode away, leaving me to rejoin my command. And so, almost instantly, the previous scene was repeated. Staff officers galloped, as if for life, with the General's compliments and a desire to know what I was doing; to gallop back again, with my reply, that I was marching, having received no order to do otherwise. This brought matters to a crisis; and I soon received and issued the welcome order to "halt." The line was now re-established, and all of *us* were enjoying a *rest*, while the general officers were occupied in riding from the right, stopping at each regiment to exchange words with the officers at their head. Our turn came at length. "Colonel," said the A. B. G., as he reined up at my side, "on the whole, this has been a very satisfactory drill; but it is very hot this afternoon, and the remaining hours had better be devoted to Battalion movements!" "Do I understand by that, General, that the 34th is dismissed to my command?" "Certainly, Colonel; and I congratulate you upon having so splendid a regiment!" and he rode off to the head of his own old regiment. Under all the circumstances,— the excessive heat of the weather, and our own universally conceded superiority,—I felt no disposition to burden the boys with much battalion drill; so, moving to the shade of a neighboring grove, arms were stacked and the men allowed to rest. *Wells* now came up! "How are you, by this time, Colonel, and what have you been about? Where's your brigade drill? I have seen a movement or two by the 34th, as a battalion; and a good deal of running about, in a confused sort of way, by the other regiments; but *where is your brigade drill?*" The state of affairs, as above written, was explained to him. "And so the rest of the afternoon is to be devoted to battalion movements! But I haven't seen the 34th engaged in any, of late!" "Why, yes, Colonel, the 34th is now engaged in the important one of *resting.*" And so, lazily we spent the time, till suddenly Wells exclaimed, "You're in for it, Colonel!" and pointed towards the body of general officers who were dashing from the far off right, straight down upon our position. To seize our arms, and gain our encampment, at a double quick, was short work. Moving on to our parade, we stood at "open order" as the general officers rode up. Never did the boys appear to better advantage; and, as the parade was dismissed, mingling with the cheers of the men of the other regiments, could be heard the clapping of hands by the Generals and the officers accompanying them.

And so ended the day, for most of us; but not for me! My explanation was yet to be made at headquarters. While waiting for the pleasure of the General, I was a good deal amused at the comments upon the 34th, made by the different officers there assembled.

"For my part," said a Field Officer, "I think the great strength of the 34th is in their Battalion drills! Not only the officers, but each man seems to know the detail of every move-

ment! and even to anticipate orders before they are given."
"Yes," said another, "their Battalion drills are splendid; but, after all, their particular strong point is their skirmish drill; there's nothing like it! You haven't seen it? well, you ought to! from beginning to end not a word is spoken; but the whole line moves like machinery, at the mere call from their bugles. It's perfectly splendid! We'll ask the Colonel to take them out to-morrow." "After all," broke in another, a Staff Officer, "after all, admirable and excellent as the regiment is in its drill, it is on parade that it most excels. Nothing I have ever seen approaches it there! To-night, for instance, could ever anything be more perfect?"

I was now called to the presence of the General, who sat surrounded by his immediate military family. Saluting, I commenced my explanation. "No matter! no matter about that, Colonel," he broke in, "it's all right; you have got a splendid regiment, admirably drilled, and I only wish I had others half as good!" and so that matter ended.

8th. The weather to-day is excessively hot, and the men suffer much.

An order from Maj. Gen. B. F Butler, is just received, dismissing from his command, *Field*, late of our G, who was *discharged* from the 34th some time since, to enable him to accept a commission in the "Corps d'Afrique." The order directs that his discharge from the 34th be cancelled, and *he* be returned to duty with us in the ranks. Field, who has reported himself, has been informed that our claim upon him ceased, upon his being mustered out of the service as a private in our ranks; and that, as far as we are concerned, he is free to go where, and as, he likes; — unless he would like to re-enlist.

Deserters come in daily. They represent that there is no considerable force in the valley; everything having been sent to strengthen Lee.

Orders are out for our movement from here at 6 A. M. to-morrow. Our transportation is cut down to three army wagons, and, in consequence, everything not absolutely indispensible is sent back to Martinsburg.

10th. Yesterday, after we had literally stripped ourselves in consequence of the order reducing our transportation, and when they could be of no possible use to us, the teams taken from us a few days since were returned; but not as they went. We have managed, up to the present time, to retain *horses* with our wagons. Now, instead of them, we are furnished with *mules.* It's hard to tell whether these animals cause the most laughing or swearing. Our teamsters, sitting upon their boxes and drawing the reins over four good looking, well behaved horses, have worn a lordly air, as, cracking their long whips, and giving their leaders a gentle flick of the lash, they have rolled into camp at a rattling gait. You would not recognize them now as the same fellows, to see them astride the near wheeler, *yipping*, and *yahing*, and jerking the *one* line, in their attempts to get their teams somewhere near where they are wanted. Perhaps the shouts and halloos of the young devils, who, seeing their trouble in managing the teams, skirmish around the leading mules, first on one side, and then on the other, don't help the matter any. Be that as it may, nothing can deprive us of the fun we've already had from the change.

CHAPTER XXVII.

SIGEL'S CAMPAIGN.

MARCH TO STRASBURG — GENERAL ORDERS — WOODSTOCK — A HALT — TUMBLING CREEK — OUR SUTLERS — OUR CAMP — A QUEER STORY — ROAST VEAL — THE ASSEMBLY — A FORCED MARCH — AN ARTILLERY DUEL — IN BIVOUAC.

Strasburg, May 10th. At 6 A. M. yesterday, the 34th having the advance, the column moved out on to the pike, and at about 1 P. M. went into camp on the bank of "Cedar Creek," about two miles short of this village. The weather was oppressively hot, the road dry and dusty; water seldom met with; and take it all in all, the march illy conducted. Two of our men fell by the way from sunstroke. We drove with us our fresh meat; our hard tack is carried; and although we have in our train more than two hundred empty wagons, not an ounce of pork is transported. Meat from cattle driven during the day, killed at night, and eaten, at the farthest, the next morning, has already produced its inevitable results — diarrhœa.

We remain in camp to-day that the engineer company may rebuild the bridge over the creek, which was destroyed when Banks and Jackson were having their little trial of speed over this race ground.

Regimental General Orders appoint Lieut. A. C. Walker to be acting Adjutant, and assign Lieut. Woods, now serving as A. A. A. G. on the staff of Max Webber, at the Ferry, to the line, in Company H.

General Orders "Army Headquarters" direct battalion drill in every command, for this afternoon; and General Orders "Headquarters Infantry Division" prohibit "the beating of drums in camp or on the march;" and "Special Orders" same Headquarters, direct "that in future" reveillé and tattoo calls "shall be sounded by bugles; and *only* by the buglers of the 34th Massachusetts Infantry Volunteers."

Lieut. Macomber, with his Engineer Corps, has been busy all day tearing down a large barn, for material for his bridge; and a detail of three hundred axemen are now employed in cutting timber to be used for the same purpose.

Woodstock, May 12th. We broke camp yesterday, at 6 A. M., and moved on to the Pike, where we were doomed to stand till past 10 o'clock, that the rest of the column might precede us; we being assigned the duty of bringing up the rear. Notwithstanding the large detail ordered to the assistance of the Engineer Corps, the bridge was incomplete, and the stream was forded.

Soon after leaving Strasburg, a halt was ordered, that our supply train, with its accompanying drove of cattle, might come up and pass to the front. The strife between our drovers and the women and children by the wayside, the one to "gobble," the others to rescue from the draft, now a single cow, and now one or more head of young stock, was amusing enough. One ragged, dirty, gaunt, grizzly, bare-legged old woman afforded us (not in authority) special amusement, as she persistently followed,— now pouring loud lamentations over her loss, into the ears of every officer she could approach; and now, diving past guards, in the hope of separating from the drove, her "one pet lamb"— a scrawny old bull. The poverty of the animal plead more in her behalf than her tears or lamentations; and after a while her old bull was separated from the drove and turned back.

About a mile beyond Strasburg our advance disturbed a party of about twenty-five Rebels, engaged in undermining, for the purpose of blowing up, the stone bridge spanning "Tumbling Creek." No other effect was produced than to cause a halt, while the overhanging crest could be scouted. Rain fell in torrents from this time till we went into camp. Occasional shots were fired into the column by skulking bushwhackers on the roadside, but without injury to any in the command.

We are now being stripped again, for the work, whatever it may be, which is before us.

All Sutlers are ordered *back*, save *one for each Brigade*, to be designated by the A. B. G. thereof. In our case, the Sutler of the 1st West Virginia, a one legged man, with a two horse team, has been selected to accompany the column.

The rain still continues, but spite of it, and our contracted accommodations, we make ourselves comfortable.

We are encamped in a most lovely spot; and the view from our own Headquarters is beautiful, indeed. The Red bud, or Judas tree, with its mantle of flaming scarlet, contrasts with the clear white of the flowering Dogwood, upon the rich green background of oak and hickory foliage. At our feet are parked the wagons of our train; beyond, the horses of the Cavalry are revelling in a field of rye, now in full head; to the right, the beeves, upon which we are to subsist, are lazily chewing their cud of contentment, while every knoll and hillside is thickly dotted with the shelter tents of the men. The air resounds with the lowing of cattle, the neighing of horses, and the braying of mules. From afar, comes the shrill trumpet call; while from our own encampment the mellow bugle note falls upon the ear. Occasionally the hearty laugh of some light hearted "boy" is heard. Strange! not a bird is seen! nor has the note of one been heard!

12th. We still hold our position, and furnish guards for the posts to the rear.

A queer story is current this morning, in explanation of the dull, heavy rumble of moving wagons, which, first heard in the evening, was continued far into the night. It was understood yesterday that a "train was to be sent down the valley;" and in the afternoon, many teams were to to be seen winding along the different encampments, and drawing up, in long line, upon the Pike. By evening the head of this train had passed the guards immediately about the camp. The officer in charge of the post in our rear arrested the further progress of the train, and sent in *to us* for instructions. As he reported the train to be in charge of the Division Wagon Master, he was instructed to offer no obstruction to its further progress; and slowly it passed from sight. Soon the Chief Quartermaster, who had been accidentally delayed at Army Headquarters, rode up to the post and inquired for the train. Informed that it had passed on its way down the Pike, he dashed in pursuit, overtook, and caused its return to camp. It was *en route, without any escort.* Inquiring now into the circumstances of its setting forth, he learned that *a note,* to a casual observer, in his own hand-writing, directing the train to be put in motion, and stating that he, with an escort, would soon overtake it, had been delivered to the Wagon Master in charge, by a horseman wearing the Union blue. A neat little trick! which, but for its timely discovery, inasmuch as Mosby and McNeil and others are below us, would have cost us largely in animals and wagons; and would have given to the Rebels an amount of transportation which they are sadly in need of.

14*th.* The odor of roast veal greeted our nostrils in the early air of the morning; and the sight of three of our drummer boys, as they stood ranged in front of Regimental Headquarters, told us plainly the source of this addition to our mess table. Rather hard upon them! after a night's successful catering, to stand, and see others devour the fruits of their chase!

At Guard mounting, *three* Co's, Capt. Fox commanding, were detailed to seize, and bring into camp, some bacon and flour, discovered by a scouting party, concealed in a mill a few miles back from our encampment.

The quiet, which settled down upon us at their departure, was unexpectedly, at about 11 A. M., broken by the sounding of "the assembly," from our Bugles. There was arming in hot haste as the voice of the Col. was heard, ordering the Companies on to the parade, at double-quick. There was no waiting for ceremony. The line was hardly formed, when the order "*right face,*" was given; and filing on to the pike, and turning to the left, we headed up the Valley. Through the encampment; past the remaining Infantry, and Artillery; along the nearly deserted streets of Woodstock; beyond the advanced pickets; out into the enemy's country, we marched. On,— still on; officers and men alike speculating as to the object of the movement — our Col., grim and taciturn as death! Now the sun burned with intense heat; now the clouds poured their contents like a deluge. Heated by the rapidity of the march in the close, muggy air, without water in their canteens, the Boys began to falter. But, deaf to all expostulations, our Col. cries out, "forward." On,— still on; with no abatement in speed; no halt for rest, or to recover breath. For the first time our men fall out; and some of our officers falter,— but no halt is ordered! Still forward; past our friends of the 12th W Va., who, drawn up by the wayside, salute, and afterwards, give us a ringing cheer as we move by. The air is oppressively hot and close; the men are faint; and the ranks are getting thinned. Officers beg for water, their pride alone keeping them from falling out; but there is no sign of halting. "Mount Jackson" comes into sight;— is reached;— is passed; still our leader cries only *"forward!"* Still on;— beyond support; past hope of help, if help should be needed. Now, one Union soldier is seen, hurrying to our little column; soon another,— soon more; some dismounted, others upon horses blown, and covered with sweat. All, as they catch sight of our flag, hasten to its protection. What does it all mean? These men are of Boyd's (1st) New York Cavalry; our gallant companions in last winter's expedition, over this same route. Now Boyd himself appears; on foot — heated — and giving evidence of having had a "lively time." We are halted, that he may tell his story. He had been ordered, on the Wednesday previous, to make a detour through the "Luray Valley," and come into camp, on this day, (Saturday), at New Market. He had accomplished the first part of his order; and, attempting the latter part, saw, as he was descending the mountain's pass, spread out in the Valley at his feet, an encampment, which, from his orders to come into camp, at this place, (New Market), on this day, he took to be of our own force. Undeceived, he pressed forward. The enemy had, however, discovered him, and sent a force through the woods; which, passing his flanks, reached his rear, and barricaded the pass behind him. As he debouched from the gap, an overwhelming force was hurled against him. To advance was impossible, so great was the odds; to fight was madness:— Safety laid only in retreat. But the barricades in

21

his rear rendered this impracticable; and each trooper, left to his own resources, sought safety in the woods and under-brush of the side hills. What now were *we* to do? We had been hurried forward, under orders to "report to Col. Moore of the 28th Ohio Volunteer Infantry." We had heard nothing of or from him since we left our encampment. Boyd knew nothing of him. All our inquiries were futile. No one had seen, or if they had, would they acknowledge to have seen, any Union troops, other than our own little body. We were beyond support. While the men were resting, the staff rode out to reconnoitre; but nothing came of it. We could hear nothing of Col. Moore; and, obedient to our orders, resumed our march. The bridge, which spanned the north fork of the Shenandoah, was crossed. So reckless seemed the movement, that it was almost as if we left hope behind. As we rose the crest of "Rhude's Hill," the boom of distant Artillery was heard. Eyes brightened, and steps were quickened. A shriek over head,— and a dull thud, was heard, as a shell dropped along side the column, but doing no greater injury than splashing with mud some of the men of "I" and "B." A side step to the right, took us out of direct range. And while officers rode out to reconnoitre, the men rested upon their arms. A spiteful crack was now heard on our left, from which direction, Acting Adjutant A. C. Walker, was seen galloping towards us. He had come upon one section of Artillery, belonging to the Union army, posted upon rising ground to the left of the pike, but without support. We moved to its aid, and the men were allowed to rest, partially sheltered, in open timber to its rear.

A sharp, but short artillery duel now followed; the enemy's shot going over our heads, and striking far in our rear; while the shells from our pieces could be plainly seen to explode over the Rebel Battery. From the increasing darkness or other causes, the enemy's fire soon ceased; and, after some delay, the 34th was moved forward upon the hill where the enemy's guns had been posted. Advancing by regimental front, we entered the woods, and were halted. "A" and "G," Captains Willard and Leach, were thrown forward to picket our front, and upon the establishment of their line, the men were ordered to lie down upon their arms. No fires were allowed; the lighting of pipes, even, was prohibited; and, *without supper*, the command prepared to bivouac in the rain and mud, as, without dinner, it had made the march, in the rain and heat of the day. Nothing, save the rain, as it pattered upon the leaves, broke the profound silence. Such few orders as it was necessary to issue were given in whispers. Time—it seemed, in the anxiety and suspense, as if hours—passed. With no previous warning, a single shot was heard, a few scattering ones followed, and then a deafening volley broke the almost death-like stillness. With the first report the men sprung up, as they had laid down, *in line*. A whispered "what is it?" was heard in the ranks. Messengers who were quickly sent out, returned, reporting that our picket line was undisturbed—save by this fire in their rear. But, beyond this, nothing could be learned; and, after an interval of weary waiting, the men were allowed to lie down again. But not long did they remain undisturbed. As before, the single discharge, then scattering shots were heard, quickly followed by repeated vollies, this time the balls cutting small branches from the trees under which we were again standing. Who and what is it? was again whispered among us. An officer who had gone far to our left, in which direction the firing was heard, soon returned, bringing information that Col. Moore, to whom we had been ordered to report, and whom we had been vainly seeking all the day previous, in endeavoring to establish his picket line, on ground to our left, had, in the darkness, stumbled upon the Rebels, similarly engaged; and the fire was from the forces thus unexpectedly brought together. From this time on, the night passed quietly. Before dawn the command was roused, and stood to their arms; and about daybreak Capt. Fox reached us, with his foraging party, having marched all night to come up with us.

CHAPTER XXVIII.

SIGEL'S CAMPAIGN—BATTLE OF NEW MARKET.

Our arms were now stacked, rations issued, and preparation made for cooking breakfast. It was not eaten, however, before Col. Moore, in person, rode up and directed us to retire some two miles, and there form in line of battle. This route led us through fields of young wheat, the soft, sticky mud of which, nearly ankle deep, rendered the movement exceedingly fatiguing. Some of our boys lost their shoes in this mud, and thereafter fought and retreated in stockinged feet.

Our line was hardly formed in compliance with this order, when an A. D. C. brought directions that we should resume our former ground. When this was reached, Companies " B " and " I," Capt. Potter, commanding, were detached and sent as skirmishers to cover our front; and the remaining Companies were ordered to form across a neighboring ravine. While the regiment was occupied in this movement, the order was countermanded, and the Colonel was directed to re-occupy, with his entire command, the ground upon which we had formed our first line of battle. Capt. Potter was re-called from the skirmish line, where, ably seconded by Capt. Soley, he had so skilfully distributed and so admirably handled his small party, as to have checked the advance of the Rebel force, many times his superior. He overtook us on our retrograde movement and the regiment thus united, soon after formed in column of companies, on the right of the pike, about midway from Rhude's Hill to New Market. We were soon, however, deployed into line, to the right. At this point the pike runs nearly in a south-easterly direction. On its right, up to and beyond the Village of New Market, the country was much broken. High hills, heavily timbered, rise on the west of the village, which are intersected by deep and somewhat rocky ravines, running at right angles with the highway. On the left of the pike the ground, though rolling and somewhat broken, was comparatively easy.

In the early morning Col. Moore had "formed his command "along a high hill on the west side of the town, and checked "for a while the enemy's advance." "But Maj. Gen. Stahl rode up and assumed command." Sigel, also, arrived soon after. Moore now, in obedience to orders, fell back some eight hundred yards, to the rear of the position he had himself taken, and formed "the 123d Ohio and 18th Connecticut on the left of a cottage;" the "other two Regiments," 1st West Virginia and 34th Massachusetts, being detached and sent to "join their own Brigade, way in the rear." Thus weakened, but having a small supporting force of Cavalry, Moore held what may be called our first line; against which, Moore reports, "the Rebels "advanced, heralding their approach by their peculiar yells, "coming up in two strong lines, far overlapping my own; my "skirmishers were driven in, and after a short, but resolute "struggle, this line was forced to the rear, which created some "confusion in the 18th Connecticut, owing to knee deep mud, "out-houses and stables close to their rear, and the insufficient "number of officers to control their movements." Meanwhile the troops composing the 2d Brigade, which in reality formed our *only* line of battle, were placed in position, under the immediate direction of Gen. Sigel himself. "On the extreme right "were two Batteries (Snow's and Carlin's), close to the woods "reaching down to the river. Von Kleyser's on an eminence in "the centre, a little advanced; and Ewing's on a ridge, on our "extreme left; the Cavalry behind our right and left centre. "The 34th Massachusetts was formed first into line, its right "resting near the two batteries mentioned; then the 1st Vir-"ginia and 54th Pennsylvania. The 12th West Virginia was "ordered to form in double column, behind the right, and took "its position in rear of the 34th Regiment, as a reserve. One "Company of the 34th (C., Capt. Chauncey), was ordered to "cover our right flank, in the woods, towards the river; and "four or five companies of the 12th Virginia, mentioned above, "to protect the two batteries on the right." This line stretched along a ravine extending toward the pike, and was partially covered from the enemy by a hill, which, rising gradually, extended some distance in its front. While it was awaiting the advance of the enemy, the men of Moore's line came back "on "the double quick, some of them running through and over our "lines, nor stopped till they met and joined the 28th and 116th "Ohio, which two Regiments, under charge of Col. Washburn, "were left in charge of the train, and had been halted at Mount "Jackson, by some Staff officer."

The advance of the Rebels, before which Moore's line had given way, was steady and continued. The air was filled with bullets and bursting shells; but, as yet, *we* had sustained no harm. Colonel Wells took his position at the left, sending Lieut. Colonel Lincoln up to the right of the Regiment Now Company G, Capt. Leach, was detached, and sent forward as skirmishers to cover our front. "It went forward, deploying about 200 yards in advance, with a precision and steadiness never surpassed on drill;" but, upon reaching the crest of the hill, was recalled, and, passing through our lines, formed in rear of their proper place in regimental line. Spent bullets were falling thickly among and around us, but inflicting no injury. Now, from some unexplained cause, the 12th Virginia opened fire, over the heads of our men, causing the first casualties of the day; and it was only by the most active efforts of Gen. Sigel, and our own Lieutenant Colonel, who rode among their lines to aid their own officers, that the seeming demoralization of this command was checked, and order restored. A charge of the whole line was now ordered. *Our* men sprang forward with a cheer. Our dogs, of whom we had a small army, ran frolicking and barking before us, as they had so often done, on drill. Receiving the fire of both lines, they were nearly all killed. Here, at the very front of our advance, fell Lieut. R. W Walker, of A, as was then supposed, mortally wounded. We poured a rapid and well directed fire into the enemy; which, aided by the heavy enfilading fire from our artillery, checked his advance. For a moment he staggered, appeared to give way, and the day seemed ours. The rain was falling in torrents; and this, with the smoke, which settled down thick upon us, hid the field from observation. Gallant as was our own charge, the order had met with a feeble response on our left, where the troops, turning, went back, suffering little loss, and inflicting less upon the enemy. While Breckenridge was moving his main force against our front, Imboden galloped down on our left, and opened his artillery within point blank range. Exposed to this flank fire, the 54th Pennsylvania, after a short but stout resistance, was led from the field by its brave commander, upon his own responsibility.

An order to retreat came up to *us from the left*. We fell back slowly, and in good order; the men, as well as the officers crying out, "Steady! Keep your line! Don't run, 34th!" It was impossible to see to any considerable distance, so thick was the smoke and rain. Suddenly, Bacon's voice was heard, calling upon his men to stand by the colors; and in response to what was supposed to be a general movement of the line, the right companies were halted, faced about, and became again warmly engaged. A determined charge upon our front, and a withering fire poured into *our left flank*, and *rear*, from the now contracting lines of the Rebels, was too much. The Color Company turned; its gallant Captain received his death wound, and the companies of the right wing followed their comrades of the left, in retreat. Just at this moment our Lieutenant Colonel fell, severely hit by shot, and shell, and, unable to continue in retreat, was left in the hands of the enemy. Our troops kept on in slow and sullen retreat till they reached Rhude's Hill, some five miles from where the battle began. Here, meeting the troops which had not been engaged, and the cavalry which had not suffered in the battle, they were rallied. The vigor of Breckenridge's pursuit abated, and Sigel withdrew his force, crossing the Shenandoah, and burning the bridge behind him.

Col. Wells, of the 34th, tells the story with more minuteness, in the following official communication to His Excellency, Gov. Andrew:

HEADQUARTERS ADVANCE FORCES IN FRONT OF STRASBURG,
May 21st, 1864.

Saturday we broke camp, in the rear of Woodstock, and marched to New Market, a distance of twenty-one miles, in seven hours, and with but ten minutes' halt. Our force consisted of a small amount of cavalry, artillery, and infantry, under Col. Moore. We had a small artillery fight at New Market; and after dark, laid down in the woods occupied by the enemy. After some skirmishing, the enemy evacuated, and, by morning, had withdrawn entirely from our front. By nine o'clock, however, they began an advance in force.

Three Companies of the 34th, under Capt. Potter, were sent far forward, upon a commanding hill; and, by skilful deployment, led the enemy to believe our whole force was there. He massed heavy columns on the right; and with three lines of battle, and with much yelling, advanced upon the line, only to find it empty. This manœuvring gave us two or three hours' time, in which Gen. Sigel, with a part of the remainder of the army, arrived on the field. After considerable manœuvring, our line was formed, about where it was the night before—the Artillery on the right, on rising ground, resting on the river; the 34th in line, its right on the Battery, its left touching the pike; other regiments on our left, and *one* in column in our rear. In front was rolling ground, on the other slope of which were two regiments of Infantry, with Infantry and Cavalry skirmishers. The Rebels advanced in *three lines of battle;* each, I think, as heavy as ours, with masses on the right and left. The ground was perfectly open, not a tree or shrub to obstruct the view. Nothing could be finer than their advance. Their yelling grew steadily nearer, and skirmishers, our Infantry in front, came back on the double quick, some of them *running through and over my lines!*

The air was filled with bullets and bursting shells, and my men began to fall. I was ordered to deploy one company, across my front, as skirmishers; and Capt. Leach, with Company "G," went forward; and his groups halted and deployed in the tumult, about two hundred yards in advance; each man taking his exact interval, and deploying to the right, as steadily as on drill. The officers, in the line, were giving their orders in low tones; and every man stood, his gun at the ready, his finger on the trigger, waiting to see the face of his foe. It was a marvel to me then, and is now, how men, who almost never before had heard the Rebel yell, and the terrible din of the battle field, could be so entirely calm and self-possessed. Soon, our men in front were, by the confusion, cleared away, the Rebel lines were plainly seen, and the battle began. Our front fire was heavy; and the Artillery had an enfilading fire, under which their first line went down. They staggered, went back, and their whole advance halted. Their fire ceased to be effective. A cheer ran along our line, and the first success was ours. I gave the order to "cease firing." Just then, Col. Thoburn, Brigade Commander, rode along the lines, telling the men to "prepare to charge." He rode by me, shouting some order I could not catch, and went to the regiment on my left, which immediately charged. I supposed this to be his order to me, and commanded to fix bayonets, and charge. The men fairly sprang forward. As we neared the crest of the hill, the regiment on my left, which first met the fire, turned and went back, leaving the 34th rushing alone into the enemy's line. I shouted to them to halt, but could not make a single man hear or heed me; and it was not until they had climbed an intervening fence, and were rushing ahead on the other side, that I was able to run along the lines, and, seizing the color bearer by the shoulder, hold him fast, as the only way of stopping the regiment. The wings surged ahead, but, losing sight of the colors, halted. The alignment rectified, we faced about, and marched back to our position, in *common time.* I could hear the officers saying to the men, and the men to each other, "Don't run!" — "Keep your line!" — "Common time!" &c. On reaching our position, the regiment was halted, faced about, and resumed its fire. The path of the regiment, between our line and the fence, was sadly strewn with our fallen. Just as we halted, Lieut. Col. Lincoln fell. The loss of his invaluable services, and the impossibility of making my voice heard in the din, rendered it necessary for me to go along the whole line, to make the men understand what was wanted. The alignment perfected, and the men well at work, I was able to look about the field, and saw, to my surprise, that the Artillery had limbered up, and was moving off the field; and that the Infantry had gone, save one regiment, which was gallantly holding the ground, far to the left. The Rebel line advanced, until I could see, above the smoke, the battle flags on the hill where the artillery had been posted. I ordered a retreat, but they either could not hear or would not heed the order. I was finally obliged to take hold of the color bearer, face him about, and tell him to follow me, in order to get the regiment off the field. They fell back slowly, firing in retreat, and encouraging each other not to run.

But the Rebels were coming on at the double quick, and concentrating their whole fire upon us. I told the men to run, and get out of fire as quickly as possible, and rally behind the first cavalry line found to the rear. The colors were halted several times, by different officers, in positions where it was impossible to make a stand, and would only start again at my direct order. I felt much relieved on receiving an order from Gen. Sullivan, who was conspicuous on the field, that the line would be formed on the ridge, and no stand made before it was reached. I directed the color bearer to march directly there, without halting; and, after getting out of fire, rode to the rear, and went round into the pike, and towards the front, looking for stragglers. I saw none; and, meeting the colors, found most of the regiment with them. The new line was formed under the personal supervision of Gens. Sigel, Stahl, and Sullivan. The pursuit of the enemy was checked; and the command was gallantly withdrawn along the single road, and across the narrow bridge, into Mount Jackson, in most admirable order, and without a single casualty. That night we stood in line until about nine o'clock, marching, behind the wagon train, till six o'clock the next morning, and reached Strasburg about 5 P. M. of Monday, having been fifty-five hours almost continuously marching, or under arms, in a constant and pouring storm. The march in that time was fifty-two miles. I can only say for the regiment, that the coolness and gallantry of the officers filled me with admiration; and I cannot recall, without deep emotion, the cheerful endurance by the men of the extraordinary hardships of the march, and the spontaneous and hearty devotion with which they offered their lives to the country. The same willing and cheerful obedience which has always characterized them in camp, distinguished them in the field; while they added to it a fire and heroism which cannot be excelled. I cannot particularize, where all did so well. Conspicuous, only, perhaps, from their more exposed position, were Color Sergeant John E. Calligan; Corporal Pepper, bearer of the State flag, hit four times, and struck to the ground; Corporal Wishart, who took the colors from his hands, and bore them the remainder of the day; and Capt. Bacon, of the Color Company, who fell directly behind his colors, while keeping his ranks steady as on parade.

I am under deep obligations to Lieut. Col. Lincoln and Adjt. A. C. Walker for their efficient services and great gallantry on the field.

As many of the officers were on detached service, I subjoin a list of those on the field:

Col. George D. Wells; Lieut.-Col. Lincoln, (wounded and a prisoner); Surgeon R. R. Clarke; Adjt. A. C. Walker; Assistant Surgeon Smith; Assistant Surgeon Allen (left in care of wounded at Mount Jackson); Capts. Potter, Thompson, Fox (killed), *wounded and a prisoner;* Soley, Willard (wounded), Bacon (killed), Leach, Lovell, Chauncey (prisoner),; 1st Lieuts. Goodrich (wounded), Elwell, Ripley; 2d Lieuts. R. W. Walker, (killed), *wounded and a prisoner;* Ammidon (captured), Dempsey, M. E. Walker, Belser, Murdock (wounded), Kinnicutt (wounded); and Major Pratt, on Gen. Stahl's staff; Lieut. Bacon, on Col. Thoburn's staff; and Lieut. Macomber, in Division Pioneer Corps. Company C was sent off to skirmish on the right of the line, and lost half its numbers prisoners, together with its two officers. I believe these are the only men left unwounded in the enemy's hands. The detaching of this Company, with other details, left me about four hundred and fifty muskets in line. Of these, the casualties foot up over two hundred killed and wounded. *Five out of every six who went in have the marks of bullets somewhere.* Dr. Clarke has sent Dr. Dale a list of casualties, as near as can be ascertained. Our wounded, left behind, are very comfortable, and well treated.

I have to regret the loss of some of the most noble and gallant spirits of my command. Gen. Sigel was on his horse, on the right of our line, during most of the engagement, and in the hottest of the fire. How he escaped is a mystery to me. He has done the regiment the honor to compliment it in very high terms.

I have the honor to be, very respectfully,

Your obedient servant,

GEO. D. WELLS.

Col. 34th Mass. Infantry.

Hon. JOHN A. ANDREW, *Governor of Massachusetts.*

I add to this the following extracts from the Rebel General Imboden's official report of the engagement, as not without interest:

"Breckenridge now resolved to attack, and disposed his troops accordingly, placing the brigades of Echols and Wharton in the centre of his line, on the west of the turnpike, while McLaughlin, with the bulk of the artillery, occupied the highest ground of the bold ridge that runs parallel with the turnpike, and giving Imboden permission *to go ahead as he* deemed best, on the east of the pike. Accordingly, Imboden moved at a gallop, with a part of his force, to Smith's creek, down which he kept to the bridge on the "Luray" road, where he re-crossed to the west side, with two guns, and all his troops, except the 13th Regiment, which he sent down on the east side, as if aiming at Sigel's rear. The two guns were run up within point blank range of Sigel's left cavalry flank, and opened on him. Simultaneously, Breckenridge pressed forward. Sigel's entire line retired slowly. His artillery was especially damaging, and he (Breckenridge) determined to silence at least one, and the most mischievous, battery, directly in front of the centre of his line; and Col. Smith, of the 62d Virginia, and Col. Skip, with his Cadets, were ordered to charge and take it. When the charge commenced, the ardor of the Cadets took them across the ravine, a little in advance of the old veteran regiment. As soon as Col. Skip saw this, though then under cannister fire, he ordered his corps of boys to "halt," and "mark time;" which they did, till Smith came up; when the two Colonels gave the order to charge, and the battery was taken, but with fearful loss on both sides. The gunners stood by their pieces till bayoneted, and the 34th Massachusetts, under Lieut. Col. Lincoln, supporting the guns, fought hand to hand, till their gallant commander fell, as was supposed, mortally wounded; though he subsequently recovered whilst a prisoner.

"After the capture of these guns, Sigel commenced a slow and sullen retreat, reaching Rhude's hill, nearly five miles from where the battle commenced in the morning, late in the afternoon, and there offered a stubborn resistance.

"Breckenridge's infantry had nearly exhausted their ammunition, and he ordered the entire line to halt for nearly an hour, to enable the men to fill their cartridge boxes from the ordnance train, which was brought on to the field for that purpose. Meanwhile the artillery kept up a vigorous fire. Night was drawing on apace; and when Breckenridge was prepared to advance again, Sigel suddenly disappeared from Rhude's hill, and by the time the Confederates gained its summit, the rear of Sigel's army was crossing the bridge over the Shenandoah, at Mount Jackson, which he immediately fired and destroyed, thus baffling further pursuit.

"The victory of the Confederates was complete. Over fifteen hundred dead and wounded, with as many stands of arms, fell into their hands, together with six pieces of artillery. Their loss in killed and wounded was also heavy. The 62d Regiment alone, of Imboden's command, reported two hundred and forty-one killed and wounded, including seven of the ten Captains, three of whom were killed in the charge on the captured battery. The corps of Cadets lost eight, killed and four officers and forty-seven privates, wounded, out of a total force of two hundred and fifty engaged. Gen. Echols' casualties were nearly three hundred, including the Cadets, mostly wounded. The artillery did not lose over eight or ten, killed and wounded. Except the 62d Regiment, attached to Wharton's brigade, the casualties were small. And such was the case with the Cavalry. Six hundred would probably embrace all casualties; of which, less than one hundred were fatal. The losses sustained by Sigel were nearly three times as great, including killed, wounded, and captured, and arose chiefly from the larger force he had engaged."

The following figures from official sources will show how erroneous were Imboden's conclusions as to the strength of the opposing armies, and the comparative loss sustained.

The official reports made to Gen. Breckenridge, on the morning of the 16th of May, show the aggregate then present to be:

In Wharton's brigade, Infantry,	1309
" Echols' " "	1488
" North West, "	983
" Battalion Cadets, "	221
" Engineer Corps,	46
" McLaughlin's Artillery,	235
Total, Infantry and Artillery,	4282

Imboden, in his report, gives the total as: Infantry, 3440; Cavalry, 800; and, Artillery, 350, with 18 guns; total, 4590.

"Of this number it appears there were killed, 34; wounded, 484; missing, 13. Total, 531." "No casualty in the Cavalry."

A field report of a special inspection of the Infantry of Sigel's army, made at Martinsburg, *April* 25, 1864, and the latest at my command, gives as then present:

In Thoburn's Brigade— Officers,	77	Rank and File	1746
" Moore's " "	41	" " "	1625
Total,	128		3371

Or, in all, 3499. Deduct from this the 28th and 116th Ohio, which two regiments were not even on the battle field, 740;

and the 18th Connecticut and ·123d Ohio, 926, which, as Col. Moore reports, were literally "overrun at once by the overwhelming force of the enemy," and which, according to Col. Wells, "came back on the double quick," some time before the Rebel line struck Thoburn's little brigade, and there remains but 1,833 as the strength of the Union infantry actually engaged. I have no means of ascertaining the strength of our artillery engaged. A field return, under date of the 19th of May, gives it as 548, with 19 guns. The strength of the cavalry is also unknown. Whatever it was, it contributed little or nothing to avert the disaster to our arms. According to the official returns, the total Union loss during the day was: killed, 93; wounded, 482; captured, 70; and missing, 186; total, 831." Of this total, our own regiment sustained nearly one-third. Capt. William B. Bacon and 26 men died a "soldier's death" upon the field; Lieut. Col. Lincoln, Capt. H. P. Fox and Lieut. R. W Walker, with 32 men, were severely wounded and left in the hands of the enemy. Capt. C. R. Chauncey and Lieut. M. Ammidon, with 19 men, were cut off and taken prisoners. In addition, Col. Wells, Capt. Willard, Lieuts. Goodrich, Kinnicutt and Murdock, with 134 men, were wounded, but were able to make their way from the field with the command.

Writes Major Pratt, of the 34th, Acting Inspector General at the time, on the staff of Major General Stahl, second in command, and who, from his position, may well enough be believed to have had accurate information of the strength of *our own army:*

"We were compelled to fight under most adverse circumstances, and were therefore defeated. During the entire fight we had but 1500 infantry engaged, as we were unable to bring up the column then on the road; and this little force was attacked by at least 8000 of the enemy. Nor were these green troops, but veterans. 'T was a magnificent sight to witness the enemy as he came down from the heights, advancing in *three** splendid lines. I now remember that in the afternoon, during the thickest of the fight, while listening to the thunder of the Artillery and the rattle of the musketry, I imagined *you* all at church, or quietly at home, little dreaming of the murderous scenes being enacted in this beautiful valley. It is said by old and experienced officers that the entire war has witnessed no severer contest. In the 1st Infantry Division, out of 1500 men, all there was engaged, 781 were either killed or wounded. *Praise of the 34th is on the lips of all;* and the regiment deserves it; for

---

* Two, according to Imboden.

all accounts agree that it fought with a splendid daring and a cool courage, rarely equalled. Yesterday, Maj. Gen. Sigel, who commanded in person during the battle, and witnessed their conduct all through the fight, in a public speech, made at a flag raising, said, speaking of the 34th and its commander, Col. Wells, 'that it was the best regiment and had the best regimental commander he had ever seen.' I give his exact words. Capt. Bacon, who was killed, was only twenty-one years of age, I believe, yet he died like a hero. Standing by the colors, he refused to retreat when the order was given, and bravely died facing the foe.

"*Massachusetts never lost a better soldier, nor old Worcester a nobler son.*"

It will be noticed that Major Pratt falls into the error that Col. Wells did, of reporting the Rebel advance as made in three distinct lines; Imboden asserting that there were only *two*. The probable explanation is, that the line of advance being diagonal to our own line of formation, throwing the approach into an apparent echelon movement, had a tendency to mislead.

All accounts agree that the advance of the Rebels was in magnificent form. Imboden gives the 34th credit for gallant and persistent fighting, and Col. Wells compliments one regiment, (the 54th Pennsylvania,) for gallant conduct. The artillery was well served. How, then, came the disaster? First, Col. Moore, in his report, complains that, after being assigned to the command of the troops, on the 14th of May, he "asked for scouts or a reliable map of the Valley, as I [he] had no knowledge of the place at all; but nobody could furnish either." He also states, "that it was a great mistake, not to let him take the regiments of his own brigade," and complains that at the very commencement of the battle, his own force, vastly outnumbered by the enemy, was further weakened by "the 1st Virginia and 34th Massachusetts being detached from his own command, and sent to the rear to hunt up their own brigade." Altogether, Moore's complaint seems to be well grounded. Second, The true cause of the disaster seems to be found in the bad judgment which led to accepting the chances of a battlefield without any, or, at least, without sufficient preparation.

Moore was stripped of one half of his original command, and left with two small Regiments, insufficiently officered, to meet the first shock of arms; and the battle was fought, on our side, by one-half of our Army, already exhausted by the marching and counter-marching of the morning, while the other half were held, miles away, at the rear. True, Sigel supposed these troops were up and constituted his left wing, as he had ordered, and as had been reported to him. In fact, however, they were lying upon the ground, miles away, in charge of our train, by order of some Staff Officer.

The summary removal of Gen. Sigel from command, before any official report of the day's doings had been made, leaves it uncertain upon whom the responsibility for this condition of affairs should rest.

As will have been noticed in the report of Col. Wells, a last line of battle was formed at Rhude's Hill; from which, after some delay, our exhausted troops were skilfully withdrawn, in good order, and without loss.

Entering Mt. Jackson, the bridge over the Shenandoah, by which we crossed, was fired and destroyed; and further pursuit checked. Here a halt was ordered. The men ate their suppers while the injured were looked up, their wounds examined and dressed, and the slightly injured placed in ambulances for transportation. Those more severely wounded were disposed of in the hospital buildings in Mt. Jackson, and left under charge of Asst. Surgeon Allen, of the 34th. These arrangements completed, at about 9 P. M., the column was again put in motion, the 34th bringing up the rear. After a sad and tiresome all night's march, Edinboro' was reached about 7 o'clock the next morning. Here a two hours' halt was given the men, in which to cook their coffee and take the rest which was much needed. Then, resuming the march, it was continued till about 5 P. M., when camp was made on the hills overlooking Strasburg. Early the next morning we were again in motion; and having crossed Cedar Creek, rested on the ground on which we had encamped on our way up the Valley.

18*th*. Early this morning the 34th, Capt. Potter commanding, and the 12th West Virginia, Col. Curtis, with one section of Battery B, 5th U. S. A., and a squadron of Cavalry, the whole under command of Col. Wells, of the 34th, were marched back through Strasburg to Fisher's Hill, where we took up position; the Rebel pickets retiring before our advance. Our stay here was short, as, on the next day, orders reached us directing the entire force to fall back to Strasburg. We moved without delay, and took up the new position designated; the Battery occupying the old earthworks on the hill overlooking the town, and the Infantry pitching their tents about half way down the hill in the rear. Here a *scant issue of clothing* was made, the most needy, only, being supplied. Several deserters from the Rebel Army came in; and a few Guerillas were brought in during our stay in the place.

Major Pratt, who had been serving on the staff of Gen. Stahl, and who now was relieved to return to his command, was welcomed most heartily. Adjt. Woods surprised and gladdened all hearts by his unexpected appearance. Hearing of our losses, he resigned his position on Max. Webber's staff, and hastened to join his comrades. Of course he was restored to his old place on the Regimental Staff. We were reinforced, also, by the arrival of the officers and men whom we left behind at Martinsburg upon our first advance.

CHAPTER XXIX.

"GEN. HUNTER IN COMMAND"—GENERAL ORDERS NO. 29—INSPECTION—MARCHING ORDERS—A FROLIC—AN ADVANCE—OUR WOUNDED AT MT. JACKSON—RHUDE'S HILL—OUR STRENGTH—NEW MARKET—MRS. RUPERT—OUR DEAD—"THE FIELD"—FORAGING—HARRISONBURG—OUR WOUNDED—THE HOSPITAL—MARCHING ORDERS—PORT REPUBLIC.

22*d*. General orders of to-day announce that the command of this army is assumed by Maj. Gen. Hunter; vice Maj. Gen. Sigel, relieved. The iron hand of the new Commander is already felt, as his order, just issued, and which follows, shows:

HEADQUARTERS DEPARTMENT WEST VIRGINIA,
IN THE FIELD, NEAR CEDAR CREEK,
May 22*d*, 1864.

GENERAL ORDERS No. 29.

"It is of the utmost importance that this army be placed in a situation for immediate efficiency. We are contending against an enemy who is in earnest, and, if we expect success, we, too, must be in earnest. We must be willing to make sacrifices, willing to suffer for a short time, that a glorious result may crown out efforts.

"The country is expecting every man to do his duty; and this done, an ever kind Providence will certainly grant us a complete success.

"I. Every tent will be immediately turned in, for transportation to Martinsburg; and all baggage not expressly allowed by this order, will be at once sent to the rear. There will be but *one* wagon allowed to each Regiment, and this will only be used to transport spare ammunition, camp kettles, tools and mess-pans. Every wagon will have *eight picked* horses or mules, *two* drivers, and *two* saddles. One wagon, and one ambulance will be allowed to Department Headquarters; and the same to Division, and Brigade Headquarters. The other ambulances will be under the immediate orders of the Medical Director.

"II. For the expedition on hand, the clothes each soldier has on his back, with *one pair* of extra shoes, and socks, are amply sufficient. Everything else, in the shape of clothing, will be packed to-day, and sent to the rear. Each knapsack will contain *one hundred rounds* of ammunition. carefully packed; *four pounds* of hard bread, to last *eight* days; *ten* rations of coffee, sugar, and salt; one pair of shoes and socks, and nothing else.

"III. Brigade and all other Commanders will be held strictly responsible that their commands are supplied from the country. Cattle, sheep, and hogs, and, if necessary, horses and mules must be taken, and slaughtered. These supplies will be seized under the direction of officers duly authorized, and upon a system which will hereafter be regulated. No straggling or pillaging will be allowed. Brigade and other Commanders will be held responsible that there is no waste; and that there is a proper and orderly division amongst their men, of the supplies taken for our use.

"IV Commanders will attend personally to the prompt execution of this order, so that we may move to-morrow morning. They will see that in passing through a country, in this way, depending upon it for forage and supplies, great additional vigilance is required, on the part of every officer in the command of men, for the enforcement of discipline.

"V The Commanding General expects from every officer and soldier of the army in the field, an earnest and unhesitating support; and relies with confidence upon an ever kind Providence for the result. The Lieutenant General commanding the armies of the United States, who is now victoriously pressing back the enemy, upon their last stronghold, expects much from the Army of the Shenandoah; and he must not be disappointed.

"VI. In conclusion, the Major General commanding, while holding every officer to the strictest responsibility of his position, and prepared to enforce discipline, with severity, when necessary, will never cease to urge the prompt promotion of all officers, non commissioned officers, and enlisted men, who earn recognition by their gallantry and good conduct.

By command of

MAJOR GENERAL HUNTER.

CHAS. G. HALPINE,
    Assistant Adjutant General."

In our Brigade, one shelter tent, only, is allowed for the official use of both Adjutant General and Quartermaster. But it is graciously permitted to them to have such supply of pens, ink, paper and office blanks, as they can induce their clerks to carry in their haversacks.

In seasonable correspondence with these new orders, our knapsacks, packed as when they were sent back from Winchester, were brought up and delivered to us, at inspection to-day. To empty them of clothing, and repack them in accordance with the new order, was the work nearest our hands. That done, our clothing was packed in boxes and delivered to the Quartermaster for transportation to the rear.

26th. Orders issued during the past night directed the march of the army at 10:30 A. M. to-day. Just previous to getting under arms, an accident happened in the 34th which cast a gloom over the command. While waiting the order to "fall in," Corporals Blanchard and Hubbard of H engaged in a frolic, when the latter seized a musket which was supposed to be unloaded, and, levelling it at the former with a playful remark, pulled the trigger. The piece was discharged, and the ball entering Blanchard's forehead near his right eye, killed him instantly. He died with hardly a moan.

29th. Woodstock. We have been encamped just outside the village for the last two days. This morning at 5 o'clock we broke camp and resumed our advance up the valley. We halted at Mt. Jackson long enough to enable the boys to exchange greetings with our wounded in hospital there. Most of them, we were glad to find, were doing well. A goodly number of those left there by us on the night of our retreat from New Market, had been removed to hospitals, or prisons further south. Dr. Allen had gone up to Harrisonburg to look after those of ours who had been sent up there.

We reached "Rhude's Hill" early in the afternoon, and made our bivouac near where we formed our last line, and made our final stand on the 15th inst. Many solid shot and shells, the latter unexploded, were *lying around loose.* The body of "Boston Bar," the Colonel's old bay, was easily recognized.

Here we were *mustered;* our rolls showing present for duty:

Officers, twenty-one; enlisted men, six hundred and four. Prisoners of war — officers, six; enlisted men, sixty-six. Absent, sick — officers, three; enlisted men, one hundred and forty-five. Died in action, or of wounds received — officers, one; enlisted men, twenty-six.

June 3d. New Market. We have gone over the battle-field, near this village. Many of our wounded still laid in the barns and out-houses near where they fell; others have been taken into the town where they could be better cared for by the humane among the citizens. Some of them have found a ministering angel in a *Mrs. Rupert,* who, almost alone of the ladies of the village, has been untiring in her deeds of kindness. In a slight hollow of the field, the bodies of our dead, thrown indiscriminately into a pile, and but partially covered with earth, presented a sickening sight. Feet, arms, and heads, were protruding at all points of this festering mass. The body of Capt. Bacon, lying, as he had fallen, among his men, was readily identified, and was removed and buried in a separate grave. A suitable mound was reared over the remaining brave. The grove of cedar trees standing in rear of the ground which our regiment held, and the huge oak on the right of our line, gave impressive evidence of the fury of the storm against which we had endeavored to stand. Hardly an inch of the trunks of these trees but showed the scars of bullets; and the stumps of the great limbs, which had been shot from the oak, gave terrible proof of the awful artillery fire directed against us. During our short stay here, the regiment was sent on a foraging expedition into the neighboring country, and brought in ten head of beeves, sixty-six sheep, five good horses, and two wagon loads of wheat, corn, and flour. This, as *official purveyors,* by virtue of general orders, under the authority of the General commanding, and for the benefit of the column. *Something* was confiscated for individual account, of which no particular return was made. While here news reached us that a supply train from Martinsburg, destined for our column, was "gobbled" by Harry Gilmor, while on its way through "Newtown;" and among those of "ours" captured, was Lieut. Platt, of K. Poor fellow! he will find Dixie a hard road to travel.

We received reliable information, also, that Bigelow and Pellisier, of E., who "fell out" on our march hither, were captured by some prowling bushwhackers, and shot; though this shooting proved not to be correct, as they subsequently returned to their Company.

June 3d. Harrisonburg. Breaking camp at New Market yesterday, at 5 A. M., we marched through the village to the music of our Band; our men exchanging cheers with such of their wounded comrades as were able to drag themselves to the doors, or windows of their temporary hospitals. A march of about twenty-two miles brought us to this place, which we reached at about 5 P. M. Our advance charged upon, and drove Imboden's rear guard from the village. We found here Lieut. Col. Lincoln, and 2d Lieut. R. W Walker, of the 34th, and about ninety of our army, more or less disabled by wounds received on the 15th ult. They were under the care of Assistant Surgeon Allen, of the 34th. We also found about 150 Rebel wounded; our advance having been too rapid to allow of their being removed. A Provost guard was at once established, and strong Patrols detailed to search the village for stores of any kind which would replenish our commissariat. The special order of the General commanding, exempted from this search, the houses of such of the citizens, as in return for their kind attentions to our wounded, had been given protection by Col. Lincoln. Conspicuous among them were the families of Col. Asa S. Gray, by whom our wounded had been fed and kindly nursed; Dr. Geo. K. Gilmer, a Mr. Lewis, and Mr. Baker; the last, our old acquaintance of last Winter's campaign. We secured a considerable quantity of flour, bacon, wheat and tobacco. A printing press, with its font of type, was unearthed from its hiding place in the ground, where it had been buried. This, because of the rank treason of its owner, was destroyed.

The hospitals were visited by Departmental, Division, and both Brigade Headquarters. Our wounded were found to be suffering for want of supplies of every kind. No medicines, no bandages, nothing, in fact, which their condition required, had been at any time furnished by the Rebel authorities. They were dependent upon the generosity of a few warm hearted

Union families for every article of food consumed, save, in the language of the country, coarse "sheep meat." And, except as tender-hearted ladies contributed articles of underwear to be torn up for bandages, they had none. An ample supply of stores,* such as tea, coffee, sugar, rice and flour, from the Quartermaster's stores, and a liberal contribution of the most indispensible articles from the medical department and the Sanitary Commission, was left for their use. Also, boots, under clothing, and a uniform complete for each of their number. The Rebel hospital was also visited, its inmates paroled, and their wants, not only present, but prospective, amply provided for.

Better than all these supplies, however, so far as good effect upon our wounded was concerned, was Gen. Hunter's solemn assurance that upon his arrival at Stanton, he would send a train of ambulances, in which those poor fellows should have transportation back to Martinsburg—a promise he failed to keep—as he sent it to our lines by way of Beverly. It may well enough be added here, that life went out with some, as day by day, hope of release vanished.

During the stay here, there was much signalling, with rockets, from the high ground at Headquarters. There was hope, in this way, of opening communication with Generals Crook and Averill, both of whom, it was thought, might be in the neighborhood of "Stanton." No answering signals were seen, however. Instead of the hoped-for messages from these officers, we were given reliable information that our direct route to Stanton was blocked at "Mt. Crawford," about seven miles distant, where strong earthworks had been thrown up, behind which no inconsiderable force of Rebel soldiers lay encamped.

4th. We resumed our march at 5 o'clock this morning, moving through the village, to the music of our several bands and drum corps. Many citizens followed the column, moved

---

* On the following Tuesday, a party of Rebel soldiers, commanded by one who announced himself as Capt. Jourdan, and who claimed to belong to General Rosser's Brigade, entered the hospital and robbed it, as they had previously the one at New Market, of all the chloroform, morphine and quinine it contained; all the spirits, sugar, coffee, they could carry off in their blankets; besides boots and articles of under clothing, and an entire uniform suit for each man of the party.

perhaps partly from curiosity as to the exact route we might take, and partly from anxiety as to the fate which was in store for us; some, confessedly for plunder, which they hoped to secure along the line of march. Very soon after leaving Harrisonburg, the column was sub-divided; the cavalry and artillery keeping along the pike, as if with the purpose of marching directly against the earthworks at Mt. Crawford; one column of infantry diverging to the left, while ours was urged rapidly toward, and over the old battle ground of Cross Keys, and so on to "Port Republic." On the march we overtook and burned a train of wagons, which, loaded with material of war, had been driven from Harrisonburg, as we approached that place. Very curiously, the authorities there had thought it best to remove the records and public papers from the various county offices, and had had them loaded upon these wagons. Of course they were destroyed in the general burning.

At Port Republic, a large establishment, occupied for the manufacture of clothing for the Rebel army, was burned. With the building a large amount of clothing was destroyed.

At this place we crossed Middle River, upon a bridge thrown over it by our Pioneers. Then fording a small creek, we marched through a small village, and went into camp about a mile and a half beyond, in the direction towards Stanton. It was late when we reached the ground on which we were to bivouac. The rain was falling in torrents; and this, and the darkness of the night, and the absence of our train, which was behind somewhere, rendered our condition anything but pleasant.

CHAPTER XXX.

HUNTER'S EXPEDITION.

BATTLE OF PIEDMONT—A MAN OF E—TWO OF F'S MEN—A GALLANT AFFAIR—STANTON—PROPERTY DESTROYED—COL. WELLS, A. B. G.—DETAILS OF OFFICERS.

5th. Reveillé was sounded at 4 o'clock this morning, and about an hour afterwards we were in motion. Crossing the road, we moved in the direction of Stanton; the 1st brigade on the right, the 2d (ours) on the left, marching across the fields, and through the woods, leaving the roads to be occupied by the cavalry and artillery, which had now rejoined us. The enemy was soon in sight, and there was much manœuvring for position, on the part of the infantry. The cavalry soon became engaged; and the artillery opened fire, though at long range. About 7 o'clock we sent forward a strong line of skirmishers, which pressed the enemy sharply. He advanced in turn, to the music of the Marsellaise Hymn, beautifully rendered by his bands. His artillery had got our exact range, and the action soon became general. We gradually gained ground. The enemy fell back slowly towards Piedmont. Here we found his main force strongly entrenched behind rail barricades. Now he concentrated his strength against the right of our line, and pressed it hard. Our brigade was moved over to its support. Upon nearing the enemy, the 34th "was detached from its brigade, and ordered to move, by the left flank, through the fields, to a hollow,—then to advance in line, facing the woods occupied by the enemy." This movement threatened the enemy's flank. As we, having gained the hollow, raised the crest of the hill beyond, a volley was poured into us, which killed four, and wounded others, among whom was our color bearer, Sergeant Calligan fell; but Corporal Hubbard seized the colors before they touched the ground, and they were gallantly borne by Corporal Wishart during the remainder of the day. Here, at scant twenty yards distance, we delivered our fire, and with a cheer, rushed on. The enemy broke back into the woods, in some confusion; our line advanced cheering, and the day was seemingly ours. But the enemy rallied, and renewed his fire with great fury. Here we had a fair stand up fight for about twenty minutes, when suddenly a heavy fire broke out on our left, against which a strong force was being brought forward. This was the enemy's reserve. Approaching down an open road, across which our two left companies now extended, it poured a withering fire into our very faces *In less than five minutes, we lost our Major, Adjutant, senior Captain, and fifty-three men killed or wounded.* An oblique fire was turned upon the enemy, by other of our companies, and a part of the 54th Pennsylvania, which was itself engaged in front, and his advance was checked. Again it was a fair fight, between the two lines, for about fifteen minutes, when the enemy broke, our men dashed ahead with a cheer, and carrying the barricades, the work was done. Our line re-formed, we were ordered into the next piece of woods, where we remained during the night. In this affair, Company I, which early in the morning had been detached, and sent out on the skirmish line, was not engaged with the regiment.

The loss to the Union arms was four hundred and twenty. Of this, the 34th had thirteen killed, and ninety-seven wounded. Companies B and D of the extreme left, together losing fifty-four men. Over 1000 of the enemy, and sixty officers, among them Gen. Vaughn, were captured, Major Gen. Jones, commanding, being killed. Among our own wounded were Major Pratt, Capt. Potter, Adj't. Woods and Lieut. A. C. Walker, (both of whom subsequently died of their wounds, the latter in the enemy's hands,) and Lieut. Ripley, who received a beautiful wound on the nose, from a flying piece of shell. Late in the afternoon, a train with supplies from below, and a small mail, reached us.

An incident or two may, perhaps, be worth relating.

At New Market, one of E's men left the ranks, and made his way hurriedly to the rear. As he bore upon his person no marks of the fight, and could give no satisfactory explanation for leaving the field, charges of "cowardice in the face of the enemy" were preferred against him. He had been regarded as one of our best men. He was too good a man to lose, at any rate, by verdict of court-martial. So he was called to headquarters. "Well, H——, how's this? I am sorry to hear such report of you. I need not tell you of the serious consequences of such conduct—disgrace to your friends and the regiment, and death to yourself! What have you to say?" "Not much, Col.! not much! But still, I'm not to blame." "Not to blame! What do you mean?" "Why, Col., I had on a new pair of shoes that day; and, do all I could, I could not make them stand still; they would run away!" With an admonition to get rid of the shoes as quick as possible, as such conduct would not be overlooked again, poor H—— was dismissed; and the wisdom of the course was shown by to-day's trial, when the man stood and charged, in line, as gallantly as the most lion-hearted among us.

F, also, had a somewhat similar experience with two of its men, D. F. C——, and A. C——, brothers; recent recruits; great stalwart fellows, whom any officer would regard as an acquisition to his command. At New Market, these fellows were among the missing. The time and the manner of their going was unnoticed. They returned to their Company the next day; one without his musket, the other minus his equipments. The story they told, although unsatisfactory, could not be disproved. So they were dismissed, with a warning that they would be closely watched in future, and would be shot down on the spot, upon any attempt to steal away from any engagement. Notwithstanding the warning, A. C—— was found to be missing early in the engagement of to-day. D. F. C——, however, still kept his place. But at that critical and exciting moment, when the enemy was pressing his attack upon our left so vigorously, and every officer along our whole line was exerting himself to the utmost to hold it unbroken, Lieut. Belser was heard to shout, "There goes C——! d—n him!"

and way in the rear could be plainly seen the form of C——, as he leaped over the ground in his race from death. With a word of caution to his junior, Lieut. Elwell darted in pursuit. But he was heavily handicapped; his short legs beneath his full, round body, had no chance in a race with the long limbs and sinewy form of his runaway friend, who was leaping away like a deer. So, coming to a stop, Elwell drew his pistol, and, *aiming low, fired.* Although unhurt, C—— stopped, and, turning, walked back to his officer. "Are you wounded?" asked E. "No, Lieut." "What were you going to the rear for, then?" "I feel sick, Lieut.; so sick that I can hardly stand up!" "Not so sick but you can run away, though!" And taking C—— by the collar, Lieut. E. run him up to, and through, our lines, and about two rods in advance of his Company. Here, standing by his side, the Lieut. talked *strong;* while poor C—— loaded and fired, till, the Confederates giving way, both joined in the final charge which decided the fate of the day.

At a later hour, among a group of officers who were discussing the incidents of the day, was Lieut. Col. Linton, of the grand old 54th Pennsylvania. Slapping Lieut. E. on the shoulder, and leading him forward, he thus addressed Gen. Sullivan: "Here, General; here's an officer who ought to be made a Brigadier General!" and then related the affair with C——, which he had witnessed. "Yes," growled Sullivan, with all the superciliousness which distinguished him! "Yes; he hid behind the other man, didn't he?"

It is only to be added, that on the 18th day of the following July, this man C——, was "killed in battle" at Island Ford. Peace to his ashes! If he wasn't a gallant soldier, he poured out his life-blood beneath the Flag, and in support of the Government, in whose service he had enlisted.

His brother deserted on the 30th of the same month, and was never heard of afterward.

6th. The first work of the day was to collect and provide for the wounded; and gather, and appropriate or destroy, such trophies of our yesterday's victory, as remained upon the field. For this last work a Company of the 123d Ohio was detailed;

and inasmuch as our transportation was limited, the order required them to destroy all small arms found on the field. Muskets and rifles to the number of 1,250 were collected and disposed in alternate layers upon piles of rails; and the whole fired. Although repeatedly cautioned to lay the pieces so that their muzzles would point in the same direction, the men became careless, and some of them were seriously wounded by the discharge of the arms.

When this work of destruction was ended, our march was resumed. The 34th again brought up the rear. No opposition was offered to our progress, and we entered Stanton at about 6 P. M. Marching through the village, *our* men halted in a field of rich young clover, the two essentials of a soldier's life, running water and a nice rail fence close at hand.

The beautiful grounds and extensive buildings of the State Asylum for the deaf and dumb were occupied for hospital purposes.

The next morning, early, we were again upon the road; but after going about eight miles, getting reliable information that Gens. Crook and Averill were near Stanton, we countermarched and re-occupied our camp ground. About two hundred of our wounded were brought up from the battle field of Piedmont, and placed in hospital here. Among those too severely wounded to be moved was Lieut. A. C. Walker, of ours, who lingered till the 14th, when he died.

8th. We have been busy, all day, in searching the town for "contraband of war;" seizing and bringing into camp provisions of every description, including tobacco; and destroying all public property stored in the place, as well as the buildings used for manufacturing clothing or supplies of any kind for the enemy. Generals Averill and Crook reached the place to-day, and encamped their commands near by. To use the language of the natives, "*there's a right smart chance of Yanks in town.*"

Col. Wells is assigned to the command of the 1st Brigade, vice Moore, of the 28th Ohio, who returns with his Regiment, its term of service having expired. Our prisoners, such of our wounded as can bear transportation, and a long train of wagons are to be sent to our lines under escort of his command. In consequence of this change in command of the Brigade, the 34th, now under Capt. Thompson, is transferred to the 1st Brigade, in place of the 18th Connecticut, sent to the 2d. Thus we enjoy the gratification of seeing our Colonel's services rewarded, and of being under the command of an able soldier. Major Pratt will remain with the column; riding, for the present, in an ambulance. Adjutant Woods, wounded in the shoulder, will go home on sick leave; so will Capt. Potter. General Orders assign Lieut. Bacon to the Brigade Staff, as A. A. A. G.; and Lieut. and R. Q. M. Howland, to be A. B. Q. M. Lieut. Ripley is detailed as Acting Regimental Adjutant.

CHAPTER XXXI

Hunter's Raid.

THE WORK OF DESTRUCTION — ON THE MARCH — LEXINGTON — PROPERTY DESTROYED — REINFORCEMENTS TO BRIGADE — ON THE ROAD AGAIN — RATIONS — THE BLUE RIDGE — PEAKS OF OTTER — LIBERTY — ON THE ROAD.

10th. The work of destroying public property, tearing up railroad tracks, and the banks and locks of the canal, and gathering in provisions, and such articles as will be of value to the army, has given employment to our Boys, and those of the other commands, since our arrival. So that the enemy was despoiled, it mattered little what became of the property! Hence the men have had no hesitation in appropriating to their own use, whatever would contribute to their personal comfort.

We had been on short allowance of tobacco, for instance, for many days; and all, who used "the weed," in any form, laid in a liberal supply. No one perhaps was so greedy as Finn, of A, who, in his anxiety lest he should be on short rations again, emptied his knapsack of every article it contained, and packed it full of what, to him, was better than "victuals and drink."

The work of destruction having been completed, we started again at five o'clock this morning, on our march up the Valley. The army was divided into three separate columns. Averill moving on the left or eastern route; Crook on the western or right; while Hunter marched on roads between the others

Our destination is understood to be Lexington; distant about 36 miles from Stanton. Our route is through a most beautiful country; extensive fields of luxuriant wheat bordering each side of the roads. As we advanced, we came upon, and passed several camps, which the enemy had but just abandoned, and captured a few of his straggling soldiers. A supply train of two hundred and fifty wagons, which had succeeded in getting through from Martinsburg, overtook us on our day's march. Inasmuch as it brought, among its other good things, a large mail, we were doubly glad to see it. Reaching Fairfax, eighteen miles from Stanton, we encamped.

11*th*. Reveillé was sounded at 4 A. M., and at five, we were again in motion. Our Artillery, Cavalry, and train occupied the Pike. The 1st Brigade moving across the country on the right, and the 2d Brigade on the left, in lines parallel with the highway, tramp through wide fields of grain, so luxuriant in growth, as to hide from view the bodies of the foot soldiers. Nothing but the gleaming lines of steel betray the presence of an armed body. Nearing Lexington, and when within a few miles of it, we heard the sound of rapid Artillery firing. It came from Crook; whose men, marching by a different route, had come in, in our front. After a short engagement, the rebels hurriedly retreated, and crossing the River, (James) destroyed the bridge which spanned it. We made our bivouac on the north side of the river, near its bank, about a mile outside the town.

12*th*. About 10 A. M. orders reached us, directing our crossing of the river, and march into, and occupation of, the town. We made our camp on the hill east of the Military Academy. The work of destruction was going on as we marched in. Nevertheless we were directed to try our hands at it. Several large mills,— many warehouses, with all their contents,— the gas works, arsenal, magazine, were fired and wholly consumed. The Military Institute,* home of the Cadets, our gallant little enemies of New Market, with its library, and all the buildings connected with it, were fired and burned to the ground. The beautiful private residence of Governor Letcher was also destroyed. Washington College was raided upon, and despoiled of the beautiful marble statue of Washington, which ornamented its halls; upon what principle, it was difficult to tell, as it

---

* Our troops were fired upon from this building,

neither could give aid and comfort to the enemy, nor be of any service to our arms. Till now, this region had known nothing of the ravages of war. Neither party has occupied it, nor has it before been even visited by our forces. Of course the lamentation on the part of the white population, is both loud and deep. The negroes, on the other hand, are wild with joy, and throng our camps, giving information and proffering assistance. Many of them engaged as officer's servants; others followed with the command, actuated by the hope of a successful escape into our lines. Within sight of our encampment, are to be seen fields of wheat, the yield from which, except that our horses and mules are turned upon them, to graze, would seem to be enough to supply the wants of Lee's entire army. Lovely indeed, almost beyond conception of those who have never seen it, is this whole region!

13*th*. The weather has been pleasant since we started on this expedition. It continues delightful; though the morning air is somewhat cool. We have had an accession to the strength of our Brigade; the 152d and 161st Ohio having been added to it. The work of destruction still goes on. To-day, among other property, seven canal boats, loaded chiefly with produce, but bearing some ammunition, and having upon their decks five pieces of artillery, were captured, fired and burned. Gen. Duffee, of Crook's command, joined to-day. He has scouted to within seven miles of Lynchburg; has cut the Charlottesville Railroad in several places; and run into Imboden, capturing from that officer some eighty prisoners, five pieces of artillery, not far from 300 wagons, with many (rumor has it 700) horses and mules; blown up several locks upon the James River Canal, and destroyed a considerable number of boats, some of them laden with ammunition. *We* found and destroyed a printing press, which had been buried in the woods.

14*th*. Marching orders were received at two; and line was formed at five, although we did not actually move till six o'clock this morning. Crook has the advance; and our division guards the train, which is very large. We take with us, in our wagons, in place of hard tack and meat, the beautiful statue of Washington, removed from the college here. Some of us think that food for the body would be more legitimate spoils of war. We are aiming for "Buckhannon," which is twenty-four miles from "Lexington." The road is rough, crooked and rocky, with occasional deep holes, which cause us no little trouble, and considerable delay. Our route led us within two miles of the *Natural Bridge*, but there was no time for hunting or examining curiosities. The bridges which spanned the creeks were guarded by small parties of Rebel soldiers, and were invariably fired at our appearance. Generally, our advance was near enough to prevent their destruction. We came in sight of Buckhannon at about 8 P. M. The infantry crossed the river in boats; the cavalry and artillery forded, losing several mules and wagons, in the darkness. "We are now in a wild and mountainous country. The scenery along our route is beautiful beyond description." The land, although generally in a pretty good state of cultivation, is apparently less productive than in the lower part of the Valley.

"Our *hard tack* is now *all gone;* flour is getting scarce, "though we still have beef and mutton in plenty."

15*th*. Again early on the road; reveillé having roused us at 4 o'clock. "The weather has been very hot, and we have "suffered much. We are crossing the Blue Ridge. The "scenery along the route is magnificent; mountain is piled "high upon mountain. Far above our heads, we catch occa- "sional glimpses of the moving column, the heavy rumbling "of the artillery carriages coming to our ears, like the low mut- "tering of distant thunder; far below us, we see the wagon "train, as it winds along its slow and heavy way. The road, in "places, is very narrow, and its windings short and sharp; and "several of our wagons went down the almost precipitous sides "of the mountain, while the drivers were endeavoring to make "the passage, near the summit." Here and there, upon the road, laid stretched the body of a dead Guerrilla, shot by our advance, while ambushed for their devilish game of bushwhacking. It was matter of great surprise to us, that so little obstruction was made to our passage; so steep was the ascent of the mountain, and so narrow and difficult the road. A small and resolute band would have found it easy work to have held at bay, in the Gap, our whole column. Bubbling up from the mountain top, and from places on the pathway up its side, were springs of delicious water, which gave us much needed refreshment.

We made our night's bivouac in the gap between the "Peaks of Otter." The men were completely tired out, although our day's march had been only eleven miles. Spite of General Orders, there has been a little foraging on private account; and though our teams are behind, we shan't all suffer for want of something eatable.

16th. Reveillé again before daylight, and we on the way soon after. The road *down* the mountain was rough and uneven, which made our march very tiresome. By afternoon we reached Liberty, and passing on about five miles, came to the river. Here again, as at so many other streams, the bridge had been burned; and the Infantry crossed on a narrow foot-bridge, while the Cavalry, Artillery, and train, forded. Our march to-day was about fifteen miles, and having made the crossing, we encamped for the night. Our advance destroyed several bridges, and many miles of track of the Virginia and East Tennessee Railroad, which runs through this place. As we entered the town, we heard the sound of cannonading — proof that Averill was up with the enemy.

CHAPTER XXXII.

Hunter's Raid.

Lynchburg — Rebel Telegrams — An Engagement — Our Loss — A Retreat — Less than Half Rations — Great Suffering — Salem — March Interrupted — The Train Cut — Some One Had Blundered — A Rest.

17th. Reveillé was sounded at 3.30 this morning, and our march was taken up without delay; a part of our wagon train, under escort of two one hundred days' regiments, having been first detached and ordered to the rear. Soon after leaving camp we came up to another bridge which had been fired. Here we were delayed some four hours while the Pioneer Corps were repairing the damage. About 2 P. M. we came up with Crook and Averill, whose columns were halted and were waiting our arrival. We had a good deal of skirmishing all day, and, when within about four miles of Lynchburg, found the enemy in strong force. Averill opened upon them with his guns, but was forced to fall back upon Crook, who was posted strongly in a piece of woods, and who in his turn charged, drove the enemy back, and took from him two twenty pounder Parrotts. We heard, at intervals during the afternoon, the screeching of locomotives and the rumbling of cars as they were rolled into the city. These noises, and the loud hurrahs of the men in the enemy's lines, gave plain indication of the arrival of reinforcements. If this is true to any considerable extent, our work, hard enough before, will be still more difficult. Meanwhile, we have made our bivouac on the ground occupied by the Rebel Artillery, part of whose pieces were taken. Our pickets are within speaking distance of the Rebel line. We can hear the noise of their chopping parties, and are kept from sleep by the firing which is quite brisk between the men of the two lines. The enemy's skirmish line is made up of sharp-shooters, many of whom, armed with long range rifles, and concealed in the tree tops, do severe execution.

Slow as has been the advance of our army since it left Stanton, the Rebel Gen. Breckenridge, during the entire time, seems to have been singularly at a loss as to its whereabouts and probable destination, as the following telegrams, copied from Gen. Breckenridge's order book, found and taken at Lynchburg, at our occupation of that place, subsequent to the "surrender at Appomatox," will show.

On the 9th inst., he, then at Lynchburg, telegraphed Gen. Lee at Richmond, that:—

"'Crook and Hunter have united; are said to be strong, with great deal of Artillery;'—and from Rock Fish Gap, on the 10th, to Gen. Imboden. 'Do not allow your communications with my main body to be interrupted;'— and to Major Harry Gilmor, 'Report to me at once where you are, and what you are doing. Yesterday evening two hundred and fifty wagons of the enemy, weakly guarded, reached Stanton. You must spare a man often to communicate with me.' Again, on the 11th, he telegraphed Imboden: 'I have report at this moment of enemy's Cavalry passing through Reed's and Tye River Gaps. *Overtake, engage, and whip him. You have the force to do it.* Use great expedition.' Two days afterwards he sent the same officer a despatch, as follows; 'Communicate with me by all possible means: I wish especially to know if enemy's Cavalry and Artillery have crossed the Blue Ridge; and *where they are.*' And on the next day, as follows: 'It is reported that enemy, at Lexington, struck tents Sunday evening. *Lose no time in finding their direction.*' Again on the 15th, in evident impatience, perhaps in some ill temper, he telegraphed Imboden: 'I do not believe there is any enemy north of the James, and east of the Blue Ridge; and except a small raiding party there has been none since Sunday last. If you are north of James River, and *not in the immediate presence of the enemy, return here at once.*' He telegraphed Gen. Bragg, at Richmond, on the same date: 'Enemy reported to be advancing, in force not known, from Liberty, in Bedford County. The Cavalry, under Imboden, *doing less than nothing.* If a good General officer cannot be sent at once for them, they will go to ruin.' At 1.30 P. M. of the 16th, he telegraphed Gen. Early at Charlotteville: 'No enemy now west of Blue Ridge. There is no Cavalry of enemy north of Lynchburg, and the roads leading to Railroad and Charlottesville, are picketed.' And again, an hour later: 'I sent repeated orders, as I moved here, for the Cavalry *to see the enemy, and report facts.* But you know the habits of some of them.' To Imboden he telegraphed: 'I don't hear anything from you, or the enemy. Where is your command? and what is the news of the enemy? If he don't advance, *you might go after him,* and try to re-occupy Liberty. Send out brave and intelligent scouting parties *to see him.* I want you to find his position, and purposes, at all hazards.'

"No relief to this state of uncertainty seems to have been derived from this appeal to his subordinate officer; since at 3:30 he telegraphed Early again that he learns 'little or nothing through the Cavalry;' and has 'no information that enemy is pressing; *my fear is that he will go away.*'

"At a later hour of the same day, however, when communicating to Gen. Vaughn the fact that *he is unable to take command to-day*, and giving direction as to the disposition of troops around the city, he adds: 'There is no occasion for any disorder. The enemy is advancing slowly. We will have Gen. Early and large re-inforcements to-morrow morning, and if enemy comes in earnest, he will be destroyed.'

"Despite this confident tone, however, he despatched to Gen. Bragg, at Richmond, as late as 9 A. M., of the 17th, that he had 'some fears that the enemy (would), will not attack Lynchburg, but will move from New London towards Danville Railroad.' And his uncertainty upon that head seems not to have been removed till later in the afternoon of that day, hours after the skirmishers of the two armies had become engaged, when he despatched Gen. Vaughn an order to be 'prepared to meet the enemy at once.'"

18th. Our troops succeeded, last evening, in forcing back the enemy behind his intrenchments, and the men of both armies laid within a few hundred yards of each other. The Rebel working parties were engaged all night in strengthening their fortifications, which look to be strongly made. At about 3 A. M. we were quietly roused, and stood to our arms, in anticipation of being attacked. Crook and Averill moved their troops at an early hour; the one to the right, the other to the left, against the flanks of the enemy. About sunrise, the Rebels opened the ball, sending a shell from their earthworks in our front. Our batteries quickly replied, and for about a half hour there was quite a sharp artillery fire. "The Johnnies," having ascertained our position, ceased to shell us, and our batteries soon quieted down. Our boys, tired, sleepy, and hungry, are lying in line, in the woods, undisturbed by the occasional minié or shell which comes whizzing over their heads. We are waiting anxiously to hear from Crook or Averill, on our right or left. There it comes! Clear to the left we hear Duffie's cannon! Our scouts are coming in from the front, with the information that the Rebels are in line of battle! Now—12 M.—our skirmishers are busy. Here *they* come! closely followed by the Johnnies, who are charging, and yelling like mad! As they come into view, our batteries open upon them, with terrible effect. The shells thrown by their artillery in reply, for the most part, pass high over our heads. As the Rebels gain the hill, on the crest of which our brigade is lying, we rise, give them a volley, and, charging, drive them back to their works, re-establishing our skirmishers in advance of their former line. The fighting now became general, and was quite sharp for about two hours. Constant and heavy skirmishing was continued till after dark, especially severe on our left. From prisoners, taken by us, we learn that Breckenridge has been heavily reënforced; Early, with his corps, having reached the place, although his artillery, as yet, is not all up. *We are not whipped!* In fact, we are holding our own, and a little more. But if we wait here till morning, we shall have on our hands more than we can conveniently manage!" I quote from a letter written by Major Pratt:

"I have not time or space to describe the entire fight; but it raged for an hour and a half with a desperate fury. Before the desperate onset of the enemy, our lines seemed at first to recoil. After swaying back and forth, our entire line finally made a charge, and drove the enemy into and over his first line of works. For a moment, the stars and stripes, borne by the color bearer of the 116th Ohio, were seen waving from the enemy's breastworks; but the word was given to withdraw, and soon our troops occupied nearly their former lines."

The entire loss in this affair to the Union arms, was about two hundred. The 34th suffered severely, losing Sergeant King (orderly sergeant) of E, Woodward of D, Breene of H, and Martin of K, killed; and Capt. Lovell, seven non-commissioned officers, and thirty-eight privates, wounded. We buried our dead, and gathered in our wounded. "All fires upon the picket line are prohibited, and orders are whispered about that we are to retire from before the place." At about 8 P. M., with a caution to the men to be careful, lest the noise of their equipments should betray our movements, we started on our backward march. We left Lieut. Goodrich, with his company, upon the picket line, entirely ignorant of the intended retreat. At a later hour he drew off his command, and overtook the column during the night. At about 11 P. M., having marched about fourteen miles, we were allowed to rest for an hour. Getting on to the road again, we reached Liberty at about 3 A. M.; and, pushing on about three miles beyond the town, went into camp. A Rebel party charged our rear guard before we were fairly out of the village, and quite a severe skirmish ensued. Before ranks were broken, orders were promulgated, directing the train to continue on the road, and the men to follow in two hours. "So we lie on the ground, in readiness to move at a moment's warning."

19*th*. "With the exception of a halt for about an hour "for meals, we have been pushed ahead, without stopping, on "the road to Salem. Both men and horses are completely "jaded. Besides the loss of rest and sleep, both are suffering "from want of food and water. Less than half rations are "issued to us, and it is impossible to obtain anything by for-"aging."

20*th*. At 2 A. M. we were roused and pushed forward. The trains were started ahead, and we followed at a rapid step. "The enemy are close up, and pursuing vigorously. The men "and animals are completely worn down; men dropping by the "wayside, and animals constantly giving out. The men get "scarcely anything to eat. Our horses have hardly once been "unharnessed since the battle, and are seldom halted, except to "graze, for a short time." At about 2 P. M., having made 21 miles, we were allowed to rest. At 6, orders came to get in readiness to move. Our wagon train was started off at once; and about an hour afterwards the column was put in motion. We marched all night, reaching and passing through Salem about daylight.

"The prospect ahead of us is not very cheering. If we are "able to continue a day or two longer, we shall save ourselves "and the greater part of our material. But we are nearly "exhausted; our teams worn out; there is neither rations for "man or beast; the country is poor, and thinly settled, giving "no chance for successful foraging, even if we had the opportu-"nity, which we have not; and the enemy is giving us much "trouble." Still, while there is life there is hope of coming out all right, though the prospect of a brilliant termination of this expedition is not flattering. We suffer a good deal from the weather, which is now, as it has been for weeks, very warm; and for want of rain, of which we have had *none* for weeks.

21*st*. "Our march was interrupted this morning, when we "were within about two miles of Salem, by a fire poured into

"us by a party of about one thousand Rebels, who had con-
"cealed themselves in a piece of woods, on our right. They
"hoped, doubtless, to detain us long enough to enable another
"body of their troops to gain the Gap, on the road between
"Salem and Newcastle, *through which we must* pass, if we *pass
"at all.* Leaving this body on our right, we pushed on, and
"overtook our train, which had stopped about a mile out, to
"enable the animals to graze. About 10 o'clock we halted,
"having marched about fifteen miles.

"As Crook's division (the rear guard) came up, it became
"engaged with the force we had left. We turned two pieces
"of our artillery upon this party, to aid Crook; and woke up
"a fire from one of their pieces, in return. While this affair
"was going on, our train and artillery, for some cause, was
"hitched up and driven on. It was 12 o'clock when it occurred
"to those in authority that it was a good thing to have infantry
"somewhere near a train moving in an enemy's country; and
"orders were sent to us to move out and overtake it. We
"reached Newcastle without having overtaken it. About a
"mile beyond, word was brought us to hurry forward, as fast
"as possible; as Guerrillas had cut the train, near the entrance
"to the Gap, and were fast destroying it. We found that
"McCausland, with a party of cavalry, had shot the horses,
"attached to a part of the artillery, and was busy in destroying
"the caissons and limbers. Our approach stopped the work of
"destruction; but they had already broken up sixteen guns,
"with their appurtenances. They got away with three pieces.
"We were obliged to abandon five others, for want of spare
"horses; but we first rendered them unserviceable. *Some one
"had evidently blundered!* In this forced march we made six
"miles in an hour and a half; which, taking into consideration
"the jaded condition of "the boys," and the fact that the route
"was over a steep mountain road, we called pretty good.
"After we had overtaken the train, an hour's halt was allowed
"us. Then we pushed forward again; crossed another range
"of mountains, and went into camp, about twelve miles from
"Newcastle. The distance marched since 8:30 o'clock last
"evening was twenty-seven miles."

22d. For a wonder, we were permitted to rest last night; and, as the order of march is changed, the train to be moved in the rear, to-day, under the protection of our Brigade, we are all "lying around loose," this forenoon, enjoying ourselves as much as possible. At 1½ o'clock we got under arms. After a leisurely march, we encamped again at 10½ P. M.; distance marched, twelve miles. Before entering the Gap, last night, Crook, who had heard of the little affair of the train, arranged a little surprise party for the Johnnies, who had been hanging on to his rear. Leaving a small rear guard well behind, he placed a handsome force in ambush, by the side of the road. The Greybacks, thinking they had a sure thing, charged. Our little party retreated; and when the Johnnies had got well into the mouth of the trap set for them, our boys rose up, fired, killing eighteen; and charged, capturing eighty more of them.

CHAPTER XXXIII.

Hunter's Raid.

WAGON GUARD — "SWEET SPRINGS" — "WHITE SULPHUR SPRINGS" — FIVE DOLLARS FOR A PIECE OF HARDTACK — MAJOR PRATT'S LETTER — "MEADOW BLUFFS" — "A HEART-ACHE" — BIG SEWALL MOUNTAIN — "HOW THE BOYS ARE CHEERING" — "AN AGREEABLE CHANGE" — "IT SEEMS HARD" — GAULEY RIVER.

23d. Reveillé was sounded at 4 o'clock this morning. On the march to-day, our Brigade was distributed through the whole length of the train; one Company between every two wagons. We crossed Twelve-mile Mountain, as it is called, from its being five miles to its summit on the west side, and seven to its base on the east side. Crossing the next succeeding range, we reached "Sweet Springs" at $2\frac{1}{2}$ A. M., where we went into camp. Day's march twenty-five miles. There was neither sleep nor rest for the men, for the whole night was made noisy by the rumbling of the wagons, which were late in coming in, owing to the extreme heat, and the bad condition of the animals. We were compelled to abandon many wagons; also horses and mules in large number. As these last fell, they were shot, and with the wagons, rolled off the mountain side.

24th. We have had a good rest. Our camp is near the springs, the water of which is very delicious. This place, in *anti bellum* days, was a fashionable resort. The hotel is of brick, three stories high, about four hundred feet long, with an L of about one hundred and fifty feet. The dining room is about three hundred feet by fifty, resplendent with mirrors, which fairly cover the entire walls. Much of the furniture, which is of the richest quality, even now remains. About a mile distant is what is called "Red Sweet Springs," where there is standing another large hotel building, but of wood. Around the main buildings are many small cottages used as family residences through the summer months; bathing houses, etc. All these buildings are unoccupied, save by a few negroes who seem to be in charge. We have fairly revelled in the waters, while enjoying the short rest.

At about 3 P. M., we started on the road to "White Sulphur Springs," which place we reached about 2 A. M. The weather was intensely hot. Our route was over a fine road, running between the ranges of mountains. The march was wearisome indeed. Its monotony was relieved once or twice, by the firing at us of a few shots, after dusk, by a little party of bushwackers, who laid concealed by the wayside.

25th. The boys have been on short allowance for some days, and are now suffering, actually suffering for want of food. It is more than a week since they have had *any bread.* "I have seen a dollar offered for a cup of coffee, and a five dollar greenback for a single "hard tack." Our horses and mules are also suffering for want of forage. Vegetation here is not so far advanced as it was where we were a week ago. Cherries are scarce! Gooseberries green, and *Onions small!* We started about 3 P. M., on our weary way; reached Lewisburg about 11, and continuing on about four miles farther, halted at about 1 A. M. We passed quite near the White Sulphur Springs;— the water bubbles up from a natural basin in the center of a beautiful valley, the spring itself being sheltered by a neat summer house, built over it. The water is strongly impregnated with sulphur. The principal building, three stories high, from four to five hundred feet long, with a basement its entire length, stands nearly in the centre of this basin. Back against the sides of the hills, are numerous cottages for family occupation, with broad and well shaded piazzas, extending entirely around them, and windows springing from the floors. Some little distance from the Springs, we came to numerous well constructed earthworks. These were thrown up last December, by order of the Rebel General Echols, in order to stay Averill, on his retreat from his raid upon Saltville. They are very strong, and so placed as to be impregnable to a direct assault. Averill succeeded in flanking them, and so escaped from his pursuers. Just at dusk, we reached Green river. The scene while fording, was magnificent beyond description. The waters were spread out near two hundred yards wide, and were about two feet deep. For a distance of near a quarter of a mile, the river was fairly crowded with men. The prisoners of the division were just ahead of our brigade; and "grey backs" and "blue bellies," were mixed well together. Cavalry men were mingled here and there in the crowd, many of the horses made to carry double. The artillery and wagons crossed more by themselves. Over this scene, the sun shone clear, its beams glancing brightly from our bayonets. The whole formed a sight, which would repay one for a good deal of such fatigue, and hunger, as we have experienced.

"The men are," writes Maj. Pratt in a letter of this date, "completely exhausted, owing to a lack of food. They have had but six ounces of flour, per man, for the whole of the last *five days;* *no* hard bread. All coffee and sugar is gone; in fact, there is nothing more to issue, except fresh beef from cattle driven along with us; and we are sixty miles from Gauley, the nearest depot. The men are so completely wearied by the severity of their labors and marches, and insufficiency of food, that very many drop by the roadside, too weary and faint to keep up with the column." Of the condition of his men, at this time, said Gen. Crook: "*hundreds of my men are starving by the wayside, in the rear,*"

26th. We started at 5 o'clock this morning, passing on our way "Meadow Bluffs," and many earthworks and rifle-pits thrown up along the road. About noon a halt was ordered which lasted about four hours. This was made that the men might rest, and receive their ration of meat—from beeves driven along with us, and knocked down, killed, and distributed, upon reaching camp;—eaten, in many cases, raw and quivering. Resuming the march, we continued on till about dusk, when *we* halted for the night. We hope that a provision train may meet us to-morrow, for our boys are actually starving. The country has been stripped clean by the troops who have preceded us, and there is literally *nothing* eatable left. Except the fresh meat, and a very little coffee, there is nothing to be issued. " I saw fifty cents offered, in vain, to-day, for a narrow strip of bacon, not two inches long."

27th. Started at 3 this morning, and halted about noon for an hour, when *meat* and a *little* coffee was issued. "The boys look so gaunt, and are so hungry, it makes one's heart ache to see them." "At the halt I saw two dollars offered and refused for *one small griddle cake.*" But we are promised rations before the day closes. We are now lying at the foot of the "Big Sewall Mountain," having marched sixteen miles to-day, and come up with Headquarters of the division. Hark! how the boys are cheering! All hardships seem to have been forgotten; and men but just able to drag themselves along on the march to-day, are shouting, and dancing, and running around as if crazy. A train (now 7 P. M.,) with two days' rations of hard-tack, sugar and coffee, and bacon, is just coming up. Our Brigade teams are up to-night; but many horses have been turned out and abandoned to-day, and those now in harness are badly played out. Averill's command, which for a while has been in the rear, is passing our camp at this moment. "I am told that five of his men died to-day of *actual starvation.*" Large as has been the loss of property, and it has been very large since we commenced our retreat, it has been as nothing compared to the privation and suffering the boys have had to bear. But we trust our hardships are nearly over, as we are within one day's march of Gauley bridge, and — plenty.

28th. We were on our way again at 4 o'clock this morning. A nice rain last night, (the first since we left Stanton) laid the dust, and left about two inches of mud through which to march. But we have had so much dust as actually to enjoy the present muddy road. At noon a halt was ordered. We made a good dinner, at which hard-tack figured largely; and made a good march in the afternoon, camping for the night just west of the road leading to "Summerville," having made sixteen miles during the day.

We are beginning to get out of the woods; having passed on our day's march good farms and farm-houses; an agreeable change from occasional rough log huts, and almost interminable forests and mountains. Some of our Virginia comrades are now at home. "I saw one of them standing guard, to-day, at his father's door; and soon after stopped at the house of a Mr.

George Hunt, from whom I learned that he was a native of Franklin county, Massachusetts; and had four sons in the Union service." We are now among Union people, and henceforth there is to be no pillaging. It seeems hard! (for we have got fairly broken in, having practiced where there was little or nothing to be "scooped in,") now that the prospect looks fair, or would but for the fact that we are among friends.

29*th*. Reveillé at 5 o'clock this morning, soon after which we were on the road. Our route laid over the Gauley Mountains, about nine miles to the bridge, and the river of that name, and to the Union lines. Soon after starting, we came to the far-famed "Lover's Leap," "Maiden Bluff," and "Hawk's Nest." From this last point, a scene of indescribable beauty and grandeur greets the eye of the beholder. The road runs along within about one hundred feet of the brow of the bluff;— the cliff, so bold, and precipitous, that one can easily toss a stone into the waters of the "New River," winding nine hundred feet below. So crooked is its course, that the view does not extend more than two or three miles down the stream; and up, it is cut off by wooded mountains, piled one upon another far above. "Yesterday, I thought we were getting out of the woods; but to-day, it seems as if we were in deeper than ever. The change is, however, an agreeable one. Every step we take, some new beauty is presented to the eye. The Rhododendrons are in the full splendor of their bloom, and are very abundant. (They were fading when we crossed the Blue Ridge, ten days ago.) As we advance, we catch occasional glimpses of the river, far below us, but the descent, although steep, is nowhere so precipitous as at the "Hawk's Nest." After a while, turning a point of the mountain, far in front, and far below us, the "Great Kanawha," formed by the junction of the waters of the "New," with the "Gauley" River, bursts upon our view. Winding down the mountain side, the Cliffs, on our right, overhang and seem ready to drop upon our heads. We reached "Gauley Bridge," to find *no bridge there;* it having been burned early in the war. Our wagon train and Artillery crossed the river in ferry boats; the Infantry on a foot bridge laid from rock to rock in the bed of the stream, while the Cavalry forded. We found the Post held by some one hundred days' men.

CHAPTER XXXIV.

Hunter's Raid.

"WE BREATH EASIER"— AN INCIDENT— THE "CRITTER RODE WELL"— MAJOR PRATT— SERGEANT MAJOR BLAKE.

We are now fairly inside the Union Lines, and breathe easier. Our camp is about a mile below the Ferry, close by the great "Fall of the Kanawha;" at a point where the mountain, receding from the west bank, leaves a grassy slope between the water and the woods, about a mile long, by fifty rods wide. Here, it is given out, we are to rest for two or three days. "And a rest, a good, genuine rest, will do us any amount of good."

An incident of our last day's march is perhaps worth transcribing; as, at the time, it furnished much amusement to the lookers-on, and to the chief actor, temporary exemption from the fatigues of marching. On our route down the mountains, we had been enjoying the scenery, which, at each successive step, burst upon the view with ever increasing grandeur. As we neared the foot of the mountain, our attention was drawn to a squad of fellows, who were chasing a little, wild, but well conditioned mule. "Like a flash, it occured to me that the animal would look well *under a saddle*, with a man of my size, riding." So, asking the aid of a few friends near, we endeavored to surround him; and after chasing him about a mile, we run him in among some Cavalry, when, by a dexterous jump, I succeeded in clasping my arms round his neck. Off he started, with a loud bray, a whisk of his tail, and a dexterous fling of his heels, twitching me off my feet, and slinging me among the brush, and against the rocks. The whole column was convulsed, and laughed, and shouted, until the mule, after dragging me some eight or ten rods, finding my weight too much, gave in, and I saddled and bridled him." "*The critter rode extremely well.*"

Of this retreat, Maj. Pratt, who, wounded, rode along with Headquarters, and had less privation than would otherwise have been his lot, writes thus:

"Our retreat continued up to yesterday. We were not compelled by the enemy to continue it thus far, as he only followed us for four or five days; but we have been compelled to march day and night, as fast as our broken-down, wearied men could move, to *escape starvation*. For the greater part of our retreat, we have marched through a very thinly settled region, poorly cultivated, and almost entirely destitute of provisions. I have no heart to write of the sufferings our poor boys have endured: and endured with a courage as lofty, and a heroism as sublime as was ever exhibited on the field of battle. To increase their sufferings, the weather has been intensely hot for the past three weeks; and as we have had no rain till a day or two since, we have marched midst clouds of dust, almost suffocating alike to man and beast. Sometimes without food for twenty-four, thirty-six, and forty-eight hours, and obliged (at first to get away from the enemy, and later, to procure food) to march both night and day, with occasional halt, for an hour or two or a time, our men became so worn out, that many were unable to keep up with the column. I have several times, after going into camp about midnight, seen men crawling along in, just as the Brigade was moving out, at 5 or 6 o'clock the next morning. When making a momentary halt during the night, have seen men drop down in the middle of the road, and in an instant, seemingly, be in a sound sleep, from which the officers, though striking them with their swords, could scarcely rouse them. We had fresh meat nearly every day (killed, hot and feverish from the drive), but for the last seven days had nothing in the shape of bread but six ounces of flour per man; less than one ounce per day. Since leaving Lynchburg, have marched rising two hundred miles; have crossed the Alleghany Mountains, and numberless others of less note; have crossed creeks and forded rivers; have endured privations of almost every kind; and have reached the land of promise, or rather a region of supplies. Yesterday we had a day of rest in camp, the first for eighteen days. Our horses and mules suffered terribly for want of forage and rest, and we lost very many. In a single day, when crossing the Alleghanies, I am told, we lost several hundred. Our wagons were of course burned. And now, what have we accomplished? We have marched six hundred miles; have fought three pitched battles; got whipped at Newmarket;—gained a glorious victory at Piedmont;—defeated the enemy in a fair stand up fight at Lynchburg—have destroyed bridges innumerable, and miles of railroad tracks; burnt foundries, mills, public stores; captured many horses, some prisoners, and brought away contrabands without number, and I am inclined to think, without value, although they have received very much care from Gen. Hunter. On the other hand, we have lost in killed, wounded and missing, probably 2,500 men; while from Lynchburg to Gauley Bridge, every rod of our way is marked by burnt wagons, dead animals, and abandoned property. I am of opinion, that although this is the greatest raid made since the war commenced, it amounts to absolutely nothing, beyond its cost. To show you how hungry our poor fellows were, I will give you a little incident. During a shower three or four days ago, and the only one for a month, and before our supply trains reached us, I crawled under a wagon to keep dry, and while there, a drummer boy came along, and picked up an old *bone* which must have lain there for a long time (the meat upon which was black, hard and dry), and commenced to eat of it as though it was the sweetest morsel he ever tasted. I have often seen men go to the spot where our cattle were slaughtered, and pick little pieces of flesh from the hides, and from the ground, to satisfy their hunger."

What may be regarded at home with more repugnance, men poked among the excrements of our team animals to get and eat the undigested grain which had been voided.

In a letter to his mother, under date June 30th, Sergeant Major Blake wrote as follows: "Seven days after leaving Salem we were in the mountains and woods ; not a solitary house once in ten miles. We had no bread--no meat--no--nothing. The men grew poor and thin. When I looked in a glass for the first time in many days, I was startled at the change. You would not have known me, had you seen me. I hardly knew myself. My face was black and thin—my eyes large—and of such *queer expression!* *They looked as if they would like to eat me up!!*"

All this is past, and to all seeming, forgotten; for in the rebound of feeling occasioned by the relief of our wants, the camp is noisy with frolicking, laughing men.

CHAPTER XXXV

Hunter's Raid.

At rest—Our muster roll—Marching again—Camp Piatt—Sad news—Retrospection—An occasion for discipline and for?—"Guns must shine"—Plundering—A notable instance—It means war!—On the Kanawha and Ohio—On the march—Rations—By rail to "Cherry Run"—Waiting—Lieut. Cobb—Arrival of the command.

30*th.* A splendid morning this, made all the more enjoyable by the fact that there was no reveillé to disturb our sleep. We are not to move to-day, and the Boys are busied in washing themselves and their clothes; filthy by this long exposure. A mail reached us to-day, and we received papers as late as the 26th inst.; our last previous ones being dated the 6th. Our Muster Roll, to-day, shows "present for duty," officers, 13; *one* (Major Pratt,) sick; enlisted men, 480; sick, 6. Absent on detached duty: officers, 9; men, 55. Sick: officers, 5; men, 226. Prisoners of war; officers, 8; men, 104. Total present, 450; total absent, 407.

Col. George D. Wells commands the Brigade, and has on his Staff, Surgeon R. R. Clarke, Quarter Master Howland, and Lieut. Henry Bacon. Lieut. Col. Lincoln, Lieut. R. W Walker, and Capt. Henry P. Fox, all wounded, are in the enemy's hands. Asst. Surgeon Allen left with wounded at Mt. Jackson. Major H. W Pratt, wounded at Piedmont, "present, sick." Capt. Wells Willard, wounded at New Market, in hospital at Sandy Hook, Md. Capt. Andrew Potter, wounded at Piedmont, "on leave" in Mass. Lieut. Wm. L. Cobb, in Martinsburg, not yet recovered from wounds. Lieut. Harry T. Hall, in Signal Corps. Capt. A. D. Pratt, Provost Marshal at Harper's

Ferry. Capt. Chauncey R. Chauncey and Lieut. Malcom Ammidon, captured at New Market, prisoners of war. Lieut. G. Macomber commanding Pioneer Corps. Lieut. F. C. Kinnicutt, wounded at New Market, in hospital, at Martinsburg. Lieut. S. H. Platt, captured on his way to the Regiment, May 19, in enemy's hands. Lieut Jere Horton, Commissary of Musters, on Division Staff. Lieut. A. C. Walker, wounded, and left at Piedmont, where he died. Lieut. L. Lincoln, Jr,, on Court Martial at Harper's Ferry. Capt. John A. Lovell, wounded at Lynchburg, in hospital at Gallipolis, Ohio.

July 2d. We started at 5 o'clock this morning, marching over a good road. The weather was cool, and we made good time, having, at 12M., marched 14 miles. After a short rest, we got on to our feet again, and having marched seven miles farther, went into camp for the night; first having received orders to move at 2 A. M. to-morrow. The other Brigade has gone on.

3d. Reveillé at 1½ A.M., and at 2 o'clock we were on the road to "Piatt," which we reached at about 5 P. M. We found that nearly the entire 2d brigade had embarked, and gone on down the river. One boat was left, and another arrived soon after we did, so that Col. Wells' Headquarters, and about three hundred of the "Heavys," (5th N. Y. A.) were loaded and pushed off.

4th. Camp Piatt. The "Gen. Crook and Minnie Roberts" were along side, upon our waking this morning, having reached here some time during the night. These were loaded and sent off at once. During the day, a mail reached us, bringing the startling intelligence of the death of Adj't Woods. We cannot realize that this is true. Splendid officer, accomplished gentleman, and brave and gallant spirit; his loss will be mourned by every man in the Regiment as that of a personal friend! About 4. P. M., tired of waiting for the arrival of other boats, eight companies of the 34th were embarked upon the only one here, which was immediately sent off. We ran by Charleston, without making a stop; steamed about two miles further on, and, as it is impossible to navigate this river in the dark, we then *tied up to the bank* for the night. We left in camp, companies "A and F," Capt. Elwell commanding (whose commission reached him to-day) with orders to take the first transportation which offered, and join the main body as soon as possible.

Looking back now from this point of comparative safety, and rest, and plenty, it seems a marvel that we are here at all. Even before we had fairly started on this raid, our rations were well nigh exhausted; and had the country passed through been thickly settled, and well cultivated, which was far from being the case, the rapidity of our march was such as to have prevented the collection of supplies. "For *four days* the regiment "marched day and night, never halting more than two hours at "any one time. For *nine* days we had nothing to eat but fresh "beef and mutton, and a very little coffee." Nor, when after the arrival of our first supply train, an issue of two days rations was made, is it any wonder that they were all consumed by the men before they went to sleep? It is difficult to describe the *entire exhaustion* induced by this long privation of food, and rest, and sleep. At a halt, men dropped in their places;—were asleep instantly;—and were roused again only with great difficulty. It would have been ludicrous, had it not been so sad, to see men supported by the "touch of the elbow" of a companion, reel as if in the last stages of drunkenness, when, by any accident, that supporting touch was momentarily withdrawn. Seldom was there any occasion for discipline, and when there was, it was enforced by the officers of the respective regiments. *We*, especially, were sensitive to any outside interference in matters of this kind; and when, one day, Lieut. Belser was administering a little well merited reprimand to one of his men, he was interrupted by Gen. Sullivan with the remark, "tie him up, Lieutenant, or, by G—d, I'll tie you up," it can't be wondered at that, as a body, our officers resented the brutal and unofficer-like interference.

It could hardly be expected that much of our old time splendor should be preserved during this hurried retreat. So that the men preserved their pieces in an effective condition seemed to be all that could be reasonably asked; and away up here, hid away among the mountains, ragged, dirty, barefoot, an order that "*Guns must shine*" on the inspection, which was to come off the next day, caused much merriment. It would be idle to deny that, spite of orders to the contrary, there were occasional instances of wanton robbery from houses, lying along our line of march. Generally, the boys showed a *commendable discrimination* in this work; and few suffered, save those who had given aid and countenance to the enemy. These were the ones, however, who were loudest in their complaints against the men. A notable instance occurred, at a halt of longer duration than ordinarily happened, near Sweet Springs. Near by headquarters was one of those large brick mansions which, in Virginia, was sure indication of former opulence and aristocracy. It offered temptation too strong to be resisted; and was overrun and ransacked by the hungry men, who were not over scrupulous in their appropriation. They had been supporting life upon "the sweepings of granaries and mills;" "upon birch bark and clover blossoms;" upon scraps of raw flesh, scraped from round the butcher's block, and, still worse, upon undigested grain, picked from the droppings of horses and mules. What wonder that now everything edible, including preserves, jellies, even pickles, quickly disappeared.. For this, excuse could be found. But they couldn't eat *razors*, nor *looking-glasses*, nor *Colt's pistols*, nor *Sharpe's rifles*, nor *silver* nor *plated ware*, nor *photograph albums;* nor had they any real use for the various articles of female apparel, such as bonnets and dresses; nor of household furnishing, such as pillow cases, sheets, &c. When, therefore, upon complaint preferred, that the men were guilty of robbing this house of articles of this description, Lieut. Bacon had satisfied himself of the justice of the charge, no one who knew him, and his knightly chivalry, will wonder, that he permitted his sympathy for the suffering womankind to get the better of his love for his comrades, and in his indignation at the outrage, that he should give assurance that the full force of army discipline should fall upon the guilty, if found within our command. Nor will they be surprised that upon the inquiry by the elder lady, if he didn't "think this was terrible treatment to be given by Union "soldiers to a *sister of John B. Floyd*," the Lieutenant should remember that in the eyes of all Unionists this same John B. Floyd stood personified as the great thief of the country; and consider, on the whole, this appeal to a Union soldier from such source, should seem a little incongruous. Spite of this, the matter was looked into, and, much to the Lieutenant's relief, the robbers were not found to be of our brigade. At a later hour the A. B. G. visited these ladies, at their request; listened to the story of their losses;—sympathized with them in their wrongs;—lamented with them in their sufferings;—and to their passionate entreaty to know what it all meant, could only reply, "*Ladies, it means war!*" Of this same affair, R. C., of F, of ours, writes: " One, of whom this narrative had to do, arrived " on the scene, late, but with an excellent appetite, which a " quantity of very rich preserves, taken from under some loose " floor boards, where they were carefully stowed away, allayed " for a considerable period. He was interrupted by a cry of " 'Fall in! fall in!' when every knapsack was thoroughly ran- " sacked, and no contraband property of any kind found." " And yet," he writes, " one of the boys, a day or two after- " wards, sold to an officer, for $30, a Colt's rifle, which he hap- " pened somehow to have about him."

5*th*. There was a heavy fog lying upon the river this morning; and from this, or some other cause, it was 7 o'clock before we swung into the stream, and got fairly underweigh. About 4 o'clock P. M. we reached "Point Pleasant," at the mouth of the Ohio; and steaming up this river, stopped at "Pomroy," just before sunset. After about a half hour's stay at this place, we shoved into the stream again, and continued on our way till dark; when we tied up to the bank for the night. Our band favored us with many delightful airs on our run, during the day; and our progress along the river, was hailed with cheers, and waving handkerchiefs by the inhabitants of the various villages we passed. We passed many coal and salt mines on our way down the " Kanawha;" but, owing to the low stage of the water, and the high banks of the river, we could see but little of the country.

6*th*. Started again early this morning. Twice during the day, the men had to leave the boat to lighten her sufficiently to allow of her passing the sand bars. Just at dark, we reached "Blennerhasset's Island," where the boat was to remain over night.

7*th*. We left the boat at 3 o'clock this morning, and took up our line of march, along the Ohio shore, for the Ferry at "Parkersburg." The country passed through, looked finely. Grass and grain were ready for harvesting; cherry trees were loaded with fruit, black and tempting. We bought some cherry pies; nice, and large, at ten cents each,— a great contrast to prices in the Valley; also some nice raspberries, with sugar and cream. Reached and crossed the Ferry to "Parkersburg;" where we found a train waiting for us. Here rations were issued; and we got a large mail. "Grafton Junction" was reached about dusk; soon after which, we settled ourselves, as well as we could, for the night, in the old box cars provided for us; and, at daylight, next morning, the 8th, found ourselves entering "Piedmont," the scene of the raid of our old *friend* "McNeil," a short time before. A short run carried us to "Cumberland," where we found Lieut. Cobb, and several of our wounded, ready to join us. We proceeded on our way to "Green Spring," where we had to haul up, on account of the rebuilding of the railroad bridge, which a raiding rebel party had destroyed. This repaired sufficiently for the passage of the train, we ran down to "Cherry Run," which we reached soon after dark. Here we passed the night.

9*th*. It is dreadfully hot, this morning. General Sullivan's Headquarters have come in to-day; also Col. Wilde's; and the detachment of the 5th N. Y. Heavies. Thus far, we get no news of the "116th" Ohio, and the two Companies of the 34th, with them. Lieut. Cobb has been appointed A. D. C. upon the Staff of Acting Brigadier Wells. The river is very low, and can be forded anywhere, without difficulty. Maj. Pratt left for home, on sick leave; his wound still very troublesome.

10*th*. We get rumors this morning, which we don't credit, however, of the presence of from 25,000 to 30,000 Rebels, in and near "Frederick," Maryland; also, that a party of the 15th New York dashed into Martinsburg, this forenoon, and drove out the Rebels; which we rather like to believe is true. Orders to march at 3 P. M., were issued, but soon afterwards countermanded; the Battery, for which we have been waiting, not having arrived. The 116th Ohio, with our two Companies, also our Headquarter teams, ambulances, and wagons, have reached us; and we are to march at 4 A. M. to-morrow, as far as Martinsburg; distance 13 miles.

CHAPTER XXXVI

THE RACE GROUND.

A GLAD WELCOME — OLD FRIENDS — TO KNOXVILLE — TO HILLSBORO' — SKIRMISHING — GEN. CROOK — JOIN HIM AT PURCELLVILLE — RESTING — TO SNICKERSVILLE — A SHARP ENGAGEMENT — OUR LOSS — A BLUNDER — CROSS THE RIVER AGAIN — TO WINCHESTER — MANŒUVERING — OFF FOR MARTINSBURG — SKIRMISHING — A DUEL — "I DIDN'T HIT HIM."

11*th.* Reveillé again, this time at 3 A. M., and we started about an hour afterwards. The weather was pleasant, until the sun was high, when it became oppressively hot. At "Hedgesville," about seven miles out, we arrested all the inhabitants of secesh tendency, and took them along with us. Martinsburg was reached soon after noon, and we went into camp, on the north side of the town.

13*th.* We passed yesterday in camp willingly enough; for the weather was hot, almost beyond endurance. It is the same to-day. Notwithstanding, we had orders to hold ourselves in readiness to move,— this time for "Harper's Ferry," which is pleasant news for us-all, as we look upon that place as a sort of home. At 4 P. M., we were on our way. As we moved through the main streets of Martinsburg, we received glad welcome from the people, with whom we had made pleasant acquaintance, during our few weeks stay this spring. If anything, the boys marched with a prouder air and firmer step, than when in earlier days, they moved in parade before the same sympathizing crowd. Marching to within a mile and a half of "Duffield Station," we went into camp for the night.

14th. Breaking camp about four this morning, and passing "Duffield Station," we reached "Bolivar Heights" at about 10 A. M., where we halted. The Col. and staff rode into the Ferry. We were glad enough to meet Capt. Pratt, Lieut. Lincoln, and others of our old friends, among whom was Capt. George S. Leland, now and for a long time Post Quarter Master. If he and the others had come, empty handed, to greet us, our pleasure would have been great; but bringing with them, as they did, things good for the stomach, in large abundance, our joy was unbounded. Blessings on them! May they always feast of the fat of the land! and, what is more, may they always have appetites as sharp as ours were! "May they be," in the language of a venerable Darkey minister among us, "at all times endowed with both *appetite* and *capacity*."

About 3 P. M. the command was in motion again. As we passed on through Bolivar and the Ferry, all ran out to greet us, and bid us welcome, and good-bye. The day was memorable to us, as being the anniversary of our crossing the river and occupying the place. Since then, how many have fallen by our sides! We crossed the Potomac upon the pontoon bridge, and, keeping on through "Sandy Hook," went into camp near "Knoxville."

15th. We started again at 6 A. M., marched along the tow path of the canal nearly to "Berlin," when, rolling up our pants, we forded the Potomac, whose waters were nearly up to our waists. Then, taking a "dirt road" leading into the Leesburg pike, we passed through "Lovettsville," where we left the pike and moved towards "Hillsboro," going into camp within about a quarter of a mile of the village. During the afternoon, our advance skirmished with a portion of Jackson's force, and captured about thirty of them; also one or two wagons. We could hear nothing of the whereabouts of the main force of the rebels.

16th. The weather was very warm this morning, and we laid quietly in camp, until about noon, when we had orders to move immediately. Our brigade took the back track to the Pike, and then struck off towards "Waterford"—skirmishing occasionally with the enemy, till we reached the town, which the Rebels left hurriedly as we entered. Our reception by the inhabitants was a warm, and seemingly a hearty one. Our halt was for a couple of hours, at the end of which time we received information that "Wright," with a portion of the 6th corps, was moving on our left. At the same time, came orders from "Crook," who had to-day been put in command of the 1st Division, Army of West Virginia," for us to join *him*, without delay, at "Purcellville." We started—struck the Pike at "Harmony," about three miles from Leesburg, and reached Purcellville about 11 P. M., having marched twelve miles. Here we went into camp.

18*th*. We remained in camp all day yesterday, resting and recruiting, of which we all stood in much need. "Mulligan and Duffie were having a warm time with the Rebels at 'Snickers Gap,' some eight or ten miles from us."

Reveillé was sounded at 3 o'clock this morning, and at 4, we were on the march. We reached "Snickersville" about 9, and rested till 2, when we started on our way through the Gap. As we gained the summit, we could see the enemy in force, posted across the Shenandoah. We moved to the right, down the river, seeking a favorable place to cross. Having reached the river, we discovered two regiments of Rebels drawn up on the opposite bank. The 34th, leading the advance, pushed boldly on, forced the crossing, and forming, drove the enemy, some half a mile to the cover of some woods; taking one Capt. and some twenty privates, prisoners. The 2d brigade followed close on our heels, and extended on *our right;* while still farther in that direction was a body of dismounted cavalry. In the distance, columns of dust disclosed the advance of strong bodies of the enemy, (Gordon's and Echol's Divisions in our front, and Rhodes' to the left) which, coming up *on our right*, charged, breaking the line and driving before them the discomfitted men. Undismayed by this apparent reverse, Col. Wells swung his own right, and charging in turn, sent the enemy again to the cover of the woods. Our ammunition was getting short, in fact, was nearly exhausted, but we felt that we could hold the enemy in check, till the 6th corps, now ready to cross from the other side, could get up in support. But to our surprise and astonishment, we received orders to recross the river. This was done in good order, the men wading in the water up to their waists, and we went into camp again in the Gap. Our regiment had four killed and eleven wounded.

19th. We have remained in camp all day, feeling soured and chagrined; and have busied ourselves in speculating upon what we cannot help considering the blunder, by which, *instead of the 6th corps crossing to support us, we were ordered to abandon a field, we had already won.* We wonder who will crave the honor of giving that order! From the hills, where the batteries of the 6th corps were, and still are in position, we can easily see the Rebels now at work, gathering their wounded, and burying their dead. They also seem to be building barricades along the river bank. Their ambulance trains are in motion; and from the columns of dust rising in the direction of Winchester, we are induced to believe their whole army is moving. We can hear sharp cannonading towards "Ashby's Gap." "Duffie" is out there somewhere.

20th. Although our orders were to move early this morning, we did not leave camp till nearly noon. As we neared the river bank, we saw that the crossing was clear, the rebels having left. A heavy shower came upon us as we entered the ford, and for a half hour it literally *poured*. We have encamped close by our battle ground of the 18th. The sight is sad enough. Our poor fellows are lying half buried; heads and arms protruding through the slight covering of earth, thrown over them. We counted twenty-two graves, of men from *one* North Carolina Regiment; and there are many others all over the field. Heavy and brisk firing, towards night, in the direction of Winchester, led us to suppose that "Averill was pounding away at Early."

21st. As we supposed last evening, Averill and Early had a "little mill," with each other, near "Winchester;" with the result that the latter left on the field four twenty pound Parrots, three hundred killed and wounded, besides losing some 2,500 prisoners. *Our* day has been spent in camp, quietly.

22d. At five this morning we were roused, with orders to move at 6 o'clock. There was quite a bustling, and hurrying, as the Boys had somehow come to the conclusion that we should remain encamped here, a few days.

Taking the Pike, and passing through "Berryville," we reached "Winchester," about 4 P. M., having marched sixteen miles. Passing through the town, we occupied our old camping ground, of two months since. Col. Thoburn, 1st West Virginia, is assigned to the command of our Division; Gen. Crook having just received his second *star*, and assumed command of the "forces of this Department in the field." We hear of the rebels, as in force, at "Strasburg." We are hoping to be allowed to remain here a few days; long enough at least to enable us to draw clothing, of which we all are sadly in need.

23d. We went to sleep last night, indulging the hope that we might have rest for a few days; but early this morning a scattering fire in our front let us know the vanity of all earthly hopes, at least in time of war, with the enemy not "twenty miles away." "Fall in! fall in!" broke upon our ears, and warned us to be ready for the enemy, who, we learned, was approaching in force. We marched out about a mile to meet him. Our Brigade had the right. After a good deal of manœuvring we were posted in a piece of woods, on the right of the Pike Going to work with a will, we soon built a splendid breast-work "a la Piedmont," for cover. It formed a strong defence. The enemy not advancing, we fell back to our first position, in the edge of the town. The Cavalry and Artillery had a lively time of it, and the skirmish line of the 2d Brigade was in, for a few moments, but did not suffer much. Our shelters are up, and we are hoping for, at least, a quiet night.

24th. The morning is fine and fair, although the air is filled with smoke. About 9, orders came for us to resume our position behind the breastworks thrown up by us yesterday. The left of the line, which was across the pike, soon became heavily engaged, and *we* were advanced through the woods for nearly a mile. The fire on the left grew hotter and hotter, and our skirmishers were just getting busy when we were ordered to fall back. So back we came, up to and through our breastworks. As we crossed these, the Rebel line, widely extended, could be seen advancing across the country. Their force proving far superior to ours, a grand retreat was ordered. Our brigade did not suffer much, but some of the others lost very heavily. We continued in retreat, falling back to the west of the town; then, taking the fields, we struck across for the Martinsburg pike. Our train was making rapidly for the rear, and we were ordered up as its guard. For miles, everything went well enough. There was heavy fighting in the rear, but all was clear in our front. Suddenly, from the flank, a body of some 400 or 500 cavalry charged the train. Wells formed in line, and scattered them with a volley. But a *panic seized the teamsters*, and for miles it was a perfect route. Order was restored after a while, and about dark we reached "Bunker Hill," and made our bivouac on the south side of the creek. "The behavior of some of the troops engaged to-day has been shameful." Among our killed is Gen. Mulligan, commanding division.

25th. A severe rain storm set in about 12 o'clock last night, continuing till about 10 this forenoon. How it did pour! We turned out at daylight, wet, cold, tired, sleepy, hungry and cross; crossed the creek, formed line of battle, and had a nice little skirmish with the Rebel force, which was again pressing us. During the whole time, the rain fell in torrents. About 9 A. M., our brigade, acting as rear guard, commenced to fall back. We reached Martinsburg about noon, and again stood in line of battle. The Rebels soon appeared, and *we* became engaged. Skirmishing was continued till about 3 P. M., when we fell further back, taking a new position on the east side of the village, from which after a while we advanced, and in turn, drove the enemy through the town, and established our line, at sunset, about a mile and a half out on the Winchester Pike. About dark, we withdrew on the Williamsport Pike, and having reached the Potomac, went into camp, on the banks of the river. While the morning's skirmish was going on, a plucky incident in the duelling line occurred. A mounted confederate rode out, alone, in front of their line, directly toward ours. Instantly a man dashed from among our cavalry to meet him; and as these two got within thirty or forty yards of each other, they began to empty their revolvers. The Reb. shot the horse from under our man, who regaining our lines, mounted another, and went forward again. While these two were firing at each other, a second Johnny came riding, under cover of the hill, towards these combatants, and got one shot at our man. Seeing this fellow, and his object, Sergeant Judd of ours, crawled down under cover of some bushes, and let him have a shot. "I did n't hit him," said J., "but as he ducked his head down under his horse's neck, and galloped away, I guess he thought the ball came near enough for comfort."

CHAPTER XXXVII

THE RACE GROUND.

TO BOONSBORO — PLEASANT VALLEY — HALLTOWN — A DAY IN CAMP AND A DRILL NOT IN CASEY — TO BURKETTSVILLE — WOLFSBURG — OUR STRENGTH — THE MONOCACY — CAPTAIN POTTER — AN EXECUTION — PLEASANT VALLEY — KNOX'S FORD — BERRYVILLE — MIDDLETOWN — A SKIRMISH.

26th. We started at light this morning, and commenced crossing the river. The ford was a very good one indeed. Reached "Williamsport," which is quite a pretty little place, whose inhabitants are said to be Union; halted long enough to enable everything to be got out of town, when we started, on the "Sharpsburg Pike," and kept on till we reached "Boonsboro'" shortly before sunset. Here we went into camp, hoping for a good night's rest; distance marched, about thirteen miles.

But about 10, we were roused, and starting out, marched to Sharpsburg, which place was reached at 2 o'clock the morning of the 27th.

27th. We were on the road again at 6 this morning, and marching down into the town, halted to draw rations. Then, starting again, passing over a part of the "Antietam" battle ground, and through Harper's Ferry, and "Sandy Hook," we reached "Pleasant Valley," about 4 P. M., where we went into camp. We are just nine miles, by the pike, from our last night's camp at "Boonsboro'," but to get here we have marched over twenty miles of a dusty, weary way.

28th. The day has been very hot. As our night was quiet,

and morning undisturbed, we began to think there *could* be "rest for the weary," but at 5 P. M., orders were received directing us to cross the Potomac; so back we trudged, crossed at Harper's Ferry, and are once more encamped at "Halltown." We hear the 6th and 19th corps are close behind us, and every thing points to another trip up the valley. Well, it *can be done*, I suppose; but it will come very hard upon us, in our exhausted condition.

29th. For a wonder we remained in camp to-day; but that the boys might not be *discontented*, a drill was ordered,— one *not* laid down in Casey.

Clothing was to be issued, of which we are all much in need; for we have marched, and slept, and fought, in rain and shine, in dust and mud, without change of any single garment since we started on our raid last April; and our clothing is not only dirty, but ragged;—and not only ragged, but fairly alive with those grey-backs which stick so like brothers, when once domiciled in one's clothing.

Preceded by our band, and followed by Lieut. Lincoln, Acting Quartermaster, whose teams were loaded with a complete outfit from head to foot for every man in the command, we were marched to the banks of a small stream, and ordered to *strip*, in as few motions as possible. Standing *in puris naturalibus*, a regiment of naked men, each one grasping his piece of soap, the order was given to "charge on the river." Such shouting, and yelling, such tumbling and pushing, such ducking and splashing, such scrubbing was never before seen. Meanwhile our Quartermaster moved up his teams to the line of old clothes; the Captains receipted for the new issue; and the men, as they left the water, their skins sparkling and glowing, were given the new clothing to put on. This done, the old clothing was piled and burned; and to the tune of "Oh, dear, what can the matter be," we marched back to our quarters, clean and bright, and as ill fitted as the last arrived one hundred days men; and for a while we shall feel just as well.

The 6th and the 19th Corps have come up; and some wags among us attempted to pass the Regiment as ninety days men.

"Ninety days men is it!" said an Irishman to whom they were telling the story. "Ninety days men, is it! and faith then, a good many of yees have had the nose-bleed, and used your old Flag as a towel! Smoke that, my honeys, till the next time!"

30th. Again the night was quiet, and the forenoon undisturbed. All were beginning to think *something was wrong*, when orders came for us "to start, and be lively about it." We packed, and started towards Harper's Ferry. The weather was very oppressive; and many of the men "fell out" during the march; some of them completely exhausted by the heat; of whom one or two died. Passing through the "Ferry," "Sandy Hook," "Reamston," and "Knoxville," we struck the "Frederick Pike," which, after following a few miles, we left to the right, and at eleven P. M. halted at "Burketsville," having marched fourteen miles. We can learn nothing definite, from the citizens, of the movements of the rebel force; hearing rumors only of their presence on this side of the river.

31st. Oppressive as was the weather yesterday, it was worse this morning. Our march was resumed at 5 A. M. Our route leading us past "Burketsville," through "Middletown" and "Belleville," to within about three miles of "Wolfsburg," where we went into camp. The Boys were entirely overcome by the heat of the day, and fell out by scores. So badly were they affected, that at the halt for dinner, there were present of the 34th, but fifteen or twenty to stack arms on the color line. Bad as this was, it was worse in some of the other Regiments of the Brigade.

July 31st. Our muster rolls show "present," officers, 14; men, 391; sick, 18. Absent: officers, 9 on detached service; sick, 6; prisoners of war, 8. Enlisted men: 34 on detached service; without leave, 12; sick, 316; prisoners of war, 105. The only changes in position or duty among the officers were that Lieut. T. W Ripley had been appointed Acting Adjutant, to date from July 1, vice S. F. Woods, died of wounds received in action at Piedmont. Lieut. Lincoln to be Acting Quartermaster; Lieut. W L. Cobb to be A. A. I. G. on Brigade Staff, and the promotion of Color Sergeant John E. Calligan to be 2d

Lieutenant, vice Walker promoted. 1st Lieut. Charles W
Elwell to be Captain. 2d Lieut. R. W Walker to be 1st Lieutenant, and M. E. Walker and Wm. F. Belser to be 2d Lieutenants.

August 1st. Turning out this morning at 4½ and starting at 5, we marched a couple of miles to "Wolfsburg," and went into camp. Here we are to await orders from Gen. Hunter, who is supposed to be in or near "Frederick City." The burning of "Chambersburg," by McCausland, was made known to us, and caused no little revengeful feeling.

3d. We started at 4 o'clock this morning, in a slight rain. This soon cleared off, leaving us to the rays of a burning sun. We reached "Frederick City" about 1 o'clock, marching directly through the place to "Monocacy Bridge;" then followed down the river until we came to the ford used by the Rebs, when, a few weeks since, they drove Lew Wallace from his position there. Crossing by the same ford, we went into camp and *pitched our "A" tents!* Heavens, what luxury!!

5th. No movement yesterday; and the only thing which occurred to break the monotony of our situation, was the arrival in camp of Capt. Potter, who was just from Massachusetts, and who, although his wound is doing well, is not fit for duty, and talks some of returning home for a time. His presence was made doubly pleasant by the fact that he brought us a mail. The weather still continues *very, very hot,* and we are glad enough that we are in camp, instead of on the march.

Gen. Grant arrived at Gen. Hunter's Headquarters this afternoon, and there is much speculation as to the actual meaning and probable result of his presence. Of course no one was surprised by the sudden call, "to the colors," which was sounded about an half hour before sunset, nor for the "order for the entire regiment to turn out." Getting under arms, the troops were formed on three sides of a hollow square, the fourth side being left vacant. For the first time in our service we were to be present at a *"military execution."* The condemned man was a member of the 23d Ohio. He originally deserted from the Rebel service and enlisted in the 23d. At the battle of "Cloyd's Mountain" he deserted this new service, and rejoined the Confederates, to be captured by his own Regiment, with a musket in his hands. On his way to the rear, he escaped from his guard and went to Ohio, where, tempted by the offer of $500, he entered our service again as a substitute. On reaching the front, he was assigned to his old Regiment, and was at once recognized by his former comrades. His arrest, trial, sentence and execution followed in rapid succession, and was all the work of one day. Kneeling on his coffin (the firing detail, about ten paces in his front), he was shot through the breast, eight balls penetrating his body.

6th. Late last eve. we received orders "to march immediately." These were countermanded in a few moments; and in their place came others directing our movement at four o'clock this morning. At that hour it was raining quite hard; but by eight A. M. it cleared away. Fording the "Monocacy," we took the road leading to Harper's Ferry; passed through "Jefferson" about noon, and went into camp near our old position of last week, in Pleasant Valley. Although the heat has been excessive, the men have borne the day's march very well. We learn to-night, that General Sheridan, with his Cavalry, is somewhere in our neighborhood.

9th. Since our arrival here, we have been allowed to remain in camp; the weather then, as since, having been hot,— hotter, — hottest. At our start to-day, we passed through the "Hook," "The Ferry," and "Bolivar;" and went into camp, on the banks of the "Shenandoah," at Knox's Ford.

After reaching camp, Lieut. Ripley, and Quartermaster Howland, rode back to the Ferry, and passed some enjoyable hours. This evening all the officers, of the field and staff, have been paid off. All will feel better in consequence, as it will be easier getting supplies, if we have some money among us. When one has no money, and can't borrow, and is forbidden to forage, it is difficult, and sometimes pretty lively work for those who sport shoulder straps, to procure subsistence.

10th. We started at four this morning, up the river, in the direction of "Berryville;" keeping between the river, and the Charleston Pike, all the way. Marched over our battle ground of "Island Ford," and reached "Berryville" about sunset, going into camp just north of the town. The 19th Corps is just to the right of us, and the 6th on their right, holding the extreme right of the line. We hear, in the distance, sounds of an engagement.

11*th*. The weather this morning is pleasant, but the air hot and close. Leaving " Berryville " at five o'clock, on the " Millwood Pike," we went in the direction of " Front Royal," about two miles, and then turned towards " Winchester." There were sounds of a smart affair away off on the right. When we were within about six miles of " Winchester," we turned again and headed in the direction of " Front Royal." We passed " White Post," and went into camp opposite, and about six miles from " Middletown." There has been heavy skirmishing, a good part of the day, by Cavalry, in our front, and by Cavalry and Artillery, on our right.

12*th*. Started about six o'clock this morning, heading for " Middletown;" where we arrived about noon,— halted for coffee,— then marched out to the creek, where the whole command was soon engaged in brisk skirmishing, which continued all the afternoon. The confederates held their ground, till nearly sunset; when the 1st and 12th Virginia, way down on the left, made a brilliant charge, and drove them on a run. This gave us the entire bank this side of the creek. In our front, the "heavies," deployed as skirmishers, gained and held the farther bank; and we have gone into camp, under cover of the woods, near the Ford.

13*th*. Daylight this morning showed us the enemy still in position, but with reduced force. Our Cavalry crossed the Creek and the Rebs fell back towards " Strasburg." The 6th and 19th Corps also crossed and went into camp on the other side of the Creek. The advance had a lively time of it out towards " Fisher's Hill." At sunset the whole force, save the skirmishers, who continued to hold the line established last night, recrossed the creek. It looks as if we were " *in for it* " to-morrow; we seeming to be fated to fight on the Sabbath. Our own Brigade has laid quietly in camp all day.

CHAPTER XXXVIII

THE RACE-GROUND.

SKIRMISHING AGAIN — TO WINCHESTER AGAIN — BERRYVILLE — CHARLESTOWN — SOME RED TAPE — MAJOR PRATT — NEWS OF COL. LINCOLN'S ESCAPE — MORE SKIRMISHING — OFF FOR HALLTOWN — ANOTHER SKIRMISH — A BARRICADE — CHARLEY THURMAN — AGAIN SKIRMISHING.

14th. Contrary to yesterday's appearances, all has been quiet to-day, no movement of importance having occurred. Just before sunset, the Rebel skirmish line made an advance, under a very brisk fire, driving our skirmishers back a short distance, when reinforcements having come up, we, in turn, drove the Johnnies; our reserve, at dusk, occupying a grain field which bounds our vision towards "Strasburg;" and which has been alternately held by one or the other party since our first reaching this ground.

15th. For the past few days the weather has been very hot; to-day was exceedingly oppressive, and the men have been thankful enough for the privilege of remaining in camp. Company drills, for three hours daily, are ordered to be resumed. About 2 o'clock this afternoon, the Rebels opened upon us with artillery, throwing some fifteen or twenty shells, under cover of which they advanced their skirmishers. Our line fell back a short distance; when it charged in turn, driving the Rebs back, and we again held the stubble field, which had been so often contended for. One of our batteries has been posted to-night on the left of our camp, in readiness to greet the Johnnies if they advance again.

The 170th Ohio left us to-day, their time having expired. Advantage was taken of their going, to send back a train under their charge.

16th. It is still very hot weather, and we have laid still during the day. Longstreet's Corps, from the direction of the "Luray Valley," tried to turn our left, to-day, and in the afternoon we heard cannonading, which we learned was near "Front Royal." Everything, however, remained quiet in our front. At 8 P. M. orders were received to "march immediately, en route for Winchester." The 19th Corps was in advance; next came the 6th, and then our own; Getty's Division, of the 6th Corps, constituting the rear guard. We reached "Winchester" at about 3 A. M. where we bivouacked; distance marched, fifteen miles.

17th. We were roused at 8 A. M. and were at breakfast, when "*Fall in,*" "Fall in," was shouted. We marched through town, and out on the "Berryville Pike," reaching Berryville about 3 P. M., where we went into camp. We learned, on reaching here, that yesterday's cannonading came from an attack made by "Longstreet, upon Sheridan," at "Front Royal;" the former being whipped handsomely, losing some six hundred prisoners and three stands of colors. The prisoners are with our column to-day, and look like splendid fighting material. Cannonading is now heard in the direction of Winchester, where we suppose the 6th Corps to be. Col. Wilson, of the 123d Ohio, is sick and delirious; he is now in a stupor in a private house near by.

18th. We started at 5 o'clock this morning, the column heading for "Charlestown." Col. Wilson was better, and we took him, with us, in our ambulance. About a mile out, we stopped and issued rations to the command, from a supply train. Halted about noon, and went into camp, in a very pleasant piece of woods, near the scene of the 34th's engagement with Imboden in Oct. last. It rained nearly all the forenoon, and is now still cloudy.

19th. In camp all day; weather rainy,— ground wet and muddy. Red tape has suddenly gained the ascendancy. Orders are issued directing the *burning of all regimental books and papers;* and subordinate officers are notified that, in future, the monthly and tri-monthly returns and reports will be required *on time.*

20th. Weather still cloudy and threatening more rain. At noon, Major Pratt, a large mail, and marching orders, all reached us at the same moment. From the Major we learn that Col. Lincoln has succeeded in making his escape from the Rebels, and had reached Worcester; his health very poor, and he probably unfit for duty for a long while. The Major himself looks much improved by his visit home; and his wound has ceased troubling him, although he is still weak.

21st. Still cloudy this morning; but about 8 the clouds broke away, and the sun burned fiercely down upon his. We were engaged in changing the direction of our Brigade line this morning, having got Headquarters established, and the Pioneers were just pitching the last tent, when sharp cannonading broke out in the direction of Martinsburg, Summit Point and Berryville, and orders came to pack up and hold ourselves in readiness to move. Marching orders soon followed; and we started off "across lots," coming out about a mile and a half to the westward of Charleston. Here we encountered a sharp skirmish fire in front. The 1st Division was on our left, and the 2d formed on our right. Far away to the right of these was the 6th Corps; the 19th being between us and the 6th. Two lines of barricades reaching for a long distance through the woods have been constructed. Skirmishing is quite lively in our immediate front, while on the right and far away to the left the cannonading is brisk. We have out a very strong line of skirmishers, and everything indicates an advance upon us, by the enemy in force. 10 P. M.— We laid in the woods behind our breastworks of rails, from 3 till now, 10 P. M; when we moved away, taking the back track for Halltown, and reaching there about 3 A. M.

22d. We had a rest of about two hours after going into our bivouac of last night, or rather this morning, when we fell in and marched to the position we are now holding, which is in a good piece of woods upon the estate, and near the home of Ex-Gov. Lucas, about a mile in front of Halltown. The 19th are on our left, and the 6th to our right. Our position is a splendid one by nature, our line extending from the Potomac to the Shenandoah, and we have entrenched ourselves quite strongly. Nothing of consequence occurred during the day, although the skirmishers in our immediate front were popping away quite briskly. About an hour before dusk our Brigade, leaving the protection of their works, made a sally and drove the enemy back about a mile, killing five, capturing an equal number, and getting back without the loss of a man. There was a very heavy thunder storm this afternoon.

23*d*. We were up at day break, and in line, prepared for and expecting an attack; but none was made. All day long the skirmishers have been actively engaged, and occasionally a field piece has been called upon, on our side, to bear upon the supposed position of the enemy. The Rebels have shown no artillery; and have succeeded pretty well in concealing from us the position of their men. We have been hard at work, forming a new barricade, on our flank. It is made of heavy logs,—is very substantial,—and we think will prove to be very strong. Who should surprise us to-day, by making his appearance in camp, and reporting for duty, but Charlie Thurman, bugler of D, who *deserted* at "Upton's Hill." He has been to Germany, but returned of his own free will, and reporting in Boston, was forwarded to us here.

24*th*. Everything this morning was quiet, and the weather again intensely hot. About noon a reconnoisance in force was ordered. We drove the Rebels from their temporary cover, (some huge hay stacks, which we fired and burned,) back to where their main body was found to be in force, and strongly posted. A sharp engagement was had, commencing on the right and extending to our own front, in which our brigade captured eleven of the Johnnies. To-night all along the line, everything is quiet, but it is the quiet which precedes the storm. There must be a fight before long, as we have been *looking* at each other long enough.

CHAPTER XXXIX.

THE 'RACE GROUND.

FEELING "TIP-TOP" — OUR ROLLS — TO BERRYVILLE AND SKIRMISH — MORE SKIRMISHING — AT WORK — EVERYBODY CROSS AND UGLY — MORE CHEERFUL — TO SUMMIT POINT — ALL QUIET — UNPLEASANT WEATHER — WEATHER MIXED — WEATHER PLEASANT — ALL SORTS OF WEATHER — CONTINUES THE SAME — FORAGING PARTY LOADED — LEAVE TO "GO IN."

Aug. 31st. Our muster roll shows with the regiment present for duty: Officers, 11; enlisted men, 368. On detached service: Officers, 9; sick, 5; prisoners of war, 6; Enlisted men on detached service, 34; sick, 306; prisoners of war, 123. The resignation of Lieut and Acting Reg. Q'rm'r Levi Lincoln, based upon Surgeon's certificate of disability, was accepted; and that officer honorably discharged the service.

To-day was an eventful one to us, in that the Paymaster arrived, and settled the little obligation each of us held against our Uncle Samuel. The boys are feeling "tiptop" in the possession of their "greenbacks."

Sept. 3d. Orders to be in readiness to move at 4 o'clock this morning, reached us yesterday afternoon. Accordingly, we turned out about 3:30 A. M., and, moving along the pike, came, about noon, in sight of "Berryville." Here we halted for two or three hours, when we took to the road again, moved up close to the town, and went into camp. By the time supper was ready, we were engaged, skirmishing heavily in front, on the Winchester road. The firing was rapid and heavy, and lasted till long after dark, but without any material result. A heavy shower, which broke upon us soon after dark, put an end to the firing.

4th. Skirmishing was resumed early this morning; our boys, being well protected, sustained slight loss. Capt. Thompson and the Major each had narrow escapes. Capt. Elwell received a slight wound in the leg. Before breakfast was finished, orders came for the men to "fall in," and move to the left of the line, where, upon arriving, they were at once set to work erecting breastworks. Here, considerable skirmishing occurred, with now and then firing by the artillery. About 70 prisoners and one stand of colors were taken from the enemy. Among the prisoners was the color bearer of the 18th Mississippi. Towards evening we got our tents ["A"] pitched.

5th. The boys have been hard at work, all day, upon the fortifications, along the whole line; but were interrupted about noon, by the Johnnies, who made an advance, with two strong lines of skirmishers. Our reserve, which had been concealed in the under-brush, charged, and captured between sixty and seventy prisoners. Our line of defences is very strong; so much so, as to lead us to believe that we shall not be attacked, while enjoying its advantage.

6th. The weather, which changed last evening, when it commenced to rain and blow severely, is still rainy, and chilly. To-day has been the most disagreeable we have had for months, and everybody has been cross and ugly. The Sutler, who has just arrived, alone looks smiling. His face beams upon us, with all the freshness of a new moon. Everything has been quiet in our front.

7th. The storm, which has raged for the past twenty-four hours, broke last night, and this morning is most beautiful. Under the influence of a bright sun, the camp looks, and the men are more cheerful. All are engaged in drying blankets and clothing, both of which are "ringing wet." Except a slight Cavalry affair, down towards "Millwood," everything to-day has been quiet; and it looks as if the enemy had withdrawn from our front.

8th. About nine o'clock came marching orders. Packing, we started, and crossing the "Charleston Pike," marched along, across the country, in a line with the "Summit Point Pike," until about four P. M., when we went into camp near "Summit Point," at the extreme right of the line, about half way between "Charleston" and "Berryville." Here we were joined by Sergeant Smith, of K, who, having escaped from the rebels at "Harrisonburg," had succeeded in making his way to our lines at "New Creek." He has had a hard time of it.

9*th*. Our march yesterday was made in a pouring rain, which continued till this morning; since which, we have been favored with regular "dog-day" weather; now, a bright scorching sun,— now a violent shower, and blowing at intervals a regular gale of wind. All is quiet in front.

10*th*. The weather, which was unpleasant enough yesterday, is a little more so to-day. The morning being very warm and pleasant; raining hard at noon, and clear and bright, though chilly in the afternoon, and evening.

11*th*. The weather continues *mixed*. Everything, in our front, continues quiet; and we have got nicely settled in our present quarters.

Way off, in the direction of "Bunker Hill," there is the sound of a smart engagement; and we think perhaps "Averill is giving the rebels a warming."

12*th*. Warm and pleasant weather, for a wonder, all day long; and we are enjoying it and our rest heartily. We are kept on the *qui vive*, however, by the sound of heavy cannonading, which has fallen on our ears from the direction of the crossing of the "Opequan," and the "Winchester and Berryville pike." Torbett is said to have charged the enemy most brilliantly, and brought off one entire regiment of South Carolinians, consisting of 16 commissioned officers and 147 rank and file, with its battle flags.

13*th*. Again, rain—rain—rain; it has literally poured down the wind blowing a perfect hurricane. Everybody has kept snug in his quarters, and the entire camp has been dismal enough.

Sept. 14*th*. The morning was pleasant, but the day has been showery. New wall tents have been pitched at headquarters, which add much to the convenience, and something to the appearance of our encampment. "We get information, to-day, that commissions have been issued, constituting Sergeants Blake and Judd, Lieutenants." They won't grumble much at this.

15th. *Rainy — cloudy — windy — sunshiny — lowery — still;* in fact, there has been all sorts of weather to-day. When the sun has shone, it has fairly burned; when it has rained, it has poured, as if the flood gates were opened; and man, dressed in a little brief authority, not to be outdone, has tried his best to make our condition uncomfortable, by the issue of general and special orders, circulars, &c., which have been poured down upon our heads thick and fast.

16th. The weather continues "the same" to-day. There is nothing doing along the lines. Not to neglect the opportunities afforded by this long-continued inaction, a party of our boys went out, this morning, foraging on their own account. They came back *loaded* in more ways than one; exhibiting outwardly a good assortment of cabbages, tomatoes, squashes, potatoes, apples, peaches, and, in the line of meat, chickens in a goodly number, a large supply of pork, and *one* turkey—buzzard. This last, in some unaccountable way, by an inexplicable rule of division, was sent up to headquarters. Whatever becomes of others, it is morally certain these fellows won't starve.

17th. The weather is pleasant to-day, for a wonder. Gen. Grant came up as far as Charleston, where he and Sheridan had a meeting; and we are looking for orders to move, it being rumored that Sheridan has at length received permission to "go in."

CHAPTER XL.

THE BATTLE OF "THE OPEQUAN."

19*th*. The quiet of the last few days was broken early this morning by the movement of the entire army. At 3 A. M. we were on the march; this time *towards* the position of the Rebel army which was in and around Winchester. Writes Capt. Soley of the 34th, as follows: "Wilson led his Cavalry from the extreme left, near Berryville, by the pike to the Opequan; crossed that stream, and galloping along the gorge, gained the Rebel earthworks at its head, where he met and drove back Ramseur's Division of Rebel Infantry. The 6th and 19th Corps coming up, established themselves in line of battle where the plain opened from the head of this gorge. Torbet crossed the creek, with his Cavalry, at a point lower down, under orders to effect a junction with Averill, who was moving on the Martinsburg pike. Crook, marching his command (the Army of West Virginia), over a *dirt road*, reached the Opequan about 9 A. M., and was held in reserve on the east bank of the creek, immediately in rear of the battle-field. As we moved to this position, the boom of artillery, faint at first, but increasing in volume as we advanced, with the muffled roll of small arms was distinctly heard. This was from Averill, driving the Rebel Cavalry up along the Martinsburg pike, and Merritt forcing his crossing of the Opequan. Soon, more distinctly, from the direction in which we were moving, came the thunder of a heavier cannonading. This was from Wilson attacking Ramseur, and the Rebels shelling the 6th and 19th Corps as they were moving into position. Now, having reached the high ground upon the bank of the creek, we were halted; arms were stacked; and the men, their appetites well sharpened by their march of nine miles, since 3 A. M., were dismissed to boil their coffee. All were in high spirits. From our elevated ground, we could overlook the scene of conflict, on the other side of the stream. The 6th and 19th had attacked with great gallantry and vigor, though as yet no decided advantage had been secured.

The battle continued with changing fortune for an hour or more, when the enemy charging in force struck our centre, between the two corps, and sent it back in some confusion. At this point, Upton's Brigade of Russell's division, led by Gen. Russell in person, struck the Rebel column of attack in flank, and compelled it to fall back. From our eminence we could see the whole extent of the field. The country, from the creek at our feet, and north of the pike leading from Berryville to Winchester, was broken, dotted with occasional corn-fields and isolated pieces of wood land, and intersected with occasional lines of stone wall. Here the Rebels were formed in line of battle. From their rear, extending up to the town of Winchester, and far away on and beyond his right and left, was an open plain; the ground, gently rolling, divided by occasional walls, and broken, here and there, by patches of thick timber. Over this field a dense cloud of smoke was hanging, which in places somewhat obscured our view. Yet we saw, or thought we saw, that our force, already engaged, was insufficient for the work in hand, and somewhat impatiently waited for orders *to go in*. The sound of battle had grown from an irregular skirmish fire, to an uninterrupted roll of musketry, mingled with and at times almost drowned by the heavier roar of Artillery. The loud cheer of our men was met by the sharper *wild yell* of the enemy, as he gathered to repel our charge, or to attack our lines in turn. The contending forces had tried each others strength; each had lost heavily; and neither had gained decisive advantage. For the moment the musketry fire had somewhat slackened, but the artillery, all along the lines, was served furiously.

Most of us leisurely smoked our pipes, and discussed the situation. A young Lieutenant of ours, anxious to add a *bar* to his shoulder straps, impatiently cut down mullein stalks with his sword, and petulantly expressed his fear, that "we should have no chance to-day." "Don't be impatient" replied a veteran Captain, measuring like an Indian, the hour with his eye; there is time enough between now and night, for many a brave fellow to lose the number of his mess." And at the very instant, from the head of the column, our bugles rang out the "assembly," and every man sprang to his place. We crossed the creek, and entered the cañon leading to the field of battle. Here we met a steady and strong current of wounded men, and stragglers, from the corps already engaged with the enemy. Forcing our way through the throng, we emerged from the gorge, turned to the right, and passing up an intersecting ravine, in rear of the troops which had been engaged, formed line on their right, in open ground, partly covered in front, by a piece of thick woods.

Here we encountered the enemy's skirmishers, who were feeling their way around the right flank of the 19th corps. A lively little affair resulted in our driving the enemy out, and back to his main line, which was strongly posted behind stone walls, in another tract of timber, which extended to the open country beyond.

Duvall's Division, upon entering the defile, after crossing the Opequan, instead of following our route, had gone down the creek, to a point farther on our right, forded an intersecting stream, waist deep in water, with the purpose of coming up on our right, where, as we first felt the enemy, he was revealed in considerable strength.

No advance could be made by us, without exposure to a flank attack; and so, standing with orders to *keep ready to charge*, we waited anxiously for Duvall's approach. Suddenly his well known battle cry was heard; and his men came into view, and dashed at the enemy, pushing him with an impetuosity seldom equalled,— never surpassed. Taking up the cry, we joined in the charge. As we advanced, a deep ravine extending to our front, separated us (the 34th) from our Division on the left. The ground in our front, was broken and rough, with here and there a tract of wood-land, in which the enemy lay sheltered. Delivering our fire with coolness and precision, we pressed forward steadily, and swept him into the open fields beyond.

These were crossed by stone walls, running in various directions, where the ground, although generally smooth, was broken by gently swelling knolls. As we gained the summit of one of these little knolls, we found, that our line of direction, being too much to the right, presented our left flank to the enemy's Artillery, which had taken position in "the open," about three-fourths of a mile from us. Changing direction by a "a left half wheel," in line, we moved directly upon the guns. Duvall's line, traced by his waving battle flags only, his men completely hidden from view by the young wood, was soon seen, as it made its way through a large tract of wood-land, on our right. He had doubled back the rebel left, which, emerging from the brush, was hurrying to the shelter of a stone wall, in our own front. The enemy, well to our left also, were seeking the cover of the same wall, which extended, in that direction, to a considerable distance.

Our own Division had not yet issued from the woods, which here projected more to the front; but we could mark its advance by the prolonged cries, and cheers it always uttered during a charge, or while driving an enemy.

Now, in our immediate front, was a wide extended field, sloping gradually away for about five hundred yards; thence rising somewhat abruptly to a point about two hundred yards farther to the front, whence it continued on a dead level to the wall, behind which, by this time, the enemy had gathered in strong force. Over this ground, under a storm of shells from the rebel guns, well posted in our front, the 34th, *isolated,— alone,—* was advanced in perfect line. Duvall, on our right, and at least one-fourth of a mile to the rear, was urging his men through the tangled brush-wood; and to our left, our own Brigade, and Division, just issuing from the woods, was engaged in rectifying its broken formation.

It would have been the part of wisdom, had the 34th been halted in the slight depression of ground, which it had to pass over, where we should have been somewhat sheltered from the enemy's fire. But, ambitious to be the first to plant our standards on the wall, behind which the enemy was posted, *we went right on.* As we reached the crest of the slope, up which we were moving, and brought the *wall*, less than 200 yards distant, into clear view, a vivid sheet of fire, like the burning, blinding lightning's glare, ran along the front, and a deadly storm of grape and bullets tore through our ranks. It seemed as if half the regiment went down before that single volley. Instantaneously the mournful wail of our bugles sounded "Lie down! lie down?" But the order was a mockery. Every man, living or dying, was already buried in the grass, which the enemy's musketry was mowing closely and clean. But for the *white flag*, which, planted firmly, was waving above our lines, neither friend nor foe would have suspected our presence. The moment and the situation were critical.

We were not only alone, in advance of any other body of troops in Sheridan's whole line of battle, but the ground we occupied was swept by grape and cannister from four Napoleons hidden behind the wall in our front; while a battery of rifled guns, further to the Rebel rear, and more to our right, dropped its shells, thick and fast, into our line. A shell from one of these guns struck the knapsack of a man near me, and sent its contents flying in the air. The brave fellow looked up, and smilingly remarked to his comrades, "That was a close shave, boys;" and as he ceased, another shell struck him full in the face, and, exploding, scattered his quivering flesh over his comrades lying near. The Captain of the company on my left was struck by a fragment of the same shell. What was to be done? To remain as we were seemed impossible; to advance or retreat seemed equally out of the question. Never, even on "*general review*," did time drag so slowly, or moments seem so dilatory. *It seemed an age* — in reality, it was nearly half an hour — when Duvall's men came up. Their advance led the enemy to turn his guns partially upon that command. Now, in the partial slackening of the fire which had so galled us, "Forward!" was sounded from our bugles. All sprang to their feet, and turned their eyes to our centre; for, in the din of the contest, the notes were indistinctly heard; and we (certainly I, for one,) deemed it hardly possible that such an order could have been given. But there, by the side of our flag, stood the slight form of our brave commander (Maj. Pratt), and near to him was our chief bugler, who, in response to the former's signal, *again blew his shrill blast*. There had been no mistake! *It was,—"Forward."* We made a dash for the wall, which the enemy abandoned with a haste proportionate to our advance, leaving behind him one of his Napoleons, and a few of his men. In the dash, and as we had almost gained the wall, fell Capt. Thompson, of D, pierced through the heart with a musket ball. Brave and accomplished officer that he was, his loss dampened the joy of our success!

Our own brigade and division coming up now, connected on our left; and the enemy fell back to some old rifle pits and earthworks, which run parallel with his lately abandoned line. From our cover, behind the wall, we could look about us. Away to the right Custer, and Torbett, and Merritt, and Averill were driving the Rebel Cavalry, in a confused mass, across the open country; to the left, the 6th and 19th corps presented a splendid appearance, as issuing from the woods, they pressed hard upon the Rebel force with which they had been engaged, now falling back broken and disordered. With the coming up of these corps, the whole army moved in magnificent array; our own Division directly upon several pieces of artillery, which had hurriedly taken position in an old earthwork, on the heights, near Winchester. The fire from these pieces was terribly annoying and destructive. On duty at Division Headquarters, and riding near the person of the Division Commander, was Parker, bugler of our company "I." A shell from one of those pieces struck his horse full in the shoulder, and exploding, sent the body of the bugler high in the air, and scattered the flesh of the animal in every direction. Seeing the mischief, a Lieutenant of Dupont's battery brought one of his *pieces*, on a gallop, to the front,—unlimbered—sighted it himself,—and fired—sending up a thick cloud of dust from in front of the Rebel cannon. *We had no more trouble from that quarter*. As we advanced against the rifle pits, the enemy gave us a feeble and irregular fire,—turned in disorder,—and a cloud of eddying dust, stirred up by his flying masses, as they hastily retreated over the plain, told us the day was won. Now the Cavalry, in one unbroken line, swept down from the right, and wheeling, gathered within its circle huge masses of the flying Rebels. We ceased firing to gaze admiringly upon the scene; this final movement which brought a most brilliant victory to our arms, and sent Early "whirling through Winchester." Following this movement closely, Crook's command, moving by the left flank, entered the town, as the enemy's rear issued from it, upon the other side. It was twilight; the principal streets of the village were choked with the stragglers, and the debris of the defeated and flying enemy. An ammunition wagon struck and exploded, with all its horses dead, obstructed our passage. All the houses, save such as were already taken for hospital use, were closed; and looked as if abandoned. Not a citizen could be seen on the streets; and we moved onward with saddened hearts, yet firm tread, out, beyond the town, some two or three miles, going into bivouac near Millwood.

"Sad enough," adds Capt. Soley, "were my feelings that night, as I stood bare headed before my company. Twenty-one of my men, who advanced against the enemy that day, were *absent*. I could account for each man of them; they were lying on the bloody field;—the greater number of them in front of the *stone wall*."

Col Wells, commanding brigade, thus writes: "The officers and men of the different commands behaved magnificently. Maj. Pratt, commanding the 34th Massachusetts, and Lieut. Col. Wilds, the 116th Ohio, handled their regiments with great courage and skill, and in all the confusion of the charge, kept their commands together. I desire to call special attention to the gallant conduct of Maj. Pratt and his regiment, in the last charge. Capt. Chamberlain, commanding the 123d Ohio, lost three of his five officers; and his men became in consequence disorganized. But with the portion of the regiment he kept with him, he did splendid fighting, and was one of the first in the enemy's works. To my own staff, Lieuts. Dissoway and Cobb, I am under great obligations for their invaluable assistance. In the first charge, some young officer, of Gen. Sheridan's staff, rode in advance of the line bare headed, and cheering on the men. I regret that I am not able to give the name of this officer, whose gallant example helped much in inspiriting the men."

"I have to regret the death of Capt. Thompson, for a long time commanding the 34th Massachusetts, and a most valuable and gallant officer. (I have the honor to forward a list of casualties, and the reports of Regimental Commanders.)

Signed: GEO. D. WELLS,

Col. 34th Massachusetts Vol. Infantry,

Commanding the Brigade.

RECAPITULATION.

TROOPS.	KILLED.		WOUNDED.	
	Officers.	*Privates.*	*Officers.*	*Privates.*
34th Mass. Infantry,	1	6	6	91
5th N. Y. Artillery,		9	1	33
123d Ohio Infantry,		6	3	39
116th " "	..	4	1	27
Total	1	25	11	190

Of our wounded, ninety-seven in number, *four* died the next day. We had one man *missing*.

CHAPTER XLI.

The Battle of the Opequan.

COL. HARRIS AND CAPT. SOLEY — CAPT. ELWELL — HOSPITAL STEWARD, FAIRBANKS — DR. SMITH.

One or two incidents of the day are well worth recounting. While we were advancing over the slope, which extended between our line and the stone wall behind which the enemy had taken his new position, a tall, fine looking officer, mounted on a large sized and powerful bay horse, galloped up on our left. Swinging wildly a dragoon's sabre, he exhorted, us in a voice which could be plainly heard above the roar of battle, to *move faster,—double quick,—run!* As he rode down the line, looking the very demon of battle, he was recognized as a Colonel of a Western regiment, (Col. Harris, of the West Virginia Infantry), now commanding a Brigade in our division. He had strayed from his own command, in his effort to follow it while charging through the thick undergrowth of the woods, and, in the excitement of the occasion, had mistaken the 34th for one of his own regiments. As he galloped along our line, which, in disregard of his oft repeated orders, still moved at *quick time,* he thus addressed the writer: "Captain, take the *double quick—double quick,—march!*" "Colonel," I replied, pointing with my sword towards the centre, "*those colors are my guide;* when they move at a double quick, my men will do the same; if you wish this regiment to move faster, you will find its commander in his place, and any order from him will be cheerfully and promptly obeyed."

The Colonel's eyes followed the direction in which my sword was pointed; and as they fell upon the tattered folds of the *old White Flag* of our State (the only one in Crook's entire command), he saw his error, and, wheeling his horse, and giving him the spur, he dashed, under a perfect storm of shot and shells, to his own command, on the left.

A few days afterwards, writes Capt. Soley, I had the honor of meeting this Colonel, at Division Headquarters; and, at his request, related the incident; which, as told, caused much merriment at his (the Colonel's) expense. "Never mind, Colonel," said the Division Commander; "never mind; you've no reason "to be ashamed of that adventure; you were nearer the enemy, "and more exposed, than you would have been if you had kept "with your own brigade!" and in the laugh that followed, no one joined more heartily than the Colonel himself, who was both a brave and meritorious officer.

Capt. Elwell relates this, as a part of his experience of the day:

Just previous to the first charge of Crook's command, directly in the path of my Company, stood a clump of trees, with thick undergrowth of small brush. In passing this obstruction, I discovered, closely stowed in an old cellar hole, a party of skulkers from the fight. To my demand what they were doing there, I received the reply that "we were put here to guard these rebels." As none of the party obeyed my order to come out, I called Sergeant Hayden and a file of men to my side, and ordered them to "fire into the hole." "Hold on Capt.! don't shoot!" broke from the party, as they tumbled over one another in their haste to get away from the direction of the muskets. They were a vile set of fellows to look at; and I am sorry to say the Blue Jackets outnumbered the Grey Backs. Selecting two of the most sickly ones of our Army, as guard over the rebels who were ordered to the rear, I formed the remaining ones into a platoon, and marched them forward, as a much needed reinforcement to my own company. Being closely watched, they joined in the charge which was soon ordered. But they could not overcome their repugnance to a fight, and in a short time, every mother's son of them had succeeded in getting away.

Poor fellows! I wonder how many of them are drawing pensions for disability contracted in the service!!

And again, this: At one of those movements when, while at

a halt, we were under a sharp fire from the rebels, but a short distance in our front, I heard and *almost* felt, the zip and dull thud of a Minnié ball, which struck Hines of my Company in the groin,—passed directly through his body, and lodged in the groin of his rear rank man, Burnham. Both fell without a word or a groan;—both laid still, as if dead, for a few moments; —when Burnham attempted to crawl away on his hands and knees. Sending a man to his aid, I moved up to, and laid down by the side of Hines. The whole line was down in obedience to such order. As I laid my hand upon his head, Hines opened his eyes, and recognized me. "I'm kilt, Captain! clean kilt entirely! take care of my money, please." I took it from his pocket, counted it, and told him the amount. "Yes, Captain! I know! fourteen dollars,"—and closing his eyes again, he laid still,—quiet and peaceful as a child; not a cry, not a groan escaped him. I had in my pocket a flask, with perhaps a half pint of whisky, which, knowing what work was before us, I had kept for some occasion like this. How I did hate to spare it! not that *then* I actually needed it, but that I never was more dry; and hardly ever would a drop have tasted better! But like a hero, I rose to the occasion, and with the spirit of a martyr, devoted it to Hines. Child-like, he sucked till he drew the last drop; and with a fervent "God bless you, Captain!" and a smile like a cherub, laid back, to all appearance indifferent to all earthly things. No cheer of comrade,—no yell of defiant foe disturbed him;

"But he lay like a warrior taking his rest,"
With the roar of the battle around him.

I don't know how long he remained thus quiet and peaceful; but it seemed a long while, when, with no previous warning, he writhed and twisted in convulsive agony, and gave utterance to the most unearthly cries and groans. I tried to pacify him; —telling him that he would exhaust himself, and that his cries would have a bad effect upon his comrades. I might as well have talked to a dead man. He would not be quieted; but, in the most heart-rending tones begged me to put him out of his misery! "I've been a good soldier, Capt.! have'nt I?" "Yes,

Hines!" "And never asked a favor." "No, Hines!" "Then Capt., dear! do me a favor now, and God forever bless you!"

"Take your pistol, Capt.! and for the love of the holy mother, blow out my brains."

The Bugles blew loud and shrilly the order to charge; and I had time only to lay him upon a blanket, which was stretched over a couple of muskets, and send him to the rear. I never saw him afterwards, as he died that night; but those yells of his ring upon my ears, at this distance of time, as loud, and piercing, as when uttered on the plains of Winchester.

What a difference in the characters of these two men, killed by this one bullet! Hines, a rough, coarse, uneducated Irishman, with a keener nose for whisky than any other man living. When we had no reason to believe there was any liquor within miles of the camp, Hines, if off duty, would slink away, and soon return, full to running over. On all such occasions, he was insubordinate, and quarrelsome; resisting all authority but my own; though submitting instantly, and without a murmur, to the slightest word of mine. On duty, he was as true as steel! unyielding, as a rock, in any position of trust! He had no feeling of fear. In battle, comprehending that there was rare sport to be had, he took good care that he had his fair share. Peace to his ashes! His body lies among the unknown dead which make the soil of Virginia holy ground! The money, taken from his body, was paid over to the first Paymaster who reached us, after he was killed. With no known relatives, this money, with his wages, and well earned bounty, is still in the keeping of the Government.

Burnham was gentle, kind, and affectionate in manner; scrupulous in doing his exact duty at all times; honest to the last degree; obedient and respectful to his superiors in rank, and gentlemanly with his associates, and comrades. He lived,—in truth, the very model of a brave, conscientious, educated New England soldier; and died—true hero, and noble patriot.

Writes Hospital Steward, Fairbanks, thus: "It was the night after the battle of Winchester. While going about my duties, I came upon the officers of an Ohio regiment, and catching the words 34th Massachusetts, could but stop to learn what was said. They were recalling the incidents of the battlefield, and the encomiums paid to the men of the regiment were as unexpected as they were dear. "Did you ever," asked one, of another, "see such a regiment as the 34th? How they went "up that hill, and over that wall, and charged the enemy alone, "with no other body of troops to support them! The d—l "himself could not have withstood them." "That's so," was the reply; "and I" don't believe there's another regiment in "the whole army that could have done it."

And Dr. Smith tells a good one which, though the scene of it was at New Market, when some of our army hurried away from the field with a speed comparable only with the rapidity with which large bodies of the rebels made haste to get away to-day, is too good to be lost.

Soon after the fighting began, an 18th Connecticut man came running to the rear, as if Satan was after him. I ran up to him to turn him back; and just as I had stopped him, Maj. Pratt galloped up, pistol in hand, and, presenting it to the man's head, ordered him to join the ranks in front. The man gave a look at the Major's pistol,— turned, and threw a glance at the enemy who were fast coming up with their hideous yell, and gasping out "Good God! do you suppose, I am going to stop the whole Southern Confedracy when it is after me!" continued his flight toward the North and safety. This was too much for the gravity of the two officers, and neither of them offered any further hindrance to the man's hurried flight.

Capt. Thompson was buried by his men on the field where he fell. Later, his brother, from Maine, came for his body. Having carefully exhumed it, he was on his way to the rear, when he fell into the hands of Mosby, and was liberated only by the sacrifice of all his money, and most of his clothing. And now Mosby is honored by being chosen to represent abroad the Government he would have destroyed!

CHAPTER XLII

Battle of Fisher's Hill.

LOSSES — DEATH OF MAJ. PRATT — MARCH TO HARRISONBURG — DUTY THERE — DOWN THE VALLEY — CAMP AT CEDAR CREEK.

Sept. 22d. We have again met the enemy, and again been victorious; turning him from his entrenchments, as the plough turns the land slice in its furrow; and sending him, discomfited, and in confusion, up the Valley.

Marching orders reached us, in our encampment, on the morning of the 20th. Our route was up the Valley, in pursuit of the Rebel army; on the heels of which, our cavalry was supposed to be hanging. With occasional halts, we reached "Cedar Creek," where we bivouacked. Resuming our march at an early hour the next morning, we soon reached Strasburg, where we formed on the left of the line already occupied by the 6th and 19th corps. Early held "Fisher's Hill," a place of great natural strength. Here he had entrenched himself; and by a line of rifle pits, and heavy earthworks, which extended from the Shenandoah River, on his right, to the North Mountain, on his left, a distance of some five miles, had rendered his position almost impregnable. The hill itself, as it rises above "Tumbling Run," a small brook which crosses the Valley pike at its base, about two miles south of Strasburg, presents a face as difficult to scale as the walls of a precipice. It can be approached from the north or eastern side by the Valley pike only, which, running along the narrow river bottom, is hemmed in on one side by Flint's Hill, so-called, and on the other by the Shenandoah River. The pike is exposed, for a long distance, to a raking fire from the guns in position on the hill. From the high bluff, at the point where Tumbling run, is spanned by a stone-arched bridge, a handful of determined men might with rocks, loosened and rolled from the summit, hold an army at bay. It was literally unassailable in front. Most of the day of the 21st, therefore, was occupied by the 6th and 19th corps in manœuvring, as it might be, for position; driving in the enemy's skirmishers, and securing the high land which rose on the eastern side of the run, some distance in front of the Rebel stronghold. While this was being done, Crook's command, the Army of West Virginia, was moving, well to the rear,—so as to be screened from observation by the enemy,—from its position *on the extreme left*, to the base of the North Mountain, on *the right*. Reaching this, it was to continue its march, still keeping under cover of the woods on the mountain, till it had gained the enemy's flank and rear, when it was to assault and carry the works. The movement, so carefully planned and so boldly undertaken, was as successfully accomplished. The 2d division having passed, undiscovered, beyond the works occupied by the enemy, the whole line was faced to the front, and ordered to charge. Moving down, at a double quick, with loud cheers, our advance was upon the enemy before he had fully recovered from his surprise. "Had the heavens opened, and we been " seen descending from the clouds, no greater consternation " would have been created."

"We ran over a line of works, upon which he was even then at work; passed on about a quarter of a mile, through the woods,—overcoming all opposition,—and came out at the foot of an almost open slope, on the crest of which, and directly in our front, was a double line of strong earth works, filled with men, and in an angle of which was a rifled gun. Nothing daunted by the sight, each man yelled, if possible, louder than before; and the men of each Regiment dashed forward, ambitious to plant their own colors *first* on the works. The cannon was fired, at less distance than one hundred yards, into the 116th Ohio; but its men rushed on, capturing the piece in the very smoke of its discharge. The 34th Mass. planted its Flag, *first of all*, upon the parapet of these works; but the men of the other commands were only a second behind. Halting here a moment to gain breath, and reform our lines, we pushed on for the next hill, from which the enemy was playing upon us with their artillery. From this point, the fighting was mostly in the woods. A succession of hills, with abrupt sides, separated from each other by valleys of considerable depth, extended to the railroad nearer the pike. The enemy's line ran directly across these hills; and on each ridge was artillery, which had full play on us as we advanced. The enemy, from each crest, met us with a rapid and heavy fire of musketry and artillery; our advance would be checked; men would come up; and the battle would stand still and increase, until our line, sufficiently strengthened, would rush on, drive the enemy to the next crest, where the same effort would be repeated, with the same result. Upon all the eminences we found artillery *hot* and *smoking:* some, indeed, loaded to the muzzle with grape and cannister, but abandoned, undischarged, before the impetuosity of our advance. The men of the 2d Division, who had turned the flank, and gained the rear of the line of earthworks, could be heard cheering as they swept down behind the enemy's position. As the last ridge before reaching the railroad was reached, the men of the 6th Corps were seen coming in. Here there was a sharp contest, but it was soon over. Crossing the railroad we advanced up the right side of the pike, and in conjunction with the men of the 6th Corps on the left, and a portion of the 2d Division on the right, drove the enemy from his last hold on the ridge, and the day's work was done."

Thirty pieces of artillery, 1,100 prisoners, a large amount of ammunition, besides caissons, limbers, ambulances, army wagons, small arms, intrenching tools, all in great number, were taken.

The charge, from first to last, must have covered over a distance of more than five miles. This entire distance was passed over under a continuous fire, sometimes very severe; the men, much of the time, on the double quick. In five minutes after coming out of the woods, the 34th Mass. had its men together, and was marching forward in line, as regularly as on parade; and when the last intrenchment was won, and the day's fighting was over, the Regiment was supporting not only its own colors, but those of many of the other Infantry organizations.

It was in reference to this, that the commanding officer of a Western Regiment, marked more for its brave daring than for its drill or discipline, asked: "How happens it, Colonel, that in "all the battles of this campaign, I have never seen the 34th in "disorder! but on the contrary, whether advancing or retreat-"ing, your Regiment has always preserved its formation; and "standing or moving, has been always closed upon its colors."

Writes Col. Wells: "I cannot speak too highly of the extreme gallantry of the officers and men of the Brigade. So far as this Brigade is concerned, I feel that the success is due, more than in any other battle I know of, to the individual heroism of the men in the ranks. The field was so vast, and the confusion so great, that the officers could do little but encourage their men, and set them examples of energetic courage."

The official list of casualties in the Brigade, is as follows:

TROOPS.	KILLED.		WOUNDED.	
	Officers.	*Privates.*	*Officers.*	*Privates.*
34th Mass. Infantry,	..	..	..	18
5th N. Y. Artillery,				4
133d Ohio Infantry,		..	..	7
116th " "	..	1	..	8
Total	..	1	..	37

An accident, which happened after the day's work was done, threw a gloom over the entire Corps, of which the 34th was part. As the officers gathered to exchange congratulations upon the success of the day, a stack of arms, on the line of the 5th N.Y Heavy Artillery, from some unknown cause, fell, causing one piece to be discharged, the ball from which struck Maj. H. W Pratt, commanding the 34th, passing through both of his legs, causing his death a day or two afterwards. Thus the service lost a gallant and tried officer, and the command a bold leader and steadfast friend, of whom Col. Wells writes: "I do not review a more gallant or efficient officer."

We were occupied the next day in caring for the wounded, burying the dead, and gathering up the trophies of the battle. Meanwhile the Cavalry and the 6th and 19th Corps sharply pursued the enemy.

Our work having been accomplished, at 10 A. M. of the 24th, we resumed our march, passing through Woodstock, Edinboro, and Mount Jackson, and going into camp about two miles beyond. Day's march, twenty-seven miles. The next morning we went on through Newmarket, passing near the field of our disastrous fight of last May, and stopping to look at the traces of the battle, still plainly to be seen on the fences and trees. Reaching Harrisonburg, the Regiment was detailed as Provost Guard. Our stay was pleasant, as the duty was light. The time was improved in making out returns, completing our rolls, and straightening matters generally. On the sixth of October, we broke camp, and started on our way down the Valley. Our Brigade formed the rear of the Infantry. Behind us was the Cavalry, which was engaged in devastating the country round about. Every barn, mill, foundry, every wheat stack and hay rick was destroyed; even standing corn was cut, piled and burned; and all cattle, sheep and swine driven before us. Huge clouds of smoke, extending as far as the eye could reach to the rear, and upon each flank, attested to the thoroughness with which this work was done.

On the 11th, "Cedar Creek" was reached; and we went into camp on its east bank, occupying a line between the Shenandoah and the Pike, at which point *we* connected with the 19th Corps, which in turn connected with the 6th, the extreme right of the line being held by the Cavalry. The line was made to conform, at all points, with the topography of the country, all the natural advantages of which were made available. With our front fortified, we rested confidently, in the strength of our position.

On the 12th, a portion of Gen. Crook's command, consisting of the 5th N. Y. Heavy Artillery, 11th and 15th Va. Infantry, the whole under Col. Harris, an officer of acknowledged military skill and self possession, were despatched on a reconnoisance towards Strasburg, with a view of learning, if possible, the position of the Rebel army, This party advanced cautiously to a hill, from which Strasburg and its surrounding country could be observed. The village was found to be unoccupied by any but its own citizens. A few Cavalry videttes were seen beyond the town; but close scrutiny, through field glasses and telescopes, failed to discover any signs of the presence of the enemy, and our party returned to camp, satisfied that no considerable hostile force *could be* in the vicinity.

CHAPTER XLIII

"RECONNOISANCE"—STICKNEY'S FARM—DEATH OF COL. WELLS
—CAPTURE OF OFFICERS—LOSS OF THE REGIMENT—
RECOVERY OF THE BODY OF COL. WELLS—A LATE
PROMOTION—CAPT. ELWELL'S LETTER.

With a knowledge of the result of this reconnoisance, what was our surprise, just as our dinner call sounded on the next day, to have a shell fired, from no one could tell where, drop in our camp, near to Headquarters mess table. There was no consternation; but a lightning flash in the broad glare of a mid-day sun could not have caused more astonishment. Another soon came. This time, a puff of smoke from the piece betrayed its situation, but no one dreamed of the presence of more than a small reconnoitering party. Writes an officer of ours, present at the time, and who took part in the engagement which followed : " About noon, might have been seen five pairs of heels protruding from a shelter tent near the centre of the line of the 34th, the owners of which were deeply engaged in a game of cards, although an indifferent spectator might have supposed from their position, that they were trying to swim on dry land. The bugles had just sounded the call to dinner. Boom! Boom! suddenly broke upon our ears. Hallo, says one, there goes a salute! we must have been licking the grey-backs again! Boom! Boom! this time accompanied by the whizzing of a shell which struck the ground mid-way between the tents, and Regimental Headquarters. Nice kind of a salute that, thought we, as scrambling out, we got on to our feet, and looked round to see what it all meant. The men of the regiment next us, were straggling through our camp, bearing with them knapsacks and blankets, half eaten hard tack, and half cooked coffee in their camp kettles. Sure enough, it was a strange kind of salute! The Rebels were popping away at us, from a hill on the other side of the creek, and had our range as accurately as if they had been engaged for a long time, instead of but a few minutes. The assembly was sounded at once; and without waiting to finish our game, we took our respective positions in line. Orders came to us to move out, and ascertain the strength of the enemy. The 1st brigade, (ours) Col. Wells, was already under arms on the left of the Pike. The 2d, Col. Harris, 10th West Virginia, was ordered to move on the right. In our front, and between us and the creek, there was a piece of low open ground, about two hundred yards wide, which must be crossed.

The Rebels concentrated their fire upon this ground as we moved over it, but the old Regiment had seen too much hot work during the summer to flinch at such a time, and marching steadily on, crossed the creek, and advanced in line toward the Rebel batteries. To all appearance, a couple of batteries only, with a small supporting force of infantry, were posted on the eminence between Cedar Creek and Strasburg; their line, partly concealed by woods, crossing the hill at right angles to the Pike. Against the force thus partially screened from observation, these two Brigades advanced in line, with an intervening interval of about two hundred yards. Between the two Brigades there was a ridge of land parallel with the line of march, which cut the *left* of the 2d Brigade from the view of the *right* of the 1st. *This* contributed not a little to the disaster of the day. Our own Regiment held the right of the 1st Brigade. Our route up from the low land led us through some thick underbrush, coming out of which, about one hundred yards in front, and at short rifle range from the enemy, was a low stone wall. We hurried our pace to get the protection of this wall, leaving on the way some men, and I think, one or two officers. When we gained the cover of the wall, we opened fire. The Rebels had much the advantage of position; the low wall not affording us much protection from their plunging fire, while they were much better covered by the brow of the hill. At first, it seemed to me that the enemy was in small force; and I was anxious to have an advance ordered, feeling sure that we could rout them, and perhaps capture their guns. In this I was mistaken; as the result proved that Early had his whole force just over and behind the hill, and in and around Strasburg. Believing that the 2d Brigade was quite near, on our right, I had paid but little attention to my flank, although I was on the extreme right of our Regiment and Brigade; nor did I dream of danger from that quarter, till one of my men called my attention to a body of grey-backs advancing upon us from that direction. Calling to Capt. Elwell, next on my left, we " changed direction " and formed our men at right angles to our former line, and by a few well directed vollies repelled this movement. Instantly we wheeled forward into line again. As we did so, the Rebels made another demonstration against our flank, this time with largely increased numbers. *We* changed the direction of our two companies again, showing front to the enemy; sent word to the Colonel, of this movement by the Rebels, and poured our vollies into them. It was evident now, however, that something was wrong. Were *we* cut off from the other Brigade? Everything indicated it. Yet we stood and held our ground. We had, in reality, lost no ground, when an order came up to us from the left, directing a retreat. The Regiment fell back, by the left flank, in order to regain, more quickly, the low ground and woods to our rear, in that direction. As my company was on the right, I was among the very last to retire. While running along by the side of the wall, I saw Col. Wells lying upon the ground, wounded, and Lieut. Cobb sitting near him, whether wounded or not, I could not see. I stopped, hoping it might be possible to help the Colonel off the field. I saw soon that his wound was mortal; and learned that he had entrusted other officers with his watch, and messages to his relatives and friends. To me, he said that he was dying; that the defeat of the 1st Brigade was owing to the falling back of the 2d without giving any notice to us, thus enabling the enemy, under cover of the woods, to advance, unperceived, and outflank us." He *ordered* me to leave him and follow the Regiment. Inasmuch as Lieut. Cobb persisted in remaining with him, I started. The Regiment had got out of sight in the ravine, and the enemy, only fifteen or twenty yards distant, was coming on at a run. Disregarding many loud and oft repeated invitations to halt, I put out my best speed. I could feel their balls striking the ground at my feet, and could hear them whizzing uncomfortably near my head. But I ran, as I never ran before in my life, for about one hundred yards farther, when in crossing a rocky ravine, I stumbled and fell. My pursuers were close upon me when I regained my feet, and in fact, others from the flank were ahead of me. There was nothing to do but to surrender, which I did; and was given permission to go to the rear. Rejoining Col. Wells and Lieut. Cobb, I found the Colonel to be sinking very fast. Placing him upon a blanket, we carried him back to the hill from which the Rebel batteries were still playing upon our retreating comrades. Here we were met by Gen. Early. He asked what officer it was, and upon being told that it was Col. Wells, inquired if it was the same who commanded the forces upon the Valley expedition of December last. Upon receiving our affirmative, the General ordered up an ambulance, into which we placed the Colonel just as he breathed his last. Thus died our beloved commander; always brave and cool, strict in discipline, and thoughtful for the welfare of his soldiers, and the reputation of the Regiment."

Capt. Willard continues his narrative thus: "As I turned from helping to place the body of the Colonel in the ambulance, I received a very civil invitation to take a long walk up the Valley, under the care of an ill looking fellow, with a musket on his shoulder. Escorted into Strasburg, I was soon joined by Lieuts. Cobb and Calligan, who had received a similar invitation, and some twenty to thirty of our own men, besides others from other Regiments. In a few days we all entered the famous "Libby" prison in Richmond. As we traveled back through and among Early's men, we learned from them that their force engaged amounted to between eight and ten thousand men; so our two little Brigades might well enough retreat. Subsequently, I learned that the movement on our part was ordered only as a means of ascertaining the strength of the force before us; and that Gen. Thoburn despatched an officer early in the affair, with orders to each commander to withdraw his force; which officer, having delivered the order to the 2d Brigade, on his way to ours, had had his horse shot under him, and was cut off from Col. Wells by this flank movement of the Rebels."

The richly-earned, well-deserved, but long-delayed promotion to a Brevet Brigadiership came to the command when the Colonel had passed from the earth, and could not feel that his services had at length been appreciated and rewarded.

Our own loss in the affair was 1 officer and 8 men killed on the field, 1 officer wounded and dying on the 17th; 2 officers and 48 men wounded, and 3 officers and 39 men taken prisoners.

A flag of truce was sent out the next day for the body of Col. Wells. Upon its being given up, it was brought into camp, and with none but necessary delay was sent forward to his family in Massachusetts, under the charge of Lieuts. Macomber and Ripley.

> In reference to this affair, Capt. Elwell writes: "Col. Wells was mortally wounded in an engagement here yesterday, and left a prisoner in the hands of the enemy. Our brigade (Wells') and one other took part in the movement. The enemy was much stronger than the small force sent out by us, and we were forced to retire. The Colonel was struck by a rifle ball, nearly in the centre of his body, just below the breast-bone, piercing him through and through. He was mounted at the time, and engaged in directing the movement of his brigade. He slid directly from his horse to the ground, was immediately surrounded by his officers, and urged to remount his horse and be taken to the rear. But he would not mount, nor would he consent to be carried back. A few moments later came the order to retreat, and, the enemy being within a stone's throw of us, we were forced to retire, and leave him on the field. We did this at his own request and imperative order, as he felt his wound was mortal, he saying, 'It is of no use, gentlemen. I cannot live. Let me lie here. Take my money and watch, and save yourselves.' Lieut. Cobb, of our regiment, remained voluntarily with him, and was captured. God only knows how tenderly and sincerely we all loved him, and how grieved and heartstricken we are at his loss. The 34th has lost its idol; and the service one of the best officers that ever stood before the enemy. Our regiment has suffered very severely, as we always have whenever engaged. Capt. Soley is severely wounded by shell; Lieut Dempsey killed; Capt. Willard and Lieut Calligan missing; Lieut. Cobb, A. A. A. G., prisoner. Our list is not perfect; but as far as now known, we have *four* killed, forty wounded and sixty-four missing."
>
> An army correspondent, writing of this affair from Middletown, says: "The 34th, during this engagement, gave another striking indication of their gallantry and soldierly qualities. The 1st Brigade of the 1st division, commanded by Col. Wells, of the 34th Massachusetts regiment, though charged by the enemy repeatedly, stood their ground nobly."

The reconnoisance having thus terminated, a strong picket line was thrown out in front of the brigade. Slight firing was indulged in by the men of the two lines, until about midnight, when an advance, cautiously made, revealed the fact that the enemy had retired.

CHAPTER XLIV

BATTLE OF CEDAR CREEK.

No movement, of any importance, was made by either army for a day or two. Our own condition was one of entire inaction; the 5th New York in its turn being on the picket line. As the evening of the 18th set in, a dense fog rose which wrapt everything in a darkness which could almost be felt. So dense was it, that in the language of one present "it was difficult to distinguish a figure standing face to face." Deep quiet was upon the camp, and nothing but our watch-fires betrayed our presence. Relying upon the report of our reconnoitering party, all slept in confidence and security. But, notwithstanding that report, Early was near at hand; his entire army securely hid from observation in the woods around Strasburg. Smarting under his recent defeat, perhaps induced to venture, by the reported departure of the 6th Corps for Washington, he resolved to attack Sheridan, and to use his own language, " as I (he) was not strong enough to attack the fortified position in front, I (he) determined to get around one of the enemy's flanks, and attack him by surprise if I (he) could." His examination satisfied him that this attack could be made, with prospect of success, only upon our left flank and rear. "The plan of attack upon which I determined," writes Gen. Early, " was to send the three divisions of the 2d Corps, to wit: Gordon's, Ramseur's, and Pegram's, under Gen. Gordon, to the enemy's rear, to make the attack at 5 o'clock in the morning; to move myself with Kershaw's and Wharton's divisions, and all the Artillery, along the pike, through Strasburg, and attack the enemy on the front and left flank, as soon as Gordon should become engaged; and for Rosser to move with his own and Wickham's Brigade on the back road, across Cedar creek, and attack the enemy's Cavalry, simultaneously with Gordon's attack, while Lomax should move by Front Royal, cross the river, and come to the Valley pike, so as to strike the enemy wherever he might be, of which he was to judge by the sound of the firing."

Gordon's route was between Massanutten Mountain and the Shenandoah river, by a blind path, practicable for Infantry, but not for Artillery. Gordon moved and got into position as directed; "Kershaw's division got in sight of the enemy's fires at half-past three o'clock; at half-past four he was ordered forward, and a very short time after, the firing from Rosser on our left, and the picket firing at the ford at which Gordon was crossing, was heard." The Rebels advanced unperceived by our picket line, which was captured almost to a man, and entered Crook's camp almost without firing a shot. Now uttering their shrill yells of triumph, and opening a heavy musketry fire, he swept along our works, meeting but little opposition (many of our men still sleeping in their tents), and driving before him a confused mass of half dressed, partially armed soldiers. At the first sound of the attack, "our own regiment and brigade fell into line behind our breastworks." "The men of other brigades" failed to hear, or hearing, failed to observe the warning, and were too slow in getting in." Our flank was easily turned. "Our own brigade, the only one in the division not surprised," made such resistance as was possible; but overwhelmed by the immense superiority of the enemy, was forced to give ground. "We fell slowly back;" the broken ranks of the other brigades rallying upon our line. The men of the 19th Corps had caught the alarm, and were in line as we reached their encampment. Joining their 1st division we made a good stand, and temporarily checked the enemy's advance. But we were soon out-flanked, and were again compelled to give away. Taking a new position, on the west side of the creek, near Middletown, we renewed the action. Here the battle hung for a time, with heavy loss to each side. But we were driven again. Now keeping up a running fight for some three or four miles, we met the 6th Corps drawn up in line, with all their artillery in position.

It held a ridge to the west of Middletown, and was not easily to be dispossessed.

As before, Early attacked with vigor; directing his main effort against our left and centre, in the hope of getting between us and Winchester. The roar of Artillery and roll of musketry was incessant; these mingled with, but did not drown, the yells and cheers of the combatants.

Custer and Merritt led their squadrons against the enemy with but partial success. We now occupied a point on the north of Middletown, about three miles from the Winchester Pike, where by great efforts, under a partial relaxation of the enemy's attack, a new line of battle was formed. It was nearly noon. The scene was one of indescribable confusion. Long lines of ambulances and army wagons were being driven hurriedly along the pike, in frantic efforts to gain our rear; Artillery and Caissons were being drawn from the woods, and across intervening fields, to position in the direction of Newtown; confused crowds of non-combatants, officers' servants, wounded soldiers, stragglers,— all alike demoralized, were streaming towards Winchester; while here and there, far away, and near at hand, embodied troops, in line, and column, upon whose arms the sun shone with great brilliancy, could be seen, fast moving into position. Retreat was no longer thought of by us; and Early says "it was apparent at this time that it would not do to *press his troops farther*." Crook, on the left, now held the Winchester Pike; next came the 19th Corps, while the 6th held the right of the line. Either flank was covered by Cavalry. So stood matters when Sheridan rode on to the field. The news of his arrival quickly spread, and new spirit seemed to animate the men. Firing was now renewed, and shells from the enemy's batteries were dropped in our lines. Our own Artillery was responding briskly, though, as yet, there was nothing like a general engagement. Some few changes in the disposition of the Cavalry were ordered by Gen. Sheridan, when the order "forward, along the line," was given.

It was about half-past one. "Getty's Division of the 6th Corps, supported by the 2d Division of Crook's army of West Virginia in solid mass, their left flank protected by a large body of Cavalry, covered by a heavy fire from batteries posted on the slopes of near commanding hills, led the opening movement against the enemy." Other masses, in similar formation, followed in quick succession. A furious fire of shot and shell struck them, before which the lines faltered; but recovering, they went forward with a cheer. The enemy's ranks shook,— then swayed,— then melted away before this charge. There was a dash forward by the whole army; and so hotly was the enemy pressed, that he found it impossible to rally. He was driven out of Middletown, and by the Pike, and across the country, towards the Creek and Strasburg, over the ground he had so lately traversed in the flush of success; and so closely pursued that the rear of the flying, and the head of the pursuing forces, came together on the scene of the morning's surprise. Back through the camps which they had swept in the morning, the beaten rebels ran, throwing away arms and everything which could impede their flight. The Cavalry kept up the pursuit for miles; capturing the greater part of the enemy's Artillery, ordnance, and medical wagons; and retaking all which had been lost by us in the attack and surprise of the morning.

"We stacked our arms behind the works from which we had been driven in the morning; and slept that night, as we had fought that day, without food." Our own immediate loss was nine wounded (two mortally), and thirty-four taken prisoners.

CHAPTER XLV

CEDAR CREEK.

CAPTS. SOLEY AND DR. SMITH — "OLD ZEKE" — OUR LOST "MARKER" — AT NEWTOWN — ON THE OPEQUAN — OUR ROLLS — MARCHING ORDERS — TO THE JAMES RIVER.

Among our wounded was Captain Soley, struck by a piece of shell, which plowed its way through the thickest part of the thigh, opening a furrow in which one's arm could easily be buried. It was the Captain's good fortune to be carried to Field Hospital in Winchester, then in charge of Dr. Smith, Assistant Surgeon of the 34th, skilful practitioner, tender nurse, and kind and sympathizing friend. The Captain himself was of a cool and calculating temperament, accustomed to take things philosophically. He looked upon a wound received in action as, according to regulations, and to be borne with patience and fortitude. But long weeks of helplessness and suffering go far to destroy both mental and physical energy; and with departing strength, came diminished cheerfulness and lessened hope. Smith saw with concern the growth of the unfavorable symptoms; and set himself to counteract the increasing despondency. He told his best stories,—reported the current news and latest anecdotes,—even essayed a song, a la Willard; but to no purpose. The Captain would'nt be charmed. So, in very despair, one morning Smith, caught a honey bee, from which he carefully removed its sting, and calling the Captain's attention to it, he drew down the bed covering, and carefully placed the insect upon the naked skin of the wounded leg. Didn't "our army in Flanders" swear! No language can do justice to the Captain's invective, as he made up in strength of words for the weakness of body which prevented him from thrashing Smith on the spot. Satisfied after a while that his patient was mad, clear through, Smith again caught the bee, and thus addressed his patient: "Now, look here, you fool! See what a fuss you've been making for nothing! Before I put it into bed with you I pulled out this fellow's sting! Do you see?" and he exhibited the disarmed insect. The insult was worse than the injury that had been anticipated. The glare from the Captain's eyes and the renewed invective from his lips satisfied the Doctor that his application had been successful. So, prescribing "fifteen drops to be taken every ten minutes," Smith went his way rejoicing; and Soley took the first step on his long march to recovery. The Captain still lives; and as he tells the story, confesses that he would prefer to face the shell again, rather than endure the agony he suffered, when the bee was raiding up and down his naked flesh.

As before stated, the morning's attack was a perfect surprise; and although at the first alarm the regiment hastily armed and repaired to its proper position behind the breastworks, the non-combatants, company, and hospital cooks and attendants, less prompt to move in sudden emergencies, were many of them captured. Of these "Old Zeke" was the best known character. He was of K; was early detailed as hospital cook; and had been distinguished for the diligence with which he read his Testament daily, and traded hospital pork *nightly* with the poor widows of Bolivar, for spiritual consolation.

Who of us will ever forget him? or the grotesque appearance he made as he trudged the weary miles of Hunter's raid, dressed in the long, swallow-tailed, black dress coat which he had "drawn" on some foraging expedition; grasping in one hand his long staff, and in the other an end of the rope by which he dragged along his diminutive little mule; for all the world like Joseph journeying into Egypt, as pictured in the school books of former days. He had caught the first notes of the morning's alarm, and, securing his mule, hurried to the rear. He was safely away, when it flashed upon him that he had left behind a volume, none the less valued, because in some mysterious manner it had found its way into his knapsack, from the library in that aristocratic old mansion raided upon near the Sulphur Springs. Instantly he stopped, tied his mule to a tree, and began to retrace his steps. His comrades warned him of his danger. But he turned a deaf ear. To all remonstrances he replied only by exclaiming "I want my Life of Christ!" "I must have my Life of Christ!" He was last seen as he was swallowed up in the band of fugitives who were hurrying to the rear. Let us hope that from his recovered volume, he derived pleasure enough to console him for the weary moments of his long captivity.

Another incident of the day, illustrative of the uncertainties of the things of this life, is full of interest. While on duty in Washington, we had procured some white silk flags, bordered with heavy fringe (on which our regimental designation was marked in gold leaf), to be used as "markers;" such being in better keeping with our white gloves and well polished scales, than the ordinary ones furnished by the Government. Fastened upon short staves which were inserted in the muzzles of their muskets, they were carried by our right and left general guides. At the battle of New Market, one of these guides tore his marker from its staff, and put it in his pocket. The other guide intended to thurst the staff of his under his body belt. But he either did'nt do so, or did it so carelessly that it was lost. Naturally it was a *trophy*, not to be neglected by any rebel who might chance to see it. Of course, too, its loss was a great mortification to the whole command. Now, at the close of this day's contest, upon reoccupying the camp from which we had been so summarily ejected, stretched upon the ground, lay the body of a stalwart rebel, and by his side his knapsack, partially filled with the plunder he had gathered from our tents. A little examination disclosed to our eyes, closely folded and carefully wrapped in an outer covering of cloth, the *lost marker of the 34th*. It is needless to add that its recovery was hailed with great joy, not only by its former bearer, but by every man in the command.

The defeat of the Rebel army was complete. Disorganized and dispirited, nowhere attempting to make a stand, it melted away before our cavalry, which hung on to, and harrassed its flying remnants.

While the main army was lying idle in camp, the 34th was detailed to act as provost guard in the town of Newtown; officers and men without tents. Our stay in this place was protracted for some weeks; at the end of which time, upon the falling back of the entire force to Winchester, we rejoined our brigade, and went into camp at the railroad crossing of the Opequan.

The tiresome duty of picketing the neighboring country, and guarding the railroad bridge which crossed the creek near our encampment, mainly occupied us. Drills were resumed. So far as the officers were concerned, their time was taken up in straightening out their accounts, and making up the rolls of their companies. F company was detailed as provost guard at brigade headquarters.

Our muster rolls for October show present for duty, 9 officers and 270 enlisted men. Absent on detached service, 7 officers; on leave, 5; sick, 5; prisoners of war, 7. 38 enlisted men were on detached service; 26 absent on furlough; 4 without leave; 329 sick; and 175 prisoners of war.

Among the officers the following changes had occurred: Maj. H. W. Pratt died Sept. 26th, of wounds received Sept. 22; Col. Geo. D. Wells, killed in action, Oct. 13; Capt. Alexis C. Solcy, wounded Oct. 13, and in hospital at Winchester; Lieut. Jas. L. Dempsey, died Oct. 17th, of wounds received Oct. 13th; Capt. Wells Willard, Lieut. and A. A. A. G. Wm. L. Cobb, and Lieut. John E. Calligan, captured Oct. 13; Lieut. Fred. A. Judd and Lieut. Melville E. Walker, wounded Sept. 19th, and absent on sick leave; Lieut. Robert W Walker, paroled prisoner at Annapolis; Lieut. and Acting Adj't Thomas W Ripley and Lieut. Charles E. Cutler, absent in Massachusetts on sick leave; and Lieut. Col.William S. Lincoln, on sick leave in Massachusetts, having made his escape from the hands of the enemy.

Our November roll shows the following changes: 3 officers only were present for duty; 6 being on extra or daily duty and 1 present, sick; 2 were on detached service; one absent with leave, three absent sick, and five were prisoners of war. Of the enlisted men, two hundred and thirty were present for duty, forty-three were on extra or daily duty, and eight sick. Forty-seven were on detached duty, thirty-five paroled prisoners, one hundred and fifty-one were prisoners of war, and three hundred and nine absent, sick; five absent without leave, and four in arrest. We had lost one officer, Lieut. F. C. Kinnicutt, by dismissal; one, Lieut Ripley, by transfer; two, Capt. John A. Lovell, and Lieut. R. W Walker, by discharge; and one, Lieut. Malcolm Ammidon by disease. Fourteen men had died from wounds received in action, and one by disease.

Lieut. Col. Lincoln had been mustered in as Col., vice Wells, killed in action; Capt. Andrew Potter as Major, vice Pratt, died of wounds; and Lieut. Col., vice Lincoln promoted; and Capt. A. D. Pratt as Major, vice Potter, promoted.

Col. Lincoln was on detached service at Cumberland. Major and Surgeon R. R. Clarke was acting Medical Director on Division Staff. Lieut. and Assist. Surgeon Cyrus B. Smith was acting as Surgeon in charge of field hospital at Winchester. Capt. C. W Elwell was serving as A. A. I. G., and Lieut. Thos. W Ripley, as A. A. A. G. on Brigade Staff; Capt. F. T. Leach, acting Judge Advocate General on Court Martial. Capt. Lovell and Lieut. R. W Walker had been discharged on account of disability.

Lieuts. Van Loan and Macomber had been promoted to Captaincies. Goodrich to a 1st Lieutenancy, and detailed as Acting Adjutant; Murdock to a 1st Lieutenancy and detailed as Acting Quartermaster; 2d Lieuts. Judd, Blake, and Hall, who was now relieved from duty on the signal corps, were promoted to be 1st Lieutenants; and Sergeants E. V Lilly, Chas. I. Woods, Herbert J. Rowley, Wells B. Mitchell, and Harlan P. Houghton had received promotion to 2d Lieutenancies.

Late in November, Col. Lincoln, whose wound was still unhealed, came up, under orders "to report to the commander of the army in the field," and was ordered to detached service in Cumberland. He brought with him, and presented to the regiment in few but touching words, a beautiful new national flag of silk, which the ladies of the City of Worcester desired to exchange for that one, of their earlier gift, which had been proudly carried in so many fields of battle, and whose tattered folds, stained by the blood of its brave defenders, was so dear to *us*. The exchange was made amid the hearty cheers of the men, whose cheeks were wet by tears which could not be suppressed.

We laid at this point, undisturbed, until the 17th day of December, when, very unexpectedly, we received marching orders, which directed "the removal of the entire 1st Division of the army of West Virginia, to the army of the James," lying before Richmond. The removal was distasteful to the men of the entire command. Representations from the commanding officers of the armies in the field, were forwarded to the department at Washington, setting forth the impolicy of transferring from the valley a force intimately acquainted with the peculiarities of the country, even though, as was to be the case, the trained warriors of the 6th and 19th corps, were to remain. These representations were supported by remonstrances from the Governors of the states of Ohio and West Virginia, which were continued, even long after the transfer was effected. But all was of no avail; and on the afternoon of the 19th of December, the entire Division marched to Stevenson's Depot, and, the next day, took transportation, on the railroad, for Washington. A short stop was made at Harper's Ferry, where many old friends gave us kindly greeting. Washington was reached the next morning. Here the command embarked upon transports; the 34th, on the steamer Massachusetts, sailing with sealed orders. A violent storm drove our own and other transports into Cherry Stone inlet, where we were compelled to lie for two days. On the 23d we got under way, and reached Fortress Munroe; made City Point the next day; and on the 25th disembarked at Aiken's Landing, and, marching out to a point at the extreme right of the line of investment about Richmond, pitched our tents at "Camp Holly."

CHAPTER XLVI

BEFORE RICHMOND.

ASSIGNMENT TO POSITION — CHANGE OF COMMANDERS — COL. POTTER — DUTY REQUIRED — OUR ROLLS — "THE HEART" — TO THE CHICKAHOMINY — TO "THE LEFT" — ABOUT PETERSBURG — OUR STRENGTH.

General Orders assign us to the 24th Army Corps, Gen. John W Turner (a West Pointer), commanding the Division. We take the place of the 2d Division of that Corps, now forming a part of the expeditionary force sent against "Fort Fisher;" are designated, and are to be known as the "Independent Division, 24th Army Corps;" and are to form a part of the "Army of the James." At our arrival, snow laid upon the ground,—the mud was deep,—fuel scarce, and hard to be got,—and our condition anything but comfortable. But chopping parties were at once detailed, and our men were soon enjoying the warmth and shelter of comfortable "log houses." Our life was one of comparative inactivity. Lieut. Col. Wild, of the 116th Ohio, who had been in command of the Brigade since the death of Col. Wells, went home in January, on leave, and was succeeded by Lieut. Col. Potter, of the 34th, as A. B. G. Capt. Frank T. Leach, Co. G., assumed command of the Regiment. Frequent and rigid inspections,—squad, company and regimental drills were had during these Winter months; and every effort was made to keep the reputation of the Regiment, for drill and discipline, and of its individual members, for soldierly bearing, up to its former high standard. The duty required of us was light, and all enjoyed the comparative rest which followed our Summer's hardships and toil.

There were present, for duty, in December, eight officers: Five were on extra or daily duty, twelve absent on detached service, one absent with leave, two were absent sick, and five were prisoners of war.

Of the enlisted men, two hundred and fifty-five were present for duty; forty-two were on extra or daily duty, and five were sick; eighty-two were on detached duty; thirty-eight absent with leave; five absent without leave; two hundred and forty-four absent sick; five absent in arrest; and one hundred and forty-three were prisoners of war. The Regiment gained two recruits from depot, and one by enlistment. Lost two by discharge on account of disability; five by death from wounds received in action, and three from disease.

Lieut. Henry Bacon had been discharged for disability, and Lieut. Ammidon had died in Rebel prison.

The men of the Regiment suffered greatly, for some weeks, for want of necessary clothing, requisitions for which had been but partially filled. More especially was this true in regard to the article of shoes, for want of which "there is almost always somebody barefooted."

There were mustered this month (January), present for duty, five officers: Eight were on extra duty; thirteen absent on detached service; one with leave; one sick, and five prisoners of war. Of enlisted men, two hundred and eighty one were present for duty; forty-nine on daily or extra duty; thirteen were sick, and one in arrest. Eighty-six were on detached service; forty-one absent with leave; two without leave; two hundred and eight absent sick; two absent in arrest, and one hundred and thirty-four were prisoners of war. The Regiment had gained seven recruits from depot, and one by enlistment; two from missing in action, and one, from desertion. And it had lost by discharge on account of disability, four; by order, one; by died of wounds, three, and of disease, three.

Capt. Goodrich was in Massachusetts on leave; Lieut. H. T. Hall on special duty as Judge Advocate General; Lieut. Cutler on court martial. Lieut. M. E. Walker was promoted to a Captaincy, and 2d Lieuts. Lilley and Rowley promoted to 1st Lieutenancies. Sergeant Major Pomeroy had been promoted to a 2d Lieutenancy.

For February our muster roll shows that there were eleven officers present for duty, and two on extra or daily duty; twelve absent on detached service; one absent sick, and four prisoners of war. Of enlisted men, that two hundred and seventy-eight were present for duty; forty-nine on extra or daily duty; thirteen sick, and one in arrest. Ninety-two were absent on detached service; fifty-seven with leave; one without leave; one hundred and seventy-five sick; three absent in arrest, and one hundred and fourteen prisoners of war.

* 1st Assistant Surgeon Cyrus B. Smith was discharged to accept promotion in 11th Massachusetts. 2d Assistant Surgeon Charles G. Allen was in Massachusetts on twenty days' leave, and had been promoted to be 1st A. S. Lieuts. H. B. Rowley, Henry T. Hall and Capt. F. T. Leach were each absent, with leave, in Massachusetts. Lieut. Col. Potter was still commanding the Brigade, as since early in February; and Capt. F. W Van Loan was in command of the Regiment.

Henry J. Millard, appointed 1st Lieutenant and 2d Assistant Surgeon, had joined the Regiment. Capt. A. C. Soley had been discharged on account of disability from wounds received. Quartermaster Sergeant Charles P. Trumbull had been discharged for disability.

On the 18th day of March, the following order was issued and read to the troops:

HEADQUARTERS 24TH ARMY CORPS,
Before Richmond, Va., March 18, 1865.

GENERAL ORDERS No. 32.

By order of the Major General commanding the Army of the James, the *Heart* is adopted as the badge of the 24th Army Corps. The symbol selected is one which testifies our affec-

---

* This officer was commissioned as surgeon of the 11th (Army of Potomac), Nov. 28, 1864. During nearly all the Valley fighting was in charge of 3d Division Hospital of our Corps. After the Battle of Winchester had charge of Smith hospital; was along with the Army, and saw the Regiment nearly every day. After he went to Army of Potomac, was there in charge of hospitals. Was on the field of battle at New Market, and under fire usually with the regiment — at Lynchburg, Piedmont, Snicker's Gap, Bolivar, Opequan, &c.

tionate regard for all our brave comrades — alike the living and the dead — who have braved the perils of this mighty conflict, and our devotion to the sacred cause — a cause which entitles us to the sympathy of every brave and true heart, and the support of every strong and determined hand. The Major General commanding the Corps does not doubt that soldiers who have given their strength and blood to the fame of their former badges, will unite in rendering the present one even more renowned than those under which they have heretofore marched to battle. The 1st Division will wear the red heart;—the Independent Division the white heart,—and the third Division the blue heart.

By command of
Major General JOHN GIBBON.

A. HENRY EMBLER,
Brevet Major and A. D. C.
Acting Assist. Adj. General.

With the opening spring, indications of renewed activity appeared. Our rest was broken in March; on the twenty-fifth day of which month the entire Division marched to the Chickahominy, ten miles, to cover the crossing of that river by Sheridan, who was en route with his Cavalry from Winchester to Richmond. The movement was well-timed, as Sheridan's arrival was almost simultaneous with our own. The men of the two parties exchanged hearty cheers at the meeting; and, with little delay, we started on our return; reaching "Deep Bottom" on the next day, after a march of twelve miles. We bivouacked here for the night; and about 5 P. M. of the 27th, crossed the James, under cover of the darkness. Continuing by an all night's march, conducted in rear of the lines of the main army, we halted about 8 A. M. of the 28th, occupying ground just vacated by the men of the 2d Corps. The march was slow and tedious, because of the darkness of the night, and the deep mud of the roads. On the morning of the 29th, the 1st and Independent Divisions of the 24th, strengthened by the 1st Division of the 25th Corps, were again set in motion towards "the left;" and crossing "Hatcher's Run," were assigned to a position in the lines of investment about Petersburg, on the right of the 2d Corps. We set about the work of entrenching ourselves, without delay. The whole of the succeeding night was spent building breastworks of rails and loose stones, and digging and throwing up the earth, with our bayonets and dinner plates, for want of better intrenching tools. The rain came down incessantly, rendering the work uncomfortable enough. On the 31st, brisk skirmishing was opened between the men on the opposing lines, which was continued for a while; after which, by a determined advance, we drove the enemy, and took and occupied the lines he had lost. The loss in the Brigade was ninety; our own being *one* man killed; and Lieut. Judd, serving as Aid to Gen. Turner, and thirteen men wounded. We laid the rest of the day exposed to a sharp fire, but without sustaining loss. Our skirmishers were well advanced on this day, and a sharp fire was kept up between the two lines. Breastworks were thrown up by us, within about 200 yards of those held by the enemy, behind which we laid safely. Exhausted by the struggle and labors of the day and night previous, we laid down with guns in hand, trusting to the vigilance and strength of our picket line.

In this month there were present for duty, 9 officers; on special duty, 7; sick, 2; absent on detached service, 10; with leave, 5; sick, 2. Of enlisted men, there were present for duty, 318; on extra duty, 49; sick, 3. Absent on detached service, 96; absent with leave, 67; sick, 156; in arrest, 2; prisoners of war, 89. The regiment had lost, by discharge on account of disability, *eight* men; by death from disease, 9; and by desertion, 2 men.

Capts. Willard and Chauncey, and Lieuts. Cobb and Platt and Calligan, had been paroled, and were home on leaves of absence; Lieut. Platt having resigned, and his resignation been accepted. The regiment was under the command of Capt. Leach, Lieut. Murdock, Acting Adjutant.

CHAPTER XLVII.

BEFORE RICHMOND.

APRIL 1 — SKIRMISHING — BATTERY "GREGG" — OUR LOSS — LIEUT. ROWLEY'S LETTER — EVACUATION OF PETERSBURG — A MARCH — GENERAL ORDERS.

About 4 A. M. of the 1st day of April, we were roused by a vigorous charge made by the Rebels upon our first line. This was handsomely repulsed; and for the remainder of the day we were undisturbed, save by the firing on the skirmish line, which was kept up without intermission. At three o'clock the next morning we were quietly roused, and piling our knapsacks, canteens, &c., were moved against two slight works in our immediate front, which we gained with little loss. Advancing again, this time by the left flank, a distance of about two miles, we halted for a short space. The fight had now become general; the roar of cannon and small arms was deafening. Everything gave evidence of the serious nature of the work before us. "Battery Gregg," a strong earthwork, was immediately in front. It was *ours* to assault. Could we take it, the Rebel line was untenable.

Our formation was in column by brigade, our own brigade in advance. The order reached us at about 11 o'clock. Moving directly against the work, a terrific fire of musketry, and grape and canister struck us in front, while shells from all the neighboring works, were directed against our flanks. "When within one hundred yards of the work," writes Capt. Leach, *our gallant leader on that day*, "we were obliged to lie down, *and crawl upon our hands and knees;* the enemy, all the time pouring grape and canister into our ranks, at a furious rate. But not a man flinched, although dead and dying comrades were lying thickly strewed upon the ground. The ditch around the fort was reached at last, and although the water in it stood waist deep, the brave fellows hesitated not to jump in, and scramble up the bank of the fort, vainly attempting to rush in en masse, and end the bloody struggle. Soon the stars and stripes could be seen floating by the side of the Rebel rag; cheer after cheer rent the air,—the Rebels fighting with the desperation of madmen, and shouting to each other "never surrender! never surrender!" For twenty-seven minutes we hung upon the works, knowing we could not retreat if we wished to. One more rush and we were inside the fort, and and for a minute or two there was a hand to hand contest. The works were ours; and the garrison,—dead and alive. Not a man escaped. Capt. Goodrich, with a few men, instantly turned the captured guns upon the nearest works occupied by the enemy, and gave them a few shells we had no other use for. Very soon the other forts were abandoned by their, or captured by our men. Considering the work we of the 34th had done, our loss was light; being only three officers slightly wounded,—five men killed, and thirty-two wounded. Arms were stacked, and the men put to work upon a new line of entrenchments, that we might hold what we had gained."

Of the morning's work, Lieut. Rowley of the 34th writes:— "Before we had time to see what we had taken (the two works first assaulted), we were moved to Petersburg, got in the rear of the Rebel works, and charged Fort Gregg. This we took after the most stubborn resistance I ever saw; the very hardest fighting we have ever had. Our men charged the Fort, jumped into the deep, wide trench, and with the help of bayonets stuck into the side of the bank or walls, climbed up to the parapet; and after we had got on to the walls of the Fort, the Rebels held us there over twenty-five minutes, fighting like madmen. We found fifty-seven dead Rebels inside the Fort, besides their wounded and prisoners. The Union loss was seventy killed, and, I don't know how many, wounded."

During the night the enemy quietly withdrew from Petersburg, evacuating also Richmond, and abandoning its strong lines of defense.

April 3d. With the coming of morning we were moved in pursuit of Lee and his army; marching to "Sutherland," a little village about ten miles distant. Here we bivouacked; and on the next day marched to "Wilson's Station," fifteen miles. Starting again early on the 5th, we marched along the Southside Railroad to Burkesville, a distance of twenty-seven miles. It was 11 P. M., when, jaded and completely worn out, we were allowed to halt. Here was promulgated an order, of which the following is a copy:

HEADQUARTERS 24TH ARMY CORPS,
Behind Richmond, April 3, 1865.

GENERAL ORDERS No. 41.

"With great satisfaction the Major General commanding congratulates his gallant command upon the successful operations of the last few days. The 24th Corps has demonstrated that with a well organized and disciplined force, no military achievement is impossible. The marching has been superior to anything of the kind heretofore witnessed, and the desperate assault upon Fort Gregg, the last of the enemy's strongholds around Petersburg, entitles this command to a place along with their late gallant comrades of Fort Fisher. Your commander is proud of you."

By Command of
Major General JOHN GIBBON.

EDWARD MEADE,
Lieut. Col., and A. A. G.

CHAPTER XLVIII.

Behind Richmond.

"RICE'S STATION" — FARMSVILLE — APPOMATOX STATION — APPOMATOX COURT HOUSE — A WHITE FLAG — THE SURRENDER — GENERAL DEVENS — GENERAL ORD'S COMMAND.

We had now gathered square upon the flank of Lee's army, which was to the north of us, marching towards "Farmsville." Now on the 6th, the 54th Pennsylvania, and 123d Ohio of our Brigade, the whole under command of Col. Kellogg of the last Regiment, were detached from the Brigade; and, strengthened by a squadron of the 4th Massachusetts Cavalry, marched across the country to hold, or, if that was impossible, to destroy the bridge which spanned the "Appomatox" at "Rice's Station;" and thus cut off the enemy's retreat in that direction. The head of Lee's army was met near that point, and a sharp engagement ensued. Our force was largely outnumbered; but notwithstanding the disparity of numbers, held the enemy at bay for hours. The Cavalry charged again and again, but unavailingly. In a last desperate effort to regain the main army, they rode gallantly against the enemy, losing their commander and eleven other officers. The Infantry maintained the unequal struggle until their ammunition was exhausted, when Col. Kellogg attempted to withdraw it. Perceiving the intention, the Rebels swooped down in overwhelming force, and made the men of both Regiments prisoners. But the resistance had been long enough to enable Ord to come up with the remainder of his corps, and compel Lee to entrench. In the day's skirmishing the loss sustained by the 34th was three men wounded.

Our march was ten miles. We reached "Farmsville" on the 7th, distant across the country ten miles, and on the 8th marched to "Appomatox Station," lying down between 11 and 12 o'clock at night, after a weary tramp of 33 miles. Roused at 3 o'clock on the morning of the 9th, we moved, at a "double quick," about two miles, to "Appomatox Court House." Here we found Sheridan's troopers, dismounted, strenuously resisting the onward movement of Lee's army, which was pressing desperately, in the hope of crushing the Cavalry before the arrival of the Infantry. to the left, we formed line in rear of the Troopers. The attack Filing of the Rebels was furious and determined. As our Cavalry, giving ground, disclosedt he line of bayonets, gleaming in the rear, the Johunies apparently lost heart. In turn they gave ground before our advance; and in about an hour we had driven them back to, and upon their main army. A white flag fluttered above their ranks, and at 9 o'clock we had orders to "cease firing." For a while the men of the two armies held their respective positions. But the rumor soon spread that proposals for a surrender of the entire Rebel army were being considered, and many a cap was tossed, and many a heart beat high with hope. When, after a little while, word was passed along our lines that Gen. Lee *had* surrendered, men actually cried for great joy. Our lines were again formed, *now* within a halfmile of those of the Rebel army. Arms were again stacked, tents pitched, and we prepared to enjoy the rest we so much needed, and which, by our almost continuous marching and fighting of this last short campaign, we had so well earned. The men of the two armies, alike joyous over the capitulation, mingled freely together; more like friends than like enemies, who for so long had held each other by the throat.

Of these last days, Maj. Gen. Devens, before his comrades of the Army of the James, thus spoke: "On the morning of the 9th of April, by a march almost unprecedented in the annals of warfare, the Army of the James had placed themselves across the Lynchburg road, and closed the avenues of escape. On that morning, Lieut. Gen. Gordon, of Georgia, who commanded the advance, said to Gen. Lee that 'his way was barred.' 'It can be nothing but Cavalry,' said Gen. Lee; 'brush them away; no Cavalry can stand against Infantry.' It was done as Gen. Lee ordered; but as the Cavalry fell back, they revealed the long and gleaming line of steel, which marked the line of Infantry, of the Army of the James. There were Ord and Gibbon — there were Turner and R. S. Foster at the head of their Divisions. To throw his exhausted troops upon that wall of steel, was a madness of which the Rebel chieftain was not capable, and the sword of Lee was laid in the conquering hand of Grant."

From a Richmond paper of that month, we extract the following: "The 1st and 2d Divisions of the 24th Army Corps, who were engaged in the pursuit of Gen. Lee to Appomatox Court House, after the fall of Petersburg, returned to this city on Tuesday morning. It is reported by military men that Gen. Lee's surrender was necessitated in consequence of the severe marching and skilful manœuvring of these forces. Their marching will compare with *any* on record. For four successive days they marched respectively eighteen, twenty-three, twenty-seven and thirty-two miles. By this rapid marching they were enabled to overtake, and surround the Confederate forces. Had these two Divisions been later in getting around to the right of Gen. Lee, it is confidently believed that Gen. Lee would have made his escape."

"It was owing to Gen. Ord's energy that his troops marched thirty-eight miles from three o'clock in the morning of April 8th, to eleven o'clock on the following night, when they quietly threw themselves down upon the ground, to rest, in front of Lee's army, without the enemy's suspecting, as acknowledged on the following morning, that there was an Infantry soldier within ten miles of them; and by four o'clock on the following morning, forming in line of battle, and fighting until a flag of truce was sent from the enemy, asking for a conference. The march certainly has no parallel in the history of the Rebellion, or any war in Europe."

CHAPTER XLIX.

TO LYNCHBURG AND RICHMOND.

MARCHING ORDERS—LYNCHBURG—DESTRUCTION OF PROPERTY —MARCH TO RICHMOND—ENTRY INTO THE CITY—OUR CAMP—APRIL ROLLS—CHANGES IN THE REGIMENT—GENERAL ORDERS.

12th. We have remained in camp at this station, (Appomatox Court House,) witnesses to the formalities, and sharers of the joy incident to the surrender of the Rebel army, under Gen. Lee. But to-day, our brigade, in obedience to General Orders, moved on the road to Lynchburg. Marching seventeen miles, we went into camp. On the next day, about noon, we entered that city after a march of about six miles. Lieut. Col. Potter was appointed Provost Marshal, and the 34th was detailed for guard and patrol duty, during the occupation of the place by the Union force. The purpose of the visit was to seize, confiscate, and destroy the property of the Rebel Government, stored in the place. Immense quantities of stores were destroyed, including tobacco, large amounts of which were *thrown into the James River.* If men and officers appropriated to their own use such quantity of this latter article as they could conveniently carry with them, it was not regarded as a violation of orders, for were not the Philistines thereby despoiled? The work of destruction having been fully done, we were on the return march, on the afternoon of the 15th. The 16th at night found us at Appomatox Court House again. Marching the 17th, 18th, and 19th, forty-four miles, we reached Burkesville, where we remained in camp three days,—at the end of which time, taking to the road again, and passing via Amelia

Court House, we reached Manchester, on the 24th, after a march, since leaving Lynchburg, of one hundred and fourteen miles. The next day the Division entered the city of Richmond. It was received by Gen. Devens' Division, which constituted the garrison for the time being, and which, drawn up on the main street, honored us with a salute, as we passed by. Thousands of negroes thronged the streets through which we marched, and made the air ring with their shouts of welcome.

We encamped on the north side of the city, about four miles out. The next morning, Col. Lincoln, who had been on detached duty since joining in November last, came up, and, with him, a large detachment of convalescent and lately exchanged men. Upon reporting, he was assigned to the command of the brigade, relieving Lieut. Col. Potter, who in turn relieved Capt. Leach from command of the regiment.

Throughout this campaign the 34th "maintained its well earned reputation for marching and fighting; was noted for its discipline; and received many compliments from the General commanding. Our Band, of which we were justly proud, never failed to cheer the sick and wounded with sweet music, or render assistance to suffering comrades."

The ground first occupied by us was destitute of shade and water, and deep in dust or mud, as sunshine or rain prevailed. A search for a better location was rewarded by finding a piece of sward land, upon a gentle knoll, at the base of which was a small stream of quickly running water; which, with the consent of the Major General commanding, was soon occupied. If it had the advantage of giving us clean camping ground, (being separated from the camp of the remaining brigades), it subjected us to extra duty on the picket line. Here, just outside of the line of Rebel earthworks, within short rifle range of a barn from which Dahlgren, on his former raid, took some horses for his command, we remained while in the city. Brigade Headquarters were located on the banks of a little rivulet, running through a grove of magnificent tulip trees, just behind a four gun battery, which, on more than one occasion, had paid its shotted compliments to raiding parties, under our colors. Beautiful residences, for the most part abandoned and unoccupied, were on all sides of us. From the gardens belonging to these estates, the officers derived supplies of toothsome vegetables. "We hear of the muster out, at Annapolis, of Major Pratt, on account of disability." Although he had been recognized as Major since his promotion; at this late day, his muster in as of that rank is, by order of the War Department, set aside as irregular, and he mustered out as Captain, for the second time. Lieuts. Platt and Cobb, lately from Rebel prisons, are also discharged; while Capts. Willard and Chauncey, and Lieut. Calligan, just exchanged, have rejoined the regiment. Capt. Fox is serving as Post Adjutant at Parole Camp in Annapolis.

Our April return shows 13 officers present for duty; on extra or daily duty, 6, and one sick; absent on detached service, 8; sick, 1; with leave, 1; paroled prisoner of war, 1. Of enlisted men, 247 were present for duty; 48 on extra or daily duty; 2 were sick; 105 were absent on detached service; 147 were absent with leave; 191 were absent, sick; 4 absent, in arrest; and 53 were prisoners of war. The regiment had lost 2 officers by resignation; 11 men by discharge, by reason of disability; 8 by death from wounds; 8 by disease, and 1 by desertion. Col. Lincoln commanded the brigade; Col. Potter was serving on Military Commission in Richmond; Capt. Willard had the regiment; Lieut. Judd, A. A. A. G. on Division Staff, was absent, sick, from wounds received in action at Hatcher's Run.

May 1st. We are doing the usual ordinary camp duty—sending out small parties to picket our front, and occasionally furnishing fatigue parties to the Quartermaster's Department in the city.

Hunter of E, and Gardner of K, both of ours, have been selected from our Brigade to bear to Washington, and deliver to the War Department, the Rebel Flags captured by our Division in the late campaign.

2d. Twelve Rebels, five of whom claim to have belonged to Mosby's late command, surrendered themselves to-day, at our picket line, and were sent in to Brigade Headquarters. Three of them were officers. There was a good deal of good natured joking about the "tall walking" done by one or the other party, in the valley, on various occasions the past season. What was better, was the anxiety to take the oath of allegiance to the United States shown by all the prisoners.

6*th.* The papers of to-day brought the General Orders of the War Department, relative to the speedy disbandment of this army; and Special Orders were sent down, directing the immediate discharge of "all disabled men." Another order, looking more to our present support, directs the commanding officers of Brigades to detail a large party of men "*accustomed to seine fishing,*" that a supply of "*shad*" may be procured. *This*, directed to men from the interior of Massachusetts and Ohio, where the water courses furnish nothing larger than Perch or Bull Pouts, gives occasion for hearty laughter.

CHAPTER L.

IN RICHMOND.

HONORS TO THE 5TH CORPS — CAPT. CHAUNCEY — HONOR TO MEADE'S ARMY — CAMP INSPECTION — MORE ORDERS — "BILLET DOUX" — MUSTER OUT — CO. G — OUR RECRUITS — RE-CLOTHED — PAY ROLLS.

5th. Brigade line was formed at 7 o'clock this morning, in a *pouring rain.* General Orders directed the march of the entire Division into the city, to show full honors to the 5th Corps of the Army of the Potomac as it passed through the streets of Richmond, on its march to Washington. We had made about half the distance, when an Orderly delivered orders for our return to camp; the ceremony having been postponed on account of the storm. We were as wet as drowned rats, long before we reached *home.*

Our picket detail has been relieved by one from the 2d Brigade. Coming in with our party was a goodly number of Rebel officers and men. These, like all who have previously come in, profess great satisfaction at the close of hostilities, and accept the situation with great good humor.

Capt. Chauncey, of ours, who has been in Rebel hands, and for the greater part of the time since his capture at Newmarket, in prison at Macon, Georgia, returned to us to-day. It is useless to say that his reception was a hearty one. Poor fellow! his appearance showed, louder than words could tell, that his lot had been a hard one; and his tale of suffering and privation, of exposure and ill usage, wrung tears from all eyes. He confirmed the reports previously received by us, that he, with Lieut. Ammidon, of our "C," and other officers, were removed to

Charleston, S. C., and placed under the fire of our Batteries while engaged in shelling that city. He also certified to the death of Lieut. Ammidon, from small-pox, contracted while thus confined in that city.

7th. Yesterday, at 6.45 A. M., the men of the Brigade stood again in line, and soon after were en route to the city, which was reached at 8½. The purpose was, as before, to pay the well deserved honors of a full salute to the Veterans of Meade's Army as they made their triumphal march *through* this city. Our Brigade drew up in line, fronting the City Hall, upon the broad steps of which Generals Meade, Meigs and others, with Chief of Staff Halleck, were seated, surrounded by their respective Staff Officers. In the rear, but a little to our right, was the Capitol of the late Confederacy. Here we stood, all the long day, in the burning sun, while the bronzed veterans moved by to the music of our assembled Bands. Each Chief of Division, and each battered standard received the full honor of dipped flags and presented arms: while, ever and anon, as the well known form of some favorite officer was seen, the air resounded with hearty cheers. Most of the Brigades were led by Colonels or Lieutenant Colonels, and some of them, and many of the Regiments were under the command of Captains. The men looked and marched splendidly, and the display was imposing. The Artillery was in small force; and the Cavalry, especially weak in numbers. The poor fellows of the Infantry suffered much from heat and dust, and a good many "fell out" by the way. We were glad to welcome and grasp the hands of our former comrades and old friends, Surgeons Smith and Thorndike, with whom we exchanged hurried and hasty greeting.

The sidewalks were thronged with negroes of both sexes, whose rows of gleaming ivory attested their unalloyed joy. Crowds of Union soldiers, off duty, cheered lustily at intervals. There was a "right smart chance" of rebel uniforms in the crowd, the wearers of which, to all seeming, were not the least interested spectators of the pageant. Here and there a female form was visible; but in every instance it was that of some Northern woman engaged as a nurse in some Hospital, or enlisted in the service of the Sanitary Commission. Among these last, many of us of the 34th were glad to see and welcome the Misses Chase, of Worcester. More than one parched tongue was refreshed by the drop of cool water provided by their kindness. It was past 4 P. M., when we received the welome order of dismissal; and an hour later, when tired, dirty, heated and hungry we broke ranks in our own encampment.

11*th*. Custer's Division of Sheridan's Cavalry, passed through the city yesterday, on its way to Washington. Riding by the side of the General was his wife, who both rode and looked as if herself every inch a trooper.

Four Corps of Sherman's army are lying in and around Manchester; on the opposite side of the River. The work of re-clothing that entire command is going actively on. These troops are to make their formal entry into, and passage through this City, on the fifteenth. At least such is the present programme. The orders for which, just promulgated, direct the troops of that command to "show proper respect to the Chief of Staff of the Army," as they pass his quarters. In view of the sharp correspondence which has lately passed between these high functionaries, it will be interesting to note the proprieties of the occasion, as the column moves past the home of the officer in question.

Headquarters was highly honored to-day by the presence of a party, under escort of, and introduced by our friend Dr. Clarke, as "the two Misses Chase, *and three other ladies* from Massachusetts." The interview lost nothing of pleasure from our not knowing the names of our fair visitors.

15*th*. Gen. Gibbon, our Corps Commander, honored our camp by a close personal inspection of it to-day; at the close of which, an order, looking to the comfort of the rank and file of the command, was promulgated by his authority. This order directed the tearing down of certain designated buildings, from which the men could procure material to *floor their tents*. In what sharp contrast this, to those orders from Superior Headquarters at Harper's Ferry, which directed the arrest of the occupants of any tent in which a board could be found; and which would have consigned to the Guard House the entire command, had not notice been given of the required search, and time allowed for the *judicious shortening* of all boards in camp.

We have been buried beneath the avalanche of orders made necessary by our expected near muster out. Now, as pleasant relief to the dull formality of these orders, has come a furious interchange of *billet doux,* between Clarke, Surgeon in Chief and Acting Medical Director on Division Staff, and Assistant Surgeon Allen, Acting Chief Medical Officer on Regimental Staff. In filling out the papers necessary for the discharge of our disabled men, it is required that the nature, extent, and cause of the disability should be particularly set forth; and Allen, in making out such papers, indulges himself in the use of such expressions as "*shot by a lousy Rebel* at New Market," or elsewhere, as the place might have been. Now, however much Allen may think he is warranted by the fact, Clarke considers the use of such expressions unbecoming in an official paper, if not disrespectful; and, in the exercise of his authority, endorses upon them "Respectfully returned; the attention of Assistant Surgeon Allen is called to the unwarranted expressions used by him; he will confine himself to the statement of bare facts in the case, in making out and forwarding papers for the discharge of enlisted men." Allen insists that, as he is required to certify to the fact of the man's disability, and his opinion of its cause, he can discharge his duty in no way different from the one he has adopted; while Clarke, using his old time formula, tells him "to continue the same" at his peril. Meantime, we lookers-on, foreseeing in the dim distance greater demand for coffee than for pistols for the two, enjoy the affair immensely. But it is no joking matter for the Orderlies; as, unless some compromise is speedily affected, we shan't have enough to bear despatches between the Headquarters of the respective commands.

15th to 25th. Orders from Washington have been received at Corps Headquarters which direct the immediate preparation of all papers necessary for *our* muster out; and we learn, unofficially, that the 34th is the first organization in the Corps to be discharged. Quartermaster Howland has been despatched to Norfolk to bring up all our books and papers; they having been sent there for safe keeping, at the opening of this Spring's campaign. And, now our joy is turned into grief, and we are overwhelmed with mortification, at the announcement that one of our men, C—— G——, of "E," is a prisoner in Castle Thunder, on a charge of larceny. Upon the representation of Col. Lincoln, made to Gen. Ord, commanding department, so soon as the fact of arrest was known to him, G's release from imprisonment was ordered. Thereupon the Provost Marshal General, by whose officers G. was arrested, demanded an investigation of all the facts of the case. By order from Department Headquarters, this investigation was directed to be made by Gen. Turner, commanding the Division, who honored Col. Lincoln by charging him with the duty of ascertaining and reporting the facts in the case. It appeared, upon enquiry, that G——, upon returning from the city a few days previously, fell in with an old, ill-conditioned horse, loose, and grazing by the wayside, but a little distance from our camp. Mindful of the comfort to be derived on a march from having an animal on which to pack one's baggage, instead of being one's self a pack-horse, G—— caught the animal, led it into camp, and turned it out to graze within the lines of our sentinels. He set up no claim to the animal, nor attempted in any way to conceal its presence in camp. And for this, Gen. Patrick's officers, without enquiring into the character of the man, or into the circumstances connected with the presence of the horse in camp,—without so much as saying to the Regimental or Brigade Commander, "by your leave, sir," hurried G—— from camp, to the comforts and safe keeping of this old and filthy Rebel prison. True he was not long in custody; but it was none the less an outrage that he was in custody at all. Report of the foregoing was duly made; and Brigade orders were issued directing the arrest of any one who, in future, should attempt the arrest of any man of the command, within the limits of the brigade, without the knowledge of the Colonel commanding. G——'s freedom was not again interfered with.

We shall have to leave behind all men recruited in 1863; our order for muster out excluding all men whose period of enlistment *extends beyond October next*. We are ordered to transfer these recruits to a regiment from Illinois, forming part of the 2d Brigade, our Division, against which order a remonstrance has been forwarded, and request made that they may be transferred to the Massachusetts 24th, in which request Col. Ordway, commanding that regiment, has joined.

Capts. Willard and Belser, and Lieut. Blake, are desirous of remaining in the military service of the country; and have given notice of their intention to avail themselves of the provisions of the order, upon that subject, just issued by the War Department.

25th to June 1st. We were agreeably surprised to-day by a visit from Col. Ivers Philips, of Worcester, whose interest in us, and our welfare, was shown by his walking from the city to our camp, in a driving rain.

Col. Wetherell, of Gov. Andrew's staff, also honored us with a call.

We are, as we have been for some time, busied in completing the papers, and making other necessary arrangements requisite to our being mustered out. Our rolls have been diminished this month by more than sixty men, by death, discharge, and transfer to the Veteran Reserve Corps. And now that we are ready and almost prepared to cast off all that pertains to military life, down comes an order directing the entire command to be re-clothed, even to the extent of *new uniforms*. It is difficult to understand the reason of such order, beyond the fact that it indicates a series of inspections and reviews.

This month's muster roll shows present for duty, seventeen officers, and five on extra or daily duty;—nine absent on detached duty;—one absent sick. Of the enlisted men, two hundred and ninety-eight are present for duty,—forty-seven on daily or extra duty,—fourteen sick. Absent on detached service, one hundred and ten;—with leave twenty-six;—without leave eight;—sick, one hundred and fifty-three;—in arrest, two;—and prisoners of war, twenty-nine. The regiment has lost by discharge, on account of disability, one officer and nineteen men; *by order*, eight men. Ten men have been *transferred*; three lost by death, from wounds;—and twenty-three by disease.

Col. Lincoln still commands the Brigade, and Capt. Willard the Regiment.

Capt. Willard is on Court Martial duty

Lieut. Cobb has resigned, and his resignation has been accepted.

Lieut. Col. and Brevet Col. Potter is serving on Military Commission in the City of Richmond.

We learn, much to our gratification, that we are to be soon discharged; that we are to be mustered out in this city; and that we are to receive our final pay and discharge papers at Readville, or Galloup's Island, which is quite as much to our disgust. We have hoped that we should be discharged on the ground where we were mustered in; and efforts are being made to get such modification of our orders, as will admit of our going to, and through the City of Worcester, if we cannot be discharged there.

CHAPTER LI

RICHMOND AND MUSTER OUT.

EXAMINING BOARD—DIVISION REVIEW—BRONZE MEDALS—OUR RECRUITS—OUR ROLLS—P. OF F—CORPS REVIEW WALSH OF A—GENERAL ORDERS 24TH ARMY CORPS—"MUSTER OUT."

June 1st to 5th. Our muster out waits only for the completion of their rolls, by company commanders.

Orders, Adjutant General's office, Commonwealth of Massachusetts, require commanders of regiments, to forward recommendations for promotion to all existing vacancies in their commands; said recommendations, in all cases, to be governed by considerations which would rule, provided the commands were to be continued in service.

By orders from *this* military department, Regimental Commanders are directed to prepare lists of officers who have "particularly distinguished themselves for bravery and military qualities," and forward them through brigade, division, and corps Headquarters; the commanding officers of each of which will append their respective comments. Brigade and division commanders are required, in like manner, to report upon their respective staff officers. As if this were not enough, there is also to be organized in each division, an *Examining Board;* which board is to be charged with examining and reporting upon the qualifications of such officers, in the volunteer force, as may desire to remain in the military service of the country. This, with the ulterior view of their appointment to commissions in the regular army.

General Orders, Independent Division, appoint to this board

Col. and Acting Brig. Gen. Wm. S. Lincoln, 34th Massachusetts, President; Lieut. Col. Titus, commanding 116th Ohio; Major R. R. Clarke, Surgeon 34th Massachusetts, Surgeon in Chief, and Acting Medical Director Independent Division 24th army corps; and Capt. Frank T. Leach 34th Massachusetts; all from our brigade, and all but one from our own regiment. The duty will be delicate, and the work somewhat arduous, as many officers in the division have already applied to be examined, hoping to be continued in the service; one, a Col., expressing a strong desire to be retained, "providing he can remain with the rank he now holds." This, considering Gen. Turner, who commands our division, holds only a Capt.'s commission in the regular service, is pretty good.

Orders from Corps Headquarters directed a review of the Division, by Gen. Gibbon, on the first instant; but these were countermanded on receipt of proclamation designating that day as a day of National fasting. The ceremony actually came off on the third instant. All three Brigades passed in column of Companies, before General Gibbon, Corps Commander, who was attended by the commanders of the other Divisions, and Gen.'s Potter, and Curtis, of Fort Fisher fame. As *we* wheeled into line, an aide-de-camp brought orders for the 1st (our) Brigade to pass again, this time at a *double quick;* while the other two were dismissed, and ordered to their quarters. All were loud in commendation of the appearance of the Brigade; especially complimenting our own regiment. "A fine regiment," said Gen. Gibbon, "*and shows the close attention paid to it in its early days.*" "A fine regiment, indeed," said Gen. Potter, "and I envy you, Colonel, the taking it home." Our "muster out," or rather the preparations for it, seem to have come to a stand; partly because of an insufficient supply of the required blank forms, and partly, perhaps, by reason of the receipt of orders from the *War Department*, which direct the careful examination, by a competent Board, of every officer, in the different commands of the army.

We learn, by an announcement from Division Headquarters, that it is now determined that the 34th is to be mustered out *last* of all the regiments which constitute the Division. This, we conjecture, is because a majority of the clerks and orderlies, besides a goodly number of the General Staff at those Headquarters, are detailed from our regiment.

Heavy and frequent rains, with intense heat by day, and cool and damp weather by night, have caused considerable addition to our number of "sick in quarters." Fortunately we have no serious sickness among us as yet.

8th. The Board of Officers charged with examining such officers as desire to be continued in the service, visited our camp to-day in discharge of their duty. The regular drill was suspended; but the men were under Capts. Willard and Belser to enable those officers to show their tact in drilling Company, and Battalion. Everything went off well. Leaving our camp, the Board visited that of the —th Virginia, to examine Colonel and Acting Brigadier H———y, of that Regiment. Headquarter's guard was found marching his beat, bare-footed, in shirt sleeves, with his pants rolled up to his knees, and his suspenders hanging from his shoulders, well down his back. The Colonel himself was mounted, and leading his men, backward and forward, across a neighboring field. Being asked to get his men into a certain specified position, "What order shall I issue?" he asked; and being informed that that was a matter for his determination, "Oh, well," he replied, "I can give the necessary order, but I want my Battalion to appear well, and I have never put them through the specified movement." The result of a whole afternoon's labor was entirely lost, if it failed to convince *him* that he had a great deal to learn in the school, even of the Company. It is said that upon an examination, upon matters not purely military, he betrayed an ignorance hardly conceivable; placing New Jersey among the New England States; unable to determine in what State the Hudson River was; or to name those which bounded on the Atlantic Ocean; was ignorant of the number of pounds' which made a ton; and answered that a bushel of corn weighed fourteen pounds, and a bushel of oats twelve pounds. For any apparent errors, he apologized, by saying that he feared he might be a little rusty, as it was some years since he had graduated from (William and Mary) College; a fear which was converted into certainty, as the examination progressed.

10th. An order came down yesterday, directing a review of the 24th Corps for this afternoon. Division line was ordered for 4½;—Brigade for 4¼;—and Regimental for 4 o'clock P. M. Our distance from the field on which the ceremony was to have been had, was six long miles; the route being over the roads into and through the city, and far beyond on the other side. To-day has been intensely hot, and the sky unclouded. About 3 P. M. a dense mass of heavy black clouds, fast rising in the west, gave warning of both wind and rain. To us inferiors in rank, this gave unmistakable sign that no review would be had. But it had been ordered, and our duty was to be on the ground. So with a wise shake of the head, and a rather reluctant step, we started, warming to our work as we got fairly on the road. Long before the ground was reached, the storm burst upon us in terrible fury. Heavens! how the wind did blow! and how the rain did pour! Soon after we halted on the field, the Acting Brigadier and Staff rode up; and, under his command, we halted at our designated position in line, at three minutes past the hour mentioned in Brigade order. But of all the troops composing the Corps, our own Brigade was the only one to put in an appearance, on the field. We held our place in line till past 5 o'clock, when an Aid of Gen. Gibbon rode up and announced the indefinite postponement of the ceremony. We should have received the announcement with as much cheerfulness, if it had been made before we were so thoroughly drenched. As it was, Brigade line was dismissed; a faint cheer was given; and each command made the best of its way to its own encampment.

11th. It is officially announced, that at this Review, whenever it shall come off, bronze medals, awarded by the Department at Washington, are to be given to enlisted men distinguished for gallant conduct in the last campaign: four coming to our Brigade, and *two* to men of *our own Regiment.*

It is also given out that the order transferring our recruits to the Regiment from Illinois, is to be countermanded, and they are to be incorporated with the 24th Massachusetts, now serving as Provost Guard in this city. It is understood, also, that Capts. Willard and Macomber, and Lieuts. Belser and Horton, are to remain with them.

Lieut. Hall has been ordered to take charge of our rolls, and deliver them to the proper officer. To facilitate our final payment and discharge, he is to be despatched to "Readville," in advance of the Regiment.

And now, when every man was anxiously counting the hours which must elapse before he received his final discharge from a service which he has helped render immortal, occurred one of those acts of insubordination, which, while bringing temporary discredit upon the command, is attended with serious injury only to the party immediately concerned.

Our own Regimental discipline has always been rigid; the *esprit de corps* of the command, admirable. At all times, and in all places, our reputation has been enviable; and since our encampment in this city, in Division General Orders which censured irregularities in other Brigades, the men composing the first Brigade have been excepted from rebuke.

In order that our men might gratify their natural desire to inspect whatever was of interest in Richmond, passes have been issued, by which they could go freely to and from the city. Brigade orders, however, forbid any man leaving the limits of the command unless provided with such pass; prohibited spending the night out of camp on any pretense; and announced that trial by court martial would follow any violation of the order. And to enforce the observance of the order, a Patrol was established, and the order directed to be read at the head of each company, at retreat, daily.

Now, this evening, directly after the reading of the order in question, private Perry, of F, serving as Provost Guard at Brigade Headquarters, threw off his equipments, and went out on a little reconnoisance, on his own account. Unfortunately for him, his scouting was directly in the path of this patrol, into whose hands he fell. The result to him was *arrest, charges, trial*, and the promulgation, this morning, of "Special Orders, Headquarters Independent Division, 24th Army Corps, announcing the approval of the General commanding, of the findings and sentence of the court martial before which he was tried: which is, that "he be dishonorably discharged the service, with loss of all pay due, and final bounty."

12th. Orders came down after retreat this evening, announcing a review of the Corps, by Gen. Ord, for to-morrow, "*rain or shine;*" and it looks sure to rain. Well! if only the reviewing officers share the water with us!

We are all made sad by the announcement, to-night, of the almost certain fate of Walsh, of "A," who, poor fellow! lies now in the hospital, near to death. How singular his case! While the regiment was lying at Fort Lyon, he was accidentally shot, supposed mortally, the ball penetrating his abdomen. He recovered; went through the service of '63, and the campaign of '64 in which he was once or twice wounded; and now, at the very instant of being discharged, is stricken down by disease, with hardly a possibility of living more than a day or two.

13th—9 P. M. We are all pretty well tired—thoroughly drenched; some not a little cross, and a good deal disgusted; and yet pleased and gratified at the general result of to-day's proceedings.

The review came off as ordered—brass bands warned us to "see the conquering hero comes!"—drums were ruffled—arms presented—colors dipped at the bidding of commanding officers; and, to crown all, the men, at the request of Gen. Turner and others, and to gratify Madame, the wife of the reviewing officer, gave three lusty cheers to Gen. Ord, as he rode down the line in review. Although the rain came down as never before in our experience in this region, it "*held up,*"—and the sun shed his brightest beams upon the troops, during the actual review. There was less of that tiresome waiting, which, although not laid down in the books as a necessary, always is an incidental accompaniment of such ceremony. The column looked and marched splendidly. The appearance and bearing of the 34th drew words of praise from more than one general officer. Having completed their "march in review," the troops were drawn up, forming three sides of a square, that all might witness the ceremony of presenting the bronze medals to the men deemed most worthy of receiving them. Two of ours, Hunter of E, and Gardner of K, were made both proud and happy by receiving these testimonials to their bravery and gallantry. As a little squint-eyed corporal of another command stepped forward in answer to the call of his name, and stood, covered with blushes, while Madame, wife of the reviewing officer, pinned to his breast the coveted medal, we could hardly control ourselves at hearing the General himself admonish him "*always to wear it*, and *guard it sacredly as a precious heir-loom to your* (his) *ancestors* — I mean your *posterity* — and if you have not got any, take my advice and go right to work and get some."

Previous to the dismissal of the troops the following was issued:

"HEADQUARTERS 24TH ARMY CORPS,
"REVIEW GROUND,
"RICHMOND, VA., *June* 13, 1865.

"SOLDIERS OF THE 24TH CORPS:

"This probably is the last occasion in which you, as a corps, will be assembled. Many of you are about to re-enter civil life; to resume those domestic duties, which, by your service to the great cause of your country, have been so long neglected. Before we separate, I desire to thank you, in the name of a grateful country, for the service you have rendered her. By your discipline, long marches, and hard fighting, you have established for generations a name second to none in the army. Your badge has become an emblem of valor and patriotism, and is a source of just pride to all who wear it.

"Those of you who are entering civil life should still wear it, on all occasions, as an evidence to your brothers who remain in the service, of your pride in a badge made sacred by the blood of so many men, and of your disposition, should your country ever again call you to arms, to again assemble under that proud emblem, and revive the glory of the 24th Corps.

"To our comrades who are leaving the service we pledge a kind farewell, and a wish that their career in civil life may be as successful and prosperous as their military life has been, alike honorable to themselves and beneficial to their country.

"JOHN GIBBON,
"Major General Volunteers, Commanding Corps."

CHAPTER LII

Journey Home and Discharge.

Brigade Headquarters—Homeward March—On the James—Baltimore—Philadelphia—Cooper's Shop Refreshment Saloon—The Surgeon's Horse—New York—Quartermaster's Department — Providence — Readville—B. & A. R. Road—The Pay Master—Our Discharge.

15th. Brigade Headquarters were broken up yesterday, immediately upon the muster out of the 116th Ohio; and to-day, our own regiment was paraded and subjected to the same ceremony. At the close of the formal proceedings, the Colonel commanding was served with an order, directing him to march, with his command, at 5 A. M. to-morrow, for Readville; where final payment is to be made, and the men to receive their discharge papers. Lieut. Hall, who is charged with the custody of our muster out rolls and records, and who was to have been despatched in advance, is now directed to accompany the command. We must march, leaving poor Walsh, who is but just alive, here in hospital.

16th to 21st. Our bugles roused us at an early hour on the morning of the 16th, and soon after, in heavy marching order, with our haversacks filled to overflowing with our three days rations, we moved on our homeward way. Reaching the city, we halted long enough to leave, at the Headquarters of the 24th Massachusetts, our recruits, who, organized into two companies, under the temporary command of Capt. Macomber and Lieut. Horton, were ordered to be transferred to that regiment; and resuming our march, we soon reached "Rockett's," where we took boat for Baltimore. Steaming down the James, passing Drury's Bluff, Dutch Gap canal,—which looked like nothing but a deep ditch cut through dry land,—and the many points made famous in this long struggle for the control of the river, and the possession of Richmond,— past City Point, and Fortress Munroe, — out on to the broad bosom of the Chesapeake, through the waters of the Patapsco, and by the walls of Fort McHenry, we entered the city of Baltimore, in the early forenoon of the 17th. Here, a short delay was rendered unavoidable by the necessity of procuring, from the Post Quartermaster, orders for our further transportation. It was a pleasant surprise for us to find that our application was to be made to, and our orders to be received from our warm friend and old time comrade, Maj. Bowman, now on duty as such officer. Furnished with the needed authority, we lost no time in taking the cars provided for us, and were soon again on our way. Not now, however, as in those days of '62, met with averted head, and scowling face, but everywhere greeted with hearty cheers. A rapid run carried us to Philadelphia, which was reached as the morning sun was breaking through the fog, and smoke, and haze, which lay heavily upon the city; and to the regular, but monotonous tap, tap, of our drums, we marched to the Cooper Shop Refreshment Saloon, where a warm breakfast awaited our coming. Almost three years had passed since such a temptation had been placed in our way, and then on this very spot! But the boys were equal to the emergency. No words can describe the vigor of their first attack, nor the steady and dogged perseverance with which they continued their assault upon the tables. Not a soul faltered; and at the close of the repast, looking down the long table, we had to mourn that for once we had been unequal to the demands made upon us.

The bugles soon sounded to the color, and we reluctantly turned to leave. But the employees of the Quartermaster's department were looking, among our horses, for animals which the Government, from former ownership, might now lay claim to. All such, or at least all believed to be such, had been turned over, previous to our leaving Richmond. But alas, for our brave, warm hearted, guileless, old Surgeon! While in the valley, he had traded his own undeniably private horse, with one of Sheridan's troopers. There would have been no trouble, if the Dr. had been contented with his first trade; when he got a nice mare, stolen to be sure, in all probability, from some secesh farmer, but to which the Government, at least, could lay no title. But when in course of time, and because of embarrassment resulting from a whinnying colt, jogging along at his heels, the Dr. allowed himself to be seduced into trading with another trooper, he paved the way for his final loss. His new purchase bore the fatal "U. S." branded upon its shoulder. There were not wanting rogues among us, who advised him to set up the claim, that the fatal letters were the initials of Uriah Saunders, a noted breeder of horses, living in the valley; and perhaps certificates to the fact could have been procured. But like the Father of his country, the Dr. "couldn't tell a lie;" and he parted with commendable grace, though reluctantly, with the faithful old animal, which had born him safely on the weary marches of the past year's campaigning. This impediment to our progress being removed, we embarked and were whirled swiftly along on our journey. Our run to New York was without noticable incident. Disembarking in the early afternoon, we were conducted to Battery barracks, where we were comfortably quartered. In the temporary absence of Col. Howe, our own State military agent, the regiment was generously treated to a bountiful feast of strawberries, by ——— military agent of the State of New York.

The first person to extend greeting to us was Hon. D. Waldo Lincoln, Mayor of the City of Worcester; who, in the hope that our homeward route would include that City, had come on to give us welcome. He brought with him the National Flag presented to the regiment, by the ladies of that City, just previous to our departure for the seat of war; and which we had exchanged, at their request, for the one we had borne through this Spring's campaign. Every possible effort was now made to secure our further transportation by the Worcester route; that all might enjoy the public reception ready for us at home. An offer was made to defray any difference in cost of transportation, and a guaranty that there should be no material variance in the time of arrival at Readville, if allowed to change our route. All efforts to this end, though warmly seconded by Col. Howe, who had now reached the city, and who was indefatigable in ministering to our wants, were of no avail. The harmonious working of the Quartermaster's Department *seemed* to require that the waters of Providence, rather than New London Harbor, should be plowed by the keel of our transport boat. The comfort of the men, and the gratification of their pride, alike natural and praiseworthy, was of little comparative consequence. And yet, by the orders of this same Quartermaster, our stay in New York was prolonged for more than a day. Its irksomeness was measurably relieved by attentions shown us by warm and sympathizing friends, who in many ways contributed to make our enforced stay a pleasant one.

At length marching orders came; and on the afternoon of the 19th, in the dying glory of an unclouded sky—through streets thronged with applauding citizens—beneath flags gayly waving from windows and house-tops—amid the discharge of cannon, and the acclamations of the multitude, we made our slow progress through the city. It was an ovation which stirred the heart of every man in the command, and brought tears to the eyes of many a battle-scarred veteran. There was no delay in our embarkation or departure. Providence was reached at an early hour the next morning, and marching by the shortest route to the depot, paying to Maj. Gen. Burnside the honor of a marching salute as we passed his residence, we took our seats for this last stage of our journey. Noon found us at Readville. Upon reporting to Maj. Gen. Pierce, commanding, quarters were assigned us in camp. Other Regiments had preceded us. Theoretically these were all occupying tents in camp; practically, the camp was deserted, hardly a man in uniform being visible. Our discharge was to await the final payment and discharge of all troops, whose arrival at the rendezvous was prior to our own; and this payment awaited the leisure or the pleasure of the Paymasters. It was a dreary look for men, many of whom had not seen the face of a relative, for nigh three years, and all of whom, now at least, were anxious once again to put on citizen's dress. There was little information to be obtained at Post

Headquarters. So, Regimental General Orders directed the immediate turning over, to the proper officers of the Post, all arms and equipments, and camp and garrison equipage,—everything, in fact, for which any officer was accountable. This done, we had neither arms, with which to do guard duty,—instruments on which to sound a call, or utensils with which to cook a ration; in fact, we were paupers. What was now to be done? To remain in a camp which all other commands had vacated, when in sight of our own hearth stones,—to eat the rations of the Government, when our own home bread was prepared for us,—longer to *wear the blue*, when now that there was no farther occasion for our service it galled our backs, were questions which came up and pressed for answer. They were all solved by dismissing the regiment, to assemble again at the call of its commander. At the order, like bees swarming from their hive, the boys rushed from the camp ground, and hurrying to a train just drawing up at the station, took their seats for Boston.

Here, at the station of the Boston & Albany Road, new trouble awaited us. The Government had provided transportation for us only to Readville. Hardly one of us had a cent of money. Upon representing our condition to the president of the corporation, upon our promise that his road should be reimbursed, whenever we should be paid off, he kindly furnished passage to our respective homes.

The Regiment left the State on the 15th day of August, 1862, with an aggregate strength of 1022 men. Three hundred and eight (308) recruits joined our ranks during our service.

It has had:—

Killed, and died of wounds,	Officers,	7
Killed on the field of battle,	Enlisted men,	107
Wounded and taken prisoners,	Officers,	3
do. do. do.	Enlisted men,	85
Captured and missing,	Officers,	6
do. do.	Enlisted men,	105
Wounded and in our hands,	Officers,	21
do. do. do.	Enlisted men,	422
Discharged for disability,	Officers,	7
do. do.	Enlisted men,	110

Honorably dis. before exp. of serv. Officers,		7
Dismissed, . do.		3

The Regiment has furnished to other commands:—

For Promotion, . . Officers,		3
do. . . Enlisted men,		43
To U. S. Army, . . do.		1
Transferred to Invalid Corps, . do.		62
Deserted since date of muster, July 31, 1862, do.		55
Transferred to 24th Mass., June 16, 1865, . Officers,		2
. Enlisted men,		180

Mustered out by reason of expiration of service:—

Field and Staff,	6
Non-Com. Staff,	4
Prin. Musicians,	2
Line Officers,	23
Line Officers commissioned to Field,	2
Line Officers commissioned as such, but mustered out as Sergeants,	10
Rank and File,	385
Died in Rebel Prisons, . Officers,	1
do. do. . Enlisted men,	43

July 6th. The regiment assembled at Readville to-day, in obedience to regimental general order, published in the newspapers. At the call of his name, each man responded and received his final pay,—seventy-five dollars, the balance of Government Bounty promised at his enlistment, and his discharge papers; having served, within twenty-five days, his full term of three years. There was one notable exception, however, in the case of John E. Calligan. This man enlisted as a member of Company E; was at once appointed a Sergeant, and detailed as color bearer. For gallant conduct at New Market, he was promoted to a 2d Lieutenancy, vice Robert W. Walker, reported killed. Walker, however, was wounded and taken prisoner instead of being killed. Notwithstanding, Calligan was assigned to duty as 2d Lieutenant, and served as such, receiving his commission in July following.

Why he was not mustered in as 2d Lieutenant does not appear; as he *served* in such capacity until the engagement on the 13th of October following, when he was taken prisoner. The apparent negligence is hard to be accounted for; as during all this period he was borne upon the rolls as an officer. Of course from the time of his promotion to the line, he ceased to draw rations or clothing, as an enlisted man. In March, 1865, having been exchanged, he was recommended for and received a commission as 1st Lieutenant; but his muster to that rank was refused on the ground that his company was so reduced in numbers, as not to be entitled to such officer. He served in his new rank however. And now, when there was no time to remedy the error, the Government ignored both his commission and his service and discharged him as Sergeant; paying him as an enlisted man only, and refusing every allowance for the rations, and clothing, during the time he had provided them from his own resources. Powerless to help, his associates could only extend to him their sympathy under such gross injustice.

With the receipt of their discharge papers, the men ceased to be in the service of the country, and with hurried adieus, each went his separate way. So the 34th passed to history.

It remained only that the white flag of the State, entrusted to our keeping, should be returned to the Executive of the Commonwealth. Its tattered remnants were endeared to us by the sad but glorious memories of New Market, and Piedmont, and Lynchburg; of Winchester, and Fisher's Hill, and Cedar Creek; of Hatcher's Run, and Fort Gregg; of High Bridge, and Appomatox Court House. It was sanctified to us by the blood of Bacon, and Woods, and Walker, and Thompson, and Pratt, and Dempsey, and Wells, and all the other heroic dead of the command. Unsullied as when first committed to our keeping, it was given to the honored hands of him from whom we received it.

And now that this work is to be given to the public, justice requires that proper acknowledgment should be made to the medical officers of the staff of the value of their services. Dr. R. R. Clarke, originally commissioned as Surgeon, was, for our whole term, in the immediate charge, or had the close supervision of our Hospitals. He was subjected to much abuse while the Regiment was being organized,— abuse entirely uncalled for and undeserved,— yet it was to his good judgment and skill as a Physician, at this time, as well as afterward to his unwearied devotion to the sick and wounded — and his unremitting zeal and fidelity to the well-being of the men of the command, at all times — and in all places — that much — very much of its efficiency was due. And this is equally applicable to his Assistants—Thorndike and Smith—each of whom received promotions, in reward for faithful service — and Allen and Millard, who came to us at a later day, but who, nevertheless, rendered invaluable service.

And so of the Quartermaster's Department! Howland went out and came back with us as a plain Regimental Quartermaster; although at different times — and for long periods — he served in the same capacity on Brigade Staff. Few Regiments were served as well as — none better than our own; and this whether in the field or garrison — in camp or on the march.

Of the manner in which the duties of the Adjutant's office was discharged, too much cannot be said in praise;— more especially when Woods filled the position. Always affable — easily approached — accomplished both as gentleman and officer, — master of the duties of his office,— he won the love and respect of his associates, and the regard and admiration of those to whose staff he was detailed. Fortunate — very fortunate indeed, was the Regiment in its Staff, both Commissioned and Non-Commissioned.

ROSTER
OF THE
34TH MASSACHUSETTS INFANTRY.

Name and Rank.	Bounty.	Residence or Place Credited to.	Date of Muster.	Termination of Service and cause thereof.
Field and Staff Officers.				
George D. Wells, Colonel,		Boston,	July 11, 1862	Kill'd Oct. 13, '64, St'kney's Fm, Bvt. Br. Gen.
William S. Lincoln, Colonel,		Worcester,	October 14, 1864	June 16, 1865, ex. of ser. Bvt. Br. Gen.
William S. Lincoln, Lieut. Col.,		Worcester,	June 3, 1862	Colonel, October 14, 1864.
Henry Bowman, Major,		Clinton,	August 6, 1862	Declined Colonel 36th Infantry.
Andrew Potter, Lieut. Col.,		Pittsfield,	October 14, 1864	June 16, 1865, ex. of service, Bvt. Colonel.
Harrison W. Pratt, Major,		Worcester,	August 23, 1862	Died of wounds, September 26, 1864.
Andrew Potter, Major,		Pittsfield,	Sept. 24, 1864	Lieut. Colonel, October 14, 1864.
Alonzo D. Pratt, Major,		West Boylston,	October 14, 1864	April 18, 1865, disability, as Captain.
Wells Willard, Major,		Springfield,	May 1, 1865	June 16, 1865, exp. of service, as Captain.
Rouse R. Clark, Surgeon,		Northbridge,	July 3, 1862	June 16, 1865, expiration of service.
William Thorndike, Asst. Surg.,		Beverly,	August 11, 1862	January 22, 1864, Surgeon 38th Inf.
Cyrus B. Smith, Asst. Surg.,		Granby,	July 31, 1862	February 2, 1865, Surgeon 11th Inf.
Thomas W. Dawson, Asst. Surg.,		Boston,	March 21, 1864	Declined, Assistant Surgeon 58th Inf.
Charles G. Allen, Asst. Surg.,		Barre,	April 12, 1864	June 16, 1865, expiration of service.
Henry J. Millard, Asst. Surg.,		North Adams,	Dec. 30, 1864	" "
Edward B. Fairchild, Chaplain,		Sterling,	August 8, 1862	July 3, 1863, resigned.
Sam'l F. Woods, 1st Lt. and Adj't		Worcester,	August 18, 1862	Died of wounds, June 26, 1864.
Chas. H. Howland, 1st Lt. & Q. M.		Plymouth,	June 9, 1862	June 16, 1865, expiration of service.
Non-Commissioned Staff.				
Cutler, Charles L., Sergt. Major,		Worcester,	July 18, 1862	Second Lieut., March 16, 1864.
Blake, Charles G., Sergt. Major,		Greenfield,	March 18, 1864	Second Lieut., June 6, 1864.
Fay, Asa B., Sergt. Major,		Northborough,	Sept. 27, 1864	Second Lieut., November 25, 1864.

THIRTY-FOURTH MASSACHUSETTS INFANTRY. 423

Lemuel, Pomroy, Sergt. Major,	Pittsfield,	Nov. 29, 1864.	Second Lieut, November 29, 1864.
Charles P. Trumbull, Q. M. Sgt.,	Worcester,	June 10, 1862	February 1, 1865, disability.
Michael F. Mullen, Q. M. Sgt.,	Pittsfield,	Feb. " "	June 16, 1865, expiration of service.
George W. Marsh, Com. Sgt.,	Leominster,	June 13, 1862	June 16, 1865, " "
James R. Fairbanks, Hos. Stew.,	Pittsfield,	August 11, 1862	June 16, 1865, " "
Timothy P. Giffin, Prin. Mus.,	Leicester,	July 31, 1862	Muster out of all hands.
John H. Hebard, Prin. Mus.,	North Brookfield,	August 13, 1862	June 16, 1865, expiration of service.
Henry C. Pellett, Prin. Mus.,	Harper's Fry, Va.,	July 9, 1863	

Line Officers.

Harrison W. Pratt, Captain,	Worcester,	August 6, 1862	Major, August 23, 1862.
Andrew Potter, Captain,	Pittsfield,	" 6, 1862	Major, September 24, 1864.
Alonzo D. Pratt, Captain,	West Boylston,	" 6, 1862	Major, October 14, 1864.
George W. Thompson, Captain,	Springfield,	" 6, 1862	Killed September 19, 1864.
William B. Bacon, Captain,	Worcester,	" 6, 1862	Killed May 15, 1864.
Charles I. Chandler, Captain,	Brookline,	" 6, 1862	March 17, 1864, Lieut. Col. 40th Inf.
Dexter F. Parker, Captain,	Worcester,	" 6, 1862	August 12, 1862, Major 10th Inf.
Daniel Holden, Captain,	Ware,	" 6, 1862	November 8, 1862, resigned.
William H. Cooley, Captain,	Pittsfield,	" 6, 1862	November 24, 1863, resigned.
Wells Willard, Captain,	Springfield,	" 6, 1862	Major, May 1, 1865.
John B. Norton, Captain,	Charlestown,	" 12, 1862	Transferred August 22, 1862, to 36th Inf.
Henry P. Fox, Captain,	Worcester,	" 13, 1862	July 6, 1865, expiration of service.
Frank T. Leach, Captain,	Northborough,	" 23, 1862	June 16, 1865, " "
Alexis C. Soley, Captain,	Worcester,	Nov. 9, 1862	February 17, 1865, disability from wounds.
John A. Lovell, Captain,	Westfield,	June 25, 1863	November 8, 1864, disability "
Chauncey R. Chauncey, Captain,	Greenfield,	March 18, 1864	June 16, 1865, expiration of service.
Charles W. Elwell, Captain,	Oakham,	May 16, 1864	June 16, 1865, " "
George B. Macomber, Captain,	Pittsfield,	Sept. 20, 1864	Transferred to 24th Infantry, June 14, 1865.
Lyman W. Van Loan, Captain,	Fitchburg,	Sept. 24, 1864	June 16, 1865, expiration of service.
George E. Goodrich, Captain,	Worcester,	October 15, 1864	June 16, 1865, " "
Melville L. Walker, Captain,	Lancaster,	Nov. 9, 1864	June 16, 1865, " "
William L. Cobb, Captain,	Greenfield,	Feb. 18, 1865	May, 15, 1865, as 1st Lieut.
Henry T. Hall, Captain,	Worcester,	Feb. 18, 1865	June 16, 1865, exp. of serv. as 1st. Lieut.
William F. Belser, Captain,	West Boylston,	May 1, 1865	June 16, 1865, " "
George L. Murdock, Captain,	Pittsfield,	June 18, 1865	June 16, 1865, " "
Lafayette Butler, 1st Lieut.,	Worcester,	July 15, 1862	September 5, 1863, dishonorably.
John A. Lovell, 1st Lieut.,	Northborough,	August 6, 1862	Captain, June 25, 1863.
Frank T. Leach, 1st Lieut.,	Hadley,	" 6, 1862	Captain, August 23, 1862.
James W. Smith, 1st Lieut.,	Oakham,	" 6, 1862	July 26, 1863, resigned.
George B. Macomber, 1st Lieut.,	Greenfield,	" 6, 1862	Captain, September 20, 1864.
Charles W. Elwell, 1st Lieut.,		" 6, 1862	Captain, May 16, 1864.

Name and Rank.	Bounty.	Residence or Place Credited to.	Date of Muster.	Termination of Service and cause thereof.
Line Officers.—Continued.				
Chauncey R. Chauncey, 1st Lieut.,		Westfield,	August 6, 1862	Captain, March 18, 1864.
Henry P. Fox, 1st Lieut.,		Worcester,	" 6, 1862	Captain, August 13, 1862.
Alexis C. Soley, 1st Lieut.,		Worcester,	" 6, 1862	Captain, November 9, 1862.
Lyman W. Van Loan, 1st Lieut.,		Pittsfield,	" 6, 1862	Captain, September 24, 1864.
T. Edward Ames, 1st Lieut.,		Charlestown,	" 13, 1862	Transferred August 22, 1862, to 36th Inf.
Albert C. Walker, 1st Lieut.,		Worcester,	" 13, 1862	Died of wounds, June 14, 1864.
William L. Cobb, 1st Lieut.,		Lancaster,	" 23, 1862	Captain, February 18, 1865.
Levi Lincoln, Jr., 1st Lieut.,		Worcester,	Nov. 9, 1862	August 31, 1864, disability.
Henry Bacon, 1st Lieut.,		Worcester,	June 25, 1863	November 29, 1864, disability.
Thomas W. Ripley, 1st Lieut.,		Greenfield,	July 29, 1863	June 16, 1865, expiration of service.
George E. Goodrich, 1st Lieut.,		Fitchburg,	Sept. 6, 1863	Captain, October 18, 1864.
Samuel H. Platt, 1st Lieut.,		Pittsfield,	March 18, 1864	March, 11, 1865, resigned.
Robert W. Walker, 1st Lieut.,		Boston,	May 16, 1864	November 4, 1864, disability as 2d Lieut.
Melville E. Walker, 1st Lieut.,		Worcester,	June 6, 1864	Captain, November 9, 1864.
William F. Belsor, 1st Lieut.,		Worcester,	June 27, 1864	Captain, May 1, 1865.
James Dempsey, 1st Lieut.,		Pittsfield,	Sept. 1, 1864	Died of wounds, October 17, 1864.
George L. Murdock, 1st Lieut.,		West Boylston,	Sept. 20, 1864	Captain, June 18, 1865.
Henry T. Hall, 1st Lieut.,		Greenfield,	October 18, 1864	Captain, February 18, 1865.
Charles G. Blake, 1st Lieut.,		Greenfield,	" 18, 1864	June 16, 1865, expiration of service.
Frederick A. Judd, 1st Lieut.,		Holyoke,	" 18, 1864	"
Erastus W. Lilley, 1st Lieut.,		Huntington,	" 18, 1864	July 5, 1865.
Wells B. Mitchell, 1st Lieut.,		Adams,	Nov. 25, 1864	May 15, 1865, disability.
Herbert B. Rowley, 1st Lieut.,		Greenfield,	Nov. 25, 1864	June 16, 1865, exp. of serv., as 2d Lieut.
John E. Calligan, 1st Lieut.		Worcester,	Nov. 25, 1864	June 16, 1865, exp. of serv., as 1st Sergt.
Charles B. Cutler, 1st Lieut.		Worcester,	March 12, 1865	June 16, 1865, exp. of serv., as 2d Lieut.
Harlan P. Houghton, 1st Lieut.,		West Boylston,	May 1, 1865	" " "
Charles H. Morrill, 1st Lieut.,		Westfield,	May 15, 1865	June 16, 1865, " " "
Asa B. Fay, 1st Lieut.,		Northborough,	May 15, 1865	June 16, 1865, " " "
William F. Pepper, 1st Lieut.,		Greenfield,	June 18, 1865	June 16, 1865, " " "
Levi Lincoln, Jr., 2d Lieut.,		Worcester,	July 18, 1862	June 16, 1865, exp. of serv., as 1st Sergt.
William L. Cobb, 2d Lieut.,		Lancaster,	July 18, 1862	First Lieut., Nov. 9, 1862.
Robert W. Walker, 2d Lieut.,		Boston,	August 6, 1862	First Lieut., August 22, 1862.
Henry Bacon, 2d Lieut.,		Worcester,	" 6, 1862	First Lieut., May 16, 1864.
J. Austin Lyman, 2d Lieut.,		Springfield,	" 6, 1862	First Lieut., June 25, 1863.
Thomas W. Ripley, 2d Lieut.,		Greenfield,	" 6, 1862	Resigned, June 17, 1863.
Jere Horton, 2d Lieut.,		Westfield,	" 6, 1862	First Lieut., July 29, 1863.
				Transferred to 24th Infantry, June 14, 1865.

THIRTY-FOURTH MASSACHUSETTS INFANTRY.

Name	Residence	Mustered in	Remarks
Albert C. Walker, 2d Lieut.,	Worcester,	August 6, 1862	First Lieut. August 13, 1862.
George E. Goodrich, 2d Lieut.,	Fitchburg,	" 6, 1862	First Lieut., September 6, 1863.
Samuel H. Platt, 2d Lieut.,	Pittsfield,	" 6, 1862	First Lieut., March 18, 1864.
P. Marion Holmes, 2d Lieut.,	Charlestown,	" 8, 1862	Transferred August 26, 1862, to 36th Inf.
Malcom Ammidon, 2d Lieut.,	Southbridge,	" 13, 1862	Died October 1, 1864, in rebel prison.
Henry T. Hall, 2d Lieut.,	Greenfield,	" 23, 1862	First Lieut., October 18, 1864.
John W. Stiles, 2d Lieut.,	Worcester,	Nov. 9, 1862	June 27, 1865, dismissed.
Melville E. Walker, 2d Lieut.,	Worcester,	June 18, 1863	First Lieut., June 6, 1864
James Dempsey, 2d Lieut.,	Pittsfield,	June 25, 1863	First Lt., Sept 1, 1864; d'd of w'ds Oct. 17, '64
William Belsor, 2d Lieut.,	Worcester,	June 28, 1863	First Lieut., June 27, 1864.
Francis C. Kinnicutt, 2d Lieut.,	Worcester,	July 29, 1863	November 8, 1864, dismissed.
George L. Murdock, 2d Lieut.,	West Boylston,	Sept. 6, 1863	First Lieut. September 20, 1864.
Charles B Cutler, 2d Lieut.,	Worcester,	March 18, 1864	First Lieut., May 1, 1865.
John E. Calligan, 2d Lieut.,	Worcester,	May 16, 1864	First Lieut., March 12, 1865.
Charles G. Blake, 2d Lieut.,	Greenfield,	June 6, 1864	First Lieut., October 18, 1864.
Frederick A. Judd, 2d Lieut.,	Holyoke,	June 27, 1864	First Lieut., October 18, 1864.
Erastus V Lilley, 2d Lieut.,	Huntington,	Sept. 1, 1864	First lieut., November 25, 1864.
Charles I. Woods, 2d Lieut.,	Petersham,	Sept. 20, 1864	Killed October 13, 1864, Stickney's Farm.
Herbert B. Rowley, 2d Lieut.,	Greenfield,	October 18, 1864	First Lieut., November 25, 1864.
Wells B. Mitchell, 2d Lieut.,	Adams,	" 18, 1864	First Lieut., November 25, 1864.
Harlan P. Houghton, 2d Lieut.,	West Boylston,	" 18, 1864	First Lieut., May 15, 1865.
Charles I. Morrill, 2d Lieut.,	Westfield,	Nov. 9, 1864	First Lieut., May 15, 1865.
Alfred Dibble, 2d Lieut.,	Southwick,	Nov. 25, 1864	June 16, 1865, expiration of service.
Daniel C. Wishart, 2d Lieut.,	Westfield,	Nov. 25, 1864	"
Asa B. Fay, 2d Lieut.,	Northborough,	Nov. 29, 1864	First Lieut., May 15, 1865.
William F. Pepper, 2d Lieut.,	Greenfield,	June 18, 1865	First Lieut., June 18, 1865.
Lemuel Pomroy, 2d Lieut.,	Pittsfield,	June 16, 1865	June 16, 1865, exp. of serv., as Sergt Major.
George A. Clapp, 2d Lieut.,	Webster,	June 16, 1865	June 16, 1865, exp. of serv., as 1st Sergt.
Robert I. Gardner, 2d Lieut.,	Egremont,	June 16, 1865	June 16, 1865, " "
Ira F. Lackey, 2d Lieut.,	Leicester,	June 16, 1865	June 16, 1865, " "
Daniel M. Damon, 2d Lieut.,	Lancaster,	June 16, 1865	June 16, 1865, " "
Charles Wood, 2d Lieut.,	Ashburnham,	June 18, 1865	June 16, 1865, " "
Henry S Clark, 2d Lieut.,	Worcester,	June 18, 1865	June 16, 1865, exp. of serv., as Sergt.
Charles A Hunter, 2d Lieut.,	Spencer,	June 18, 1865	June 16, 1865, "
Walter W. Scott, 2d Lieut.	Worcester.	June 18, 1865	June 16, 1865,

Company A.

Name	Residence	Mustered in	Remarks
George A. Clapp, 1st Sgt.,	Oxford,	July 13, 1862	March 12, 1865, 2d Lieut.
John W. Stiles, 1st Sgt.,	Worcester,	June 22, 1862	November 9, 1862, 2d Lieut.
James J. Colby, Sergt.,	Millbury,	July 31, 1862	November 14, 1864, died of wounds.
Joseph J. Farwell, Sergt.,	Millbury,	July 31, 1862	December 28, 1862, Lieut. in U. S. C. T.

Name and Rank.	Bounty.	Residence or Place Credited to.	Date of Muster.	Termination of Service and cause thereof.
Company A.—Continued.				
Emory H. Hawks, Sergt.,		Shelbourne,	August 15, 1862	June 16, 1865, expiration of service.
Frederick H. Hodgman, Sergt.,		Millbury,	July 31, 1862	June 9, 1863, disability.
James R. Joselyn, Sergt.,		Brookfield,	July 31, 1862	June 16, 1865, expiration of service.
Michael Kenney, Sergt.,		South Hadley,	July 13, 1862	June 16, 1865, "
Stephen H. Rhoades, Sergt.,		Worcester,	June 22, 1862	November 14, 1863, Lieut. in U. S. C. T.
Freeman Snow, Sergt.,		Brookfield,	July 13, 1862	June 16, 1865, expiration of service.
John O. Aldrich, Corp.,	$325 00	Northbridge,	Dec. 8, 1863	June 14, 1865, to 24th Infantry.
James H. Baldwin, Corp.,		Worcester,	June 22, 1862	March 29, 1865, disability.
George A. Blood, Corp.,	439 33	Sturbridge,	July 31, 1862	Transferred to V. R. C.
Francis A. C. Chester, Corp.,		Somerville,	Dec. 18, 1863	June 14, 1865, transferred to 24th Inft.
Charles B. Flagg, Corp.,	325 00	Lancaster,	June 23, 1862	June 16, 1865, expiration of service.
James J. D. Murry, Corp.,		Greenfield,	Dec. 21, 1863	Killed September 3, 1864.
Elijah C. Pearl, Corp.,		Brookfield,	July 13, 1862	Died December 8, 1864, Andersonville, Ga.
James R. Roe, Corp.,		Millbury,	July 31, 1862	April 15, 1865, disability.
William Sherry, Corp.,		Grafton,	July 31, 1862	June 24, 1865, expiration of service.
Timothy Sullivan, Corp.,		Grafton,	July 31, 1862	June 16, 1865, "
George E. Warren, Corp.,		Worcester,	June 22, 1862	June 16, 1865, "
John H. Bartlett, Drum.,		Worcester,	June 22, 1862	June 16, 1865, "
George Carter, Drum.,		Fitchburg,	June 22, 1862	June 16, 1865, "
Orrin Stacy, Bugler,		Grafton,	June 22, 1862	June 16, 1865, "
Joseph Bolio, Wagoner,	325 00	Worcester,	July 31, 1862	June 16, 1865, "
Edwin N. Adams,		Brookfield,	Dec. 12, 1863	June 14, 1865, transferred to 24th Inft.
Edwin Allen,		Worcester,	July 31, 1862	June 16, 1865, expiration of service.
Henry Allen,		Charlton,	July 31, 1862	July 14, 1865, disability.
Waldo J. Allen,		Sturbridge,	July 31, 1862	March 14, 1863, disability.
George Arney,		Millbury,	July 31, 1862	June 16, 1865, expiration of service.
Hosea L. Barnes,		Brookfield,	July 31, 1862	June 16, 1864, died of wounds.
John Bell,		Clinton,	July 31, 1862	June 16, 1865, expiration of service.
George W. Bigelow,	325 00	Worcester,	July 31, 1862	July 13, 1865, "
Ziba A. Blodget,		Grafton,	Dec. 29, 1863	August 29, 1864, died at Andersonville.
Thomas C. Bryant,		Grafton,	July 31, 1862	June 16, 1865, expiration of service.
William Bryson,		Clinton,	July 31, 1862	June 16, 1865, "
Charles W. Burbank,		Worcester,	July 31, 1862	Missing Aug. 15, '64; died in enemy's hands.
John S. Burns,		Grafton,	July 31, 1862	July 31, 1863, disability.
Jonathan C. Burrouglis,		Northbridge,	Dec. 3, 1863	June 14, 1865, transferred to 24th Infantry.
Edmund Butler,		Milford,	June 22, 1862	May 10, 1865.

THIRTY-FOURTH MASSACHUSETTS INFANTRY. 427

Name	Bounty	Residence	Mustered in	Remarks
Patrick Casey,	325 00	Worcester,	Nov. 16, 1863	May 5, 1865, died of wounds.
Olney B. Chase,		Worcester,	August 15, 1862	June 16, 1865, expiration of service.
Lorin S. Clark,		Grafton,	July 31, 1862	June 16, 1865, "
Willard Clapp,		Grafton,	July 31, 1862	March 11, 1863, disability.
Michael Clary,		Sturbridge,	June 22, 1862	June 16, 1865, expiration of service.
Arthur S. Colburn,	325 00	Millbury,	July 31, 1863	May 11, 1865, disability.
John Collins,		Auburn,	Nov. 28, 1863	June 14, 1865, transferred to 24th Infantry.
Eben Conant,		Petersham,	July 31, 1862	June 16, 1865, expiration of service.
James P. Coolidge,		Brookfield,	July 31, 1862	June 16, 1865, "
Asa F. Crosby,		Sturbridge,	July 31, 1862	September 19, 1864, killed in battle.
Charles R. Cutler,		Worcester,	June 31, 1862	September 22, 1864, missing.
William Dee,		Boston,	July 22, 1862	June 16, 1865, expiration of service.
Dennis Donovan,		Worcester,	July 31, 1852	February 9, 1864, disability.
Edward Doner,		Millbury,	July 20, 1863	June 20, 1863, deserted.
Louis Dover,		Uxbridge,	July 31, 1862	February 18, 1864, disability.
Thomas Finn,		Millbury,	July 31, 1865	June 16, 1865, expiration of service.
William L. Fuller,		Millbury,	July 31, 1862	June 20, 1863, deserted.
Charles F. Gould,		Millbury,	July 31, 1862	June 16, 1865, expiration of service.
Henry Gover,	555 33	Brimfield,	July 31, 1862	June 16, 1865, "
Francis A. Grover,		Uxbridge,	Dec. 14, 1863	June 14, 1865, transferred to 24th Infantry.
Henry H. Graham,		Grafton,	July 31, 1862	November 24, 1862, disability.
Joseph H. Grant,		Millbury,	July 31, 1862	December 10, 1862, "
James Hancock,		Brookfield,	July 31, 1863	June 16, 1865, expiration of service.
George A. Haraden,		Millbury,	July 31, 1862	October 10, 1862, disability.
Joseph Hirst,		Millbury,	July 31, 1862	May 21, 1865, "
Henry F. Hobart,		Clinton,	July 31, 1862	June 1, 1865, "
John W. Holbrook,		Sturbridge,	July 31, 1862	April 6, 1865, killed in battle.
James Hurst,		Worcester,	June 22, 1862	May 30, 1865, disability.
Horatio C. Jameson,		Brookfield,	June 22, 1862	March 28, 1864, Promoted U. S. C. T.
John A. Josselyn,		Grafton,	July 31, 1862	May 9, 1863, disability.
Patrick Kelley,		Sturbridge,	June 22, 1862	June 16, 1865, expiration of service.
William King,		Grafton,	Oct. 17, 1863	June 14, 1865, transferred to 24th Infantry.
Benjamin W. Knights,		Millbury,	July 13, 1862	June 20, 1863, deserted.
Jesse F. Knowles,	325 00	Warren,	Dec. 19, 1863	March 13, 1865, died at Wilmington, N. C.
Oscar Marsh,	550 66	Deerfield,	July 23, 1863	June 14, 1865, transferred to 24th Infantry.
William Martin,		Boston,	July 31, 1862	August 5, 1864, died at Andersonville.
Bernard McKenny,	84 00	Wales,	Jan. 11, 1863	May 16, 1865, special order War Department
James McKnight,		Worcester,	July 31, 1862	June 5, 1864, killed in battle.
Timothy Minehan,		Sturbridge,	July 31, 1862	June 16, 1865, expiration of service.
Darius Moon,		Sturbridge,	July 31, 1862	June 16, 1865, "
James Moon,				

Company A.—Continued.

Name and Rank.	Bounty.	Residence or Place Credited to.	Date of Muster.	Termination of Service and cause thereof.
John Morton,		Worcester,	July 31, 1862	August 11, 1864, died at Andersonville.
Joseph P. Morse,		Worcester,	July 31, 1862	June 16, 1865, expiration of service.
George H. Perkins,		Brookfield,	July 31, 1862	September 2, 1864, Lieut. in U. S. C. T.
Daniel G. Pitts,		Millbury,	July 31, 1862	March 4, 1864, Lieut. in U. S. C. T.
Charles A. Porter,		Brookfield,	July 31, 1862	April 5, 1865, disability.
Richard R. Pratt,		Grafton,	July 31, 1862	May 30, 1865, "
Elliott D. Puffer,	$25 00	Sunderland,	Dec. 30, 1863	November 12, 1864, died at Andersonville.
Austin Putnam,		Grafton,	July 31, 1862	June 3, 1863, disability.
John M. Putnam, Jr.,		Brookfield,	July 31, 1862	June 16, 1865, expiration of service.
Henry A. Rawson,		Millbury,	July 31, 1862	June 1, 1865, special order War Department.
Michael Riley,		Oxford,	Nov. 25, 1863	June 14, 1865, transferred to 24th Infantry.
Ezra L. Robbins,	$25 00	Worcester,	July 17, 1862	May 27, 1865, disability.
John W. Russell,		Brookfield,	July 13, 1862	June 16, 1865, expiration of service.
George A. Ryan,		Millbury,	July 3, 1864	June 3, 1864, died of wounds.
Timothy Ryan, Jr.,		Millbury,	July 31, 1862	June 16, 1865, expiration of service.
Waterman M. Ryan,		Millbury,	July 31, 1862	June 16, 1865, "
William Sabin,	$25 00	Southbridge,	Jan. 4, 1864	July 9, 1864, died of wounds.
John Savage,		Grafton,	July 31, 1862	Missing since Oct. 19, '64; capt'd at Cedar C'k.
George F. Schrock,	50 00	Buckland,	Sept. 23, 1863	February 18, 1864, disability.
Richard Sharrock,		Sturbridge,	July 31, 1862	November 30, 1864, died of wounds.
James Shepherd,		Sturbridge,	July 31, 1862	June 16, 1865, expiration of service.
Edward A. Stone,	$25 00	Worcester,	July 31, 1862	July 16, 1864, transferred to V. R. C.
Andrew Smith,		Swanzey,	Jan. 13, 1864	June 14, 1865, transferred to 24th Infantry.
Joseph Son,		Millbury,	July 31, 1862	April 29, 1863, deserted.
Charles F. Spring,		Grafton,	July 22, 1862	June 16, 1865, expiration of service.
William A. Taft,		Millbury,	July 31, 1862	June 16, 1865, "
Rayson Tierney,		Southbridge,	July 31, 1862	June 16, 1865, "
Loring B. Vinton,		Brookfield,	July 31, 1862	February 16, 1864, transferred to V. R. C.
Charles L. Walker,		Upton,	July 31, 1862	June 16, 1865, expiration of service.
Nathaniel C. Walch,		Oxford,	July 31, 1862	June 16, 1865, died June 18, 1865.
Sylvester Webber,		Worcester,	July 31, 1862	August 30, 1862, deserted.
Caleb W. Wheeler,		Grafton,	August 4, 1862	July 15, 1864, transferred to V. R. C.
Franklin Whitney,		Grafton,	July 31, 1862	June 16, 1865, expiration of service.
Robert Wilson,		Millbury,	July 31, 1862	August 25, 1864, died at Andersonville.
John P. Wise,		Lancaster,	July 31, 1862	March 15, 1864, died of disease at Lancaster.
Orville Young,		Brookfield,	July 31, 1862	June 16, 1865, expiration of service.

THIRTY-FOURTH MASSACHUSETTS INFANTRY.

Name	Bounty	Residence	Muster-in	Remarks
Henry H. Clark, 1st Serg't,		Pittsfield,	June 22, 1862	June 16, 1865, expiration of service.
James L. Dempsey, 1st Serg't,		Pittsfield,	June 22, 1862	July 9, 1863, promoted 2d Lieutenant.
Erastus V. Lilley, 1st Serg't,		Huntington,	August 4, 1862	September 1, 1864, promoted 2d Lieutenant.
Lemuel Pomroy, 1st Serg't,		Pittsfield,	" 1, 1862	January 20, 1665, promoted Sergeant Major.
William Carr, Serg't,		Adams,	" 16, 1862	June 16, 1865, expiration of service.
William Claridge, Serg't,		Williamstown,	" 1, 1862	June 16, 1865, " "
James D. French, Serg't,		Pittsfield,	" 1, 1862	June 16, 1865, " "
Albert M. Hubbard, Serg't,		Windsor,	" 1, 1862	June 16, 1865, " "
Wells B. Mitchell, Serg't,		Adams,	" 1, 1862	October 18, 1864, promoted 2d Lieutenant.
William Cady, Corp.,		Huntington,	" 1, 1862	June 16, 1865, expiration of service.
Elisha Chapin, Corp.,		Pittsfield,	June 22, 1862	June 16, 1865, " "
Oliver Cottrell, Corp.,		Lenox,	August 1, 1863	May 16, 1865, disability.
Edward H. Davenport, Corp.,	$325 00	Buckland,	Dec. 17, 1863	June 14, 1865, transferred to 24th Infantry.
William F. Evans, Corp,		Stockbridge,	August 14, 1862	June 16, 1865, expiration of service.
Michael Meecham,		Pittsfield,	June 22, 1862	June 16, 1865, " "
Edward Meecham,		Worthington,	August 4, 1862	June 16, 1865, " "
John N. Moore,		Huntington,	" 1, 1862	June 16, 1865, " "
Charles H. Moulton,		Pittsfield,	" 1, 1862	June 16, 1865, " "
James A. Needham,	325 00	Clinton,	" 1, 1862	April 17, 1865, disability.
Emerson Newton,		Montague,	Dec. 29, 1863	June 14, 1865, transferred to 24th Infantry.
William N. Otis,		Huntington,	August 1, 1862	May 17, 1865, disability.
Warren W. Philips,		Adams,	" 1, 1864	June 26, 1864, died of wounds.
Eugene Renne,		Great Barrington,	" 1, 1862	April 15, 1865, disability.
Harlan W. Torrey,	325 00	Windsor,	" 22, 1862	December 21, 1864, disability.
Charles W. Pool, Mus,		Worcester,	June 16, 1862	June 16, 1865, expiration of service.
Adrian M. Adams,		New Marlboro,	August 1, 1862	July 3, 1865, disability.
James Anderson,		Pittsfield,	" 1, 1862	June 2, 1863, deserted to the enemy.
Francis H. Axtell,		Huntington,	" 1, 1862	July 22, 1864, died of wounds.
John Baptist,		Pittsfield,	" 1, 1862	June 16, 1865, expiration of service.
George Bass,	325 00	Cheshire,	October 21, 1863	October —, 1864, disability.
George H Bascom,		Worcester,	June 22, 1862	June 16, 1865, expiration of service.
James A. Bell,		Pittsfield,	August 1, 1862	May 26, 1863, disability.
Joseph S. Bemis,		Chester,	" 1, 1862	January 21, 1363, disability.
Charles F Bennett,		Dalton,	June 22, 1862	May 22, 1865,
Frederick E. Blanchard,	325 00	Adams,	August 1, 1862	May 9, 1863, deserted.
Edward Burns,		Pittsfield,	Nov. 27, 1863	March 20, 1865, died in hands of enemy.
Joseph B. Brown,		Adams,	August 1, 1862	June 16, 1865, expiration of service.
Napoleon Burt,		Pittsfield,	June 16, 1862	May 19, 1865, disability.
Thomas S. Burns,		Clinton,	August 22, 1862	June 10, 1864, died of wounds.
William Burns,		Pittsfield,	" 1, 1862	August 5, 1862, deserted.
George B. Cantrell,	325 00	Deerfield,	Dec. 21, 1863	June 14, 1865, transferred to 24th Infantry.

THIRTY-FOURTH MASSACHUSETTS INFANTRY.

Name and Rank.	Bounty.	Residence or Place Credited to.	Date of Muster.	Termination of Service and cause thereof.
Company B.				
Martin Canfield,		Blackstone,	August 4, 1862	May 31, 1865, disability.
John Casey,		Pittsfield,	June 22, 1862	June 5, 1864, killed in battle.
Emerson H. Chapman,		Huntington,	August 1, 1862	November 13, 1864, died at Salisbury, N. C.
Patrick Cummings,		Lenox,	" 1, 1862	October 16, 1862, deserted.
Thomas Dugan,	325 00	Claremont,	Dec. 21, 1863	June 14, 1865, transferred to 24th Infantry.
Hiram Daily,	325 00	Pittsfield,	Nov. 27, 1863	March 17, 1865, disability.
David Davis,		Adams,	August 4, 1862	June 5, 1864, killed in battle.
Joseph Desham,	325 00	Ashfield,	Jan. 12, 1864	June 14, 1865, transferred to 24th Infantry.
Charles H. Dill,		Pittsfield,	August 4, 1862	August 20, 1864, died of wounds.
Ira W. Dill,		Pittsfield,	Dec. 10, 1863	April 18, 1865, disability.
Henry W. Dodds,	325 00	Dalton,	Jan. 4, 1864	January 30, 1865, died at Annapolis, Md.
William Deland,	325 00	Shelburne,	August 4, 1862	June 16, 1865, expiration of service.
Michael Donnelly,		Windsor,	" 4, 1862	June 16, 1865, "
William E. Donnelly,		Blackstone,	" 4, 1862	September 4, 1864, died of wounds.
William H. H. Eastman,		Lenox,	" 4, 1862	June 16, 1865, expiration of service.
Asa N. Elder,		Pittsfield,	" 4, 1862	June 16, 1865, "
Joseph Fisher,		Huntington,	" 1, 1862	February 22, 1864, transferred to V. R. R.
Hamlin L. Ford,		Lenox,	" 1, 1862	June 18, 1864, died of wounds.
Patrick Gealy,	325 00	Windsor,	" 1, 1862	May 9, 1863, disability.
Patrick Gibbons,		Pittsfield,	Dec. 7, 1863	June 14, 1865, transferred to 24th Infantry.
John Grady,		Clinton,	June 22, 1862	Feb. 22, 1865, died in Rebel prison of wounds.
John Handley,		Pittsfield,	August 1, 1862	June 16, 1863, expiration of service.
William A. Hawley,		Windsor,	" 1, 1862	November 30, 1864, died of disease.
Edson J. Harrison,		Pittsfield,	June 22, 1862	June 16, 1865, expiration of service.
Nelson Harned,		Pittsfield,	June 22, 1862	January 7, 1864, died of disease.
Wilbur Hart,		Adams,	August 1, 1862	June 5, 1864, killed in battle.
Timothy Higgins,		Clinton,	" 1, 1862	January 16, 1863, disability.
William Hogan,		Pittsfield,	October 14, 1863	June 14, 1865, transferred to 24th Infantry.
Erastus M. Hubbard,	325 00	Cheshire,	August 1, 1862	August 17, 1864, died at Andersonville.
Albert L. Hunt,		Warwick,	Dec. 18, 1863	June 14, 1865, transferred to 24th Infantry.
William Jarvis,		Pittsfield,	August 1, 1862	June 16, 1865, expiration of service.
Ralph Joslyn,		Huntington,	" 1, 1862	June 16, 1865, "
William Kelly,		Pittsfield,	June 22, 1862	June 16, 1865, "
Thomas Leeson,		Pittsfield,	June 22, 1862	April 3, 1864, died of disease.
Alanson C. Lewis,		Huntington,	August 1, 1862	February 22, 1865, disability.
Johnathan A. Lilley,		Huntington,	" 1, 1862	May 13, 1865, disability.

Rufus E. Lyman,		Huntington,	August 1, 1862	June 16, 1865, expiration of service.
Patrick Maloy,		Clinton,	" "	June 16, 1865, "
Thomas Maloy,	325 00	Clinton,	Dec. 11, 1863	June 14, 1865, transferred to 24th Infantry.
William Mandige,		Pittsfield,	July 22, 1862	July —, 1864, deserted.
Jacob Martin,		Lenox,	July 31, 1862	June 16, 1865, expiration of service.
John McCarty,	325 00	Washington,	Nov. 11, 1863	June 24, 1865, transferred to 24th Infantry.
Henry R. McCullock,		Lenox,	July 31, 1862	February 22, 1864, transferred to V. R. C.
Michael McGratty,		Chester,	August 1, 1862	June 16, 1865, expiration of service.
Henry P. Merrill,		Richmond,	" "	March 26, 1864, died of disease.
Jeremiah E. Miner,	325 00	Windsor,	Jan. 14, 1864	May 31, 1865, disability.
Jonathan I. Miner,	325 00	Windsor,	Jan. 14, 1864	June 14, 1865, transferred to 24th Infantry.
John Morgan,		Adams,	August 1, 1862	December 27, 1862, disability.
Robert Morton,		Lanesboro,	July 13, 1862	February 22, 1864, transferred to V. R. C.
Stephen Monks,		Pittsfield,	June 22, 1862	October 19, 1864, wounded at Cedar Creek.
Calvin Noble,		Middlefield,	August 1, 1862	December 15, 1862, died of disease.
Henry Noble,		Middlefield,	" "	December 4, 1862, died of disease.
Richard Nokes,		Adams,	" "	June 27, 1865, expiration of service.
Thomas O'Connor,		Pittsfield,	June 22, 1862	June 16, 1865, "
Philip Otis,		Pittsfield,	June 22, 1862	May 13, 1865, disability.
Charles F. Parsons,		Great Barrington,	June 22, 1862	June 16, 1865, expiration of service.
Levi Phillips,	325 00	Huntington,	August 1, 1862	Aug. 5, 1863, transferred to V. R. C.
Edward Phillips,	325 00	Hadley,	Dec. 28, 1863	June 14, 1865, transferred to 24th Infantry.
Orrin Pratt,		Clinton,	Dec. 11, 1863	June 14, 1865, "
John Purtell,		Adams,	August 1, 1862	May 15, 1864, killed in battle.
Warren S. Read,		Richmond,	" "	December 8, 1862, died of disease.
Liberty B. Sampson,	325 00	Williamstown,	Dec. 28, 1863	Jan. 18, 1865, died in Rebel prison, Salisbury.
Joseph W. Sawyer,	325 00	Warwick,	Dec. 2, 1863	October 18, 1864, died in prison, Salisbury.
John D. Shaw,		Pittsfield,	August 1, 1862	Aug. 27, 1864, died of wounds, Stanton, Va.
Patrick Shields,		Lenox,	June 22, 1862	June 16, 1865, expiration of service.
Edward Smith,		Chicopee,	August 1, 1862	December 27, 1862, disability.
George H. Snell,		Pittsfield,	June 22, 1862	November 24, 1863, disability.
Tyler Sprague,		Huntington,	August 1, 1862	June 16, 1865, expiration of service.
Joseph Stanton, Jr,		Pittsfield,	" "	June 16, 1865, "
Louis Stearns,		Chesterfield,	" "	June 16, 1865, "
Elisha W. Tilden,		Worcester,	" "	April 8, 1863, disability.
Michael Toole,		Pittsfield,	" "	June 16, 1865, expiration of service.
Sabastian Trabold,		Adams,	" "	June 16, 1865, "
Frank M. Turner,		Windsor,	" "	June 16, 1865, "
Henry M. Whitman,		Adams,	" "	February 22, 1864, transferred to V. R. C.
Newton B. Whitman,		Windsor,	" "	February 22, 1864, "
George O. Wiley,		Adams,	June 22, 1862	March 8, 1865, disability.
John Wilmot,		Pittsfield,	June 22, 1862	July 6, 1864, captured at Winchester.

Company C.

Name and Rank.	Bounty.	Residence or Place Credited to.	Date of Muster.	Termination of Service and cause thereof.
Henry S. Clark, 1st Sergeant,	....	Worcester,	August 2, 1862	June 18, 1865, promoted Second Lieut.
Charles M. Cleaveland, 1st Sergt.	....	West Boylston,	July 31, 1862	November 24, 1862, disability.
Asa B. Fay, 1st Sergeant,	....	Northborough,	" 31, 1862	September 27, 1864, Sergeant Major.
Nelson A. Cross, Sergeant,	....	Worcester,	" 31, 1862	June 6, 1865, disability.
Joseph J. Fairbanks, Sergeant,	....	Northborough,	August 4, 1862	June 16, 1865, expiration of service.
George W. Fisher, Sergeant,	....	Sterling,	July 31, 1862	June 16, 1865, "
John M. Forbes, Sergeant,	....	Boylston,	" 31, 1862	January 13, 1865, died at Salisbury, N. C.
Hodgkins, Nathaniel, Sergeant,	....	Northborough,	" 31, 1862	September 27, 1864, died of wounds.
George L. Murdock, Sergeant,	....	West Boylston,	" 31, 1862	September 6, 1863, Second Lieut.
Cephas N. Walker, Sergeant,	....	Westborough,	" 31, 1862	July 6, 1865, expiration of service.
Theron H. Barton, Corporal,	....	Uxbridge,	" 31, 1862	June 1, 1865,
Charles E. Brigham, Corporal,	....	Westborough,	" 31, 1862	January 14, 1864, Lieut. U. S. C. T.
Dexter P. Brigham, Corporal,	....	Westborough,	August 2, 1862	June 16, 1865, expiration of service.
Jerome W. Burditt, Corporal,	....	Northborough,	July 31, 1862	June 16, 1865, "
Harrison Chase, Corporal,	....	West Boylston,	" 31, 1862	June 16, 1865, "
Charles P. Fisher, Corporal,	....	Westborough,	" 31, 1862	January 14, 1864, Lieut. U. S. C. T.
William E. Fitts, Corporal,	....	Sterling,	" 31, 1862	May 14, 1865, died of dis. in Sterling, Mass.
George S. Prouty, Corporal,	....	Northborough,	" 31, 1862	June 17, 1864, died of wounds.
William F. Sanford, Corporal,	....	Northborough,	" 31, 1862	June 16, 1865, expiration of service.
George A. Snow, Corporal,	....	West Boylston,	" 31, 1862	June 16, 1865, "
John Tucker, Corporal,	....	Boylston,	" 31, 1862	January 3, 1863, disability.
Lyman S. Walker, Corporal,	....	Westborough,	August 15, 1862	June 16, 1865, expiration of service.
James M. Wilson, Corporal,	....	Boylston,	July 31, 1862	June 9, 1865, order War Department.
Charles W. Bacon, Musician,	....	Worcester,	" 31, 1862	June 16, 1865, expiration of service.
Henry C. Ferguson, Musician,	....	Westborough,	" 31, 1862	June 16, 1865, "
Frank J. Sweeney, Musician,	....	Westborough,	" 31, 1862	July 17, 1864, disability.
Minot C. Adams,	....	Westborough,	" 31, 1863	September 15, 1864, died at Florence, S. C.
William M. Aldrich,	....	Oxford,	" 31, 1863	June 16, 1865, expiration of service.
Erastus E. Baker,	....	Boylston,	August 2, 1863	August 24, 1864, died at Andersonville, Ga.
Alonzo H. Bigelow,	....	Westborough,	July 31, 1862	May 23, 1865, disability.
William H. Blake,	....	Westborough,	" 31, 1862	June 5, '64, died of wds at Harrisonburg, Va.
Harmon H. Burpee,	....	Sterling,	" 31, 1862	June 16, 1865, expiration of service.
John M. Barr,	....	Leominster,	" 31, 1862	July 5, 1865,
Albert H. Carruth,	....	Northborough,	" 31, 1862	April 19, 1865, died at Alexandria, Va.
Charles S. Carter,	....	Westborough,	August 2, 1862	October 26, 1864, died at Florence, S. C.
Frank Carafgne,	....	Northborough,	July 31, 1862	June 16, 1865, expiration of service.

THIRTY-FOURTH MASSACHUSETTS INFANTRY. 433

Name		Residence	Date of muster	Remarks
Joseph Cassavant,		Sterling,	July 31, 1862	June 16, 1865, expiration of service.
John Carron,			Joined Ap. 26, '65	June 1, 1865, deserted.
William E. Chase,		Uxbridge,	July 31, 1862	February 16, 1864, transferred to V. R. C.
George S. Chickering,		Westborough,	August 2, 1862	November 1, 1864, died at Florence, S. C.
George S. Clark,		Holden,	July 31, 1862	June 16, 1865, expiration of service.
John H. Clark,	$325 00	Holden,	Dec. 5, 1863	June 14, 1864, transferred to 24th Infantry.
Darius Coleman,		Northborough,	July 31, 1862	December 27, 1862, disability.
William E. Cooley,		Worcester,	" 13, 1862	July 28, 1862, deserted.
John Dailey,		Sterling,	" 31, 1862	June 6, 1865, disability, S. O. W. D.
Henry J. Day,		Northborough,	July 31, 1862	June 22, 1865, expiration of service.
Byron Donavan,		Westborough,	August 2, 1862	July 1, 1865, "
John Doyle,		Sterling,	July 31, 1862	October 13, 1864, killed in battle.
Ariel B. Drake,		Mendon,	August 2, 1862	June 16, 1865, expiration of service.
Joseph Dudley,		Northborough,	July 31, 1862	April 4, 1865, died of wds. at Pt. Rocks, Va.
Joseph B. Farnsworth,		Coleraine,	Dec. 26, 1863	June 14, 1864, transferred to 24th Infantry.
George A. Ferguson,		Westborough,	July 31, 1862	June 23, 1865, disability, S. O. W. D.
Andrew Gammell,	325 00	Holden,	Dec. 10, 1863	June 14, 1865, transferred to 24th Infantry.
Peter Gamache,		Northborough,	July 31, 1862	March 8, 1865, transferred to V. R. C.
Patrick H. Gavin,		Sturbridge,	" 31, 1862	August 27, 1864, died at Andersonville, Ga.
Charles W. Gill,		Princeton,	" 31, 1862	June 16, 1865, expiration of service.
Edward B. Guild,	325 00	Millbury,	Dec. 28, 1863	June 14, 1865, transferred to 24th Infantry.
George F. Hall,		Westborough,	July 31, 1862	June 16, 1865, expiration of service.
George W. Handy,		Holden,	" 31, 1862	June 16, 1865, "
Charles H. Hardy,		Westborough,	" 31, 1862	June 16, 1865, "
Albert Henry,	50 00	Holden,	Sept. 17, 1863	June 14, 1865, transferred to 24th Infantry.
Edwin E. Henry,		Holden,	July 31, 1862	June 16, 1865, expiration of service.
John A. Hilton,		Sturbridge,	August 4, 1862	June 16, 1865, "
Orin Hodgman,		Sterling,	July 31, 1862	September 30, 1864, died at Charleston, S. C.
Charles Hooper,		Boylston,	" 31, 1862	June 10, 1865, disability, S. O. W. D.
Amasa A. Howe,		Holden,	" 31, 1862	November 25, 1864, died at Florence, S. C.
William J. Howe,		Boylston,	" 31, 1862	June 16, 1866, expiration of service.
George F. Johnson,	325 00	Worcester,	Jan. 5, 1864	Jan. 4, 1865, died of wds. at Annapolis, Md.
George A. Jordan,		Millbury,	July 31, 1862	February 15, '64, transferred to V. R. C.
Francis E. Kemp,		Westborough,	" 31, 1862	November 1, 1864, died at Millen, Ga.
Thomas F. Kennedy,		Worcester,	" 24, 1862	Deserted.
Leonard W. Keyes,		West Boylston,	" 31, 1862	June 16, 1865, expiration of service.
Charles H. Lewis,		Northborough,	" 13, 1862	June 16, 1865, "
Andrew J. Locker,		Princeton,	" 31, 1862	September 25, 1864, died at Charleston, S. C.
William W. Lombard,		Sturbridge,	August 2, 18.2	June 16, 1865, expiration of service.
John Lord,		West Boylston,	July 31, 1862	June 16, 1865, "
Frederick W. Mahan,		Sterling,	" 31, 1862	November 13, 1862, disability.

THIRTY-FOURTH MASSACHUSETTS INFANTRY.

Name and Rank.	Bounty.	Residence or Place Credited to.	Date of Muster.	Termination of Service and cause thereof.
Company C.—Continued.				
Napoleon Mallett,	325 00	Boylston,	Dec. 8, 1863	May 31, 1865, disability, S. O. W. D.
John Martin,	....	Sturbridge,	July 31, 1862	June 27, 1865, disability.
Samuel W. Mathewson,	325 00	Worcester,	Dec. 12, 1863	March 11, 1865, transferred to V. R. C.
Charles H. Maynard,	....	Sterling,	July 31, 1862	April 16, 1864, died of disease.
David Miner,	325 00	Ashfield,	Jan. 12, 1864	June 1, 1865, order War Department.
Justin Minot,	....	Northborough,	July 31, 1862	August 12, 1865, disability, wounds.
John Mockley,	....	Westborough,	"	June 16, 1865, expiration of service.
Jonathan A. Morey,	....	Boylston,	"	June 16, 1865, "
Norris Moore,	....	Spencer,	August 2, 1862	June 16, 1865, "
James W. Munroe,	....	Uxbridge,	July 31, 1862	July 5, 1865, "
Simeon G. Newton,	....	Sturbridge,	" 31, 1862	Oct. 7, 1863, died at Webster, Mass., of dis.
Oliver P. Payne,	....	Sterling,	" 31, 1862	April 1, 1863, died of disease.
William C. Perry,	....	Holden,	" 31, 1862	October 21, 1862, died of disease.
Edwin W. Pierce,	325 00	Worcester,	Jan. 5, 1864	December 26, 1864, died of wounds.
John Piper,	....	West Boylston,	August 15, 1862	February 15, 1864, transferred to V. R. C.
Simeon Potter,	....	Westborough,	July 31, 1862	June 16, 1865, expiration of service.
Michael Powers,	....	Boylston,	August 15, 1862	June 16, 1865, "
James E. Prentiss,	....	Sterling,	July 31, 1862	June 3, 1865, order War Department.
Merrick Reed,	....	Westborough,	" 31, 1862	June 16, 1865, expiration of service.
Amos Rice,	....	"	" 31, 1862	June 16, 1865, "
Edward Rivers,	554 66	Holden,	Dec. 15, 1863	June 14, 1865, transferred to 24th Infantry.
Ephraim H. Sargent,	325 00	"	Dec. 7, 1863	June 14, 1865, "
Levi F. Shepard,	....	West Boylston,	July 31, 1862	June 16, 1865, expiration of service.
James Smith,	....	Sterling,	" 31, 1862	June 16, 1865, "
Ezra J. Stevens,	325 00	Holden,	Dec. 7, 1863	June 14, 1865, transferred to 24th Infantry.
Albert Taft,	....	Uxbridge,	July 31, 1862	June 7, 1865, order War Department.
John B. Tallman,	....	West Boylston,	" 31, 1862	May 15, 1864, killed in battle.
Perry W. Towle,	558 66	Northborough,	" 31, 1862	July 13, 1863, died of disease.
Silas W. Walker,	....	Worcester,	Jan. 4, 1864	June 14, 1864, transferred to 24th Infantry.
John W. Ward,	....	Hopkinton,	July 31, 1862	December 27, 1864, died of disease.
Henry H. Welch,	....	Princeton,	" 31, 1862	December 31, 1862, deserted.
James Welch,	325 00	Worcester,	Jan. 4, 1864	November 17, 1864, died at Florence, S. C.
Chester H. Weston,	325 00	Huntington,	Jan. 4, 1864	June 14, 1865, transferred to 24th Infantry.
Charles B. Whitcomb,	....	Worcester,	July 31, 1862	May 27, 1863, disability.
Henry W. Willard,	....	Leominster,	August 2, 1862	February 26, 1863, disability.
James S. Willard,	....	Leominster,	" 4, 1862	January 3, 1863, disability.

THIRTY-FOURTH MASSACHUSETTS INFANTRY. 435

Name	Bounty	Residence	Mustered in	Remarks
Frederick A. Wiswall,		Westborough,	August 2, 1862	November 13, 1863, Lieut. in U. S. C. T.
Charles Workman,		Sterling,	July 31, 1862	September 15, 1865, disability from wounds.
Joseph M. Wright,		Boylston,	July 31, 1862	June 7, 1865, order War Department.
Company D.				
William Keefe, 1st Sergeant,		Springfield,	August 4, 1862	June 16, 1865, expiration of service.
Joseph A. Winn, 1st Sergeant,		Holyoke,	July 13, 1862	February 13, 1865, disability from wounds.
Horace W. Aldrich, Sergeant,		Holyoke,	July 31, 1862	May 19, 1865, S. O. W. D.
John Avery, Sergeant,		Holyoke,	July 31, 1862	June 16, 1865, expiration of service.
John H. Clifford, Sergeant,		Holyoke,	August 4, 1862	June 16, 1865, "
Thomas D. Dooley, Sergeant,		Holyoke,	July 31, 1862	October 10, 1863, disability.
Frederick A. Judd, Sergeant,		Holyoke,	" 31, 1862	June 27, 1864, 2d Lieutenant.
John McMahan, Sergeant,		West Springfield,	" 31, 1862	August 15, 1862, deserted.
Stephen A. Sargent, Sergeant,		Springfield,	" 31, 1862	June 16, 1865, expiration of service.
John H. Tannatt, Sergeant,		West Springfield,	" 31, 1862	April 11, 1863, 2d Lieut. New Jersey line.
Joseph G. Albee, Corporal,		Holyoke,	" 31, 1862	May 25, 1865, disabled from wounds.
George H. Atkins, Corporal,		Granville,	" 31, 1862	February 27, 1864, disabled from wounds.
Solomon Benway, Corporal,		West Springfield,	" 31, 1862	June 14, 1864, died of wounds.
Aaron Clapp, Corporal,		West Springfield,	" 31, 1862	June 5, 1864, killed in battle.
Eben G. Clark, Corporal,		Holyoke,	" 31, 1862	September 23, 1864, died of wounds.
Nelson R. Hossington, Corp'l,		West Springfield,	" 31, 1862	April 28, 1863, Lieut. U. S. C. T.
Joel Miller, Jr., Corporal,		West Springfield,	" 31, 1862	September 19, 1864, killed in battle.
Frederick Morin, Corporal,		West Springfield,	" 31, 1862	January 21, 1864, Lieut. U. S. C. T.
George C. Potwynne, Corporal,		Springfield,	" 13, 1862	May 15, 1864, killed in battle.
William H. Richards, Corporal,		West Springfield,	" 31, 1862	May 19, 1865, order War Department.
Abram Smith, Corporal,		Holyoke,	" 31, 1862	June 16, 1865, expiration of service.
George L. Warriner, Corporal,		West Springfield,	" 31, 1862	July 19, 1863, deserted.
Daniel Webster, Corporal,		Holyoke,	" 31, 1862	October 13, 1864, killed in battle.
John Winans, Corporal,		Springfield,	June 22, 1862	June 16, 1865, expiration of service.
Frank S. Hatfield, Musician,		Springfield,	July 31, 1862	June 16, 1865, "
Charles Thurman, Musician,		Clinton,	" 31, 1862	
J. H. P. Arentz, Jr.,		Boston,	Dec. 5, 1863	August —, 1864, deserted.
Nahum H. Ayres,		New Braintree,	July 31, 1862	May 18, 1865, disability from wounds.
Horace F. Ball,	$325 00	West Springfield,		June 16, 1865, expiration of service.
Joseph Balcom,	325 00	Conway,	January 7, 1864	June 14, 1864, died of wounds.
Milton Ballard,	325 00	Wendell,	Dec. 30, 1863	June 14, 1865, died of wounds.
Patrick Barry,		Brimfield,	July 13, 1862	July 30, 1864, died of wounds.
Horace E. Bellows,		West Springfield,	" 31, 1862	March 8, 1865, died of disease.
John W. Benway,	325 00	South Hadley,	Nov. 7, 1863	June 14, 1865, transferred to 24th Infantry.
William H. Bennett,	325 00	Millbury,	Dec. 26, 1863	June 14, 1865, transferred to 24th Infantry.

THIRTY-FOURTH MASSACHUSETTS INFANTRY.

Name and Rank.	Bounty.	Residence or Place Credited to.	Date of Muster.	Termination of Service and cause thereof.
Company D.—Continued.				
Charles A. Braman,	.....	Easthampton,	July 31, 1862	January 10, 1865, disability from wounds.
Edmund Broderic,	325 00	West Springfield,	" 31, 1862	June 16, 1865, expiration of service.
Uri Bradley,	.....	Colerain,	Dec. 21, 1863	June 14, 1865, transferred to 24th Infantry.
Emerson G. Brewer,	325 00	Springfield,	July 31, 1862	January 27, 1863, disability.
Leigh R. Brewer,	.....	Granville,	" 31, 1862	June 30, 1863, disability.
Robert Carroll,	325 00	Colerain,	Jan. 11, 1864	October 13, 1864, killed in battle.
George W. Caswell,	.....	West Springfield,	July 31, 1862	June 16, 1865, expiration of service.
Joseph P. Chapman,	325 00	Richmond,	August 10, 1864	June 14, 1865, transferred to 24th Infantry.
Parvin Clapp,	325 00	West Springfield,	Dec. 4, 1863	June 5, 1864, killed in battle.
Richard Clark,	.....	South Hadley,	July 31, 1862	March 12, 1863, disability.
Myron Conner,	325 00	Springfield,	Jan. 12, 1864	May 25, 1865, died from wounds.
George W. Cook,	325 00	Colerain,	August 9, 1864	June 14, 1865, transferred to 24th Infantry.
Joseph A. Copeland,	.....	Holyoke,	July 31, 1862	June 8, 1865, order War Department.
Neal Cullen,	.....	Holyoke,	" 13, 1862	May 18, 1865, order War Department.
John Cummings,	50 00	Granville,	" 31, 1862	June 16, 1865, expiration of service.
John W. Cummings,	325 00	Ware,	Sept. 22, 1863	June 16, 1865, disability from wounds.
Robert G. Curtis,	.....	Erving,	Jan. 4, 1864	June 2, 1865, " "
Benjamin Day,	.....	West Springfield,	July 31, 1862	April 9, 1865, " "
Cornelius Donahue,	.....	Holyoke,	" 31, 1862	May 15, 1864, killed in battle.
Joseph H. Efner,	325 00	West Springfield,	" 31, 1862	December 20, 1864, Lieut in U. S. C. T.
Winnick Elkins,	.....	West Springfield,	Dec. 1, 1863	June 14, 1865, transferred to 24th Infantry.
Lester C. Farnham,	.....	Blandford,	July 31, 1863	June 6, 1865, order War Department.
Roland N. Farnham,	.....	Granville,	" 31, 1862	Died in hands of enemy.
William Fitzjoseph,	.....	Springfield,	June 22, 1863	August 24, 1862, deserted.
Joseph E. Frary,	.....	Springfield,	July 25, 1862	June 16, 1865, expiration of service.
James Fry,	.....	Springfield,	" 31, 1862	June 26, 1865, disability from wounds.
Rinaldini Fuller,	.....	Holyoke,	" 31, 1862	June 16, 1865, expiration of service.
Albert H. Gaylord,	325 00	West Springfield,	Dec. 7, 1863	July 30, 1864, died of disease.
Gilbert H. Gaylord,	325 00	West Springfield,	" 7, 1863	June 14, 1865, transferred to 24th Infantry.
Dighton Goddard,	.....	Blandford,	July 31, 1862	June 16, 1865, expiration of service.
Frederick Goddard,	.....	Northampton,	" 31, 1862	November 24, 1862, disability.
Silas Goodnow,	.....	Springfield,	" 13, 1862	August 10, 1863, disability.
Thomas Gormley,	.....	Springfield,	" 13, 1862	January 18, 1865, died of wounds.
John Halbering,	325 00	Colerain,	" 31, 1862	February 23, 1864, dishonorably.
Hugh Hamilton,	325 00	Colerain,	Jan. 11, 1864	April 2, 1865, killed in battle.
Timothy M. Harrington,	.....	Heath,	Dec. 24, 1863	May 18, 1865, order War Department.

THIRTY-FOURTH MASSACHUSETTS INFANTRY.

Name		Residence	Date of Muster	Remarks
Francis C. Hayes,		Tolland,	July 31, 1862	June 16, 1865, expiration of service.
Thomas Hayes,		Tolland,	July 31, 1862	May 22, 1865, disability.
William Henry,		Springfield,	Jan. 9, 1864	March 31, 1865, killed in battle.
Charles H. Hopkins,		Holyoke,	July 31, 1862	May 21, 1863, disability.
Myron Howe,	$325 00	Wendell,	Dec. 20, 1863	June 14, 1865, transferred to 24th Infantry.
Henry Hobbard,		West Springfield,	July 31, 1862	March 15, 1863, died at Fort Lyon, Va.
Lorin Huntington,	325 00	Springfield,	July 31, 1862	June 16, 1865, expiration of service.
George W. Jennings,	398 66	Williamsburg,	August 9, 1864	June 14, 1865, transferred to 24th Infantry.
Marion Johnson,		West Springfield,	July 31, 1862	August 5, 1863, transferred to V. R. C.
William A. Jones,		West Springfield,	"	June 16, 1865, expiration of service.
George H. Justin,		Granville,	"	May 5, 1865, order War Department.
Lester Kendall,		Holyoke,	"	June 16, 1865, expiration of service.
Frank L. Kimball,	325 00	Springfield,	June 22, 1862	June 5, 1864, killed in battle.
Ludwig Klahn,		Clarksburg,	August 12, 1864	June 14, 1865, transferred to 24th Infantry.
Frederick Krollman,		Granville,	July 31, 1862	June 16, 1865, expiration of service.
Orrin Ladd,		Holyoke,	" 13, 1862	January 29, 1864, disability.
Joseph Laporte,	325 00	Holyoke,	" 31, 1862	May 19, 1865, order War department.
Philip Leahey,		West Springfield,	" 31, 1862	September 19, 1864, killed in battle.
Daniel Looney,		Holyoke,	Dec. 23, 1862	June 16, 1865, expiration of service.
Edgar F. Manning,	325 00	Brimfield,	July 31, 1862	" "
William Marshall,		South Hadley,	June 22, 1862	June 16, 1865, "
Frank Matthews,		Springfield,	Dec. 29, 1862	June 14, 1865, transferred to 24th Infantry.
Henry McElroy,	325 00	Boston,	June 22, 1862	June 16, 1865, dishonorably.
James McFarland,		Holyoke,	Dec. 23, 1863	August 21, 1864, died at Andersonville, Ga.
Bernard McGovern,	325 00	Dudley,	July 31, 1862	May 28, 1865, order War Department.
John McMahan,		Holyoke,	" 13, 1862	October 30, 1863, deserted.
Elijah Meacham,		Southwick,	Jan. 2, 1864	February 28, 1865, died at Annapolis, Md.
Franklin Meyers,	325 00	Worthington,	August 4, 1862	June 16, 1865, expiration of service.
Lewis Morgan,		West Springfield,	July 31, 1862	August 6, 1862, deserted.
Edward Murphy,		South Hadley,	" 31, 1862	June 16, 1865, expiration of service.
Isaac F. Nash,		Granville,	" 31, 1862	" "
Arthur Neal,	325 00	Holyoke,	Feb. 29, 1864	June 14, 1865, transferred to 24th Infantry.
William J. Nash,	325 00	Savoy,	Jan. 11, 1864	June 14, 1865, "
Daniel O'Keefe,	325 00	Springfield,	Jan. 4, 1864	June 14, 1865, "
Melvin Packard,		Northampton,	July 31, 1862	October 30, 1863, disability.
Frank Parsons,		Holyoke,	July 31, 1862	June 16, 1865, expiration of service.
Paul Paro,	325 00	Winchendon,	October 26, 1863	June 14, 1865, transferred to 24th Infantry.
Charles L Pennock,		Sheffield,	July 31, 1862	June 14, 1865, killed in battle.
Joseph M. Perkins,	325 00	Holyoke,	July 31, 1862	June 5, 1864, killed in battle.
Austin Pratt,	325 00	Wales,	Jan. 4, 1864	September 21, 1864, died of wounds.
Edward L. Pratt,		Colerain,	Dec. 18, 1863	June 14, 1865, transferred to 24th Infantry.

438   THIRTY-FOURTH MASSACHUSETTS INFANTRY.

NAME AND RANK.	Bounty.	Residence or Place Credited to.	Date of Muster.	Termination of Service and cause thereof.
Company D.—Continued.				
Charles Quint,		Holyoke,	July 13, 1862	June 16, 1865, expiration of service.
Samuel E. Ripley,	$325 00	Shutesbury,	Dec. 20, 1863	April 10, 1865, transferred to V. R. C.
John M. Roach,		Springfield,	July 13, 1862	February 26, 1865, died at Danville, Va.
John Roachford,		West Springfield,	" 31, 1862	January 27, 1863, disability.
Charles H. Sampson,		Holyoke,	" 31, 1872	June 7, 1864, disability.
James H. Sanders,		Granville,	" 31, 1862	June 8, 1865, disability.
John H. Savage,		Holyoke,	" 31, 1862	November 15, 1863, transferred to V. R. C.
Alfred Sill,		Holyoke,	" 31, 1862	August 24, 1862, disability.
Daniel O. Simpson,	325 00	Conway,	Jan. 12, 1864	July 24, 1864, died at Andersonville, Ga.
Joseph D. Smith,	325 00	Springfield,	August 10, 1864	June 14, 1865, transferred to 24th Infantry.
Malcolm Smith,		Holyoke,	July 31, 1862	May 15, 1864, killed in battle.
*Samuel D. Smith,		West Springfield,	August 21, 1862	May 23, 1865, order War Department.
Henry W. Soule,		Tolland,	July 31, 1862	December 27, 1863, disability.
Asa N. Sparks,	325 00	Colrain,	Dec. 10, 1863	June 5, 1864, killed in battle.
Royal Stimpson,		Warwick,	October 30, 1862	June 14, 1865, transferred to 24th Infantry.
Charles E. Thompson,		West Brookfield,	July 31, 1862	February 11, 1864, transferred to V. R. C.
Jerry Tierney,	325 00	Springfield,	August 13, 1864	May 29, 1865, disability.
Joseph D. Ufford,		West Springfield,	July 31, 1862	June 21, 1865, expiration of service.
Charles Walker,		Colrain,	Jan. 11, 1864	June 14, 1865, transferred to 24th Infantry.
Joseph Wallace,	325 00	Colrain,	Jan. 4, 1864	" " "
Charles W. Warriner,		Springfield,	July 13, 1862	Nov. 13, 1862, disability.
Charles H. West,		South Hadley,	" 31, 1862	January 29, 1864, disability.
David B. West,		South Hadley,	" 31, 1862	June 16, 1865, expiration of service.
Benjamin C. Wilbur,	325 00	Richmond,	Jan. 4, 1864	June 14, 1865, transferred to 24th Infantry.
Frederick L. Wilson,		Springfield,	July 31, 1862	June 16, 1865, expiration of service.
Samuel B. Winchell,		Granville,	" 31, 1862	November 24, 1862, disability.
William H. Winans,		Springfield,	" 31, 1862	December 29, 1862, disability.
Seth A. Woodward,		Warwick,	October 30, 1863	June 18, 1864, killed in battle.
Company E.				
William F. Belser, 1st Sergeant,		Worcester,	July 13, 1862	June 28, 1863, Second Lieut.
John E. Calligan, 1st Sergeant,		Worcester,	" 13, 1862	May 16, 1864, Second Lieut.
Harry B. King, 1st Sergeant,		Barre,	" 13, 1862	June 18, 1864, killed in battle.
Ira Lackey, 1st Sergeant,		Leicester,	" 31, 1862	May 18, 1865, Second Lieut.

* Not on Regimental Book.

THIRTY-FOURTH MASSACHUSETTS INFANTRY.

Name	Bounty	Residence	Muster Date	Remarks
Anson S. Comee, Sergeant,		Barre,	July 13, 1862	January 14, 1863, disability.
Daniel H. French, Sergeant,		Worcester,	June 21, 1862	November 13, 1864, died of wounds.
Charles A. Hunter, Sergeant,		Spencer,	July 31, 1862	June 18, 1865, Second Lieut.
Alfred James, Sergeant,		Leicester,	" 31, 1862	January 12, 1865, transferred to V. R. C.
Christopher Pennell, Sergeant,		West Stockbridge,	" 31, 1862	December 8, 1863, Lieut. U. S. C. T.
Albert J. Rugg, Sergeant,		Worcester,	" 31, 1862	June 16, 1865, expiration of service.
William W. Underwood,		Shirley,	" 31, 1862	February 18, 1865, disability,—from wounds.
Liberty W. Worthington, Sergt.,		Spencer,	" 31, 1862	June 16, 1865, expiration of service.
Emory G. Adams, Corporal,		Barre,	" 31, 1862	April 24, 1864, died of disease.
John W. Belcher, Corporal,		Spencer,	" 31, 1862	June 16, 1865, expiration of service.
Henry Bemis, Corporal,		Spencer,	" 31, 1862	June 16, 1865, " "
Henry Converse, Corporal,		Spencer,	" 31, 1862	June 16, 1865, " "
Otis E. Davis, Corporal,		Athol,	" 31, 1862	June 16, 1865, " "
M. Gardner Gage, Corporal,		Spencer,	" 13, 1862	October 18, 1863, killed in battle.
William F. Green, Corporal,		Worcester,	" 23, 1862	June 16, 1865, expiration of service.
Charles H. Johnson, Corporal,		Petersham,	" 31, 1862	May 15, 1864, killed in battle.
Henry H. Sibley, Corporal,		Spencer,	" 31, 1862	June 16, 1865, expiration of service.
Arthur M. Stone, Corporal,		Spencer,	" 31, 1862	June 16, 1865, " "
John Wheeler, Corporal,		Shirley,	" 31, 1862	March 25, 1865, died of Typhoid Fever.
Joseph H. Burnham, Musician,	$325 00	Holyoke,	Dec. 1, 1863	June 14, 1865, transferred to 24th Infantry.
Alexander Comrie, Musician,		Worcester,	July 13, 1862	June 16, 1865, expiration of service.
Timothy P. Giffin, Musician,		Leicester,	" 31, 1862	June 16, '65, ex. of serv. May 1, '63, prin. mus.
Frank Seymour, Wag.,		Worcester,	" 31, 1862	June 16, 1865, expiration of service.
Franklin Adams,		Auburn,	August 5, 1862	June 8, 1865, disability from wounds.
George H. Angell,	50 00	Worcester,	Sept. 30, 1863	February 11, 1864, transferred to V. R. C.
John H. Archibald,		Barre,	July 31, 1862	November 25, 1863, disability.
Caleb H. Babbitt,		Barre,	" 31, 1862	December 28, 1863, "
Joseph H. Bacon,		Barre,	" 31, 1862	July 5, 1865, expiration of service.
Horace A. Balcolm,		Shirley,	" 31, 1862	October 10, 1862, disability.
William R. Barr,	325 00	Oakham,	Dec. 10, 1863	June 14, 1865, transferred to 24th Infantry.
George H. Beard,		Shirley,	July 31, 1862	June 16, 1865, expiration of service.
Oscar R. Bemis,		Spencer,	" 31, 1862	August 26, 1862, died of disease.
Alexander Benway,		Leicester,	" 31, 1862	November 20, 1862, disability.
Joseph Benjamin,	325 00	Spencer,	Dec. 1, 1863	June 14, 1865, transferred to 24th Infantry.
George L. Bigelow,		West Boylston,	Dec. 30, 1863	September 30, 1864, died at Andersonville.
James G. Bigelow,	325 00	Spencer,	Dec. 7, 1863	June 14, 1865, transferred to 24th Infantry.
Andrew Blood,		Shirley,	July 31, 1862	June 16, 1865, expiration of service.
Henry H. Bowman,		Spencer,	" 31, 1862	May 25, 1865, " "
Edward Boyne,		Spencer,	" 31, 1862	May 4, 1863, deserted.
Frank M. Boynton,		Shirley,	" 31, 1862	June 16, 1865, expiration of service.
Lewis Brosseau,	325 00	Barre,	Dec. 8, 1863	June 14, 1865, transferred to 24th Infantry.

Company E.—Continued.

NAME AND RANK.	Bounty.	Residence or Place Credited to.	Date of Muster.	Termination of Service and cause thereof.
Peter Brosseau,		Barre,	July 31, 1862	October 13, 1864, killed in battle.
James I. Brown,		Worcester,	Dec. 8, 1863	June 14, 1865, transferred to 24th Infantry.
Walter R. Brown,		Spencer,	July 31, 1862	June 1, 1865, disability.
William Butler,		Greenfield,	Dec. 3, 1863	June 14, 1865, transferred to 24th Infantry.
Rensselaer Butler,		Spencer,	July 31, 1862	June 16, 1865, expiration of service.
John Cambo,		Barre,	"	June 16, 1865, "
Dwight Chickering,		Spencer,	"	July 18, 1864, killed in battle.
Henry G. Chickering,		Spencer,	"	Feb. '65, lost from transp't at Wilm'ton, N.C.
George P. Clark,		Spencer,	"	April 19, 1865, disability.
Henry R. Clark,		Spencer,	"	June 16, 1865, expiration of service.
Newton H. Clark,		Swampscot,	"	September 19, 1864, killed in battle.
William H. Clark,		Swampscot,	"	February 17, 1865, disability.
Patrick W. Clifford,	$325 00	Northfield,	Dec. 28, 1863	May 15, 1864, killed in battle.
John R. Cobleigh,		Barre,	July 31, 1862	July 19, 1863, died of disease.
John R. Cobleigh, Jr.,		Barre,	"	June 16, 1865, expiration of service.
George H. Farmer,		Shirley,	"	June 16, 1865, "
William H. Farmer,		Shirley,	"	May 15, 1864, killed in battle.
Joseph A. Farnsworth	325 00	Shirley,	"	January 12, 1865, transferred to V. R. C.
Charles L. Fay,		Spencer,	Dec. 1, 1863	June 14, 1865, transferred to 24th Infantry.
James W. H. Gage,		Spencer,	July 13, 1862	June 15, 1865, expiration of service. Corp.
Francis Galen,		Worcester,	13, 1862	February 2, 1863, deserter.
Gardner Galen,		Dana,	13, 1862	June 2, 1863, deserter.
Henry Gardner,		Worcester,	13, 1862	February 14, 1864, transferred to V. R. C.
James W. Garrity,		Worcester,	13, 1862	March 7, 1863, deserter.
Patrick Gately,		Shirley,	13, 1862	February 14, 1864, transferred to V. R. C.
Charles H. Giffin,		Spencer,	31, 1862	July 5, 1865, expiration of service.
Stephen E. Gifford,	579 99	Lee,	Nov. 9, 1863	June 14, 1865, transferred to 24th Infantry.
Micah Graves,		Barre,	July 13, 1862	December 12, 1863, disability.
James W. Green,		Spencer,	" 31, 1862	April 4, 1865, "
Amos H. Hale,		Spencer,	"	November 20, 1862, "
Henry A. Hale,		Spencer,	"	May 1, 1863, "
James Haley,		Shirley,	"	June 16, 1865, expiration of service.
George W. Harding,		New Salem,	August 11, 1862	July 5, 1865, "
Leroy Hawes,		Spencer,	July 31, 1862	April 3, 1865, died of wounds.
Edwin Holden,		Leicester,	" 31, 1862	June 16, 1865, expiration of service.
George F. Howe,	289 99	Stow,	Jan. 7, 1864	June 3, 1865, order War Department.

George W. Howe,			Barre,	July 31, 1862	May 31, 1864, died of wounds.
Otis M. Hinter,			Spencer,	July 31, 1862	Apr. 10, '64, dr'n'd while on duty at Har. Fer.
* Joseph W. Howard,			Athol,	March 31, 1864	
Lincoln L. Johnson,			Leicester,	July 31, 1862	August 1, 1864, died of wounds.
Edson P. Kidder,			Barre,	Dec. 31, 1862	June 15, 1863, died of disease.
Alexander O. Kingman,	$325 00		Northbridge,	Dec. 21, 1863	June 14, 1865, transferred to 24th Infantry.
John B. Lapierre,			Shirley,	July 31, 1862	November 24, 1862, disability.
Joseph Legacy,			Milford,	" "	December 20, 1862, "
Walton Livermore,			Spencer,	" "	June 16, 1865, expiration of service.
John M. Lyndes,			Spencer,	" "	May 21, 1865, disability.
Walter Mahan,			Milford,	" "	August 24, 1864, died of disease.
William C. Manning,	325 00		Worcester,	Jan. 5, 1864	June 14, 1865, transferred to 24th Infantry.
Isaac A. McDaniels,			Shirley,	July 31, 1862	December, 1864, died at Richmond, Va.
John F. Methven,	325 00		Worcester,	Jan. 5, 1864	April 21, 1865, Lieut. in U. S. C. T.
Roland E. Neff,	50 00		Worcester,	Sept. 30, 1863	June 14, 1865, transferred to 24th Infantry.
Abel Nicholas,			Shirley,	July 31, 1862	June 16, 1865, expiration of service.
Erastus Orcutt,	325 00		Orange,	Dec. 10, 1863	November 6, 1864, died of wounds.
Hammond W. Page,			Spencer,	July 31, 1862	June 16, 1865, expiration of service.
Robert D. Parker,	325 00		Worcester,	Dec. 21, 1863	February 10, 1865, transferred to V. R. C.
Francis Pellissier,	325 00		Greenfield,	Dec. 17, 1863	June 14, 1865, transferred to 24th Infantry.
Arba Pierce,			Worcester,	July 31, 1862	November 1, 1862, deserted.
John A. Pratt,	325 00		Spencer,	Jan. 15, 1864	February 18, 1865, transferred to V. R. C.
Orville W. Prouty,			Barre,	July 31, 1862	June 16, 1865, expiration of service.
George E. Rice,			Orange,	" "	June 16, 1865, "
True L. Rice,	325 00		Barre,	Dec. 14, 1863	January 24, 1864, transferred to V. R. C.
Porter W. Robinson,			Deerfield,	July 31, 1862	May 15, 1864, killed in battle.
Edward Savage,	391 32		Richmond,	Dec. 31, 1863	June 14, 1865, transferred to 24th Infantry.
John Shaughnessy,	325 00		Leicester,	Dec. 21, 1863	April 2, 1865, killed in battle.
James Shean,			Barre,	July 17, 1862	June 17, 1865, disability. O. W. D.
Joseph W. Smith,			Leicester,	" 31, 1862	November 1, 1864, died at Florence, S. C.
Owen Smith,			Shirley,	" "	January 18, 1864, deserted.
Lorenzo Spalding,			Warren,	" "	June 26, 1865, expiration of service.
John Sweeney,	325 00		Wendell,	Dec. 19, 1863	June 6, 1865, O. W. D.
William J. Taylor,	325 00		Uxbridge,	Dec. 24, 1863	Dec. 24, 1864, died at Richmond, Va.
Charles H. Thompson,			Spencer,	July 13, 1862	October 17, 1864, died at Andersonville.
Charles E. Usher,			Spencer,	" 31, 1862	June 16, 1865, expiration of service.
William D. Usher,			Dana,	" "	June 16, 1865, "
Joseph F. Ward,			Barre,	" "	June 16, 1865, "
John B. Webber,				" "	January 18, 1864, deserted.
Joseph H. Whittier,				" "	June 16, 1865, expiration of service.

* Not on Regimental Book.

THIRTY-FOURTH MASSACHUSETTS INFANTRY.

NAME AND RANK.	Bounty.	Residence or Place Credited to.	Date of Muster.	Termination of Service and cause thereof.
Company E.—Continued.				
John G. White,	....	Shirley,	July 31, 1862	June 16, 1865, expiration of service.
Joseph M. Winslow,	$325 00	Barre,	" 31, 1862	June 16, 1865, "
Benjamin C. Wilbur,	....	Richmond,	Jan. 4, 1864	June 14, 1865, transferred to 24th Infantry.
Richard Young,	....	Becket,	July 31, 1862	June 16, 1865, expiration of service.
Company F.				
Henry T. Hall, 1st Sergeant,	....	Greenfield,	July 31, 1862	August 23, 1862, Second Lieut.
William F. Pepper, 1st Sergeant,	....	Greenfield,	" 31, 1863	November 29, 1864, Second Lieut.
Charles G. Blake, Sergeant,	....	Greenfield,	" 31, 1862	June 6, 1864, Second Lieut.
Roswell L. Church, Sergeant,	....	Greenfield,	" 31, 1862	June 16, 1865, expiration of service.
John L. Hawks, Sergeant,	....	Heath,	" 31, 1862	August 24, 1863, disability.
Frederick N. Hayden, Sergeant,	....	Greenfield,	" 31, 1862	November 8, 1864, died from wounds.
Foster Meekins, Sergeant,	....	Whately,	" 31, 1862	June 16, 1865, expiration of service.
Herbert B. Rowley, Sergeant,	....	Greenfield,	" 31, 1862	October 18, 1864, Second Lieut.
Charles Stowell, Sergeant,	....	Deerfield,	" 31, 1862	June 16, 1865, expiration of service.
Horace W. Walsh, Sergeant,	....	Oxford,	August 2, 1862	June 16, 1865, "
John Buchanan, Corporal,	....	Greenfield,	July 13, 1862	May 28, 1865, disability.
Peter Ely, Corporal,	....	Shelburne,	" 31, 1862	June 16, 1865, expiration of service.
Edward M. Fuller, Corporal,	....	Clinton,	August 9, 1862	March 21, 1864, Lieut. in U. S. C. T.
Samuel M. Hall, Corporal,	....	Hawley,	July 31, 1862	June 5, 1864, killed in battle.
William J. Hilton, Corporal,	....	Deerfield,	August 2, 1862	December 18, 1862, deserted.
Felix Mallette, Corporal,	$325 00	Ashfield,	Jan. 12, 1864	June 14, 1865, transferred to 24th Infantry.
Julius A. Parkhurst, Corporal,	....	Southbridge,	July 31, 1862	June 16, 1865, expiration of service.
Joseph L. Phillips, Corporal,	....	Buckland,	" 31, 1862	June 16, 1865, "
Charles S. Smith, Corporal,	....	Greenfield,	" 31, 1862	June 16, 1865, "
Edwin L. Tobey, Corporal,	....	Buckland,	" 31, 1862	June 16, 1865, "
George Ward, Corporal,	....	Ashfield,	" 31, 1862	June 16, 1865, "
Samuel S. Waterman, Corporal,	....	Montague,	August 7, 1862	May 15, 1864, killed in battle.
Edward W. Wheelock, Corporal,	....	Greenfield,	July 13, 1862	June 16, 1865, expiration of service.
Leonard Wright, Corporal,	....	Millbury,	" 31, 1862	May 8, 1863, disability.
George E. Plumley, Musician,	....	Greenfield,	" 31, 1862	June 16, 1865, expiration of service.
Lawson Dunnell, Wagoner,	....	Charlemont,	" 31, 1862	June 16, 1865, "
Franklin Allen,	....	Greenfield,	" 31, 1862	November 13, 1863, deserted.
James M. Allen,	....	Deerfield,	" 13, 1862	February 2, 1863, transferred to V. R. C.
John R. Amidon,	....	Southbridge,	August 2, 1862	May 21, 1863, disability.

THIRTY-FOURTH MASSACHUSETTS INFANTRY.

Name	Residence	Bounty	Date	Remarks
Samuel Ashton,	Colrain,	$325 00	Jan. 4, 1864	June 14, 1865, transferred to 24th Infantry.
Peter L. Baker,	Hawley,	....	July 31, 1862	June 16, 1865, expiration of service.
John E. Bent,	Worcester,	....	August 9, 1862	June 16, 1865, "
Chandler H. Blanchard,	Hawley,	325 00	July 31, 1862	December 12, 1864, disability.
Everett W. Blanchard,	Hawley,	....	Nov. 12, 1863	September 12, 1864, died of disease.
Charles J. Botsford,	Po'keepsie, N.Y.,	....	Oct. 6, 1862	October 26, 1863, disability.
Henry Bowers,	Greenfield,	325 00	Dec. 14, 1863	September 19, 1864, killed in battle.
Henry J. Bowers,	Greenfield,	325 00	" 15, 1863	October 12, 1864, died from wounds.
William J. Bowers,	Greenfield,	325 00	" 14, 1863	December 28, 1864, died of disease.
Martin O. Brown,	Colrain,	....	July 31, 1862	April 21, 1863, disability.
William H. Bradley,	Heath,	....	" 13, 1862	June 16, 1865, expiration of service.
Charles K. Burnham,	Montague,	....	" 13, 1862	June 16, 1865, "
George A. Burnham,	Greenfield,	....	" 31, 1862	September 19, 1864, killed in battle.
James Burke,	Shelbourne,	....	Oct. 27, 1863	June 14, 1865, transferred to 24th Infantry.
Robert Calligan,	Worcester,	....	August 4, 1862	October 10, 1863, dishonorably.
Franklin W. Carson,	Oxford,	325 00	July 31, 1862	June 14, 1865, transferred to 24th Infantry.
Patrick Casey,	Greenfield,	....	Nov. 25, 1863	November 17, 1862, disability.
Joseph M. Chase,	Greenfield,	....	July 31, 1862	June 16, 1865, expiration of service.
Norris E. Chapin,	Ashfield,	....	" 31, 1862	June 16, 1865, "
Alphonso Church,	Greenfield,	....	" 31, 1862	May 17, 1865, dssability.
Henry G. Clark,	Deerfield,	325 00	Nov. 19, 1863	June 14, 1865, transferred to 24th Infantry.
Alonzo Coates,	Charlemont,	50 00	Sept. 24, 1863	July 30, 1864, deserted.
David F. Coates,	Charlemont,	325 00	Dec. 31, 1863	July 18, 1864, killed in battle.
Henry S. Coolidge,	Greenfield,	325 00	Oct. 21, 1863	June 10, 1864, died from wounds.
Michael Corliss,	Greenfield,	....	Dec. 10, 1863	June 16, 1865, expiration of service.
Otis Damon,	Charlemont,	325 00	" 10, 1863	May 25, 1865, order War Department.
Walter Dunbar,	Greenfield,	....	July 31, 1862	June 16, 1865, expiration of service.
Lafayette Eddy,	Ashfield,	....	" 31, 1862	February 22, 1865, died at Salisbury, N. C.
Lucius J. Eddy,	Greenfield,	50 00	Sept. 25, 1863	June 14, 1865, transferred to 24th Infantry.
John Eberlin,	Greenfield,	325 00	Feb. 23, 1864	June 14, 1865, "
Lysander Estee,	Heath,	....	July 31, 1862	March 14, 1865, disability.
John Fitzgerald,	Charlemont,	....	" 31, 1862	July 10, 1863, killed accid'y, Relay Ho, Md.
Ernest E. Freeman,	Worcester,	325 00	Dec. 2, 1863	March 11, 1865, disability.
Sumner Frink,	Deerfield,	....	July 31, 1862	June 16, 1865, expiration of service.
Patrick Galivan,	Conway,	....	" 31, 1862	June 16, 1865, "
Abijah W. Gleason,	Charlemont,	....	" 31, 1862	September 1, 1863, transferred to V. R. C.
Adoniram J. Gleason,	Rowe,	....	" 31, 1862	February 28, 1863, died of disease.
Michael Gorro,	Ashfield,	325 00	Jan. 12, 1864	May 15, 1864, killed in battle.
James E. Green,	Shutesbury,	100 00	Sept. 5, 1864	June 16, 1865, expiration of service.
Joseph B. Green,	Erving,	....	August 7, 1862	June 16, 1865, "
Peter Hackett,	Conway,	....	July 31, 1862	October 10, 1862, disability.

THIRTY-FOURTH MASSACHUSETTS INFANTRY.

NAME AND RANK.	Bounty.	Residence or Place Credited to.	Date of Muster.	Termination of Service and cause thereof.
Company F.—Continued.				
Henry C. Hallett,	$50 00	Holyoke,	July 31, 1862	June 16, 1865, expiration of service.
John Harrington,		Worcester,	Sept. 16, 1863	June 14, 1865, transferred to 24th Infantry.
Alonzo Helme,		Hawley,	July 31, 1862	May 23, 1863, disability.
William Hildreth,		Barre,	August 6, 1862	June 30, 1865, expiration of service.
John Hines,	325 00	Worcester,	Nov. 19, 1863	September 19, 1864, killed in battle.
Ira N. Hitchcock,		Holyoke,	July 31, 1862	April 8, 1865, disability from wounds.
Alexis R. Hubbard,		Deerfield,	"	May 23, 1865, disability.
Henry B. Isham,		Greenfield,	" 31, 1862	June 16, 1865, expiration of service.
Alden C. Jackman,		Greenfield,	" 31, 1862	"
Andrew F. Jackson,		Brookfield,	" 31, 1862	April 24, 1863, disability.
David Jillson, 2d,		Colrain,	" 31, 1862	June 16, 1865, expiration of service.
Lewis Jillson,		Colrain,	" 31, 1862	June 16, 1865, "
Samuel C. Jillson,		Hawley,	" 31, 1862	February 29, 1864, disability.
Erastus Kenney,		Greenfield,	" 31, 1862	October 18, 1864, transferred to V. R. C.
John Kennedy,	325 00	Deerfield,	" 31, 1862	May 5, 1863, disability.
William Leonard,		Southbridge,	Jan. 2, 1864	June 14, 1865, transferred to 24th Infantry.
Joseph H. Lombard,		Southbridge,	August 3, 1862	June 16, 1865, expiration of service.
John Mack,		Worcester,	August 2, 1862	June 16, 1865, "
Daniel B. Mahoney,	325 00	Montague,	August 4, 1863	October 10, 1862, disability.
Cyrus Marsh,		Ashfield,	July 31, 1862	December 27, 1862, disability.
Andy McClelland,		Greenfield,	Jan. 12, 1864	May 15, 1864, killed in battle.
George E. Mitchell,		Erving,	August 7, 1862	January 22, 1864, disability.
John Murphy,		Erving,	July 31, 1862	October 19, 1864, died from wounds.
Michael Murphy,		Greenfield,	" 13, 1862	June 16, 1865, expiration of service.
Allen Newton,		Springfield,	" 31, 1362	June 16, 1865, "
Marcus M. Newton,		Colrain,	" 31, 1862	February 15, 1864, transferred to V. R. C.
Walter C. Nichols,	325 00	Ashfield,	Jan. 12, 1864	June 16, 1865, expiration of service.
Samuel O'Neil,		Erving,	July 13, 1862	June 14, 1865, transferred to 24th Infantry.
Ferdinand G. Packard,		Erving,	" 13, 1862	June 16, 1865, expiration of service.
Frank B. Packard, Jr.	325 00	Deerfield,	Jan. 22, 1864	Sept. 15, 1863, died of disease.
William R. Parker,		Shelburne,	July 13, 1862	June 14, 1865, transferred to 24th Infantry.
Charles J. Perry,		Charlemont,	" 31, 1862	June 10, 1865, dishonorably.
William A. Phipps,		Montague,	" 13, 1862	October 13, 1864, killed in battle.
Walter Pierce,		Greenfield,	Dec. 12, 1863	June 16, 1865, expiration of service.
Warren J. Potter,	325 00	Orange,	Nov. 16, 1863	June 14, 1865, transferred to 24th Infantry.
Nathan B. Putnam,				June 14, 1865, transferred to 24th Infantry.

THIRTY-FOURTH MASSACHUSETTS INFANTRY. 445

Name		Residence	Date		Remarks
Ralph H. Ranney,	....	Ashfield,	August	9, 1862	June 16, 1865, expiration of service.
Charles M. Remington,	....	Greenfield,	July	31, 1862	March 27, 1863, disability.
James F. Remington,	....	Greenfield,	August	5, 1862	October 16, 1862, disability.
Lucius Reniff,	....	Buckland,	August	9, 1862	February 15, 1864, transferred to V. R. C.
Peter Richards,	....	Erving,	July	31, 1862	June 16, 1865, expiration of service.
John W. Rowley,	....	Greenfield,	"	13, 1862	" " "
William H. Seeley,	....	Greenfield,	"	13, 1862	May 19, 1863, disability.
Gilbert E. Siegars,	325 00	Worcester,	Jan.	5, 1864	June 14, 1866, transferred to 24th Infantry.
Charles M. Sheffield,	325 00	Hopkinton,	Dec.	10, 1863	Deserted.
William R. Smith,	50 00	Conway,	Sept.	16, 1863	June 14, 1865, transferred to 24th Infantry.
Charles H. Stowell,	325 00	Shutesbury,	Nov.	16, 1863	June 14, 1865, transferred to 24th Infantry.
Jerry Sullivan,	....	Greenfield,	August	2, 1862	June 16, 1865, expiration of service.
Thomas A. Taylor,	....	Charlemont,	July	31, 1862	" "
Henry W. Temple,	325 00	Deerfield,	Dec.	21, 1863	June 14, 1865, transferred to 24th Infantry.
Salem J. Tiffany,	....	Southbridge,	August	13, 1862	September 1, 1864, died at Andersonville, Ga.
John Tulley,	....	Charlton,	August	6, 1862	November 23, 1862, disability.
Horatio E. Turner,	325 00	Clinton,	August	2, 1862	September 8, 1864, died at Andersonville, Ga.
Elias E. Vebber,	....	Charlemont,	Dec.	25, 1863	June 14, 1865, transferred to 24th Infantry.
Thomas B. Warren,	....	Boylston,	August	4, 1862	January 18, 1865, transferred to V. R. C.
Benjamin D. Waterman,	325 00	Shelburne,	Nov.	23, 1863	June 14, 1865, transferred to 24th Infantry.
Franklin D. Waterman,	100 00	Shutesbury,	Sept.	3, 1863	May 18, 1865, order War Department.
Horton Waterman,	325 00	Shutesbury,	Feb.	4, 1864	June 14, 1865, transferred to 24th Infantry.
Charles E. Whittaker,	....	Greenfield,	July	13, 1862	March 9, 1865, disability, wounds.
Ebenezer E. Whitney,	....	Deerfield,	"	31, 1862	May 19, 1865, disability, wounds.
Charles Wilson,	....	Deerfield,	"	31, 1862	July 14, 1863, died of disease.
Enos B. Williams,	....	Charlemont,	"	31, 1862	February 17, 1864, disability.
Martin V. Williams,	....	Deerfield,	August	2, 1862	January 3, 1863, disability.
Lewis L. Wood,	50 00	Colrain,	Sept.	24, 1863	October 19, 1864, died of wounds.
Charles H. Wright,	....	Millbury,	August	5, 1862	February 15, 1864, transferred to V. R. C.

Company G.

Name		Residence	Date		Remarks
Edwin B. Smith, 1st Sergeant,	....	Westfield,	July	31, 1862	June 16, 1865, exp. of service, absent wounded.
Alfred Dibble, Sergeant,	....	Southwick,	"	31, 1862	November 9, 1864, 2d Lieutenant.
Frederick W. B. Fleming, Serg't,	....	Westfield,	"	31, 1862	June 16, 1865, expiration of service.
James H. Gaylord, Sergeant,	....	Westfield,	"	31, 1862	October 13, 1864, killed in battle.
Carl Hock, Sergeant,	....	Worcester,	"	31, 1862	June 16, 1865, expiration of service.
David H. McIver, Sergeant,	....	Westfield,	"	31, 1862	December 26, 1864, disability.
Charles H. Morrill, Sergeant,	....	Westfield,	"	31, 1862	November 9, 1864, 2d Lieutenant.
William H. Mosher, Sergeant,	....	Westfield,	"	31, 1862	June 16, 1865, expiration of service.
Otis R. Reed, Sergeant,	....	Westfield,	"	31, 1862	February 8, 1864, transferred to V. R. C.

THIRTY-FOURTH MASSACHUSETTS INFANTRY.

NAME AND RANK.	Bounty.	Residence or Place Credited to.	Date of Muster.	Termination of Service and cause thereof.
Company G.—Continued.				
William R. Stocking, Sergeant,		Westfield,	July 31, 1862	June 16, 1865, expiration of service.
Daniel C. Wishart, Sergeant,		Westfield,	" 31, 1862	November 25, 1864, 2d Lieutenant.
William W. Bemis, Corporal,		Worcester,	" 31, 1862	June 16, 1865, exp. of serv.
Henry O. Clark, Corporal,		Westfield,	" 31, 1862	June 16, 1865, "
Edmund Cooper, Corporal,		Westfield,	" 31, 1862	June 16, 1865, "
John E. Dickson, Corporal,		Westfield,	" 31, 1862	June 15, 1864, died of wounds.
William Foos, Corporal,		Westfield,	" 31, 1862	May 15, 1864, killed in battle.
George Gandy, Corporal,		Westfield,	" 31, 1862	June 16, 1865, expiration of service.
Manheim Gershell, Corporal,		Westfield,	" 31, 1862	November 24, 1863, disability.
Orssamer Kenfield, Corporal,		Brimfield,	" 31, 1862	June 16, 1865, expiration of service.
George B. King, Corporal,		Westfield,	" 31, 1862	December 3, 1862, disability.
William M. Kinney, Corporal,		Westfield,	" 31, 1862	December 8, 1862, died of disease.
Bernard Marth, Corporal,		Westfield,	" 31, 1862	July 9, 1863, deserted.
Thomas Meadon, Corporal,		Westfield,	" 31, 1862	January 30, 1865, disability.
Thomas J. Smith, Corporal,		Westfield,	" 31, 1862	June 16, 1865, expiration of service.
John J. Warner, Corporal,		Westfield,	" 31, 1862	November 4, 1862, died of disease.
John E. Grant, Musician,		Westfield,	" 31, 1862	June 16, 1865, expiration of service.
George F. Moody, Musician,		Westfield,	" 31, 1862	November 24, 1862, disability.
James H. Atwater, Wagoner,		Westfield,	July 31, 1862	June 16, 1865, expiration of service.
Oscar E. Adams,		Auburn,	August 5, 1862	June 16, 1865, "
Marshall Alden,	$325 00	Greenwich,	July 31, 1862	May 9, 1865.
Thomas Archibald,		Sunderland,	Jan. 2, 1864	April 26, 1865, died of wounds.
William A. Ballou,	325 00	Worcester,	Dec. 12, 1863	November 6, 1864, died at Annapolis, Md.
Hiram A. Bancroft,	325 00	Greenfield,	October 26, 1863	June 14, 1865, transferred to 24th Regiment.
Lorey J. Bancroft,	325 00	Greenfield,	October 27, 1863	" "
Charles D. Barnes,		Westfield,	July 31, 1862	June 14, 1865, "
Thomas Beebo,	325 00	Conway,	Jan. 12, 1864	June 16, 1865, expiration of service.
John Boyle,		Westfield,	July 31, 1862	January 13, 1865, order War Department.
Henry E. Briggs,	325 00	Deerfield,	Dec. 8, 1863	March 18, 1865, "
Andrew Brock,	325 00	Buckland,	Jan. 12, 1864	June 14, 1865, transferred to 24th Infantry.
George W. Brown,		Southwick,	July 31, 1862	January 25, 1864, transferred to V. R. C.
Thomas J. Brown,		Westfield,	" 31, 1862	November 3, 1862, died of disease.
Fred. J. Bryant,		Phillipston,	Feb. 14, 1864	December 15, 1864, disability.
James H. Carr,		Westfield,	July 31, 1862	Promoted in New Jersey Volunteers.
John Carroll,		Blackstone,	August 5, 1862	August 8, 1862, deserted.
Dwight Chapman,		Westfield,	July 31, 1862	October 13, 1864, killed in battle.

THIRTY-FOURTH MASSACHUSETTS INFANTRY. 447

Name		Residence	Date		Remarks
James P. Chapman,		Russell,	July	31, 1862	January 23, 1864, transferred to V. R. C.
George W. Church,		Granville,	Dec.	31, 1862	December 23, 1862, died of disease.
Irving Clapp,		Leverett,	Dec.	28, 1863	June 14, 1865, transferred to 24th Infantry.
Andrew J. Curtis,	380 00	Warwick,	Dec.	30, 1863	" " "
William Colgrove,	325 00	Brimfield,	July	31, 1862	June 16, 1865, expiration of service.
Henry J. Cooley,		Westfield,	"	31, 1862	October 12, 1864, died at Andersonville, Ga.
Arthur J. Cushman,		Southwick,	"	31, 1862	January 7, 1863, deserted.
John Davis,		Westfield,	"	31, 1862	February 12, 1864, Hospital Steward, U.S.A.
Andrew Day,	325 00	Colrain,	Jan.	4, 1864	June 14, 1865, transferred to 24th Infantry.
Frederick M. Day,		Southwick,	July	31, 1862	June 16, 1865, expiration of service.
Joseph Deering,	325 00	Deerfield,	Dec.	15, 1863	June 14, 1865, transferred to 24th Infantry.
Dwight L. Dickinson,		Westfield,	July	31, 1862	June 16, 1865, expiration of service.
James H. Elliott,		Westfield,	"	31, 1862	February 4, 1865, disability.
Joseph M. Ellis,		Westfield,	"	33, 1862	June 16, 1865, "
Samuel D. Ely,		Westfield,	"	21, 1862	June 16, 1865, "
Charles T. Everton,	325 00	Westfield,	"	31, 1862	June 16, 1865, expiration of service.
Thomas Faron,		Millbury,	Jan.	5, 1864	June 14, 1865, transferred to 24th Infantry.
Henry M. Field,		Southwick,	July	31, 1862	April '64, for prom'n as Lieut., 36th U.S.C.T.
Homer F. Fox,		Westfield,	"	21, 1862	February 25, 1864.
Lucius G. Fox,		Westfield,	"	31, 1862	June 16, 1865, expiration of service.
Eli J. Gardner,		Brimfield,	"	31, 1862	June 14, 1865, disability.
Francis S. Gardner,	190 00	Brimfield,	"	31, 1862	May 23, 1865, disability from wounds.
Horace M. Gardner,		Southwick,	Sept.	2, 1863	
Amos Gaylord,		Westfield,	July	31, 1862	December 16, 1864, died at Annapolis, Md.
Joseph H. Gibbens,		Westfield,	"	31, 1862	December 19, 1862, died of disease.
Solomon S. Giddings,		Westfield,	"	31, 1862	May 25, 1865, order War Department.
Christopher Goddard,		New Braintree,	August	5, 1862	February 8, 1863.
John H. Goetz,		Westfield,	July	31, 1862	May 15, 1864, killed in battle.
Marcus M. Goodell,	325 00	Brimfield,	"	31, 1862	June 16, 1865, expiration of service.
Thomas Harty,		Phillipston,	Feb.	15, 1860	June 14, 1865, transferred to 24th Infantry.
Franklin Hayden,		Westfield,	August	5, 1862	April 12, 1865, died at Annapolis, Md.
Edward W. Hitchcock,		Brimfield,	July	31, 1862	June 16, 1865, expiration of service.
James Hogan,		Russell,	"	31, 1862	"
John R. Houghton,		Greenwich,	"	31, 1862	December 11, 1862, died of disease.
Daniel Hurley,	325 00	Worcester,	August	2, 1862	February 11, 1864, died Harper's Ferry, Va.
Ariel Hutchins,	325 00	Springfield,	Dec.	30, 1863	June 14, 1865, transferred to 24th Infantry.
Arad Johnson,		New Salem,	Dec.	2, 1863	May 15, 1864, killed in battle.
William Johnson,		Southwick,	July	31, 1862	August 13, 1864, died at Andersonville, Ga.
Ransom C. Kenny,	325 00	Hawley,	August	30, 1864	June 14, 1865, transferred to 24th Infantry.
David A. Kingman,	402 66	Northbridge,	Dec.	31, 1863	"
George Knapp, Jr.		Westfield,	Dec.	29, 1683	June 14, 1865, "

THIRTY-FOURTH MASSACHUSETTS INFANTRY.

Company D.—Continued.

NAME AND RANK.	Bounty.	Residence or Place Credited to.	Date of Muster.	Termination of Service and cause thereof.
John T. Knox,	....	Southwick,	July 31, 1862	June 16, 1865, expiration of service.
Charles D. Lamson,	....	Westfield,	July 31, 1862	June 16, 1865, " "
William J. Lamb,	....	Phillipston,	August 5, 1862	January 25, 1864, transferred to V. R. C.
John A. Lewis,	....	Worcester,	July 31, 1862	November 16, 1863, died of disease.
Moses B. Loomis,	....	Westfield,	July 31, 1862	January 7, 1863, deserted.
Charles D. Manning,	325 00	Springfield,	Dec. 30, 1863	June 14, 1865, transferred to 24th Infantry.
Julius Miller,	....	Westfield,	July 31, 1862	May 15, 1864, wounded and captured.
Wesley Mixter,	....	Westfield,	July 31, 1862	June 16, 1865, expiration of service.
James Morse,	....	Westfield,	July 31, 1862	August 17, 1862, deserted.
Charles D. Mullett,	460 00	Barre,	Dec. 9, 1863	February 22, 1865, died at Annapolis, Md.
Peter Myoue,	....	New Braintree,	July 31, 1862	May 20, 1865, order War Department.
Patrick O'Brien,	....	Westfield,	July 31, 1862	February 4, 1865, disability from wounds.
Frederick S. Phelps,	....	Brimfield,	July 31, 1862	June 16, 1865, expiration of service.
Augustus Plant,	....	Russell,	July 31, 1862	June 16, 1865, " "
George Pratt,	325 00	Clinton,	Jan. 4, 1864	June 14, 1865, transferred to 24th Infantry.
Roland Rising,	....	Westfield,	July 31, 1862	June 16, 1865, expiration of service.
Samuel P. Robbins,	....	Greenwich,	July 31, 1862	February 8, 1864, transferred to V. R. C.
Homer Russell,	....	Westfield,	July 31, 1862	November 11, 1862, disability.
Rising Rutan,	....	Brimfield,	July 31, 1862	February 8, 1864, transferred to V. R. C.
Henry H. Saunders,	....	Southwick,	July 31, 1862	June 16, 1865, expiration of service.
Bernard Schledin,	....	Northborough,	July 31, 1862	June 22, 1865, " "
Lewis Seymour,	....	Westfield,	August 5, 1862	April 25, 1863, disability.
Alfred A. Sibley,	....	Rowe,	July 31, 1862	June 16, 1865, expiration of service.
Philo Sibley, Jr.,	325 00	Westfield,	Dec. 15, 1863	June 14, 1865, transferred to 24th Infantry.
Richard Smy,	....	Southwick,	July 31, 1862	September 19, 1864, killed in battle.
James Snow,	....	Westfield,	July 31, 1862	June 3, 1865, disability.
Martin D. Sperry,	....	North Adams,	July 31, 1862	May 23, 1863, "
John W. Stafford,	325 00	Rowe,	August 5, 1862	September 16, 1862, deserted.
Luther Stafford,	....	Southwick,	Dec. 8, 1863	January 22, 1865, died at Salisbury, N. C.
Pierson S. Stillman,	325 00	Brimfield,	July 31, 1862	June 12, 1865, order War Department.
William G. Stone,	....	Greenfield,	July 31, 1862	June 16, 1865, expiration of service.
Paul J. Tatro,	325 00	Westfield,	October 5, 1863	June 3, 1865, order War Department.
Morris A. Toomey,	....	Westfield,	July 31, 1862	November 19, 1863, disability.
Charles L. Trask,	....	Worcester,	October 20, 1863	January 25, 1864, transferred to V. R. C.
Francis L. Verona,	325 00	Westfield,	July 31, 1862	June 14, 1865, transferred to 24th Infantry.
Thomas Wagner,	....	Westfield,	July 31, 1862	October 13, 1864, killed in battle.

THIRTY-FOURTH MASSACHUSETTS INFANTRY. 449

Name		Residence			
John Walsh,		Shelburne,	Jan. 15, 1864	325 00	June 14, 1865, transferred to 24th Infantry.
Simeon Ward,		Westfield,	August 5, 1862	....	June 16, 1865, expiration of service.
Henry Wells,		Westfield,	July 31, 1862	....	January 4, 1863, disability.
Henry Whitman,		Montgomery,	" 31, 1862	325 00	April 2, 1865, killed in battle.
Alonzo M. Wilson,		Rowe,	Dec. 8, 1863	190 00	June 14, 1865, transferred to 24th Infantry.
* Horace J. Williams		Oxford,	Sept. 2, 1864		

Company H.

Name		Residence			
Daniel M. Damon, 1st Sergeant,		Lancaster,	July 31, 1862	....	May 15, 1865, 2d Lieutenant.
Melville E. Walker, 1st Sergeant,		Worcester,	" 31, 1862	....	June 18, 1863, 2d Lieutenant.
Charles Wood, 1st Sergeant,		Ashburnham,	" 31, 1862	....	May 15, 1865, 2d Lieutenant.
Malcolm Ammidon, Sergeant,		Southbridge,	" 31, 1862	....	August 13, 1862, 2d Lieutenant.
Stephen Blackmer, Sergeant,		Southbridge,	" 31, 1862	....	March 4, 1864, died at Harper's Ferry.
Daniel Buckley, Sergeant,		Webster,	" 31, 1862	....	May 25, 1865, disability.
George Congdon, Sergeant,		Southbridge,	" 31, 1862	....	March 23, 1865, disability.
Joseph B. Corey, Sergeant,		Southbridge,	" 31, 1862	....	June 16, 1865, expiration of service.
George H. Dean, Sergeant,		Southbridge,	" 31, 1862	....	June 16, 1865, "
Harlan P. Houghton, Sergeant,		West Boylston,	" 31, 1862	....	October 18, 1864, 2d Lieutenant.
Frank C. Kinnicutt, Sergeant,		Worcester,	" 31, 1862	....	July 29, 1863, 2d Lieutenant.
Robert B. Sinclair, Sergeant,		Worcester,	June 22, 1862	....	February 19, 1863, disability.
George W. Corey, Corporal,		Southbridge,	July 31, 1862	....	June 16, 1865, expiration of service.
Albert O. Blanchard, Corporal,		Southbridge,	" 31, 1862	....	May 26, 1864, accidentally shot and killed.
Charles E. Blackman, Corporal,		Southbridge,	" 31, 1862	....	June 16, 1865, expiration of service.
Solon W. Chaplin, Corporal,		Lancaster,	" 31, 1862	....	July 5, 1864, killed in battle.
John A. Farnsworth, Corporal,		Lancaster,	" 31, 1862	....	May 18, 1865, order War Department.
John E. Farnsworth, Corporal,		Southbridge,	" 31, 1862	....	June 16, 1865, expiration of service.
George E. Hubbard, Corporal,		Leicester,	" 31, 1862	....	June 16, 1865, "
Rufus H. Newton, Corporal,		Southbridge,	" 31, 1862	....	Sept. 6, 1865, exp. service, dis. from wounds.
Eber C. Pratt, Corporal,		Lancaster,	" 31, 1862	....	August 26, 1863, Lieut. in U. S. C. T.
Charles B. Tisdale, Corporal,		Leicester,	" 31, 1862	....	January 8, 1863, disability.
Henry E. Williams, Corporal,		Worcester,	" 31, 1862	....	May 25, 1865, "
William K. Morse, Musician,		Ashburnham,	" 31, 1862	....	June 16, 1865, expiration of service.
Walter O. Parker,		Worcester,	" 31, 1862	....	June 16, 1865, "
Benjamin Adams,		Southbridge,	Nov. 12, 1863	$325 00	February 2, 1865, transferred to V. R. C.
Linus C. Albee,		Upton,	July 31, 1862	....	June 16, 1865, expiration of service.
Charles W. Aldrich,		Uxbridge,	" 31, 1862	....	February 11, 1864, transferred to V. R. C.
Henry Anson,		Southbridge,	" 31, 1862	325 00	Transferred to V. R. C.
Nathan B. Angell,		Southbridge,	Feb. 25, 1864	....	June 14, 1865, transferred to 24th Infantry.
Franklin Arms,		Southbridge,	July 31, 1862	....	January 8, 1863, disability.

* Not on Regimental Book.

450   THIRTY-FOURTH MASSACHUSETTS INFANTRY.

Name and Rank.	Bounty.	Residence or Place Credited to.	Date of Muster.	Termination of Service and cause thereof.
Company H.—Continued.				
Harrison G. O. Bacon,		Webster,	July 31, 1862	July 3, 1863, disability.
John A. Barr,		Leicester,	" 31, 1862	February 11, 1864, transferred to V. R. C.
Edwin S. Beecher,		Southbridge,	" 31, 1862	June 16, 1865, expiration of service.
Edwin Bennett,		Southbridge,	" 31, 1862	December 20, 1862, disability.
Sumner W. Black,		Ashburnham,	" 31, 1862	November 20, 1863, died of disease.
Charles E. Blood,	325 00	Lancaster,	Dec. 19, 1863	June 14, 1865, transferred to 24th Infantry.
Michael Bowler,		Southbridge,	July 31, 1862	June 16, 1865, expiration of service.
Dennis Breen,	325 00	Webster,	" 31, 1862	June 18, 1864, killed in battle.
James A. Bridge,		Lancaster,	Dec. 19, 1863	May 15, 1864, killed in battle.
Jonas H. Brown,		Lancaster,	July 31, 1862	June 16, 1865, expiration of service.
Sanford Broadbent,		Southbridge,	" 31, 1862	June 5, 1865, disability.
John Bryson,		Southbridge,	" 31, 1862	June 1, 1865, disability.
James Buckley,		Webster,	" 31, 1862	February 11, 1864, transferred to V. R. C.
Levi B. Burbank,		Lancaster,	" 31, 1862	February 27, 1864, disability.
Elisha W. Buxton,		Chariton,	" 31, 1862	September 4, 1862, died of disease.
Arnold Capron,		Southbridge,	" 31, 1862	June 5, 1864, killed in battle.
Edward G. Carey,		Monson,	" 31, 1862	May 26, 1865, disability.
Alfred Castle,		Ashburnham,	" 31, 1862	February 11, 1865, order War Department.
William H. Cheney,		Southbridge,	" 31, 1862	June 16, 1865, expiration of service.
George B. Colburn,		Lancaster,	" 31, 1862	May 16, 1865, disability.
Patrick Coffay,		Webster,	" 31, 1862	May 20, 1863, disability.
Thomas Comerford,	325 00	Webster,	Dec. 7, 1863	June 14, 1865, transferred to 24th Infantry.
Walter B. Cutting,		Southbridge,	July 31, 1862	October 13, 1864, killed in battle.
Joseph N. Day,	325 00	Lancaster,	Jan. 4, 1864	June 14, 1865, transferred to 24th Infantry.
James Daily,		Lancaster,	July 31, 1862	June 16, 1865, expiration of service.
Joseph Duprey,		Webster,	" 31, 1862	"
James Dillon,		Lancaster,	" 31, 1862	April 7, 1863, disability.
David Fairfield,		Southbridge,	" 31, 1862	June 17, 1865, expiration of service.
Francis H. Fairbanks,	325 00	Lancaster,	" 31, 1862	January 5, 1865, died at Salisbury, N. C.
George W. Farnsworth,		Lancaster,	Jan. 4, 1864	June 8, 1865, disability.
Richard Farrell,		Dudley,	July 31, 1862	February 11, 1864, transferred to V. R. C.
Daniel Finn,	325 00	Deerfield,	Jan. 15, 1864	January 15, 1865, "
Francis L. Flanley,	325 00	Worcester,	Oct. 19, 1863	June 11, 1865, disability from wounds.
Arthur L. Fox,	325 00	Worcester,	Jan. 5, 1864	June 5, 1864, killed in battle.
John L. Fox,	325 00	Boston,	Dec. 16, 1863	June 14, 1865, transferred to 24th Infantry.
Michael H. Furey,		Lancaster,	July 31, 1862	August 5, 1865, expiration of service.

THIRTY-FOURTH MASSACHUSETTS INFANTRY.

Name	Bounty	Town	Date		Remarks
Thomas Gallagher,	325 00	Clinton,	Dec.	7, 1863	June 14, 1865, transferred to 24th Infantry.
Martin Grady,		Webster,	June	22, 1862	June 16, 1863, expiration of service.
Stephen W. Gray,		Lancaster,	July	31, 1862	April 2, 1864, died of disease.
Henry G. Green,		Southbridge,	"	31, 1862	March 19, 1864, disability.
Horace M. Green,		Oakham,	"	13, 1862	June 16, 1865, expiration of service.
Martin V. B. Grimes,		Ashburnham,	"	31, 1862	February 16, 1865, disability.
Alfred H. Hall,		Upton,	"	31, 1862	September 18, 1863, disability.
William F. Harding	325 00	Amesbury,	Nov.	12, 1863	June 14, 1865, transferred to 24th Infantry.
James Hill,		Auburn,	July	13, 1862	May 25, 1863, disability.
William C. Hoard,		Uxbridge,	"	31, 1862	August 10, 1862, deserted.
Michael Hogan,	325 00	Dudley,	Dec.	15, 1863	June 14, 1865, transferred to 24th Infantry.
Frederick L. Holmes,		Southbridge,	July	31, 1862	July 8, 1865, expiration of service.
George O. Holman,		Worcester,	"	13, 1862	June 16, 1865, " " "
George G. Horton,	325 00	Huntington,	January	4, 1864	June 14, 1865, transferred to 24th Infantry.
James Houghton,	540 33	West Boylston,	"	4, 1864	June 14, 1865, " " "
Andrew Hoyle,		Webster,	July	31, 1862	May 31, 1865, disability.
Edwin Hoyle,		Millbury,	August	4, 1862	June 16, 1865, expiration of service.
Thomas A. G. Hunting,		Lancaster,	July	31, 1862	May 23, 1865, disability.
John H. Jordan,		Dudley,	August	4, 1862	June 16, 1865, expiration of service.
Thomas Keating,		Webster,	July	31, 1862	June 16, 1865, " " "
Edward Keough,		Canton,	June	22, 1862	August 10, 1862, deserted.
Franklin B. King,		Leicester,	July	31, 1862	February 11, 1864, transferred to V. R. C.
Henry C. Lamberton,		Ware,	"	31, 1862	May 19, 1865, disability.
Ebenezer Leach,		Southbridge,	"	13, 1862	December 27, 1862, disability.
David T. T. Litchfield,		Southbridge,	"	31, 1862	June 16, 1865, expiration of service.
Michael Mahan,		Webster,	"	31, 1862	February 11, 1864, transferred to V. R. C.
Mathew Malloy,		Leicester,	"	13, 1862	February 11, 1864, " " "
David Marcy,		Southbridge,	"	31, 1862	June 16, 1865, expiration of service.
Samuel Marsh,		Webster,	"	31, 1862	June 16, 1865, " " "
David W. Matthews,	50 00	Lancaster,	Sept.	19, 1863	June 14, 1865, transferred to 24th Infantry.
George W. Matthews,	50 00	Lancaster,	"	31, 1863	June 1, 1865, disability.
Morris McNancy,		Monson,	July	11, 1863	Feb. 8, 1865, died at Salisbury, S. C.
Enos Messier,	325 00	Clinton,	Dec.	31, 1863	Sept. 23, 1864, died at Andersonville, Ga.
William H. Miller,		Lancaster,	July	22, 1862	Jan. 19, 1865, transferred to V. R. C.
Patrick Moriarty,		Webster,	June	31, 1864	June 16, 1865, transferred to 24th Infantry.
Andrew H. Morse,	325 00	Southbridge,	March	21, 1863	June 14, 1865, " " "
William Partenhiemer,	325 00	Greenfield,	Jan.	28, 1864	August 14, 1864, died at Frederic City, Md.
Edwin Pendergrast,		Webster,	July	31, 1862	June 16, 1865, expiration of service.
Solomon Pippin,		Webster,	"	31, 1862	May 2, 1863, disability.
Karl Pohlman,	325 00	Greenfield,	Feb.	13, 1864	June 13, 1865, disability.

THIRTY-FOURTH MASSACHUSETTS INFANTRY.

NAME AND RANK.	Bounty.	Residence or Place Credited to.	Date of Muster.	Termination of Service and cause thereof.
Company H.—Continued.				
Frank Pollard,	325 00	Leicester,	Jan. 4, 1864	Nov. 19, 1865, disability from wounds.
David Power,	325 00	Millbury,	Dec. 29, 1863	May 25, 1865, order War Department.
Michael Powers,		Webster,	July 31, 1862	June 9, 1865, "
Maurice Reynolds,	325 00	Southbridge,	July 31, 1862	June 16, 1865, expiration of service.
Louis Rivers,		Southbridge,	March 4, 1864	June 14, 1865, transferred to 24th Infantry.
Robert Robinson,	325 00	Webster,	July 31, 1862	Feb. 11, 1864, transferred to V. R. C.
Henry Buddy,	325 00	Deerfield,	Jan. 25, 1864	Feb. 11, 1864, transferred to 24th Infantry.
Lawrence Ryan,		Dudley,	Dec. 7, 1863	June 14, 1865, transferred to 24th Infantry.
James Ryan,		Southbridge,	July 13, 1863	June 16, 1865, expiration of service.
Malachi Ryan,		Webster,	" 31, 1862	Feb. 11, 1863, deserted.
Joseph D. Schofield,		Webster,	" 31, 1862	Feb. 26, 1863, died of disease.
William A. Sears,	325 00	Southbridge,	" 7, 1862	June 20, 1864, died of wounds.
Patrick Sherry,		Lancaster,	Jan. 5, 1864	June 14, 1865, transferred to 24th Infantry.
Paul Soubrie,		Webster,	July 31, 1862	June 16, 1865, expiration of service.
Woodbury C. Smith,		Worcester,	" 31, 1862	January 10, 1864, for promotion.
Henry F. Southwick,	325 00	Leicester,	Jan. 1, 1864	June 14, 1865, transferred to 24th Infantry.
Chauncey Stafford, Jr.	325 00	Rowe,	Dec. 8, 1862	June 14, 1865, "
Charles E. Tisdale,		Charlton,	July 19, 1862	January 8, 1863, disability.
Alexander Wald,		Southbridge,	" 31, 1862	December 18, 1863, disability.
Lorin A. Walker,		Upton,	" 31, 1862	May 15, 1864, killed in battle.
Joshua A. Webber,		Charlton,	" 31, 1862	August 18, 1862, deserted.
George E. Wiley,	325 00	Lancaster,	Jan. 1, 1864	June 14, 1865, transferred to 24th Infantry.
George H. Wild,		Worcester,	July 31, 1862	June 20, 1865, expiration of service.
Company I.				
Joseph N. Clark, 1st Sergeant,		South Hadley,	July 31, 1862	June 13, 1865, disability.
Robert J. Hamilton, 1st Serg't.		Springfield,	" 13, 1862	May 25, 1863, Captain 55th Infantry.
Charles I. Woods, 1st Sergeant,		Worcester,	" 31, 1862	September 20, 1864, 2d Lieutenant.
William A. Barton, Sergeant,		Ware,	" 13, 1862	November 24, 1862, disability.
Thomas Conner, Sergeant,		Barre,	" 31, 1862	June 16, 1865, expiration of service.
Thomas E. Emery, Sergeant,		Springfield,	" 31, 1862	May 31, 1865, disability.
Leander E. Fisher, Sergeant,		Holyoke,	" 31, 1862	February 15, 1864, transferred to V. R. C.
Allen E. King, Sergeant,		Barre,	" 13, 1862	June 6, 1863, disability.
William A. Phetteplace, Serg't.		Wales,	" 31, 1862	October 19, 1864, killed in battle.
Walter W. Scott, Sergeant,		Leicester,	" 31, 1862	June 18, 1865, 2d Lieutenant.

THIRTY-FOURTH MASSACHUSETTS INFANTRY. 453

Name			Residence	Date of Muster		Remarks
Albert C. Spear, Sergeant,	.	.	Worcester,	July	31, 1862	June 16, 1865, expiration of service.
Joseph W. Webber, Sergeant,	.	.	Worcester,	"	31, 1862	September 19, 1864, killed in battle.
Azur W. Barlow, Corporal,	.	.	Worcester,	"	31, 1862	June 16, 1865, expiration of service.
Michael Carney, Corporal,	.	.	Barre,	"	13, 1862	February 2, '65, transferred to V. R. C.
Willard Darling, Corporal,	.	.	Palmer,	"	31, 1862	June 16, 1865, expiration of service.
William M. Fay, Corporal,	.	.	Warren,	"	31, 1862	May 20, 1863, died of wounds.
George H Gilbert, Corporal,	.	.	Worcester,	"	31, 1862	May 4, 1865, died of wounds.
Lucien Gilbert, Corporal,	.	.	Warren,	"	31, 1862	June 16, 1865, expiration of service.
John Kirkpatrick, Corporal,	.	.	South Hadley,	"	31, 1862	June 16, 1865, "
Reuben G. Tuttle, Corporal,	.	.	Springfield,	"	31, 1862	Transferred to V. R. C.
William A. White, Corporal,	.	.	Barre,	"	13, 1862	June 15, 1865, expiration of service.
John H. Wiswell, Corporal,	.	.	Warren,	"	31, 1862	March 23, 1865, died at Wilmington, N. C.
Henry A. Crocker, Musician,	.	.	Ware,	June	23, 1862	June 21, 1864, died of wounds.
Edward L. Drake, Musician,	.	.	West Brookfield,	June	22, 1862	May 29, 1865, order War Department.
Elias A. Bassett, Wagoner,	.	.	Ware,	July	22, 1862	June 16, 1865, expiration of service.
George E. Adams,	.	.	West Brookfield,	"	31, 1862	May 15, 1864, killed in battle.
John W. Adams,	.	.	West Brookfield,	"	31, 1862	April 19, 1865, disability.
Elbridge B. Ainsworth,	.	.	Warren,	"	31, 1862	May 29, 1863, disability.
Albert A. Aldrich,	.	.	West Brookfield,	"	31, 1862	May 7, 1863, disability.
Charles H. Allen,	.	.	Brookfield,	"	31, 1862	January 14, 1863, disability.
Edward G. Babcock,	.	.	Ware,	Dec.	13, 1862	June 16, 1865, exp. of service, absent sick.
Edwin A. Barr,	$325 00	.	Worcester,	July	12, 1863	March 1, 1864, died of disease.
Edwin W. Barlow,	325 00	.	West Brookfield,	"	31, 1862	July 18, 1864, killed in battle.
Sylvanus Barlow,	.	.	South Hadley,	Jan.	2, 1864	May 29, 1865, disability.
Peter Baum,	.	.	Ware,	August	4, 1862	June 16, 1865, expiration of service.
Charles I. Bemis,	.	.	Springfield,	July	31, 1862	June 16, 1865, "
Joseph M. Blake,	.	.	Warren,	"	31, 1862	June 14, 1865, transferred to 24th Infantry.
George Bliss,	.	.	Worcester,	Nov.	23, 1862	December 26, 1862, disability.
Charles H. Bliss,	.	.	Ware,	July	31, 1862	V. R. C.
Daniel Bliss,	.	.	Ware,	"	31, 1862	December 11, 1864, died at Danville, Va.
Daniel Boyle,	.	.	Leicester,	"	31, 1862	August 28, 1863, transferred to V. R. C.
Joseph R. Brooks,	.	.	Worcester,	"	31, 1862	January 29, 1863, disability.
John Buckley,	325 00	.	Barre,	Jan.	13, 1862	June 14, 1865, transferred to 24th Infantry.
Casper Burkhardt,	325 00	.	Deerfield,	July	22, 1864	June 16, 1865, expiration of service.
Pliny F. Barr,	.	.	Worcester,	Nov.	31, 1862	June 14, 1865, transferred to 24th Infantry.
Joseph H. Campbell,	.	.	Greenfield,	July	5, 1863	June 16, 1865, expiration of service.
Ephraim C. Carey,	.	.	Worcester,	"	31, 1862	June 16, 1865, "
Almon R. Caswell,	.	.	Worcester,	"	31, 1862	June 16, 1865, "
Lorenzo Chickering,	.	.	West Brookfield,	"	31, 1862	Sept. 19, 1864, killed in battle.
Daniel W. Cole,	.	.	Wales,	"	31, 1862	June 27, 1865, expiration of service.
James Connell,	.	.	Ware,	"	13, 1862	February 18, 1864, transferred to V. R. C.

35

THIRTY-FOURTH MASSACHUSETTS INFANTRY.

Company I.—Continued.

Name and Rank.	Bounty.	Residence or Place Credited to.	Date of Muster.	Termination of Service and cause thereof.
Edwin L. Crouch,	325 00	Wales,	Jan. 1, 1864	May 21, 1864, died of wounds.
*Charles Cutler,	325 00	West Brookfield,	March 15, 1864	July 30, 1864, died.
George W. Darling,	....	Palmer,	July 13, 1862	June 8, 1863, disability.
Gardner E. Davis,	....	Barre,	" 13, 1862	June 16, 1865, expiration of service.
Christopher L. Delmage,	....	Holyoke,	" 31, 1862	December 7, 1862, deserted.
Francis J. Denny,	....	Ware,	" 31, 1862	Sept. 20, 1864, died at Andersonville, Ga.
Theodore Dodge,	....	Warren,	June 22, 1862	June 16, 1865, expiration of service.
Michael Donnelly,	....	Holyoke,	July 13, 1862	"
John Farley,	....	Worcester,	" 31, 1862	June 19, 1865, dishonorably.
George H. Fellows,	325 00	New Marlborough,	Nov. 18, 1863	June 14, 1865, transferred to 24th Infantry.
Samuel L. Perry,	....	Palmer,	July 13, 1862	June 16, 1865, expiration of service.
John H. Foley,	325 00	South Hadley,	Jan. 4, 1864	June 14, 1865, transferred to 24th Infantry.
William Foley,	325 00	Warren,	" 1, 1864	May 15, 1864, killed in battle.
Harvey Gilbert,	....	Worcester,	July 31, 1862	June 16, 1865, expiration of service.
Dominick Goodson,	....	Springfield,	" 31, 1862	"
Frank W. Gordon,	....	Palmer,	" 31, 1862	May 7, 1863, disability.
Lewis Gravoll,	325 00	Warren,	Dec. 19, 1863	March 14, 1865, disability.
Charles E. Hannum,	....	Ware,	June 22, 1862	June 16, 1865, expiration of service.
Charles B. Harback,	325 00	Warren,	Dec. 26, 1863	June 14, 1865, transferred to 24th Infantry.
Maurice Hartnett,	325 00	Warren,	Dec. 30, 1863	Aug. 27, 1864, died at Andersonville, Ga.
Michael Harrington,	....	Wales,	July 31, 1862	June 2, 1863, deserted.
George D. Haven,	325 00	South Hadley,	" 31, 1862	November 23, 1863, disability.
Andrew Herman,	....	Deerfield,	Jan. 24, 1864	October 19, 1864, killed in battle.
Edwin Hobbs,	....	Wales,	July 31, 1862	June 16, 1865, expiration of service.
Otis D. Holden,	....	Ware,	" 31, 1862	June 16, 1865, "
Bradford R. Holmes,	....	Worcester,	" 31, 1862	July 28, 1865, "
William A. Howard,	....	Ware,	" 31, 1862	February 18, 1864, transferred to V. R. C.
Charles L. Johnston,	....	Enfield,	" 31, 1862	June 16, 1866, expiration of service.
Andrew J. James,	....	South Hadley,	" 13, 1862	March 4, 1864, transferred to V. R. C.
James Kenney,	50 00	South Hadley,	Sept. 21, 1863	May 7, 1863, disability.
Michael Kennedy,	....	Monson,	June 22, 1862	June 14, 1865, transferred to 24th Infantry.
George H. Lester,	50 00	Pittsfield,	Sept. 29, 1863	May 15, 1864, killed in battle.
Jerry Logan,	....	Warren,	July 31, 1862	May 31, 1865, disability.
Eleazer May,	....	Worcester,	" 31, 1862	May 13, 1865, disability.
John McClusky,	....	Worcester,	" 31, 1862	May 18, 1863, disability.
George McComb,	....	South Hadley,	" 31, 1862	May 18, 1865, order War Department.

THIRTY-FOURTH MASSACHUSETTS INFANTRY.

Name		Bounty	Residence	Date	Remarks
Charles Moore,	. . .	. . .	Roxbury,	October 5, 1864	June 14, 1865, transferred to 24th Infantry.
Edwin H. Moore,	. . .	$325 00	Worcester,	June 22, 1862	June 16, 1865, expiration of service.
George Moran,	. . .	. . .	Worcester,	June 17, 1862	July 30, 1864, died of sun stroke.
Patrick Moriarty,	. . .	325 00	South Hadley,	Dec. 2, 1863	June 14, 1865, transferred to 24th Infantry.
James Mundell,	. . .	. . .	Worcester,	July 31, 1862	June 16, 1865, expiration of service.
John A. Needham,	. . .	. . .	Worcester,	" 31, 1862	" " "
Willard B. Needham,	. . .	325 00	Wales,	Dec. 30, 1863	October 13, 1864, killed in battle.
James O'Neil,	. . .	325 00	Warren,	Dec. 18, 1863	May 15, '64, died in enemy's hands of wds.
John O'Neil,	. . .	325 00	Warren,	Dec. 28, 1863	February 18, 1865, disability.
Joseph B. Quivillon,	. . .	. . .	Worcester,	July 31, 1862	June 14, 1865, transferred to 24th Infantry.
Michael Rice,	. . .	. . .	Ware,	" 13, 1862	May 7, 1863, disability.
Henry L. Ross,	. . .	. . .	Leicester,	" 13, 1862	July 28, 1865, expiration of service.
Frank Sherman,	. . .	. . .	Worcester,	" 31, 1862	June 16, 1865, " "
Thomas P. Shumway,	. . .	. . .	Warren,	" 31, 1862	February 15, 1864, transferred to V. R. C.
Charles H. Skidmore,	. . .	325 00	South Hadley,	Dec. 31, 1862	June 16, 1865, expiration of service.
David A. Smith,	. . .	. . .	Monson,	" 21, 1863	July 6, 1865, " "
Dennis Smith,	. . .	325 00	Worcester,	July 31, 1862	July 31, 1864, died of wounds.
Samuel Smith,	. . .	. . .	West Brookfield,	Jan. 2, 1864	June 16, 1865, expiration of service.
Daniel C. Spear,	. . .	. . .	Ware,	July 31, 1862	June 14, 1865, transferred to 24th Infantry.
William H. Spear,	. . .	. . .	Worcester,	" 31, 1862	October 10, 1862, deserted.
Samuel St. Peter,	. . .	. . .	Monson,	Dec. 21, 1863	February 18, 1864, transferred to V. R. C.
Albert M. Stewart,	. . .	. . .	Worcester,	July 31, 1862	May 20, 1864, died of wounds.
Charles A. Stebbins,	. . .	. . .	Worcester,	" 31, 1862	August 10, 1862, deserted.
Charles Stockwell,	. . .	325 00	South Hadley,	" 31, 1862	May 15, 1864, killed in battle.
Harry B. Stone,	. . .	. . .	Greenfield,	Nov. 9, 1863	March 27, 1865, disability from wounds.
Harry C. Truesdell,	. . .	. . .	Worcester,	July 31, 1862	June 14, 1865, transferred to 24th Infantry.
John Wagner,	. . .	. . .	Worcester,	" 31, 1862	April 2, 1865, killed in battle.
Charles Walker,	. . .	325 00	South Hadley,	" 31, 1862	March 7, 1864, died of disease.
Charles H. Walker,	. . .	325 00	Colerain,	Jan. 11, 1864	June 16, 1865, expiration of service.
Alfred D. Washburn,	. . .	. . .	Wales,	Dec. 30, 1863	June 14, 1865, transferred to 24th Infantry.
Charles L. White,	. . .	. . .	Worcester,	July 31, 1862	April 1, 1865, transferred to V. R. C.
John T. White,	. . .	. . .	Barre,	" 13, 1862	July 24, 1864, died of disease.
Austin F. Wilson,	. . .	. . .	Barre,	" 13, 1862	June 16, 1865, expiration of service.
George G. Williams,	. . .	. . .	Warren,	" 31, 1862	November 28, 1864, disability.
Abner Wolcott,	. . .	325 00	Wales,	" 31, 1862	June 16, 1865, expiration of service.
Edward J. Wright,	. . .	325 00	Worcester,	" 31, 1863	May 29, 1865, disability.
Franklin T. Wright,	. . .	. . .	Worcester,	" 31, 1862	June 16, 1865, expiration of service.
					August 12, 1863, disability.

Company K.

Name and Rank.	Bounty.	Residence or Place Credited to.	Date of Muster.	Termination of Service and cause thereof.
Cornelius Burley, 1st Sergeant,		Pittsfield,	July 31, 1862	December 16, 1864, disability.
Robert J. Gardner, 1st Sergeant,		Egremont,	" 31, 1862	May 1, 1865, 2d Lieutenant.
Abram M. Chapman, Sergeant,		Becket,	" 31, 1862	May 18, 1865, disability.
William B. Clark, Sergeant,		Granby,	" 31, 1862	January 21, 1864, Lieut., U. S. C. T.
Edward R. Emerson, Sergeant,		Pittsfield,	" 31, 1862	June 6, 1863, Lieut., 54th Infantry.
Franklin W. Hull, Sergeant,		Hancock,	" 31, 1862	November 2, 1863, Lieut., U. S. C. T.
Arthur Marks, Sergeant,		Pittsfield,	" 31, 1862	January 1, 1864, Lieut., U. S. C. T.
Horace Putnam, Sergeant,		Millbury,	August 5, 1862	May 25, 1865, disability.
George W. Robinson, Sergeant,		Worthington,	July 13, 1862	June 16, 1865, expiration of service.
Robert M. Smith, Sergeant,		Granby,	" 31, 1862	June 14, 1865, disability.
Edward W. Chapin, Corporal,		Richmond,	" 31, 1862	March 22, 1865, disability.
Ephriam B. Church, Corporal,		Egremont,	" 31, 1862	June 16, 1865, expiration of service.
Harvey Clapp, Corporal,		Millbury,	August 5, 1862	June 16, 1865, "
Noah A. Clark, Corporal,		Pittsfield,	July 31, 1862	October 18, 1863, killed in battle.
James Cowan, Corporal,		Pittsfield,	" 31, 1862	May 4, 1865, disability.
Orrin H. Granville, Corporal,		Boston,	" 31, 1862	November 2, 1863, promoted in U. S. C. T.
Thomas J. Phillips, Corporal,		Hancock,	" 31, 1862	August 31, 1865, disability.
William H. Porter, Corporal,		Pittsfield,	" 31, 1862	June 16, 1865, expiration of service.
James Rawdon, Corporal,		Leicester,	" 13, 1862	April 8, 1865, died of wounds April 2.
Nathan L. Robinson, Corporal,		Pittsfield,	" 31, 1862	June 16, 1865, expiration of service.
Ensign M. Smith, Corporal,		Dalton,	" 31, 1862	June 16, 1865, "
William H. Tucker,		Hardwick,	" 31, 1862	June 16, 1865, exp. service, absent wounded.
George H. Carpenter, Musician,		Pittsfield,	" 31, 1862	June 16, 1865, expiration of service.
Edgar P. Fairbanks, Musician,		Pittsfield,	" 31, 1862	November —, 1862, died of disease.
Julius F. Rockwell, Wag.,		Pittsfield,	" 31, 1862	June 16, 1865, expiration of service.
Edward B. Anthony,		Pittsfield,	" 31, 1862	Dec. 12, 1864, disability.
John M. Anthony,		Peru,	" 31, 1862	May 29, 1865, disability.
Charles G. Askey,		Hinsdale,	" 31, 1862	February 11, 1864, transferred to V. R. C.
John P. Bambush,		Holden,	" 31, 1862	June 16, 1865, expiration of service.
Charles H. Boyden,	$325 00	Brookfield,	Dec. 2, 1863	June 14, 1865, transferred to 24th Infantry.
Francis T. Bartlett,		Worthington,	July 31, 1862	December 31, 1863, died of disease.
Russell Bartlett,		Granby,	" 31, 1862	June 16, 1865, expiration of service.
William Bartlett,		Leicester,	" 31, 1862	June 8, 1864, died of wounds.
Frederick S. Blodgett,		Pittsfield,	" 31, 1862	June 16, 1865, expiration of service.
Charles J. Bridgman,		Pittsfield,	" 31, 1862	January 23, 1864, disability.
Henry D. Brockway,		Hancock,	" 31, 1862	June 26, 1864, died of wounds.

THIRTY-FOURTH MASSACHUSETTS INFANTRY. 457

Name					Residence		Date		Remarks
James F. Brodie,	.	.	.	.	Lanesborough,	July	31,	1862	June 16, 1865, exp. of serv., absent prisoner.
Samuel F. Buck,	$325 00	.	.	.	Hinsdale,	"	31,	1862	June 16, 1865, expiration of service.
Edwin D. Burgess,	.	.	.	.	Worcester,	Dec.	31,	1863	May 15, 1864, killed in battle.
Abram C. Cady,	.	.	.	.	Dalton,	July	31,	1863	May 17, 1864, died of wounds.
Henry C. Cady,	.	.	.	.	Pittsfield,	"	31,	1862	June 16, 1865, expiration of service.
George A. Carlton,	.	.	.	.	Hancock,	"	31,	1862	" "
Aaron B. Chapman,	.	.	.	.	Pittsfield,	"	31,	1862	March 21, 1864, disability.
Nathaniel C. Chapman,	.	.	.	.	Pittsfield,	"	31,	1862	December 27, 1862, disability.
William H. Chase,	.	.	.	.	Pittsfield,	"	31,	1862	February 14, 1863, disability.
Dwight Cleveland,	325 00	.	.	.	Hardwick,	Nov.	11,	1864	July 16, 1865, expiration of service.
Charles Deland,	.	.	.	.	South Hadley,	July	31,	1862	June 14, 1865, transferred to 24th Infantry.
William Dennis,	.	.	.	.	Great Barrington,	"	31,	1862	November 22, 1862, died of disease.
William Doren,	.	.	.	.	Lenox,	"	31,	1862	June 16, 1865, expiration of service.
Silas W. Edgarton,	.	.	.	.	Dalton,	"	31,	1862	July 21, 1864, promoted, U. S. C. T.
*Samuel Frank,	.	.	.	.	Westfield,	Nov.	23,	1863	June 14, 1865, transferred to 24th Infantry.
Nathan A. Freeland,	325 00	.	.	.	Peru,	July	31,	1862	April 25, 1863, disability.
David N. Gilmore,	.	.	.	.	Shutesbury,	Dec.	26,	1863	May 15, 1864, killed in battle.
John T. Gloyd,	.	.	.	.	Dalton,	July	31,	1865	February 11, 1864, transferred to V. R. C.
Sereno E. Gloyd,	325 00	.	.	.	Worthington,	"	28,	1863	October 5, 1864, died of disease.
Loren E. Goldthwait,	.	.	.	.	Granby,	Dec.	17,	1863	May 26, 1865, disability.
Darius N. Goodell,	.	.	.	.	New Ashford,	July	31,	1862	January 20, 1863, disability.
Michael Haggerty,	.	.	.	.	Pittsfield,	"	31,	1862	June 16, 1865, expiration of service.
Henry C. Harmstead,	.	.	.	.	Egremont,	"	31,	1862	February 11, 1864, transferred to V. R. C.
William B. Haskins,	325 00	.	.	.	Adams,	Dec.	14,	1863	June 14, 1865, transferred to 24th Infantry.
George W. Hicox,	.	.	.	.	Great Barrington,	July	31,	1862	June 19, 1865, disability.
Henry G. Hinds,	.	.	.	.	Lanesborough,	"	31,	1862	June 5, 1864, killed in battle.
Albert Howe,	.	.	.	.	New Ashford,	"	31,	1862	February 11, 1864, transferred to V. R. C.
Conrad Houmps,	.	.	.	.	Hancock,	Dec.	4,	1863	September 19, 1864, killed in battle.
Otis H. Hyer,	.	.	.	.	Pittsfield,	July	31,	1862	June 8, 1865, disability.
Samuel H. Hubbard,	.	.	.	.	Dalton,	"	31,	1862	June 16, 1865, expiration of service.
George F. Ingraham,	.	.	.	.	New Ashford,	"	31,	1862	July 31, 1865, disability.
John H. Jones,	.	.	.	.	Richmond,	"	31,	1862	June 16, 1865, expiration of service.
Ezekiel P. Kempton,	.	.	.	.	Brookfield,	"	31,	1862	June 1, 1865, disability.
John H. Kippe,	.	.	.	.	Pittsfield,	"	31,	1862	December 27, 1862, disability.
Robert Killand,	325 00	.	.	.	Brookfield,	"	31,	1862	February 11, 1864, transferred to V. R. C.
Henry King,	.	.	.	.	Pittsfield,	Dec.	20,	1863	June 14, 1865, transferred to 24th Infantry.
Robert G. Kirke,	.	.	.	.	Hancock,	July	31,	1862	May 25, 1865, disability.
Marshall C. Knapp,	325 00	.	.	.	Hancock,	"	31,	1863	October 15, 1864, died of wounds.
Henry F. Knox,	.	.	.	.	Holden,	Dec.	2,	1863	June 14, 1865, transferred to 24th Infantry.
Franklin F. Knox,	.	.	.	.	Brookfield,	July	31,	1862	June 16, 1865, expiration of service.

* Not on Regimental Book.

458   THIRTY-FOURTH MASSACHUSETTS INFANTRY.

NAME AND RANK.	Bounty.	Residence or Place Credited to.	Date of Muster.		Termination of Service and cause thereof.
Company K.—Continued.					
Fultine Lape,		Lanesborough,	July	31, 1862	March 21, 1865, disability.
Milo Lawrence,	$50 00	Great Barrington,	Oct.	5, 1863	July —, 1864, died at Florence, S. C.
John B. Loomis,		Egremont,	July	31, 1862	January 19, 1864, disability.
James Lynch,	325 00	Pittsfield,	Nov.	28, 1863	June 14, 1865, transferred to 24th Infantry.
George Malcolm,	325 00	Pittsfield,	Jan.	9, 1864	June 14, 1865, "
Francis Martin,	325 00	Conway,	"	12, 1864	"
Morton Maynard,		Dalton,	July	31, 1862	June 13, 1864, killed in battle.
Charles E. Mason,	325 00	Lanesborough,	"	31, 1862	June 11, 1865, expiration of service.
Barney McFeely,		Hancock,	Dec.	10, 1863	June 8, 1865, disability.
Henry McGilp,		Pittsfield,	July	31, 1862	January 23, 1865, transferred to V. R. C.
William Mink,		Pittsfield,	"	31, 1862	June 16, 1865, ex. of service, absent w'n'd.
Michael F. Mullen,		Pittsfield,	"	31, 1862	May 26, 1865, disability.
Freeman Newton,	325 00	Montague,	Dec.	27, 1863	Feb. 1, 1865, Quarter-master Sergeant.
Rufus S. Newton,		Brookfield,	July	31, 1862	May 19, 1865, disability.
William F. Newell,		Dalton,	"	31, 1862	Oct. 29, 1862, disability.
Edward H. Norton,		Richmond,	"	31, 1862	June 16, 1865, expiration of service.
Marion Onderdonk,	288 66	Granby,	Jan.	4, 1864	May 16, 1865, disability.
John Owen,		Hinsdale,	July	31, 1862	June 14, 1865, transferred to 21th Infantry.
William F. Pease,		Hardwick,	"	31, 1862	May 15, 1864, killed in battle.
Samuel D. Peck,		Granby,	"	31, 1862	Nov. 11, 1862, died of disease.
Joseph Philander,		Deerfield,	Jan.	21, 1864	June 14, 1868, transferred to 24th Infantry.
Joshua Phillips,		Lanesborough.	July	31, 1862	April 23, 1865, drowned at Potomac Cr'k, Va.
Thomas J. Phillips,		Hancock,	Dec.	4, 1863	August 31, 1865, disability, ex. of service.
Elijah Plass,		Lenox,	Jan.	31, 1862	Jan. 16, 1863, died of disease.
Thomas Powell,	325 00	Pittsfield,	"	31, 1862	June 14, 1865, disability.
Michael Quinn,	325 00	Pittsfield,	Nov.	28, 1863	June 14, 1865, transferred to 24th Infantry.
George L. Rice,	325 00	Wendell,	Dec.	8, 1863	June 14, 1865, "
Frank Samuel,	325 00	Westfield,	Nov.	28, 1863	June 14, 1865, "
Henry Sawyer,		Hancock,	Dec.	10, 1863	June 14, 1865, "
Edwin Shumway,	325 00	Peru,	July	31, 1862	April 10, 1865, disability.
John H. Skinner,		Worcester,	Jan.	5, 1864	June 14, 1865, transferred to 24th Infantry.
George A. Smith,		Hinsdale,	July	31, 1862	June 16, 1865, expiration of service.
James Smith,		Pittsfield,	"	31, 1862	June 16, 1865, "
James S. Smith,		Dalton,	"	31, 1862	Feb. 11, 1864, transferred to V. R. C.
John D. Smith,		Dalton,	"	31, 1862	June 16, 1865, expiraiton of service.
Joel Sprague,	325 00	Conway,	Jan.	15, 1864	June 14, 1865, transferred to 24th Infantry.

THIRTY-FOURTH MASSACHUSETTS INFANTRY.

Name	Residence	Bounty	Mustered in	Remarks
William B. Starke,	Egremont,	. .	July 31, 1862	June 16, 1865, expiration of service.
Joseph S. Stephens,	Hinsdale,	$325 00	Dec. 3, 1863	June 14, 1865, transferred to 44th Infantry.
Harlan P. Stowell,	Hinsdale,	. .	July 31, 1862	June 5, 1864, killed in battle.
Newell P. Stone, Jr.,	Peru,	. .	" 31, 1862	March 12, 1863, died of disease.
Hugh Stuart,	Lanesborough,	. .	" 31, 1862	June 16, 1865, expiration of service.
Dexter Taylor,	Hancock,	. .	" 31, 1862	Oct. 5, 1864, died of wounds.
James M. Taylor,	Hancock,	. .	" 31, 1862	June 16, 1865, expiration of service.
Freeman N. Upham,	Brookfield,	. .	" 31, 1862	June 16, 1865, "
Caleb S. Vickery,	Hancock,	325 00	" 31, 1862	Nov. 18, 1862, died of disease.
Charles H. Walker,	Richmond,	. .	Jan. 4, 1864	June 14, 1864, transferred to 24th Infantry.
Chapin J. Warner, Jr.,	Granby,	. .	July 31, 1862	June 16, 1865, expiration of service.
Jacob Watson,	Brookfield,	. .	" 31, 1862	Feb. 11, 1864, transferred to V. R. C.
Willis P. Worden,	Pittsfield,	325 00	Nov. 28, 1863	June 30, 1865, disability.
Charles H. Wilson,	Worcester,	50 00	Sept. 21, 1863	May 22, 1865, disability.
George Witherwax,	Greenfield,	325 00	Jan. 15, 1864	August 31, 1864, died at Baltimore, Md.
Israel Wood,	Conway,			June 14, 1865, transferred to 24th Infantry.

IMPRISONMENT AND ESCAPE

OF

LIEUT. COLONEL LINCOLN.

The close of the 15th of May, 1864, left me, with many of my companions in arms, wounded and in the hands of the enemy. We had marched, the day before, a distance of twenty-one miles in seven hours, with but one halt, and that of only *ten* minutes. Now the sun had sent down his fiercest rays, now the clouds had poured their contents, in torrents, upon our devoted heads. Tired, wet through, and hungry, —for we had not a morsel to eat with us,—in the thick darkness of the overhanging woods, we laid down, in line of battle, upon our arms. *Twice* the vollies of musketry from opposing parties on our left had caused us to spring up in line; and again, we had been roused, before dawn, by our own officers, and held in readiness for any movement which might be made. Later on in the morning, we had passed hours in marching and countermarching for position, and still later had met the attack of the enemy, and after a sharp and severe fight, had been badly beaten. As the day closed, some sixty of us found ourselves stretched in and around an old barn, near the battlefield, closely guarded by Rebel soldiers. During the early hours of the evening, and well into the night, our party received accessions from such wounded Union soldiers as were able to make their way unaided; or, too severely wounded to walk, were brought in by the enemy. Occasionally, by the light of a lantern, some Rebel officer would examine us. "Are there any Confederate wounded here?" was asked by Major Meem, Medical Director on the staff of Gen. Breckenbridge, as he stood at the head of a goodly sized party of Rebel surgeons. No answer was returned by any of us, as the question was addressed to no one in particular. "I say, you d——d Yankee sons of b——s, are there any Confederate wounded here?" "No, sir!" was the reply. "Then this is no place for us, gentlemen!" said the Major; and he turned away. Among the wounded was Capt. Graham of the 54th Pennsylvania. He had been shot directly through the right lung, and each breath he drew sent the air *whistling* through the wound, disturbing the dying, who laid near. "I wish, Major," said I to Meem, "you would give a look to this officer, before you go." "We've got enough to do to attend to the confederate wounded," said he; but spite of the remark turned to comply with the request. As he drew the shirt from the wound in the Captain's breast, he broke out with "All he wants is a *d——d good horn of whiskey*," and walked off. All his companions followed, save one, (I wish I knew and could give his name), who, lingering behind, closed the wound with a piece of plaster, and gave him to drink from a jug in the hands of an Orderly.

With the morning light we were able to recognize, and enquire as to each others condition. Another night passed, with the addition of a few more to our number, among whom was Capt. Fox of ours, from whom we learned of the death of Capt. Bacon, of our color company.

Late in the afternoon of this day (Tuesday), with an armed Rebel on each side of us, Capt. Fox and myself made a slow march into town, and to the office of the Provost Marshal. Here our names and rank were registered, and we were directed to report ourselves at the hospital. At this place our wounds were examined and partially dressed; a thick slice of bread (the only food which either of us had had since Sunday morning), was given to each, and we were told that we might "look out for ourselves" till we were wanted. We procured lodgings at the Village hotel, where we staid till Thursday, when we were informed that we were wanted again at the hospital. Reporting, we found drawn up before the door of the building a long wagon, without cover, without springs, with no seat, and not even straw upon which to sit or lie, into which we were directed to get, as we were to be sent, in this way, to Harrisonburg, some twenty miles away. We were now joined by Lieut. Ammidon, of ours, who had been captured, but fortunately not wounded. Our journey was a sad and tiresome one. But it had an end; and late in the afternoon, when our teams stopped in the middle of the main street of Harrisonburg, opposite the Court House, we stepped down and out, at the invitation of our guard. It was a curious coincidence, that *here*, as on the battlefield, the first question asked me by the guard was the *whispered one*, "*Are you a Mason?*" In the light of subsequent experience, I can't help thinking that I should have fared better, while a prisoner, if I could have answered this question in the affirmative. Here we took a sad farewell of Ammidon, who was at once hurried on further south to Andersonville, *and his death*. We were now escorted to the hospital which was established in the buildings of the Academy, at the outskirts of the town, and reporting to the Surgeon, were by him ordered to report to the officer in charge of prisoners at the Court House. Entering, we were warmly greeted by Lieut. Walker and some forty or fifty of our own wounded men who had preceded us. We were assigned to the upper story of the building. There was the *bare floor* to sleep on; no straw was furnished us. Our blankets, tin cups, canteens, indeed everything of the kind had previously been taken from us. Three times a day, coffee, bread and *sheep meat*, as the Rebel soldiers called it, cut in cubes about two by two, were brought us. It so happened that my place on the floor, was next the door, as the room was entered. The coffee was brought in a large water pail, a small tin cup floating in it, from which we were to drink. As the bearer entered, he turned to me. Filling the cup I put it to my lips, to take it away again with my thirst unquenched. My lips were blistered by the boiling liquid. And when, after going the rounds of the room, the soldier was at the door, on his way out, I reached again for the cup, I was met with the *pleasant* remark, "Let that alone, you've had your chance before." And so it *happened* always. We had many visitors, most of them apparently coming to see how we looked, as they exchanged no words with us. Some came, however, from interest in the cause for which we suffered; or drawn by sympathy for us, on account of our wounds. Among the latter was a Mrs. Lewis, wife of a prominent merchant in the place, whose kindness of heart overbalanced the contempt in which she held the "myrmidons of the Tyrant Lincoln," and who furnished to many of us supplies from her own table as long as we remained in the Court House. Among the former was Col. Asa S. Gray, and his daughter, Miss Orra Gray, staunch lovers of the Union, both of them; ministering angels in our hours of despondency, of want, of suffering, and of death! To their unwearied attention, and unstinted supply of whatever they could procure, which in any way would contribute to our welfare, all of us were indebted for comfort, and some of us for restored health and life. Dr. George H. Gilmer, a physician of the town, not only visited us, but attended to our wounds, till the arrival of Dr. Allen, assistant Surgeon on the Staff of the 34th regiment; and in other ways did much to relieve us. *Capt.* McNiel, too, old Guerilla that he was, called often, and showed us much kindness, after his fashion.

"Have you written home, Colonel?" asked he one day. "Yes, Captain!" "How did you send your letter?" "By way of Richmond and flag of truce boat." "Pshaw!" said he, "your folks will never hear from you by that route! Here," said he, "here is some paper; I see you've got pen and ink; write a letter if you want to;—pay for a Confederate Post Office stamp,—I must make you contribute that much to our cause,—give me your word that you won't write anything you ought not to—seal it up and give it to me—and I'll put it into one of *your* post offices for you, though, mind, I don't promise that I won't rob it *first*." He was as good as his word; and, of all the letters written home by me while a prisoner, all of which were forwarded via Richmond and flag of truce boat, this one was the only one which reached its destination. Major Meem too, called occasionally. Once, before our surgeon came up, as he entered the room, I asked him if he would not look at a little fellow of ours, whose wrist was terribly shattered by a Minie ball. "I suppose you wan't I should look at you, too! Why the devil didu't you leave one of your own surgeons to take care of you?" said he: but the little fellow had already taken off his handkerchief, and held out his wrist, swollen, mangled, and of a *dark, deep red color*. "Erysipelas there, Major, isn't there?" "Yes." "His arm will have to be amputated, won't it?" "Yes." "Won't you operate?" "We can't be troubled with your men, Colonel! we've got our hands full with our own," said the Major, as he turned and walked away. So life went on with us; till, on the afternoon of the 25th, *ten days* after the battle, we were gladdened by the arrival of Dr. Allen, one of our own surgeons, who had come up to take care of our wounds. Finding that we were packed too closely, he at once applied himself to securing other and more airy, and comfortable quarters; and having effected our removal, set about examining our wounds. The little fellow, whose wrist was so badly shattered, and whose arm Major Meem had at a later day amputated, was among the first to receive attention. Upon removing the bandage from the stump, the *bone was found to project three and one-half inches beyond the "flap:"* this, by actual measurement. Was this accidental? or was it in furtherance of the *interest*, as explained below, in the case of Ryan, whose left knee joint was shattered badly, and who now was low and sinking. "This man," said Dr. Allen to Major Meem, "ought to have had his leg amputated immediately after being wounded." "Yes!" said the Major, "I thought so." "You saw him, then?" "Oh yes!" "Well, why didn't you operate?" "Oh, Doctor!" was the reply, "*you know its for our interest to kill all your men we can*"—and the conversation ended.

After Dr. Allen's arrival, and before he had removed us to our new quarters, and while he was temporarily absent, from the Court House, an ambulance was driven up, and a guard, getting out, announced that "Col. Lincoln, Capt. Fox, Capt. Graham, and Lieut. Walker would take seats in it," as they were about to be started off South. To hear was to obey. In the effort to comply with the order, Lieut. Walker fainted, before he had reached the ground floor ; Col. Lincoln managed to get down, and part way to the ambulance; while the two Captains succeeded in reaching and taking their seats in the vehicle. At this stage in the movement, Dr. Allen made his appearance. In much excitement, he remonstrated at the cruelty of the order; and obtained a promise of delay, till he could find the proper authorities, and remonstrate against its execution. He might as well have whistled against the wind, for all the effect he produced. The order had been issued, and would not be countermanded. Discouraged, he was returning, when he accidentally met Major *Hunter Johnson, Acting Post Quartermaster*, who hearing his representation that the removal of Col. Lincoln and Lieut. Walker would greatly endanger their lives, took the responsibility of countermanding the order, so far as those officers were concerned. He could not save the two Captains, however, and they were driven away. The days dragged their slow length along. Nothing but an occasional death varied the monotony of our life; till one morning we were visited by a rebel officer, who asked us for our *parole*. We demurred, till, upon his solemn assurance that there was no Union force nearer than

Cedar Creek, and at present, not the most remote possibility of our being recaptured, we yielded, and gave the required pledge. The *next day*, however, Hunter, with his army, marched into town! Before marching away, he visited the hospital — cheered us by his promise, that, upon reaching Stanton, he would send down a train with ambulances enough to take us all to Martinsburg; and left with us liberal supplies of flour, coffee, tea, sugar, &c., morphine, quinine, chloroform, stimulants and other medicines, and bandages sufficient for *our* wants. He left a large supply of all these articles for the rebel wounded, of whom there were more than two hundred in town. He left also clothing, stockings, uniforms and boots for all of our men. He had hardly gone, before the hospital was entered by a party of soldiers, headed by a man in rebel uniform, who gave his name as *Capt. Jourdan* of Rosser's command, and who robbed it of *all* the liquors, *all* the morphine, quinine, and chloroform *we had;* all the coffee, sugar, and tea they could carry off; each man taking *one* and some *two* suits of uniforms, and one or more pairs of boots. Days passed; and as with their passage, without the appearance of the train promised by Hunter, hope of speedy liberation fled, some of our men lost courage, drooped, and died!

We were denied the privilege of burying our dead in the village cemetery; and it was only by the persevering energy of *Miss Gray*, that permission was given us to deposit their remains in the long disused graveyard belonging to the Methodist society of the town.

In the absence of any better astringent, Allen sent out the nurses to cut down the only wild cherry tree we knew of; and to dig up, and bring in the roots of blackberry bushes, of which to make tea.

The Rebel authorities, who had run off at Hunter's approach, now returned, and resumed control. To our surprise, and indignation, we found that a guard was again stationed over us. We demanded its removal. Maj. Johnson replied that the question of the validity of our parole had been referred to Richmond for determination. He removed the guard, till he should be informed of the decision. Meanwhile, Early came down the valley with his army; and the guard was replaced over us.

In consequence, a note was written and sent to Maj. Johnson, Acting Post Commandant, setting forth that our paroles were *valid*, — or of no binding force; that if valid, there was neither propriety or right in keeping us under guard; that if they were deemed invalid, we had no cause of complaint; but, that unless the guard was withdrawn, we should consider ourselves discharged from the obligations which the parole imposed. Although no reply was made to our note, the guard was *continued* over the hospital, and we left to draw our own inferences from such continuance.

During this period, occasionally one or more of our wounded, now convalescent, made their escape from the hospital in the village. No attempt at escape was made at our own, however. Maj. Meem, at this time, re-appeared in the village. With his return, an effort was made to send away such of us as were well enough to bear the journey south. The means of transportation were limited, however. If the regular stage coach, from Winchester and below, came up empty, they would load in fourteen of us; if it was filled with passengers, our party would have to wait a more convenient season for their journey. Up to this time it had been left to Dr. Allen to determine *who must go :* he being directed only as to the *number* to be sent. But now Allen announced that he had orders to send off the next day, fourteen of us; "and Colonel," said he, "*you are named as one to be ready*. I told Major Meem," said Allen, "that you were in no condition to travel yet, and he is coming up to see you, and judge for himself." And so we were prepared when he made his appearance that morning. "Pshaw!" said he, as he replaced my shirt, after making his examination, "Why *in hell* don't you get well, Colonel! I reckon you don't try very hard, do you? But you'll have to go! Don't you think now, you could take the journey if it was to your home?" "*I'd try to, Major*," was my reply. "Well, this is to Richmond!" "By the way of Lynchburg? as Capt. Fox went," asked I. "How did you know anything about that?" "Oh! I didn't dream it." "Well, get well!" said he, "we'll let you off this time, but we can't keep you here forever, you know." "I don't want to stay that long," I replied, and the subject was dropped. "By the way Allen," he rejoined, "did you get your whiskey, to-day?" This, in allusion to the fact, that since Rosser's captain had robbed the hospital of every thing of the kind, he (Meem) had undertaken to supply us with what was needed. "I got what you sent me, Major!" said Allen, "but its *queer whiskey!* Lincoln here, had rather take his quinine clear, than in that stuff" "Where is it? get a tumbler, and let's try it," said the Major. He did so: not *once* only, but twice, and not by tasting merely, but by drinking, till he emptied *one* of the *two* bottles he had filled for our sick. He left us after a while, much to *my relief*, if to that of no one else. My respite was short however: for not many days afterward, upon Allen's return from the lower hospital, he again announced, that he was ordered to get another party ready to be sent away, and that I was again included among those to go. As before, so now, Major Meem was to come up, in the evening, to examine my condition for himself.

Allen, Lieut. Walker, and myself, were the only occupants of one of the rooms, and as the Doctor left to make up his list of those best able to bear the journey, I made known to Walker, (who, poor fellow! was on crutches and could not go), my determination of trying to effect my escape that night. He tried to dissuade me, on the ground that, weak as I was from my wounds and long confinement, I could not possibly succeed. But I felt that if I could get beyond the guards, I could manage it some how. Of course, I placed my chief reliance upon the aid I confidently expected to receive from any negroes I should meet on my way; and preferred the risk incurred in the attempt, to the entertainment which would be furnished me at any of the rebel prisons farther South. So I cast about for a companion, and calling Snow, of our G, to my side, made known my plans, and sent him out with some money, to hunt up the "Old Auntie" who had done our washing, and get from her some suits of clothes with which to disguise ourselves. He returned, having procured for himself, only, the suit required. While he was gone, I had enlisted another recruit, in the person of Doherty, a man of the 54th Pennsylvania. Snow was again despatched, with instructions to tell the old "mammy" what I intended to do; and also that she *must* send me a suit of her "old man's" clothes; no matter how ragged; and get him to meet us *that night*, at a spot designated, to guide us on our way. I had enquired of our visitors, at different times, as carefully as possible, of the direction of the different roads in sight from the hospital; the nature of the country, and the character and disposition of the people along each route; and now pitched upon the road leading by Rawley Springs, through Pendleton County, to Beverly, within the Union lines, as the most safe to be taken. But we wanted a guide at any rate, till we were fairly in the mountains. Snow's second attempt resulted in his bringing in a complete suit of well worn Grey for Doherty: an old white hat, *minus crown and part of its brim*, for me; and a promise from the old negress, that her husband should go to the rendezvous agreed upon, that night, and wait for us; and should take with him a suit of *old clothes* for me to wear.

So we waited with comparative composure for the appearance of Major Meem. He came at last; bringing with him a Dr. King, also a rebel surgeon. They examined me thoroughly, but gave no intimation of the opinion they reached. The Major discussed his whiskey as before; and *between drinks*, indulged in reminiscences of his life, while studying his profession at the Northern colleges, and confessed to having had many a good time among the Yankees. "Do you know, Colonel, how much pleasure it would give me to dine with you at your own home?" he asked. "How I should like, Major, to extend an invitation to you *now*, if I could only fix upon a *particular day*," was my reply. "Well," said he laughing, "it does look as if there was a little difficulty about that, doesn't it?" "By the way, Allen," said he, "Haven't you got a *pair of boots for me?* mine are almost gone !" "I'm afraid," said Allen, "I've none that will fit you. There are none left smaller than nines, *and you wear*"——"*fives*," said the Major; "but we can't be too nice about the fit!" So Snow was directed to bring in a pair. Meem literally stepped into them, they were so large, but nevertheless was pleased: so much so that he insisted that King should also have a pair, and Allen sent for another one, which gave equal satisfaction, though none the less a *misfit*. Still they kept their seats! What else did they want? I was becoming nervous: now wondering whether Snow had not been careless, and now whether the *old "Auntie"* had not been treacherous, when Meem got up, and taking me by the hand, and wishing me a pleasant journey, went away with his friend King and their *new loves*, the Boots. Allen now closed the hospital, and crawled between his blankets; and, contrary to his usual custom, laid still, and almost instantly fell asleep. Nothing broke the quiet that settled down upon us, save an occasional snore from some heavy sleeper, or the measured tread of the sentinels around the building in which we were confined. We had planned to attempt our escape at as early an hour as possible. To aid it, one of *our fellows*, good singer, and capital story teller that he was (he had lost a leg and could not travel), volunteered to go out by the front door, and entertain the guard, in the hope that the sentinels, stopping occasionally to listen, would get irregular on their beats, and thus give us a chance to slip from the back of the building, *between them*. Another comrade, on his bunk at a back window, was to give a low whistle when the *coast was clear*. Close to the rear of the hospital was a small shed, which was to be the first step of our flight; a little way beyond was a board fence, our second step; while beyond, and till we reached the cover of the cornfield, all was open to observation. Well in among the growing corn was the white oak tree agreed upon as the place of rendezvous. Doherty was to try his luck first, I next, and Snow was to follow last. Warned by Allen's low and regular breathing that he was asleep, I got up carefully, and, giving Walker's hand a hearty grasp as I passed him, left the room. My appearance was the signal for the others to set about their work. Almost instantly we heard the rich voice of our one-legged comrade, as he charmed our friends, the guards. With but little intervals the low whistle of our other friend was heard, and Doherty slipped out! I soon followed, and with but little delay gained the rendezvous, where I found Doherty. Snow soon joined us. But there was no guide! What should we do? Snow and Doherty in their suits of homespun grey were capitally disguised; but for myself, if once seen in our own blue, detection and capture was almost sure. Still, I was the most unwilling to remain where we were. With the directions which Dr. Gilmer (to whom late in the afternoon I had confided my intention of trying to escape) had given me, I felt confident of finding the house of a negro, in whom we could trust; and, finding him, of obtaining somehow, whatever disguise was necessary for my wants. But Snow was so confident that our guide would soon make his appearance that he absolutely refused to move from the spot. So, with an injunction to him not to wait a great while, Doherty and I left him, and made our way up to a corner of the field, abutting upon a piece of wood-land, where we could better conceal ourselves. While waiting somewhat impatiently for Snow to join us, we were startled by a musket shot, from the direction of the hospital; quickly followed by loud talking, and the sound of horses in quick gallop along the road near us. Had our escape been so soon discovered? Why is not Snow alarmed? and what keeps him from joining us? were questions each asked of the other. Every minute of waiting seemed an age; and after much urging, Doherty consented to go down, keeping covered by the fence, with a message to Snow to join us immediately. In his absence, I fancied the voices were getting nearer and nearer, and was much relieved by the hurried tread of Doherty, who came up with the story that beneath the tree where we had left Snow he had caught sight of from *six* to *eight* persons, who were talking loud and angrily together. I may as well say here, what I afterward learned from Snow, (who, tired of waiting, attempted to find us, and failing in that, succeeded in making his way back into the hospital again, from which, at a later day, he succeeded in escaping,) that the shot which so alarmed us *was an accidental one*, from a falling stack ; that the loud talking we heard was in a detachment of Cavalry men on their way down the pike to join Early's army ; and that at no time in the night, after we left, was there anybody but himself under *the tree.* But this we did not *then* know ; and jumping to the conclusion that our escape had been discovered, and Snow already retaken, we also came to the conclusion, that our only hope of final escape laid in immediate flight. So we struck across the fields in a *southerly* direction, under cover of woods wherever practicable. Our plan was to reach the road which led, via Rawley Springs, to Beverley, in our lines ; traveling by a line paralell to it, *through the fields and woods*, as far as possible. Dr. Gilmer, who alone of all my new made friends, knew of my intention to escape, had given some general directions as to the route, and also, the names of one or two persons whom I could safely trust, provided, (and there was the difficulty) I could succeed in reaching their houses. We continued our way, crossing one or two roads, which we left, because not answering the description of the one we were in search of. Morning came upon us, literally wanderers in a strange land. If we could only have found a "little cabin inhabited by a negro family, with a wheelwright's shop, by the banks of a little creek," we should have found *safe hiding place, something to eat,* and *faithful guide* on our way ! ! As it was however, we hunted for, and found some thick underbrush, under cover of which we laid down and slept. Voices, in loud conversation, woke us late in the morning ; but, satisfied that we were well screened, we took another nap ! By noon we were awake again. We now held a long consultation ; but as we did not know *where we were ;* as it was not safe to attempt to move while it was light ; and as we were both dry and hungry, it was thought best to get another nap, if possible. We did not wake again till near sundown ! To while away the time, Doherty cut and trimmed a good hickory stick for each of us ; while I laid still, husbanding what strength I had, for our coming night's march. My wound was very painful ; and though *I* suffered much from thirst, *Doherty* professed to want nothing but food. Each of us was supported by the hope that we should yet find the house which had been fixed upon, as our refuge, after our first night's travel ; (wherein dwelt our much needed guide across the mountains,) and which we hoped Snow might have reached ; and when it was dusk, we left our cover, and with undiminished courage resumed our tramp, still keeping the direction of our previous night's route. We carefully felt among the stubble of a large wheat-field in our way, for any chance heads of grain with which to satisfy our hunger ; and we quarrelled with an old sow for the possession of a stagnant pool, in which she was peacefully reclining, that we might satisfy our thirst. Here we held council again. Looking south-west over the town, from our place of confinement in Harrisonburg, a solitary hill, sugar-loaf in shape, rose high above the surrounding country. From the information we had, we ought, upon looking to our rear to have seen this hill on *our right*, but we did see it on our *left* ; and we were forced to the conclusion, that, by some mistake, we had crossed the road which led to the Springs. It had been represented as *widely laid out, thrown up in turnpike shape*, and pretty well travelled. So, taking another drink, (*it didn't taste so well this time*) we turned our faces northward, and kept on till we came to a road, which, in the belief that it was the one we sought, we followed for a while under some of the pines by its side. This seemed to run out into a mere wood's path, when we left it, and keeping still more to the north, across the fields, soon came out into another road, along which we kept till the morning light warned us to take to the mountains, and hide. Hunger, and thirst, and anxiety as to our whereabouts prevented sleep ; and crawling beneath the shelter of some thick underbrush, we spent the day in watching the farm-houses which dotted the plain below, in hopes of catching sight of some *"contraband."* At times, we speculated as to what had become of Snow, and what effect our escape had had on the fate of our comrades left at Harrisonburg. The sight of Rebel Cavalrymen near, riding from house to house below us, and holding short colloquy with the inmates of each, did not add to our peace. Our day watch came to an end at last; and at dusk, flanking the houses at our feet, we descended the mountain for the purpose of obtaining food, and, if possible, information as to our whereabouts. Our watch of the day had shown us that the house near by had no inmates, save the aged and grey-headed couple, who had responded to the calls of the Rebel horsemen during the day.

Of course, dressed as I was in my own proper uniform, save that a private's blouse had been substituted for the regulation coat; with my arm confined, and useless, by reason of my wound, it was not prudent for me to show myself. So Doherty left me seated with my back to a stone wall, and went up to the house alone. He soon rejoined me, having in one hand a pitcher of milk, and in the other *two* slices of bread, which we attacked without ceremony. The old man had followed Doherty, unperceived; and now, while we were eating, reached over the wall and placed his hands on my shoulder. "Who are you? Where do you come from? Where are you going? and what are you doing here, at this time of night," he asked. Too many questions to answer at once; so he was told merely that we were *Conscripts*, on our way to report at Harrisonburg, to the Rebel commandant. There had been a late conscription; and all conscripts had been ordered to report the day *after* we left. "You ought to have reported yesterday." "Yes! but we lost our way in crossing the mountains!" "Where did you come from?" "Moorfield." "How did you pass the picket at Brock's Gap?" "We wan't challenged!" "That's strange!" There was a good deal of like questioning and answer; the result of it being to give us the information that we were on the road to "Brock's Gap," instead of "Rawley Springs," and that we were only *nine miles* from Harrisonburg. Having eaten our supper, we rose and followed the man as far as his house, *on the way* to Harrisonburg. Here we exchanged with him a pleasant good night, and continued our way in apparent unconcern. But, so soon as we were fairly screened from his observation, we retraced our steps. Having re-passed his house, we sat down to discuss our situation. Here we were, on a road we knew to be a very dangerous one, for (McNeil's company was at "Moorfield,") and parties of his men were continually passing between that place and Harrisonburg. Besides, while prisoners, in conversation with our guards, as well as those well disposed toward us, we had learned that in many respects an unsafe road to take. Still I could not make up my mind to turn back, in search of another route. My feet were already very sore, and inflamed, and I dreaded any increase of travel.

At length, with much difficulty, I persuaded Doherty it was best to *keep on.* It was nearly morning when we neared the entrance to the Gap. We were walking after the fashion of the country, *Doherty leading a few paces,* when, at a turn in the road, I caught sight of the light of a picket fire, which Doherty had not seemed to notice. My low whistle, or the snapping of a twig, upon which Doherty had incautiously stepped, attracted attention; and a sharp "who goes there," followed. We each threw ourselves upon the ground, close to the bushes which lined the road, and after a little delay, crawled through the brush to the river bank, (the Shenandoah) plunged into the water, which we forded somehow; and, climbing the mountain, hid in a thick clump of evergreens. Here we passed the next day undisturbed. Heavy clouds gathered in the afternoon sky, but we started at dusk, in spite of the rain which had begun to fall. At the foot of the mountain, we found a creek running across our way. We forded it safely, carefully feeling the way with our canes, and sat down on its bank to empty the water from our boots, and wring it out of our stockings. We had not finished, when the tread of horses' feet, and rattling of sabres, warned us of near danger. How my heart beat, as the foremost rider pulled up his horse, (a step farther and he would have been actually upon me,) to settle with his companion the dispute between them, whether or not they were at the Ford. Fortunately for us they concluded that it was at a point lower down the creek, and reining round their horses, they rode away. Of course we moved as soon as they were fairly off; and after a little waiting, every thing being still, put on our boots, and walked away. But a new trouble met us soon after. We came to where the road forked. In the darkness of the night we could hardly see a hand before us; so, kneeling, we tried, by careful feeling of the road, to ascertain which was the most traveled, meaning to take it. But we could not satisfy ourselves, and concluded to hide again and wait for the morning. So we climbed the mountain, and laid down to rest and sleep. It was late when we woke, cold and stiff, and of course wet through, for it was raining hard, as it had all the night long. All day we watched the roads in sight, hoping that some of McNeil's men would pass, and so we be able to select our route; for we had now determined to make for "Romney" and "Moorefield," and *our lines* at "Cumberland." Late in the afternoon, it having cleared away, we descended the mountain part way, and hid in a thick clump of laurel bushes, almost directly *over* the road. After long waiting and watching, we caught sight of two Rebel soldiers, slowly riding toward Harrisonburg; and as they passed, heard: "Well, they can't be on this road, for the Colonel was never out of the hospital till the night he got away; and he could not have traveled so far;" and recognized in one of the party, a soldier who had been guard over us for weeks.

We *knew* now that we had been pursued; and that our pursuers, *on this road*, unable to hear anything of us in advance, were returning, satisfied that we must have taken some other route. Of course we felt greatly relieved at what we had just seen and heard; and waited, with a good deal of impatience, for the coming on of evening, that we might resume our journey. At near dusk we picked our way to the foot of the mountain, and soon after started. Our road wound up and round the side of the mountain; it was narrow, bordered on each side by tall trees growing thickly together, which made it pretty dark; and we trudged along with a good degree of confidence, greatly relieved by the knowledge that we were no longer being pursued. Once or twice, we stopped to consult at a divergent path, but were not tempted to wander from our better travelled road. Hours had passed, and we were still climbing; the road had been gradually getting worse, and worse; we occasionally stumbling over projecting roots, and stumps; when, all at once, we stood on the summit of the mountain, *face to face* with the newly risen moon! It should have been at our *backs!* How had we gone astray? and how far from our true route had we been led? Alas! there was no opportunity to enquire, if enquiry would have been safe; and with feelings a good deal depressed, we turned to retrace our steps, carefully examining the way, as we walked on, to determine, if possible, at what point we had wandered. Morning broke upon us, while still upon our backward way; and we went into the woods, for concealment, a good deal dispirited. We were roused from sleep by the crowing of cocks, and the barking of dogs, in the door-yard of a house not far away; and which had been *unnoticed* before. The clear notes of a bugle, sounding the reveille, drew our attention to a party of Rebel horsemen in another direction, who were engaged grooming their "cattle." We were almost in "the *open,*" so far as this party was concerned; and, digging our heels into the ground, slowly but carefully worked ourselves, upon our backs, *under cover*. We watched anxiously the departure of these soldiers; and, relieved by their riding away, were amused later in the day, by observing the females and children of the family near us, as, with *straight poles* for flails, they kept hard at work pounding out their crop of wheat. Way off, in another direction, by itself, and apparently in the middle of a large field of grain, was a small, one-story house, at which we determined we would apply for food, when night should come.

We felt gloomy enough! My own condition called for all the nerve I was possessed of. My wound, from want of attention, was extremely painful, and besides, my feet were so badly swollen, and blistered, that I could hardly walk. In addition, I was weak from want of food, and suffering for water. Doherty, not having been wounded, was in better condition; still he suffered a good deal. Notwithstanding all this, we started as soon as it was dark; and going up to the house, Doherty obtained a *couple of slices of bread, well-covered* with *apple butter*, and, what *he did not want so much*, the company of the owner of the place, out to where I was seated. Of course it was natural that we should be questioned, and perhaps equally natural that we should not tell *all* the truth, or *nothing but* the truth. Again we passed ourselves off as Rebel soldiers, this time as returning from furlough; and were not a little startled to find that we *had been* on the road to Franklin County. Professing to belong to Imboden's command, our friend kindly undertook to pilot us across the country, to a road which led to *Winchester*, where Imboden was. We followed him until we reached a road, which he assured us led direct to Winchester; thanked him for his kindness, and paid him for his bread, and left him. Now here was a dilemma! If we did not want to go to "Franklin," neither did we wish to go to Winchester, which we had good reason to believe must now be occupied by Early and his army. Still, in the uncertainty of being able to find the road from which we had strayed in some unaccountable manner, it seemed the best course to keep on. By keeping to the mountains, we believed we could avoid all the Rebel pickets; and there would be but little more danger in taking this route, than the one by "Romney." True, if retaken, we should fare better at the hands of McNiel, than in the keeping of Mosby or Harry Gilmor. Besides, the distance to Martinsburg was less than to any point in our lines by way of Romney.

So we accepted our new situation with comparative cheerfulness. Once in the course of the night, we were brought to a stand-still, by the apparent *running out* of the road, in the thick brush, at what appeared to be the bed of a mountain brook, now completely dried. On our hands and knees we felt, (for in the darkness we could see nothing) for the foot marks of horses, or *fresh horse dung*, which would be a guide. But we failed to find either; and after long hunting, came into a foot path, which gradually widened out and gave us a way of escape from the difficulty which threatened us. Warned by the coming daylight, we again hid on the mountain. After a sound sleep, we woke, and cautiously made our way through the woods to a point, from which we could plainly see what was going on in a farm house beneath. We were interested in watching the Rebel soldiers, who occasionally stopped on their way to chat with the young girls of the family, and in endeavoring to hear what was said. We heard enough to satisfy us that there had been a late battle between the two armies in the valley; but not enough to learn at what place it was fought, or which party were victors.

Early in the afternoon, Doherty announced his determination of going to the house, for food. Although we could plainly enough see that there were no males about the house, I tried to dissuade him from venturing — at any rate, while it was daylight; but he declared he *should die* unless he had *something to eat*, and off he started. I was relieved at seeing him reach the house, make known his wants (as I well knew by seeing one of the girls go to the "spring house"), and leave with some bread in his hands. But I was equally disturbed when, as soon as he was fairly away, one of the girls sounded a *conch*, and I saw a man, who was cradling oats in a field not far off, start on a run for the house. Hurrying to meet Doherty, we climbed the mountain, flanked the house, and, keeping under cover of the woods, continued our flight, till warned by the setting of the sun of the danger of again losing our way.

Seating ourselves, each discussed his *single slice of bread*. Now, Doherty found leisure to tell the cause of his rapid retreat from the house. He had asked for a larger allowance of bread than was first given him; and while incautiously asking his way, and the distance to Winchester, one of the girls accused him of being a *runaway prisoner from Harrisonburg*, and, in his confusion, he left without waiting for the additional supply he had asked for. But he learned that the road we had been traveling did not lead to Winchester. *So we had lost our way again!* Nothing daunted, however, we started as soon as it was dark. Morning saw us once more in hiding, with no house in sight. We slept pretty much through the day; and were on our road again as soon as it was prudent to travel. It had now become very hard work for me to walk. Not only were the soles of my feet badly blistered, but the toes were much swollen and festered, *and the nails of some of them had come off;* so that when day began to break, warning us to seek a hiding place, I felt really unable to climb so far as prudence dictated; and, entirely exhausted, threw myself down along side a fallen tree, in some underbrush, not half way up the mountain side. The violent barking of a hound which had found us out disturbed us. How mad I was as the whelp stood there, with glaring eyes and standing hair, regarding none of my coaxings! The voices of children crying out "Watch 'em, Brave!"— the speculation as to what "Brave" *had found;* and the promise of the father, that, after breakfast, they would go up and see, admonished us of our imprudence. But flight, at the moment, would only make matters worse; so we laid quiet, in hope that "Brave" would soon tire of his barking watch—as he did. When his yelping ceased, we rose, hurried to another part of the mountain, and, with a prayer for safety, laid down, and, after a while, slept soundly. In this manner, traveling by night, hiding by day, avoiding every house, except when driven to one by the pangs of hunger, we made our way for eleven successive nights; once becoming so hopelessly lost as to feel compelled, by very despair, to rouse the inmates of a farmhouse, to get directions as to our route. Fortunately, here again, the only occupants of the dwelling were aged people. The suspicion of the old man, who, in answer to our request, good-naturedly got up from his bed to put us on our way, was allayed by our telling him that *we belonged to McNeil's command, and were in a hurry to get to Moorfield, as we had overstayed our leave of absence.* "Then you don't want to go to Moorefield," said he, "for McNeil moved to Romney yesterday." "It's *McNeil*, and not *Moorefield* or *Romney* that we are after," said we; and, changing his direction, the old fellow led us through the bushes, and putting us on a road, which he said led to Romney, *forty miles distant,* left us with a hearty wish for success. Our situation was thus much bettered. We not only knew where we were, but the distance between us and our lines at "Clear Spring," for which place we now determined to aim; but had the more important information that McNeil was directly in our path. Our progress *had been*, and must still necessarily be, slow; owing not only to my feeble condition, but also because the weather was intensely hot, and, owing to the drought, water seldom to be met with; and it was dangerous to ask for food. We had depended upon finding berries in plenty; and running across a contraband occasionally. But we had seen neither during any part of our journey. As for water, there was almost literally none. The bed of every stream was dry; and we came across no springs. Never shall I forget my feelings at seeing, one night, by the faint light of a just rising moon, the glimmer of water a short distance ahead of us! We made short work of reaching it, and driving out a hog, which had made his bed in it! Sitting down, Doherty filled our canteen. It had been *two nights and two days since either of us had had a drop to drink!* I emptied the canteen at a draught! and Doherty, after filling it again, did the same! We sat a while to rest and cool ourselves, for the night was exceeding hot. Before starting, we thought best to take another drink; but now both taste and smell were sickening! Neither of us could swallow a drop! But we filled the canteen, lest we should find no more, and started again. I am amused now, as I recall the calculations we made of our probable progress. *Three nights* more, and we should be safe beneath the "old flag"! The 54th Penn. had been stationed in the neighborhood of "Romney;" and Doherty claimed to know every cross-road and mountain path between that place and Clear Spring. Alas! how vain all our calculations proved! On our next night's travel we came to a fork of the road which puzzled us. After reconnoitering a house near by, and finding it occupied by *women only*, we enquired of them, and learned that we were but eighteen miles from "Romney" by either road; and that there was little choice between the two.

Our route led up over the range which divided two valleys. The way was steep, and the latter part of it rough and uneven. I had been for some time anxious to stop for the night; when suddenly the loud baying of hounds warned us of our nearness to some house, and a step or two opened into a clearing, and showed us plainly to the gaze of its owner, standing at the just opened door of his cabin. It would only excite suspicion to retreat; so we boldly announced our desire to join McNeil at Romney, expressing a fear that we had lost our true road. Sure enough, we had. The old man kindly gave us directions by which to regain our route, and, following them, we soon got out of his sight, when we took to the woods for concealment. It had been cloudy, which, perhaps, was one cause of our going astray. At night we were again on the road, taking now the right, now the left hand path; and in the morning laid ourselves down beside a fence in a thick piece of woods which bordered upon the roadside. A dense fog laid heavily upon the land, and hid from us a house standing but a short distance from our resting place. We were both so nearly exhausted, and our feet were so sore from repeated blisters, that we took no more steps than we felt to be absolutely necessary. Still, had not the fog so completely hid the house, we should not have dared to have laid down where we did. We had not slept, when we were roused by the dropping of a set of bars,—the passing by of some cows,—and a good-natured voice asking us what we were doing there. It was the same class of man we had encountered twice before—old, gray-headed, long past his prime. There seemed to be no others in this country! He was a Philadelphia lawyer for questions, some of which were hard to be evaded. Our old story, that we were McNeil's men, anxious to rejoin him, and traveling at night because we had overstayed our time of absence, seemed to satisfy him. He insisted upon our going to his house with him, which we did, thinking on the whole it would be safer to do so than to refuse. Seeing how difficult it was for us to walk, he became suspicious again at my explanation of blistered feet. "Why, you soldiers ought to be toughened to it," said he. "You forget that we are mounted soldiers," said I. "That's so," said he. We each got a slice of bread of the old fellow, and learned that we had again lost our way, being now *twenty-six miles* from Romney, instead of *eighteen*, as two nights before. I am ashamed to say that I *stole* from the house a piece of bar soap, as a dressing for my sore and inflamed feet. I would have bought it; but I had nothing but greenbacks, and was afraid to show them. Leaving the old man and his aged partner, we took to the road again, and, as soon as hidden by the fog, took to the cover of the heavy timber.

Never could anything afford greater relief than this soap gave, spread *in thick slices* over *the raw spots* on my feet! I slept nearly all day. At night we got along with no accident; and by morning came out on to the pike leading from Winchester to Romney, about *five miles* from the latter place. Here we begged a drink from a young girl who was milking by the roadside; and turned to the hill again for hiding.

The day was spent in speculating as to the probable presence of McNeil at Romney; the danger of being seen by any of his scouting parties, or of falling upon any of his pickets; and my ability, if not interrupted, of walking the distance remaining before us during the coming night. Doherty repeated, over and over again, the fact of his intimate acquaintance with the surrounding country, and his perfect knowledge of all the mountain paths and roads in the neighborhood. So that at night we started with increased confidence of success. We traveled slowly, and with great care; stopping frequently to listen for any noise which would indicate the approach of any party, and to peer through the darkness for the faintest glimpse of any picket fire. We had no cause for alarm till we came in sight of Romney; but it seemed as if every house in that village was lighted up; and, after a moment for consultation, Doherty led the way across the fields, leaving the town well to the left—I following as fast as my crippled condition would allow. Each of us had many, but no serious, falls, in this cross cut over the uneven country. We struck the road again about a mile and a half north and east of the town. It was necessary to do this; because, directly ahead, ran the south branch of the Potomac, which we must cross on the bridge which spanned it there, or be compelled to keep on along the mountains, for, we did not know how many more, days and nights.

It was a night "as dark as Egypt," and we were tramping along, Doherty leading and I following as fast as I was able, when suddenly, from the darkness ahead, came the startling "halt! who comes there?" Before I could get up and interpose, Doherty answered "refugees." But to the next question I answered, giving my Christian and omitting my *surname*, as, on the whole, somewhat dangerous. To all the other questions, I answered with just the *least grain of truth*, drawing from the sentinel the somewhat doubtful "Well! I suppose it is all right, isn't it?" and in a confident tone my own "Yes, you d——d fool, do you suppose we should be here, with McNeil just in front, if it was'nt?" The sentinel (for such he was) made some reply, but in a tone of voice *too low* to be heard plainly. "*Let's run*," said Doherty. "No," said I, "He'll alarm the camp if we do; and there will be an end of me, if not of both of us." The sentinel's cross "what are you standing there for?" "are you going to keep me here all night?" admonished us, and we started towards him. It was too dark to enable either of us to see the other with any distinctness. Evidently, however, our new friend had some misgivings; for he joined us as we came up, and walked some distance, questioning us somewhat closely, particularly as to *where* we came *from*, and *where going*. As he left us to go back to his post, a most unaccountable noise, on our left, gave us new alarm; and it took some time and careful examination before we could determine that it came from a body of horses champing their rations of whole corn. A good deal relieved by this discovery, we came to the conclusion that the party had bivouacked in the woods, leaving a sentinel only on the road; and that we had successfully passed all danger. Doherty still wanted to take to the fields and run; but I wouldn't, for I couldn't; so we continued on the highway. A few steps brought us to a sharp turn of the road, where was a collection of *long* low buildings; among them a large barn. As we made the turn the scene which broke suddenly upon us, sent the blood curdling to our hearts, and almost completely paralyzed us. Directly in our front was a large mansion, brilliantly lighted from ground floor to garret, filled with a merry party of both sexes, enjoying themselves with music and dancing; while in the grounds around, groups of rebel soldiers, gathered about their camp fires, were busily engaged in cooking. Fortunately for us, we had not passed from the shade of the barn; and still more fortunately, the water, at some previous rains, had worn a gully across the road, at the very spot where our flight had been thus arrested. Instinctively we threw ourselves upon the ground, hardly daring to breath, fearing each moment that we might be discovered. The sentinel who had allowed us to pass, now rode by, and asked of one of his comrades if he had " seen anything of two strange men." "I hain't seen nobody," was the reply. "Is that you, Bill?" was asked in turn. "Yes!" "Well, you'd better go back to your post; for if the old man finds out you've left it, you'll catch hell!" "Well, I don't know as I done right in letting them pass!" "No matter; they can't get out if they have got in;" and, comforted by this assurance, our friend rode back to his post. Soon the order to "fall in for supper" drew the whole party round the fires; and under cover of the darkness, caused by this movement, *we crawled on our hands and knees* across the road, in the gully in which we had been concealed, to what we thought a safe distance up the mountain side. We laid there a long while, listening anxiously for each sound from the party below. At length there was a lull in the music; a *heavy tread* on the piazza floor, and a *voice which was recognized at once as McNeil's*, called "Sergeant Allen." "Aye, aye, Sir," responded the Sergeant. "Wake up Lieuts. Bradshaw and Scott, and then saddle." There were a few moments busy preparation; and then the same voice, with these preliminary words, "half-past four is the time, boys," gave the order to "march." It seemed an age after the command filed away, before all was quiet in and around the house. During all the time, no persons ever *hugged the ground* with a closer embrace than we did. The noise of closing doors at length satisfied us that everybody had left. We raised ourselves to a sitting position, and "*which way did they go?*" was asked by each of the other at the same time. One knew no more than the other; and in this uncertainty neither of us cared to move. Three miles ahead, upon our projected route, was a wire suspension bridge across the south branch of the Potomac; and McNeil, as we well knew, whichever way he went, was too wary a soldier to leave *that* unpicketed. There was nothing left for us, but abandoning all hope of escape that night, to take to the mountains again for safety. So we did; and made our bed in earthworks thrown up in the first year of the war. Here we enjoyed a sound sleep. At daybreak, Doherty, looking out upon the valley below us, informed me that the large brick building at our feet, where the "sound of revelry by night" had so startled us, was upon an estate owned by a Mr. Inskip, a well-known rebel. "I know," said he, "every path across these mountains; have taken them thousands of times on my way to and from picket. There is a house a little way off, where we can get a *good, square meal*. I have had many a one in it; and I wan't to get on to 'Hanging Rock,' (so called from its projecting part way over the pike beneath it) while it is light, and see if there is any picket on the bridge." I acknowledged that these were all good reasons, but still I told him I would not move; it was dangerous enough at night, as our last night's experience proved; it would be much more so in the day; and besides, after getting safely so far, I should feel ashamed enough to be caught, as it were, within sight of home. And to convince him that I was in earnest, I stretched myself out for another nap. When I awoke, Doherty resumed the subject, and after hesitating long, I consented to start. The movement came near being a fatal one for us, however; for all at once, without anything to give us warning, we came out upon a clearing where *young men* — the only ones we had seen on our whole tramp — were engaged in mowing. As we came out from the woods, they caught sight of us, and dropping their scythes, made for their horses, which, saddled, were hitched to the fence. We dodged back to the protection of the woods, and bending to the right, hurried away as fast as we could. Whether they searched for us or not we could not tell. We kept on with all the speed we could muster, till in making our way down a mountain, we came to a deep gully, bordered on each side by high blackberry bushes, at the bottom of which ran a stream of beautifully clear water. We had now been out thirteen days, and had had but *six slices of bread* (each) to eat; and we had suffered more than I can tell for want of water. So we gave ourselves up to this indulgence; eat and drank, and drank and eat, till we could hold no more. With a parting sip, we turned away, having first filled our "canteen." We were now making our last climb before coming to "Hanging Rock." "I thought you told me that there was but one or two houses about here," said I to Doherty. "So I did," said he. "What's all this noise then, of driving cattle?" asked I. He could not tell, and we made our way more slowly, and with greater caution.

Just before sundown we reached the top of the mountain, made our way carefully to "Hanging Rock," from which we were to get a sight of the bridge, and, to our dismay saw that the flats near it, on both sides of the river, were filled with cattle, horses, and wagons, all within a line of Rebel sentinels. Evidently our situation was not a safe one: and we started at once in search of a secure hiding place, and, deeming ourselves safe from observtaion, laid down among some bushes. Hardly had we done so, when our attention was attracted by the sound of voices, and the tread of a picket guard, as it passed on its way to some point in our rear, higher up the mountain. It marched past so near, and we saw them so distinctly, it seemed impossible they should not see us. But, thank God! they did not discover us! So soon as they were out of hearing, crawling close to the ground, and stepping with the utmost care, we descended the mountain, and squeezed ourselves in between some huge rocks, whose sides rose far above our heads. From here we could catch a glimpse of the soldiers on the opposite side of the river, and could plainly hear what was said by those who passed on the road beneath us. In this way we learned that the party was McNeil's; which, having made a raid on "Oldtown," in Maryland, the night before, was now returning with their plunder. Feeling that we were safe, we moved the loose stones which interfered with our comfort, and resting our backs against the rocks, which hid us from observation, gave ourselves to sleep.

Morning dawned, and showed us that this party was still encamped. Towards noon all had gone, save a party (a picket, probably), who, although not visible, we could hear conversing beneath us. Nothing disturbed us during the day or night. We were wakened the next morning by the sound of distant cannonading, which fell faintly but with perfect distinctness upon our ears. Doherty, who alone, from his service in this region, might have made something of it, could not locate it. Before long, a small party of Rebel Cavalry came in sight. Soon a larger party appeared, wounded men in carriages, supporting each other, or held up by comrades apparently unwounded, army wagons, pieces of artillery, ambulances, caissons, all mingled in confusion, and a party of mounted Infantry, each man having a large bundle of straw strapped behind him, and all urging their animals to a speed unusual on a march. What did it all mean? The sound of the cannonading, and the sight of the wounded men, plainly enough indicated that the party had been engaged. Which party was victorious was a matter of more concern to us; and we strained our ears to catch, if possible, some word which would relieve our anxiety. At length the voice of some one urging his horse along the road and past the confused mass, enquiring "Where's the General? Where's McCausland?" gave us a knowledge of whose the command was. The anxious enquiry by one, of "Where do you suppose Averill is?" was met by the taunting reply, "Don't you fret; you'll see him as soon as you want to!" The question by one, "Where do you suppose McNeil is?" was answered by another, who gave the confident assurance that "He promised he would tear up the railroad, and he never yet had disappointed them." All these things, and many others, were full of interest to us, but did little to relieve our anxiety. The column had passed by, and the perfect silence below and above us was leading to the belief that the pickets had been withdrawn, when the rapid tread, on the pike below, of a horse coming from the direction of Romney; the sharp question, "Where are you going, Major?" and the reply, "Over to the other Brigade," drove from the minds of each of us all thoughts of further travel that night. We had learned at Harrisonburg, on the march of the Rebel army down the Valley, that McCausland was brigaded with Bradley Johnson; and now the inference was irresistible that the "other Brigade" was Johnson's—probably at Springfield, across the river.. So another night's confinement was before us, and still longer acute suffering (for such it had now become) from hunger and thirst. With the early morning the rear guard of this force marched away, and all became silent as death. This silence was so long and unbroken, that Doherty urged our leaving at once. I refused to stir. "Look down there, Colonel," said he; pointing to a house on the flat below us; "I have eaten many a good meal at that house, and *I shall die* if I don't get something to eat right away. Come, now! We can't either of us stand this longer! Let's start!" But I refused, and urged him strongly to bear our condition till evening. It was to no purpose, however; and with a promise on his part to be very careful in making his way out from our hiding place, we shook hands, and, with a wish for mutual success, parted. Left thus alone,

I was wondering whether I had not been foolish to consent to the separation, when Doherty's hurried return roused me. He had, while still within the protection of the woods, caught sight of the glimmer of the bayonets of a picket, on the mountain. *He was n't now so hungry as he had been!* and, if only he had not been seen, was willing to stay in hiding as long as I pleased.

We remained closely hid all day, nothing occurring which gave us any uneasiness. Late in the afternoon, a horseman jogged along below us, unchallenged. In the belief that our way was now clear, we crept from our hiding place, and cautiously made our way down the mountain, and skirted its base till we reached a point opposite the bridge. There was no picket stationed at it. But what seemed worse was the fact that its suspension wires had been thrown off their supporting piers, *on one side;* and it was hanging by the strands of the wire ropes of one side alone. It didn't seem possible to cross it, if we waited for night, if, indeed, we could pass it anyhow; and in very desperation we determined to attempt the matter at once. Our footing was the railing on the side of the bridge. Steadying ourselves as well as we could, by grasping the connecting stay rods, we *did* cross. (I could not have done it with my one serviceable arm, had not Doherty helped me.) Almost immediately we came full upon a party of men, by the side of the road, whose nods and whisperings alarmed us much. There was nothing for us but to march by as unconcernedly as possible, and, once out of their sight, to take to the woods and hide again. It was near morning when we started again; and having succeeded in flanking Springfield, turned away for our last rest before reaching our lines. We were now nearing a new danger. The old soldiers, who had been detailed to guard the bridges and stations along the Baltimore and Ohio Railroad, had been drawn off by Sigel and Hunter, for their expedition up the Valley; and their places had been filled by the 100 days men, as they were called, who were neither well drilled or disciplined. There was danger on approaching the outposts, at any of these stations, after dark, lest the sentinel, in the nervousness springing from his inexperience, should *fire before he challenged*. So, in view of this danger, we started early in the afternoon, kept the cover of the woods for a while, and when within two or three miles of our journey's end, came out upon the pike, which we boldly followed. No sign of life disturbed us as we limped along. We reached the smouldering fires and smoking ruins which marked where a railroad station had been, unchallenged. *One house only* of the little village was standing; at the door of which stood *two females* exulting over the destruction. An application for admittance to the house, and for food, was *denied*; and we turned away, to cross the Potomac into "Oldtown," Maryland. The foot bridge had been also destroyed; and Doherty led the way to the "ford" below. We entered the water, which sent a chill through our bodies. The stream was swift, and it was with great difficulty that we made way against the force of the current. The crossing made, we sat down on the bank, to wring the water from our clothes. That done, we set out for the village. "Halt there!" sang out a long-legged fellow, dressed in the uniform of our cavalry, and who came out of a house near by, and made his way to us. But we did not care to stop; and he soon overtook us. "Where are you going?" he asked. "Up to a tavern, if there is any here," was answered, and he led the way. It was quite dark; so that, unnoticed by us, quite a crowd followed on after.

Just as we reached the door of the hotel, the old landlady was about shutting up for the night. Our civil request to be furnished with supper brought the ungracious response "that we could not have any." "Why not, my dear Madame?" "It's too late to be cooking supper for anybody, to-night." "You can give us some bread and milk, can't you? we are very hungry." "No." "Why not?" "That d——d McNeil has driven away all my cows." "Well, you can give us some bread and butter, surely!" "Yes; I suppose I can do that," and off she went on the errand. The crowd which had followed us, now pressed round, clamorous to know our names, and business, and destination, and where we came from; to but few of which questions were any direct replies made. Matters were fast getting unpleasant for us, when the old lady announced that our supper was ready. We ate it without ceremony; and almost stifled by the closeness of the room (every window being shut down) and unsuspicious of any pending trouble, stepped to the door for a breath of fresh air. A crowd of some eighty to one hundred people stood crowding around the door, and shouts of "*make them answer*" greeted us as we made our appearance. A little bantam of a fellow, with a musket almost as large as he was, touching me on the shoulder, demanded to be informed who we were, etc. "*Friends*," I answered. "But that won't do," he said. "Where did you come from?" "Romney." "Where are you going?" "Martinsburg,"—(most unfortunate answer for Early held the place, a fact which at the time was unknown to us.) "What do you want there." "That's none of your business," and thereupon the crowd shouted "They are spies, take them to the guard house." It was getting serious; and I offered if there was a decent man among them, who would come into the house and listen, that I would tell our story, and satisfy him that there was nothing to fear from us; but that I would not talk to the crowd around. So a spruce, gentlemanly-looking man was pushed to the front, who led the way into a side room, wherein lay a wounded rebel officer, victim of the little affair of the Tuesday before, the cannonading from which had awakened us in our retreat. To this man, I told, without reservation, the whole history of our escape, and everything connected with it; and I confess was indignant when I concluded, to hear him say "that he reckoned it was all right, but he "was *peculiarly situated*, and he didn't think he could satisfy the people outside." Of course, nothing more could be done on our part, and so we followed him to the door. He did nothing to try and relieve us; and again my little friend with the musket, ordered us to go with him to the guard house. We still refused; and some one in the crowd sang out "*Where's Thresher?* send for Thresher!" A short, thick-set man soon made his appearance, to whom I gave our history as before, and from whom I received a hearty grasp of the hand, and an assurance that he would set all right. He did so in a few words, and the crowd at once dispersed. It was now past one o'clock, and I turned to the landlady with a request for a bed. "You can't sleep in this house to-night," she said. "Why, what's the matter, now?" I asked. "Why, McNeil may come back to-night; and if he should, and you were in the house, you could not get away so easily," was her answer. "Well, come Doherty, its only one night more; let us be off!" But as I turned, this Mr. Thresher announced his intention of going into the woods with us. Waiting for him to go after a covering, we followed as he led the way into the mountains, where already some twenty of the citizens of the place, afraid to remain at their homes, were soundly sleeping. A dense fog had settled down upon the earth. We lay and shivered, but *could not sleep;* and at the early dawn, made our way to the tavern which had been so inhospitably closed against us the night before. Here, at breakfast, we met Capt. Squires, of the —— Virginia Cavalry, down from Cumberland, in command of a small scouting party. We learned from him the situation of affairs in the Valley, and by his advice concluded to make our way to Cumberland. It was nineteen miles there, and neither of us were in condition to walk any farther. But horses were not to be obtained for *love or money.* All that McNeil had not robbed these people of, had been driven into the mountains for safety. We must walk or stay where we were. So taking directions from Capt. Squires, we got on to the tow path of the canal, and started. It wanted a few minutes to seven o'clock when we set forth. Nobody can imagine how we suffered, as we struggled on in this, our first exposure for months to the rays of the sun. At half-past two we were at the mouth of Patterson's Creek, only seven miles from our starting place, and looking across the river, caught sight of a repair party at work upon a partially burned railroad bridge; and what seemed better, something which we took to be a locomotive engine. So, spite of the shouts and gestures of the working party, who watched us narrowly, we plunged into the river, and after many tumbles and much trouble, succeeded in crossing. Our friends had been endeavoring to make us understand, by their gestures, etc., that the river was not fordable; but we could not hear what was said, till it seemed easier to keep on than to return. As we came up from the river, faint and exhausted, our appearance attracted the attention of three gentlemen who were enjoying the shade of some large trees at the station house. I had called a young boy to me, and sent him off to get us some milk. At his departure one of these gentlemen came up to where we were sitting, with the remark "You are pretty well played out, I see; how far have you been traveling?" "From Oldtown." "That would not have worn you so!" "The sun is dreadfully hot, and we are n't used to it." Eyeing us still more sharply — " You are soldiers!" he said. " Well, that's a good one," said I. " Oh, you need not deny it; I can see that plainly enough! But you need not be afraid of me, if you are in Virginia. My name is Everett. I'm a cousin of Edward Everett, who was Governor of Massachusetts; you've heard of him, I reckon, and I am a thorough-going Union man. You want to go to Cumberland? Well, come up to my house, eat dinner with me, and to-night, when the engine comes down to take back these men here, I'll get a place for you on the train." I met this frank speech with equal plainness, and told him our story. As we were on the way to his house, we met the boy (his son) with a pitcher of milk. "Don't drink that now," said he, "wait and, have some whiskey first, and then, with your dinner, you may have all the milk you want. That's my advice as a medical man." And so we went to his house, drank his whiskey, ate his dinner, took his milk, and engaged in conversation till the noise of the engine warned us it was time to separate. Accompanying us to the train, he helped us on board, shook hands as he bid us good-bye, with a wish for our success, and we steamed away.

Reaching Cumberland, I reported at Department Headquarters. "How are you, Colonel? how did you get here? and where, in heaven's name, have you been?" exclaimed Gen. Kelley, as, jumping from his seat, he grasped my hand. "I heard of you, long ago, as having escaped; and not *seeing* you, or *hearing* anything of you, concluded you had been retaken, or had died on your way." "Heard of me, General! How could that have been?" "Some one of our men, who got away when you did, came in more than ten days ago, and reported!" The mystery was soon solved, by the appearance of our hospital cook. He had been allowed by the guard to pass and repass at all hours; was out of the hospital when we left; at his return, looked first for Doherty, and then for Snow, neither of whom could he find; recalled the fact that they had been consulting closely the day before; came to the conclusion that they had escaped; turned on his heels, was allowed to pass out, went to a neighboring house, where lived a young girl he had been making love to; roused her, and exchanged his clothes for an old suit of her father's, which she threw out of the window; started off; walked all night; and, after a good nap, started the next day, in broad daylight; was halted by one of a party of loyal men called ————, organized to resist conscription in their region; was conducted to the officer in command, to whom he told his story; was taken to a neighboring house, where he was given his meals, and kept secreted till night;—then mounted on horseback and guided safely on his way till morning;—when he was again ushered into a farmhouse, where he was fed and kept through the day, as before; when, mounted upon another horse, he was again guided on his way. And so, concealed and well-cared for by day,—and riding from station to station by night,—he made, in *a week's time*, a pleasant journey; while we, unaided, had had seventeen days of toil, exposure, suffering and danger.

Seeing my enfeebled condition, Gen. Kelley sent for Dr. Lewis, surgeon at the General Hospital at Claryville, to whom he gave me in charge. Here I was given the luxury of a warm bath:—was furnished with a change of underclothing, after my wounds, which were in a sad state, were dressed;—and, refreshed by a delicious supper and the cool breezes of the mountain, I rested in the quiet enjoyment of my accomplished escape.

www.ingramcontent.com/pod-product-compliance
Lightning Source LLC
Chambersburg PA
CBHW021316020526
44114CB00052B/794